Rev. John Edmund Cox

The annals of St. Helen's Bishopsgate, London

Rev. John Edmund Cox

The annals of St. Helen's Bishopsgate, London

ISBN/EAN: 9783743372917

Manufactured in Europe, USA, Canada, Australia, Japa

Cover: Foto ©Lupo / pixelio.de

Manufactured and distributed by brebook publishing software (www.brebook.com)

Rev. John Edmund Cox

The annals of St. Helen's Bishopsgate, London

INTERIOR OF ST. HELEN'S, AS RESTORED, A.D. 1865-8.

THE ANNALS

OF

ST. HELEN'S, BISHOPSGATE,

LONDON.

EDITED BY THE

REV. JOHN EDMUND COX, D.D.

(OF ALL SOULS' COLLEGE, OXFORD),

VICAR IN CHARGE.

LONDON:
TINSLEY BROTHERS, 8, CATHERINE STREET, STRAND.
1876.

[*All rights of Translation and Reproduction are reserved.*]

Dedication.

TO

THE MOST WORSHIPFUL THE MASTER, WARDENS,
AND COURT OF ASSISTANTS

OF

THE GUILD OF MERCHANT TAYLORS',

THIS VOLUME,

ENTITLED

"THE ANNALS OF ST. HELEN'S, BISHOPSGATE,"

PREPARED BY THEIR DESIRE,

AND ASSISTED, AS TO PUBLICATION, BY THEIR LIBERALITY,

IS

Most Gratefully Dedicated,

BY THEIR

TRULY OBLIGED AND FAITHFUL SERVANT,

JOHN EDMUND COX, D.D.

*Vicar in Charge of the United Parish of St. Helen's, Bishopsgate,
and St. Martin Outwich.*

PREFACE.

During the twenty-seven years of my connection with the parish of St. Helen's, Bishopsgate, first as the incumbent of that parish, and now as "Vicar in charge," since its union by her Majesty's Order in Council, May 5th, 1873, with the adjacent parish of St. Martin Outwich, it has been a desire on my part to give to the world an account of the considerable historical interest with which its ancient Church and surroundings must ever be associated. The difficulties of fulfilling that desire had, however, been found to be insuperable until the Merchant Taylors' Company—now the patrons of the United Parish, as they have been from time immemorial of St. Martin Outwich—encouraged me to undertake the task, which I was well aware would be one of difficulty, but of the full amount of which I had formed but a very inadequate idea previously to my attempt to overcome it; and but that the researches of the late Mr. William Meade Williams, a former parishioner well known for his antiquarian and archæological attainments, were most liberally and considerately placed at my disposal by his son, I have no hesitation in saying that I must have withdrawn from the task on its immediate commencement, in despair of ever being able to accomplish it. Mr. William Meade Williams's researches—the result of a long and well-spent life—are incorporated in two thick quarto volumes, each of which has been elaborately illustrated by an immense collection of engravings, obtained after much trouble and at considerable outlay. Inasmuch, however, as the literary matter in those volumes was not intended, or prepared, with a view to publication, although brimful of information, its numerous details required careful examination, patient research, and almost entire reconstruction. Very nearly two years have been spent in the effort to bring this invaluable "rude matter into due form;" and it is now presented both to the Worshipful Company of Merchant Taylors and the public, in the hope that, "with all its imperfections on its head," it may be received with some amount of favour, and with the admission that the subject itself is not unworthy of the pains that have been taken to make it generally acceptable.

Of the pre-Reformation History of the Parish of St. Helen's, Bishopsgate, nothing more remains than is incorporated in the first chapter of this work. Had there been more information extant to throw light upon the nearly three centuries' existence of the Convent and Parish Church of St. Helen's prior to that period, it is impossible that it could have escaped the unwearied investigation and patient research of the Rev. Thomas Hugo, M.A., F.S.A.—one of the most accomplished antiquaries and archæologists of his time. That gentleman had also the advantage of being assisted by the late Dr. Black in his investigations—an authority of the very highest repute; but nothing more could be discovered by either of those painstaking examiners than will be found embodied in a paper, read by the former gentleman eleven years ago before the Archæological Society, of which I have availed myself, with his full consent. And here I would tender to Mr. Hugo my very best thanks for the abundant means he has afforded for lightening my labours, and assisting my researches; for without his exhaustive paper—which hitherto has had but a limited circulation—I should scarcely have known where to turn for much of the information he had so abundantly and adequately supplied. To many other friends I must also offer my warmest acknowledgments both for advice and assistance, but to no one of them more so than to Charles Mathew Clode, Esq., one of the members, and a late Master of the Merchant Taylors' Company, and the accomplished author of "Memorials of the Guild of Merchant Taylors in the City of London, &c.;" to J. B. Monckton, Esq., Town Clerk of the Corporation of the City of London, by whose permission and aid I have been permitted to furnish a copy of the will of Adam Fraunces, preserved in the archives of the Town Clerk's office, and never before printed; to Mr. H. C. Overall, of the same office, by whom that will has been deciphered and copied; to Mr. Tedder, the Librarian of the Athenæum Club; to Mr. Williams, to whose liberality and co-operation I have already referred; to Col. Joseph L. Chester, who had previously collated the Parish Registers; and to Messrs. Wadmore and Baker, of Great St. Helen's, the architects of the Restoration of St. Helen's, 1865-8, by whom the architectural details of the Church have been supplied, and from whom the frontispiece of the interior has been obtained. I should also be greatly wanting in gratitude were I not to acknowledge the invaluable information concerning the Cæsar family, which, unsolicited on my part, was most kindly afforded me by Miss Cottrell-Dormer, of Danes-Dyke, Flamborough. That lady, being herself descended from the Cæsar family, and having accidentally heard of the work I had in hand, at once communicated the valuable information for my use, which will be found under the narrative of Sir Julius Cæsar Adelmare, and his descendants.

JOHN EDMUND COX, D.D.

ST. HELEN'S, BISHOPSGATE,
October 9th, 1876.

TABLE OF CONTENTS.

CHAPTER I.

Birth and character of St. Helena—Finding of the true Cross—First Roman Colony in Britain—Edmund the Martyr—Priory of St. Helen's—Foundation of Priory—William Basing's Will—Kentwode's Constitutions—Directions to Prioress and Convent—Dancing and Revelling forbidden—Names of Three Prioresses—Will of Elizabeth Rollesley—Court of Augmentations—Thomas Cromwell—Common Seal of St. Helen's—Demise of Reginald Goodman—Leases of Tenements—"Valor" of Ecclesiastical Property—Thomas Benolt, Clarenceux Herald—Sundry Grants of Property—Anthony Bonvixi, Merchant—John Rollesley's Annuity—Grants of Sundry Annuities—Annuities and Leases—Last Act of the Prioress and Convent—Edward Alleyne—Adam Fraunces—Cardinal Pole's Pension Book—Survey of the King's Officers—Site of the Priory—Plan of Buildings—Curious Hagioscope—Grant of the Site—Lease of Crosby Place—Surrender of Priory—Leathersellers' Company—Ancient Crypts . . . . pp. 1—37

CHAPTER II.

St. Helen's Church—The Parish and Convent Churches—Architectural Details—Merchant Taylors' Company—The Nuns' Grate—Sir John Lawrence—Church Windows—Coats of Arms . . . pp. 38—45

CHAPTER III.

Tithes and Impropriators of St. Helen's—Pope Nicholas IV.—Advowson of Vicarage—Grant by Queen Elizabeth—Michael and Edward Stanhope—Sir John Langham—Appeal to the House of Lords—The Macdougall Family—Ministers, Curates, and Lecturers of St. Helen's, from A.D. 1571 to A.D. 1876 . . . . pp. 46—56

CHAPTER IV.

Monuments and their Uses—Robinson and Kerwin Monuments—Dame Abigail Lawrence—Francis Bancroft—Smith and Kuhff—Captain Martin Bond—William and Esther Finch—Bond, "Flos mercatorum," and Drax—Sir Thomas Gresham—Sir Andrew Judd—Sir William Pickering—Sir John and Lady Crosby—Sir Julius Cæsar Adelmare—Sir John and Lady Spencer—Alderman Bernard and Gervash Reresby—Alderman Chambrelan—Monumental Brasses—Benolte, Windsor Herald . . . . pp. 57—74

CHAPTER V.

Benefactors—Robinson and Fenner Gifts—Prior's Bequest—Cicely Cyoll's Will—Abraham Chambrelan—Sir Martin Lumley—The Lumley Lectureship—Robinson and Fenner Gifts—Joyce Featly—Daniel Williams—Bond, Langham, and Tryon—Sundry Bequests—Mary Clapham's Will—Baker, Roe, and Dingley Bequests—Christ's Hospital—The latest Bequest . . . . pp. 75—89

CHAPTER VI.

Marriage, Baptism, and Burial Registers . . . . . . pp. 90—99

CHAPTER VII.

Vestry Records from A.D. 1558 to A.D. 1812—Extracts from Church Wardens' Accounts, &c. . . . . pp. 100—226

CHAPTER VIII.

"Worthies" connected with St. Helen's—Sir John Crosby—John Leventhorpe—Sir William Holles—Richard Williams—Thomas Benolte—Antonio Bonvixi—Nicholas Harpsfield—Sir Andrew Judde—Sir William Pickering—Sir John Spencer—Daniel Featley—Sir Thomas Gresham—Cæsar Adelmare—The Cæsar Family—Matthew and Alberigo Gentilis—Edward Brerewood—Peter Maunsell—Richard Ball—Arthur Barham—Thomas Horton—Jonathan Goddard—Robert Hooke—Sir Martin Lumley—Sir John Langham—Sir John Lawrence—Sir Philip Boteler—Sir John Eyles, Sen.—Sir Francis Eyles—Sir John Eyles, Jun. . . . . pp. 227—328

CHAPTER IX.

Crosby Place — Richard, Duke of Gloucester, Lord Protector, and afterwards King—Sir Bartholomew Read—Antonio Bonvixi—German Cioll — Alderman Bond—Divers Ambassadors Resident — Crosby House a prison for the Royalists in the Civil Wars—Sir John Langham—Appropriated to Nonconformists in the Reign of Charles II. —Bernard Edward Howard, 15th Duke of Norfolk—Crosby Hall a Warehouse of the East India Company—Messrs. Holmes and Hall—Restoration of the Hall—Alderman Copeland—Miss Hackett

pp. 329—337

CHAPTER X.

Nonconformist Divines, Occupants of Crosby Hall, from A.D. 1662 to A.D. 176- . . . . pp. 338—358

APPENDIX.

Basing's Will—Benedictine Rules — Kentwode's Constitutions — Adam Fraunces' Will—Restoration, 1865-8—London Tithes Acts—Special Commission—Queen Anne's Bounty—The Advowson of St. Helen's —William Bond—Thomas Benolte—Mayor of the Staple—Merchant Adventurers—Sir Thomas Gresham's Will—Gresham College Act—Francis Bancroft's Will—St. Martin Outwich and St. Antholin

pp. 359—436

ILLUSTRATIONS.

Interior of St. Helen's as restored, A.D. 1865–8 . . . . . *Frontispiece*
Seal of the Convent of St. Helen's . . . . . . *Title-page and Cover*
Plan of St. Helen's, Conventual Buildings, &c. . . . . . . Page 31
Ruins of "St. Helen's Nunnery," A.D. 1799 34
The Crypt of "St. Helen's Nunnery," destroyed A.D. 1799 . . . 36
Plan of Nunnery 37
West Front, St. Helen's, A.D. 1806 38
Monument of John Robinson, A.D. 1609 59
Monument of Martin Bond, A.D. 1643 63
Monument of William Bond, A.D. 1576 64
Monument of Sir Andrew Judde, A.D. 1558 66
Monument of Sir William Pickering, A.D 1574 67
Monument of Sir John and Lady Crosby, A.D. 1475 68
Monument of Sir Julius Cæsar Adelmare, A.D. 1634 69
Monument of Sir John and Lady Spencer, A.D. 1609 70
Plan of the Church of St. Helen's 355

ERRATA.

Page 6. Foot-note*, *for* "Monascon," *read* "Monasticon."

,, 11. *Dele from* "Reynold Kentwode, Dean of St. Paul's," *to* "at the end of this volume"—this paragraph having been retained in the text by an oversight.

,, 41. Foot note*, *for* "Kirman," *read* "Kirkman."

,, 59. Headline, *for* "Kirwin," *read* "Kerwin."

,, 59. Line 9, *for* "Thon Robinson," *read* "Jhon Robinson."

,, 265. Line 9, *for* "March 30," *read* "March 3."

,, 301. Foot note, line 25, *for* "Charles," *read* "Henry."

OF

ST. HELEN'S, BISHOPSGATE,

WITHIN THE

CITY OF LONDON.

CHAPTER I.

TRADITION reports that ST. HELENA, the patron saint of this Church, was born at Colchester A.D. 242, and was the daughter of Coel II., Prince of Britain and king of that district. Having revolted against the Romans, Constantius Chlorus, the Roman general then in Spain, who was afterwards Emperor, was sent to reduce Coel to obedience, and for that end besieged Colchester. After some time the siege was raised, and on Constantius betrothing Helen, from that marriage was born, in the year 265, Constantine, the first Roman Emperor who made public profession of the Christian religion and protected and encouraged it by wholesome laws. His father had secretly favoured the Christians and retarded the persecution against them, but Constantine declared himself their protector, and jointly with Licinius published an edict in their favour at Milan, A.D. 313.

Helena was considered the most beautiful woman of her time, was extremely well skilled in music, and adorned with many other accomplishments. Her father having no other child had caused her to be educated in such a manner as might best fit her to govern. Withal she was a woman of great charity and piety, and although it has been stated that she gave her son a Christian education, we are assured by Baronius,* upon, as he reports, the authority of Eusebius, that she herself was indebted to Constantine for her conversion to Christianity. At the advanced age of eighty, being desirous of visiting the place where our Saviour had suffered, she is reported

---

* Annal. Eccl., Tom. iii. p. 594. Ed. Lucæ, 1738.

B

to have made a voyage to the Holy Land, and, during her journey, to have dispensed very considerable benefactions to many persons, towns, and societies. Finding that the heathens (offended at the superstitious veneration paid to the place of our Saviour's burial) had covered the tomb with earth, and erected over it a temple dedicated to Venus, she ordered that building to be demolished and the earth to be removed in order to build there a magnificent church, and by the eager desire and fervent piety of those who laboured in the work of preparing the place for the foundation, on May 3, 319, three crosses are said to have been discovered deeply buried in the ground, being those on which the Redeemer and the two thieves were crucified, as also the tablet whereon Pilate had written that Christ was crucified King of the Jews! The true cross is reported to have been selected by the miraculous power it displayed of restoring the dead to life. The corpse of a female some time deceased was placed alternately upon the three crosses. The two first that were tried produced no effect, but the third instantly raised the body to a state of reanimation! The true cross being thus discovered was divided and subdivided into innumerable fragments, so that the pieces thus distributed amounted to treble the quantity of wood contained in the original; yet, through some holy miracle it was said to have remained entire and unimpaired! Some of the fragments were encased in gold, and some in gems, and conveyed to Europe, the principal portion being left in the charge of the Bishop of Jerusalem, who exhibited it annually at Easter until Chosroes, King of Persia, plundered that city and took away the holy relic. The cross was subsequently recovered and solemnly deposited in the great church of the Twelve Apostles, at Constantinople!*

St. Helena having built a gorgeous church over the sepulchre, and called it New Jerusalem, then erected a second at Bethlehem, where Christ was born, as also a third church upon the Mount of Olives, whence Christ ascended to the Father. Many things she gave to churches and to poor people, and, after a godly and religious life, died at Rome in the arms of her son, Aug. 18, A.D. 327, where her festival is kept yearly on that day.

Richard, the Monk of Westminster, in writing of Britain says, " Our arrangement brings us to that province which was called by

---

* Clavis Calendaria, i. 340; ii. 155.

the Romans 'Flavia,' but whence it received that name, whether from Flavia Julia Helena, the mother of Constantine the Great, who was born at this place, or from the Roman family of the Flavii, length of time prevents us from determining, which also prevents our firm conviction in the truth of certain things which monuments of antiquity would indicate.—Near the Cassii where the Thames flows into the ocean was the country of the Trinobantes, a people, who not only placed themselves of their own accord under the friendship of the Romans, but also proposed to them to colonize their metropolis London and Maldon, which were situate near the sea. They say that in this city (London) was born Flavia Julia Helena, the most pious wife of Constantius Chlorus and the mother of Constantine the Great, being descended from the Kings of Britain. This also was the first of the Roman colonies in Britain, and was renowned for the temple of Claudius, the image of Victory, &c. London was first called Trinovantum, afterwards Augusta, and then London again. According to old chronicles it is of greater antiquity than Rome. It was fortified by the most pious Empress Helena, the most holy discoverer of the cross." Stow also states, on the authority of Simon of Durham, that "she builded the walls about the cities of London and Colchester."*

---

* " St. Peter's Rome. The third chapel has over the altar the statue of St. Helena, the work of Boggi, an excellent sculptor." In the church of St. John de Lateran, is "a magnificent monument of St. Helen of porphyrie." "We came to St. Crosse of Jerusalem, built by Constantine over the demolition of the temple of Venus and Cupid, which he threw down; and 'twas here they report he deposited the wood of the true Crosse found by his mother Helena, in honour whereof this church was built. Here is a chapel dedicated to St. Helena, the floore whereof is of earth brought from Jerusalem. They suffer no women to enter, save once a year."—Evelyn's Mem., vol i. pp. 111, 116, 160.

"Also besyde the queer of the Chirche at the ryght syde as men comen downward 16 greces (steps) is the place where our Lord was born: that is fulle well dyghte of marble, and fulle richely peynted with gold, sylver, azure, and other coloures. And 3 paas (paces) besyde, is the crybbe of the ox, and the asse. And besyde that is the place where the sterre felle that ledde the three kynges."—The Voyage and Travaile of Sir John Maundeville Knight in the 14th Century.

Sandys adds "that at the upper end of the subterranean chapel of the Nativity, in an arched concave, stands the Altar of the Nativity: under this is a semi-circle; the sole (flooring) set with stones of several colours in the form of a star, and in the midst a serpentine, there set to preserve the memory of that place where our Saviour was born."—A Relation of a Journey begun 1610, by Geo. Sandys. 1670.

The original church of St. Helen in London was dedicated to the Empress Helena, and is said to have been erected to her memory by her son Constantine.*

In the year 1010 Alwyne, Bishop of Helmcham, removed the remains of King Edmund the Martyr from St. Edmundsbury to London, and deposited them in this church for three years, until the depredations committed by the Danes in East Anglia ceased.†

"In a court on the east side of Bishopsgate Street, in Bishopsgate Ward," Newcourt reports, "stands the fair church of St. Helen, sometime a priory of Black Nuns, and in the same, the Parish Church of St. Helen."‡ That there was a church here before the founding of the said priory, which was granted to the canons of St. Paul's by Ranulph and Robert his son, appears by the following document:—

"This agreement between the Dean of St. Pauls, and Ranulph and Robert his son, Witnesseth, that the said Ranulph and Robert do grant to the Canons of St. Pauls, the church of St. Helen, yet so that they shall hold the same during the term of their natural lives, upon the payment of twelve pence yearly. . . . But on their decease a third person of their body (or from their friends) whom they shall have chosen, shall hold the aforesaid church, on the payment of two shillings per annum, to the said canons; but upon his decease the said church shall remain in the full, free, and undisturbed possession of the said canons. . . . Ranulph also obtained from his brethren that every year they should celebrate the anniversary of Turstin, Archbishop of York."§

To this agreement the following were witnesses:—

William the Archdeacon.
Richard & Richard his brothers.

Robert de Cadomo, Robert de Aco, Nicholas Gaufrid the younger, William the master, Henry Walter, Gaufrid the constable, William de Caln, Theodore, Richard de Amond, Baldwin, Robert the younger, Walfrid, Hubert Hugo the master, Radulf, Richard

---

* Europ. Mag., vol. xlviii. p. 173.
† Entick's Lond., vol. iii. p. 398. Hughson, vol. ii. p. 420.
‡ Newcourt's Repertorium, vol. i. p. 263 (Reg. Dec. & Cap. lib. A. f. 32).
§ "Hæc est conventio inter Capitulum S. Pauli et Ranulfum, et Robertum filium ejus, scil. Quod Ranulfus et Robertus concedunt Canonicis S. Pauli Ecclesiam S. Helena, ita tamen quod eandem tenebunt toto tempore vitæ suæ, reddendo singulis annis xiid. Quibus autem defunctis, tertius

de Winton, Albinus the Priest, Richard Malatri, Fulk the Younger, Brun, Osbert, Becha.

After this, in 1181 (the first year of Ralph de Diceto, he being Dean), in the state of the manors and churches belonging to the said Dean and Chapter, it is thus recorded :—" Ecclesia S. Helena est Canonicorum, et reddit eis xx. sol per manum Magist. Cipriani, solvit Synodalia xij^d. Achidiacono xij^d. Habet cœmiterium."*

After the church fell into the hands of the dean and chapter by the death of the several parties, they granted the right of patronage to one William, the son of William the Goldsmith, who afterwards applying to Alard the dean, and the chapter of St. Paul's, had leave of them to found a priory of nuns there, as appears by the following instrument :†—

"PRIORY OF ST. HELENS next the way of Bishopsgate Street, in the City of London.‡

" Of the constituting of Nuns in the same.

"Know all present and to come, that I, Alardus, dean of the church of St. Paul, London, and the chapter of the same church, do grant to William the Son of William the Goldsmith,§ patron of the church of St. Helen, London, that he may constitute Nuns in the same church for the perpetual service of God therein, and may bestow on the society of the same, the right of patronage to the said church, as the same was granted to him by our predecessors; provided that the prioress or other governing such house (after election made by the same), do make presentation thereof to the dean and chapter of London and swear fidelity to the same Dean and Chapter, as well for such Church as for a pension or annuity of half a mark, payable within eight days of Easter . . . and they do

---

suorum quem elegerint, tenebit supradictam Ecclesiam reddendo duos sol. per Ann. eisdem fratribus: Illo autem defuncto remanebit eadem Ecclesia Canonicis soluta et quieta et libera. Etiam Ranulfus obtinuit à fratribus suis, quod singulis annis anniversarium Turstini Eborac, Archiep. celebrabunt. Ad hanc conventionem fuerunt isti Archidiaconi, &c. &c."

* Newcourt (Reg. Dec. and Cap. lib. A. f. 37, vol. i. p. 363).

† Stow (Survey of London, p. 430. Ed. Lond. 1754) says "founded by William de Basing, Dean of St. Paul's."

‡ For the original Latin Document, see Appendix A.

§ Lineally descended from William the Founder was Sir William Fitzwilliam, merchant tailor, and servant to Cardinal Wolsey, Alderman of Bread Street Ward, 1506, from whom is descended the present Earl Fitzwilliam.

further swear not to alienate such before mentioned patronage or to subject their convent to any other control. And we do moreover grant as far as in us lies, that the said society or convent, so to be erected may appropriate and convert to their own use all revenues belonging to the said Church, excepting the aforesaid pension, they discharging all episcopal dues appertaining to the said church; and if it shall happen that the Nuns of such convent shall conduct themselves improperly, We grant the same to men of religion, to hold without molestation, in the same manner as is mentioned with respect to such Nuns; And the Dean and Chapter bind themselves similarly towards them; and that this our grant and concession and all other engagements may be held in perpetual remembrance and firmly observed, we have caused the same to be done in the form of a handwriting: the one part whereof to be kept by us, and the other by the said William and the said Nuns, and have mutually sealed the same &c.*

"Witness, Alardus, Dean of London and others."

This foundation of the priory was probably about the year 1212, in the latter part of the reign of King John, for Alardus de Burnham, Dean of St. Paul's, died on the 14th August, 1216.†

The nuns were of the Benedictine order, and wore a black habit with a cloak, cowl, and veil.‡

William Basing, one of the sheriffs of London in 1308, 2 Edward II., was a great benefactor to this priory, which he augmented both in building and revenue, for which probably he was also holden to be a founder.§ Not long after the time of the above William Basing, one Henry Gloucester was interred here, descended from him, by the mother's side, whose will and testament are here inserted :—

"In the name of the Father, of the Son, and of the Holy Ghost, Amen.

"I Henry de Gloucester, Citizen and Goldsmith of London, do make my Will and Testament as follows. I leave my body to be buried at St. Helens, London, in such place as the Prioress

---

* Dugdale, Monascon Angl., vol. iv. p. 553. Ed. Lond. 1817-30.
† Newcourt's Repertorium, vol. 1. p. 364.
‡ For the Rules of the Benedictine Order, see Appendix B.
§ Weever's Fun. Monts., p. 421.

and Nuns of that Convent shall direct. I also leave to my daughter Elizabeth a Nun in the said convent of St. Helens, six shillings. I also leave to the prioress and convent of St. Helens, Eleven Marks of Silver annually, for the purpose of providing two monks to perform divine service in the said church of St. Helen for my soul, for the soul of Margaret formerly my Wife and for the souls of William my father and of Wilhelmina my mother, daughter of Thomas de Basings brother of William de Basings the founder &c. The remainder I leave for the maintenance of my son John; and if my said son John shall die without any offspring, the whole shall remain to my daughter Johanna, and the heirs of her body lawfully begotten. I also leave to my niece Johanna Adynet five shillings: Given and executed at London on Thursday next after the feast of St. Andrew the Apostle. Anno Dom. 1332 in the sixth year of the reign of King Edward III."*

A Cottonian manuscript, a large sheet of parchment, contains the following regulations, drawn up A.D. 1439, to be observed by the nuns of the convent, to which is appended a very small piece, containing a petition from the convent. The seal is much broken. A perfect impression of the seal appendant to a deed, dated 1534, 26 Hen. VIII., is among the records of the Leathersellers' Company.†

---

* Probate of this will was made January 15, 1332, 6 Edward III.—MSS. in Bib. Cotton. Weever, Fun. Monts., p. 421.

The original is in Latin as follows:—

"In nomine patris, et filii et spiritus sancti, Amen. Ego, Henricus de Gloucestre, civis et aurifaber London, condo testamentum meum in hunc modum, Lego corpus meum ad sepeliendum apud Sanctam Elenam, London; ubi priorissa et conventus eiusdem domus ibidem eligere voluerint. Item lego Elizabeth filie mee, Moniali eiusdem domus, sancte Elene, sex solid. Item lego Priorisse et Conventui Sancte Elene undecim marcas argenti annuatim ad inuenend. duos Capellanos Divina celebrare in eadem Ecclesia Sancte Elene, pro anima mia, et anima Margarete quondam uxoris mee, ac pro animabus Willelmi patris mei, et Willelme, matris mee, fil Thome de Basings, fratris Willelmi de Basings, Fundatoris, &c. Residuum vero lego ad sustentationem Johannis filii mei. Etsi idem Johannes filius meus sine prole obierit, integre remaneat Johanne filie mee et heredibus de corpore suo legitime procreatis. Item lego Elizabeth filie mee, duas schopas abenas. Item lego Johanne Adynet nepte mee, quinque solidos. Dat et act, London die Jovis prox . post festum. Sancti Andree . Apostoli . Ann . Dom . 1332. Reg Regis Ed. 3. 6."   † Malcolm's Lond. Rediviv., vol. iii. p. 548.

"Constitutiones per Decanum et Capitulum Ecclesiæ Cathedralis S. Pauli, Lond. factæ, Moniales Cœnobii S. Helenæ prope Bishopsgate infra civitatem London. tangentes :*—

"Reynold Kentwode, Dean and Chapeter of the Church of Poules, to the religious women, Prioress and Covent of the priory of Seynt Eleyns, of owre patronage and jurisdictyon immediat, and every nunne of the said priory, gretyng in God with desyre of religyous observances and devocyon. For as moche as in oure visitacyon ordinarye in your priorye boothe in the hedde, and in the membris late actually exersyd, we have founden many defautes and excesses, the whiche nedythe notory correccyon and reformacyon, we, wyllyng vertu to be cherished, and holy relygion for to be kepte as in the rules of your ordyerre, we ordeyne and make certeyne Ordenauns and Injunccyons, weche we sende you wrete and seelyd undir owre commone seele, for to be kepte in forme as thei ben articled and wretyn unto you.

"Firste. We ordeyne and enjoyne you, that deveyne servyce be don by you duly nyghte and day, and silence duly kepte in due time and place, after the observance of youre religione.

"Also we ordayne and enjoyne you Prioresse and Covente, and eche of you syngerly, that ye make due and hole confession to the confessor assigned be us.

"Also we enjoyne you Prioresse and Covent, that ye ordeyne conveuyent place of firmarye, in the wiche your seeke sustres may be honestly kepte and releyed withe the costes and expences of youre house, accustomed in the relygion durynge the tyme of heere sikenesse.

"Also we enjoyne you Prioresse that ye kepe youre dortour, and by thereinne by nythe, aftyr observaunce of your relygion, without that the case be suche that the lawe and the observaunce of youre religione suffreth you to do the contraye.

"Also we ordeyne and injoyne you Prioresse and Covent, that noo seculere be lokkyd withinne the boundes of the cloystere; ne no seculere persones come withinne aftyr the bell of complyne, except wymment servantes and mayde childeryne lerners, also admitte no one sojournauntes wymment withoute lycence of us.

"Also we ordeyne and enjoyne you Prioresse and Covent, that

---

* Dugdale, Monasticon Angl., vol. iv. p. 553. Ed. Lond. 1817-30 [Hodie Rot. antiq. Cotton. Mus.] Ex ipso autogr. in Bibl. Hatton.

ye, ne noone of youre sustres use nor haunte any place withinne the Priory, thoroghe the wiche evel suspeccyione or sclaundere mythe aryse; wyche places for certeyne causes that move us, we wryte not here inne our present injunccyone, but wole notyfie to your Prioress: nor have no lokyng nor spectacles owtewarde, thorght the which ye mythe falle in worldlye delectacyone.

"Also we ordeyne and enjoyne you Prioresse and Covent, that some sadde woman and discrete of the seyde religione, honest, well named, be assigned to the shittyng of the cloyster dorys, and kepyng of the keyes, that none persone have entre ne issu into the place aftyr complyne belle; nethir in noo other tyme be the wiche the place may be disclaundered in tyme comying.

"Also we ordeyne and enjoyne you Prioresse and Covent, that noo seculere wymmen slepe be nythe withinne the dortour, with owte specialle graunte hadde in the chapeter House, among you alle.

"Also we ordeyne and enjoyne you, that noone of you speke ne comone with no seculere personne ne sende ne receyve letteres, myssyres or geftes of any seculere personne, withowte lycence of the Prioresse: and that there be an other of youre sustres present, assigned be the Prioresse to here and record the honeste of bothe partyes, in such communycation; and such letteres or geftes, sent or receyved may turn into honeste and wurchepe, and none into vilanye, ne disclaundered of youre honeste and religyone.

"Also we ordeyne and enjoyne you Prioresse and Covent, that none of youre sustres be admitted to noone office but that they be of gode name and fame.

"Also we ordeyne and enjoyne you, that ye ordeyne and chese on youre sustres, honeste, abille, and cunnyng of discreyone, the weche can, may, and schall have the charge of teching and informacyone of youre sustres that ben uncunnyng, for to teche hem here service and the rule of here religione.

"Also for as moche that diverce fees, perpetuelle corrodies, and lyvers have be graunted before this tyme to diverce officers of youre house, and other persones, weche have hurt the house, and be cause of delapidacyone of the godys of youre seyde house, we ordeyne and enjoyne you, that ye reserve noone officere to no perpetuelle fee of office, ne graunte, ne annuete, corody, ne lyvery, withoute specialle assent of us.

"Also we enjoyne you, that alle daunsyng and revelyng be utterly forborne among you, except Christmasse and other honest tymys of recreacyone, among youre selfe usyd, in absence of seculers in alle wyse.

"Also we enjoyne you Prioresse that there may be a doore at the noone's quere, that noone straungeres may looke on them, nor they on the straungeres, wanne thei bene at divyne service. Also we ordeyne and enjoyne you Prioresse, that there be made a hache of conabyll* heythe, crestyd withe pykys of herne, to fore the entre of youre kechyne, that noo straunge pepille may entre wethe certeyne elekctts avysed be you and be youre steward to suche persouys as you and hem thynk onest and conabell.

"Also we enjoyne you Prioresse, that non nonnes have no Keyes of the posterne doore that gothe oute of the cloystere into the churcheyerd but the Prioresse for there is moche comyng in and oute unlefulle tymes.

"Also we ordeyne and enjoyne, that no nonnes have, ne receyve noo schuldrin wyth them into the house forseyde, but yf that the profite of the comonys turne to the vayle of the same house.

"These Ordenauns and Injunccyons, and iche of them, as thei be rehersid above, we send unto you Prioresse and Covent, chargyng and commaunding you and iche of you alle to kepe hem truly aud holy in vertu of obedience, and upon peyne of contempte; and that ye doo them be redde and declared foure tymes of the yeere in youre chapele before you, and that thei may be hadde in mynde, and kepte under peyne of excommunicacyone, and other lawfulle peynes, to be yove into the persone of you Prioresse, and into singuler persones of the Covent, wheche we purpose to use agens you, in case that ye desobeye us: reservyng to us and oure successors poure these forsayde ordinaunces and injunctiouns to chaunge, adde, and diminue, and with hem despence, as ofte as the case requirethe and it is needfulle. In to which witnesse we sette oure common seele, govyn in oure Chapitter House, the XXI day of the monyth of June the yere of oure Lord MCCCCXXXIX. et anno regni Regis Henrici Sexti, post Conquæstum decimo septimo."

"The Nuns endeavoured, during the reigns of Henry III. and Edward I., to stop up the lane or passage through the court of

---

* "Reasonable," or rather, convenient, suitable.

their House, from Bishopsgate Street to S. Mary-Axe. In the thirty-third year of the former King they obtained a licence to include a lane lying across their ground, inasmuch as it had been found by inquest that no damage would accrue thereby to the citizens of London. The licence was dated at Westminster, the 24th March, 33 Henry III. 1248-9.* Some resistance, as it appears, was made to this inclusion, for in several subsequent inquests the jurors describe the lane as a common thoroughfare, from the Gate of the Nuns of S. Elen to the Church of S. Mary at Ax, called 'Seint Eleyne Lane,' through which there was always in ancient times a common passage for carts and horsemen, as well as for foot passengers.† Their obstruction was at least partially successful, and, as such, has descended to our own time. There is still no thoroughfare for carriages.

"Reynold Kentwode, Dean of S. Paul's (1422—1441), together with his Chapter, made a number of Constitutions for the Nuns, dated the 21st of June, 1439.‡ Many of these are extremely curious, and furnish us with most descriptive illustrations of conventual life. These have been accurately transcribed from the original document, now among the Cottonian Rolls, and are placed in the Appendix at the end of this volume.

"The names of the three Prioresses which are given by the last editors of Dugdale, are Eleanor de Wyncestre or Winton, in the 7th and 12th of Henry III.; Alice Asshfeld, who granted a lease to Sir John Crosby, the builder of Crosby Hall, in 1466;§ and Mary Rollesley, the last Prioress. To these four others may be added, D——, Alice Wodehous, Alice Tracthall, and Isabel Stampe.‖ The first-mentioned lady is believed to have been the first Prioress. She addressed a petition, which is given in the Appendix, to Alard de Burnham, dean of S. Paul's, and Walter Fitzwalter, archdeacon of London, in or some short time previously

---

* Pat. 33 Hen. III. m. 7.
† Rot. Hundred, i. 409, 410, 420, 425, 426, 431.   ‡ Rot. Cott. v. 6.
§ "See the particulars in the Rev. T. Hugo's History of Crosby Hall, Transactions of the Lond. and Midd. Archæol. Soc., vol. i. p. 40."
‖ "By will dated 26th April, A.D. 1469—Philip Malpas, merchant, citizen, &c., bequeaths to the Prioress of St. Helen's, 20s.; and to Dame Alice Woodhows, nun there, 20s., and also to every other nun professed in the same house 6s. 8d. to pray for his soul.—Extract from a Paper by B. B. Orridge, Esq., Transactions Lond. and Midd., vol. iii. p. 9, pp. 290."

to the year 1216. The second was the immediate predecessor of Alice Asshfeld, and granted to Sir John Crosby a lease of the house in which he resided when he obtained from the latter that of the same and adjoining premises, on which he subsequently built his magnificent mansion. It is presumed that she resigned her office of Prioress, as a lady of the same name and probably herself stands first of the eleven present and consenting Sisters in the document of 1466. The third, Alice Tracthall, leased some premises in Birchin Lane, about which more details will be given, to Thomas Knyght, by indenture dated the 20th March, 13 Henry VII., 1497-8. The fourth, Isabel Stampe, was the last Prioress but one. When she succeeded to her office cannot be determined, nor the time of her decease or resignation; but she granted leases of some of her conventual property on the 3rd of December, 1512, and on the 1st of November, 1526.*

"The will of Elizabeth Rollesley, who would appear to have been the mother of the last Prioress, is given by Maddox in his *Formulare*. It was dated the 23rd August, 1513, 5 Henry VIII.; and, among other bequests, directs:—'Item; I bequeth to the Prioress and Covent of S. Elyns in London, v li. Item; I bequeth to Dame Mary, my dowter, being a Nonne of the same place, v li.' Another daughter, Alice, was a Nun of Dartford, and to her was left a similar legacy.†

"On the 26th January, 19th Hen. VIII. 1527-8, the Prioress, Mary Rollesley, and Convent leased to Richard Berde a tenement in the parish of S. Ethelburga, for a term of forty years, at an annual rent of xx s.‡

"On the 21st December, 20th Hen. VIII. 1528, they leased to Robert Nesham, citizen and baker, and Agnes his wife, one bake-

---

* See p. 11. For the following details, as for much other reliable information, I am very largely indebted to the Rev. Thomas Hugo's, M.A., Lecture read at Ironmongers' Hall, March 10th, 1864; he having collected the details from the Conventual Leases, the Ministers' Accounts, the Valor, the Surrenders, the Particulars for Grants, the Orders and Decrees, Pension Lists, Surveys, and other Records of the Court of Augmentations, the Patent and Originalia Rolls, and several collections of Rolls and Charters, or documents usually called by that name, &c. &c.

† Madox's Formulare Anglicanum, p. 440.

‡ Ministers' Accounts, 31-32 Hen. VIII. No. 112.

house, with appurtenances, in the parish of S. Andrew Undershafte, for a term of forty years from the following Christmas, at a yearly rent of lxxiij s. iiij d. The repairs were to be done by the farmer.*

"On the 20th May, 21st Hen. VIII. 1529, they leased to Richard Staverton a tenement in the parish of S. Mary Magdalene in the Old Fishmarket for a term of sixty years, at a yearly rent of xxxiij s. iiij d.†

"On the 20th September, 23rd Hen. VIII. 1531, the Prioress and Convent leased two tenements, with two gardens adjoining to the same, within their close, to William Shelton, from the Michaelmas following, for twelve years, and, after the expiration of those years, for a term of fourscore and nineteen years, at a rent of 1s. a year, payable at the four usual terms. The repairs were to be done by the farmer aforesaid.‡

"On the 26th January, 23rd Hen. VIII. 1531-2, they leased to Richard Berde aforesaid, and Alice his wife a tenement in the parish of S. Ethelburga for a term of sixty years, at a yearly rent xlv s. Repairs by the farmers.§

"On the 10th of June, 25th Hen. VIII. 1533, Mary Rollesley, Prioress and Convent entered into an agreement with Richard Berde aforesaid, citizen and girdler of London, by which, inasmuch as the late Prioress of S. Helen's, Dame Isabell Stampe, had, by a deed bearing date 1st November, in the 18th Hen. VIII. 1526, granted and let to Thomas Larke, citizen and Merchant Tailor, their great tenement or inn called the Black Bull, with cellars, &c., in the parish of S. Alburghe, in the Ward of Bishopsgate, and two adjoining tenements, for one and twenty years, from Midsummer following, at a yearly rent of 9l. 14s. sterling, they transferred the same to the said Richard at the same rent. If unpaid six weeks after due, the Prioress might enter and distrain. The agreement was allowed by the Court of Augmentations, on the 5th Jan., 32nd Hen. VIII. 1540-1.‖

"On the 10th of July, 25th Hen. VIII. 1533, they leased to the aforesaid William Shelton a tenement with appurtenances in

---

* London Conventual Leases, No. 24. Ministers' Accounts.
† Ministers' Accounts. ‡ Ibid. § Ibid.
‖ Conventual Leases, No. 17. Orders and Decrees, vii. f. 35 b.

their close, for a term of four score and eighteen years from the next following feast of the Nativity of S. John the Baptist, at a yearly rent of x s. payable at the four terms. Repairs by the farmer.*

"Among Dean Kentwode's orders, previously referred to,† is the following regulation:

"'Also for as moche that diñce fees ppetuett corrodies and lyuers have be grauntyd be for this tyme to diuerce officers of ȝowre house and other' psones whecħ have hurt the house and be cause of delapidacyoñ of the godys of ȝowre seyde house we ordeyne and jnioyne ȝow that ȝe reseyve noon officer' to noo ppetuett ffee of office ne graunte noo annuete corody ne lyuery without speciatt assent of vs.'

"On the 10th September, 26th Hen. VIII. 1534, the Prioress and Convent gave to Thomas Crumwell, the then secretary of the king, afterwards Earl of Essex, an annuity of four marcs, issuing from their lands and tenements in London, for the term of his life, payable yearly at Michaelmas. If in arrear for three weeks, the said annuitant might enter and distrain. Four pence were paid immediately, as earnest and parcel of the annuity. This was allowed by the Court of Augmentations, with arrears from the dissolution of the House, on the 8th of February, 30th Hen. VIII. 1538-9.‡

"On the 10th September, 1534, they also leased to Richard Berde aforesaid a tenement in the parish of S. Alborough, in the ward of Bishopsgate, for a term of three score years, from Michaelmas next ensuing, at a yearly rent of xvj s. sterling, payable at two terms of the year. If in arrear for six weeks, the Prioress and Convent might enter and distrain.§

"On the 1st of October, 26th Hen. VIII. 1534, Dame Mary Rollesley, Prioress, and Convent granted and leased to fee farm to John Rollesley, gent. all their manor of Burston or Bruston, in the county of Middlesex, with all the lands, tenements, woods, underwoods, court-leets, profits of courts, fines, amerciaments and other profits and commodities whatsoever appertaining to the same manor, from the Michaelmas last past to the end of fourscore years next ensuing, at a yearly rent of 9*l*. payable at Lady Day and Michaelmas, in equal portions. Repairs were to be made by

---

* Ministers' Accounts. † See p. 8.
‡ Orders and Decrees, x. f. 131. § Conventual Leases, No. 25.

the aforesaid farmer. If the aforesaid rent or any parcel thereof were in arrear for forty days, the Prioress and Convent were to enter and distrain. This was allowed by the Court of Augmentations, on the 8th of November, 34 Hen. VIII. 1542.* The original of this lease still exists among the documents of the Augmentation Office, and has appended to it the common seal of the House, representing S. Helen, in agreement with the most important fact of her history, standing under the Cross which she embraces with her left arm, and holding in her left hand the three nails of the Passion. On the right, opposite to the empress, is a multitude of women with extended arms and upraised countenances. Beneath is a trefoiled niche, and under it a woman's (?) head and left arm in the same attitude as that of the figures above. The legend is SIGILL. MONIALIVM. SANCTE. HELENE. LONDONIARVM. a representation of this seal has been given by Malcolm, and has been reproduced for this volume.†

"On the 2nd December, 26th Hen. VIII. 1534, the Prioress and Convent leased to Alan Hawte, his executors and assigns, a messuage with a garden within their close for a term of fourscore and nineteen years, at a yearly rent of 1s. payable at Lady Day and Michaelmas in equal portions. Repairs by the farmer.‡

"On the 24th December, 26th Hen. VIII. 1534, the Prioress and Convent appointed Sir James Bolleyne, knt., to be steward of their lands and tenements in London and elsewhere, the duties to be performed either by himself or a sufficient deputy, during the life of the said James, at a stipend of forty shillings a year, payable at Christmas. If in arrear for six weeks, the said James might enter and distrain. Allowed, with arrears from the Dissolution, by the Court of Augmentations, on the 10th of February, 30th Hen. VIII. 1538-9.§

"On the 1st January, 26th Hen. VIII. 1534-5, Mary Rollesley, Prioress, and Convent made Richard Berde aforesaid, their seneschal, receiver and collector of all their manors, &c. by charter under the conventual seal, dated as aforesaid, for the term of his life from the date of the instrument, with a fee or stipend of 12*l.*

---

* Ministers' Accounts. Orders and Decrees, xiii. f. 14 b.
† Malcolm's Lond. Rediv. iii. 548.
‡ Ministers' Accounts.   § Orders and Decrees, x. f. 141 b.

sterling, and 20s. for his livery : also with eatables and drinkables, two cartloads of fuel and ten quarters of charcoal a year allowed and delivered to him, and the use and occupation of one chamber, and of a certain parlour appertaining to the same, within the precinct of the Priory, with free ingress to and egress from the same at all convenient and lawful times during his life.*

"On the 20th of January, 1534-5, 26th Hen. VIII., the Prioress and Convent granted, demised, and let to Regnald or Rouland Goodman, citizen and fishmonger, their lands or great gardens, with a 'Shedd' and other appurtenances, with free entry and issue, incoming and outgoing at all times convenient, requisite, and necessary, into and from the same, by and through the next way now used, had, and occupied, lying and being in the parish of S. Botolph without Bysshoppesgate, in the tenure of John Newton, 'pulter,' from Michaelmas, 1540, for fourscore years, at a yearly rent of four marcs sterling, payable at Ladyday and Michaelmas, in equal portions. The said Rowland to keep and maintain competently all the fences of the said lands or gardens. If in arrear for a quarter of a year, the Prioress or Convent to have again and repossess their premises, as in their former estate. Allowed by the Court of Augmentations, on the 26th of November, 31st Hen. VIII. 1539.†

"On the 10th of December, 27th Hen. VIII. 1535, they leased

---

* Conventual Leases, No. 20 ; Ministers' Accounts.

† Ministers' Accounts. Orders and Decrees, vi. f. 27. Mr. Hugo remarks, "Among the documents in the possession of the Leathersellers' Company is one of the same year as the seven last described, 1534, and probably the counterpart of one of them. I regret that I cannot give positive information on this point inasmuch as to my application to the Court of the Company for permission to inspect it for a few minutes, in order to include its details in the present memoir, that body thought fit to issue a refusal ! It is difficult to understand the reason of such a repulse, further than that it appears to be a sort of tradition with the Company to resist all such solicitations. So long ago as the year 1803 Malcolm complained that he 'received no encouragement in his enquiries.' 'As it is,' he adds, 'what can be viewed by the passenger I shall describe ; but further this deponent cannot say.' (iii. 562.) This jealous custody and concealment of documents, which are now possessed simply of historical and archæological interest, I had almost hoped were among the follies which have passed away—or, at any rate, that it would not have found an apparently perpetual lodgment in a worshipful Company of the City of London."

to John Rollesleye their messuage or mansion place, with the gardens, cellars, solars, &c. appertaining to the same, lately in the tenure of Nicholas late Bishop of Landaff, situated between the tenements of Sir John Russell, knt. and Alen Hawte, within the close of S. Helen's, from the Christmas following, for four score years, at a yearly rent of xlvj s. viij d. sterling, payable at the four terms in even portions. If in arrear for thirteen weeks, the Prioress and Convent might enter and distrain. Repairs to be done by the farmer. As in the other instances given in the notes, the original lease still exists.*

"On the 20th December, 27th Hen. VIII. 1535, they leased to Thomas Pett, citizen and grocer, a messuage in the parish of S. Ethelberga for a term of twenty years at a yearly rent of xlv s.†

"On the 7th of April, in the 27th year of Hen. VIII. 1536, the Prioress and Convent granted, demised, and let to John Rolesley ten tenements, with gardens thereunto adjoining, and three chambers, with their appurtenances, situated within the close and tenements aforesaid; the tenements in the holding respectively of Richard Parker, Guy Crayford, Edward Waghan, Edward Bryscley, Margaret Dalton, widow, John Bernard, Richard Harman, John Harrocke, and Andrew Byscombe; and the chambers, one on the ground, in the tenure of Emma Lowe, widow, and the other two up the stairs, over the chambers of the said Emma, in the tenure of William Damerhawle; together with the alley, tenements, cellars, and solars, to the said alley appertaining, situated in the same close, (except a tenement or chamber in the said alley, wherein Johane Heyward then dwelt,) and another tenement outside the close, wherein Thomas Rancoke then dwelt, from Michaelmas last past for threescore years ensuing, at a yearly rent of £15, payable at the four usual terms of the year. The said John to keep the said premises in good and sufficient repair. If the rent were in arrear for six months after any of the said feasts, and no sufficient distress for the arrears could be found, the Prioress and Convent might re-enter and repossess. This was allowed by the Court of Augmentations, on the 17th April, 31st Hen. VIII. 1540.‡

---

* Conventual Leases, No. 14.   † Ministers' Accounts.
‡ Conventual Leases, No. 15. Ministers' Accounts. Orders and Decrees, v. f. 1.

"On the same day the Prioress and Convent granted and let to the same John their tenements with appurtenances in the parish of S. Alphe in 'Muggewell Strete,' and S. Olave in 'Silver Strete by Crepulgate,' from Michaelmas next coming for a term of fourscore years, at a yearly rent of £7 sterling, payable at the usual terms. The said John to keep the premises in competent and sufficient repair. If the rent were in arrear for six weeks, the Prioress and Convent were to have power to enter and distrain. If for a quarter of a year, or if the repairs were not accomplished in avoiding rain and other extreme weather, they might re-enter and repossess themselves wholly of the property. This was allowed by the Court of Augmentations on the 20th April, 31st Hen. VIII. 1540.*

"On the same day, the Prioress and Convent leased to John Rollesleye, his executors and assigns, two tenements in the parish of S. Elen's outside the close, one in the tenure of William Shurburne, citizen and barber-surgeon, and a marsh called the 'Hare Marsshe' in the parish of Stebunheth in the county of Middlesex, for a term of sixty years, at a rent of viij li. xv s. iiij d. payable at the four usual terms.†

"In the 27th of Hen. VIII. the 'Valor' was taken of all ecclesiastical property, to determine the tenth which was henceforth ordered to be paid to the King for the support of his dignity of Supreme Head of the Church of England. The yearly value of all the possessions of the House was £376 6s., in rents from tenements in the city of London, the rectory of S. Helen's, tenements in Bordeston and Edelmeton in Middlesex, Eyworth in Bedfordshire, Barmeling in Kent, Balamesmede and Marck in Essex, Ware in Hertford, and Dachet in Buckingham. Out of this sum various rents for lands in several parishes of the city were to be deducted, together with the stipends of Sir James Bulleyn, knight, chief steward, Richard Berde, receiver, and John Dodington, auditor; and pensions to David Netley, chaplain of the perpetual chantry of the B. V. M. in the Church of S. Helen's; Thomas Criche, chaplain of the chantry of the Holy Ghost, in the same church; the churchwardens of S. Mary Botowe; the

---

* Ministers' Accounts. Orders and Decrees, v. f. 2.
† Conventual Leases, No. 9. Ministers' Accounts.

wardens of a fraternity in Bow Church; Thomas More, chaplain of a chantry in S. Michael's, Cornhill; poor people at the anniversaries of Adam Fraunces, Robert Knolls, and Hugh Wynarde, in the Church of S. Helen's; the vicar of Eyworth; the Bishop of Lincoln, for sinodals and procurations; and the Abbess and Convent of Barking. These amounted to £55 10s. 3½d., leaving clear £320 15s. 8½d.; the tenth to be deducted from which was £32 1s. 7d.*

"On the 6th October, 28th Hen. VIII. 1536, they leased to John Dodington a tenement called 'the Sterre' at Ware, with all its chambers, cellars, solars, &c. for a term of sixty years from the next following Michaelmas, at a yearly rent of xl s. payable at Lady Day and Michaelmas, in equal portions. Repairs to be done by the aforesaid farmer.†

"On the 20th of May, 29th Hen. VIII. 1537, the Prioress and Convent granted to Richard Wolverston, yeoman, for sundry good services, an annuity of twenty shillings sterling, issuing as before, for the term of his life, payable in equal portions at Christmas and Midsummer. If in arrear for six weeks, the said Richard might enter and distrain. Allowed, with arrears from the Dissolution, by the Court of Augmentations, on the 12th of February, 30th Hen. VIII. 1538-9.‡

"On the 30th of May, 29th Hen. VIII. 1537, they leased to John Thurgood, his executors and assigns, a tenement with shops, cellars, solars, &c. in Ivelane, in the parish of S. Faith in Paternoster Rowe, for a term of fifty-one years from the Lady Day of that year, at a yearly rent of liij s. iiij d. payable at the four usual terms. Repairs by the farmer.§

"On the 1st of July, 29th Hen. VIII. 1537, they leased to Richard Stafferton a tenement, with shops, cellars, solars, &c. in the parish of S. Mary Wolnoth, for a term of fifty years, at a yearly rent of xxiij s. iiij d. payable at the four terms.‖

"On the 1st of December, 29th Hen. VIII. 1537, they leased to Sir Arthur Darcy, knt. a messuage within their close, late in the occupation of Thomas Benolt the herald, from Michaelmas last

---

* Val. Eccl. v. i. pp. 392, 393.
† Conventual Leases, No. 18. Ministers' Accounts.
‡ Orders and Decrees, x. f. 164 b. § Ministers' Accounts. ‖ Ibid.

past, for a term of four score and sixteen years, at a rent of xl s., payable at the four usual terms. Repairs by the farmer.*

"On the 1st of December, 29th (?) Hen. VIII. 1537, the Prioress and Convent granted to John Dodington an annuity of xl s. for the term of his life, payable in equal portions at Easter and Michaelmas.†

"On the 2nd of December, 29th Hen. VIII. 1537, they leased to Elizabeth Hawte, widow, their tenement or messuage, with cellars, solars, gardens, woodhouses, stables, &c. 'abbutting vpon the well yarde in the said P^s orye on the westt, one other parte therof ending at the gate called the tymber halle gate buttyng vpon the Inner dorter on the East pte, the other pte therof w^t the gardeyne therto adioynyng stretching alonge the ffrater on the sowthe parte, and the other parte therof lyeng alonge the cartewaye goyng into the tymber yarde on the north parte,' from the Christmas following for fifty years, at a yearly rent of xx s. sterling, payable at the four terms. The Prioress and Convent to keep in repair.‡

"On the 20th of December, 29th Hen. VIII. 1537, the Prioress and Convent granted to John Dodyngton, gent. aforesaid, auditor of their accounts, to have the first advowson, nomination, and presentation of their vicarage of Eyworth, in the county of Bedford and diocese of Lincoln, for one single turn, whenever the said vicarage should by death, resignation, promotion, or in any other way, chance to be vacant, as fully and entirely as they themselves the patrons. Allowed by the Court of Augmentations on the 9th of February, 35th Hen. VIII. 1543-4.§

"On the 21st of January, 29th Hen. VIII. 1537-8, the Prioress and Convent granted to John Sewstre, gent., for good counsel, past and future, an annual pension of four mares, issuing as before, for the term of his life, in equal portions at Lady Day and Michaelmas. If in arrear for five weeks, the said John to have power to enter and distrain. Allowed, with arrears, by the Court of Augmentations on the 12th of February, 30th Hen. VIII. 1538-9.‖

---

* Conventual Leases, No. 11.   † Ministers' Accounts.
‡ Conventual Leases, No. 16.   § Orders and Decrees, xiv. f. 78.
‖ Ministers' Accounts. Orders and Decrees, x. f. 149.

"On the 16th of March, 29th Hen. VIII. 1537-8, they leased to Nicholas De la Mare, priest, one little tenement on the north side of the close or churchyard, from Lady Day following, for the term of the ensuing forty years, at a yearly rent of x s. payable at Michaelmas and Lady Day. If in arrear for half a year, the Prioress and Convent might enter and distrain. The lessors were to do all necessary repairs. If the said Nicholas died before the end of the aforesaid term, a month after his decease the lease to be void, and of no effect.*

"On the same 16th of March, 29th Hen. VIII. 1537-8, they leased a tenement to David Necton, for a term of forty years from the following Lady Day, at a yearly rent of x s., payable at Lady Day and Michaelmas in equal portions.†

"On the 20th of March, 1537-8, they granted to Thomas Percye, citizen and skinner, the renewal of a lease, which Alice Tracthall a former Prioress, had granted to Thomas Knyght, by indenture dated the 20th of March, 13th Hen. VII. 1497-8, of a tenement or 'brue hous called the Scomer vpon the Hope, sett and being in Byrchin Lane, and a plour sett on the northe syde of the hatte dore of the said tent Bruehous towardť the Strete,' &c. from Lady Day, 1547, when that lease would expire, to the end of a term of three score years, at a yearly rent of vj li. xiij s. iiij d. sterling, payable at the four terms. If in arrear for six weeks, the Prioress and Convent to enter and distrain; if for fourteen weeks to repossess. Repairs by the farmer. The lessors or their deputies might examine the premises twice in every year, to see that the farmer fulfilled his engagement.‡

"On the 28th of March, 29th Hen. VIII. 1538, they leased to Antony Bouvixi, merchant, their great messuage, with all houses, solars, cellars, gardens, &c. called Crosbyes Place, together with nine messuages belonging to the same, for a term of seventy-one years, immediately after the end and completion of a term of ninety-nine years to John Crosbye, citizen and grocer of London, viz., from the feast of the Nativity of S. John the Baptist, 1565, at a yearly rent of xj li. vj s. viij d. payable at the usual terms.§

---

* Conventual Leases, No. 12.   † Ministers' Accounts.
‡ Conventual Leases, No. 6.
§ Ibid., No. 10. Part. for grants, Antony Bouvyxe. Ministers' Accounts.

"On the 30th of March, 29th Hen. VIII. 1538, the Prioress and Convent granted to Edward Rollesley, gent., in consideration of good and faithful service, an annuity of forty shillings sterling, issuing as before, for the time of his life, payable at Lady Day and Michaelmas in equal portions. If in arrear, the said Edward might enter and distrain. The said Edward was put into possession by a payment to him of fourpence. Allowed by the Court of Augmentations, with arrears from the Dissolution, on the 26th of October, 31st Hen. VIII. 1539.*

"On the 12th of April, 29th Hen. VIII. 1538, they leased to Robert Owterede, citizen and cordwainer, two tenements outside the close, for a term of thirty years, at a rent of xlvj s. viij d. payable at the usual terms.†

"On the 17th of April, 1538, they renewed to Domenic Lomelyn a lease formerly made to him by Isabell Stampe, Prioress of S. Helen's, dated the 3rd of December, 4th Hen. VIII. 1512, of a tenement in S. Elen's, for four score and eleven years, at a yearly rent of x li. x s. sterling. If in arrear for six weeks, the Prioress and Convent to enter and distrain.‡

"On the 20th of June, 30th Hen. VIII. 1538, they leased to John Melshame a tenement in Chepesyde, in the parish of S. Matthew in Ffrydaye Strete, with shops, solars, cellars, &c., 'wherof one shoppe hath the signe of the Mylke mayde w^t tankarde on her hedde, and the other shoppe hath the signe of the Cowe,' from the Midsummer following, for a term of forty years, at a yearly rent of vj li. xiij s. iiij d. payable at the four usual terms.§

"On the 26th of June, 30th Hen. VIII. 1538, the Prioress and Convent granted to John Rollesley, gent., for good counsel past and future, an annuity of four marcs sterling, issuing as before, for the term of his life, payable in equal portions, at Lady Day and Michaelmas. If in arrear for one month, the said John might enter and distrain. Allowed, with arrears from the Dissolution, by the Court of Augmentations, on the 24th of April, 31st Hen. VIII. 1539.||

---

* Orders and Decrees, vi. f. 47 b. † Ministers' Accounts.
‡ Conventual Leases, No. 26.
§ Conventual Leases, No. 8. Ministers' Accounts.
|| Orders and Decrees, x. f. 298 b.

"On the 30th of June, 30th Hen. VIII. 1538, Mary, the Prioress and Convent gave to Henry Bowsell, gentleman, of London, a certain annuity or annual rent of ten shillings, issuing from their lands and tenements in the city of London. It was granted in reward of good counsel given previously, and to be rendered in time to come, and was to be paid in equal portions at Christmas and Midsummer. If it were unpaid for the time of six weeks, the said Henry might enter and distrain. This was allowed by the Court of Augmentations on the 28th of January, 34th Hen. VIII. 1542-3.*

"On the same day the Prioress and Convent granted to Henry Bowsfell, gent., for good counsel, &c., and certain other considerations then moving them, a certain annuity or annual rent of twenty-six shillings and eightpence sterling, issuing from their property in London and elsewhere, for the term of his life, payable yearly at Christmas and Midsummer, in equal portions. If in arrear, in part or in whole, for six weeks, the aforesaid Henry might enter and distrain. Allowed, with arrears from the Dissolution, by the Court of Augmentations, on the 17th of October, 31st Hen. VIII. 1539.†

"On the 1st of July, 30th Hen. VIII. 1538, they leased to William Shyrborne a tenement with cellars, solars, &c., outside the close, from the feast of the Nativity of S. John the Baptist in that year, for a term of thirty years, at a yearly rent of xx s. payable at the usual terms.‡

"On the 2nd of July, 30th Hen. VIII. 1538, they leased to William Shelton two tenements in the parish of S. Mary at Naxe, for a term of fourscore years from the following Michaelmas, at a yearly rent of xl s. payable at the four terms. If in arrear for a quarter of a year, the Prioress and Convent might enter and distrain. Repairs by the farmer.§

"On the 9th of July, 30th Hen. VIII. 1538, the Prioress and Convent granted to Jerome Shelton, gent., for good counsel past and future, an annuity or annual rent of four marcs sterling, issuing from their tenements in the city of London or elsewhere, for the term of his life, payable at Christmas and Midsummer, in equal portions. If in arrear for forty days, the said Jerome

---

* Orders and Decrees, xiii. f. 126 b.   † Ibid. vi. f. 114 b.
‡ Ministers' Accounts.
§ Conventual Leases, No. 7. Ministers' Accounts.

might enter and distrain. The Court of Augmentations continued this payment to the said Jerome, with arrears from the Dissolution of the House, on the 12th of February, 30th Hen. VIII. 1538-9.*

"On the same day, the Prioress and Convent granted to Roger Hall, for good and faithful service, an annuity of twenty shillings, issuing as before, for the term of his life, payable at Christmas and Midsummer. If in arrear for five weeks, the said Roger might enter and distrain. Allowed, with arrears from the Dissolution, by the Court of Augmentations, on the 19th of November, 32nd Hen. VIII. 1540.†

"On the same day, the Prioress and Convent granted to John Staverton, gent., for good counsel, &c., an annuity of four marcs sterling, issuing as before, for the term of his life, payable at Christmas and Midsummer, in equal portions. If in arrear for fourteen days, the said John might enter and distrain. Allowed, with arrears from the Dissolution, by the Court of Augmentations, on the 20th of November, 32nd Hen. VIII. 1540.‡

"On the 1st of August, 30th Hen. VIII. 1538, they leased to John Rollesley their manor of Marke, with all and singular its appurtenances, situated in the parishes of Leyton and Walcombestowe, in the county of Essex, together with all its lands, tenements, rents, services, &c., for a term of fourscore years from the next following Michaelmas, at a yearly rent of viij li. payable at Lady Day and Michaelmas in equal portions. Repairs to be done by the aforesaid farmer.§

"On the 20th of August, 30th Hen. VIII. 1538, they leased to Thomas Persey one messuage with shops, cellars, solars, &c. in the parish of S. Martin Owtewiche, for a term of sixty years, at a yearly rent of liij s. iiij d. payable at the four usual terms.||

"On the 1st of September, 30th Hen. VIII. 1538, they leased to Richard Staverton a messuage with appurtenances in the parish of S. Mary Magdalene in the Old Fishmarket, for a term of fourscore years, at a yearly rent of lxvj s. viij d.¶

"On the 10th of September, 30th Hen. VIII. 1538, they

---

* Orders and Decrees, x. f. 127.   † Ibid. viii. f. 56 b.
‡ Ibid. viii. f. 89 b.   § Conventual Leases, No. 21.   Ministers' Accounts.
|| Ministers' Accounts.   ¶ Ibid.

leased to Richard Staverton aforesaid, his executors and assigns two tenements outside the close for a term of fourscore years from the Michaelmas of the same year, at a rent of xlvj s. viij d. payable at the usual terms.*

"On the same day they leased to Richard Staverton aforesaid a tenement in the parish of S. Matthew in ffrydayestrete, for a term of fourscore years, at a yearly rent of lxvj s. viij d. payable at the four usual terms.†

"On the same day they leased to the aforesaid Richard Staverton, his executors and assigns, two tenements in the parish of S. John in Walbrooke, for a term of fourscore years, at a rent of lxxvj s. viij d. payable at the four terms.‡

"On the 1st of October, 30th Hen. VIII. 1538, the Prioress and Convent granted to John Melsham, gent., for good counsel, &c., an annuity of twenty shillings, issuing as before, for the term of his life, payable at Lady Day and Michaelmas, in equal portions. If in arrear for five weeks, the aforesaid John might enter and distrain. Allowed by the Court of Augmentations on the 22nd of November, 32nd Hen. VIII. 1540.§

"On the 4th of October, 30th Hen. VIII. 1538, they leased to Antony Bonvixi, his executors and assigns, a tenement with solars, cellars, &c., situated in a certain alley within their close, over the 'larder-house' and the 'cole-house' of the said Antony, and lately in the tenure of Julian Fraunces, for a term of fourscore years from the feast of Michaelmas in that year, at a yearly rent of x s. payable at the usual terms. Repairs were to be made by the farmer.‖

"This was the last act of the Prioress and Convent before the event which removed from them the power of entering into any similar engagements for the time to come. In less than two months afterwards the storm had fallen upon them, and all was over. The unhappy Sisters, like hundreds of others in similar establishments, were then ruthlessly expelled from their ancient home, to encounter the dangers of a world of which they had

---

* Ministers' Accounts.   † Ibid.   ‡ Ibid.
§ Orders and Decrees, viii. f. 81.
‖ Conventual Leases, No. 22. Part. for grants, Antony Bonvyxe, and Ministers' Accounts.

hitherto little or no experience. The original deed of Surrender still exists in the Record Office. There are no signatures to this document, which was forced on the sufferers against their will, already prepared before it was submitted to their acceptance, and slightly concealing, under a flimsy disguise of law, an act of the basest and most shameless despotism. The common seal of the Priory was appended; but only a fragment of it now remains. The document bears date the 25th of November, 30th Hen. VIII. 1538—not 1539, as the editors of Dugdale have stated in error.

"The names of the last Prioress and Sisters, so far as they have been recovered, were Mary Rollesley, Prioress, and Margaret Sampson, Elizabeth Graye, Katherine Glassappe, Joan Pamplyn, Elionor Hanham, and Ann Alleyne, Sisters. The latter were surviving in 1556. It is probable that half were by that time dead. But there is no certain account of the number who witnessed the destruction of their House.

"It is probable that the last named Sister was daughter of the John Aleyn and Agnes his wife to whom the Prioress and Convent, on the 19th of July, 12th Hen. VIII. 1520, leased a tenement in the parish of S. Olave by London Bridge, called the 'Sonne,' alias the 'Salutacyon,' and a messuage adjacent to the same, for the term of the life of the survivor, at a yearly rent of six pounds thirteen shillings and fourpence.* It is surmised that she was related also to the famous Bishopsgate benefactor, the munificent Edward Alleyne, born in the parish of S. Botolph, September 1st, 1566, and founder of Dulwich College in 1619 (?).

"Roger Hall, already mentioned, was janitor of the west gate of the close, and with Alice his wife was at the Dissolution of the Priory in possession of a house worth 10s. a year.†

"At the time of the Suppression the Prioress received a gratuity of xxx li. and the grant of an annual pension of x li. ;‡ and four annuities, or 'perpetual pensions,' in behalf of the dissolved House, amounting yearly to the sum of cxij s. ij d. ob. were paid by the Government to 'the Deane and Chapiter of Pawles' in the 34th, 35th, 36th, 37th, and 38th years of Hen. VIII.§

---

* Ministers' Accounts. † Ibid.
‡ Misc. Books, Off. Aug. vol. 245, n. 228.
§ Misc. Books, Off. Aug. vols. 248, 249, 250, 256, 262.

"In the year 1556 the annuities and pensions paid to the former officers and inmates of the Priory were as follows:—

S. HELEN'S LATE PRIORY.

Annuities.

Edward Rowlesley	xl s.	
John Rowlesley	liij s.	iij d
Richard Berde	xl s.	
John Melsham	xx s.	

Pensions.

Margaret Sampson	liij s.	iiij d.
Elizabeth Graye	liij s.	iiij d.
Katherine Glassappe	liij s.	iiij d.
Joan Pamplyn	lxvj s.	viij d.
Elionor Hanham	liij s.	iiij d.
Ann Aleyne	liij s.	iiij d.*

"There were two Chantries† in the Church of S. Helen's, the priests of which received annual stipends from the Priory. These incumbents at the time of the 'Valor,' in 1536, were

David Netley, B. V. M.	viij li.
Thomas Criche, Holy Ghost	vij li.

"In the Ministers' Accounts, 31-32 Hen. VIII. we find

Nicholas de la Mer, B. V. M. founded for the soul of Adam Fraunces	viij li.
Thomas Ryson, Holy Ghost, founded for the soul of Adam Fraunces,	vij li.
Thomas Wynestaneley, Nuns' chaplain .	vj li. xiij s. iiij d.

"In the Certificate of Chauntries and Fraternities, 2nd Edward VI. the names of the last incumbents are thus given, with their previous stipends and post-Dissolution pensions:—

S. Ellens.

Thomas Wynston, vj li. xiij s. iiij d.	pension	c s.
Thomas Robson vij li.	,,	c s.

---

* Cardinal Pole's Pension Book, f. iii.

† These Chantries have lately been discovered, and restored, for a description of which, see p. 41. The will of Adam Fraunces is inserted in the Appendix.

" In the Particulars for the sale of the Chantry Lands it is stated that certain property in S. Helen's of this nature was sold on the 24th of December, 3 Edward VI. 1549, and on the 26th of January, 3 Edward VI. 1549-50, to John Roulande, page of the King's wardrobe, and was 'past in the names of John Dodington and William Warde, as parcel of the sum of Mcclxxv li. iiij s. viij d.'*

" Lastly, from Cardinal Pole's Pension Book we learn that the priests before mentioned were still living in 1556.

CHANTRIES IN THE CHURCH OF S. HELEN'S.

Pensions.

Thomas Robson, lately incumbent there . .	c s.
Thomas Wynstanley, lately incumbent there .	c s.†

" Of the scene of these transactions, not a stone remains to tell of the House and its glories. A view of the place as it existed at the close of the last century, which is furnished by Wilkinson in his *Lond. Illust.*, represents the ruins of edifices whose main portions and features are of the Early English period, and which were probably coeval with the foundation of the Priory. These he calls the 'Remains of the Fratry.' Having had the advantage of a personal examination of these beautiful memorials, he says : 'The door leading from the cloister to the fratry, which the writer of this well remembers to have seen at the late demolition of it, was particularly elegant, the mouldings of the upper part being filled with roses of stone painted scarlet and gilt ; the windows of the fratry itself also, which were nearly lancet-shaped, were extremely beautiful.' He also gives two views of the beautiful 'crypt,' and one of the hall above it ; the former of which is in the Early English style, while the latter has ornamental additions of post-Dissoultion times. It appears by his plan that there were at least two 'crypts,' one under the hall, and another to the south, under what would be called the withdrawing room. It is the former which is represented in his engravings.

" Of contemporary descriptions," Mr. Hugo remarks, " that contained in the 'Valor' simply makes mention of the 'scite of the Priory, with the court-yards and little gardens, with divers houses

---

* Parts. for Sale of Chantries, vol. i. p. 270 b.
† Cardinal Pole's Pension Book, f. iiii.

situated within the precinct.' And the Ministers' Accounts are similarly meagre. A few particulars, already given from several of the leases, necessarily refer to the adjoining premises rather than to the Priory itself. Stow, Howel, and others furnish us with nothing to supply the deficiency. Truly valuable, therefore, and by far the most interesting description of the House with which I am acquainted, is the following Survey of the King's Officers, preliminary to the disposal of the property. It is a picture of the place as the Nuns left it, and before the changes which soon afterwards ensued:—

"'The late Priorye of Saint Elenes within the Citye of London. The View and Surveye ther taken the xxist daye of June, in the xxxiij Yeare of the raigne of our Soveraigne Lord Kinge Henrye the viijth, by Thomas Mildmay, one of the King's Auditors thereunto assigned. That is to saye,

"'The Parisshe of Saint Elenes, within the Citie of London, and the Scite of the late Priory therin.

"'Fyrste, the cheaf entre or cominge in to the same late Priory ys in and by the street gate lyying in the pishe of St Elenes, in Bysshopsgate Streat, which leadeth to a little cowrte next adioyning to the same gate, havinge chambers, howses, and buyldinges, environinge the same, out of wch cowrte there is an entre leadinge to an inner cowrte, wch on the North side is also likewise environed wth edificyons and buyldings, called the Stewardes lodging, with a Countinge house apperteninge to the same. Item, next to the same cowrte ther ys a faire Kechinge, withe a pastery house, larder houses, and other howses of office, apperteninge to the same; and at the Est ende of the same Kechyn and entre leadinge to the same hall, wth a litle plor adioyning, having under the same hall and plor sondrie howses of office, next adioyning to the Cloyster ther, and one howse called the Covent plor. Item, iij fair Chambers adioyninge to the hall, whearof the one over the entree leadinge to the cloyster, thother over the Buttree, and the third over the larder. Item, from the said entre by the hall, to the Cloyster, wch cloyster yet remaneth holly leaded, and at the North side of the same cloyster a fare long howse called the Fratree. Item, at thest end of the same Cloyster, a lodginge called the Suppryors lodging, wth a litle gardin lieng to the same. And by the same lodginge a pare of staires leading to the Dortor, at the

Southend whearof ther is a litle hows, wherein the Evidence of the said hows nowe dou remayne, wth all howses and lodginges vnder the same Dorter. Item, at the Westende of the same cloyster, a done leadinge in to the nuñes late Quire, extending from the dore out of the churche yarde unto the lampe or pticyon deviding the priorye from the pisshe, wch is holly leaded. Item, at thest ende of the said cloyster, an entre leading to a little Garden, and out of the same littell garden to a faire garden called the Covent Garden, cōteninge by estimacū half an acre. And, at the Northend of the said garden, a dore leading to another garden called the Kechin garden; and at the Westende of the same ther is a Dove-howsshe; and in the same garden a dore to a faire Woodyerd, wth howses, pticōns, and gardens, wth in the same Woodyerd a tenement, wth a garden, a stable, and other thapptances to the same belonginge, called Elizabeth Hawtes lodginge. All which p̃misses ben rated, extentyd, and valued, The Kings highnesse to be discharged of the repacōns, of the yerely value of

vj li. xiij s. iiij d.

"'Item, one Tenement their in, in the hold of Willm. Baker, by the yeare, xx s.

"'Item, one other Tenement, in the hold of Jane Julian, by the yeare, xiij s. iiij d.

"'Item, one other Tenement ther, in the hold of Edmūde Brewer, by the yeare, xiij s. iiij d.

"'Item, one other Tenement ther, in the hold of Eye Sturdye, by the yeare, xiij s. iiij d.

"'Item, one other Tenement ther, in the hold of Lanclott Harryson, by the yeare, xiij s. iiij d.

viij li. xiij s. iiij d.
Sm^a x li. vj s. viij d.

Ex^m p me Thomam Mildmaie, Auditor.'*

"The House was evidently a large and goodly collection of edifices. You entered from Bishopsgate Street by a gateway into a court surrounded by the more humble buildings of the community, and from thence into an inner court which contained some of the more important offices, the steward's lodging and

---

* Archæol. xvi. 29.   Malcolm's Lond. Red. iii. 550, 551.

counting-house, the kitchen, pastry-house, larder, and other apartments, the entrance to the hall and an adjoining parlour, with offices below them, as well as that to the cloister and the Convent parlour. The entrance to the cloister, the buttery, and larder had

each an elegant chamber above them adjoining the hall. Next came the Cloister, on the north of which was a long and goodly building, called the Fratry, and on the east the lodging of the Sub-prioress with its garden. Adjoining this a flight of stairs led to the dormitory, south of which was a small house, in which were deposited the various leases and other legal documents connected with the conventual property. West of the cloister a door led to the Nuns' church. An entry on the east side, by the Sub-prioress's lodging and the dormitory, introduced you to a little garden, and thence to the fair pleasure-garden of the house. At the north end of this a door led to the kitchen-garden, with a dove-house at its western end; and a further door communicated with a capacious wood yard, which embraced various enclosures, tenements, gardens, a stable, and other appurtenances. Such was the home of the Nuns of S. Helen's.

"The north aisle of the Church of S. Helen's was 'the Nunnes Quire,' and was divided, by a screen from pier to pier of the arcade, from the part appropriated to the parish. One of the fastenings, or a piece of iron popularly considered so to be, until the restoration of 1867, was to be seen occupying its original position on the east side of one of the piers. In the north wall of this aisle is a curious hagioscope, which at first sight looks like an altar-tomb. Its base is ornamented with panels, and through these, which although now filled up behind, were pierced with oblique openings, an altar at the east end of the same aisle might have been seen from the so-called 'crypt,' which, I believe, was used by the nuns as a cloister."

With reference to the dispersion of the spoil, so far as regards the site of the house, and of the various adjoining tenements in and about the close, Mr. Hugo has supplied the following highly important information in his lecture above referred to:*—

"On the 21st of April, 30th Hen. VIII. 1539, the King granted to Balthazar Gwercy, of the city of London, surgeon, and Joan his wife, certain tenements, gardens, &c. in the parishes of S. Mary at Nax and S. Andrew Undershafte in consideration of £71 10s. the property to be held of the King in chief by the service of a twentieth part of one knight's fee, and a yearly rent of xxvj s. viij d. payable at Michaelmas.†

"On the 3rd of October, 31st Hen. VIII. 1539, the King granted to Guy Crafford, Esq. and Joan his wife, in consideration of the sum of £54, a messuage or tenement, with cellars, solars, stables, gardens, &c., situated in the parish of S. Helen's, and within the close of the late Priory, formerly in the tenure of Thomas Benolt, then in that of Sir Arthur Darcy, knt. and lastly in that of the aforesaid Guy. Also another messuage adjoining the same on the west, and lately in the tenure of George Taylour, gent. Both were among the possessions of the late Priory, and were to be held from Lady Day last past by the service of a twentieth part of one knight's fee, and a yearly rent of six shillings and eight pence by name of tithe payable at Michaelmas. The grant was made without fine great or small, and was dated, witness the King at Westminster, on the day aforesaid.‡

"On the 3rd of March, 31st Hen. VIII. 1539-40, the King granted to William Crane, Esq. and Margaret his wife, and their heirs, ten tenements, within the close and circuit of the late Priory of S. Helen's, then in the tenure of John Parker, Guy

---
* See p. 12.
† Ministers' Accounts. Pat. 30th Hen. VIII. p. 8, mm. 8 (20), 7 (21).
‡ Pat. 31st Hen. VIII. p. 4, m. (35) 20. Orig. 31st Hen. VIII. p. 1, r. lv.

Crayford, Hugh Vaughan, Edward Brysseley, Margaret Dalton, John Barnard, Richard Herman, John Harrope, and Adrian Bryscombe; three chambers, in the tenure of William Damaral, and Emma Lawe, within the close; and six chambers in the tenure of Richard Atkyns, Alice Paule, Reginald Deane, Elizabeth Watson, and the aforesaid William, situated in a certain alley within the close; a tenement in the tenure of John Parker within the close, in the parish of S. Andrew Undershaft; and another tenement in the tenure of the said William within the close, all belonging to the said late Priory, and leased to John Rollesley. The property was to be held by the service of a twentieth part of one knight's fee, and a yearly rent of thirty-four shillings and eightpence. The grant is dated at Westminster on the day above mentioned.*

"Then came the grant of the site of the House itself.

"On the 29th of March, 33rd Hen. VIII. 1542, the King granted to Sir Richard Williams, knt., alias Crumwell, in exchange for the manors of Brampton and Hemyngford Grey, in the county of Huntingdon, and for the sum of 731l. 0s. 7½d. sterling, various lands in the counties of Glamorgan, Herts, Huntingdon, Bedford, Norfolk, &c. Also the whole of the site, sept, circuit, and precinct of the late Priory of S. Helen's the church vulgarly called 'the Nonnes Churche of Seynt Helyns,' and all and singular messuages, houses, buildings, &c. &c., belonging to the said site. Also certain messuages in the tenure or occupation of William Baker, Jane Julyan, Edmund Brewer, Guy Sturdye, and Lancelot Harrison, or their assigns. Added to this horrible amount of sacrilege, other lands in the counties of Devon, Herts, Huntingdon, and others, lately belonging to the dissolved monasteries of Ramsey, Nethe, S. Alban's, Huntingdon, Forde, Yermouth, &c. The property was to be held in chief, by the service of a tenth part of one knight's fee and the payment of various yearly rents for the different portions, that for the S. Helen's property amounting to thirty-nine shillings and nine pence farthing sterling, for all services and demands. The grant bears date, witness the King, at Westminster, on the day above mentioned.†

---

* Pat. 31 Hen. VIII. p. 7, m. 1 (32). Orig. 31st Hen. VIII. p. 2, r. ccv.

† Pat. 33 Hen. VIII. p. 6, mm. 37 (18)—34 (19). Orig. 33rd Hen. VIII. p. 3, r. xxi.

"On the 9th September, 34th Henry VIII. 1542, the King granted to Antony Bonvixi, merchant, in return for the sum of 207*l*. 18*s*. 4*d*. together with certain property in Essex, the reversion of Crosbyes Place, and all solars, cellars, gardens, lanes, messuages, tenements, void pieces of ground, and all other appurtenances thereunto belonging. It had been already leased to him, as we have seen, by indenture dated 28th March, 29th Hen. VIII. 1538. Also various curtilages in the parish of S. Mary at Naxe, leased to the same on the 4th October, 30th Hen. VIII. 1538. Crosbyes Place with appurtenances was valued at the clear yearly sum of 11*l*. 16*s*. 8*d*. and the property in the adjoining parish at that of 12*s*. The former was to held in chief, by the service of a fortieth part of one knight's fee and the payment of a yearly rent of twenty-three shillings and eight pence of lawful money of England payable at Michaelmas by name of tithe. The latter also in chief, by the service of a hundredth part of one knight's fee, and a similar rent of 15*d*. payable at Michaelmas. The grant was dated, witness the King, at Westminster, the 9th December, 1542.*

"On the 16th July, 35th Hen. VIII. 1543, the King granted to Roland Goodman, citizen of London, for 146*l*. 0*s*. 6*d*., the property formerly leased to him, a tenement called 'le Shedd,' lately in the tenure of John Newton, with a garden and three closes of land, in the parish of S. Botolph without Bishopsgate, and belonging to the Priory. Property belonging to other houses accompanied the aforesaid. That of S. Helen's was to be held in chief by the service of a hundredth part of one knight's fee and a yearly rent of five shillings and four pence. The grant was dated, witness the King, at Terling, on the day before named.†
The original instrument is still preserved among the Harleian Charters, a large sheet of parchment, with a pen and ink miniature of the royal dealer in the upper left-hand corner, and

---

* Pat. 34 Hen. VIII. p. 1, mm. 14 (13)—12 (15). Orig. 34th Hen. VIII. p. 1, r. xvi.

† Pat. 35 Hen. VIII. p. 9, mm. 14 (26), 13 (27). Orig. 35th Hen. VIII. p. 4, r. iiij xv.

RUINS OF "ST. HELEN'S NUNNERY," A.D. 1799.

a tolerable impression of the Great Seal appendant at the foot.*

"On the 24th September, 36th Henry VIII. 1544, the King granted to Roger Higham and William Grene, among other possessions of various London houses, divers tenements in the parish of S. Helen's lately in the tenure of William Shirborne, Robert Owtred, William Plumpton, Richard Kyrton, William Hunte 'wever,' John Dymmocke, and Richard Staverton, with other tenements in the parish of S. Ethelburga and elsewhere, belonging to the late Priory. The annual value of these amounted to the sum of 19*l.* 12*s.* 8*d.* and they were to be held in free burgage for all services and demands. The grant was dated, witness Katherine, Queen of England, and General Ruler of the same, at Westminster on the day named above.†

"The more distant portions of the possessions were granted to Henry Lord Audley, William Gurle, Sir Martin Bowes, Christopher Campion, John Rollesley, Richard Tate, John Pope, Robert Curson, John Gates, William Bodye, John Small, Thomas Goodwyn, Dominic Lomelyn, Robert Harrys, Richard Taverner and others."

At the dissolution of religious houses the priory was surrendered (30 Hen. VIII.), and, according to the foregoing declaration, was valued according to Speed at 376*l.* 6*s.*; Dugdale gives the valuation at 314*l.* 2*s.* 6*d.*

After the suppression, King Henry VIII.,‡ in the 33rd year of his reign, gave the site of the priory and its church (called the Nuns' Church) § to Richard Williams, alias Cromwell, and the whole church, the partition betwixt the Nuns' Church and the Parish Church being taken down, now remaineth to the parish.‖ It is a Gothic structure of the lighter kind, consisting of a plain body with large windows. The steeple was not built until the year 1669, and is wrought with rustic at the corners, with a turret and dome. It appears, according to Stow, that Sir Thomas Gresham

---

* Harl. Cart. 51 H. 21.
† Part. for Grants, William Grene. Pat. 36 Hen. VIII. p. 14, mm. 37 (3)—34 (6). Orig. 36 Hen. VIII. p. 5, r. i.
‡ Newcourt's Repert. Eccles. Lond. 1708, vol. ii. p. 314.
§ Coll. Magist. Grimes. ‖ Stow's Survey, Ed. 1754, vol. i. p. 430.

had promised to build a steeple, in recompense for the ground occupied by the erection of his monument in the Church; but by an oversight, it is presumed, in his will, no provision was made for that purpose.

The Nun's Hall, and other houses thereto appertaining, were, after the dissolution, purchased by the Leathersellers' Company— a society incorporated by letters patent (22 Hen. VI., anno 1442) by the name of the Wardens and Society of the Mystery or Art of Leathersellers of the City of London—who converted the Nuns' Hall into a common hall, for the purpose of holding their meetings, and it continued in such use until it was demolished, with the other remnants of the old Priory, in 1799, to make way for the present St. Helen's Place.

The general view given of the ruins of this ancient Priory, as represented in the prospect delineated S.E., reminds us rather of some romantic fragment of antiquity to be found in distant counties, than of one situated in the very centre of the populous city of London. The drawing was made on the spot in 1799.

The Nuns' dining-hall or refectory, a view of which is represented over that of the two crypts at the south end, was formed of the best joiner's and plasterer's work in the kingdom; the screen was most elegantly worked, having six columns of the Ionic order, richly adorned; and the curiously fret-worked ceiling, panelled wainscot, richly-worked window abutments, Gothic recesses, and grand stone-work arched entrance, rendered the whole, when perfect, a scene truly striking, and sublimely grand. Enough is preserved in the view of the great south window to ascertain its immense magnitude; and, from the number of the other windows that ornamented this apartment, sufficient light must have been admitted to dispel the gloom which pervades most ancient buildings.

The two crypts under the great hall communicating with each other, were probably in occasional use by the Nuns for devotional exercise and meditation. The view of the second crypt, looking from the south, was taken immediately after the demolition of the hall and other buildings above, and in the same plate are represented specimens of the architecture of the building, which is Norman. The parts delineated are the piscina on the west side of the double

THE CRYPT OF "ST. HELEN'S NUNNERY," DESTROYED A.D. 1799.

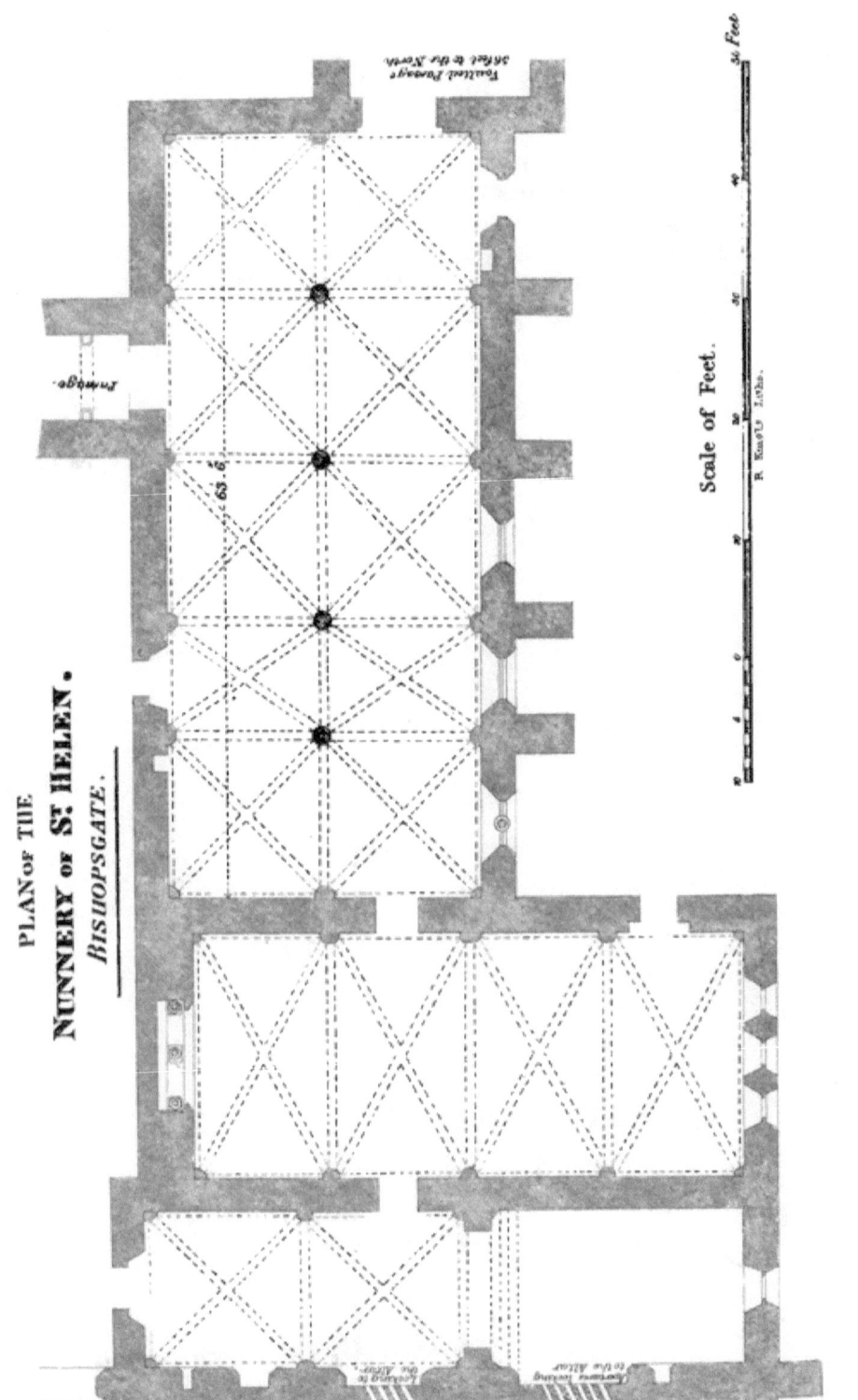

range of vaulting, the springer to the arched head of the passage, the arched head of the passage on the west side of the double range of vaulting, elevation of the base, and plan of one of the columns and springers which support the arched roof. In the plan of the nunnery are shown the entrances to the crypts by the vaulted passages, one of which was fifty-six feet in extent, looking to the north. It will also be observed that the crypt to the north was considerably larger than that at the southern end of the building.*

---

* Malcolm's Lond. Rediviv., vol. iii. p. 554.

CHAPTER II.

ST. HELEN'S CHURCH.

THERE are but few of the ancient structures in London that convey any idea of their former solemnity. S. Helen's is an exception.* When entering, the tall and graceful Gothic impresses the beholder with veneration for past times, heightened by the altar tombs and recumbent figures in the chancel. Some of the most remote memorials are gone, and others mutilated, but the general effect is remarkably striking.

As to the exterior, the west front has been covered with cement. It presents, therefore, but inconsiderable features of the original architecture. The angles at each end have been strengthened by double buttresses, of which the northern ones are destroyed, and the front is divided, by a single buttress in the centre, into two portions, in each of which is a window of five lights, under a low pointed arch. The mullions have arched heads, but are destitute of cuspings. Beneath each window was formerly a doorway; the northernmost has been walled up; the southern still remains, and is the principal entrance to the Church; it is covered with a pent-house, and the original workmanship is hidden by a frontispiece of carved woodwork. On a panel above the arch is the following inscription:—

"Worship the Lord in the beauty of holiness."

The original finish of the elevation has been destroyed, and battlements of a bad style substituted. Above the centre rises a mean turret covered with cement, and finished with a cupola. The south side of the Church contains three windows of three lights each; the mullions resemble those of the west front, and have equally suffered from the hands of repairers. A single buttress remains between two of the windows, and below the second from the

---

* It is one amongst the few churches which escaped destruction at the Great Fire of London, A.D. 1666.

WEST FRONT, ST. HELEN'S, A.D. 1808.

west is a low doorway with a semicircular arch enclosed in a heavy Doric frontispiece with the date of its erection, 1633.* This front, like the west, is covered with cement, and finished with a modern embattled parapet. The northern side has four windows of the same character and description as the others. The eastern end of the Church has four windows, all of which have been restored and filled with stained glass.† To understand the peculiar arrangement of this Church it should be borne in mind that the portion northward of the arches running along the centre was formerly the Nuns' Choir. This was added to the Parish Church for the use of the inmates of the adjoining Convent, probably about the year 1216, and was separated from it by a continuous screen until the dissolution of the Convent at the Reformation, when this screen was taken down, and the whole space thrown into the Parish Church. To the south of the nave is a transept and two chapels, the northern dedicated to the Holy Ghost, and the southernmost to the Virgin.

The Parish Church must have been in existence previously to the year 1010, as appears from a circumstance recorded, that in this year the remains of King Edmund the Martyr were removed from St. Edmundsbury, and deposited herein for three years, until the depredations by the Danes had ceased. The earliest portions now remaining are of the 13th century. Of this date are the lancet windows of the transept, now blocked up, the staircase door in the south-east corner, the second arch north of the chancel, an ambry under the pulpit, the doorway which led into the Convent on the north side of the Nuns' Choir, with the two openings formerly guarded with gratings, and a lancet window at the west end of the same side. At this date the floor of the Church must have been much lower than at present, and it was raised at each alteration of the Church until it became four feet higher than the original level. This was discovered at the restoration of the Church (1865-8), and is still visible at the north side, and at the staircase of the transept. Entering the Church by the western doorway, an oak porch internally covering the entrance is the first

---

* All these windows were repaired during the restoration of 1865-8, and filled with stained glass.

† Restoration 1865-8. For subjects and donors, see Appendix.

object of attention. It is enriched with Corinthian pilasters and a profusion of carving,* with this inscription—

> "This is none other than the howse of God.
> This is the gate of Heaven."

Against the entrance on the north side of the parochial nave is the poor box, supported on a terminal figure, representing a beggar soliciting alms. The southern doorway has, internally, a smaller porch, of Elizabethan work, the pilasters of the Ionic order. The shells and Cherubim, which, with the pediment, were removed from the east end of the Church, present very early specimens of Italian architecture in this country. At a small distance northward of the western doorway may be seen the staircase, which has received the finish of the mean bell turret. The portion which is within the church is constructed of wood, in imitation of rustic work, and shows in height successively three orders of architecture in pilasters, and each story has an oval window.

The arcade which divides the church lengthwise into two portions, displays two different styles of architecture; it contains in all six arches, the first four from the west end rest on clustered columns, with four centred Tudor arches of a date between the early-pointed arch, the second from the east of the arcade, and the flat-pointed ones of the windows; they were probably erected in the fifteenth century,† the two easternmost arches being of different altitudes. To the internal jambs of the higher arch are attached two semi-octangular columns which support a chamfered equilateral arch of considerable elevation, but not equal in height to the others already described. The extreme eastern arch only differs from the westernmost in respect of altitude, springing considerably lower, and resting on one side on a half-round column—the most conspicuous remains of the earliest Church (erected A.D. 1210). The northern aisle is lighted at the east end by a window of five lights, circumscribed by a fairly-proportioned pointed arch, the tracery of which, until the restoration of 1865-8, was almost entirely destroyed. The form of the arch and other remains showed that this window was the workmanship of the

---

* The work of Inigo Jones, during the restoration of 1633.
† After the death of Sir John Crosby, 1475.

fourteenth century, a period when the pointed style was in the highest state of perfection. The east end of the nave had a window of seven lights; the arch was of the low pointed form like the generality of those before described, and with the rest of the windows of this Church, had been despoiled of its tracery.* The transept is separated from the body of the Church by a handsome low pointed arch of a very considerable span. On its east side are also two pointed Tudor arches, springing from clustered columns, and opening into the chapels of the Holy Ghost and Virgin Mary. In the southeast angle is a door leading to a winding stair of early work. The remainder of this side of the transept, and the south and western walls are plain, with only one window,† opened a few years since, but without any ornament. In the south wall this window was ornamented originally with tasteful mullions and tracery, which, at some former period, had been walled up, and in 1807 it was completely destroyed. It was, however, very imperfectly utilized a few years since. The small chapels eastward of the transept are separated from it by the arches, just noticed, and from the Church by a similar arch. They are lighted by two windows of three lights each in the eastern wall. In the eastern wall are several small niches and piscinas, all of which, as well as the roof, were restored in 1874, by the munificence of the Merchant Taylors' Company. From the style of architecture of these chapels and the adjoining transept, it may be satisfactorily concluded that these portions were erected in the fourteenth century. As now restored, they exhibit beautiful specimens of pointed Gothic, *temp.* Henry VII., and are probably a restoration of the original work, dating back to *temp.* Edward III.

The Vestry, which was most probably of the time of James I., had been built within the Lady chapel, which was cruelly mutilated for that purpose. This has been entirely removed, and the beauty of

---

* Each of these windows was discovered to be in such a ruinous condition at the restoration of 1865-8, that they had to be replaced with new work, and were fitted with stained glass, the former by the Gresham Committee in memory of Sir Thomas Gresham, and the latter by Messrs. Kirman and Stewart Hodgson, in memory of their parents, whose remains are interred within the Church.

† There were originally three lancet windows on the south side and two on the west; one is still to be traced, although not available for use.

the two chapels brought out in its original perfection. Within the Lady chapel, upon a bracket, there is a small sitting statue of a female in the act of reading from a book which rests on her knee, and is supported by her right hand. It is evidently a Roman Sibyl, although it has been said to represent the Patron Saint of the Church. It is reported that large sums of money on several occasions have been offered for it. It has been thoroughly cleansed of numerous coats of black paint, and proves to be of alabaster, of rare Italian workmanship, previously to the time of Michael Angelo, and very little injured. How it came into the possession of the parish cannot be ascertained, no record having been ever discovered. The ceiling of the Church is composed of flat arched beams, resting on corbels, to which are attached shields, most of which are greatly mutilated. The spaces between the beams, which were originally of brown oak, are plastered; and, together with the beams, were, until 1865-8, whitewashed, and repaired with plaster of Paris! They were then carefully restored. The two compartments over the eastern end are painted with clouds, and an angelic choir—probably of the date of the porches, A.D. 1663. The roof of the northern aisle, or Nuns' quire, was thoroughly renewed, agreeably with the general characteristics of the building in 1865. At this restoration two windows—one of two lights, and the other deeply indented in the wall—were discovered. They have been restored, and filled with stained glass. The smaller is, doubtless, one of the most ancient features of the building existing before the demolition of the convent—in the remaining walls of which three most unsuitable windows were pierced, possibly under the direction of Inigo Jones, during the restoration of 1633. In the northern wall were likewise discovered the entrance doorway to the cloister and dormitory of the convent, with portions of the stone steps remaining uninjured. At this point the three levels of the floor may be now distinctly traced.

On the same side of the Church the Nuns' Grate is still existing. Its general appearance is that of an altar tomb, but more lofty. The base of the square pedestal is adorned with upright open niches, and the canopy, which is a low pointed arch, has its soffit richly panelled. The whole is surmounted by an embattlement, the frieze richly sculptured. At the angles of the cornice are two shields, having arms, but no longer discernible, and the upper member of the cornice has a row of conventional strawberry leaves set upright upon it.

Although the Church is not remarkable for either magnitude or architectural beauty, it will be gathered from the preceding description that it contains specimens of almost every variation of the pointed style, from the commencement of the thirteenth century to the last declension of its use, when it yielded to the newly-imported architecture of Italy, one of the earliest specimens of which is also to be seen in the woodwork of this building. The Church was until 1865–8 divided by a screen, erected in 1744, which crossed it at the second pillar from the west end, making a small ante-chapel. That screen was partially surmounted by a gallery, on which the organ was placed. This unsightly obstruction was then demolished, and the organ removed into the south transept. The remainder of the Church eastward of this screen was pewed and appropriated to the use of the parishioners, but these were at the same time cleared away, open oak benches being substituted in their room. A quaint piece of carved work, which had been set up to sustain the Lord Mayor's sword and mace, was removed to the pillar dividing the choir from the chapel of the Holy Ghost at the same time. It consists of two twisted Corinthian columns, supporting an entablature highly enriched, and an attic panel. The shafts of the columns are set off with a wreath of foliage running round them. On the frieze are the following arms. Ar. a cross, Raguly. Gu. and a dexter canton. Ermine—the arms of Sir John Lawrence, Lord Mayor, 1665. In the attic is the City Arms, and the whole structure is crowned with the arms of Charles II., supported by two gilt angels, and surmounted with the royal crown. On the south side of the Church is the pulpit, an elaborate piece of carving of the seventeenth century, with a large sounding-board,* supposed to

---

* Some of the windows and other details were found to be so dilapidated that it is difficult to assign a date to them. This applies particularly to the east window of the Nuns' choir, and of the chapels and south window of the transept, which have all been recently restored, as well as to the choir seats which, until the late repairs, were placed against the north wall. They belonged probably to the fourteenth century. At his death in 1475, Sir John Crosby bequeathed to the Parish the sum of five hundred marks for the repair of the Church, and it must have been almost rebuilt soon after that date, for to this

have been designed by Inigo Jones. There is also an elaborate rest for the insignia of the Lord Mayor in wrought iron, with the Royal, the Mercers, and another Company's arms emblazoned.

The woodwork of the Church is of various degrees of antiquity. Within the chancel a series of antique stalls, but without Misereres, are now placed for the choir. These stalls had been appropriated to the poor of the parish, on the northern side of the Nuns' quire; they were in all probability formerly the Nuns' seats. In construction they are very simple, and without ornaments, being merely separated by sweeping elbows, and are without canopies. From the same side of the Church, several pews, which show the workmanship of the early part of the seventeenth century, were removed, and arranged so as to form desks for the minister and choir. The altar screen of the Wren period, which was adorned with two Corinthian columns and two Antæ, sustaining an entablature and cornice, being totally out of character with the architecture of the Church, and thoroughly rotten, was replaced by a neat stone *reredos*. The centre of the cornice, consisting of two scrolls disposed pedimentally at the side of the royal arms (probably those of Charles I.), and which are supported by angels recumbent upon the scrolls, was removed to the south entrance door in 1865.*

In the several windows of the Church, previously to 1868, were many shields of arms in stained glass; most of these were reglazed elsewhere and utilized. Those in the window above the communion table were introduced into the window of the chapel of the Holy Ghost, and skilfully blended with modern stained glass. They

---

period belong the arches on the north side of the nave, and those east of the transept. The east window of the chancel, and the south windows of the Lady chapel, the roofs of the nave and of the Nuns' choir are probably of this period, as well as the doorway of stairs leading to the convent. Of the sixteenth century are the eastern sepulchre and the niches of the chapels, those windows of the Church which are not already noticed, and the arch over the monument of Sir William Pickering, who died 1574. In the year 1631, the Church having again fallen into decay, was repaired at considerable expense, and the works completed in 1663; the south porch under the superintendence of Inigo Jones. The tiles discovered in 1865-8 were reproduced by Messrs Minton, and used for paving the chancel, and are not only singular but unique, the subject of a portion of them being a double-headed eagle, with evident reference to Constantine the Great.

* See p. 40.

consist of eight coats, viz.: 1. the City Arms; 2. the Grocers' Company; 3. Sir John Crosbie; 4. the Leathersellers' Company; 5. the Merchants' Mark; 6. Lady Crosby; 7. Sir John and Lady Crosbie's impaled together; 8. Barry nebulle, Az. and Ar. a Chief of the last, supposed to be the arms of Sir Ralph Astry, Lord Mayor in 1493, in which case the Chief should be Gules, and charged with three bezants—the former colour has probably faded in this instance, as it has done in other shields in the present Church. The whole of these coats of arms—excepting those of the Leathersellers' Company, which are more modern—are enclosed in ornamental quatrefoils. The first window of the north aisle has four shields, held by angels. The arms are those of the City, the Mercers' Company, Sir Thomas Gresham's, and the family of Chicheley.

CHAPTER III.

TITHES AND IMPROPRIETORS OF ST. HELEN'S.

"Among the early Christians the payment of tithes was regarded as a matter of conscience, and no laws were passed for its enforcement until the Council of Macon, Oct. 23, A.D. 585." In Britain, "the custom of devoting a tenth part of all property to the service of the clergy is mentioned in the Canons of Egbert, Archbishop of York in A.D. 750, and in the Ordinance of the Council of Celchyth in A.D. 787.* In A.D. 794, Offa, King of Mercia, endowed the Church with tithes of all his kingdom, and Charlemagne made several laws regulating their payment about A.D. 800." The whole tithe system appears to have been "sanctioned and amended by the General Lateran Council in A.D. 1215." The order of Roger Niger, Bishop of London, in 1228, was "that the citizens should pay of every pound's rent by the year, of all houses, shops, &c., the sum of 3s. 4d., as time out of mind had been paid."†

"In the thirty-seventh year of Henry VIII., the sum of two shillings and ninepence in the pound was agreed to be paid by the citizens of London to the clergy. This was a great diminution from what had been before; but so many were the evasions made, that the clergy, in the reign of James, had been obliged to have recourse to the Exchequer, by which court it was decided that this tithe of the houses justly belonged to the benefice. But, with the rise of Puritanism, the opposition became great and almost insurmountable. The clergy, reduced to poverty, declared that they had no means to discover the true value of their rents. The case, at first submitted to the King (Charles I.), was by him referred to the Archbishop (Laud), and the other members of

---

* See Townsend's Manual of Dates, p. 974. Ed. Lond. 1874.
† Hook's Lives of the Archbishops of Canterbury, vol. vi., New Series, pp. 257-8.

the council, and when Bishop Juxon became Lord Treasurer, the condition of the clergy was certainly improved. No doubt the Archbishop would have carried the improvement further had not the troubles of the times increased upon him. His attempt thus to benefit the clergy was one of the crimes laid to his charge at his trial."* Dr. Hook says, "the 25th year of Henry VIII.," but this is an error, as the Act itself, as set out in the Appendix, testifies.

In the year 1288 Pope Nicholas IV. granted the tenths to King Edward I. for six years, towards defraying the expense of an expedition to the Holy Land, and that they might be collected at their full value, a taxation by the King's precept was begun in that year, and finished as to the province of Canterbury in 1291, and as to that of York in the following year. This taxation is a most important record, because all the taxes, as well to our Kings as the Popes, were regulated by it, until the survey made 26th Henry VIII., and because the statutes of colleges, which were founded before the Reformation, are also interpreted by this criterion, according to which their benefices, under a certain value, are exempted from the restriction in the Statute 21st Henry VIII. concerning pluralities.†

After the dissolution of the monasteries, King Henry VIII. granted (March, 1537-8) the Priory of St. Helen's, as already noticed,‡ with many other castles, lordships, and manors, the annual value of which was estimated at 30,000*l.*, to Richard Williams, alias Cromwell, in consideration of his good service and the payment of 4963*l.* 4*s.* 2*d.*

Edward VI., in the fourth year of his reign (1551), by his letters patent, bearing date the 1st of April, gave (*inter alia*) the jurisdiction of this place to the Bishop of London (Nicholas Ridley)

---

* Hook's Lives of the Archbishops of Canterbury (Second Series), vol vi. pp. 257-8.

† Liber Regis, p. 572. St. Helen not in charge in the King's books, or to the payment of first fruits and tenths. As to what amount of tithes, or if any at all, paid by the parishioners of St. Helen's previously to the Reformation, there is no record. The impression seems to be that the Chantry Priests (see above, p. 28) discharged both the conventual and parochial duties.

‡ See p. 33.

and his successors, which was afterwards confirmed by Queen Mary by her letters patent, dated March 2, in the first year of her reign (1554), Edmund Bonner being then restored to the Bishopric.

Sir John Harrington, High Sheriff of Rutland,* 12th, 25th, and 32nd Henry VIII., and again in 6th Edward VI., "dying within St. Helens, London, in 1552, was, on Monday the 4th September, carried into his country, in a horse litter, to be interred, with his standard and pennon; mass and dirge having every day been sung for him; that is, from the 18th day of August, on which he died, to the day of his remove."† This appears to have been the first celebration of the funeral mass after the accession of Queen Mary (Edward VI. died July 6), and on the 21st August the minister of St. Ethelburga, with others, was set in the pillory and his ears nailed to it, for heinous and seditious words spoken against the Queen, and having spoken more words to the same effect, was set in the pillory again, August 23, which was the first day mass began to be said in a church.

In the year 1568, Queen Elizabeth granted a lease to Cæsar Aldermarie (Adelmare), Esq., and Thomas Colcel or Colshill, parishioners and inhabitants of St. Helens, for, and in the name of all the parishioners and inhabitants there, upon their desire to them granted of the rectory of the said parish, for that intent and purpose, that the rents, issues, and profits of the same, shall, from time to time, rise, grow, and increase, to the use, profit, and commodity of the parishioners there. Therefore, in consideration of 17*l*. 12*s*. 3*d*. paid by the said Cæsar Aldermarie and Thomas Colcel, at the receipt of the Exchequer, she (the said Queen) granted and deviseth to them all that rectory and parsonage and Church of St. Helen's, except and reserved to her Majesty and her heirs, the advowson of the vicarage there. To have and to hold the said rectory, parish, and church, messuages, houses, tithes, and oblations, and other profits, to the said Cæsar and Thomas, their executors and assigns, from the feast of St. Michael the archangel, unto the term of twenty-one years, yielding and paying therefore yearly to her, her heirs and successors, the sum of 8*l*.16*s*.1*d*. The said Cæsar and Thomas to pay as well the priest's wages there doing

---

* Betham's Baronetage, vol. i. p. 107.
† Strype's Memorials, vol. iii. pt. 1. p. 34. Ed. Oxford, 1822.

service, and all other sums of money for bread and wine, and other necessaries in the Church to be expended and paid.

There was also a clause that the said "farmers" shall repair the chancel and housing to the said rectory belonging; and likewise a clause that after such reasonable sums of money, received, paid, and deducted, as they laid out, as well for the expense of this lease, or otherwise, about the sum, and obtaining the same, or of these letters patent, and from thenceforth all such issues and profits, coming and issuing of the same parsonage, all charges of the said parsonage being deducted, they shall convert and dispose to the use and commodity of the parishioners; dated May 27, in the 10th year of her reign.

About the year 1588 the Queen proposed to grant a lease to one Captain Oseley, for his good service against the Spaniards. This Oseley being in Spain in those eventful and dangerous times, had sent very good intelligence thence, and likewise in the fight against the Spanish Fleet in 1588, whereupon Howard, Lord-Admiral, sent a letter in his behalf to the Lord Treasurer, that, for the causes mentioned, it was the Queen's pleasure that he should so stay the same parsonage, that no lease of it in the meanwhile should be granted out of the Exchequer, which should prevent the reward of one, who had so well deserved in adventuring his life so many ways in her Majesty's service.

By deed dated April 11, 1589, in the 31st year of her reign, Queen Elizabeth lett to farme to the Churchwardens of St. Helens, to the public use of all the parishioners, the Rectory and Church, with their rights, &c., belonging to the late priory of St. Helens, reserving to her Majesty and her heirs the advowson of the vicarage for the term of 21 years, paying yearly the sum of 8*l*. 16*s*. 4*d*. at the receipt of Exchequer. The parish to provide and pay as well the stipend of the minister, and also all charges for bread, wine, and other necessaries in the said church. The said Churchwardens, after all reasonable expenses, shall give yearly 20*l*.* to a sufficient preacher, to be allowed by the Bishop of

---

* This amount still remains as the sole endowment from the tithes of St. Helen's, for the remuneration of the minister. The value of the tithes was for a considerable period 60*l*. per annum. It is, therefore, clear that the intention was that the stipend of the minister should be a *third of the whole sum*. Unfortunately those, who thus fixed that sum, had no idea that

London. The remainder of the profitts, &c., for the use and commodity of the parishioners; and further, the said Churchwardens, for themselves and their assigns, do covenant that no greater rate of value of the houses or tenements within the parish than heretofore has been used or accustomed, shall be assessed or taxed without the consent of our Treasurer of England, or the Chancellor of our Court of Exchequer for the tyme being thereunto first, obtained. The Chauncell of the Church, and all houses, &c., belonging to the Rectory to have all necessary repairs, and in the default of the rent to her Majesty, or nonfulfilment of the above conditions, the lease to be avoid.*

In the year 1599 the Queen sold the Rectory to Michael Stanhope, Esq., one of the Grooms of the Privy Chamber, and Edward Stanhope, LL.D.,† and one of the Masters in Chancery, to be held by them, their heirs and assigns, in consideration of their having paid to her Majesty the sum of 610*l*. 18*s*. 7*d*., granting to them the whole Rectory and Church of St. Helens, with their rights, members, and appurtenances, late belonging to the priory of St. Helen; and all the messuages, houses, edifices, gardens, tithes, oblations, rents, fruits, profits, commodities, advantages, &c., belonging to the said rectory and Church; and the annual rent of 8*l*. 16*s*. 1*d*., formerly belonging to the said priory, and parcel of the

---

any change in the value of money would ever take place in the future, and, in consequence, whilst the whole of the tithes have increased in an immense ratio, those who have been possessed of them have appropriated all the increase to their own benefit and advantage, and continued, what they could not escape, the payment of 20*l*. per annum, and added not a single farthing more. This system, however, is not confined to St. Helen's. It has obtained in almost every impropriation through the length and breadth of the kingdom, and in every capitular body where the Deans and Chapters, having paid themselves and all the inferior members the sums fixed by their statutes, then divided the handsome surplus over and above among themselves, with scarcely any reference whatever to Minor Canons, Lay Vicars, or Clerks, Choristers, &c. In taking the Decanal and Capitular Funds into their hands recently, the Ecclesiastical Commissioners, whilst providing in every respect for the Members of the Chapter, have almost wholly ignored the condition of the poorer members of the body.

* See Appendix.

† Edward Seymour, Duke of Somerset, Lord Protector, married Ann, daughter of Sir Edward Stanhope, Kt., a lady of high mind and undaunted spirit.

possessions; which priory, rectory, and church is extended to the clear yearly value of 8*l*. 16*s*. 1*d*. To hold by fealty, in free and common soccage, and not *in capite*, nor by military service. And, moreover, the Queen gave all the rents, profits, and revenues, &c., of all the premises, from the Feast of the Annunciation of our Blessed Lady last past. Twenty pounds to be issuing from the said Rectory for a sufficient preacher of God's Word within the said Church, to preach from time to time, to be allowed by the Bishop of London for the time being, to be paid him quarterly, by equal portions, and from the said payments to free and indemnify her and her successors." Dated at Westminster, September 13, 1599, in the 41st year of her reign.

Since the above period it appears to have been granted back, and also the advowson of the Church to the Dean and Chapter of St. Paul's, who became both patrons and ordinaries of the place, and collated to the Church as a vicarage.

In 1636 there was a return made of this Church, viz.: an Impropriation belonging to the Earl of Northampton, worth sixty pounds per annum.*

In 1662, Sir John Langham, Bart., became farmer of the Rectory of St. Helen, and filed a bill in Chancery, Michs. 14 Charles II., against Sir John Lawrence† and others, parishioners, setting forth that he was entitled to some certain rate or customary payment of tithes in the City of London of 2*s*. 9*d*. for every 20*s*. rent, confirmed by Act of Parliament, 37 Hen. VIII. But that the defendants had combined and refused to pay any tithes, or any other customary payment, although they had often been requested in a friendly manner, and the plaintiff being but lately entitled to the said rectory, is not only a stranger to the duties which ought to be so paid, but also to the true rents of the respective houses, &c. The said plaintiff being without remedy, save only in a Court of Equity, was willing to have accepted the customary payments, but the defendants refused to inform him. The defendants, in their answer, stated the cus-

---

* Newcourt's Repert. Lond., vol. i. p. 364. (Sion Coll. MS.)
† Lord Mayor of London, A.D. 1665-6, who resided in a mansion within Great St. Helen's, built under the supervision of Inigo Jones, the front of which yet remains much the same as during his mayoralty.

tomary payments time out of mind. And it was decreed, with the consent of the plaintiff and all the defendants, that they shall pay the several sums of money, according to the several rates and customary payments by them set forth in their several respective answers, and shall continue the payment for so long as the said plaintiff shall continue Impropriator of the said Rectory, and the said defendants shall continue inhabitants of their respective houses.

A.D. 1734.— —— Freeman, Esq., was rated at 64*l.* 12*s.* 7*d.* in the King's books, as Impropriator, and was succeeded, A.D. 1739 by one William Parker. How long this Impropriator stood possessed of the tithes there are no records to show, or at what date he was succeeded by Edward Bradley. It is not stated what the purchase-money paid on the different changes was, but it has always been understood in the parish that Bradley, who was a parishioner, offered to sell the tithes to the parish for 700*l.*

A.D. 1805, the tithes were purchased by the Rev. Edward Cook, whose real purchase-money was not more than 700*l.* The actual sum paid by this purchaser was 1300*l.* Three per Cent. Consols, then very low in price; and no sooner had he become the possessor of them than he set to work to exact tithes from the occupiers of Crosby Square and others who had been exempt, and increasing others. What he then said to dissentients was that he knew the law of tithes as well as any Chief Baron of the Exchequer, and thus frightened them and raised the income considerably, although far below the rating of 2*s.* 9*d.* in the pound. In the year 1822, "The Tythes of the Parish were sold by Mr. Cooke to Mr. Alexander McDougall for 6000 guineas." This sale was by public auction, and there is a list of the then tithes extant as acknowledged and paid, and that list with some of the particulars of sale in the parish, were produced and used in a suit between Mr. Alexander McDougall and the parishioners before the Master of the Rolls, and afterwards on appeal to the House of Lords, in which the claims of the former were established.

After the decease of Mr. Alexander McDougall, Nov. 1835, the tithes were devised to the members of his family, their management being in the hands of his eldest son, Alexander John McDougall.

On his decease, in April, 1867, a division of their father's property was determined upon, and in order to effect this it was determined to dispose of the Impropriator's tithes by private contract. This was effected by a sale of those attached to that portion of the parish, which was originally the property of Sir Thomas Gresham, and after his decease became the site of Gresham College, agreeably to the tenour of his will; afterwards passing to the Crown, and being used as the Excise Office, in the courtyard of which the business of the Royal Exchange was transacted, until the re-building of that establishment after the fire of 1839. The accommodation for the transactions of the Excise not being sufficiently commodious, the site was bought by a Company, and upon it was built what is now known as "Gresham House," a huge and ugly pile of buildings wholly occupied by merchants, &c. as offices. After a considerable amount of litigation between Mr. Alexander John McDougall as to the amount payable for tithes, the matter was terminated, on his decease, by their entire and perpetual redemption for 5000*l*. Soon afterwards, the Leathersellers' Company in like manner redeemed the tithes upon their valuable property in St. Helen's Place for 7000*l*. The remainder, being very considerably diminished in amount by these sales, was purchased by Mr. Edwin Newman, solicitor, for 2250*l*., in 1875. This sale, in combination with those already mentioned since the death of Mr. Alexander John McDougall, as well as by several others previously made by his father, must have realized very nearly 20,000*l*.; yet no further endowment for the minister than the 20*l*. per annum fixed by Queen Elizabeth, A.D. 1589,* was ever made. A proposition to raise this amount to 200*l*. per annum, contingent upon the success of Mr. Alexander John McDougall's litigation with the Gresham House proprietors, was indeed made, but it was frustrated by his death. The McDougall family afterwards proposed to purchase an annuity of 200*l*. for the then incumbent,† but it came to nothing after a considerable amount of negotiation, and the minister's stipend would still have remained 20*l*. per annum had not the amalgamation of the two parishes of St. Helen and St. Martin Outwich taken place, A.D. 1873, by Order of

---

* See p. 49. † The Rev. Dr. Cox.

Council, to which reference will be fully made in a future chapter.

The following is a list of the ministers or vicars, as also of the curates, lecturers, and readers, &c.; and also of Sir M. Lumley's lecturers:—

VICARS.	CURATES.	LECTURERS.
1571. Thomas Sir,* died 1576.		
1575. Olivar, John.	1576. Thos. Barbor.	
1586. Lewis.	1580. Gardener.	
1600. Hughes, Lewis.	1586. Lewis.	
1603. Ball, Richard.		
1613. Downing, Thomas.		
1618. Evans, Thomas.		
1619. Lawrence, William.		
1621. Brown, Joseph.		
1635. Maden, Richard, Author of Sermons of Christ's love towards Jerusalem. Lond. 1637.	1636. Townsend.	1636. Walker.
1639. Milward, Matthias.	1639. Broadstreet.	
1642. Edwards, Thomas.		
1645. Willes, Samuel.		
1647. Barham, Arthur.	1647. A. Barham.	
1663. Sybbald, John, A.M., Oct. 5.†		1655. Cooper.
1666. Horton, Thoˢ, S.T.P.,‡ June 13.		
1674. Pelling, Edw., A.M.,§ Maii 11.		

---

* Such of the clergy as were under the degree of doctor were commonly called Sir. (Heylin's History of the Reformation, vol. i. p. 197, ed. Lond.) (Robertson, Eccl. Hist. Soc.), 1849.

† See Newcourt's Repert. Lond., vol. i. p. 365, edit. Lond. 1708.

‡ Tho. Horton, Doctor of Divinity of Cambridge, and Master of Queen's College there, was incorporated in the same Degree in Convocation at Oxford, Aug. 9, 1652. He was born in London, bred in Emanuel College, of which he became Fellow, and a noted Tutor to young Presbyterian scholars. In 1637 he was constituted one of the publick Preachers of the University of Cambridge, and in 1638, or thereabouts, he became minister of S. Mary Cole-Church, London (a Donative in the Mercers' Company), afterwards he was Preacher to the Society of Gray's Inn, Reader of Divinity in Gresham College, a Holder-forth sometimes before the Long Parliament, one of the Triers or Commissioners appointed for the Approbation of publick Preachers and Vicar of this parish of S. Helen's, as my author saith [Ath. Ox., vol. ii. p. 779]. However, after the Restauration, upon the Resignation of Sybbald, it appears that in 1666, June 13, he was collated to this Vicarage by the Dean and Chapter of St. Paul's, which he held till his Death. (June 13, 1674.)

§ Edw. Pelling on appointment to S. Martin, Ludgate.

Ministers of St. Helen's. 55

VICARS.	CURATES.	LECTURERS.
1678. Hesketh, Henry, A.M., Nov. 11, res. Chosen by Parish, by consent of Dean & Chapter. Bishop of Killala, 1689-90.*	1678. Plymley.	1685. Dr Fuller.
	1689. John Dalgarno.	
1694. Willis, Thomas, A.M., Jan. 23. Died. Chosen as above.		
1701. Estwicke, Sampson, June 4. Chosen as above. Impropriator's right allowed.		1700. Thos Haws.
1712. Butler, William, LL.D.†		
1715. James Ptolemy, M.A.‡		
1729. Gaithorne, John. Called Sequestrator.	1726. Ric^d Boud.	
1731. Haywood, Valentine, A.M.§	1731. Allen.	
		1741. Simpson.
1745. Coulton, George.	1758. G. Toovey, D.D.	1745. Smith.
1773. Naish, John, Feby 13. Presented by Impropriator and collated by Dean and Chapter.	Wm. Edmonds. Assistant.	1760. Mapletoft.
		1763. Carey.
1795. Watts, Robert, M.A., Nov. 2. Res^d Collated by Dean and Chapter against Impropriator's recommendation.	1795. J. J. Ellis.	1774. Middleton.
1799. Blenkarne, James, M.A.‖ Oct. 13. Died.		1805. Blenkarne.

* Henry Hesketh, although nominated Bishop of Killala, does not appear to have been consecrated, William Lloyd, a Welshman, but of Trinity College, Dublin, Precentor of Killala, and Dean of Anchrory, having succeeded Dr. Richard Tennison, translated to Clogher. See Cotton's Fasti Eccl. Hibern., vol. iv. p. 73. Ed. Dublin, 1848-51.

† Rector of St. Anne's, Aldersgate, and Prebendary of St. Paul's, published a sermon, "Thanks for Victory," 1704, 4to, Esth. iv. 14; Fast sermon, 1712, 4to, Prov. xxi. 30; Assize, 1715, 4to, Titus iii. 1; "Vice the destruction of the Soul," 1719, 4to, Matthew, viii. 22; "Reformation of Manners," 1722, 8vo, Eph. v. 11; Visitation, 1723, 4to, Ex. xx. 7; election of Lord Mayor, 1724, 4to, Neh. v. 19; election of Lord Mayor, 1729, 4to, Ex. xviii. 21.

‡ Of Christ Church, Oxford, A.M., 1694, Prebendary of St. Paul's, preached a sermon on the funeral of Mr. Durley, 1717, 4to, Psalm xxvii. 15; LL.B. of St. John's College, Cambridge, 1715.

§ A.M. of St. John's College, Oxford, 1781.

‖ See Malcolm's History of London, vol. iii. p. 552., ed. London, 1803.

Ministers of St. Helen's.

VICARS.

1835. Charles Mackenzie, M.A., resigned* 1847.

1847. J. M. L. Le Mesurier, M.A., Archdeacon of Gibraltar, resigned.

1849. John Edmund Cox, M.A., afterwards D.D. Jan. 19, 1849. Resigned May 22, 1873, on amalgamation of St Martin Outwich with St. Helen's.

1873. John Bathurst Dean, M.A., Rector of St. Martin's Outwich, was instituted Vicar, on resignation of Dr. Cox.

LECTURERS.

1835. C. Mackenzie.

1847. Albert Alston, M.A., afterwards D.D., died Dec. 1871.

1872. J. E. Cox, Jany 6th.

Vicar in charge, by Order of Council, John Edmund Cox, D.D., May 5th, 1873.

---

* On appointment to St. Benet, Gracechurch.

CHAPTER IV.

MONUMENTS.

"Monuments were denominated *a muniendo*, because they were at the first erected to defend the bodies of the dead from the savage brutishness of wild beasts, which otherwise might have destroyed the bodies in their graves; for in those days all were buried in the fields near some way, or at the feet or top of mountains, as now in Turkey, and the eastern parts of the world; about which time it was the usage in England to inter their dead upon the ridges of hills, or spacious plains, fortified or fenced about with pointed stones, pyramids, pillars, or such like monuments, as Stonehenge on Salisbury Plain, &c., to put passengers in mind of their mortality; and though the British cities had churches from the beginning of Christianity, yet the Christians always buried their dead without the walls of towns and cities until the time of Gregory the Great, who was Bishop of Rome, anno 590, when the monks, friars, and priests began to offer sacrifices for the souls departed. At length they obtained churchyards for places to bury their dead for the advantage of their profit; and in process of time, license to bury in churches, that so often as their relations came to those holy places and beheld their sepulture, they might remember, and earnestly pray to the Lord for them; for which reason Constantine was buried in the porch of the Apostles in Constantinople, Honorus in the porch of St. Peter at Rome, and the Empress in the church: and in England Augustine the Monk, Bishop of Canterbury, was buried in the porch of the Church of St. Peter and St. Paul, near Canterbury a religious house of his own foundation, without the city, and the six next succeeding Bishops of the same Province were interred near him.

"Cuthbert, the eleventh Archbishop of Canterbury, consecrated anno 741, obtained a dispensation about the year 758, from the Pope, to make cemeteries and churchyards in England for the burial of their dead ; for before his time the bodies of the Kings and Archbishops in England were not buried in cities, for in those days they followed the example of our Saviour who was buried without the gate, and this Archbishop was the first that was interred in Christ's Church. Shortly after, gravestones were made and tombs erected with inscriptions engraved upon them declaring briefly, with a kind of commiseration, the name, age, merit, dignity, state, praise, time, fortune, and manner of the death of the party interred which was called an epitaph, and have always been accounted the greatest mark of respect, because they express a great love to the deceased person, and preserves his memory to posterity, which was a comfort to his friends and relations, and put them in mind of his mortality.

"The invention of these epitaphs proceeded from the presage or sense of immortality implanted naturally in all men, and is attributed to the scholars of Linus the Theban poet (who flourished about the year of the world 2700. For they first bewailing this Linus their master in doleful verses when he was slain, those verses were called from him Ælinum, afterwards Epitaphia, because they were first sung at burials, and afterwards engraved upon the sepulchres ; which may be called monuments *a memoria*, for that they are memorials to put men in mind of their frail condition and their deceased friends; or *a monendo* to warn men of their mortality, and to excite their inward thoughts by the sight of death to a better life; and these monuments were accounted so sacred, that such as violated them were heretofore punished with death, banishment, condemnation to the mines, or loss of members, according to the circumstance of fact and person.

"These monuments serve for four uses or ends: 1. They are evidences to prove descents and pedigrees. 2. To show the time when the party deceased. 3. They are examples to follow the good, and eschew the evil. 4. Memorials to put the living in mind of their mortality."*

It would occupy far too much space to enumerate the numerous monuments which exist within the walls of St. Helen's—such, for example, as tablets, footstones, &c. The following descriptions, therefore, are confined to those most especially worthy of notice

---

* Sir H. Chauncey's Historical Antiquities of Herts, p. 554. Ed. Lond., 1700.

JHON ROBINSON, A.D. 1600.

and consideration. They will be taken into consideration, not according to their respective dates of erection, but according to their position, beginning from the north wall of the Nuns' Quire.

The first that claims attention is that of Thon Robinson, merchant of the staple of London, and merchant-taylor; an elaborate specimen of its period—husband, wife, and children being placed, according to sex, on each side of an altar-table, with the following inscription :—

Within this Monument lye the earthly parts of THON ROBINSON, Marchant of ye Staple of England, free of ye Cōpany of Marchant Talors, and sometymes Alderman of Londō, and Christian his Wife, Eldest daughter of Tho Anderson, Grocer. They spent together 36 Yeares in holy Wedlock, and were happy besides other worldly blessings in nyne sonnes and seaven daughters. She changde her mortall habitation for a heavenly on the 24th of April, 1592, Her husband following her on the 19th of February, 1599. Both much beloved in theire lives, and more lamented at theire deaths especially by the Poore to whome theire good deedes (being alive) begott many prayers and now (being dead) many teares. The glasse of his life held three score and ten yeares, and then ran out. To live long and happy is an honor, but to die happy a greater glory. Boeth these aspired to boeth. Heaven (no doubt) hath theire soules, and this howse of stone theire bodyes, where they sleepe in peace till the sōmons of a glorious resurrection wakens them.

Upon entering the Church by the west door, an altar-tomb, of somewhat small proportions, immediately attracts attention, for its simplicity in structure, no less than for the quaintness of its inscription, which is as follows :—

Here lyeth the bodie of WILLIAM KERWIN of this Cittie of London, Free Mason, whoe departed this lyfe the 26th daye of December, Aū° Dō. 1594.

    Ædibus Attalicis, Londinum qui decoravi;
    Me duce surgebant aliis regalia tecta
    Exiguam tribuunt hanc mihi fata Domō.
    Me duce conficitur, ossibus vinc meis.[*]

And here alsoe lyeth the bodie of MAGDALEN KIRWIN his Wife by whom he had issue 3 sonnes and 2 daughters shee deceased the XXIIIth August, 1592.

---

[*] The fates have afforded this narrow house to me, who have adorned London with noble buildings. By me, royal palaces were built for others. By me, this tomb is erected for my bones.

> Magdalena jacet, virtus post fata supstes,
> Corpus humo tectum, Christo veniente resurget
> Conjugiique fides, Religioque manent.
> Ut mentis consors astra suprema colat.
> Nos quos certus amor primis conjunxit abbanis
> Junxit idem Tumulus, junxit idemque Polus.*

BENJAMIN KIRWIN yᵉ sonne of WILLIAM KIRWIN, deceased yᵉ 12th of July An. Dom.—1621, whoe had issue 7 sonnes and 5 daughters whereof 5 of them are buried in this Vault.

> Christus mihi vita
> Mors mihi lucrum.†

On the right-hand side, or the south wall of the Church, is the following monument:—

> En Memory
>
> Of Dame ABIGAIL LAWRENCE
>
> Late Wife of Sʳ JOHN LAWRENCE, Kt & Alderman heere interrᵈ
> was this tomb Erected
> Shee was the tender Mother of ten Children
> the nine first being all daughters
> she suckled at her owne breasts
> they all lived to be of age,
> her last a son died an Infant
> Shee lived a married wife thirty nine years
> three and twenty whereof
> Shee was an exemplary matron of this Cittie
> dying in the 59ᵗʰ year of her age
> being the 6 June
> 1682.

Returning to the Nuns' Quire, at a very small intervening space from the Robinson monument,‡ the spectator is startled by the appearance of a huge, incongruous, and ugly piece of masonry—a tomb in the very worst taste, and so unsightly as to mar the entire ecclesiastical proportions of this part of the building. It is to the memory of Francis Bancroft, and bears the following inscription:—

---

* Magdalen lies here! Thou virtue survivest the tomb. Her body now covered with earth shall rise again at the coming of Christ: To her Husband, Faith and Religion still remain that when deprived of life, he may dwell in the loftiest heaven.

The same Tomb has joined and the same Heaven has united us, whom an unvaried love connected from our earliest years.

† To me to live is Christ, to die is gain.

‡ See p. 59.

> The ground whereon this Tomb stands was
> Purchased of this Parish in MDCCXXIII by
> **FRANCIS BANCROFT Esq'**
> for the interrment of himself and friends only
> (and was Confirm'd to him by a Faculty from the
> Dean and Chapter of St Paul's
> London the same year) and in his Lifetime he
> erected this tomb, Anno, 1726 and settled part of
> his Estate in London and Middlesex for the
> Beautifying and Keeping the same
> in Repair for ever.

Francis Bancroft left behind him a very singular will, in which the most curious directions were specified for the interment of his remains.* The reputation this individual bore during his lifetime was not of the best. He was a descendant of Archbishop Bancroft, and in early life is reported to have been in poor circumstances. He obtained the appointment of Lord Mayor's officer, of which there were at the time four, two seniors and two juniors. It appears that the juniors had the enviable (!) privilege of laying informations, and of obtaining half the fines that were levied upon those who had infringed the law. They were, in fact, informers. In the natural order of things, the junior officers became seniors. Thrice, it is said, this promotion fell to Francis Bancroft's lot, and thrice did he buy back the junior office, in order to carry on the process by which he realized his money. So unpopular was he in the City of London, it is recorded, that when he was buried the populace mobbed his remains, attempted to upset the coffin, and rung the bells, which were then located above the entrance to Great St. Helen's.† With the property left to the disposition and management of the Drapers' Company, the Bancroft Hospital was founded in Mile-End Road, for the benefit of twenty-four almsmen, and the education, clothing, and maintenance of one hundred poor boys. The funds, most carefully and consistently husbanded, have very largely increased; the value of the charity, in every particular, is reckoned only second to Christ's Hospital, Newgate Street. An application has been recently made to the Drapers' Company who, as will be seen by the monumental inscription upon the tomb, have the custody and charge of its maintenance and repair, by the testator's will, for ever—to

---

* For Francis Bancroft's Will, see Appendix.
† See Stow's Survey, p. 278. Ed. Lond. 1754.

remove this hideous specimen of bad taste and ridiculous vanity to another spot, under the great west window of the Nuns' Quire, unhappily without effect, it being supposed that a consent to comply with the request may invalidate the terms of Francis Bancroft's will. In compliance with the directions of that document, a sermon is preached in commemoration of his "Act and deed," for which, and for reading the prayers, the sum of 1*l*. 11*s*. 6*d*., liberally increased of late years to 5*l*. 5*s*., has to be paid to the officiating minister, 7*s*. 6*d*. to the parish clerk, and 5*s*. to the sexton.

Passing from the consideration of Francis Bancroft and his tomb, the eye is caught by a plain tablet—

> In Memory of
> JOHN SMITH, Esqre
> of this Parish who died June 29th 1783 Aged 80
> By Strict Probity
> Sincerity and Benevolence
> he endeared himself to
> ALL
> who knew him.
> But more especially to the Poor and Needy
> by kind Condescension & boundless
> CHARITY.
> Reader Go and do thou likewise."

Adjoining the above is another equally plain and simple tablet, bearing the following inscription :—

> Near this Spot are deposited the remains of
> HENRY PETER KUHFF, Esquire*
> who departed this life
> October the 10th 1796
> in the 70th year of his age
> of
> PETER KUHFF, his Son
> who died January the 10th 1786
> in his 7th year
> of
> FREDERICK CHARLES KUHFF, Esquire
> who died March 11th 1792
> Aged 50 Years

---

* 1796, Oct. 10, at Highgate in his 70th year, Henry Peter Kuhff, Esq. An eminent merchant, and many years a Director of the Royal Assurance Co.—*Gentleman's Mag.*, p. 883.

MARTIN BOND, A.D. 1643.

We next approach one of the most remarkable amongst the many remarkable monuments for which this Church has obtained the appellation of "The Westminster Abbey of the City"—that of Martin Bond, Captain of the City Train-bands in 1588, when that body of citizen soldiers were reviewed by Queen Elizabeth at Tilbury, in preparation against the threatened invasion of the Spanish Armada. It is placed on the north wall of the Nuns' choir, and represents an encampment. In the foreground is a large open tent, within which he is represented sitting in a thoughtful posture at a table. At the side of the tent a page holds his horse, and in the front are two sentinels with partisans, in large boots and slouched hats. The whole is enclosed in a frontispiece, consisting of two composite columns, sustaining an entablature and pediment, the cornice broken to admit the arms; below the sculpture is the inscription, from which we learn that all this military display is for a captain of the Trained Bands.* The monument is, however, invaluable as displaying to perfection the costume of the times. This was covered with numerous coats of black paint, which have recently been removed by the care of the Haberdashers' Company, to show that the materials of which the monument is composed consists of black marble and alabaster. The inscription is as peculiar as the monument itself is remarkable:—

𝔐emoriæ Sacrum.

Neere this place resteth ye body of ye worthy

Cittizen and Soldier

MARTIN BOND Esqr.

Son of Willm Bond, Sherief and Alderman of London

He was Captaine in ye yeare 1588 at ye Camp at Tilbury and after remained

Cheief Captaine of ye trained bandes of this Cittiy until his death.

He was a marchant adventurer and free of ye Company of Haberdashers.

he lived to the age of 85 yeares

and dyed in May 1643.

His pyety, prudence, courage and honesty have left

behinde him, a never dyeing monument.

---

* Trained Band for Aldersgate. Afterwards in the Artillery.

> Quam prudens hic Miles erat, quam Nobile Pectus
> Noverunt Princeps, Patria, Castra, Duces,
> Civi quanta fuit Pietas, quam larga Manusq ;
> Pauperis agnoscunt Viscera, Templa Togæ.
> Miles hic et Civis qualem Vix millibus Unum
> Sæcla referre queant, nec meminisse Parem.
> Patruo bene merito Gulielmus Bond, Armiger Posvit.*

To the right of this monument, but at a lower level, is a monument to the father of Captain Martin Bond, who was designated, as appears by the inscription, the *Flos mercatorum* of his times.

On the floor of the north aisle is a slab, on which the effigy of the deceased—name unknown—and several shields, &c. are cut on the stone in the manner of a brass. Such memorials are rather uncommon.

Immediately adjacent to the monument of Captain Bond is a somewhat ugly structure, to which reference is made simply on account of the singularity of its inscription, which runs to the following effect :—

> Siste Gradum
> Peripatetice, & paulisper contemplare,
> Ornatissimi microcosmi heu ! breves reliquias
> Nunc in pulverem redacti olim
> GULIELMI FINCH, Armigeri antiqua &
> in Agro Cantij Familia oriundi
> Naturæ & Gratiæ dotibus egregie nobilitate Ad Oris Corporisq. venustatem accessit major Animæ pulchritudo optimis virtutibus insignitæ Quas in Christianæ Religionis testimonium et decus luculenter usque exeruit.
> Eximia in Deum. O. M. Pietate erga Sacros Pastores summa Reverentia Fidelitate in Principem, Justitia in Proximum Conjugali Paternaq Indulgentia Singulari in Familiares affectu integgerrimo propensa in Omnes Benevolentia; Linguâ castus et candidus, manu supra fidem Liberalis ; Nemini turpiter obloqui, aut, obtrectare solitus omnibus benifacere, inprimis Egenis absq^b, præcinente buccina, Eleemosynis pariter ac Thesauris plenus, quo probe accumulatas in Terra plurimos prudens Mercator in Cœlo recondidit, Vitam tandem commutandis aliquandiu mercibus prospere transactam 42 Ætatis annum emensus Jun 27. 1672. Meliori quæstu cum Morte comutavit.
> Relictis & bonæ Spei Parvulis cum dilectissima et amantissima Uxore quæ in perpetuam tam chari Capitis Memoriam Monumentum hoc constantissimi Amoris Pignus, extruendum curavit, Ipsa interim mœrore cum Illo consepulta Abiiam attonitus Viator & mirare tam probum in tam pravo seculo **Virum,** aut vivere potuisse, aut debuisse
> MORI.

---

* How prudent was this soldier, and how noble his mind, his prince, his country, and his superior officers knew. How great his piety, how extensive his liberality the poor can testify, as also religion and the pensioners on his bounty This soldier and citizen ages cannot produce one out of a thousand to equal, nor is his like remembered. William Bond, Esq. has erected this as a memorial of his uncle's worth.

WILLIAM BOND, A.D. 1576.

ESTHER FINCH, Fœmina castissima, Viro morigera et curæ domesticæ dulce levamen liberorum (quos septem reliquit) Mater provida, Sincera pietate, alacri erga tenuiores benignitate, liberalitate in omnes, morum denique sanctitate conspicua. Viri (dum in vivis esset) decus simul et solamen, defuncti Vidua supra quamdici potest moestissima. Vixit annos 41. Menses 5. demptis diebus 11. Obiit Maii die 4 Anno Salutis 1673.*

Within very small intervening space another singular epitaph is worth consideration. It runs thus :—

Epitaph

On the lamented death of his honored Friend
WILLIAM DRAX

Esq. who exchanged this life for immortality Decem 17 1669 in the 63 yeare of his Age.

To thy dear memory blest soule i paie
This humble tribuit though in such a way
As reather doth proclaime my want of skill
Than any want of love of heart and will
True to thy trust none in our memory
Can charge the more or less with treuchery
Bring forth the p'son, Rich, poore, old or younge
That can justly say he ever did them wrong
In others weal or woe thy heart
Would sympathies and take its part
Oh what's more like the Deity
Than blessed hoary piety
A soul fitted for heaven when glorious Grace
Triumphs with him in his sure restinge-place
But is he dead Can I beleeve
That he should die and we should live
Methinks we may the knot untie
Better to live fitter to dye
Now death I see doth wisely chuse
The gold but doth the dross refuse
Weepe not as without hope cry not alas
Hees better where he is than where he was
Hearke, is not that his voice doth not he say
Heaven's meanest mansion, is worth this globe of clay
Who so doth live and doe and die like thee
His fame shall last to all eternity.

---

* Stop! O passenger, and for awhile contemplate philosophically the remains of that Microcosm, formerly most adorned, alas, now reduced to dust. William Finch, Esq., sprung from an ancient and illustrious family of Kent. To the beauty of his countenance and shape of body (gifts of Nature), as well as to nobility of birth, he added the beauty of a soul adorned with the best virtues, which he constantly used in testimony, and for the honour of the Christian Religion.

Of great piety towards God (our greatest good), reverence for his pastors,

Northward of this is the tomb of the great City merchant, Sir Thomas Gresham, concerning whom the following information may for the present suffice, as an account of his remarkable career appears under the head of "Worthies" connected with St. Helen's. It consists of a large altar-tomb of rich Sienna marble, covered with a ledger of black marble, the dado of which is richly ornamented with various mouldings appertaining to Italian architecture, and Sir Thomas's arms, in a more chaste style than the usual works of the period. It has recently been thoroughly cleaned and restored at the expense of the Gresham Committee and Mercers' Company. Above this tomb a helmet is placed upon a bracket, in the angle of the window—restored and filled with stained glass during the restoration of 1865-8, at the charge of the Gresham Committee of the Corporation of the City of London—which helmet, tradition intimates, was borne before the corpse on the night of Sir Thomas Gresham's funeral.

In like manner, with reference to Sir Andrew Judd, whose monument is fixed upon the opposite side of the same window, the inscription of his monument is only given; the further particulars

---

fidelity towards his prince, justice to his neighbours, indulgence to his wife and children, affection for his friends, and benevolence to all, chaste and sincere in language, and of incredible liberality of sentiment, he never reproached or disparaged anyone, but was accustomed to do good to all, particularly to the needy, without sounding a trumpet before him; abounding in alms, as well as in wealth, which honestly accumulated on earth, as a prudent merchant he laid up in heaven. At length, June 27, 1672, having completed the forty-second year of his age, he bartered with death, a prosperous life for a better possession.

He was much lamented by those he had left behind him. His children of good promise, and his most beloved and most loving wife, who, for a perpetual memorial of his dear self, and as a pledge of her unvaried love, has caused this monument to be erected; she having in the meantime died through grief, is buried together with him. Go now, astonished traveller, and wonder that a man so good, could have lived in so depraved an age, or ought to have died.

Esther Finch, a most chaste woman, obedient to her husband, and a sweet soother of his domestic cares, a careful mother of her children (of whom she has seven), of sincere piety, great benignity towards her inferiors, and of liberality to all. In short, conspicuous for the sanctity of her manners, and at the same time the glory and comfort of her husband when alive, but now dead. A widow more sorrowful than can be expressed, lived 41 years, 5 months, wanting 11 days, and died May 4, 1673.

SIR ANDREW JUDDE, A.D. 1588.

SIR WILLIAM PICKERING, A.D. 1574.

of his career, &c., being inserted in the chapter devoted to the "Worthies" of St. Helen's.

> To Russia and Muscoua
> To Spayne Gynny withoute fable
> Traveld he by land and sea
> Bothe mayre of London and Staple
> The Commenwelthe he norished
> So worthelie in all his days
> That ech state fullwell him loved
> To his perpetuall prayes.
> Three wives he had : one was Mary
> Fower sunes one mayde had he by her
> Annys had none by him truly
> By Dame Mary he had one dowghtier
> Thus in the month of September
> A thowsande fyve hundred fiftey
> And eight died this worthie Stapler
> Worshipynge his posterytye.
> Sr ANDREW JUDD K^{nt}.

The magnificent **Tomb of Sir William Pickering**, who died at Pickering House, St. Mary Axe, in 1574, aged 58, is situated under the north-east arch of the choir. For splendour of decoration, no monument in London, out of Westminster Abbey, can compare with it. It consists of an altar-tomb, panelled into compartments, sustaining on the ledger six Corinthian columns and two arches at the head and foot of the tomb, which jointly support a canopy formed of two arches resting on the entablature above the columns by way of impost, the soffits of the arches being filled with sunk panels, containing roses and fleur de lis alternately. The canopy is surrounded by an ornamental circle, sustained by two chimeræ, and enclosing the arms of the knight—viz., SA. a chevron, between three fleur de lis, OR. Within this canopy, upon the altar-tomb, lies extended the effigy of the knight, the size of life, bareheaded, in complete armour with trunk breeches, his head resting on a rolled mat, and a ruff surrounding his neck. The countenance is open and full of animation, the nose Roman, and the whole bespeaks a very handsome man, worthy to be the favourite of the discriminating Elizabeth ; at the feet of the figure is a fleur de lis. Attached to a pillar near the monument is a tablet with an inscription : "To the memory of Sir William, and his father, —— Pickering." The monument bears the following inscription :—

> Quiescit hic GULIELMUS PIKERINGUS, Pater, Equestris
> Ordinis vir, Miles Mariscallus. Qui obiit 19 Maii, Anno
> Salutis à Christo.
> MDXLII.
>
> Jacet hic etiam, GULIELMUS PIKERINGUS, Filius, Miles,
> Corporis Animiq; bonis insigniter ornatus; Literis excul-
> tus, et Religione sincerus: Linguas exacte percalluit.
> Quatuor Principibus summa cum laude inservivit: Hen-
> rico scilicet octavo, Militari virtute: Eduardo sexto,
> Legatione Gallica: Reginæ Mariæ, negotiatione Ger-
> manica: Elizabethæ, Principi omnium illustrissimæ,
> summis officiis devotissimus, Obiit Londini, in ædibus
> Pikeringiis, Ætate LVIII Anno Gratiæ, MDLXXIIII
> Januarii Quarto.
>
> Cujus Memoriæ, Thomas Henneagius, Miles, Cameræ
> Regiæ Thesaurarius; Johannes Astley, Armiger,
> jocalium Magister: Drugo Drureius, et Thomas
> Wottonus Armig., Testamenti sui Executores, Monu-
> mentum hoc posuere.*

In the Chapel of the Holy Ghost, on the south side of the choir, is a monument of Purbeck marble (A.D. 1475), with the figures of Sir John Crosby and his first wife, Anneys. He is represented in plated armour, with a mantle gathered up on his right shoulder, and falling over on his left, under his back, with a standing cape, and over it a Yorkist collar of rondeaux. On the little finger of the right hand is a ring, and others on the little and third fingers of the left hand: his hair is cropt and parted. Under his head is a helmet, the crest gone. He has a dagger at his right side, fastened by a singular belt, but no sword. His knee-pieces are riveted on the inside, and there is a fold or parting on his greaves. At his feet is a lion looking up to him. His lady is in a mantle, and very close-bodied gown, in which her feet are folded up, with long tight

---

* Here lies William Pickering the elder, Knight, Field Marshal, who died the 19th of May, in the year of our salvation by Christ 1542.

Here also lieth William Pickering the younger; a true soldier, remarkably endowed with good things, versed in literature, and a sincere Christian; he was singularly skilled in languages; and served four sovereigns in the most honourable manner; Henry the VIIIth in his military capacity. Edward the VIth in an embassy to France. Queen Mary in a negotiation with Germany; and the most illustrious Princess Elizabeth, by the greatest devotedness to duties of the highest moment. He died in London at Pickering House, January 4. In the year of grace 1574, aged 58. To his memory Thomas Henneagius, soldier and Treasurer of the Royal Household; John Astley, Esq., Master of the Jewels; Drugo Drury, soldier; and Thomas Wotton, Esq., have placed this monument.

SIR JOHN AND LADY CROSBY, A.D. 1475.

HIC REQVIESCIT ... *NA CÆSAR VIDVATA HÆC MARMORA POSVIT ET SEPVL* ...

Omnibus χρι fidelibus ad quos hpῦ presens Scriptum peruenerit: Ætatis, me Julium Adelmare alias Cæsarem militem, virtutis Curiæ Cortoʒum Elisabethæ Reginæ supremæ curiæ dominalitatis Judicem, et vnum è Magistris libellorum: Jacobo Regiæ priuatis consilijs Cancellarium scriarij et Cartoʒum Cʒonioʒum Magistrum hac presenti Carta mea Confirmasse me annuente Diuino numine naturæ debitum libenter soluturum quam primū Deo placuerit. In cuius rei Testimonium manum meam et sigillum opposui. datum 28vij februarij Aᵒ Dᵐⁱ MDCXXXV.

Jul. Cæsar

per ipsum, tempore morts suæ, CAROLO REGI a priuatis Co... ailijs, nec non Rotuloʒ rum Magistrum, ... vere pium, Apprime literatum, pauperibus ... im positi Charitatis re ceptaculum, patriæ fili... is et Amicis suis percharissimum solutum est. Obijt 18 Die Aprilis A°. Dᵐⁱ 1636 ÆTATIS Suæ. 79

IRROTVLATVR CÆLO.

IN CVIVS MEMORIAM DOM'NA

sleeves down to her wrists. Over the back of her hand passes a singular band: she has a ring on her fore and little fingers, and round her neck a collar of roses; a small cordon hangs on her right hip from a belt sloping from the left side; her cap is fitted close to her ears, and the hair tucked up under it, a veil falling off the cushion under her head, which is supported by two angels. At her feet lie two little dogs. The inscription, directed by his Will to be put on the ledge of this monument, has been long since removed, but in quatrefoils, surrounded by niches in two stories—one of which, until recently, was below the level of the floor and pavement—at the sides of the altar-tombs, are shields with the arms of Crosbie. Sable, a chevron ermine, between three rams trippant. Argent, armed and hoofed. Or.

The following is the inscription, on brass, that was originally placed upon the edge of the table whereon the effigies are recumbent :—

> Orate pro animabus JOHANNIS CROSBY, Militis, Ald. atque tempore vite Majoris Staple ville Caleis; et AGNETIS Uxoris sue, ac THOME, RICHARDI JOHANNIS, JOHANNIS, MARGARETE, et JOHANNE liberorum ejusdem JOHANNIS CROSBY, Militis. Ille obiit 1475 et Illa 1466. Quorum animabus propitietur Deus.*

Near this monument, in the south transept, is the singular altar-tomb of Sir Julius Cæsar Adelmare, who, feeling the ruling passion strong in death, moulded his epitaph in the form of a deed, to which he affixed his broad seal, which is "railed," and also its enrolment in a court—however, superior to that in which he used to preside.

The following is the inscription :—

> To all faithful Christian People to whom this writing may come. Know ye, that I JULIUS ADELMARE alias CÆSAR, Knight, Doctor of Laws, Judge of the Supreme Court of Admiralty of Queen Elizabeth, One of the Masters of Requests to King James, and of his Privy Council, Chancellor of the Exchequer and Master of the Rolls, by this my act and deed, confirm, with my full consent that by the Divine aid, I will willingly pay the debt of Nature as soon as it may please God. In witness whereof I have fixed my hand seal. Feb^r 27. 1634
> JUL. CÆSAR.

---

* Pray for the souls of John Crosby, Soldier, Alderman and during a ....tion of his life Mayor of the Staple of the town of Calais, and of Agnes his w..e, of Thomas, Richard John, John, Margaret and Johanna, Children of the same John Crosby, Soldier. He died in 1475 and she in 1466. On whose souls may God have mercy.—Weever's Fun. Monum., p. 421, ed. London, 1631.

He paid this debt, being at the time of his death, of the Privy Council of King Charles, also Master of the Rolls: truly pious, particularly learned, a refuge to the poor, abounding in love, most dear to his country, his children, and his friends.

He died April 18, 1636, in the 79th year of his age. It is enrolled in Heaven. His Widow, Lady Ann Cæsar, has erected this monument to his memory and here rests with him.

Against the south wall of the parochial nave, the splendid monument of Sir John Spencer is now placed. At the restoration of 1865-8, it was removed from the south transept to this spot by the Marquis of Northampton, by whose care, and at whose expence it was cleansed from numerous coats of white paint, and found to consist of a magnificent specimen of the purest alabaster. Upon this tomb are placed the recumbent figures of Sir John and his wife in the habits of the times in which they lived, the size of life, and at their feet is the figure of their daughter, in the attitude of prayer. The monument is covered with a sumptuous arched canopy, ornamented with pyramids.

The following is the inscription:

| HIC SITUS EST JOANNES SPENCER EQUES AURATUS CIVIS & SENATOR LONDINENSIS, EJUSDEMQ CIVITATIS PRÆTOR ANNO DM. MDXCIIII QUI EX ALICIA BROMFELDIA UXORE UNICAMRELIQUIT FILIAM ELIZABETH GUILIELMO BARONI COMPTON ENUPTAM OBIIT 3º MARTII DIE ANNO SALUTIS MDCIX[*] | SOCERO BENE MERITO GULIELMUS BARO COMPTON GENER POSVIT |

A full account of this great City merchant and trader is incorporated amongst the "Worthies of St. Helen's."

On the floor of the north aisle is a slab, on which the effigy of the deceased (unknown), and the ornamentation are cut on the stone in the manner of a brass. Such memorials are rather uncommon.

Removed from the old vestry wall to a spot immediately adja-

---

[*] Here lies John Spencer, Knight, Citizen and Member of Parliament for London. Lord Mayor of the same City A.D. 1594. By Alicia Bromfeld his wife he left an only daughter, who was married to William Baron Compton. He died March 3 in the year of our salvation 1609. To his most excellent father-in-law, this was erected by William Baron Compton.

SIR JOHN AND LADY SPENCER, A.D. 1609

cent to the tomb of Sir Julius Cæsar, is a monument of Italian marble, which attracts attention. The following inscription records whose memory it is intended to preserve :—

In a Vault near this place are deposited the remains of
WALTER BERNARD, Esq.
Alderman* & late Sheriff of this City
in both which stations He acted to the General satisfaction
of his Fellow Citizens
His private as well as publick character was truely amiable
He was a sincere Christian
A Faithfull Husband, a kind master and a true Friend
And as the whole Conduct of his life
was agreeable to the principles of true Religion and virtue
so his death was universally Lamented.
He dyed May the 4. 1746 Aged 51.

A singularly beautiful tablet in the adjacent wall cannot be left unnoticed, the workmanship being in every particular worthy of consideration. It bears the annexed epitaph :—

Hic Jacet
Quod Mortale erat GERVASH RERESBY.
Antiquissima ejusdem nominis familia
Eborancensi oriundi
Qui cum triginta plus annos in Hispania
fide indelibatâ sum moque honore
vixisset
In Angliam tandem
rediit
atque animâ mente inconcussâ
Salvatori reddidit
Anº Doṁ MDCCIV.
Hoc Patri optimo
Filius posuit unicus.†
Mercy Jesu.

Another elaborate specimen deserves consideration :—

---

* Alderman of Broad Street Ward.—*Gentleman's Mag.*, vol. xvi. p. 272.

† Here lies the mortal remains of Gervash Reresby, of a most ancient family of the same name, originally from Yorkshire, who, after he had lived for more than thirty years in Spain in the greatest estimation, and with the highest honour, returned to England, and, with an unshaken faith, delivered up his soul to his Saviour, Anno Dom. 1704. His only son erected this (monument) to his most excellent parent.

M. S.

CHARLES CHAMBRELAN, ESQ.,
Alderman of this City,
in testimony of his true affection
and sorrow for their deaths,
hath consecrated this Monument
to the memory of his dearly beloved wife

RACHEL

(the daughter of Sr John Lawrence, K{t}
Lord Mayor of London, 1665),
who died August the 21st, 1687,
soon after her delivery of her 10th child.
And of his fourth daughter, Hester,
who dyed the 9th of June, 1687,
at the age of 6 years, 8 months,
Both whose Bodies are here deposited in a Vault
near this place
(belonging to his Ancestors),
In expectation of a joyful resurrection
at the last day.

M. S.

In the same Vault with his dear Wife and daughter
(And with like hopes of a joyful resurrection together),
yeth the body of CHARLES CHAMBRELAIN, Esq., Alderman of this City,
who departed this life Jan. 29th, 1704, aged 65 Years,
having nowhere left behind him either a Merchant better accomplished
or a Gentleman more compleatly adorned with all sorts of
useful knowledge.
In memory of her most affectionate
and entirely beloved Father,
Abigail, his sorrowful Daughter and sole executrix
(the wife of Lemying Rebow, Esq.),
caused this Monument to be enlarged.

This monument conceals an Early English window, similar to one adjacent, which, although opened at the recent restoration, as to the interior, could not be utilized on account of a set of offices having been built upon the Church.

BRASSES.

St. Helen's is by no means rich in monumental brasses, but those which exist are generally believed to be excellent specimens of the several periods whose dates they bear. For the sake of safety, as well as of preservation, they have all been recently transferred to the two restored chapels of the Holy Ghost and Virgin Mary. They date back to A.D. 1393, but in the more remarkable instances of a later period, A.D. 1400, the representation of a priest in full canonicals, and a female figure, there is no record to indicate to whom they refer.*

Not so with regard to one adjacent—containing the effigies of a London merchant and his wife, in the costume of the period, to the memory of Thomas and Margaret Williams, with the following inscription :—

> Hic jacet THOMAS WILLIAMS, generos, et MARGARETA Uxor ejus
> qui   Thomas obiit XVI. die mensi Januarij a dn̄i 1495,
> Et   Margareta obiit die   mensi
> Quoram animabus propitietur Deus. Amen.†

The most elaborate and perfect of all the specimens is that of some distinguished gentlewoman of the style of the latter part of the reign of Henry VII., whose costume is that which was worn by those aged ladies of that day who not unfrequently ended life in a nunnery as lady abbesses, or even as mere sisters, to the no small emolument of the Church.‡

The next, belonging to the sixteenth century, in tolerable preservation, is to the memory of John Leventhorpe, Esq., a figure clothed in complete armour, bearing underneath the following record :—

> Hic jacet JOHANNES LEENTHORP Armig nup unus quatuor hostiarior camere dom reg Henri septum, qui obiit VI die Augusti aº dn̄i mº Vº X cuie die ppicietur deus amē.§

A similar brass, five years later.

> Humbly prayeth you of your charitie to pray for the souls of Mr. Roṅᵗ. ROCHESTER, Esq., late Srgeant of the Pantry of our Sovrain Lord King Henry the VIII., which dep-d this p-sent lyff the first day of May, the yere of oure Lord God a thousand five hundredth and fourteen. On whose soul ihū of his i-fynite grace have mercy. Amen.

A plain strip of brass—the oldest memorial in the Church—records that it has reference to—

> ROBERT COTESBROK gist ycy morust . . . . . . le xj jò de Maris, l'an de g'ce
> Mil ccc lxxxxiij ce. ||

---

* See Fairholt's "Costumes," p. 183, ed. Lond. 1846.

† Here lies Thomas Williams, gentleman, and Margaret his wife. The said Thomas died Jan. 16, 1495, and the said Margaret . . . . . . May God have mercy on their souls. Amen.

‡ See Fairholt's "Costumes," p. 238.

§ Here lies John Leventhorp, Esq., one of the four Keepers of the Chamber to King Henry VII., who died August 6th, 1510. To whose soul God be gracious. Amen.

|| Robert Cotesbrok lies here . . . . . . died the 11th day of March, the year of grace, 1393.

Two brasses, of which the drawings are still extant, although they themselves have altogether disappeared from their respective matrices, were to the memory of—

> JOANE daughter of Henry Seamer, and wife to Richard, Son and Heir of Robert Lord Poynings.*

Thomas Benolte (A.D. 1534), Windsor Herald, and his two wives, the execution of which must have been exceedingly beautiful. The inscription, as follows, has been preserved:—

> Here under lieth the Bodi of THOMAS BENOLTE, Squyer, sometyme servant and offycer of Armes, by the name of Windsor Herault, unto the right high, and most mighty Prince of . . . . most drade Souverayne Lord Kyng Henry the VIII: which Thomas Benolte, otherwyes namyd Clarenceux Kyng of Armes, decesid the Viii day of May, in the year of our Lord God MVCXXXIIIJ, in xxvi yere of our said Soverayne Lord.

---

* "The account of this monument, given in Stow's Survey of London, from the first to the last edition, adds 'she died a virgin, 1420.' This figure is now lost, but an impression of it . . . taken by the late Mr. E. R. Mores, when it was preserved in the church chest, represents her habited in a mantle, surcot, and kirtle with mitten sleeves, and on her breast, ihu mercy; her head-dress is of the veil kind, with the bosses of reticulated hair above her ears. . . . . . Mr. Mores has written under it, 'Obiit virgo, 1420.'—Gough's Sepulchral Monuments, vol. ii. part 2, p. 55, ed. Lond. 1786–96. See also Stow's Survey of Lond., vol. i. p. 431.

"In this Church their was a figure of the Trinity, and a high altar of S Helen; to w^h much devotion was paid. In the year 1488, Rafe Mackin, Esq., of this parish, made his will, to be buried before the Trinity, in St Helen's Parish, in Bishopsgate-Street, &c. *Item*, I bequeath to the Church a blake velvet gown, and a blake velvet cloke. *Item*, I bequeath to the high aultare of St Ellen's a fyne Diaper Tabull Cloath."—Stow's Survey of London: vol. i. p. 431, ed. Lond., 1754–55.

CHAPTER V.

BENEFACTORS.

The Benefactors belonging to this parish are numerous, as the following list—obtained from authentic parochial documents—fully proves, and cannot fail to be acceptable as a record of the pious benevolence of our forefathers by the antiquarian and archæologist.

1579, May 16.—Margaret Dane bequeathed to the Master, Wardens and Company of Ironmongers the sum of 2000*l*., on condition that they should lend to twenty young men of the Company 100*l*. each at 5*l*. per cent. for the space of three years, on sufficient security, and on repayment that it should be lent out again from time to time for ever, and that in consideration of the benefit thereof the Company should put in sufficient security to pay yearly 100*l*. as follows: to Christ's Hospital, St. Bartholomew's, and St. Thomas's Hospital, 10*l*. each; to twenty poor maids at their marriage 10*l*.; to the Universities of Oxford and Cambridge 5*l*. each, for the relief and bringing up in learning two poor scholars; 10*l*. to be distributed in bread and beef amongst poor prisoners in Newgate, &c.; 5*l*. towards the maintenance of a school at Bishop's Stortford; 10*l*. for a dinner in their hall on the anniversary of her death, and to provide twelve thousand faggots every year, to be equally distributed to each ward. . . . . The sum of 25*l*. is paid yearly, in lieu of faggots, to the aldermen of twenty-four of the wards of London, 1*l*. 0*s*. 10*d*. to each for distribution among the poor of their respective wards. . . . . The amount annually received by this parish is two shillings.

1599, July 12.—John Robinson, Senr., Merchant of the Staple, by his will gave to his son Arthur a tenement in the parish of St. Olave, near the Tower of London; and his will is, "that for ever shall be paid out of the said Capital house, to the Parson and Churchwardens, by quarterly payments, 5*l*. 4*s*., which they shall distribute weekly by two shillings, every Sunday morning in bread to the poor people inhabiting in this parish, with a clause for distress if unpaid after the space of forty days." . . . .

The premises charged with this payment, consisting of a house in Crutched Friars, afterwards became the property of the Carpenters' Company. They are now held by the East India Company, who have taken down the house and erected on the site thereof a part of their warehouses in that street, on which is placed the arms of the Carpenters' Company, by whom the annuity is paid.*

1603, Sep. 29.—EDWARD FENNER, of this parish, citizen and carpenter, by his Will did order and dispose of his messuage or tenement, wherein he dwelt, being No. 40 Bishopsgate Street, in this parish, to several persons for their respective lives, and after their decease, the reversion thereof to the minister and churchwardens of this parish for the time being; and to the master and wardens of the Company of Carpenters and their successors for ever, to the end that they, within four years after that they shall be possessed thereof, pay his next heir then living 20l., he requiring or demanding the same, and to be paid at the said messuage by quarterly payments, and then after that all such rents after made be divided in two equal parts, whereof one equal half part to be distributed yearly for ever to the poor of this parish, and the other equal half part among the poor of the said Company of Carpenters. . . . .

This house was let on lease, Sept. 12, 1671, for thirty-four years, at the rent of ten pounds per annum. It was afterwards let to William Poole, sadler, at thirty pounds per annum, for twenty-one years from Lady-day, 1705, the first year at a peppercorn rent, on account of the repairs. This lease was renewed to Mr. Poole for the like period from Lady-day, 1726, at the same rent, with an allowance of 40l. for repairs.

Oct. 2, 1777.—A lease was granted to Mr. H. Ward for twenty-one years from Lady-day, 1779, at 34l. per annum, the first year's rent being allowed on his undertaking to keep the house in good repair, and to expend 80l. thereon within two years. This lease was delivered up at Lady-day, 1793, and a new lease

---

* Commissioners' Report on Public Charities, p. 322.

was granted to H. W. Ward for the term of forty years, at 34*l.* per annum, on his agreement to spend 250*l.* in repairs, the parish allowing him the first year's rent in part thereof, at the expiration of which period, March 25, 1833, a new lease was granted to Mr. Stone, at 52*l.* 10*s.* per annum, Mr. Stone putting the house into complete repair, and paying all taxes and insurances.

1607, March 11.—WILLIAM PRIOR, citizen and pewterer, of London, by his Testament willed, after the decease of his wife, the yearly rent of his house, No. 27, Bishopsgate Street, to be paid to the churchwardens for the time being, and to be by them laid out yearly for ever, viz., 8*l.* of the said rent to be bestowed on sea-coals, and given to the poor of this parish, and also for two sermons to be preached yearly for ever, viz., on the first Thursday in clean Lent, one sermon, and the other on the day of his burial (which was March 27, 1608), for which sermons he gave thirteen shillings and fourpence out of the said rent; and to the minister, churchwardens, and parishioners for the time being 2*l.* yearly for "a drinking," to be spent on the day the said first sermon shall be preached; and the rest of the said yearly rent to be to the use of the poor of the said parish; and if the said trust is not executed in the manner aforesaid, the messuage to go to St. Ethelburga parish, with remainder to the Pewterers' Company. . . . .

The house was let on lease, June 4, 1697, for twenty-one years from Lady-day, 1699, to Mr. Math. Chewter, at 30*l.* per annum, and a present fine of 50*l.*, with agreement not to let it to a tallow chandler, a cook, a victualler, a blacksmith, or a baker; and Mr. Chewter paid Mr. Churchwarden Woods five shillings in part of the fifty pounds fine, which he acknowledged the receipt of. . . . .

June 2, 1720.—A lease was granted to Mrs. Ireson for twenty-one years, at 40*l.* per annum, with a fine of sixty pounds ("Mr. W. Palmer, a parishioner, had offered to take a lease for fifty years, at 45*l.* per annum, and fifty pounds fine, but retracted therefrom and eluded the vestry, whereby this vestry has deemed him injurious, troublesome, and impertinent"). At the expiration of the above period, Midsummer, 1741, a lease was granted to Mr. Nathl. Ware, for the like term of twenty-one years, at the same rent, the parish allowing one year's rent for repairs, and Mr. Ware paid one shilling to the churchwarden to bind him to his agreement.

Lady-day, 1784.—The same house was let on lease to Mr. Thomas Delafield for twenty-one years, at 42*l.* per annum, on his expending 115*l.* in repairs, towards which the parish allowed the first year's rent. A new lease was granted, October 27, 1803, to Mr. Whittenbury, for twenty-one years, at 42*l.* per annum. The premises were then taken by Mr. Edward Arman, on a building lease, for sixty years, from Lady-day, 1819, at the rent of 40*l.* per annum, and a further charge of 3*l.* 16*s.* per annum for land-tax, which was redeemed by the parish in the year 1800, at an expense of 126*l.* 16*s.* Mr. Arman also purchased from the parish the tithes of his house during the duration of his lease for 12*l.* 12*s.*

1608, Aug. 25.—CICELY CYOLL, Widow of German Cyoll, Merchant, "considering the fickle and uncertain state and condition of this present lyfe, and having observed what contentions and controversies doe many times arise amongst deere friends for the goods and possessions of such as leave their estates undisposed, being either prevented by suddaine death or by protracting tyme until such feebleness and debility of body and memory overtake them, that they cannot set any certaine course or order therein, I leave my body to be buried in my late father's vault in St. Michael Bassishaw, and at my buriall I wish a sermon to be preached by my loving friend Mr. Ball, preacher at St. Hellens, unto whom I leave as a legacy 6*l.* 13*s.* 4*d.* . . I will that there be given to fourscore poor women, fourscore gowns of the value of 1*l.* 6*s.* 8*d.* apiece, twenty of the poor women to be of the parish of St. Hellens, and other twenty of St. Michael Bassishaw, and the others as my executors shall appoint. And to every of the said poor women twelve pence apiece. And for a dynner for the entertainment of my kindred and friends such as shall resort to my buriall, and I do limit the sume fifty pounds to be bestowed and the dinner to be kept in my dwelling house in Bishopsgate Street. . . . .

. . . . . "I will and ordain and do give and dispose the sum of One Hundred and Twenty pounds to be bestowed within convenient time after my decease by my executors upon some convenient purchase of lands, tenements or hereditaments within the City of London of the yearly value of Six pounds at the least and likely to hold the same value for ever, and the same purchase so found to be assured to certain ffeoffees of the said several parishes of St. Michael Bassishaw and St. Hellens. And to be continued in assurance to the said parishes for ever to the end that the Church Wardens of the said several Parishes from time to time for ever, shall by and with the revenues of the lands so purchased, distribute weekly for ever to as many poor widows or sole women of their parishes to be equally chosen by a like number in either parish, such as the said parishioners shall think meet to receive the same benevolence every Sabbath day in the morning as the rent or revenues of the said purchase shall extend, to give to every of them two pence a piece in white bread."

1612.— —— FOUNTAIN gave 10*l*. to the poor of this parish.

1614.—EDWARD BRYERWOOD, Reader of the Astronomy Lecture at Gresham College, bequeathed the sum of 10*l*. to the poor of this parish.

1614.— —— OLIVAR gave 2*l*. to the poor of this parish.

1630, June 10.—ABRAHAM CHAMBRELAN, merchant, in consideration of the sum of 60*l*. paid him by Sir Henry Rowe, executor of Mrs. Cyoll, with the consent of the parishioners of St. Helen's, granted unto the said parishioners an annuity or rent-charge of 3*l*. per annum for ever on two messuages, situate in Great St. Helen's, to be distributed according to the will of Mrs. Cyoll: and by the will of Mr. Chambrelan, dated December 15, 1640, he bequeathed 100*l*., to remain as a stock, for the use of the poor of St. Helen's for ever, on condition that the parish will allow a vault to be made in the Church for a burial place for himself, wife, and posterity: and within six months after his decease receive and take in the above sum of 60*l*.

The said sum now forms part of the parish stock.

1631, Sep. 1.—Sir MARTIN LUMLEY, knight, and alderman of London, by his will, gave to the churchwardens and their successors for ever one annuity or rent-charge of 20*l*. issuing out of his messuage or tenement in the parish of St. John the Evangelist, London, called the Black Boy, at two payments—Christmas and Lady-day (?)—by even and equal portions, upon trust, for the establishing a lecture or sermon for ever, to be preached in this Parish Church on Tuesday evenings weekly, from Michaelmas to Lady-day, to the honour and glory of God and comfort of the auditors: the churchwardens to pay the same to a godly divine for his pains in preaching; the said sermon or lecture to begin about five o'clock in the evening: and to the said churchwardens likewise one other amount or rent-charge of 4*l*. per annum, issuing out of the said messuage, for the use of the poor householders of this parish at Christmas and Lady-day by even and equal portions.

The heirs and successors of Sir Martin Lumley were to have full power and authority for ever in appointing or displacing the said minister. No claim to the appointment having been made by the heirs for many years past, the parishioners in vestry have usually appointed the vicar. Attendance was always given on the proper days at *three* o'clock, instead of the evening, and it is said that if a congregation of three persons attended, the lecture would be preached. It must be stated, however, to the credit of the Rev. Charles Mackenzie, the vicar from 1835 to 1847, that he altered it again to evening service, as ordered by the donor, commencing at half-past six o'clock, and continued yearly to a comparatively numerous congregation, during the whole time he held the living.

The annuity of 4*l*., together with those of W. Pennoyre and Thomas Hanson, is given away about Christmas to poor housekeepers not receiving parish relief, at the discretion of the churchwardens.

At a court for determination of differences touching houses destroyed by the fire of London, held in Clifford's Inn Hall, June 28, 1667—on the petition of Rebecca Garrett, respecting the tenement left by Sir Martin Lumley, known by the sign of the Black Boy (afterwards called the Bear and Ragged Staff) in Watling Street, charged with the payment of 24*l*. per annum to the Parish of St. Helen's: and that the rebuilding of the said tenement will cost 1500*l*., the parish utterly refusing to contribute thereto, and that the ground as it lies will not pay the said annuities, the churchwardens being summoned to appear in court, after great debate touching the contribution—it was decreed: That the petitioner should rebuild the said tenement with all convenient speed, and that the payment of the 4*l*. shall cease until Christmas, 1668, and that the payment of the annuity of 20*l*. per annum be forborne and cease for thirteen years from Michaelmas, 1668; and all arrears from the time of the fire are hereby acquitted; and after the expiration of the said thirteen years, the payment of the said annuity of 20*l*. to revive and continue to be paid, and the payment of the said annuity of 4*l*. to continue without ceasing when the messuage shall be rebuilt.

1633.— —— Meynon left 10*l*. to the poor.

—— Masters left 10*l*. to the poor.

Item.—There is a payment of 3*l*. per annum unto the vicar of this parish, issuing out of a messuage some time in the occupation of Charles Perkins. This is said to have been anciently the Vicarage House, and of late was claimed by the Skinners' Company.

1633, Oct. 14.—William Robinson, late of this parish, citizen and mercer, by his deed enrolled in Chancery, charged a messuage or tenement, and two yard lands, and a quarter of a yard land in Staverton-upon-the-Hill, in Northamptonshire, and all his lands there, with one annuity of 2*l*. 12*s*. after his decease, for ever to be paid to the churchwardens and overseers of the poor of this parish at Lady-day, to be distributed among the poor pensioners of this parish, by 12*d*. per week, in good sweet wheaten bread every Sabbath-day after morning sermon or dinner service in the said Church. The property, thus charged, now belongs to the Manor of Staverton; the annuity is regularly paid at the Banking-house of Messrs. Glyn and Company, and forms part of the fund for the distribution of bread on Sundays.

1635, Feb. 8.—Thomas Fenner, citizen of London, by his will, gave all his messuage and tenement in this parish, after the decease of his wife and brother, unto the parson and churchwardens of this parish, upon trust that they shall, "out of the rent and profit thereof, yearly distribute, among seven poor women of this parish in most want, 7*l*., and shall cause one sermon yearly to be preached in this church on the day of his burial (March 2, 1635,) by some godly preacher, and shall give to him for his pains for every sermon ten shillings, and that the churchwardens may take other ten shillings yearly for their travell and paines taken in and about the premises; and all the rest of the rents and profits shall be to the use of the poor of the said parish."

The house devised by the above will was let on a building lease, June 1, 1687, to Thomas Kirkes, for 25 years at 8*l*. per annum, and on May 7, 1689, a further term of 25 years was added to the lease. At the expiration of that period, March 25, 1739, a new lease was granted to Mrs. Elizabeth Kirk for 21 years, to pay 10 guineas fine, 12*l*. per annum rent, clear of all taxes, and to lay out 60*l*. in repairs.

In 1760 a surveyor being engaged to value certain premises in order to an exchange between the parish and Mr. Eyre, reported that Mr. Eyre should have all the premises over and against the gateway leading into Great St. Helen's, the parish taking the premises on the north-side, No. 38, Bishopsgate Street, and paying him the sum of 20*l*. 10*s*. . . . . Advertisements having been inserted in the daily papers to let the premises exchanged with Mr. Eyre, on a building lease, several proposals were received, and on August 27, 1761, a lease was granted to James Stone for 61 years at a yearly rent of twelve guineas, Mr. Stone also agreeing to give five guineas for the use of the poor. . . . . In 1805 an additional term of seven years was added to this lease, then in the possession of Mr. Greenaway, at the same rent, in consideration of his long residence and services as churchwarden and continual overseer. The additional term was afterwards surrendered to the vestry, and they resolved to grant him a new lease for 21 years from the expiration of the original term, at the rent of 60*l*. per annum, the tenant paying the land-tax and insuring the premises. . . . . The new lease bore date June 24, 1822.

1636, April 20.—JOYCE FEATLY,* by her will, did "appoint that, after the death of her husband, Dr. Daniel Featly and herself, yearly to be paid out of the rents and profits of a messuage in the parish of Lambeth in Surrey (being copyhold of the Manor of

---

* "Commission Issued 21 Feby 23d Chas. 1st.
"Executed 5th Dec. follg.
"found that Danl Featley and Joyce his wife both Dec^d were thentofore seized in Fee in right of s^d Joyce accord^g to the Custom of the Manor of Kennington in Co. of Surrey of one Messu. and Garden with the appurts. sit. in Lambeth, of the Yearly Value of £20.
"That s^d Danl and Joyce in or ab^t Apl. in the 12th year of his s^d Majesty's Reign according to the Custom of the Manor Surrender the Premes. as herein ment^d
"That s^d Joyce with consent of her Husband, by a writing Dated the 20 day of Ap^l in the 12th year of his s^d Majesty's Reign, did limit and appoint that after the Death of herself and Husband the use of the s^d surrender of the Premises sho^d be to the use of Wm Kerwin her nephew and his Heirs upon Trust as therein men^d. That the s^d Joyce shortly after mak^g s^d writ^g Died and was Buried in St. Helen's Church on the 3^d Oct., 1637. That the s^d Danl her husband her survived, and enjoyed the Premis. That s^d Danl Died on or ab^t 21 Ap^l 1645, and that Andrew Kerwan Pretended Title to the Premises."

Kennington), for ever 4*l.* per annum to be paid to the vicar and churchwardens of this parish by quarterly payments upon trust to distribute 12*d.* thereof weekly every Sunday in bread, and 20*s.* thereof yearly to the minister to preach on the day of her burial (which was October 3, 1637), and in default of such sermon the said 20*s.* to go to the poor of the parish, and 6*s.* per annum to be bestowed in repairing her father's tomb (KERWIN's) and the other 2*s.* yearly to the sexton for keeping the same tomb clean. Upon the death of Dr. Featly, April 21, 1645, the heirs of the said Joyce refusing to pay the said annuity, the vicar and churchwardens sued out an inquisition upon the statute for charitable uses, and in December, 1648, obtained a decree for the payment, but the Manor of Kennington being vested in the Crown, and in consequence of the change of Government and confusion in those times, the said decree was never put in execution or revived until the year 1702, when the vicar and churchwardens sued out a writ of Scire Facias to revive the said decree; to which one Nicholas Lampon and others in possession of the premises put in exceptions, and the cause being heard before the Lord Keeper, November 13, 1703, his lordship ordered payment of the said annuity from Michaelmas 1703, with a remittance of all arrears by consent and each party paying their own costs; which order was made a final decree of the Court of Chancery and enrolled in the Petty Bag Office, March, 1703-4. The money spent in this suit for the recovery of this annuity was 70*l.* 2*s.* 8*d.* The premises thus charged, consist of three houses in Kennington Lane, and belong respectively to—

Mr. Slade, of Doctors' Commons, who pays	£2	0	7
Mr. Cook, of Water Lane, Tower Street	1	3	2
And Mr. Hunter, of St. Martin's Lane	0	16	3

as their respective portions of this annuity."

1636.—Sir JULIUS CÆSAR left the sum of 5*l.* for the use of the poor.

1636, Dec. 16.—DANIEL WILLIAMS, merchant, bequeathed 50*l.* to be distributed amongst such poor housekeepers, whose wants make them labour hard to get a poor living, inhabitants of the parish of St. Stephen, Coleman Street, where he was born; St. Peter the Poor, where he was apprenticed; St. Andrew Undershaft and St. Helen, as his executors, in their discretion shall, by advice and information of the churchwardens of the said parishes, think fit to distribute the same. And a further sum of 200*l*. to be laid out in lands, one half thereof for the benefit of the poor of the parish of St. Stephen, Coleman Street, and the other half to the use of the poor of St. Helen's and St. Andrew Undershaft to be equally divided between them.

1643.—Captain MARTIN BOND bequeathed the sum of 25*l*. to the poor.

1646, April 21.—THOMAS HUTCHINS, Merchant Taylor, by his will directs "that the sum of 50*l*. shall be paid by my executors to the churchwardens of the parish of St. Helen's where I now dwell, to the intent, and upon trust and confidence that they with the other parishioners shall make such provision and assurance that fifteen penny loaves of wheaten bread shall be weekly for ever given and distributed amongst the poor of the said parish, whereof the almsfolk there to be first preferred."

1647.—THOMAS AUDLEY left 30*l*. to the poor.

1649.—JOHN EYLES left 20*l*. to buy coals for the poor.

1649.—Alderman LANGHAM gave 5*l*. to be given in bread to the poor.

1652, Sep. 14.—MOSES TRYON bequeathed to this parish the sum of 100*l*. to remain as a stock for the said parish for ever; the benefit and increase thereof arising, to be disposed of for the benefit of the poor of the said parish for ever, or otherwise as the churchwardens and vestry should think fit, in confidence that they and their successors would for ever thereafter observe and perform the grants and agreements contained in an order of vestry, October 25, 1643, touching a burial place in the said Church, thereby granted to him, his heirs and posterity for ever; and if at any time hereafter the said vestry should infringe the said order, then the same legacy to be given to the parish of St. Nicholas Acons in London for the benefit of the poor of that parish.

1654.—Mrs. CHAMBERLAIN gave 10*l*. to the poor.

1656.—Mr. GILES left 20*l*. to buy coals for the poor.

1656, March 23.—ADAM LAWRENCE bequeathed "to the relief of the poor of the parish of St. Hellens the sum of 10*l*., to be distributed amongst the said poor by and at the discretion of my executor, with the advice of the minister and churchwardens. I give to Mr. Barham, minister of St. Hellens, the sum of 10*l*. I give to my executor the sum of 100*l*., to be layd out by him to and for such charitable use as he shall like and approve, either for the encouragment of the minister, or relief of the poor of that parish, or both, having consulted with the vestry of the parishioners on that behalf." His nephew, Sir John Lawrence, sole executor, by an indenture dated May 16, 1684, obliged himself, his heirs, &c., to pay the said legacy of 100*l*., and the sum of 150*l*. due for interest thereof, and also to pay 100*l*. more for leave to make a vault in the parish church for the use of himself and his family. The said Sir John Lawrence did by the same indenture, therefore grant to several persons and their heirs forever, in trust for the Parish, one annuity or rent charge of 20*l*. per annum, to be issuing out of a messuage or tenement in this parish, late in the occupation of John Seagre, with a clause for distress, redeemable upon the payment of 350*l*.

This annuity was redeemed by Mrs. Dorothy Lawrence, April 29, 1736, for the said sum of 350*l*. Of this sum 150*l*. was borrowed by the Parish, June 7, 1744, for the finishing of the workhouse, and the remainder was invested, and now forms part of the parish stock.

 1658.—H. HILL gave 20*l*. to the poor.
  „ — WILDS gave 2*l*. to the poor.
  „ — BYARD left 5*l*. to the poor.

 1670, May 25.—WILLIAM PENNOYER bequeathed the sum of 100*l*. to be paid into the hands of the overseers of the poor for the parish of Great St. Helen's, to be by them put out and invested in good security for the relief of three poor housekeepers there forever.

 1670, November 1.—JOHN LANGHAM.—" I give and bequeath for the use of the poore of St. Hellen's, London, the sum of 100*l*., to be kept in my executors' hands, to be by them, the ministers and churchwardens of the same parish for the time being, distributed to twenty of the poorest ffamilyes or widdowes of the same parish, of the best name and ffame, by 20*s*. a-piece, every St. Thomas's day, for the next five years after my decease."

 1672, June 4.—WILLIAM FINCH bequeathed 50*l*. towards building a new steeple.

 1673, July 25.—HENRY WHITTINGHAM, by his will: " I give

and bequeath unto the poor of the parish of St. Hellens, where I do dwell, and have long lived, the sum of 25*l*."

1682, May 23.—DIANA ASTREY, of this parish, widow, did by her will give 10*s*. yearly, to the world's end, to the minister of this parish, for better encouragement to preach ; and to the clerk 2*s*. 6*d*. yearly to the world's end, to be paid yearly in the month of November, to be an example for others to do the like.

1683.—Sir THOMAS VINER left 10*l*. to the poor.

1687.—Mrs. TRYON left 10*l*. to the poor.

1692.—Mrs. PAIGE left 20*l*. to the use of this parish.

1702.—ABRAHAM CHITTY left 5*l*. to the poor.

1702.———— SPURSTOW left 5*l*. to the poor.

1704, April 13.—Alderman WOOLFE gave a carpet and cushions for the use of the communion table.

1705, May 13.—GERVASH RERESBY left 10*l*. to the poor.

1707.—Mrs. PRIDEAUX gave vallens of crimson velvet, with a large gold fringe thereto, as an addition to the cushion provided for the pulpit.

1711.———— FOOTE left 20*l*. to the poor.

1718.—JOHN WRIGHT gave 5*l*. to the poor.

1719.—GEORGE BODDINGTON left 10*l*. to the poor.

1720, June 18.—ISAAC BERKLEY, late of Calcutta, did by his will give to this parish the sum of 4000 rupees, the produce thereof, amounting to 500*l*., was remitted to this country by the East India Company, and received by the parish July 25, 1723. It was then ordered to be laid out in South Sea Stock. A Bill in Chancery was filed by the minister against the churchwardens, relating to the disposal thereof, to which an answer being made, and a decree by the Master of the Rolls, it was resolved, June 10, 1725, that the said stock shall be laid out in the erection of an organ in the Church.

1735, December 18.—MARY CLAPHAM by her will gave to the ministers and churchwardens of the parish of St. Helen's the sum of 100*l*., to be by them laid out in the purchase of freehold lands, or in some of the public stocks or securities, and directed that out of the clear annual rents and profits arising thereby, her late father's (Joseph Sem) monument should be repaired as occasion should require, and that the residue of such rents and profits should, yearly upon Christmas Eve, be distributed amongst the poor of the said parish, in such proportions as the minister and churchwardens shall think fit.

By order of Vestry, April 29, 1736, the above sum was invested in the Three per cent. annuities, and on April 20, 1737, it was ordered to be sold out to pay off the sum of 100*l.*, which had been borrowed for the use of the parish at 4½ per cent., the Vestry agreeing to indemnify the minister and churchwardens, for the time being, touching the several uses for which the said legacy was left to the parish.

1736.—JOHN BAKER left 10*l.* to the poor.

1742. Dec. 15.———— ROE, by his will produced at a vestry, "Gave to the parish of St. Helen towards purchasing a Parsonage house in the said parish for the Minister to reside in constantly and not for him to make any advantage of by letting it out to another, but for his own proper habitation and place of abode that he may be ready at hand on occasion, and provided a Parsonage house be purchased in the said parish and inhabited by the Minister within the space of three years after my decease: on this condition I give to the said parish of St. Helen 100*l.* to be paid to the Churchwardens then being : and in case a parsonage house should be purchased in the said parish and constantly inhabited by the Minister before my decease—then this 100*l.* shall be towards keeping the said house in repair, but if a Parsonage house be not so purchased and so occupied before my decease, nor within the space of three years after as aforesaid, Then I will, that this 100*l.* shall go to the Incorporated Society for propagating the Gospel in Foreign Parts."

1748. Mar. 28.—ROBERT DINGLEY having previously informed the parish that his mother had died intestate, and knowing that it was her intention that something should be given for the benefit of the poor, presented Thirty Pounds, on condition that the following entry should be made on the Table of Donations : "Mrs. Susannah Dingley gave 30*l.* to this parish, that two shillings be distributed in Bread every first Sunday in the month for ever to twelve poor parishioners who are most constant at the sacrament over and above their usual allowance."

1749.— ——— GRIGMAN left 20*l.* to the poor.

1768. April 30.—THOMAS HANSON bequeathed to the Minister and Churchwardens of this parish for the time being and their successors the sum of 500*l*., upon trust to invest the same in the public stock or funds of this kingdom, and pay and apply the interest thereof, unto and among such indigent and industrious inhabitants and parishioners (if any such there be) of the said parish who shall not receive alms therefrom.

1776.—JOHN SMITH, of Great St. Helen's, by deed, dated Sept. 25, 1776, transferred to the governors of Christ's Hospital the sum of 2500*l*. Three per Cent. South Sea Annuities on condition that they should pay to his nephew, William Webber, of Fursley, in the county of Devon, aged 43 years, an annuity of 100*l*. during his life, and after his decease that they should from time to time for ever, maintain and educate in the said hospital two children of persons who shall be inhabitants of this parish, to be chosen by a majority of the vestry of the said parish, and on the death or discharge or other removal of every such child or children, within three months to receive and admit other or others, in his, her, or their room. Provided that the parent or parents of such child or children so to be maintained and educated, shall have been an inhabitant or inhabitants of the said parish one whole year next immediately before such choice shall be made, and every child so to be chosen shall be upwards of seven years of age, born in lawful wedlock, of honest and reputable parents. And the Minister and Churchwardens shall comply with and be subject to the forms generally in use for the admission of children into the said hospital.

The following records of Mr. John Smith's benevolence also appear in the parish books:—

Sept. 27, 1770.—The thanks of the vestry were given to John Smith, Esq. for the service he has done this parish in getting several children into Christ's Hospital.

May 29, 1777.—The thanks of this vestry were given to John Smith, Esq. for having had painted at his own expense the doors and doorcases of the church, and also the iron rails round the church yard.

April 23, 1778.—The thanks of the vestry were given to John Smith, Esq. for having promised to get Charles Oxtoby, a poor boy belonging to this parish, into Christ's Hospital, and for having given the churchwardens five guineas to divide among the poor pensioners.

August 27, 1778.—The thanks of the vestry were given to John Smith, Esq. for having presented the parish with a large folio bible and also a silver cup and cover.

June 15, 1780.—The thanks of the vestry were given to John Smith, Esq., for having presented the parish with three new bells and the hanging thereof in the steeple of this parish church.

Feb. 12, 1784.—John Smith, Esq., having by his will left the sum of 20*l.* to be distributed amongst the most necessitous poor inhabitants of this parish at the discretion of a vestry to be called for that purpose, it was this day distributed accordingly.

1823. March 6.—THOMAS TRUNDLE, of Crosby Square, late vestry clerk, bequeathed to this parish the sum of 25*l.* Three per Cent. Consols in trust to pay the annual interest thereof to the poor women belonging to the parish that usually attend Divine service on a Sunday in the said church, and to receive bread and other gifts in manner following :—One moiety thereof on Sunday next after Christmas Day, and the other moiety on the first Sunday after Whit Sunday in every year.

CHAPTER VI.

REGISTERS.

The parish registers of St. Helen's unfortunately do not commence at the earliest date of those records. The volume, or volumes, containing the entries for 1538, when they were first ordered, down to 1575, is, or are, hopelessly lost. Those in existence, however, have a respectable antiquity, as they embrace the personal annals of the parish during the last three hundred years. The volumes now remaining are in good condition, and, in some instances, the original rough drafts have been preserved, which sometimes furnish more particulars than are given in the official copy. They should both be consulted when any inquiry is made within their period.

As St. Helen's appears to have been the most aristocratic parish of Old London—St. Olave, Hart Street, probably ranking next—it follows that the registers are full of entries respecting the early history of families that have since become connected with the nobility and gentry of the country, and, in many instances, been ennobled themselves. The names of many historical personages will be found among them, and altogether, according to the testimony of a gentleman,* who has had great experience among parish registers, they are perhaps as interesting a series as will be found in any parish in the kingdom. The church appears always to have been a popular one for marriages, before the existence of Lord Hardwicke's Act, and down to 1754, numerous entries will be found of parties from places most remote, whose names do not, perhaps, again appear in the registers. The baptisms are also

---

* Col. Joseph L. Chester, an American antiquary and archæologist, who has collected and arranged the immense stores of Registers, MSS., &c. of Westminster Abbey, the value of which work may be inferred by its being printed by the Harleian Society.

extremely interesting, and the records of burials within the church, for a long period before the registers commence, and a considerable time afterwards, afford abundant data for the genealogist, biographer, and historian.

It is somewhat difficult, therefore, to make such a selection of entries from the registers as will furnish an adequate idea of their character, which could only be accomplished by printing them in full; but the following, taken almost at random, may be regarded as fair examples :—

Marriages.

1575, April 17.—John Pitway and Anne Bindle. [The first marriage in the earliest volume.]

1596-7, Jan. 10.—Michael Stanhope and Ann Reade. [He was of the family of the Earls of Chesterfield. She is usually called Elizabeth in the peerages.]

1600, April 7.—Sir Anthony Cope, Kt., and the Lady Anne L'Estrange.

1604, Nov. 20.—Sir Robert Bosville, Kt., and Elizabeth Pelishall, mayd.

1606, July 12.—Sir George Snellinge, Kt., and Cicily Sherly.

1608, May 3.—John Howland, of Gray's Inn, Esq., son of Sir Giles Howland, of Streatham, in Surrey, Kt., and Cislye Suzan, of this parish.

1608-9, Feb. last.—Charles Somerset, Esq., son of the Right Hon. Edward, Earl of Worcester, and Elizabeth Powell, maiden, daughter of Sir William Powell, of Monmouth, in Wales, Knight, were married at Worcester House, in the Strand, by virtue of a special dispensation under the hand of my Lord of Canterbury, and by a licence from the Faculties, dated February 25th. [This entry occurs among the burials in the original register, or rough draft, only, and has lines drawn across it, but is probably the only record existing of the marriage.]

1610, April 10.—Thomas Coventry, of the Inner Temple, Esq., and Elizabeth Pitchford, of this parish, widow, late wife of William Pitchford, apothecary, deceased. [This was the second marriage of the celebrated Lord-Keeper Coventry, created Lord Coventry in 1628.]

1617, July 21.—Thomas Ascough, of Gray's Inn, Esq., and Anne Sterne, of Maulton, co. Cambridge, widow, late wife of Robert Sterne, Gent., deceased.

1619, April 22.—Felix Tindal, of Queen's College, Cambridge, Clerk, and Suzan Bradshawe, of St. Stephen's, Coleman Street, late wife of Obadiah Bradshawe, Clerk, deceased.

1624, June 17.—Richard Leigh, of Acton Burnell, in Shropshire, Gent., and Elizabeth Allen, daughter of Mr. Edward Allen, Alderman of London.

1629, Nov. 23.—Richard Prowze, of the City of Exeter, Gent., and Frances Carewe, of Huntingdon, co. Essex, widow.

1635, Sep. 3.—Phillipp De Goltes, Gent., and Hellen Bootes, "virgo Hagensis," by a certificate from the Dutch congregation.

Marriages continued.

1644, Dec. 26.—John Cudden, of Westminster, widower, and Dame Lady Catherine Essex.

1647, Oct. 6.—Sir Arthur Ingram, Kt., and Dame Catherine Boynton, widow.

1648-9, March 13.—Philip Boteler, Esq., son and heir of John Boteler, of Woodhall, Herts, Kt. of the Bath, and Elizabeth Langham, daughter to John Langham, Esq., Alderman of London : there being present the said Sir John Boteler and Alderman Langham, together with about forty more of their friends as witnesses.

1552-3, Jan. 20.—George Smithson, of Kipling, co. York, Esq., and Ellinor Fairfax, daughter of Charles Fairfax, of Menston, in the same county, Esq.

1660-1, Feb. 21.—Sir Thomas Hussey, Kt. and Bart., of Honington, co. Lincoln, and Dame Sarah Langham, of this parish : married by Dr. Sanderson, Bishop of Lincoln.

1670, July 7.—Henry Booth, eldest son to the Lord Dalamore, of Cheshire, and Mrs. Mary Langham, of this parish, spinster.

1675, Dec. 4.—William Morgan of Tredegar, co. Monmouth, Esq., and Elizabeth the Lady Darrell.

1683, Sep. 18.—Joseph Haskinstells, of Amsterdam, merchant, and Sarah Eyles, of this parish.

1693, June 8.—Thomas Warr and Dorothy Iregonwell, both of St. Margaret's, Westminster.

1703, Aug. 20.—Francis Gastrell, Dr. of Divinity, of Lincoln's Inn, and Elizabeth Mapletoff, of Greenwich, Kent.

1706, Aug. 15.—Thomas Turner, of Lincoln's Inn, Gent., and Dame Mary Stoughton, *alias* Payler, of St. Giles' in the Fields.

1714, Oct. 18.—Martin Folkes, of Nafferton, Yorkshire, Gent., and Lucretia Bradshawe, of St. Andrew's, Holborn.

1727, Aug. 13.—The Honourable Charles Compton, Esq., and Mrs. Mary Lucy.

1738, April 27.—Thomas Foxley, M.A., Rector of Great Rollright, co. Oxon, bachelor, and Elizabeth Rawdon, of Stratford Bow, co. Middlesex, spinster.

1749, Aug. 3.—Thomas Croft, Esq., bachelor, and Lucy Thompson, spinster, both of this parish.

1755, Jan. 16.—Peter Gaussen, of this parish, bachelor, and Anna-Maria Bosanquet, of St. Gregory's, spinster, a minor.

1759, April 29.—Willoughby Arundel, of Hackney, Middlesex, bachelor, and Mary Wright, of this parish, spinster.

1762, June 24.—Richard Hoare, of Boreham, in Essex, bachelor, and Susannah-Cecilia Dingley, of this parish, spinster.

1766, April 6.—Richard Pepys, of this parish, widower, and Mary Sanderson, of the same, spinster.

1771, Nov. 7.—John Peter Du Roveray and Jane Scott, both single, and of this parish.

1774, Nov. 3.—Henry Boulton, Esq., of this parish, bachelor, and Juliana Raymond, of Barking, Essex, spinster.

1780, Dec. 14.—Thomas Cope, of this parish, bachelor, and Mary Mountain, of St. Mary, Aldermanbury, spinster.

1783, Oct. 23.—John-Peter Du Roveray, Esq., widower, and Réné-Marguerite Bonard, spinster, both of this parish.

1789, April 4.—John-Henry Rougemont, of this parish, bachelor, and Frances-Mary-Rachael Rivaz, of St. Botolph Bishopsgate, spinster.

1791, June 14.—Charles Mayo, Esq., of this parish, bachelor, and Elizabeth Knowlys, of St. Dunstan in the East, spinster.

1794, Jan. 14.—The Rev. John Davis, of Waltham Holy Cross, co. Essex, widower, and Sarah Davis, of this parish, widow.

1795, Dec. 16.—Francis-David de la Chaumette, of St. Mary's, Newington, Midx., Esquire, bachelor, and Olympia-Charlotte Page, of this parish, spinster, a minor, with consent of her father, John Page.

1797, Feb. 23.—The Rev. Thomas Sikes, Clerk, of Gilsborough, co. Northampton, bachelor, and Susannah Powell, of this parish, spinster.

1800, Jan. 11.—Bunce Curling, M.D., of St. Pancras, Midx., bachelor, and Harriet Hutchinson, of this parish, spinster.

1806, May 22.—David Colby, Esq., of St. Martin in the Fields, bachelor, and Ann Costin, of this parish, widow.

Baptisms.

1575, July 30.—George, son of Anthony Howse. [The first entry of baptisms in the existing registers.]

1576-7, Jan. 2.—**Ann**, daughter of Edward Stanhope.

1577, Dec. 31.—**William**, son of William Reade, Gent.

1579-8, March 10.—**John**, son of John Jeckell [? Jekyll], Gent.

1581, Nov. 22.—**Michaell**, son of Edward Stanhope, Gent.

1587, June 23.—**John**, son of John Bowcher, Gent.

1589, Aug. 27.—**Anne**, daughter of Edward Dudley.

1591, Aug. 15.—**Elizabeth**, daughter of Peter Delavale, merchant.

1595, July 31.—**Ferdinando**, son of Richard Tayler, Dr. in Physic.

1597, July 25.—**Bridget**, daughter of Peter Turner, Dr. in Physic.

1600, July 28.—**Anne**, daughter of Thomas Morley, Gent., and Suzan.

1600-1, Feb. 15.—**Hester**, daughter of Albericus Gentyle, a civilian, and Hester.

1602, July 5.—**Pembrook**, daughter of Sir Henry Leonard, Knt., and Chrisogon : out of Dr. Turnor's.

1603, Dec. 11.—**Mathewe**, son of Albericus Gentyle, Doctor of the Civil Law, and Hester.

1604-5, Jan. 8.—**Elizabeth**, daughter of Sir Michael Stanhope, Kt., and Dame Anne.

1607-8, Feb. 4.—**George**, son of Thomas Greene, Gent., of Canterbury, and Alice.

1608-9, Jan. 2.—**William**, son of Sir Rotherham Willoughby, Kt., and the Lady Anne, his wife.

1611, May 26.—**David**, son of Abraham Chamberlen, merchant, and Hester.

1611, July 1.—**Elizabeth**, daughter of Sir Henry Baker, Kt., and Dame Katharine.

1611, Sep. 1.—" *Job rakt out of the Asshes*, being borne the last of August, in the lane going to Sir John Spencer's back gate, and there laide in a heape of Seacole Asshes, was baptised the ffirst daye of September following, and dyed the next day after."

1613, July 28.—Jaell, daughter of Roger Manwaring, Preacher.
1614, Sep. 18.—Humfry, son of Philip Gifford, Gent., and Suzan.
1616-7, Jan. 6.—Rebecca, daughter of Richard Ball, Parson of St. Helen's, and Elizabeth.
1619, March 26.—John Fawkner, reputed son of George Fawkner, Gent., servant to the Duke of Lennox, and Mary Peirce, servant to Edmund Peirsen, scrivener.
1621, June 27.—James, son of Sir Henry Fynes, Kt., and Dame Hellen; in Dr. Crooke's house.
1621-2, Jan. 6.—Hilkiah, son of Hilkiah Crooke, Dr. in Physic, and Anne.
1623, Sep. 12.—Lettes, daughter of Sir Fouke Grevell, Kt., and Dame Anne.
1626, Oct. 18.—Benjamin, son of Joseph Browne, Clerk, and Minister of this parish, and Suzan.
1631, June 29.—Margaret, daughter of Mr. Thomas Wiseman, Gent., and Elizabeth.
1634, July 2.—Samuel, son of Herriott Washbourne, Sugar Baker, and Agnes.
1635, June 18.—Patrick, son of Willoby Skipwith, Esq., and Honnor his wife.
1637-8, Feb. 19.—Anne, daughter of the Right. Hon. Spencer, Earl of Northampton, and the Right Hon. Countess, his wife.
1638, May 26.—Robert, son of Sir Gilbert Jarrett, Kt. and Bart., and Dame Lady Mary.
1643, May 15.—Edward, son of Myles Corbett, Esq., and Mary.
1647, Nov. 16.—Edward, son of Edward Cooke, Dr. in Physic, and Mary.
1649, Aug. 9.—Joane, daughter of Richard Wylde, Esq., and Rebecca: born Aug. 3rd.
1650, April 26.—Elizabeth, daughter of Robert Warberton, Esq., and Elizabeth: born 13th.
1651, June 18.—Samuel, son of Boulstrod Whitlock, Lord Commissioner of the Great Seal of England, and Dame Ladie Mary his wife.
1653, June 16.—John, son of Arthur Barham, our Minister, and Mary.
1654-5, Feb. 3.—Bigley, son of Samuel Carleton and Martha: born Feb. 2, baptized by Mr. Barham, in the Tower of London.
1656, Nov. 6.—Rowland, son of Rowland Hill, merchant, and Grace.
1658, July 8.—Rebecca, daughter of Alderman John Lawrence, and Abigail: born July 6th.
1659, Aug. 12.—Stephen, son of Stephen Langham, merchant, and Mary.
1661, Dec. 31.—John, son of Sir John Lawrence, Kt. and Alderman, and Abigail his Lady: born Dec. 11th.
1666, Aug. 17.—Anthony, son of Thomas Henchman, D.D., and Mary.
1669, March 28.—Richard, son of Thomas Garraway, Coffee-man, and Elizabeth.
1670, Oct. 9.—Charles, son of Sir Francis Clarke, Kt., and Lady Elizabeth.
1674, Dec. 5.—Elizabeth, daughter of Gilbert Aspinwall, Esq., and Mary.
1676, June 3.—Joseph, son of Brewen Rives, merchant.
1677-8, Jan. 8.—George, son of George Shuckburgh, Esq., and Anne.
1678, Oct. 1.—Stephen, son of Sir Stephen Anderson.
1680, Oct. 1.—Charlotte, daughter of Michael Biddulph, Esq., and Mary.
1682, April 11.—Angell, daughter of Sir Nicholas Butler, Kt., and Jane.

1685-6, March 16.—Dudley, son of Dudley Crue [Crewe], and Dorothy.
1687, Nov. 3.—Winifred, daughter of Alexander Pitfield, Esq., and Elizabeth.
1691, June 12.—Norbury, son of Richard Tennison, Lord Bishop of Clougher, and Ann : born June 10th.
1695, Aug. 26.—Joseph, son of Thomas Willis, clerk, and Elizabeth.
1697-8, Feb. 28.—Elizabeth, daughter of Edward Sayer, Esq., and Sarah.
1698, Dec. 20.—Martha, daughter of Charles Gresham, Esq., and Mary.
1700, April 22.—George, son of Mr. Charles Burdett, and Mary.
1700, May 26.—Edward, son of Robert Eyer, Esq., and Elizabeth, in St. Andrew Undershaft.
1700, Aug. 4.—Ann, daughter of Mr. William Atwell, banker, and Mary.
1702, Sep. 21.—Edward, son of Mr. Clement Boeheme, merchant, and Ann.
1703-4, Jan. 18.—Mary, daughter of Captain Peyton Nelson, and Mary.
1704, Sep. 7.—William, son of Dr. John Hawes and Margaret.
1706, July 15.—Henry, son of Robert Newton, clerk, and Margaret.
1708, Aug. 5.—" Anne, the natural daughter of Granado Chester, by Anne [blank] wife of [blank], shee cohabiting with the said Chester in continent, *as being sold by her said husband to Chester*, according to common fame."
1711, Dec. 8.—Epiphanus, son of Epiphanus Holland, clerk, and Susanna.
1713, May 29.—Attwell, son of Sir Bybie Lake, and Mary.
1715, Nov. 25.—" Granodo, son of Granodo Chester, and Mary his wife."
1716, May 21.—John, son of John Parsons, a Quaker, of Pinner, Middlesex, and Mary.
1717, Oct. 31.—William, son of Christopher Feake, merchant, from Jamaica, and Catherine.
1719, June 24.—Martha, daughter of Sir John Lock and Dame Martha.
1722, Oct. 21.—Cornelius, son of Abraham Van Mildert, and Anne.
1725-6, Feb. 24.—Richard, son of Captain Francis Goslin, and Sarah.
1730, June 14.—Charles, son of Charles Duncomb, and Hannah.
1735-6, Feb. 5.—Richard, son of John Gascoyne, and Anne.
1742-3, Jan. 26.—John, son of Rev. Thomas Winfeild, and Frances.
1748-9, Jan. 11.—James-David, son of Elisha Auriol, and Margaret : born 22nd December, 1748.
1755, Nov. 21.—Esther, daughter of Charles Rebotier, and Magdalen.
1760, May 31.—John-Nicholas, son of John-Baptist Durand, and Ann : born 6th May.
1769, Oct. 13.—Martha, daughter of John-Spencer Colepeper, and Martha : born 17th September.
1772, April 15.—James-John-Charles, son of Lewis Agassiz, and Mary : born 8th March.
1778, Oct. 1.—John, son of John Dawson and Sarah, of the province of New York, America.
1784, Jan. 12.—(Born) Thomas, son of George Bertie, and Mary.
1787, Sep. 16.—Maria Ann, daughter of John Fenwick, and Maria : born 16th August.
1792, June 7.—Martha, daughter of Bryan Troughton, and Martha : born 24th April.
1796, April 10.—Henry-William, son of Henry Chichester, and Eleanor : born 12th March.

1798, May 29.—William, son of William Brent, and Amelia: born 5th April.
1800, May 12.—Susan-Lydia, daughter of Henry-William Ward, and Susan: born 22nd February.
1805, April 14.—Richard Beresford, son of John Jarvis, and Anne: born 25th February.
1810, March 22.—Frederick, son of Thomas Danvers, and Lucy: born 22nd February.

Burials.

1575, April 7.—John Byngle [the first entry of burials in the existing registers].
1575, Dec. 4.—Sir John Pollard, Kt.
1575, Dec. 9.—Paulina Adylmar (doubtless one of the family afterwards taking the name of Cæsar).
1576, June 14.—Mr. William Bond, alderman.
1578, Dec. 3.—Mr. John Gresham, gent.
1579, Dec. 15.—Sir Thomas Gresham, Kt.
1585, April 3.—The Lady Pollard, wife of Sir John Pollard, Kt.
1586, Dec. 5.—Charles, son of Doctor Cæsar.
1592, Sep. 23.—Nicholas Fylio, Secretary to the French Embassador—buried by the Pardon door.
1593, Oct. 23.—Peter, son of Baldwyn *Eightshilling* (several others of this name buried).
1595, July 14.—Sir Thomas Reade, Kt.: in Sir Thomas Gresham's vault.
1596, Dec. 14.—The Ladye Anne Gresham, wydowe.
1602, June 4.—Mathew Gentyle, physician.
1603, Sep. 9.—Abraham, son of William Framebreaking, a nurse child.
1605, Dec. 3.—Gertrude Reade, the Lady, wife of Sir William Reade, Kt.: died Oct. 24th; buried in Sir Thomas Gresham's vault.
1608, April 2.—Dorcas, wife of Thomas Sanderson, Esq., and daughter to Sir Julius Cæsar, Kt.
1608, June 21.—Alberick Gentyle, Doctor of the Civil Lawes, King's Professor of the Civil Law at Oxford.
1609, May 4.—Dame Helen, wife of Sir William Willoughby, Kt.; buried at St. Peter le Poor.
1609-10, March 22.—Sir John Spencer, Kt.: in a new vault by the vestry door; died March 3rd.
1610, April 7.—Dame Alice Spencer, widow: in her husband's vault; died March 27.
1610, July 18.—Sir Thomas Cæsar, Kt., one of the Barons of the King's Māties Exchequer: died the same day in his house in Chancery Lane.
1612, Sept. 2.—" *Job Rakt out of the Ashes*, as is mencofied in the Register of Christnings."
1612, Dec. 4.—Walter Hastings, Esq., Master of the Horse to the Right Honourable Earl of Worcester.
1614, May 24.—Dame Alice Cæsar, wife of Sir Julius Cæsar, Kt., Chancellor of the Exchequer, and one of the Privy Council.
1615, Oct. 18.—Peter Mounsell, Reader of the Phisick Lecture in Gresham College.

Burials continued.

1619-20, Jan. 20.—Mrs. Margery, wife of Mr. Martyne Lumley, Alderman.

1620-1, Jan. 30.—Samuel Calvert, Gent., and secretary to the Turkye Company of Merchants.

1623, Dec. 2.—Lettis, daughter of Sir Fouke Greuell (Sir Fulke Greville), Kt., and Dame Anne.

1625, Nov. 21.—Bridget, daughter of Mr. Edmond Allin, Alderman, and Hellen: buried in Bow Church.

1629-30, Jan. 19.—Ann Peck, an aged widow, and sister to the Right Hon. Sir Julius Cæsar, Kt.: under the Communion Table.

1631, July 16.—Abraham Aurelius, a French Minister.

1632-3, Feb. 13.—Richard Broughton, Gent., from Sir Julius Cæsar's.

1634, Aug. 7.—Sir Martin Lumley, Kt., and late Alderman; buried in the Church, wrapped in lead, within a coffin, under his ancestors' stone close to the reading pew, about a yard deep.

1636, April 18.—Sir Julius Ceasar, knighte, M^r of the Roules, and one of the King's Māties most honourable Privie Counsell, was buried under Mr. William's stone by the Communion Table, on Easter Monday night, being the xviii.th day of Aprill.

1637, Aug. 30.—Dame Lady Anne Ceasar was buryed in the vault by her late husband, Sir Julius Ceasar, Knighte.

1637, Oct. 3.—Joice, wife of Daniel Featly, Doctor in Divinitie, in the vault of her late father, William Kirwin.

1637, Nov. 9.—Robert Ceaser, Esquier: under Mr. William's stone, by the Communion Table.

1639-40, March 2.—Patrick Murry, son of the Right Hon. Patrick, Earl of Tully Barden: in Sir Julius Ceasar's vault.

1643, May 11.—Martin Bond, Esq., from Creechurch parish: in the Church.

1646, Oct. 22.—Elizabeth Wiseman, in the Church.

1649, Dec. 26.—Peter Tryon, in the vault of Mr. Moses Tryon, his grandfather.

1652-3, March 1.—William Berkley, sometymes Alderman, free of the Haberdashers, in the Church.

1655, July 19.—Thomas Gresham, Gent.: died in the parish of St. Andrew Undershaft: buried near Sir Thomas Gresham's monument.

1656-7, Feb. 5.—Julian, daughter of Alderman Backhouse: in their vault.

1660, June 6.—Richard, son of Sir Foucke Grevill: in the Church.

1660, Sep. 11.—Dame Mary, wife of Sir James Langham, Kt.: in the Chancel.

1662, June 18.—John, son of Sir John Lawrence: in the Church.

1662, Sept. 13.—Sir Foucke Grevill: in the Church, on his son.

1663-4, Feb. 17.—Doctor Langham's wife: in the Chancel.

1666, June 28.—Mrs. Susanna, wife of Alderman Spurstow: in the North Aisle.

1668, June 4.—Captain Isaac Jurine.

1669, May 11.—Captain Edward Bartlett: in the North Quire.

1669, Dec. 31.—Sir Edward Alstone: in the Chancel, near his daughter the Lady Langham.

1670, Aug. 3.—The Lady Alstone: in the Church, in her husband's grave.

1671, March 30.—Mrs. Jane Eaton: in the north quire; and her little son, who was ript out of her body.

H

Burials continued.

1672, July 4.—Mr. William Finch: in the north quire.
1673, Sep. 18.—The Lady Foster: in the north ile, under the stone of Mr. Briggs, her former husband.
1675, March 27.—Dr. Jonathan Goddard: in the chancel.
1677, Aug. 20.—Mr. Edward Drayton: in the north quire.
1681, June 16.—The Lady Abigall Lawrence: in the Church, in Mrs. Tryon's vault.
1683, May 3.—Sir Thomas Viner: in the south quire.
1686-7, Jan. 6.—John Standish, Dr. of Divinity: on the south side of the altar.
1689, Sep. 19.—Mr. Peter Culling: in Madam Tryon's vault.
1690, April 13.—Sir Francis Clarke: in the Church.
1691-2, Jan. 29.—Sir John Lawrence: in the family vault.
1691-2, March 10.—Mr. Arthur Barham, clerk: in the south isle.
1695-6, Jan. 17.—Capt. George Goddard: in the Church.
1698, Dec. 30.—Henry Spurstow, Esq.: in the north aisle.
1700, Sep. 29.—Francis Clarke, Esq.: in the Church.
1701, May 4.—Mr. Thomas Willis, minister of this parish: in the chancel, on the north side of the communion table.
1702, Aug. 24.—Ann, daughter of Mr. Edmund Prideaux, merchant: in Julius Cæsar's vault, in the south quire.
1703, April 11.—Sir John Woolfe: in the vault by the vestry door.
1703, July 6.—Sir John Eyles, Kt.: in his vault in the Church.
1705, Sep. 14.—Dame Sarah Eyles, widow, relict of Sir John Eyles, Kt., deceased: in the vault belonging to that family in the Church.
1707, Aug. 8.—Madam Anne Carter, widow: in the north quire.
1708-9, Jan. 31.—Jacob De Lillers, merchant: in the south isle.
1710, Nov. 23.—Elizabeth Spencer, widow: in the Church.
1711, Sep. 19.—Sir Joseph Woolfe: in a vault in the choir.
1713, Aug. 27.—Mary Bowyer, widow: in the chancel, in Mr. Robert Foot's vault.
1714, June 2.—Joseph Woolfe, Esq.: in Sir John Woolfe's vault.
1715, Aug. 31.—James Penrice, Esq.: in the north quire.
1716, June 5.—Sir Francis Eyles: in their vault.
1718, Oct. 11.—Francis, son of Joseph Eyles, Esq.: in their vault.
1718, Nov. 27.—Dame Mary Robinson, late wife of Dr. John Robinson: in Mr. Robinson's vault.
1719, May 16.—George Boddington, Esq.: in a vault in the north aisle.
1720, Sep. 13.—Madam Ann Foot: in their vault in the chancel.
1721-2, Feb. 25.—Madam Sarah Styles: in Mr. Eyles' vault in the Church.
1723, April 22.—Lady Catharine Lawrence: in their vault.
1724, Sep. 3.—Sir Samuel Stanyer: in the north aisle.
1728, March 29.—Francis Bancroft, Esq.: in his tomb.
1728, Sep. 10.—The Hon. Lady Ann Coventry: in the chancel.
1731, July 1.—Mrs. Dorothy Crispe: in the south quire.
1732-3, Jan. 15.—General George Kellum: in the Church.
1735, April 22.—Dame Elizabeth, Lady Eyles: in the family vault.
1735, Nov. 23.—Dame Mary Eyles, late wife of Sir John Eyles, Bart.: in the family vault.
1735-6, March 18.—Richard Good-Inch: in the churchyard.

Burials continued.

1738, Oct. 27.—John-Brette Sherbrooke, Esq.: in the south quire, in the Church, near the vestry.
1738-9, Feb. 22.—James Buck, Esq.: in the Impropriator's vault.
1739-40, Feb. 15.—Sir Joseph Eyles: in the family vault.
1742, May 25.—The Rev. Matthias Symson: in the churchyard.
1743, Oct. 23.—The Rev. Mr. James Ansty: in the churchyard.
1743-4, Feb. 17.—The Rev. Mr. Haywood: in the Church.
1744-5, March 17.—Sir John Eyles: in the family vault in the Church.
1746, May 12.—Walter Barnard, Esq., Alderman of Broad Street Ward: in Mr. Jones's vault in the chancel.
1746, Sep. 17.—John Lewis Auriol: in the churchyard.
1748, May 18.—Edward Brown, Esq.: in the Church.
1752, Nov. 4.—Catherine Lawrence: in Lady Lawrence's vault.
1753, Oct. 17.—The Rev. Mr. Peter Sympson: in the churchyard.
1754, April 25.—Elizabeth, wife of Charles Dingley, Esq.: in the family vault.
1759, Sep. 24.—Peter Gaussen, Esq.: in the chancel.
1761, April 27.—Dame Sarah Eyles: in their vault.
1767, Jan. 20.—Henry Hall, Esq.: in the quire.
1768, Nov. 5.—Sir John Haskyns Eyles Stiles: in the family vault.
1772, June 25.—Richard Sherbrook: in the south quire.
1772, Dec. 7.—Rev. Charles Burdett, D.D.: in the Church.
1776, Dec. 12.—Susanna Townsend: in the Dingley family vault.
1781, June 16.—Arthur Stert, Esq.: in the choir.
1785, July 6.—John William Smith, Esq.: in Mr. Woolf's vault in the chancel.
1787, June 25.—William Boles Pilkington: in the chancel.
1788, Nov. 28.—Peter Gaussen, Esq.: in the chancel.
1792, Sep. 17.—Mr. Richard Goodhall: in Mr. Foot's vault in the chancel.
1795, Aug. (—).—Rev. John Naish, Vicar of this parish, aged 71: in the chancel.
1796, Nov. 5.—Hector De Dompierre, aged 58: in the Church.
1804, Dec. 14.—Anna Maria Gaussen, aged 70: in the chancel.
1810, March 23.—Mary Ann Blenkarne, aged 6 years: in Mr. Eyles' vault in the south aisle.

CHAPTER VII.

VESTRY RECORDS.*

At a Vestrye kept by the pshioners of S\[t] Hellens upon Sonedaie the seconde day of Octobre A\[o] Domini 1558.

Imprimis. It is ordeyned that a booke of paper be prepared wherein all orders concluded at any Vestrye may be entred and put in writinge.

Item. That the yongest Church Warden for time being shal be bound to entre or cause to be entred the saied orders in the saied booke within xiiii. daies after upon paine of v $s.$

Item. That the saide pshioners. shall yerelye assemble together upon the Sonedaie next after the feast of S\[t] Michall the Archangell to ellecte and chose the Church Wardens for the yere following, the saied assemble to be duelye called by the Church Wardens upon the paine of v $s.$

Item. That the Olde Church Wardens shall make yerelie a good and a perfect accompte of their office before the said pshioners upon Sonedaie next after the feaste of All Saints upon payne to forfeit and paye the some iii $s.$ iiii $d.$ yf he have no lawfull excuse. And anye Sonedaie after asmuche untill they have made their saied accompte. The saide some or somes of money to be levyed to the use of the saide prsh Church.

Item. That when at this Iasper Umpton, Henrye Browne and Robert Spencer have found themselves greved with their assessement to the Clarke's Wages. It is agreed that at the next Vestrye to be kept, the matter shall be further ordeyned.

Item. That yf any prshner of the saied prshe be duelie warned by the Church Wardens to come to any vestrye to be

---

* The Vestry Records of St. Helen's from A.D. 1558 to A.D. 1812 contain so many parochial references of interest that they are here given in their entirety without note or comment. Those between A.D. 1812 and the present time, containing very little matter of importance, are omitted.

kept by the saied parishners, and doe make defalte, That then he or they having no good lawful excuse, shall forfeite for anye suche defalt the some of ii $d.$ to the use of the parishe.

Item. That the Clarke that now serveth shall depart at Christemas next, and then to have a qters. wages, and in the meane season to provide an other.

At a Vestrye holden the vi[th] of ffebruarie A° 1558.

Imprimis. It is agreade that Richard ffortune shalbe Church Warden for this yere followinge.

Item. It is agreade that Iermyne Ciolle, Will[m] Hagar, Blase Saunders, and Iasper Umpton shall take the accompte of Mr. Browne betwene this and Sonedaie next, and then to make reporte thereof. And also to take accompte of the Collector of the XV and of the strangers, so that the remayner thereof may be brought in to the use of the parishe church.

Item. It is agreade that Gregory Bacon shalle serve in the Quyer as a Conducte to playe and singe there, and to have £iiii by the yere for his wage to begynne at Christemas last, and that he shall give the prshe a yeres warnynge afore his departure.

Item. That Thomas Parker shall serve the parish as Clarke at all tymes havinge yerelie xx $s.$ to begynne at Christemas last, w[t] all comodities to the same except the Great Bell.

Item. That Steven Derrom shall serve as Sexton, and have xx $s.$ a yere to begynne at Christemas last paste.

Item. That Thomas Parker shall washe the clothes of the Church and kepe the Clocke and have xiii $s.$ iiii $d.$ for the same.

Item. That Will[m] and George Graye shall shutte up their doores wth they have latelye made out of their houses into the close.

Item. That W[m] Hagar shall paye for his absence at this Vestrye ii $d.$

At a Vestrye holden the Sondaie the xx[th] of Octobre A° 1560.

It is this daie ordered that M[r] Goddolphyn and Iohn Edwards shall be Church Wardens for this yere followinge. And that M[r] Goddolphyn shall have the charge of the Money this yere, and to go out at Michaelmas next, and the saied Edwards to remayne for the yere following wth another to be chosen to him.

At a Vestrie holden the iiiith daie of Maye. A° 1561.

Thomas Odyll and George Lodge are elected to be Collectors for the poor people for this yere following.

At a Vestrie holden the xxith daie of December. A° 1561.

This daie were chosen comon officers for the yere following, viz.

    Thomas Colshill   for the Comon Counsell.
    Richard Kirke } For the Wardmote Quest.
    Edmund Stone }
    John Edwards   Constable.
    George Gray   Scavenger.
    Kylbye   Bedell.

At a Vestrie holden the xxiith daie of ffebruarie A° 1561.

Raffe Skeres and John Edwards were elected to be Collectors for the secunde fiftene, which was granted towards re-edifyinge of Powles Church.

It is also agreade at the said Vestrye that Mr Colshill, Mr Cioll, Mr Saunders, Mr Hagar, Mr Lodge, Mr Goddolphyn and Mr Watson, shall upon the Wednesdaie then next following goe to the Leathersellers Hall, and ther to confer wth the Wardens and Assistants of the saied Leathersellers concerning the repairing and amendement of certaine decayde places on the outside of the North Ile of the Church.

The xxviiith of October 1563.

At this Vestrie Willm Knyll is choesen and appointed to be conducte in place of John Hailes to plaie on the Organes and to singe in the Quyer for the same Wage that hath heretofore bene accustomed from Michelmas last past.

At the same Vestrie it is agread by consent of the prshonrs of this parish and the companye of the laborers that they shall contynue their resorte to this parishe church yerely on Trynitye Sonedaie as heretofore they have done, paying to the Parishe Church yerelie ii *s.* to the Church Wardens for the tyme beinge.

The xxviith of June 1563.

It is ordered and agreed that Rice Austen, Clockmaker shall have yerelye for thamendinge and lookinge to the Clocke the some of v s. and that he shall have xv d. for his paynes allreedie taken therein.

The vth daie of Mairche 1563.

It is ordered from hencefurthe that none shal be buryed within the Churche or Churcheyarde of this parishe beinge not of the parishe and not departing this worlde within the parish unles it be otherwise ordered by consent of the parishe holden at a Vestrie.

Item. That non shal be buryed within the Church unles the dead corpse be coffened in wood, and also pay the ordeynarie charges to the Churche for the rynginge and tollinge of the Great Bell.

Item. That Thomas Parker shall appear before the Auditors at the next Audit to be kept, ther to answer unto such things as shall be objected against him, and also to be ordered by the said Auditors.

The xth of Julie 1564.

It is agread by the worshipfull of the parishe w^t other, that Thomas Parker, Clarke, now beinge not dwellinge in the parishe depted shalbe buryed in the Church porche paieing the dutcies belonging thereunto.

The xxxth daie of Julie 1564.

It is agreade that Thomas Underwood shall serve in the place of the Clerke, until Michelmas next havinge vi s. viii d. for his Wage and other advantage incident for the same.

The first daie of October 1564.

It is agreade that Thomas Underwood shall serve in the place of the Clarke untill Easter next having xx s. for his wage and all other advantage incident for the same.

Quarto ffebruary 1564.

It is agreade by the assent of the whole parish, that the Leas of the parsonage already granted to the use of the parishe shalbe sued furth, and the charge thereof to be paid by the Church Wardens out of the stock of the Church. And also they have appoynted Mr Colshill, Mr Saunders, Mr Howe, Mr Skegge, Mr Hagar, and Mr Watson to consider howe the said lease may be well assured to the use of the parish, and also to dispose how the profitts of the same from tyme to tyme shalbe collected and to determyn in all things concerninge the same lease.

The xxth daie of Marche 1564.
A° Septimo R. Elizabeth.

It is agreade the said daie and yere, that for the first two yeres recepte of the revenues of the profitte of the psonnage. of this Church of St Hellen, begyninge at the feast of St Michaell the Archangell last past, shalbe collected and gathered by Mr Thomas Colshill and Mr. Blase Saunders or their sufficient deputye or deputyes, and they to paie as well the Quenes grace rent as yt shalbe due goynge out of the same psonage, as also to paie the Curate and other ordynary charge from tyme to tyme as shalbe due. And the same to be allowed yerelie in their accompte, wch accompte shalbe yerelie made at the feast of St Michaell tharchangell or wtin x daies then next ensuinge at the farthest.

Item. It is agread that the Curate shall furthwith make a perfect booke of all the names of the howsholders of this parishe wt their wyfe, children and servaunte, viz., suche as be of the age of xvi yeres or above, and the same booke, or a true copie thereof to be delivered to the said Mr Colshill and Mr Saunders.

Item. It is agreade that Mr Howe shall deliver unto Mr Colshill out of the Church Stocke remayinge in his hands the some of Twentie Pounds towards the charge of the Lease and fyne for the said parsonage.

xiiii January, A° Domini 1564.

At a Vestry holden the saied daie and yere, It is ordered and agreade be the whole assent of the parishioners here present that the residue of owre roode lofte yet standinge at this daie shalbe taken downe accordinge to the forme of a certain writing made and subscried by Mr. Mollyns, Archdeacon of London* by the comandemt of my Lord Bishoppe of London† and others the Quenes maties comissionrs. And further that the place where the same doeth stande shalbe comelie and devoutlie made and garnished againe like to St Magnus Church or St Dunstone in the East as to the descrecon of the Church Wardens shall seme good.

---

* John Mullins, Molens, or Molins, S.T.P., Prebendary of Kentish-town, collated December 13th, 1559, and died May 22, 1591.—Le Neve's Fasti, vol. ii. p. 323. Ed. Oxford (Hardy), 1854.

† Edmund Grindal, S.T.P., elected July 26th, consecrated Dec. 21st, 1559; translated to York, May 16th, 1570; translated to Canterbury Jan. 10th, 1575-6; died July 6th, 1583, ætat. 63. Id. vol. i. p. 26; vol. ii. p. 301. See above, p. 55.

Quarto November, 1565.

It is ordered that the Clarke shall have yerely for washinge the Church Clothes viiis.

Item. It is ordered that no Vaulte nor Tombe hereafter to be made in any parte of the Church without composition had and made with the Church Wardens and parishe upon payne for breach thereof that the Church Wardens for the tyme beinge shall forfeit for every tyme in this offending £x. to be paid to the use of the Church.

Item. That any person which shalbe buryed within the Church above the steppes, that is to say betwyne Sir Thomas Gresham's pew and the Vestrie dore, shall paye xvs. And betwyne the steppes unto the Quire dore in all the iles xs. And in the rest of the boddie of the Church vis. viii$d$. And in the Church porch iiis. iiii.

It is ordered that none shall drye any clothes in the Church Yard.

It is ordered that he or they that shall have the custodie and profitt of the little gardens about the Crosse shall see this last order for the drying of clothes executed accordingly upon payment to lose the keping of the said garden, and another to be placed in the same.

The xx daye of Marche 1568.

At a Vestry holden thys daye ytt was bargayned and agreyd that ffyttler the Carpenter showlde have for mendyng the Church Roffe at the West ende of the Churche, and for the new greatt beame and for the wood plate and the tryander that lyeth uppon ytt and for so manye boardes as shalbe fownde rotten under the leade for all hys woorke in the same and for removing of the cloke howse to sett ytt upon the corner of the wall so as ytt shall be borne uppon the wall and not to beare any p^t of ytt on the roofe of the Churche all which thyngs he must do at his own charge as well nayles as tymber & boordes so as the parish shalbe att no other charge butt onlye the leaddyng of ytt agayne, and for all the sayed worke, the sayed ffyttler must have syxteene nobles and besyde one noble thatt he hathe alreaddye in ernest.

The xxvth daie of februarie a° 1575.

It is agread that Willi^m Kynll the Clarke shall have daie and tyme until the sixth daie of March next comynge to enquire and searche for the Register of the parish which as he sayth he lost neckligently.

It is agread that the Church Wardens shall give notice to Mr. Colshill for to bring the books of accompte for the parish that they may remayne in the keping of the same Church Wardens and that the parishe desier to know how Mr. Colshill holdeth the lease of the parsonage.

It is further accorded that there shalbe kepte on the first Sondaie of each Monethe one Communyon, wch Communyon shalbe so monethlie kept from tyme to tyme and that the Church Wardens wth two or three of them shall devide the prshe so equallie as to their discressions shall seeme expedient.

It is also agread that vi. v. or fowre of the M^{rs} of the parishe shall cess the Curate and Clarke's duties as well for Marriages as burialls, and to have nothinge for Christnynge. Moreover

It is agread that the Church Wardens shall repair to the Parishioners of the pshe to what and howe much evre Man will contribute and paie for and towards a reader of a Lector; to be said in the same parish twice in the Weke and the surplussage of the Clarke's Wage to go to the same.

It is informed that the parish priest receiveth the offeringe of the leathersellers & others wch of right ought to come to the poor men's box, of the wch he must make restytution and from henceforthe to receave no such offeringes.

The xith of Aprill a° 1576.

At a Vestrye holden the same daie and yere, It is agread that M Thomas Barbor, or some learned Man shall evre Wednesdaie & fridaie duringe the whole yere reade a lecture in owre Churche the same lecture to begynne at v of the clock in the afternoone, & ende at Six of the Clocke. This however to be kept from our Ladye daie in March untill Mychelmas daie, and from Mychelmas to our Ladye daie, the same readinge to begyn at fowre of the Clock and to ende at fyve. And the said Mr Barbor to have for his paines xx markes by the yere to be paid hym Quarterlye, the biggest bell to be knolled by the Sexton one Quarter of an howre before the Lector.

It is also agread that there shalbe convenient railes and benches wth matts uppon them set in the chancell for them that shall receave the communyon to kneele and rest uppon after such order as it is at St Magnus.

It is also agreed that the Organes and the scaffolde they stande on shalbe taken downe.

It is also agreed that the two upper steppes where the Alters did stande shalbe taken awaie and made levell with the third stepp ymediatelie after Easter.

The last daie of Septembre a° 1576.

It is agread that Willm Donne the Sexton shall have for his paynes takinge more then he was wont to doo, by reason of our lecture vi*s* viii*d* the yere begynnynge at Mydsomer last a 1576.

A Vestry holden the vth daie of Octobre beynge the first Sondaie after Mychelmas daie 1578.

Item. Yf anye of the parishe will buy the Organes betwene thys and Alhallow daie next, thaye to have them before any other gevinge as the Church Wardens and he can agree, and yf none of the parishe do betwene this and hollandtyde buye them as afore sayd then the Church Wardens after the sayed daie to sell them as they can for the benefit of the parishe.

Item. The old roape to be soulde by the Church Wardens and a comlye clothe to be boughte for the pulpitt.

Item for parishe clarke ytt ys agreyd that Robert Austyn shall serve for thys yere ensuying and so long after as ytt shall please the parishe, and to have for his wage thys yere four pounds from Mychellmas laste and the orddnarye proffytts.

The xxvi of October 1578.

At a Vestrye holden this daie tthat there shalbe a petition made unto the Governors of Chrysts Hospitall for to receave a chylde of Elizabeth Brownes w^h Elizabeth was borne in thys parishe and her parents wear of long contynuans therein and yf the sayed chylde may be relieved in the sayed hospitall, the said parish wyll take order for relievyng of the sayed Elizabeth who wth her chylde are in sutche extreme povertye thatt yf she and her chylde have nott present helpe they are lyke bothe to dye in the streets

[The Vestry Records between 1578 and 1676 are lost.]

676. May 4. Proposed by Thomas Williamson, Upper Church Warden.

That there be a Register Book wherein may be registered the Parish Accounts, the Gifts, Legacies, Bonds, &c.

That there be appointed a Chest to remain in the Vestry, with three locks and keys, wherein the Register Books and Books of Accounts, and Bonds and other writings shall be kept. Ordered.

That some fitt person be desired to peruse the writings now in the Vestry, that gifts, and legacies, and other rights may be discovered.

That the Vestry will be pleased to appoint where the Church Plate shall be kept, that the Church Warden may not be damnified. Ordered. That Mr Williamson shall keep the Church Plate at his own house without any detriment upon any casualty.

1676. December 15. That three keys be bought for the Chest and the Deputy to have one, and the Upper Church Warden one, Mr Westcomb one, and when they are fixed, the bonds and all other things thereunto belonging be putt into it.

1677. December 17. That the interest for the 100*l*. left by Mr Adam Lawrence twenty years since for charitable use and still remaining in the hands of Sir John Lawrence the Executor to Mr Adam Lawrence be refered to the generosity of Sir John Lawrence to give such sums of money as he shall think fitting for the damage thereof for these twenty years past.

1678. April 12. That Mr Pelling shall have ten shillings a sermon for all the gift sermons, that is to say, the two sermons of Mr Pryor and the one of M^r ffenner.

That if Mr Lemm doth not within a months time give Mr Pelling satisfaction for the Vault he lately made in the Church Yard (the property thereof lying in the said E. Pelling as his glebe) and order a Tombe or Gravestone to be desently layd according to the good likeinge of the Church Wardens, that then the said Vault shall be filled up with earth and all things to be as they were before.

September 27. That the Church Wardens do wait on the Dean and Chapter of St Pauls, and acquaint them with the present vacancy (Mr Pelling having left the parish) and to pray them for to admit the inhabitants to nominate a Minister to them for their approbation and choice.

November 11. Mr Hesketh chosen Minister having 18 votes out of 21.

1679. February 26. That Mr Hesketh shall have £20 given (him) by this Vestry, in consideration of the loss in subscription.

1682. March 29. Twenty shillings be paid to Mr Houghton the Registrar of St Pauls, for the draughts of the leases that were formerly made for two parcels of ground in the Church Yard, to build upon.

1683. December 22. Upon the proposal by Mr Hesketh for the setting up of an Organ in the Church, he giving encouragement to hope that it may be purchased, and sett up without diminishing the stock of the parish: The parishioners in Vestry declare their consent to the setting up of an Organ as is proposed. And they doe order a Comittee of the Parish to treat with Mr Hesketh upon all occasions about the sayd Organ, and to conclude the whole matter relating to it, if they find good cause, and if any obstruction happen in the same to consult the Vestry for their further Order what to doe. The Gentlemen appointed for the said Comittee are these that follow:—

> Langley } *Church Wardens.*
> Baker
> Paige, Coventry, Shutt,
> ffinch, Izard, *or any five of them.*

1684. April 3. That no more than fifty shillings shall be allowed by the Parish to be spent upon Ascension days.

1685. December 18. That a doore bee made to the street goinge into Whyt Horse Ally, and that it be constantly lockt up, when it shall be dark, at the charge of John Gordon, and that there be keys for ye severall Inhabitants livinge therein.

1686. January 26. Joseph Lem deceased Executor had leave to lay a gravestone on him in the Church Yard.

1687. June 1. Lease for 25 years to Mr. Curke to build his house in Bishopsgate Street at £8 p^r annum. N° 48.

December 30. Robert Mulcaster elected Parish Clerk with the consent and approbation of the Minister.

1688. November 21. Gate next St Mary Axe repaired at the parish charge.

February 15. The question being put, Whether upon the death of Mr John Mead late Church Warden (Upper) another should be chosen in his place. It was ordered, That none shall be chosen before Easter.

1689. May 7. That the Church Wardens for the tyme to come charge the parish only with £10 for the Ascension Dinner, and they give the parish creditt for the halfcrowns they receive of the

Parishioners contributed by them towards the expense of the dinner.

That in consideration of the great charge Mr Kirk hath been at, in defending the right of the parish in obtaining a stack of chimneys encroached on by Mr Bateman being the next house adjoining, they had conditioned to ad to his lease 25 years more.

1689. October 28. That the charge of covering the graves shall be discharged by the friends or executors of the deceased, and not to be at ye charge of the parish, and that intimation be given to the relations or executors whereby they may not pretend for want of notice.

That the present Church Wardens provide in this Vacancy of a Minister, such able Ministers to preach at the charge of the parish as the Church Wardens shall think fitt, and that the severall parishioners then present were contented to pay their subscriptions for this Crissmas Quarter which was to the late Mr Hesketh towards the discharge of the same.

December 6. Mr Hesketh's letter being read : It was agreed for a subscription and every one to subscribe whereby a competent sum may be raised for a subsistence for him, that he may be induced to preach constantly and remain Vicar of the parish of St Helens.

December 23. That a subscription be made for the Bishop of Killally for one year, provided that he is pleased so long to reside with us.

That Mr Paige, M^r ffoot, Mr Allen, and Mr Coventry Church Warden doe wait on the Bishop of Killally to acquaint him that Mr Hesketh is contented that he shall supply the cure during his residence in the parish of S^t. Helens and receive all the profitts.

1690. April 11. That the surplus which was collected in the last Xmas Quarter towards supplying the cure as also the other rents &c. due to the Vicar, be given to the Lord Bishop of Killalla towards the charge of a Reader.

April 24. The Right Reverend the Lord Bishop of Killalla our Minister Chairman.

October 6. That all strangers that shall come to bury in St Helen's Church or Church Yard, that before ever the grave be made, they shall pay double dues to the Clerk or upon refusal of the same they shall not bury their corpse here.

1691. April 28. That Mr Coventry doe pay to the Lord Bishop of

Killalla out of the parish money in his hands the sum of twenty pounds for a year's allowance due from the impropriator M^r ffreeman as by a decree in chancery and the said impropriator to be charged therewith, as also for a quarter's allowance more due from him at Christmas last, and the Church Wardens makedem and thereof.

1691. August 13. That fifteen pounds be given unto my Lord Bishop of Clogher* as his dues from Capt ffreeman and three pounds as a gratuity besydes.

December 18. Mr Hesketh presided.

1692. June 29. Legacy of £20 from Mr. Paige.

April 1. That Mr Charnack shall have power to reimburs Mr Joseph Lewis his five pounds seven shillings six pence, given by him to be excused from being Churchwarden.

1694. January 23. That the Dean and Chapter of St. Paul's, having on the 20th day of January sent for the Churchwardens and acquainted them that Mr Henry Hesketh had resigned the Vicaridge of S Hellens into their hands and that the place was voide, and the Church Wardens as was usuall having desired leave for the parishioners to recommend and choose a person to be admitted by them for their Minister, and leave being granted for the parishioners to proceed to an election, accordingly on this day, in a full Vestry called for that purpose, Dr John Williams and Mr Thomas Willis being put in nomination, Mr Thomas Willis had the majority by about fifty persons.

March 29. That the Church Wardens' accounts be audited within three months after his time is out at furthest.

Warder's Coat not to exceed 30s.

May 24. That it be a standing rule at all times to be observed, that the Orders agreed upon in any Vestry shall be read over at the opening of the next Vestry, and that no order made in any Vestry shall be binding or valid without it be in the next succeeding Vestry ratified and confirmed.

That the Engine be brought into the Church, and that the old Engine House be pulled down for the better accommodation in burying the dead.

---

* Richard Tennison, D.D., Dean of Clogher, became Bishop of Killala and Achonry, Feb. 18th, 1681-2, was translated to Clogher, Feb. 26, 1690-1, and to Meath, June 25th, 1697; he died July 29th, 1705.—Cotton's Fasti Eccl. Hibern., vol. iii. p. 80; vol. iv. pp. 71-2, 120. Ed. Dublin, 1848-51.

That the Inhabitants on the north side of the Churchyard have liberty at their own charges (that wall being to be pulled down) to build a wall and pallisadoes, provided they come no further with the foundation wall than the first row of trees upon the Churchyard.

1694. May 30. The above standing order was unanimously confirmed.

December 18. That the Comon Counsellmen, with the two Church Wardens, do se the parish wrightings brought and put into the chest in the Vestry, and that they doe inspect and examen the same.

1696. March 28. That Mr William Goodwin have leave to make use of the ground where the Stocks now stand for a conveniency to work in during the pleasure of the parish, leaving the same when required as he found it.

April 17. A Motion was made and negatived, that one Mr Armstrong, who is building a piece of ground in the street by St Helen's Gate, is willing to purchase at an annual rent and present fine, the place where the Bells hang over St Helen's Gate.

That for the time to come, no Church Warden shall, upon any one extraordinary occasion, disburse above the sum of 40s. upon the Parish account without the consent of the Parishioners first consulted with in Vestry in order to it.

That for the future the Church Warden do sumon the Parishioners to the Vestry to be consulted with once in two months at least, and as much oftner as he please and see fitting, And that whenever the Parishioners are so sumoned printed ticketts be left at every person's house intimating the time when that Vestry is to be holden, the day before it is held.

April 20. That the Parish should admit of a fine for the service of the office of Churchwarden.

That the fine for Churchwarden and Overseer of the Poor shall be £30.

That Mr. Robt ffoot, Churchwarden elected, shall not be allowed a deputy.

April 28. That Mr. Robt ffoot shall pay £20 for a fine for Churchwarden and Overseer of the Poor, or else he shall be confined to hold itt himself, and the said moneys shall be appropriated to the repare of the Church.

That the Steeple over against St Hellen's Gate be lett by lease at the discretion of a Committee (there named), with power to treat and conclude with Mr. Armstrong concerning it.

May 8. Mr. Churchwarden Woods acquainted this Vestry that Mr. Robt ffoote, Churchwarden Elect, had paid him the fine of £20 for that office which was set on him by the last Vestry.

Mr. John Woolfe was then chosen in his stead.

May 15. Mr. John Wolf, Churchwarden Elect, appeared and submitted to the fine of £20 for that office, which being accepted, the Vestry proceeded to a new Election.

Mr. Dan Allen was then chosen.

May 22. Mr. Churchwarden Woods acquainted the Vestry that Mr. D. Allen, Churchwarden Elect, had p^d his ffine of £20 for ye s^d office according to a former order of Vestry for admitting Gentlemen to fine for the office of Churchwarden and Overseer of the poor. Mr. Abraham Chitty was then chosen, who being present submitted to the fine of £20, and Mr. Churchwarden Woods acknowledged the receipt of it.

That the Gentlemen who have already or hereafter shall pay ye fine of £20 for the Office of Overseer of the Poor and Churchwarden shall have the liberty to pay a ffine of £10 for the Office of Constable and Scavenger when it comes to their turn, and that no other persons thall have the same liberty.

That Mr. Abraham Chittey having paid his ffine of £20 for the Office of Overseer of ye Poor and Churchwarden, this Vestry do proceed immediately to the choice of a new Churchwarden.

Mr. ffrancis Benzelin being chosen submitted to the ffine of £20, and Mr. Churchwarden Woods acknowledged the receipt of it.

That Mr. ffrancis Benzelin having paid his ffine of £20 for the office of Overseer of the Poor and Churchwarden, this Vestry do proceed immediately to ye choice of a new Churchwarden.

Mr. ffrancis Eyles was then chosen.

May 25. Mr. Churchwarden Woods acquainted the Vestry that Mr. ffrancis Eyles had paid his ffine of £20 for the said office.

Mr. Ed^m Prideaux was then chosen.

That the Gentlemen following, or any three of them, ye Churchwarden being one, doe wait upon the Gentlemen afternamed, to know what they please to give towards the repair of the

Church in order to their being excused frō yͤ office of Overseer of yͤ Poor and Churchwarden.

Committee of eight persons, with a list of twenty others who are to be waited upon for the above purpose.

1696. June 3. The agreement between the Parishioners of Sᵗ Helen's and Mʳ Armstrong of Sᵗ Margaret's, Westminster, Gent.

It is agreed by and between the Church Wardens and Parishioners of Sᵗ Helen's, London, and Thomas Armstrong, that he, the said Thomas Armstrong, upon paying to yͤ Church Warden yͤ sum of One Hundred Pounds, and taking down the Bells, Wheels, and Ropes in the Bellfrey, and delivering them safe and sound into yͤ parish church of Sᵗ Helen's, at his own charge, shall have a lease of yͤ said Bellfrey for Sixty One Years, to comence from Michaelmas next, at yͤ yearly rent of Ten Shillings payable annually at yͤ Church Warden's House, and it is agreed that yͤ passage shall not be made any narrower than now it is, or any lower than yͤ passage going into Crosby Square is between yͤ pavement and ceiling, or brestsumer, and that he the said Armstrong pave yͤ passage under yͤ said gateway, and keep the same so paved at his charge, and to the chanel in the street.

    Thomas Woods.   George Bodington.   Abraham Chittey.
    Clement Kettle.   Tho. Hawes.   George Heath.
          Robert Charnock.   Rich. Bromley.

The passage is to be eight ffoot, two inches and a quarter of an inch wide measuring the front to the street from inside to inside; and eight ffoot three inches and half an inch wide measuring yͤ back part towards Sᵗ Helen's; and ten ffoot and eight inches high from the under side of yͤ Brest Sumer to yͤ pavement.

Mr. Willis the Vicar, and Mr. Edmund Prideaux were then added to the Comittee and Ordered, That all the Gentlemen of the Comittee sign the Lease when to be signed by Mr. Armstrong.

June 18. That the Vault wherein Sir John Spencer was buryed (the Earl of Northampton taking no care for the repayre of it) be appropriated to the use of yͤ Parish.

That three of the four Bells delivered into the Church by Mr Armstrong be sold towards the repayre of yͤ Church, and the best of the four to be kept for the use of yͤ Parish.

That Iron Pallisadoes be made round y[e] Churchyard by the Parishioners living thereabouts if they please without any charge to the Parish, like to those of Allhallows Church Yard in Lombard Street, and to be painted in oyle colours once in three years.

1696. June 20. The Parishioners living near the Churchyard were to have six months time to consider and resolve in, whether they will be at the charge of the Iron Pallisadoes or not.

That the Minister and Churchwardens be requested and desired to search the Court Rolls of Kennington Mannors, in the County of Surrey, at the Parish charge, in order to the discovery of a Gift some time since to our Parish by Joyce Featly, wife of the late Dr. ffeatly of Lambeth, and which has not yet been paid.

At a Meeting held Oct. 8, 1696, It was agreed that Sir Christopher Wren be consulted about the repairs of the Church, and the Parliament be petitioned for an Act to repair the Church.

July 8. A Comittee chosen to assist the Church Wardens with their councell, advice, and directions in the repayre of the Church.

Dec. 17. A report being made that the lease of Mr. Cropper's dwelling house was near expired, a Committee was appointed to enquire into the lease of y[e] said Mr. Cropper's House, and to make report thereof to y[e] next Vestry, and to view y[e] said House and consider how it may for y[e] future be best lett for the service of y[e] parish.

Dec. 18. That Mr. Williams shall have liberty to lay a Tombstone upon his ffather's grave even to the pavement, gratis. But in opposition to this order it was alledged that Mr. Williams was willing to give Ten Pounds to the Parish. However, carried in y[e] affirmative that he may lay one gratis if he please.

169$\frac{6}{7}$. ffeb. 7. That an humble petition be presented to the Honourable House of Comons for some allowance out of y[e] duty to be laid on coals towards y[e] finishing the repairs of St. Helen's Church, and that those of the parishioners that are not now present to sign the said petition this day be waited on at their respective houses in order to their signing of it. . . . The Minister and Church Wardens, with seven other inhabitants, be desired to go with the petition to-morrow morning to the Parliament House and take care it be presented.

March 4. A Lease of the House lately occupied by Mr. Tho[s] Cropper was agreed to be granted to Mr. Nathaniel

Chewter for twenty-one years at £30 per annum Rent, and a present ffine of £50, and not to let it to a Tallow Chandler, a Cook, a Victualler, a Blacksmith, or a Baker.

Mr Nathaniel Chewter paid Mr Church Warden Woods ffive shillings in part of the ffivety pounds ffine which he acknowledged the receipt of.

1697. April 20. A Committee was appointed To audit the accounts of the Church Wardens whose accounts are not yet audited, and the ensuing year are to be so.

That an Inventory be taken of all Plate, Books, or other things belonging to the parish of St Helens, and that it be entered in ye parish book where the Church Wardens Accounts are entered, and that every New Church Warden upon receipt of them subscribe his name to ye said inventory.

May 20. That a rate of Six Pence in ye pound on Houses in ye parish of St Helens be raised in order to the finishing ye repayres of ye Church and that ye Assessment be according to ye present rates of ye several Houses in the King's Tax, and that ye moneys so to be raised be paid by ye parishioners to ye Church Warden before ye ffeast of St John Baptist next.

June 5. That Mr Thomas Woods late Church Warden having been oft called upon to adjust his Accounts with ye parish as Church Warden for ye year last past, and not having yet done it, do gett his said accounts ready to be audited by ye first day of July next, or else be prosecuted for not doing so by ye present Church Warden in ye behalf of the parish.

July 23. The accounts not being audited, the Church Warden was ordered to prefer a Bill in Chancery if they are not brought in before the 2 day of August.

December 16. That the Church Warden do provide a Coat for the Warder and pay for it not exceeding forty shillings.

The Auditors reported that they had examined the accounts of Mr Hardy and Mr Woods late Church Wardens and find that the sum of Twenty Nine Pounds and Two Pence is due to Mr Hardy and that the sum of fforty Pounds is due to the parish from Mr Woods. Ordered. That the sum of fforty Pounds be paid presently by Mr Woods, or that the present Church Warden take care to recover it at the parish charge, and that Mr Hardy be paid out of the same money when it is received.

1697. December 18. That Mr Nathl Chewter doth give his Note for the payment of £20 in six months time to ye Churchwarden for a fine to be excused from serving the office of Churchwarden and Overseer of the Poor which he complied with accordingly.

That Mr Nathl Chewter do pay to ye Churchwarden Prideaux next weeke the sum of Ten Pounds for a fine in excusing him from ye office of Constable and Scavenger for ye year ensuing.

1698. April 28. A Petition of Mr Robert Mulcaster ye Parish Clerk was presented to ye Vestry and read, praying he might have an yearly salary settled on him for executing ye said office. The consideration of which was referred to the next Vestry. . . . . No further—appears to have been taken upon it.

December 16. That the Gates of St Hellens towards St Mary Axe be kept and repayred, and that the present Churchwardens doe desire Mr Jones to repair the same, and in default thereof, to prosecute the same at ye charge of ye parish.

1698/9. January 19. That it be a standing rule that the Bricklayer shall have five Shillings for every grave in ye Church, he keeping the pavement levell, and the Iles whole, and that at the end of every year before his bill be paid the whole pavement be viewed by the Comon Councellmen and Churchwardens. This standing order to be fairly written and hung up in the Vestry.

January 25. A Motion was made that a Watchman should be kept at the parish Charge at St Helen's Gate leading to St Mary Ax. Referred to another vestry.

April 13. That for ye futer all uper Churchwardens give one hundred pounds security within fourteen days after he is elected to some person of ye parish who shall be appointed to receive and keep ye said bond and to deliver up ye said bond again to ye obleidged when his accounts are audited and ajusted.

That a Book be provided in which shall be entered an Inventory of all the Wrightings, Plate, and other Movables belonging to the Church and Parish ye which Book for ye futer shall be delivered to all succeeding Churchwardens for the time being.

April 25. That Mr Decosta do pay as a fine for all Offices both of ye Parish and Ward, Twenty Five Pounds, by reason he has given warning to go out of his house at Michaelmass next and y^t he gave a Noate of his hand to pay the said sum immediately.

That the Belfry and Church be repaired and a Bell hung up

to give notice of Burials, and that ye Common Councell Men be desired to assist the Churchwardens in the same.

1699. August 9. That Mr Heath ye Churchwarden have a Key to ye Church; y^t he may at any time come at ye Engine.

August 28. A Vault being designed to be made in ye Chancell for a burying place for Mr Joseph Jones of this parish and his family by ye sole order of Mr Tho Willis the present Minister without ye knowledge or approbation of ye parishioners, and a debate ensuing thereon the question was put . . . . Whether the Minister of this parish has a right to dispose of ye ground in ye Chancell to make a Vault and appropriate it to particular persons without ye consent of ye parishioners assembled in ye Vestry, and it was carried that ye Minister has no such right.

September 1. Mr Thomas Willis, Minister of this Parish appearing at the Vestry, and desiring the consent of this Vestry that Mr Joseph Jones might build a Vault in ye Chancell for himself and family. . . . . Ordered. That upon Mr Willis his request, this Vestry doe consent Mr Jones may build a Vault in ye Chancell, provided he satisfy Mr Willis and for ye future at all tymes he keep ye pews and pavement over ye said vault in good and sufficient repair.

Mem. Sir Tho Pinfold, Ordinary to the Dean and Chapter of St Pauls on ye 15 of December following this vestry viewed the abovesaid Vault after it was made, and then told Mr Willis that he nor any Vicar of St Helens had a right of appropriating any part of ye ground of ye Church or ye Chancell to any person or family.

November 16. Upon ye request of ye President, Governours & Assistants of ye Corporation for ye poor of ye City of London to ye Parishioners of this Parish; that they would grant a place in ye Church for their Servants and Children to sitt together in during ye tyme of divine worship—Ordered unanimously, That the President, Governors & Assistants of ye said Corporation shall have a convenient part of ye long pews on ye North Side of ye Church, for ye abovesaid use, Provided, That ye Parish be not put to any cost or charge, and that ye said Governors give ye Parish a Covenant under their Common Seal to putt ye said pews into ye same condition they are now in, if hereafter they should discontinue to use ye same.

Be it remembered y^t ye Pewes which are to be altered are in ye same fashion as those are, which are to ye Eastward in ye same range; only y^t they are in three divisions; a passage going up between those two divisions next ye West End of the Church.

December 15. Upon a Motion made to ascertain ye Church Wardens Expenses on Publick Entertainments the ffollowing Orders were unanimously made and agreed unto and ordered to be fairly writt and hung up in ye Vestry. Viz. :

That all the parishioners (paying Scott & Lott) be invited twice a year without any charge or contribution, viz, on ye first clean Thursday in every Lent to an Entertainment in ye Evening after Sermon, and on every Ascension Day to dinner.

That ye Expenses on ye said Entertainment in Lent do not exceed fforty shillings.

That ye Expenses on Ascension Day doe not exceed Twelve Pounds, and y^t ye charge of ye points, Bread and Drink ffor ye Children be included in ye said Twelve Pounds.

January 3. That the Church Wardens, with ye assistance of ye Common Councellmen, doe forthwith hang up ye Gates of St Helens leading into St Mary Axe, or upon any opposition to ye contrary, take such course at law as shall seem proper.

April 5. A Motion being made by Mr Thos Willis, our Minister, y^t there might be allowed him a Reader to read prayers, the matter was referred to ye next Vestry.

The order of Vestry of ye 13th of Aprill, 1699, being read, importing that for ye future all Upper Church Wardens shall give One Hundred Pounds security, Ordered, That for ye future ye Upper Church Warden Elect doe give such Bond of One Hundred Pounds, and lodge in ye hands of some one Inhabitant of ye Parish apointed by ye Vestry, before he be presented at Doctors Commons to be sworn.

That Mr John Hanbury, Upper Church Warden elect, doe give a Bond of Security as above, and deliver it (to be kept) into ye hands of Mr Geo. Boddington.

June 4. That the sum of fforty shillings be payd towards defraying the charges of ye suit against Giles Hall, watchman, by Mr Graham, and at ye Sessions against ye said Graham and Turner ye sayd Watchman's charges there also disbursed and payd.

September 20. Mr Bromley, Constable of this precinct, complained that ye Parish was taxed to ye Watchmen double to what is paid to them, and ye remainder sunk or converted to other uses, and that this part of ye Ward is not duly watched as it ought to be. A Committee was appointed to enquire into the same, and report thereon to the next Vestry.

The Churchwarden also reported that, according to the Order of Vestry, he had sett up the Gates in that part of St Helens leading to St Mary Axe, and put locks on the same for ye use of ye Parish, and that Mr Joseph Jones, though he had a key of ye same delivered to him, break off ye said Lock in contempt of ye order.

That the Church Wardens procure another lock and put on ye said Gates in the room of those thus broken, and that Mr Church-Warden Hanbrey doe goe to Mr Joseph Jones and acquaint him that if he please to pay for the said new lock, the Parish are soe kind as to pass by this offence, and if the said Jones doe refuse to do this, the said Church Warden have liberty to take such course at law against the said Joseph Jones as he shall be advised.

That Knight and Jenkens be two whole bearers for the buriall of the dead, and have whole pay, and that the other four be at the nomination and apointed by the Clerk and Sexton, and if it so at any time happen that there be but two bearers employed, that the Clerk and Sexton have half pay, and they the other half.

That the Minister be requested for to bring in the old Psalms, that they may be sung again in the Church.

1700. December 18. That the Church Warden do pay unto Mr Robt Mulcaster the sum of Three Pounds towards the buying him a fitt and decent gown, provided the said Robt Mulcaster will read the severall lines of ye Psalms to be publickly sung, before they are sung, till contradicted by Order of Vestry.

1701. April. That whereas Dr Fuller, lately deceased, who preached the Winter Lecture in St Helen's Church (viz.: every Tuesday in the evening from Mich{s} to Lady Day following) being the gift of Sir Martin Lumley. It was moved in Vestry by the Inhabitants then there, That some persons of the sayd Parish should be nominated to goe to Sir Martin Lumley and make application to him in behalf of Mr Willis, present Minister of this parish, to be admitted and settled to preach the sayd Lecture Sermons for the future.

That Mr Hanbury be the Bricklayer for the Parish of St Helen doing the work as is expressed in the Orders hung up in the Vestry, at reasonable prices.

April 17. A Bond given to Mr Heath, late Church Warden, for £72 balance due to him from the Parish. Signed by the present Church Wardens, who are indemnified by the Vestry.

May 7. A Committee appointed to wait on the Impropriator to acquaint him with the death of Mr Willis, the late Minister, and inform them where ye right of presentation is.

That for the future at all Vestrys ye Minnits that are taken be read and agreed to, and entered in the same words afterwards in the Vestry books and compared with the minnits.

May 10. The above Committee having been with the Impropriator, reported his answer, viz.: That ye right of presentation is in him, and said as the Parish is willing to let him quietly possess his right, he should always endeavour to gratify the Parish in their ancient usages of electing a Minister.

Votes of thanks to the Committee, and their charges, £1 10s., allowed them.

A message being sent to this Vestry from Dr Harwood, that y Dean of St Pauls* would in the vacancy provide persons to officiate and particularly to-morrow morning and evening:

This Vestry has ordered ye two Church Wardens, with Dr Hawes and Mr Heath, to wait on ye Dean or his Commissary, and acquaint him that the Impropriator had ordered Mr Cook to officiate to-morrow morning, and no other, except ye Dean be pleased to preach himself.

June 4. In nomination for Vicar.

Mr Cooke.　　Mr Canham.　　Mr Pritchard.
Mr Estwicke.　Mr Holkomb.　Mr Hilliard.
Mr Sampson Estwicke chosen.

That the two Churchwardens, with Mr Allen, Dr Hawes, and Mr Heath do wait upon the Dean of St Paul's and 'M^r ffreeman, to acquaint them of the choice of Mr Estwicke.

That the Parish Rates for Leathersellers' Hall be agreed with according to the discretion of the Common Councilmen.

---

* "William Sherlock, S.T.P., Prebendary of St. Pancras, was nominated 25th April, and elected 12th June, 1691, and installed on the 15th of the same month. He died at Hampstead in Middlesex 19th June, 1707, ætat. 67, and was buried in St. Paul's."—Le Neve's Fasti Eccl. Anglican., vol. ii. p. 316. Ed. Oxford (Hardy), 1854.

1701. October 10. A Committee appointed to collect subscriptions for Mr Estwicke.

December 17. That the sum of Five Pounds be paid unto Mr Soulby's daughter for wrighting the (parish) Books this year.

1702. April 7. Mr Aylward, elected Church Warden, excused all offices on paying the fine of £30, the question having been put whether it should be £25 or £30.

April 10. Mr Crispe elected; excused on the same conditions.

April 13. Mr Thos ffinch elected; excused on the same conditions.

April 15. Mr Cotton elected; excused on the same conditions.

April 13. That Mr. ffrancis Eyles shall have liberty, at his own charge, to make a vault in the Church underneath the Christning Pew, he paying of £30 for the use of the Parish, and the dimensions of the said vault are to be left to the discretion of the two Common Councilmen and the Church Wardens.

That Mr Geo. Heath appearing this day with his Bond of £72 principle, and £4 6s. interest, Ordered, That the same be paid, which was done immediately, and the Bond cancelled.

May 22. This Vestry being convened to consider of the condition of this Parish with respect to the books, deeds, and writings belonging to the same, and as to severall gifts, devizes, and bequests to this Parish and the poor thereof, and as to the number, condition, and charge of the poor. And the three keys belonging to the Parish Chest being lost, it is thereupon Ordered, That the said Chest now remaining in the Vestry be forthwith broken open, which was accordingly done. And in the said chest are found several deeds and writings belonging to the Parish, but upon strict search and enquiry, some of the Books relating to Vestry proceedings in this Parish for many years past are wanting. It is therefore ordered:

That strict enquiry be made thereof, and that a Committee be appointed to inspect the Parish writings and concerns now laid open, and report thereon to the next Vestry. That there be three locks and keys (as was usual) for the said chest, the Minister and two Church Wardens each to keep one, and that from time to time it shall be sett down (on every removal of the said keys) into whose hands they are put.

That Mr Stephen Locker, Clerk to the Leathersellers Company be assisting to the said Committee, to reduce the writings into good order and to make a Catalogue and what else may be necessary concerning the same. And it is also ordered:

That the said Mr Stephen Locker be chosen to be Clerk for the drawing up and entering into the Vestry Book the proceedings of the Vestry, and for the stating and making up the Accompts and Books relating to this Parish.

1702. June 16. Mr Churchwarden Bromley reported, as relating to the £4 p^r Annum given for ever by the Will of Mrs Joyce Featley, That he with Stephen Locker had searched the Court Books of the Mannor of Kennington and that he had discovered the Houses and Lands subject to the payment of the said £4 p^r Ann. and produced Extracts he took out of the said Court Books, and also particulars of the said Houses and Lands which now are of the yearly value of £75 p^r Ann. And hath taken Copies out of the Petty Bag Office, of the Inquisition and Decree made thereon. The matter was then referred to the Committee to prosecute and sue at law the persons liable to pay the said £4 p^r Annum and for all arrears thereof. It is also ordered:

That the said Committee shall take into their care and management the demand this parish hath upon the impropriator for £20 p^r Annum and reserved in a Grant from the Crown to the Preacher of this Church & do therein as they shall think fit and be advised.

August 20. Mr Edmond Prideaux being desirous to interr his deceased daughter in Sir Julius Cæsar's Vault: Ordered, That he shall have leave, on condition that he shall give Bond to the Parish for £200 to save harmless the Parish against all Suits, &c. which may arise in consequence of such interment.

December 16. Mrs Aldworth prays a renewal of her lease for the term of her life, for a reasonable fine.

1703. March 25. The Churchwardens reported that they had inspected the Will of Edward Fenner, by which is given the Moiety of the rents and profits of the house now held by lease heretofore made to Deputy Thomas Aldworth at £10 p^r Annum. And find the said house rested in the Minister and Church Wardens of St Helens, and the Master and Wardens of the Carpenters Company and their successors for ever, " for such good uses as hereafter mentioned, viz. That all such rents, issues and profits, that shall from henceforth for ever after be had or made, shall be from time to time parted and divided into two equal parts and portions; Whereof one equal part and portion I will that it be distributed yearly for ever to and amongst the poor people of the said parish. And the other equal half part and portion, I will that it be distributed yearly for ever, to and amongst the poor of the said Company of Carpenters." And they do further find that the said house is now let by lease under Mr Aldworth at the rent of £32 p^r Ann. And they are advised that the anticipating the full yearly rents & profits of the said house by taking a fine is repugnant to the intent of the donor's said Will and a breach of trust, and is injurious to the poor of this parish and the poor of the Carpenters Company. And they do further find that in the lease of the said house granted to the said Deputy Thomas Aldworth, dated September 12, 1671, under which his widow claims, the Minister of St Helens was no party, though the first person appointed a Trustee by the said Will.

An Accompt was given to this Vestry that the part of the Ward within Bishopsgate pays for but twelve watchmen which at three shillings and six pence p^r week each man comes to £109.4 p^r Ann. Of which sum this parish only is rated and pays near £60 p^r Ann. and as appears by the Beadle's Book tho' they have not above four Watchmen and these not entirely belonging to the service of the said parish, whose pay according to the abovesaid rate amounts to but £36.8 p^r Annum. And there being a necessity for one Watchman more at the East Gate of St Helens, for the better securing that part of the parish: It is Ordered, That the Beadle of the Ward (who at this time collects the money rated upon every Inhabitant for the Watch) shall pay such Watchman or Men, as is, or shall be placed at the said gate, And in case he refuse so to do: It is further Ordered, That the Constable of the Parish for the time being shall collect the several rates assessed on the Inhabitants of this parish and apply and pay the same to the respective watchmen who do duty for this parish. And that the Beadle of the Ward have a Copy of this Order.

1703. June 18. The Auditors directed to enquire into several abuses &c. practised by the Clerk and Sexton and of the perquisites and salaries claimed or received by them.

Referred to the Churchwardens to give leave to erect a Monument to Mr White on the South Wall, behind the Font on payment of not less than £5 for the use of the parish before the Monument be put up.

1703. December 17. That Mr Locker be paid Ten Pounds for such his Service done to this time, and that Six Pounds p^r Annum be allowed to the said Mr Locker so long as he shall duly perform the office of Vestry Clerk of this Parish.

December 18. That no person whatsoever shall be admitted to fine for any Parish or Ward Office without Special Order of the Vestry of this Parish in that behalf had, and made.

1704. April 20. That the number and charge of the Poor be entered in a Book, Entitled, "The Poors Book of this Parish" and that the Poors & Scavengers Rates be entered in the said Book to remain as a Register of such matters. That from henceforth there shall be paid Ten Shillings for every person not being a parishioner of this parish who shall be buried in the Church Yard of this parish: And, That no person shall be buried in the Church or Church Yard without notice thereof be first given to the Church Warden by the Clerk or Sexton of this parish. And That in case the said Clerk or Sexton shall neglect or refuse to give Notice to the Church Warden before the burial of any person in the Church or Church Yard, he or they shall for every such offence be suspended and discharged frō his or their place or office. And That this Order shall be written fair & fixed in the Vestry House.

The Decretal Order in Chancery touching the Gift of Joyce Featley being read:

It was Ordered, that the Vicar shall be paid Twenty Shillings p^r Annum for preaching a Sermon on the 3rd October yearly being the day on which the said Joyce Featley was buried in this Church pursuant to her Will.

That henceforth Tent Wine shall be had and used in this Church for the Sacrament of the Lord's Supper, and the charge thereof exceeding, or over and above Eighteen Pence Per Quart shall be paid by the Church Warden.

June 21. That the Sexton shall be chosen yearly at Easter when the other yearly officers are chosen.

That a Man, not a Woman shall be now chosen Sexton for the year ensuing until Easter next.

December 5. The order of 13 April 1699 relating to the

Upper Church Warden giving security being read: Ordered That every Church Warden shall give Bond in like manner within fourteen days next after he is chosen.

Agreement for a lease of the House in Bishopsgate late Mr Aldworth to William Poole for £30 p^r Annum from Lady Day 1705 for 21 years. First Year at a Pepper Corn on account of repairs. Half the rent to the Carpenters Co.

That the Clerk shall not have a key to the Church and that the key he hath shall be delivered to the Church Warden.

Permission granted to lay a Stone on Henry Rispe's grave in North Isle on payment of Two Guineas. The Stone to be about three feet long.

1704. December 18. That none shall have the keeping of a Key to the Church save only the Minister and Church Wardens, and such as they shall direct or give leave to have it.

1705. February 9. Mr Richard Bromley chosen Church Warden until Easter, in place of Mr Roger Wardman, deceased.

That upon payment of Twenty Five Pounds, the Vault of C. Chamberlain may be enlarged, and made not exceeding three feet longer and two feet wider, so that it does not intrench upon any particular vault.

That Pallisadoes shall be set up on both sides of the walk in the middle of the Churchyard from the gate to the Church door, and a Committee appointed to agree upon the doing thereof.

March 19. That the wall at the west part of the Churchyard, which was this morning taken down without any order or privity of Vestry, shall be rebuilt again in the same condition it was, at the cost and charge of those who did take it down, or cause the same to be taken down.

April 13. The Committee concerning the new Rales in the Churchyard report the work done, Ordered and Declared by this Vestry the approbation thereof.

Thanks is given by this Vestry to Alderman Woolfe for the carpet and cushion he lately gave for the use of the Communion Table.

A request being made to the Vestry on behalf of Mr Reresby for a Monument against the wall of the Vestry for his father, who gave by his will a legacy of Ten Pounds to this Parish, it is Ordered, That the said Mr Reresby be attended by the Church

Warden with the answer of this Vestry, That he may set up a Monument, but this Vestry doth expect some acknowledgment or sum to be given as he himself shall think fit.

1705. December 19. That the degree relating to the Tithes payable by the Inhabitants of this Parish, dated 9 February, 1662, and the rate now settled for the Tithes shall be both entered in the Book of Memorials and Bequests of this Parish, and a note of reference to the same shall be set up in the Vestry.

1706. January 2. The Quest having chosen a Chaplain who is a stranger, and noways concerned in officiating in any Parish within this Ward, and in respect thereof, request or caution was given to the Foreman of the Quest, That the Minister of this Parish, or his Deputy, hath time out of mind done such office for the Quest, and ought to have done it now, this precinct being by much the most considerable in the whole Ward Within.

Resolved unanimously, That this Vestry do resent it, and resolve not to go to this Court of Inquest.

July 5. Mr Chewter had leave to sink a place for laying in of dung or scavage in the ground on the north side of the Churchyard wall next to Sir Joseph Woolfe's, and to enjoy the same during the pleasure of this Parish.

October 16. Mr Chewter ordered to pay one shilling per annum for the above place.

December 23. This Vestry taking into consideration whether this precinct of St Helen will go in a body to the Court of Inquest this year and attend them as formerly, and it being put to the Vote, it was unanimously resolved in the negative. And it was also resolved and ordered, That the Common Councilmen and Church Wardens of this Parish do wait upon the said Inquest the first day of their sitting to acquaint them that this Parish doth take notice of and resents the proceedings of the said Inquest in their deviating from the ancient custom of the Inquests of this Ward in the choice of a Foreman not of this Precinct.

1707. September 18. That the Church Warden do take care and order the necessary repairs of the Church as he shall think fit.

That the Buckets for Fire belonging to the Church being but few and out of repair, be repaired and made up to the number of three dozen.

That the Church Warden provide a decent cushion for the pulpit.

1708. April 8. Reported: That Mrs Prideaux had given to adorn the Pulpit, Vallens of Crimson Velvet, with a large gold fringe thereto, as an addition to the cushion which the Church Warden had provided for the Pulpit. Ordered, That the Church Wardens do wait upon the said Mrs. Prideaux, and give to her the thanks of this Vestry for her kind present.

The Church Warden also reported to this Vestry that he had paid Thirty Shillings to Thomas Picketts, gardener, for putting into good and decent order the Churchyard and the trees planted therein, and had also agreed with the said gardener (if this Vestry approved) to pay him thirty shillings per annum for keeping it in like order. And has likewise agreed with —— Younge, clockmaker, for twenty shillings per annum to be paid him for his keeping in good order of repair the Church Clock. The same agreements are by this Vestry ordered to stand confirmed.

That twenty shillings shall be allowed to the Sexton yearly for his labour in winding up the clock and looking after it.

That the Church Wardens for the time to come, before they shall be sworn into their office, do each of them give Bond of One Hundred Pounds penalty, with some fitting person as his respective surety (not being a parishioner of this parish), for his fidelity and rendering account for, and touching his receipts and payments and doings in the affairs and concerns of this Parish.

See next Vestry.

Number and incident charge of the Poor as it was—

March 27, 1706—£64, 16s.
1707—£55, 14s.
1708—£61, 4s.

April 21. The above resolution for Church Wardens giving security was altered as follows :—

That the Church Wardens for the future shall each give his own Bond of the penalty of two hundred pounds, without other security, for fidelity, &c. &c. &c.

May 5. Mr Churchwarden Hathaway having bespoke a small Engine for the sum of Eight Pounds, this Vestry doth approve thereof.

That the Church Wardens do enquire of the Town Clerk concerning agreement made by the proprietors in the Thames Water for their supplying Fire Cocks with their water, for publick benefit, gratis.

1708. September 14. The Great Engine ordered to be repaired.

Inventory of Goods, Books, Ornaments, &c., ordered to be entered in the Parish Book.

1709. April 29. That an Ejectment be commenced and brought for the Houses in lease from this Parish to Nathaniel Chewter in respect of the arrears due and owing to this Parish upon account of rent of the same premises.

The Church Warden to contract with Mr Warren for keeping the Engines in repair.

Mr Locker, Vestry Clerk, presented a Bill for business extraordinary done by him for the service of the Parish, referred to the Auditors to report thereon.

September 30. The report of the auditors concerning Mr Lockers being read, the same being in three Bills, several of which had the same sums entered in them, the same was fully considered by the Vestry, and the sum of ten pounds eight shillings and one penny being agreed upon by the same to be due to Mr Locker to this day for all demands, besides what is due to him as Vestry Clerk, being this day three pounds, which said sums making together the sum of £13 8s. 1d., to be paid to Mr Locker, he giving therefore a discharge in full of all accounts to this day. And whereas the Parish are in arrears for several sums to be paid by them occasioned by some extraordinary charges, It is ordered, That Mr Locker be discharged from his service as Vestry Clerk for the future.

December 15. That £10 be lent to Mr John Bellows to carry on his trade, as the only means to prevent his wife and children becoming chargeable to the Parish.

That Robert Mulcaster, Parish Clerk, do attend the Vestry, and enter the Orders.

1710. May 25. Mr Richard Durley had leave to make use of part of the Churchyard to lay his timber in; provided any damage done he should make it good.

October 23. The Church having been repaired at a charge of £155 10s., the question was put whether it should be paid by a poors' rate or a pound rate. It was agreed for a pound rate at ninepence in the pound.

1711. December 13. That four pounds be paid to Mr Munchaster for his service as Vestry Clerk to Christmas. Twenty shillings also to be given to the Sexton, as a gift, for keeping the way clean to the Church.

March 15. Mr Robert Foot had leave to make a vault in the Church on payment of £35. The vault to be made 7 feet by 8 feet clear.

December 7. Copy of grant of a piece of ground for Robt Foot's vault at the upper end of the middle isle on the south side thereof, near the communion table, over which ground the two pews adjacent to the communion table are erected.

December 18. That four pounds be paid to Robert Mulcaster for his attendance as Vestry Clerk.

1712. March 17. Upon the representation of the Physicians of St Bartholomew's Hospital, that a pauper of this parish cannot be cured without his going to Bath, it was ordered, That a sum not exceeding four pounds be paid to the Treasurer of the said Hospital for the charge of the same.

April 24. Upon the complaint of John Glover against Mr Gibson for making the house next to him a public house, whereby his business is very much declined, It is ordered, That if the said Glover and Gibson cannot accommodate and adjust the difference, that the said Gibson be prosecuted at the charge of the Parish for drawing drink without a licence.

December 17. Four pounds to Robt Mulcaster as Vestry Clerk.

1714. March 3. The children now in the Workhouse belonging to this Parish be continued there at two shillings and sixpence per week, until they can be provided for otherways.

R. Churchhill and Charles Ball having given their Bond to the President, &c., of Bethlem Hospital to defray the charge of burying, &c., William Miller, in case he should die there, and to provide for him in case he should be discharged, the Church Wardens were ordered to give their Bond in behalf of the Parish to indemnify them from any charge, &c., that may happen to them on account of the said W. Miller.

April 22. Mr. Thomas Hall had leave to take down the Parish Boundary Stone in his wall, upon condition to put it up in the same place in the new wall which he designs to build.

That the Church Wardens do order the padlock which is now on the door betwixt Mr. Hall's yard and the Churchyard to be taken off, and Mʳ Hall have leave to pass and repass during the pleasure of this Parish.

1714. May 21. That the Church Wardens do wait on Mʳ Hanger and Mʳ Lepiper and let them know that this Parish do expect an acknowledgment for permission of burying of Joseph Woolfe, Esq., now expected from France in ordered to be interred here.

June 2. That Ten Guineas (exclusive of all dues) should be the sum paid for permission of Joseph Woolfe, Esq., to be interred in the vault where his father was buried, upon which Mʳ Woolfe's friends promised to pay the said ten guineas.

June 5. A motion being made that Madam Hanah Wakeman (daughter of George Boddington, Esq., of this Parish) being dead, it is presumed that her father designs to have her buried in a vault which was Alderman Backhurst's in the North Isle. The question was put whether the consideration for leave should be Eight or Sixteen Guineas, and it was agreed, That Sixteen Guineas should be paid for the use of this Parish.

December 24. Order in Chancery. That the several sums due from Joyce Featley's Gift should be paid at the Vicar's House or upon the Tomb Stone of William Kerwyn her Father in the Church of Sᵗ Helens.

December 16. Mʳ Backwell desiring to lay a Grave Stone where his Wife was interred near the Reading Desk, The Church Warden was ordered to treat and agree with him on the best terms.

That if Mʳ Boddington will please to remove his daughter Wakeman from the place where she was buried into the Vault which was Alderman Backhurst, the consideration for leave should be but Eight Guineas and not Sixteen Guineas as was ordered in the Vestry June 5 last past.

That the Modes or Accounts of Tythes payable quarterly to the Improprietor by the Inhabitants of this parish be transcribed and hung up in the Vestry that the said Inhabitants at any time may have recourse unto.

1715. February 10. That Mʳ Seayers late Church Warden be paid Interest on the balance of his account (£28 11s. 5d.) from the time his account was audited and passed, to the time the balance due to him was paid, being from 8 Dec. 1713 to Dec. 1714.

The Vestry returned M Durley thanks for presenting them with Ten Pounds to be excused from serving Constable and Scavenger when it came in course for him to serve.

A Committee appointed to examine what damage the Great Engine had sustained at the fire in Thames Street.

1715. February 23. Agreed to be repaired for Three Guineas.

Complaint was made to this Vestry respecting Mr George Stinton the present Sexton of this Parish, and —— White (who was employed to clean the Church) . . . . Mr Barrett the Reader acquainted the Vestry that he had examined both, and by their confession the charge appeared to be fact. Upon which it is Ordered, That the said Mr Stinton be forbid coming to this Church to officiate as sexton for the future.

That Mr Mulcaster the Clerk do assist M^m Stinton in opening the pews &c. during the ensuing Lent, and until the time for chusing the Parish officers at Easter, and that the profits which shall arise by preaching the Lent Sermons in this Church shall be equally divided, share and share alike.

April 21. If any which may be chosen for the Office of Church Warden shall think fitt to pay to be excused of serving said office, It was agreed To take Fines of any not exceeding Six Persons.

A Letter was received from Mr Stinton who complains that several false reports have been spread abroad of him, desires the Christian Compassion of this Vestry. The Church Warden ordered to go and let him known that he shall have all necessary assistance.

May 3. Mr Manoel Ximenes complains of being elected Church Warden having been only three Years in the Parish, but offers Twenty Five Pounds to be excused from all offices, which was accepted; the Church Warden stating he knew Mr X. was looking out for a larger house and might remove very shortly.

May 9. Mr William Dare applied for leave to make a Vault in the Church Yard, which was refused.

June 3. Edward Gibbins, Church Warden Elect, The present

Church Warden, Ordered to take proper method to oblige him to serve the said office for this parish.

1715. June 16. Edward Gibbius being present, It was agreed in consideration of his being Church Warden of Putney to excuse him the said office here, upon his paying Ten Guineas, and if he continues Five Years in this Parish then to make up the Ten Guineas Twenty Pounds.

1716. April 6. John Stone requested to fine for all offices; which was allowed on payment of Thirty Pounds.

October 17. John Shreife Upper Church Warden died.

1717. July 29. The Auditors reported that having examined the Accounts of Mr. Wright late Church Warden, they find he has charged the parish with £7 2s. 6d. paid for one Boardman; and they find no order of Vestry for his paying more than £3 10s. 0d. A further som of £14 5s. paid for beautifying the Church Warden's and Minister's Pew, and that £12 9s. 1d. is particularly for the Church Warden's Pew, and they find £1 13s. overcharged for Wine. The two first of these articles the Vestry voted to be allowed, but the allowance not to be a precedent for the future and that no Church Warden shall be allowed to lay out more than forty shillings at one time upon the parish without an Order of Vestry.

August 14. The Vestry ordered a twelve month's extraordinary rate on the Inhabitants, for defraying the debts of the parish, and other duties arising touching the poor and the poor's rate, and that the assessment of such rate be made by the persons mentioned in the Warrant for making the assessment for the present Year.

1718. April 17. That no parishioner or stranger that are brought to be buried in the parish of St Helen's in the Church or Church Yard after the hour of Ten O'Clock at night from Lady Day to Michaelmas, but what shall pay double dues.

That no parishioner or stranger that are brought to be buried here after the hour of Nine O'Clock at night from Michaelmas to Lady Day but shall pay double dues.

Mr Leithulein desiring to bury his lady in the same vault with her father Sir Joseph Woolfe, It was agreed: That he should be allowed to do so, on payment of Fifty Pounds, the parish dues included.

M̅ʳ Churchill appointed to look after the Engines at a salary of 30s. pʳ annum.

1719. April 2. Several parishioners that have served some offices being desirous to fine to be excused from all other offices, as the Parish is in debt and wants money—It is agreed to take Twenty Pounds of each of the following Gentlemen for that purpose: Mʳ Edward Harris, Mʳ Richard Reddaway, and Mʳ Robert Dingley.

Thanks were voted to Mʳ Charles Goodman for taking the trouble to view the parish books, writings, &c., and making a register or memorial of the same in a parchment Book.

May 1. —— Chesters allowed to build a Family Vault on North Side of Church, Ten Foot Long and Eight Foot Broad on payment of Forty Pounds.

May 16. George Boddington having left Ten Pounds to the parish allowed to be buried in the same vault with his wife on payment of the usual dutys.

December 16. Mʳ John May, Mʳ Thomas How, Mʳ William Simmons, & Mʳ John Horseley allowed to fine for all offices, Twenty Pounds each.

1720. June 2. Lease of (qy. 27 Bishopsgate) granted to Mʳˢ Iveson for Twenty One Years at £40 a Year with a fine of Sixty Pounds.

Mʳ William Palmer a Parishioner had offered to take a lease for fifty years at £45 pʳ annum and fifty pounds fine. But he retracted therefrom and eluded the vestry, whereby this Vestry has deemed him, Injurious, Troublesome and Impertinent.

The Church Wardens to pay and apply the sum of Ten Pounds to the use of Thomas Mashedo a distressed inhabitant as they shall think fit.

That John Scott an Attorney be elected Vestry Clerk at a Salary of Four Pounds a year to commence at Midsummer next during the pleasure and good liking of this Vestry.

That the Church Warden or Wardens be empowered to spend at this Vestry and every future vestry Ten Shillings and place the same to the parish charge and accounts.

Then the Church Wardens in the name of this Vestry by their order returned their Thanks to Mʳ Ptolomy James, Minister of this parish, for his care, kindness, and liberality in procuring the two branches belonging to and hanging in this Church.

December 20. Edward Gibbon having been elected scavenger,

was desirous of paying the usual fine for that office and constable, to which it was objected that he had not paid the balance of the fine for churchwarden, as agreed June 16, 1715, but Mr Richard Stert engaging that the several sums should be paid, Mr Gibbon was excused from serving all offices whatsoever, after such payment thereof.

1721. February 28. Mr Isaac Boddington, formerly an inhabitant, to be allowed to bury his deceased wife in a vault in this Church wherein several of his relatives are buried, on paying such sum as he shall think fit, and also paying the usual dues and fees in such cases.

April 13. Mr Henry White, Mr John Dare, and Mr Gilbert were nominated for Upper Church Warden. Mr White being elected, Mr Dare, and Mr Gilbert, and Mr Colt were then nominated for under Church Warden ; Mr Gilbert elected.

November 18. That proper methods be taken to have and get 4000 rupees given by the will of Mr Isaac Berkeley, who died in Calcutta, returned or remitted hither in pounds sterling by the East India Company.

December 18. Four pounds to be paid to Mr Mulcaster for or in lieu of salary claimed by him for acting as Vestry Clerk.

Thanks given to Mr Isaac Boddington for the sum of four guineas paid by him for liberty to bury his wife in a vault in the Church, as above.

1722. March 22. Benjamin Thompson and Henry Barnwell chosen Engineers in the room of Mr Churchill, deceased, who are to exercise the office and have the salary annually by turns; Mr Thompson the first year.

May 7. Mr Thomas Edwards having at the last Vestry offered eight guineas for leave to lay a stone over his father's grave near the Pulpit, in the South Isle, which was referred back for inquiry as to the dimensions of the stone, It was at this Vestry resolved That Mr Edwards have leave to lay a stone, six foot two inches long, and two foot six inches broad, on payment of the sum of ten guineas and the charge of this Vestry.

That John Scott be discharged from being Vestry Clerk at Midsummer next, and that his salary do then cease.

May 22. The Church ordered to be repaired at an estimate of £127, and a rate made for raising the money for such repairs.

May 31. That the Church Wardens do employ such workmen

as they shall think fit for the repairs of the Church, so that they employ those who will do their work best and cheapest, and preference to be given to such workmen as live in this Parish.

That Iron Gates and Palisadoes be made and set up at the Front or West End of the Church Yard.

That the money for repairing the Church and making and setting up the said Gates and Palisadoes be raised by a Pound Rate wherein each Parishioner is to be rated Ten Pence for every pound of the Annual Rent he or she pays for what he or she rents or occupies in this Parish.

That Isaac Hellen be made free of this City at the charge of this Parish.

1722. October 11. The Bills for the repairs of the Church amounting to £242 8s. 2d. were allowed and approved, and a rate of Twelve Pence in the pound made for the payment thereof.

Mr Samuel Guyon, late Church Warden, chosen Vestry Clerk till Easter.

October 22. The Church Warden proposed that a Committee should be chosen to survey the late repairs. A Committee appointed accordingly.

October 31. The Committee reported that they had met together with Mr Browne the City Bricklayer, and all are of opinion that the Tradesmen employed have done honestly and justly by the Parish, and that the Church Wardens have been diligent, industrious and frugal in the management of this affair committed to their care, which report was confirmed by the Vestry.

December 17. Mr Richard Loyd excused from serving his Ward Offices on payment of Ten Guineas in consideration that by his business he is obliged to live chiefly out of town.

1723. April 9. Mr Bedell appeared to treat with this Vestry on behalf of Francis Bancroft, Esq., for leave for the said Bancroft to build a Vault (a previous application had been made by Mr Bedell, April 13, 1721, but without name or particulars, when Mr B. was requested to deliver a proposal in writing stating the dimensions, &c.) for himself and such friends and relations as he shall under his seal appoint by his handwriting and to no others. It was agreed That Mr Bancroft paying to the Church Warden the sum of Ninety Five Pounds shall have leave to make a Vault in the said Church, the walls to be 18 inches thick and the Vault to be

9 foot square within, and to erect a monument over the Vault and to fix such ironrails as he shall think fit, not exceeding 8 foot high all at his own charges, and the said Mr Bancroft to make everything good that is altered in making the said Vault, &c. The Vault to be made as near Mr Robinson's Vault as conveniently can be under the seats where the workhouse children useth to sit. Mr Bancroft to have free liberty to repair the Vault, &c. when he will.

1723. May 2. That the above Monument shall not exceed Eight foot in height and that the rails shall not exceed the height of Six foot, and that a sufficient space shall be left on the West Side to carry a corpse into the said Vault without obstruction.

July 25. The Church Warden reported that he had received a Bill of Exchange for Five Hundred Pounds being the produce of Mr Berkeley's legacy which it was agreed should be invested in South Sea Stock until it should be settled how to lay it out in the strictest manner according to the will of the donor.

Decr 5. The Church Warden reported that the Five Hundred Pounds had been laid out in South Sea Stock at 102⅝ Per Cent. and that the Minister had filed a Bill in Chancery against the two Church Wardens relating to the disposal thereof. Upon which a Committee was appointed to take the advice of Counsel and that the case which the Church Wardens had stated to Counsellor Edwards with his opinion be copied into the . . . . Book of this parish.

1724. March 24. A deputation attended from the parish of St Botolph Bishopsgate to request that this parish would accommodate them with seats &c. during the time of the rebuilding their Church upon such terms as shall be agreed to by a Committee to be chosen for each parish; which was agreed to unanimously and the Committee appointed.

April 9. The Bill and Answer which was lately given to the Court of Chancery respecting Mr Berkeley's Will being read, The Vestry was well satisfied with the Church Wardens' answer to the said Bill.

April 13. Mr Penara excused all offices on payment of thirty pounds and the charges of the Vestry. The Ten Shillings charges fterwards allowed.

April 16. Sir Biby Lake having been elected Church Warden

informed them that he has been a Barrister at Law above twenty years and therefore excused from serving any Parish or Ward Offices. But in regard that he has a great respect for the parish, he would make them a present of Twenty pounds on condition that they give him no further trouble respecting parish or ward offices for the future. This offer was immediately accepted and thanks voted for his kind and generous present.

1724. Decr 18. Lease granted jointly with the Carpenters' Company to Mr Poole for 21 Years from Lady 1726 at £30 per annum £40 to be allowed for repairs.

The Churchwarden ordered to proceed against the Leatherseller's Co^y for the payment of the rate made for the repairs of the Church amounting to £6 10s. 0d. as they shall be advised by Counsell learned in the law.

Nathaniel Poole chosen Vestry Clerk (in the room of Mr Samuel Guyon deceased) during the pleasure of the Vestry.

1725. April 2. Committee appointed to consider of the decree made by Sir Joseph Jekyll Master of the rolls relating to Mr Berkeley's legacy and to give their opinion in what manner, and for what use the money so given shall be laid out and applied.

April 29. The Committee considered that it would be well to allow the money to continue as at present invested until they shall agree how to lay out the same according to the intent of the donor. Excepting so much as shall be necessary to pay the costs of this suit.

June 10. That the Five Hundred pounds given by Mr Isaac Berkeley and the profits thereof, shall (as soon as conveniently may be) be laid out in the erecting and putting up an Organ in this Church, and that a proposal pursuant to the said resolution be drawn up, and the Churchwardens do wait on Mr Lightbourn the Master in Chancery to whom the matter concerning the said legacy stands referred for his opinion touching the same.

June 14. That the Churchwardens and their successors shall not deliver out of their Custody any Books, papers, or writings to any person or persons whatsoever without taking a receipt for the same.

Nov. 8. That the dividends on £500 be applied to the payment of Costs of Suit and the principal money remain till its increase or the benevolence of the parishioners can and will enable the said Parish to build an Organ loft and Organ.

1725. Dec. 1. The said South Sea Stock to be sold and so much South Sea Annuities to be purchased, the surplus Stock and interest to be applied in discharge of the law expenses.

1726. April 27. John Gould excused all offices on payment of Thirty Pounds.

All Under Church Wardens are hereby ordered to bring in their first Years account and state of the poor at the expiration of their first year.

May 4. Moses Raper having been chosen Churchwarden informed them that he had let his House and was going out of the parish. Sir John Lock then being in nomination with other Gentlemen did freely, generously and voluntarily and before he was chosen, pay to the Churchwardens Thirty Pounds to be exempted from all offices, which was accepted with the thanks for his generous act.

Thanks to Mr Tame Church Warden for his care and diligence in serving the parish.

Five Guineas voted as a present to the Vestry Clerk for his great trouble in copying accounts not his business and many attendances on Committees &c.

May 16. Mr Peter Merchant proposed to give £25 as a fine for all offices, thereupon the Vestry considering that they were in want of money to reimburse Mr Colt late Churchwarden who has been a long time out of his money (1724), and that they cannot chuse Mr Merchant on any office 'till Xmas or Easter next, agree to accept his offer.

Mr Henry Hamerton also offered Ten Pounds as a fine for Churchwarden, he having served all other offices. Thereupon the Vestry, considering his large family, accepted thereof. Mr Colt's balance amounting to £32 18s. 9d., to be paid with interest.

The Under Churchwarden allowed to take charge of the parish plate. The Upper not having a conveniency to take care of it.

July 15. Henry Desleborough of the parish of Lambeth having married the Widow of the late *Warder*, on the promise of the Church Warden to give him £5 with her The said £5 ordered to be paid on his bringing a Certificate from Lambeth parish that he has a legal settlement with them.

Oct. 18. The Under Church Warden having removed out of the parish, a new one chosen for the remainder of the Year.

1726. Dec. 15. That the Under Church Warden do provide for all the Pensioners of this parish proper Badges as the Law directs, and to give each pensioner a Badge, and order them to sow the same on each of their outward garment. And in case such pensioner after such Order shall not wear or refuse to wear such Badge at the time of receiving their pension, and at all other times, the said Churchwarden shall and may refuse paying such pensioner their pension.

That in case the said Churchwarden shall pay to any pensioners their respective pension without his, her, or their badge as aforesaid, shall be prosecuted as the law directs at the expense of the Parish.

1727. April 6. M* Dufresney elected Churchwarden. Excused all offices on payment of £30, with the thanks of Vestry for his generous act.

June 7. Mr. Dufresney not being so generous as the friend who had agreed to pay the £30 thought him, would only give £28. It was therefore put to the vote whether his friend Captain Tame should pay the £30 or only the £28 which he had received. It was agreed to excuse him the said 40 shillings, considering the good intent the said Captain Tame meant for the parish.

A Man named Blackburn proposed to marry Mrs Hanks, who is a very troublesome and chargeable pensioner to this parish, in case this parish would give with her Ten Guineas as a marriage portion, And that he would also take the said Mrs Hanks' daughter as an Apprentice and by that means free the parish from any further expense; whereupon it was ordered, That the Churchwarden do upon the solemnization of the said marriage, and when the said Mrs Hanks's daughter is bound apprentice to the said Blackburn pay him Ten Guineas as a consideration for his natural love and affection which he bears to the said Mrs Hanks.

Dec. 15. The Churchwarden ordered to repair the pump and a Committee appointed to see that it is well and sufficiently repaired.

Complaint against Mr. Mulcaster, the Clerk, for opening of Vaults and other grounds without asking of the consent of the Churchwardens.

1728. Feb. 21. A Fire Cock ordered to be made and fixed in the upper part of Great St Helens.

1728. Oct. 17. A motion was made by Mr Jackson one of the Church Wardens that he should have liberty to enter a Caveat against any person that should be now chosen Parish Clerk, and that such person so chosen shall give such security to the Minister & Church Wardens as the parishioners in Vestry assembled, at any subsequent Vestry shall think fitt to order. Thereupon it was agreed and ordered That a Caveat be forthwith entered, and the person chosen Parish Clerk shall give such security to the Minister & Churchwardens as the Vestry shall think fitt to order.

A motion was now made and the question put, That Mr James the Minister would nominate and appoint a parish Clerk, Thereupon he sincerely desired to be excused, and gave this reason, because he would disoblige none.

Ordered, That the Election of a parish Clerk be by ballot and he that hath the majority on the first ballot shall be duly elected. .... The Vestry proceeded to the Election of a Parish Clerk in the room of Mr Robt Muleaster when there appeared for Thomas Wooles 18, for Ja^s Ladyman 16, for J. Butler 15, R. Day 10 and for Richard Lowe, none. Thomas Wooles being declared to have the majority. Mr James the Minister being then asked whether he agreed thereto, he approved of the same.

1729. April 10. The Church Warden reported that a surplus being due from Mr Alex^r Boucher on the Scavengers Rate collected by him in 1727 and he refusing to account with the Auditors for the surplus, he had summoned him before the Comm^{rs} of Sewers, when he pretended he had lost his Book, whereupon the Comm^{rs} had fined him £10 pursuant to Act of Parliament. The Auditors are now desired to make such end with the said Mr Boucher as they shall think fit in relation to the said surplus.

That for the future no Church Warden shall expend above Forty Shillings for the Oyster Feast, that being the gift of Mr Prior to this parish.

That the Church Wardens for the future shall not expend above £12 on Ascension day to defray all charges.

May 7. The Bill of Costs relating to Mr Berkley's legacy ordered to be taxed before a Master in Chancery.

1730. January 28. Whereas at the Election of Parish Clerk, Oct. 17, 1728, the Church Warden had liberty to enter a Caveat against any person that should be then chosen, and a Caveat was then entered against Thomas Wooles accordingly. Now this Vestry considering the said T. W. capable of serving this Parish as Parish Clerk, do hereby desire and order the present Church Warden and the Vestry Clerk to attend with the said Thomas Wooles at Doctors Commons and take off the said Caveat, That he may be at liberty to be sworn in Parish Clerk, and that the Church Warden do give him any Certificate that may be necessary.

1730. April 2. Samuel Green having been chosen Warder at the last Vestry, desired to decline the office, which was agreed to.

Mr Blackburn agreed to wind up the Clock and keep it in good repair for £4 ℞ ann.

April 10. Mr Ruck fined £20 for Church Warden.

That the Church Warden do pay Mr Gathurn, the Sequestrator, the half of Sir John Lawrence's Money, being £8 15s. as a present for serving the parish.

April 15. Mr Palmer fined £20 for Church Warden.

1731. Mar. 1. Mr Webb having fined 40s. for Scavenger and Mr Garrett having fined Twelve Pounds for Inquest, Constable and Scavenger, It was proposed, That they should give their notes of hand to serve the office of Church Warden when elected, the Vestry rather chose to have a minute made in the Vestry Book of their acknowledgment.

Complaint being made against Thomas Wooles the Parish Clerk for misbehaviour in the duty of his office. It is ordered, That the order of the 28 Jany last year be dissolved, And that the said Caveat do still remain till further orders of this Vestry.

July 14. Application was made on behalf of Richard Backwell for leave to put up a Monument between the Pulpit and the South Window annexed not exceeding 4 f^t wide, 6f^t high, and the projection not to exceed 9 inches. Agreed, That he should have leave on payment of Twenty Guineas. His Agent being informed thereof refused to comply and offered Ten Guineas, which this Vestry rejected.

July 29. Mr Backwell's Agent again attended and paid the Twenty Guineas, He making good all damages that shall be done by reason and consideration thereof.

1732. Feb. 9. Ten Guineas to be paid to Mr Haywood, the Minister, as a voluntary present from this Parish.

That the Church Wardens do endeavour to suppress the supposed disorderly house called the Mitre.

1732. March 10. A request being made by Mr Nathl Gould, a parishioner, that this Vestry would grant to him and his family the liberty of sitting in the uppermost pew on the left hand of the middle Isle next the Communion Table; It was resolved, That permission be granted during the pleasure of the parish, but when the said N. Gould or his family shall not be at Church, then the said pew shall be filled at the discretion of the Churchwardens for the time being.

April 13. The Caveat entered against Thomas Wooles ordered to be withdrawn, and the Church Wardens to sign any Certificate for discharging the said Caveat.

That the Church Wardens take proper measures to oblige one David Knight to provide for a bastard child supposed to be his, which was some time since dropped in this parish.

July 31. A fire in Little St. Helen's having been extinguished by the industry of Mr Thos Wooles and other persons, It is ordered That a reward of Three Guineas be given to them for their exertions.

Complaint being made that the graves were not dug deep enough and therefore were very offensive. It is ordered That for the future every grave shall be dug Seven feet deep, and that the gravedigger shall have two shillings for his trouble.

That the Pavement from the Pump to the corner of the Church Wall shall be paved, and that the Church Warden do pay for the same so far as belongs to the Parish.

1733. Jany 24. The Church Warden ordered to pay the sum of £24 17s. 8d. to the Treasurer of the London Workhouse, pursuant to an Act of Common Council Dec. 14 last past for raising the sum of £2443 14s. 0d. towards the further employing the poor of the City of London.

Considering that a Workhouse would be the means of easing the rates and lessen the expense of the Poor, a Committee was appointed to look out for a convenient house for the purpose.

March 29. That the Churchwardens for the future have liberty to expend the sum of Six Pounds at the Oyster Feast yearly (including the forty shillings left by Mr Prior for that purpose).

May 10. A Committee appointed to treat with the Church

Wardens, &c., of St. Pulcher's Parish, touching their receiving and providing for the poor of this parish in their Workhouse.

1733. Dec. 17. Forty Shillings not being considered sufficient to buy a good Coat and Hat for the Warder, It was agreed That the sum of Three Pounds be allowed for that purpose.

That the bill of Mr Poole, the Vestry Clerk touching the appeal of Ann Price being £4 1s. 0d. be paid.

1734. Feb. 5. Mr Clark, Executor to Major Genl Kellum applied for leave to lay a Black Marble Stone over his grave, 6f^t long and 4f^t broad, and to erect a monument on the South Wall 5f^t high and 3f^t broad. Permission was granted on payment of Thirty Guineas of which Mr Clark took time to consider. The parish to have the liberty to bury any other person in the same grave.

March 6. As Mr Clark would not comply to give thirty guineas. It was agreed, That Mr Clark should have leave on payment of Twenty Guineas to which he agreed.

That for the future no person (except a parishioner) shall have liberty to lay down any grave stone in the Church without reserving to the parish the right of laying any other person under such grave stone.

That Five Guineas be given to Mr. Haywood the Minister as a present, but with this particular order that it be no precedent.

April 18. On the petition of the Vestry Clerk begging the favour of this Vestry to augment his Salary from £4 to £6 ℔ annum The question being put whether he should have such advance, it was agreed to.

It being reported that the Poor's Rates are not sufficient to support the Poor, by means whereof this Parish has been subject to overrates It is ordered, That the quarterly rates be raised from 10s. ℔ Ann. to 15s. ℔ Ann. and so in proportion in order to prevent the trouble of making overrates for the future.

July 19. Mr Clark attended and gave the Parish Ten Guineas on condition that no other person whatsoever should ever hereafter be buried in the same grave where Major Genl Kellum now lies interred.

July 26. That Two Guineas out of the above Ten Guineas be given to the Revd Mr Haywood with this particular order that it be no precedent.

1734. July 31. That the Iron Gates and Rails round the Church Yard be new painted.

September 19. Application was made on behalf of Mrs Mary Newland for leave to lay a Stone over the grave of her late husband Mr Isaac Newland in the Church Yard and offered for such liberty the sum of Three Guineas which was accepted.

September 26. An agreement was entered into with Mr Thruckstone to receive and maintain all the parish poor, present and to come, and provide them good wholesome Meat and drink, Washing, lodging, Clothes, Physic and all other necessaries whatsoever; and to put the Children out as Apprentices and pay premiums with them—to indemnify the parish from all suits or charges concerning the provision or settlement of the poor or other matter in any wise relating to them. The Church Wardens and other parishioners to have liberty to inspect the House and see that the said poor are well and sufficiently provided for, at all times. They also agree to pay the said Thruckstone £130 p^r Ann. for performing the above covenants, and if any of the poor shall die at his house, he is to be at the expense of burying them. All such poor as may be hereafter settled on the parish to be sent to his house. This agreement to be in force for twelve months and at its expiration the poor to be at liberty to depart with all the wearing apparel they have been provided with and to keep the same for their own use, and in case of any dispute between the said Thruckstone and the Parish, the case to be referred to the Lord Mayor, whose decision is to be binding on both parties.

Bill of Fare.

For dinners. Sunday. Hot Meat, Bread & Broth.
Monday. Cold Meat Bread & Cheese or Butter.
Tuesday. Boiled Wheat with Butter & Sugar.
Wednesday as Sunday.
Thursday as Monday.
Friday. Thick Milk or ffirmity.
Saturday. Bread & Cheese or Butter.

Milk Porridge for Breakfast, Bread & Cheese or Butter for Supper.

1735. April 10. That two Surplices be provided for the Revd Mr Haywood.

Decr 18. Twelve Months given to Mr Thruckstone of their intention to take away the poor.

Legacy of £100 left to the Parish by Mrs Clapham.

Mr John Dare elected Parish Clerk in the room of Thos Wooles, deceased, the Revd Mr Haywood consenting thereto.

1736. March 18. Notice was given that Mrs Dorothy Lawrence would pay off the £350 and Int^t left by Sir John Lawrence on which it was agreed that Mrs Lawrence should be requested to retain the money on the same security and pay the parish but 4 p^r Cent.

An order given for borrowing £100 at 4½ p^r Cent. to pay off the debts of the Parish.

That four black neats leather chairs be bought for the Vestry and that one of them be an elbow chair.

April 29. The Church Warden reported that he had received the above £350 and £8 15s. 0d. Int^t which together with the £100 legacy of Mrs Clapham's were ordered to be invested in the 3 p^r Cent Annuities.

That two dozen of good buckets be provided for the use of this Parish.

May 28. A Committee having been appointed at the last Vestry to receive proposals for the several repairs wanting to be done to the Church and the several estimates or proposals being produced, It was ordered, That the Committee be impowered to treat with the several workmen in the best and cheapest manner they can, And that such workmen who shall be chosen shall be tyed down to perform his work according to such proposal.

The pavement of the Church ordered to be thoroughly repaired.

July 28. The Grave Stones to be put down in their proper places as before.

August 13. A Legacy of £10 left by Mr John Baker to be distributed among the poor was given forthwith among fifteen Persons as follows, 4 at £1, 3 at 15s., 7 at 10s., and 1 at 5s.

Notice ordered to be advertised twice in the daily Advertiser and London Evening Post, To persons claiming a right to any of the Monuments in the Church and are minded forthwith to send

Workmen to repair and beautify the same at their own expense, may have liberty from the Church Wardens to do so.

That application be made to the Lord Chancellor for leave to apply the £500 left by Mr Berkley for and towards the building of on Organ and erecting an Organ Loft in this Church.

1736. October 15. The Committee appointed for the repairs of the Church presented the several Bills which they had carefully examined amounting to £550 3s. 1d. which were referred back to the said Committee in order to have some abatement made on such Bills as seem to them unreasonable.

That the above Sum be raised by a pound rate at   in the £ of the Annual Rent each parishioner pays for what he or she occupies in this parish and that the said rate so intended to be made, shall be made in the vestry room of this Parish, and that all the parishioners are to be summoned to be present, who are desired to come prepared to give an account what rent they pay, by reason no inhabitant shall be dissatisfied with what they shall be rated.

October 20. The above Church Rate made at 2s. 6d. in the £.

November 24. That the Rev Mr Haywood have Nine Pounds out of the interest of Sir John Lawrence's money.

1737. January 7. A Committee appointed to agree with some other Parish for the clothing and maintaining the poor of this parish in their Workhouse at a price not exceeding Four Shillings ⅌ Week for each person.

That the Sextoness be paid in future the same sum for ringing the Bell for a burial in the Church as in the Church Yard, being Two Shillings and Sixpence.

That a Table with the names of the Benefactors to this parish, done in gold letters be put up in the Church.

That a surplice of strong holland be provided for the common use of this parish.

That the Church Warden do take up or remove such Trees in the Church Yard and plant others in their room as he shall think fit.

That the Minutes of every Vestry for the future be read over at the breaking up of the Vestry and signed by one of the Church Wardens for the time being.

February 3. The Committee appointed at the last Vestry reported that they had entered into an agreement with the Church Warden and Overseers of the Parish of St Sepulchre for the maintenance of the poor in their Workhouse at four shillings each weekly. This parish to provide clothing and medicines. The agreement may be broken after the expiration of twelve months on giving three months notice. And for the due performance of the several contracts, the parties severally bind themselves in the penalty of Fifty Pounds. Which Agreement this Vestry do concur and agree to accordingly.

The Church Warden reported the Leathersellers' Company and others had refused to pay the Church Rate. Upon which he was ordered to take such lawful ways and means as he shall be advised to oblige them.

1737. April 20. Nathl Gould paid £20 as a fine for Church Warden.

That the £100 legacy left by Mrs Clapham and invested in the 3 ⅌ Cent. Bank annuities be sold out to pay off the £100 borrowed at 4½ per cent. March 18, 1735-6. And that this Parish shall indemnify the Minister and Church Wardens for the time being, touching the several uses for which the said legacy was left to this Parish.

August 4. That Mr Burdett and Mr Parker be allowed to pay only half of the Church Rate in full of the whole, they having both gone out of the Parish.

October 21. The Gresham Committee having refused to pay £15 the sum which they were assessed for Church Rate and offered £10 in lieu thereof, the Churchwarden was ordered to proceed against them for the recovery thereof, should they refuse on his again applying to them for that purpose. The opinion of Counsel had been taken by the Gresham Committee which was given in favour of the Parish.

That a new Lease should be granted to Mr Nathl Ware of the house he now lives in belonging to this parish for the term of twenty-one years from the expiration of his old lease which will be at Mids^r 1741, and to continue to pay the rent of £40 p^r ann. The parish to allow one year's rent for repairs, which being agreed to, Mr Ware paid One Shilling to the Church Warden for the use of the poor to bind him to his agreement.

A new lease also agreed to be granted to Mrs Eliz^h Kirk for twenty-one Years. To pay Ten Guineas fine, Twelve pounds p^r

annum rent clear of Taxes and to lay out Sixty pounds in repairs, to commence from the expiration of the present lease at Lady Day 1739.

The Vestry Clerk to prepare the Leases at the expense of the several tenants.

1738. April 6. That the Tuesday's Lecture be continued from Lady Day last to Michaelmas next, but this parish is not to be at any expense for such continuance. The Church Warden taking such security as he shall think proper to make good all damages which may be done to the Church.

August 11. Mr Maynard had leave to build a Vault under his pew in the North Isle on payment of £20—£5 5s. of which money to be given to Mr Haywood.

September 28. An account of Mr Berkeley's Legacy amounting with interest to £521 6s. 4d. and a Committee appointed to examine all papers and vouchers that have been paid touching the said legacy.

1739. February 9. A Motion being made whether the Women had a right to vote for a parish Clerk or not, and debates arising thereon, this Vestry was dissolved.

February 15. Mr Haywood having given his consent The Vestry proceeded to the Election of a parish Clerk in the room of Mr John Dare, deceased, and It was agreed by a great majority That the Election should be by balloting and to be balloted for three times.

Upon the first ballot there were for Ja^s Ladyman 25 Thos Hill 29 Thos Cole 10 Chas Garrett 8 who having the least number was left out on the second ballot when there were for James Ladyman 28 Thomas Hill 32 Thomas Cole 9 who having the least number was left out on the third ballot when there were for James Ladyman 45 Thos Hill 32. Whereupon the said Ja^s Ladyman was declared duly elected.

March 8. The Committee appointed to examine Mr Colt's account touching Mr Berkeley's legacy reported that the sum of £2 13s. 0d. was due from Mr Colt, but there still remains unpaid to Mr Emerson the Solicitor £21 0s. 3d. and to Mr Wilson the Solicitor £7 17s. 0d. which Sums Mr Colt was desired to pay as soon as the interest on the £500 Stock was sufficient to pay the same.

A motion being made whether the Tuesday's Lectures should be continued during this Summer Half Year, a division was demanded and there appeared for the Lecture 21 and the Teller, and against the Lecture 22 and the Teller, the Majority was therefore declared against the Lecture.

Alderman Bernar, Church Warden.

1739. April 26. The question being whether this Vestry would allow Mr Ladyman the Parish Clerk a certain Salary or not It was carried by a great majority that he should have a salary. It was then agreed That the Salary should be Eight Pounds a Year, but only during the pleasure of the Vestry.

October 18. That the Church Warden do provide Mr Gynand with a proper pew at his discretion with this reservation, that if the Vestry shall not think it a proper pew, then they may be at liberty to displace the said family again.

1740. February 28. Committee appointed to examine the Old Engine and if they find it as bad as represented, to sell it and contract for a new Engine of the modern fashion with all necessary utensils for working the same.

Committee appointed to draw up a case touching the several decrees on Mr Berkeley's Legacy and take some eminent counsel's opinion thereon.

April 10. On the report of the above Committee y^e £500 was ordered to be invested in the names of the Minister and Church Wardens.

That a Church Rate be made of Two Pence in the £

April 22. It being represented to this Vestry, That Mr Andrew Dehoes who was chosen Under Church Warden at the last Vestry is a Jew by religion and a very unfit person to execute that office It was agreed that he should be excused from serving the said office upon payment of Fifteen Guineas.

April 25. Mr Hodges paid the fine of £20 to be excused from serving the office of Church Warden on condition that he should not be nominated for any other Ward offices previous to Christmas 1743, having been elected Church Warden before his real turn according to seniority. Mr Sparrow was then elected and not being at home to give an answer whether he would serve, the Vestry adjourned to Eight o'clock to-morrow morning.

April 26. Mr Sparrow sent a note for £25 to be excused from serving the offices of Churchwarden, Constable and Scavenger, which offer was rejected, and it was carried That he should be excused on payment of £28, which Mr Bernard undertook for Mr Sparrow should be complied with, and Mr Smith was chosen Under Churchwarden.

1740. June 19. But notwithstanding the said undertaking of M. Bernard the said Mr Sparrow would not agree to pay any more than £25 and insisted on being sworn into the office of Churchwarden which he accordingly was on the 26th of April last——Therefore this Vestry doth excuse the said undertaking of Mr Bernard it being done in a friendly manner to serve Mr Sparrow, and do also dissolve and declare void the said Election of Mr William Smiths being chosen Under Churchwarden for the reason abovementioned.

Whereas a debate arose at this Vestry touching the Bearers for Funerals. For the better regulation of them this Vestry doth order the Bearers shall be settled in the following manner viz. That the Clerk shall have 3 when 8, 3 when 6 and 2 when 4. The Sextoness to have 3 when 8 2 when 6 and 1 when 4. The Warder 2 when 8, 1 when 6 and 1 when 4.

August 14. Ordered that a New Rate be made for the supply of the poor not to exceed the sum of £65 for every quarter.

Committee appointed to inquire after a proper house for the reception of the poor.

October 21. Committee reported that they had agreed with the Churchwardens of St Olave, after viewing five little tenements in Gunpowder Alley in Crutched Fryars to take a lease for Seven, Eleven, or Fourteen Years, at the yearly rent of Twenty One Pounds, clear of all taxes for a Workhouse for this Parish, and recommend that one Mrs Dodd who has a yard and washhouse part of the said premises may continue tenant who now pays £6 10s. ℔ Ann^m which will reduce the rent to £14 10s. ℔ ann.

To which the Vestry agreed and ordered a lease to be prepared accordingly.

1741. April 2. The Churchwarden ordered to sell out £130 £3 ℔ C^t Ann^s for the furnishing of the Workhouse &c.

The legacy of £500 left by Mr Berkley ordered to be laid out in South Sea Stock for the safety and benefit of the Parish.

Full copies of all the Orders of Vestry and decrees on this subject.

1741. April 5. Robert Dingley J^r requested leave to make a Vault for his father and family in the footway in the Churchyard 12 feet long by 8 feet wide. Permission granted on payment of £20, the Rev. Mr Haywood to have £6 10s. thereof.

July 23. The Workmen's Bills for fitting up the Workhouse amounting to about £160 ordered to be paid.

Twenty-four poor in the Workhouse. Committee appointed to meet at the Workhouse every Wednesday.

A Bill of Fare for the Workhouse produced by Mr Hunt the Master thereof and approved.

December 17. A Matron appointed at 30s. ℙ Quarter during the pleasure of the Workhouse Committee.

March 11. A Committee appointed to receive Subscriptions and proposals for the building an Organ and Organ-loft to be built from the pillar of the North side of the Churchwardens to the South wall. Proposals received from Mr Griffin and Mr Jordan.

Mr Griffin's proposal.

I propose to build, (at my own proper cost & charge) set up, and completely finish a new Organ value Five Hundred Pounds and to consist of the following Stops and each stop of the number of pipes following.

In the Great Organ.		In the Choir Organ.	
One Stopt diapason	56	One Stopt diapason ⎫	by
Open do.	56	Open do. ⎬	communi-
do. principal	56	do. principal ⎭	cation.
do. twelfth	56	do. Flute	56
do. fifteenth	56	do. Vox humane	56
do. Terce	56		112
do. Trumpet	56		
do. Clarion	56	In the Ecco and Swell.	
do. Sesquialtra five ranks	280	One Stopt diapason	32
do. Cornet ,,	135	Open do.	32
	863	do. Cornet five ranks	160
Choir Organ	112	do. Trumpet	32
Ecco & Swell	288	do. Clarion	32
	1263		288

That in the said Organ there shall be three new strong sounding boards, and three new rolling boards, and three new strong pair of bellows, of such length and breadth as to give wind sufficient to make the Chorus plump and bold, without any faintings, And that all the pipes and all the other materials of the said Organ shall be entirely new and such as have not already been made use of in any organ whatsoever.

That the Keys shall be handsomely made and that the Touch shall be easy and free and not hard or deep.

Item. There shall be an entire separate frame of sufficient strength to support the sounding boards, and all other the inside work, and all the pipes Except those pipes of the open diapason and other pipes which appear in front and are to be affixed in the outside Case or Frame, and that all the conveyances of wind from the sounding boards to the front pipes or from the Sounding boards to the Cornet or any other conveyances of wind from the sounding boards to any other pipes or stops, shall be of the most proper.

And for the better security and preservation of the said organ, all parts of the said work which may at any time be necessary to be opened or taken asunder for the better cleaning, repairing, or amending the said Organ shall be fastened with Screws or Buttons without any Nails.

Item. I will make or cause to be made a Compleat Butifull outside case or frame of Mahogany, the work to be masterly finished with Beads, Mouldings, Carvings, frees, Cornishes and other ornaments, and that the front of the said Organ shall be of the shape and finished in the same manner as the inclosed plan.

Item. I will make or cause to be made all the pipes which are to compose this Organ to imitate the natural tone of the several instruments and the Humane voice, and that all the stops in the said organ shall have the fulness of body, sweetness, and justness of tone which is proper to the said several different stops, and all other the several parts of the said Organ shall be so masterly finished as to render it a compleat instrument, and when finished will submit it to the judgment of such Organists as shall be agreed on.

Item. I propose to keep the said Organ in tune, in repair, and to perform on it, or cause it to be performed on to the satisfaction of the parishioners, or the major part of them during the time of my natural life, for and in consideration of the sum of £250, to be paid within   after the Organ is opened, and £25 ℔ Annum during the said term of my natural life ; and in case it should at any time happen that the said Organ should not be played on to the satisfaction of the Parishioners, and notice thereof given or left in writing pursuant to an Order of Vestry of the said parish, That then and for that time only, the said annuity shall cease and not be paid 'till the said Organ shall be played upon again to the satisfaction of the said parish.

By your most obedient humble Servant

Thos. Griffin

P.S. The pipes in the front of the Organ to be guilt with Gold.

The proposals of Abra Jordan, Organ Builder, John Harris & Co. to the Rev^d the Minister and the Gentlemen of St. Helens for a New Organ to be erected in their Church.

On the Great Organ the compass is from GG to E in Alt being 54 Keys &c.

			On the Chair or Choir Organ :—
An open diapazon	. .	54 speaking.	
Stopt do.	. .	54 do.	Open diapazon . . . 21 pipes
Principal	. . . .	54 do.	by communication . 33 otherwise.
Great twelfth	. . .	54 do.	Stop'd diapazon . . 29 pipes
Fifteenth	. . . .	54 do.	by communication & 25 otherwise.
Bass Sexquialtra of			Principal 21
four ranks	. . .	104	by communication & 33 otherwise.
Cornet of four ranks		112	Flute 54
Trumpet		54	Vox humane 54
		540	199

Eccho's and swelling on ye third sett of Keys.

Open diapazon	29 pipes
Stop'd do.	29
Trumpet	29
Hautboy	29
	116

Tis to be observed that this Organ contains 855 valuable speaking pipes besides the advantage of 71 more that speak by communication. Here are no mixtures or supplemental stops of small pipes which serve for little else than to make the appearance of a number of pipes which will be subject to be out of Tune upon the least variation of the wind of the Bellows and are of little value and strength to an Organ. The above Organ if after you have heard it meets with your approbation, we will sett up free of all other charges ye gallery being prepared for the sum of £350.

We are Gent
Y^r very humble Serv^{ts}

Budge Row March ye 2 A. Jordan & Comp.
  1741.

1742. April 22. On the report of the Committee, the Vestry Clerk was ordered to prepare the draft of the Agreement between the Minister and Churchwardens on the part of the parish with Mr Thomas Griffin, the Committee having contracted and agreed with him, for the building of the Organ, &c.

December 15. Bond given to Mr Alderman Barnard for the balance of his Accounts as Churchwarden £154 17s. 7d. Interest at 4 ℔ Cent ℔ Annum.

Committee appointed concerning a legacy of £100 left by Mr Roe for the purchase or keeping in repair of a Parsonage House to be constantly inhabited by the Minister.

Whereas severall poor persons who are not willing to go into the workhouse, have been very troublesome to the Churchwardens and have likewise applied to this Vestry for relief; This Vestry considering such practices detrimental to the Parish, Order That the present Churchwardens and all succeeding Churchwardens for the future shall not at any time or times hereafter, give any Sum or Sums of money whatsoever to any poor person belonging to this parish who shall not be in the parish Workhouse; And this to be a Standing Order.

1743. November 3. The Committee concerning Mr Rowe's Legacy reported that they had waited on Mr. Beechcraft Ex'or to the said Mr Rowe who advised them that it would be proper to apply to Counsel touching the same, for that in his opinion they were deprived by the Mortmain Act to receive it. The Committe were then directed to apply to Counsel and to Act and do as they shall think proper, and if the said Committee think proper to pay £200 to the Augmentation of Queen Anne's Bounty, this Vestry do desire Mr. Alderman Barnard and Mr. John Lodge to lend £100 each to this parish at 4 ⅌ Cent ⅌ Annum, the Churchwardens to give two separate Bonds for the same.

Church Rate to be made of 2ᵈ in the pound.

Faculty to be procured for opening the organ.

1744. March 29. Committee appointed to consider of ways and means to discharge the parish debts.

Ordered. That the Churchwardens do give directions to the Parish Clerk to give publick notice in the Church the Sunday morning before they intend to call a Vestry the week following, and also of the business intended to be done at such Vestry.

William Carvell being in attendance, the Churchwarden reported that his wife and children were in the workhouse in consequence of his having run away from them to live with another woman: Whereupon It was agreed that he should be immediately taken into Custody and carried to the Compter that night as a Vagrant. The said Carvell was then charged with a Constable and taken to the Compter accordingly.

June 7. N.B. £130 has been borrowed from Sir John Lawrence's money for the finishing the workhouse.

On the application of Mrs. Sprackling the Sextoness it was agreed to raise her salary from £4 ⅌ Ann. to £6 ⅌ Ann.

August 2. Robert Bradley chosen Organ Blower at a Salary of Forty Shillings ⅌ Ann.

Alderman Cokayne Churchwarden.*

December 12. Revᵈ Mʳ Willmott attended this and several following Vestrys for Revᵈ Mʳ Colton.

1745. December 16. Election for Parish Clerk in the room of John Ladyman deceased.

Ordered. That the Election be by holding up of hands. In nomination, Thomas Hill and Thomas Londindine. It appearing to this Vestry that Thomas Hill had a very great Majority of Votes was now declared by Mr. Alderman Cokayne to be duly

---

* Francis Cokayne, Aldⁿ of Cornhill Ward, Sheriff 1746, Mayor 1751, Died 1767. "A Court of Aldermen was held at Guildhall, 17 Novʳ 1767, when £100 was ordered to be paid to the Widow of the late worthy Alderman Cockayne, as a testimony of the sense they entertained of his ever being ready and willing to serve his fellow Citizens."—*Gent. Mag.*, vol. xxxvii. p. 560.

elected Parish Clerk who being called in promised to behave well in his office.

1745. February 17. This Vestry called to consider what method to take to make good the deficiences of Mr. Churchwarden Stevens, he being now under misfortunes. The Vestry Clerk reported that by desire of the Upper Churchwarden he had waited on Mr Stevens to settle the account between him and the Parish, and it now appears by the said account laid before this Vestry, that Mr Stevens had collected half a year on his Poor Rate which amounted to £118 4s. 0d. and had paid on account of the parish the sum of £61 18s. 5d. the balance whereof amounting to £56 5s. 7d. he is not at present able to pay, but desires time to pay the same. Mr Stevens also delivered up the Poor Rate Book and desired to be concerned no further in the collection thereof.

Mr Church Warden Cokayne and Mr Tuff were requested to meet Mr Stevens's Creditors and impowered to act as they shall think proper for the benefit of the Parish.

Mr Tuff also agreed to collect the remaining half-year's Poor Rate.

1746. December 15. Whereas at a Vestry held the 17th day of February last it appears by an entry then made that the balance on Mr Churchwarden Stevens's account to this parish was £56 6s. 7d. but upon Mr Alderman Cokayne's settling the said account with Mr Stevens he made it appear that there was but £47 12s. 8d. due from him to the parish, and Mr Alderman Cokayne being present at this Vestry reported that he had received the sum of £16 13s. 0d. by way of composition for the use of the parish in full for the said £47 12s. 8d. and that he had given a receipt in full for the same on the behalf of this Vestry, which this Vestry now consents and agrees to, and accordingly this Vestry now returns the said Mr Alderman Cokayne and Mr Tuff thanks for the trouble they have had on this occasion.

January 20. Vestry summoned at the request and expense of John Cooke who desired to take a new lease of the house he occupied formerly granted to Mr Poole. Complaint and objection was made by several parishioners that the said Cooke fed and kept great numbers of Cattle in the Cellar and killed the same on the said premises and also suffered the Hides and Skins to lay in the shop for several days which occasioned a very great stench ;

all which proceedings this Vestry think a very great nuisance. On which Mʳ Cooke agreed to enter into a penalty in the said lease not to have any kind of Cattle killed on the said premises, nor to allow any Hides or Skins to lay there. Debate arising thereon, It was carried, Nemine Contradicente, That they would not let the house to the said Cooke, or to any other Butcher whatsoever, It being deemed by this Vestry that the carrying on such a trade in a public street is a great nuisance. And therefore it is ordered by this Vestry, that in case any person shall sett up and follow the trade of a Butcher in this parish for the future, he or she shall be prosecuted for the same as the Law directs at the expense and charge of this parish.

1747. May 1. Mʳˢ Bernard, widow of Alderman Bernard a worthy Inhabitant of this parish, desired leave to erect a Monument at her own expense in memory of her late Husband, against the Wall adjoining to the Vestry Door. But a debate arising whether that part of the church was in the chancell or not It was agreed That if the parish have a right, to make Mʳˢ Bernard a present of the said Grant, and that she have leave to erect a Monument there (subject to the above proviso) of the following dimensions— viz. 8 ft. in length, to project 2 ft. 10 in. and to be 15 ft. and a half in height.

The Churchwardens were ordered to wait on Mʳˢ Bernard with the above order, and (to inform her) that some Gentlemen think there is a more convenient place to erect the said Monument and to offer her a place against the wall between Mʳ Alderman Chamberlain's Monument and the pulpit.*

September 10. Election for Sextoness determined by a great majority that it should be by balloting, and to be determined by one Ballot.   Mary Green elected.

October 28. Letter sent to the Churchwardens by Mʳ Robᵗ Dingley stating that his mother had died intestate, but as he knew it was her intention that something should be given for the benefit of the Poor Proposed to give Twenty Guineas on their agreeing to allow twelve twopenny loaves to the twelve most

---

* The monument was erected against the wall adjoining the Vestry door; but, singular to say, during the restoration of the two Chapels of the Holy Ghost, and of the Virgin, in 1874, it was removed very nearly to the spot above mentioned.

worthy persons every Sacrament Sunday for ever, over and above their present allowance. Also for permission to place a Tablet against the wall of the lower end of the Church not exceeding three foot square.

It being considered that the interest of the said Twenty Guineas was not a sufficient allowance to defray the expense of the provision of Bread, that part of his proposal was rejected, and it was agreed, that he should be at liberty to erect the said Tablet whenever he pleased Gratis.

1747. December 17. It was reported that Mr Dingley was willing to make some additions to his proposal : whereupon It was resolved That if Mr Dingley would purchase so much Stock in the 3 ⅌ C^t annuities that the annual interest thereof should bring in Twenty-four Shillings ⅌ ann. clear to the Parish, the same should be laid out according to his proposals But would not accept the trust on any other Terms.

Leave granted to Mr Thomas Payne to place a Stone in the North Wall of the Church, between the Bread Table and the Old Tomb, the dimensions about 3 f^t by 2 f^t.

1748. March 3. The above permission to Mr Payne was excepted against at this Vestry and not confirmed ; and it is now Ordered That the said order be revoked.

April 14. Leave given to the Trustees of Charity Schools for the Children to come to a public rehearsal to this Church. To make good all damage, and also to be at the expense of cleaning the Church.

May 19. Vestry summoned to prevent disputes between the Churchwarden and the Widow Blackborow who had the cleaning and taking   of the Church Clock, which the Churchwarden considered he ought to do, being a Clockmaker. Leave given to him.

December 15. The Fire Cock by the Pump ordered to be removed to another place and repaired.

Robert Dingley by Letter now offered Thirty Pounds to the Parish on condition that the following entry be made on the Table of Donations.

" Mrs Susannah Dingley gave Thirty Pounds to this Parish that two shillings be distributed in Bread every first Sunday in the month for ever to twelve poor parishioners who are most constant at the Sacrament, over and above their usual allowance."

This proposal being taken into consideration was unanimously agreed to.

1749. March 28. The above sum of Thirty Pounds laid out in New South Sea Annuities.

Mr Walker had leave to lay down a Stone over his late wife in the passage to the Church, the Vestry reserving their right to the ground to bury any other person.

Mr Guynand fined £20 to be excused serving Under Chwarden. October 26. Revd Mr Perfect for Revd Mr Colton who has only attended one Vestry (April 3, 1746). Mr Willimott previously.

R. Margerum chosen Master of Workhouse at Twelve Guineas ₱ Ann. in room of Mr Hunt who had Fifteen Guineas.

December 14. Richard Boyfield chosen Vestry Clerk.

1750. January 16. That Mr Tuff late Churchwarden do pay the balance of this (his) account £52 16s. 2d. (Mr Tuff went out of office April 1747). Question being put that he should pay One Years Interest thereon was negatived.

Rate made towards paying the debts of the Parish the said debts amounting to £259 6s. 10d.

April 19. Mr Marchant had leave to lay a flat Stone over the Grave of his late wife, reserving to the parish the right of the ground.

Mr Hale also had leave to lay a flat stone over his daughter's grave on the same conditions.

December 18. This Vestry taking into consideration a method to regulate the holding of Vestrys for this Parish for the time to come, Do hereby Order, That for the future a Vestry to be held within fourteen days after every Quarter day in every Year except Lady Day quarter.

1751. January 14. Mr J. L. Berchere had leave to lay a Stone on the grave of his late wife, on the above conditions.

February 19. Mr Robert Dingley applied for leave to make a Vault in the footway in the Church yard Six feet and a half wide and Nine feet and a half from out to out, and in regard that Mr Ward was not an Inhabitant, It is ordered, That upon Mr Dingley's paying the sum of Forty Pounds, he may have liberty to make such vault. . . . Mr Dingley refused to comply therewith.

Mr Tuff acquainted the Vestry that the R^t Honble Francis Cockayne, Esq., the present Lord Mayor (Churchwarden 1745), intends coming to this Parish Church on Sunday the 24th of March to hear a Charity Sermon. And therefore moved That a proper Stand for the Sword of State with his Lordship's Arms be erected at the expense of this Parish. Which is ordered accordingly to be erected agreeable to the directions of the Churchwardens and Common Councilmen.

1751. April 11. The Committee appointed to enquire into the affairs of the workhouse reported that for three years last past the average expenditure had been £239 13s. 8d. ℔ ann. That the Annual Expenses of maintaining the Poor according to the agreement with one John Thruckstone amounted £195. The Committee directed to enquire if the parish of St Olave's will make any abatement of the rent of the workhouse.

1752. January 8. Revd Mr Looker for Mr Colton.

Mr John Lodge had leave to make a Vault in the Church under those two pews in the South Choir near the Chapel in the passage going to the Pulpit, eleven foot long and eleven foot wide from out to out, and eight foot long by seven foot wide clear inside and ten foot deep below the pavement of the Church on payment of Twenty Pounds.

April 2. Mr Chandler reported that he had searched the ground and that a Vault might be made agreeable to the foregoing order.

October 19. Ordered That the duty of Constable be paid by the parish.

1753. July 26. The various sums of Money lying in different Stocks the property of the parish having been ordered to be transferred into one general account, and laid out in the purchase of Three ℔ C^t Bank Annuities, the account thereof was now produced as follows.

£110 3s. 2d. South Sea S^t^{k} sold at 120 ℔ C^t. . 132 3 10		Bought £550 Bank Ann^s 1726 at 104½ ℔ C^t. . . 572 13 9		
£389 16s. 10d. New South Sea Ann^s sold at 106 ℔ C^t. 413 4 7		Brokerage 13 6		
£30 New South Sea Ann^s sold at 106 ℔ C^t. . . 31 16 0				
577 4 5				
Less Transfer & Brokerage 1 5 0		Balance to Ch^h Warden . 2 12 2		
£575 19 5		£575 19 5		

£200 had been previously transfered by Ald^m Bernard's Exe^{rs} making the whole of the parish Stock £750 3 ⅌ C^t Bk. Ann^s 1726.

1754. January 10. Mr Payne had leave to lay a Stone over his Wife's grave on the usual conditions.

That all Certificates granted by this Parish be for the future registered in a Book.

January 24. Committee appointed to treat for a new lease of the workhouse or for other premises suitable for the purpose.

April 18. The above Committee reported that they had agreed with the Parish of St Olave Hart Street for a lease of the Workhouse for Seven, Eleven or Fourteen Years at £21 ⅌ ann.

June 27. The Workhouse Committee agreed with Mr Hawes an Apothecary for his attendance and medicines for the poor of this parish at £10 ⅌ ann.

At the request of some of the Parishioners It was moved, That the Revd Mr Romaine might have the use of this Church for the reading of prayers and preaching a Sermon One day in a week. Consideration thereof adjourned to the next Vestry.

October 10. The above Motion was given up by the Gentlemen on whose behalf it was made.

The Upper Church Warden Clarke having removed out of the parish, the Under Warden Mr Scattergood was elected Upper Churchwarden, and Mr Knox and Mr Craghead were successively elected Under Churchwardens for the remainder of the year and were excused on paying their fines.

October 24. Mr William Walker elected Under Churchwarden.

Committee appointed to meet and agree with Mr Joseph Eyre about a new Lease of the premises over the Gateway upon the best terms they can for the advantage of this parish.

1755. April 3. Election for Sextoness, To be determined by one Ballot and the highest number upon the said Ballot to be the Sextoness in the room of Mary Green deceased.

For Catharine Green	50
Margaret Lonondine	9
Amy Gwillan	2
Elizabeth Read	0

Mr Henry Guynand Senr applied for leave to build a Vault in the Church near Bancroft's Monument which was granted on condition that he should pay the sum of Thirty Pounds and also have leave to fix a Tombstone flat against the North Wall.

At the next Vestry this Order was revoked in consequence of Mʳ Guynand refusing to comply therewith.

Ordered. That when and as often as there shall be occasion for opening any Vault or Vaults belonging to any person or persons who heretofore have had or who hereafter shall or may have liberty to make a Vault or Vaults, the person or persons giving directions for the opening such Vault or Vaults shall from time to time pay such and the like expense of breaking the groun.. and also pay such other fees as are usual and customary to be paid on the burial of every other person not having a Vault in this parish.

1755. April 15. Ordered. That no person or persons shall for the future have liberty to build a Vault in the Church or Church Yard unless they pay £30 for the same.

Mʳ Dingley applied for leave to lengthen his Vault in the Church Yard, 7 foot 6 in. which was agreed to on his paying Twelve Pounds for the use of the Parish.

That the Parish Clerk, Sextoness and Beadle have Twenty Shillings a year added to their Salaries in lieu of the Sacrament Money and Bread usually given them.

October 9. Mʳ Warrand complained of being overrated in the last rate made for the use of the Poor, on which the question was put Whether he should pay Fourteen Shillings or Eleven Shillings ; and on holding up of Hands it appeared that the majority are of opinion that Mʳ Warrand should pay Fourteen Shillings which was accordingly ordered.

Mʳ Boulter also complained of being overrated and the question was put whether he should pay Twenty Shillings or Sixteen Shillings. The majority decided that he should pay Twenty Shillings.

1756. January 15. Mʳ Lord chosen Master of the Workhouse, in the room of Mʳ Marjorum, deceased.

That the Churchwardens distrain the goods of Benjamin Evans for a year's poor rate and a year's overrate due to this parish and that Mʳ Boyfield (Vestry Clerk) do attend the Churchwardens at the time of making the said distress.

1756. April 22. The above order annulled.

October 14. Mr Gardner had leave to lay a flat stone over his child's grave in the Church Yard; the parish reserving the right of burying there.

Mrs Hawkins had leave to lay a flat stone over her late husband's grave in the Church Yard on the same condition.

Notice ordered to be given to Mr Lord the Master of the Workhouse to quit the service of the parish at Xmas.

Mr Edward Bradley a practitioner offered to succeed Mr Lord. Chosen at the next Vestry.

Ordered, That the sense of the next Vestry be taken with respect to the Burial of Strangers in the Church Yard.

1757. January 13. Ordered. That if any application shall hereafter be made on behalf of any person having a Husband or Wife Son or Daughter before interred in this parish to be buried in or near their grave, then such fees shall be paid for opening the ground as customary, but if an application should be made on behalf of any person having any relation (except as above) before interred in this Parish to be buried in or near their grave, in such case double fees shall be paid for opening the ground, and if any application should be made for any person having no relation before interred in this Parish, then the sum of Four Pounds shall be paid for opening the ground in the Church and the sum of Forty Shillings for opening the ground in the Church Yard.

That the Parish Clerk or his Successors shall not break or cause to be broke any ground in the Church or Church Yard for the burial of any person or persons without leave for that purpose first had and obtained from the Upper Church Warden and further That every grave where the ground will admit, shall be dug Seven feet at least from the surface of the Earth.

Mary Moreton appointed a Searcher in the room of Mrs Saunders deceased.

April 14. That the Table of Fees for Burials Christnings and Marriages be wrote in a strong legible hand and hung up in the Vestry Room.

The Orders relating to the burial of Strangers and restraining the Parish Clerk also Ordered to be written in a strong legible hand and hung up in the Vestry.

October 13. The Order of Decr 1750 relating to holding of

Vestrys repealed and it is Ordered That the Churchwardens shall and may for the future summon and call a Vestry or Vestrys at such time as they shall think proper.

1758. March 30. Ordered. That a fine of £30 shall for the future be paid by every person refusing to serve or desiring to be excused from serving the office of Church Warden of this parish.

1759. January 11. That the Vestry Clerk do wait on Mr Farley and inform him that unless he sends the accounts of his late Churchwardenship to be audited and settled forthwith this parish must take proper measures to compel him.

June 28. Edward Bradley chosen Parish Clerk unanimously in the room of Thomas Hill, deceased.

1760. January 31. Mr Walker resigned the office of Engineer.

April 10. Samuel Osborn chosen Engineer at the yearly Salary of Thirty Shillings and to have 5s. a Quarter to play the Engine four times every year to keep the same in order and the further sum of Ten Shillings and Six pence each time he shall be assisting at any fire besides the expenses he may be at upon any such occasion.

That for the future the Upper Churchwarden for the time being shall have the care and management of the Poor and that the Under Churchwarden for the time being shall have the care and management of the Church so far as relates to the receipts and payments thereof.

That for the future a Copy of the Minutes of every Vestry held for this Parish be delivered to the Churchwardens for the time being.

July 10. Letter from the Comptroller of City Lands that the ground on which the workhouse stands will be required in making a Street 50 feet wide from Crutched Friars into the Minories, and requesting them to make a valuation thereof which they estimate at Sixty Pounds for the remainder of their Lease. And a Contract was entered into Octr 30 with Mr Solomon Pepper of Hoxton to farm the Poor. No further communication appears to have been made by the City Land Committee and on January 22 1761 the Goods &c. in the workhouse in Crutched Friars belonging to this Parish were ordered to be forthwith sold, and (Mar. 26) the Church Wardens are desired to treat with any persons for the disposal of the remainder of the Lease for such price as they shall think proper, and in case they cannot dispose of the same before Midsummer day, they are then to give notice to the Parish of St Olaves to determine the said lease at Christmas day next ensuing.

1761. April 9. That a fine of Forty Shillings shall be paid by every person refusing to serve or desiring to be excused from serving the office of Sideman of this Parish.

Mr Thomas Maynard proposed to fine for the Office of Churchwarden notwithstanding his turn by rotation may not happen these Seven Years. It was agreed that he should be excused serving the said office on paying the sum of £25.

May 28. Mr Dingley had leave to add a small border of Nine Inches round the Monument erected by him some years since to the memory of his family.

Mr Mills had leave to lay a flat stone over the Grave of a relation.

August 27. Advertisements having been inserted in the daily papers to lett the premises lately exchanged with Mr Eyre on a Building lease, several proposals were received and a lease was agreed to be granted to James Stone being the highest bidder for 61 years at a yearly rent of Twelve Guineas, Mr Stone also agreeing to give Five Guineas for the use of the Poor.

October 30. A Surveyor having been engaged to value certain premises to be exchanged with the parish and Mr Eyre, reported that Mr Eyre should have all the premises over and against the Gateway leading into Great St Helens. The parish taking the premises on the North Side and paying him the sum of £20 10s.

1762. January 14. Mr Jacob Hodgson had leave to lay a flat Stone over his Wife's grave, for which favour he gave Half a Guinea for the use of the Poor.

The question was put and Negatived, That three children of Mr Durand (a parishioner) buried in the Church Yard might be removed and buried in the Church.

April 15. That for the future no part of the money that may be collected in the Bason for the use of the Poor on any occasion whatever shall be given to the Parish Clerk, Sextoness or Beadle. And further that the money given them out of the Collection received at the last Fast day for the Poor be refunded.

That for the future there shall be no swearing in dinner provided at the expense of this Parish (Swearing in Ch^h War^n).

Revoked at the next Vestry.

Motion Negatived, That the Procession on Ascension Day be once in three Years only.

That such Procession be continued annually and that instead of 2s. 6d. usually collected of the parishioners upon that day, a sum of Five Shillings be collected. The last part of this Order was repealed at the next Vestry.

1763. April 7. That an Inventory and Account of the several Writings, Plate, Books, and Papers, belonging to this Parish be made and taken by the Vestry Clerk and entered into a Book to be provided for that purpose, and delivered to the Under Church Warden and by him to his Successor in that Office and so from time to time upon any election of an Under Church Warden, such Book to be delivered to the person so elected, to the end that such Book may remain in the custody of the Under Church Warden for the time being.

July 26. That the Church Wardens do forthwith proceed against Mr Chas Chandler late Church Warden for the recovery of the Moneys due from him to this Parish.

October 6. Committee appointed to inspect the repairs of the Church reported, That the expense thereof would be £1000 or thereabouts, Whereupon it was ordered, That the Church be thoroughly repaired and the said Committee do raise the money necessary for that purpose by way of Annuities for Lives or otherwise as may appear most for the advantage of this Parish.

Estimate to be taken and laid before the next Vestry of the expense of putting up a Screen or Partition (for keeping the Church warm at the lower end) under the Organ Loft.

This Order revoked at the next Vestry.

1764. January 10. It is ordered, That Mr Chandler have till the 1st day of March to pay the arrears due from (him) to this Parish and if not paid in that time This Vestry doth order the Church Wardens for the time being to proceed against him for the recovery of such arrears and that the Vestry Clerk acquaint him by Letter of this resolution.

April 26. Saml Osborn and Isaac Moses were elected Sidesmen, but in case the said Mr Moses shall desire to be excused from serving the said office, This Vestry doth consent thereto on his paying the fine of forty shillings. And in such case this Vestry doth declare Mr Thomas Coward to be duly elected Sidesman in the room of the said Mr Moses.

That there be no procession, nor any Taggs, Cakes and Ale given away on next Ascension Day, on account of the repairing of the Church, but the parishioners to dine together as usual.

That the Money for repairing the Church be raised by Annuities upon Lives on the following terms, viz.—

40 Years	to	45 Years	at	£7	0s.	℔ C^t
45	,,	50	,,	7	5s.	,,
55	,,	55	,,	7	10s.	,,
55	,,	60	,,	7	15s.	,,
60	,,	63	,,	8	0s.	,,
63	,,	65	,,	8	10s.	,,
65	,,	68	,,	8	15s.	,,
68	,,	70	,,	9	0s.	,,

and it is further Ordered, That in granting such Annuities preference shall be given to the parishioners of this Parish in case they or any of them shall be desirous to advance any money upon the terms aforesaid.

Repealed January 3, 1765.

1764. July 12. Motion made to put up a Clock on the *outside* and a dial on the *inside* of the Church, Ordered That there should only be a dial put up in the inside of the Church in the front of the Organ loft, similar to the dial lately put up in the Church of St Andrew Undershaft.

August 7. Proposal of Mr Thomas Smith.

To make a dial under the Organ with a Silvered dial plate 18 inches diameter, a Mahogany Moulding to the case with carved and gilt ornaments like that of St Mary Axe and in a good and workmanlike manner £9.9.0.

Another estimate was received from Edward Pashley for the sum of £11.11.0.

Mr Smith's proposal was agreed to.

Committee of Ten Gentlemen having been appointed to superintend the repairs of the Church. Five of them to be a quorum, This Vestry being informed of the difficulty there is to get Five of the said Committee to meet upon business, It is ordered That any three of the said Committee have power to act.

1764. September. 13. Mʳ John Dale had leave to lay a flat stone with an inscription over his Children's grave in the Church on the usual conditions.

It was moved in the name of the Revᵈ Mʳ Toovey, That the New Version of the Translation of the Psalms of David might for the future be sung in the Church, which was ordered accordingly.

Mʳ John Lodge in behalf of himself and Several other Inhabitants residing in Little Sᵗ Helens desired leave of this Vestry to open a door out of the Garden belonging to Leathersellers Hall into the Church at the East End thereof at their own expense which was granted accordingly.

October 11. Particulars for rebuilding the Walls of the Church Yard on the North and South Sides and the East End thereof will come to £61.10.

To take down and clear away the Brick Walls on the North and South Sides and East End and the Iron Work and dwarf Wall at the West End of the Church Yard and to pave the whole with Purbeck Squares to be done for £260.10.

To take down the old Brick Walls on the North and South Sides and East end of the Church Yard and building New dwarf Walls, 3 feet high, and cope them with Portland Stone, and put new Iron Railing upon all the New Walls and paint it four times in Oil Colour will come to £189
               Oak Posts & Planks   20
                                 £209

The Churchwarden informed the Vestry that a Subscription was opened by several of the inhabitants in case this Vestry should order the said Church Yard Walls to be taken down and a new dwarf wall with iron rails to be built, towards defraying part of the extra expenses thereof.

Resolved, That the Committee agree in such manner as they shall think fit, for and about the taking down the said Church Yard Walls and building new dwarf Walls with new Iron Railing, provided the Subscription beforementioned be not less than Seventy Pounds.

October 19. Resolved that Mr. John Maynard (who was going to quit the Parish and therefore could no longer be of the Committee for the repairs of the Church without the consent of the Vestry) might be continued one of the said Committee till the repairs of the Church were finished.

1765. January 3. This Vestry being informed of the difficulty of raising money upon the terms of the order of the 26th April last, do agree that the said order be repealed.

That the Committee be empowered to raise such sums as they shall think necessary for completing the repairs of the Church upon the Parish Security by granting Annuities upon two or more lives not under the age of 40 Years.

January 16. Mr. Jacob Marsom had leave to make a vault seven foot long and five foot wide in the clear and the walls to be one brick and a half thick, and to place a flat Tomb Stone even with the pavement over the said Vault in the Chancel of the Church on payment of the sum of £30.

February 19. To the Churchwardens, &c.

Gentlemen

The advanced price of all sorts of provisions & all other necessarys obliges us to offer our present Situation to your consideration, and as every individual is acquainted with the truth of it, we don't doubt of relief.

For twelve months past and daily advancing by which we have been considerable sufferers by maintaining your poor at the present prices, and which we cannot continue without manifestly hurting ourselves and expending the small matter we have got by care and industry.

Therefore we humbly hope you'll grant us something extra for the time past and as soon as the price of provisions are fallen we shall willingly accept of our usual price.

We are Gentlemen with respect
Your most obedient humble servants
JOHN HUGHES.
Hoxton, ffeb. 16th 1765. WILLIAM PHILLIPS.

This Vestry taking the said Petition into consideration and also the great dearness of provisions, Ordered That a gratuity of £20 be paid to the said Messrs Hughes and Phillips.

The Church Warden acquainted the Vestry that the Rev. Mr. Toovey requested they would give leave for the Parish Clerk to have a Gown. It was ordered that a proper gown be provided for the Parish Clerk to wear during the time of Divine Service.

That deal folding doors glazed be put up under the Organ Gallery and also a *Schreen* from the Sidesmen's Pew to the North Wall so high as to range with the under side of the said gallery.

1765. April 11. M Burdett had leave to put a flatt stone against the North Wall of the Church in memory of his late Father and Mother.

That in case any Churchwarden or Wardens shall for the future neglect to receive of any parishioner or parishioners any rate or rates that shall or may hereafter be made or assessed, or shall omit to take and pursue all legal methods for recovering and receiving such rate or rates of and from any Parishioner or Parishioners who shall refuse to pay the same, That then and in either of the said cases, such Churchwarden or Churchwardens shall make good and pay to this parish all and every deficiency or deficiencys that shall or may happen in such rate or rates by such neglect or omission.

October 24. That a New Surplice be provided for the Revd Mr Toovey.

That for the future after every Vestry One Guinea be spent instead of Ten Shillings.

November 13. That Mr Chas Chandler (Churchwarden 1761-2-3) be applied to, to know whether he has given in the accounts of his late Churchwardenship and to whom. And if he has not given in any, that he be required to deliver them to be audited forthwith.

That Mr George (Churchwarden 1762-4) be required to deliver in the accounts of his Churchwardenship within One Month.

(Here endeth **Book A.**)

1766. April 3. Mr Thomas Smith a parishioner who put up the Dial in the inside of the Church and has looked after the same for One Year Gratis Applied for a salary of 40s. a Year for winding up the same, cleaning it when necessary and keeping the same in good repair, which was agreed to.

Mr Lubton proposed to clean the windows of the Church and Vestry room Once a Year at 36s. p^r annum which was Negatived.

Elizabeth Moseley who was lately delivered of a Bastard Child applied for relief, and it appearing that the parish had received a sum of money from the person to whom the Child had been sworn, for the care and maintenance of the said child, and that the said bastard child had died soon after its birth, It was ordered, That the Church Warden do give her the sum of Five Guineas.

1766. April 29. The late Churchwarden ordered to pay out of the surplus of the monies now in his hands, £50 a-piece to the present Churchwardens.

Church Rate ordered of One Shilling in the £.

September 4. Petition of Messrs Hughes & Philips, Farmers of the poor, requesting on account of the dearness of provisions to have the price advanced from 3s. 6d. to 4s. ℔ week which was agreed to.

1767. January 15. Churchwarden Wells moved That the Order of Vestry of 30th March 1758 imposing a fine of £30 on persons refusing or desiring to be excused from serving the office of Church Warden be repealed, which was unanimously agreed to, And it was Ordered, That in future a fine of £20 shall be paid by every person refusing or desiring to be excused from serving the said office.

June 18. On the application of Mr Mills to be allowed to pay the sum of £18 to be excused serving the office of Church Warden, the Vestry considering that his election into that office may be some years hence, agreed to accept thereof.

July 2. The late Peter Gaussen deceased did in the year 1747 apply for leave to make a Vault in the Chancel but there being no room such application was rejected, but leave was given to the said Peter Gaussen to make a Brick Grave in the chancel, and in consideration thereof and as he did not by his Will bequeath anything to this parish, Mr Peter Gaussen offered the Vestry £40 which was accepted. . . . . Mr Peter Gaussen then applied for leave to put up a monument; and it was Ordered, That Mr Peter Gaussen or any of his family shall have leave at any time hereafter, at his, or their expense to put up a Monument in the Church either against the North Wall between the monuments of Captain Bond and William Finch, or on the North Side of the pillar next Sir W. Pickering's Monument, or in any other vacant part of the Church Walls as with consent of a Vestry may be agreed on.

The Churchwarden ordered to enquire whether Mr Johnson is not liable to be prosecuted for refusing to take upon him the office of Sidesman, and the Vestry authorized the Churchwarden to carry on such prosecution against him as he shall be advised.

1768. June 2. Whereas by a former Order of Vestry, the number of persons appointed to constitute a Vestry was limited to 13. And it has been found that the business is often retarded or rendered difficult to be completed for want of such a number to attend at such Vestrys. It was agreed that such Order be repealed, and that for the future, Nine persons, inhabitants and householders of the said parish, be, and are hereby enabled to form and constitute a Vestry and are hereby authorized and impowered to make such Orders and Regulations as shall or may be judged necessary or advisable to be made or done at any future vestries held for the said parish.

Ordered. That before Gresham College is pulled down, some person or persons be employed to measure the ground on which the said College and the Houses in front thereof stand.

June 16. That a flat stone with an inscription thereon be put over the grave wherein Wm Browne Esq. and his late Wife are interred, reserving to this parish the property of the ground over which the said stone shall be put and the right to bury therein.

October 6. Churchwardens and Overseers Ordered to take proper measures for levying and recovering the Parish Taxes chargeable on the house in the tenure or occupation of Green, situate in Little St Helens.

1769. January 5. That the Fire Engine shall not be taken out to assist at any Fire, except in the Wards of Bishopsgate Broad Street, Cornhill and Lime Street and that Bradley the Engineer be acquainted therewith.

May 18. The Churchwarden ordered to pay Mr Bishop the Proctor £20 on account of the cause Wells & Bartlett against Kendall.

1770. April 19. Mr William Clarke was appointed to look after and take care of the Church Clock at the yearly salary of 40s., and it is ordered that the same be wound up at least once a week.

Thomas Hanson Esq. late of Crosby Square deceased, by his Will bequeathed to the Minister and Church Wardens of this parish for the time being and their successors the sum of £500 upon trust to invest the same in the Public Stock or funds of this Kingdom, and pay and apply the interest thereof, unto and among such indigent and industrious inhabitants and parishioners (if any such there be) of the said parish who shall not receive Alms.

The said Mr Hanson's Benefaction ordered to be inserted in the list of Benefactions to this parish and to be entered in the Green Book.

1770. September 6. Election for Vestry Clerk in the room of Robert Boyfield deceased.

Candidates Thomas Trundle who had 42 Votes and Richard Atkinson who had 40 Votes.

Election by Ballot. Mr Trundle declared duly elected.

September 27. Thanks of the Vestry given to John Smith Esq. of Great St Helens for the service he has done this parish in getting several Children into Christ's Hospital.

December 20. Resolved on the motion of the Church Wardens that there be no Ribon and Laces given to the Inhabitants of this parish on any Ascension day for the future.

Minute ordered to be made in the parish books on the motion of Mr Churchwarden Wells, That he had cited Mr Henry Kendall in the year 1767 for not paying the Church Rate due to this parish, and that he had obtained a Judgment and decree on such Citation for the arrears of the Church rate due, and the sum of £88 for Costs.

1771. April 4. Resolved, That Mr Churchwarden Wells be allowed the sum of Twelve Pounds to serve the office of Upper Churchwarden for the year ensuing. . . . . Mr Wells having been in office from April 1766.

Agreement to pay   Dod the sum of Two Guineas to cut the Trees and dig up the Church Yard and sow the same with Grass for one year.

Copy of the decree, Wells and Bartlett against Kendall.

Extracted from the registry of the Arches Court of Canterbury, Nov. 3 1770. Before the Right Worshipful Dr George Hay, Official, Principal of the Arches Court &c. sitting in Judgment in the presence of John Green, Deputy Register.

For information and sentence at the Petition of Bishop,[*] On which day the Judge having heard the Proofs read and Counsel on

---

[*] The Parish Proctor.

behalf of Bishop's Clients did at the petition of Bishop by this his interlocutory decree (having the force and effect of a definite sentence) in writing pronounce the rates Libellate to be just rates & condemned Henry Kendall, Althan's Client in the sum of Four Pounds Four shillings for such rates and also in the costs of Suit made and to be made on the part and behalf of Bishop's Client as well in the first as the second instance of this cause. Then Bishop *porrected* a Bill of Expenses and prayed, and the Judge at his petition taxed the same at the sum of Eighty Eight Pounds of lawfull money of Great Britain besides the sum of fourteen Shillings and Ten Pence of like lawful money for the expenses of the Monition and Execution thereof, and Bishop made oath that his Clients had and must necessarily expend the said sum taxed and prayed and the Judge at his petition decreed a Monition to issue under Seal against Althan's said Client to pay or cause to be paid to Bishop or his Clients the said sorts Principal and Costs taxed as aforesaid within fifteen days after the service of the Monition on him for that purpose under pain of the service of the greater excommunication. Present Althan dissenting. But the Judge ordered the said Monition not to go out in Fifteen days from this day which being done Bishop prayed and the Judge at his Petition decreed the Church Rates marked A B C, the five Books of Account numbered 1 2 3 4 5, and the two Vestry Books heretofore to Wit on the Byday after Hilary Term last brought into the Registry of this Court to be delivered out to Bishop or his Clients the said rates being first registered. Present Althans dissenting.

J^{no} GREENE, Dep. Reg^r.

1771. May 16.   Church Rate Ninepence in the £.

Situation of Organist being vacant by the death of Mr Thomas Griffin, his nephew Mr George Griffin proposed to play, tune, and keep the Organ in repair for the sum of Twenty Five Pounds ℔ annum, and was thereupon duly elected.

Motion negatived, That there be provided some Warming Machine for warming the Church.

June 5.   Election for Churchwarden in the room of Mr Wells deceased.

1772. February 19.   That John Brown do nail up leads upon the walls and other places in and about the Excise Office to denote the bounds of this parish there, and that the same be placed as near the places where they were formerly nailed as may be.

Leave given to lay a flat Stone over the grave of Thomas Burdett, Esq. on the offer of the sum of Five Guineas reserving to the parish the right of the ground, and also over the grave of John Tristram for the like sum of Five Guineas and on the same condition.

Motion negatived, For a Warming Machine to warm the Church.

1772. May 7. New Damask Curtains ordered for the Organ Loft.

June 11. Question being put whether the Buildings belonging to the Excise Office in this parish should be assessed at £1600 or £2000 ℔ Annum. It was resolved That it should be at £2000.

October 7. Messrs Phillips & Hughes applied to be allowed the further sum of Threepence ℔ Head for the poor of this parish which was agreed to.

That the old curtains belonging to the Organ Loft be given to Mrs Green the Sextoness.

1773. January 28. Churchwardens ordered to proceed against Mr Booth the late Churchwarden unless he delivers his account within seven days from this time.

Charles Chandler, Unanimously elected Beadle, Engineer and Organ Blower in the room of Robert Bradley, deceased.

February 19. Some doubts having arisen as to the right of this parish to appoint a Minister for Sir Martin Lumley's Tuesday Evening Lecture vacant by the death of the Revd Mr Mapletoft An extract from Sir Martin Lumley's Will was read, by which it appears that the right of appointing the Lecturer is in the Heirs of Sir Martin Lumley and not in this parish.

Some doubts having also arisen as to the right of chusing a Vicar for this parish in the room of the Revd Mr Coulton also deceased The Vestry Clerk reported that he had not been able to get a Copy of the Grant made by Queen Elizabeth to Michael and Edward Stanhope of this parish Church out of the office. The Churchwardens then informed the Vestry that they had searched the several Vestry Books belonging to this parish, and that it appears that this parish had chosen several Vicars, and that they had attended the Dean of S^t. Pauls* with extracts from the said Books and requested that he would be pleased to give the parish leave to proceed to the choice of a Vicar, who informed them that the Impropriators had presented the Revd Mr Naish to him, and that he had promised to approve him, that he was sorry he could not comply with their request and that in case they had applied to him first, he would have paid regard to their recommendation.

Mr Churchwarden Fasson also informed the Vestry that the Revd Mr Naish took possession of this parish Church on Saturday last and informed him that he was properly authorised to do so. The Vestry Clerk then stated that in pursuance of an order from the Churchwarden who had been informed that a petition had been preferred to the Lord Chancellor† in order to obtain his Lordship's order to confirm the presentation of the Impropriators he had searched at the office of the Secretary of Presentations and found that no such petition had been preferred, and that he had attended Mr Collins in Doctors Commons who (as he had been informed) is Deputy to the Dean of S^t. Pauls and enquired of him by what authority Mr Naish had taken possession of the parish church, when the said Mr Collins informed him that the Dean sent for Mr Naish on Saturday last and informed him that in case he would take immediate possession of this parish Church he would collate him thereto, that Mr Naish agreed so to do, and the Dean thereupon collated him accordingly, that he then asked the said Mr Collins if the Dean had collated the said Mr Naish in his own right or on the presentation of the Impropriators, to which Mr Collins answered in his own right. Mr John Lodge then informed the Vestry that the Impropriators intended to take the opinion of a Civilian in respect to their right of presentation, and in case they shall be advised that the right of presentation is in them, they intend to commence an action of Ejectment, to eject Mr Naish

---

* "Thomas Newton, D.D., Bishop of Bristol (elected Dec. 8th, 1761, confirmed on the 24th, and consecrated on the 28th of the same month), appointed Prebendary of Westminster, March 22nd, 1757, Dean of St. Paul's, Oct. 8th, 1768, and died Feb. 14th, 1782, ætat. 77." See Le Neve's Fasti, vol. i. p. 220, vol. ii. p. 317, and vol. iii. p. 336. Ed. Oxford (Hardy), 1854.

† "A.D. 1771. The Hon. Henry Bathurst, created Lord Apsley, Lord Chancellor, Jan. 23. Succeeded his father as Earl Bathurst, A.D. 1775; resigned A.D. 1778." See Haydn's Book of Dignities, p. 105. Ed. Lond. 1851.

from this parish Church. The further consideration of this subject was therefore adjourned.

1773. March 15. Mʳ John Jennings had leave to make a Vault in the Church 7 ft. long and 2 ft. 6 in. wide at each end and 3 ft. in the centre, and also of fixing a Monument on the pillar of the Church next the Vault. The Monument not to exceed 21 inches in breadth, on payment of Twenty Guineas.

That a sett of Ladders be provided and kept in the most convenient place in this Church.

April 15. —— Dod to have a gratuity of ten shillings over and above the two guineas allowed him for digging and sowing the Church Yard &c. for the last year.

Mʳ William Clark had leave to lay a flatt Stone in the church over the grave of his late wife, the parish reserving the right to the ground.

That the Lord Mayor's Arms put up in this Parish Church be erased.

June 10. Church Rate Sixpence in the £.

Iron Rails round Church Yard to be painted.

June 29. Present, Revᵈ James Naish, Minister.

Resolved, That this parish do request Mʳ Naish to continue Mʳ Toovey his Curate upon the same terms he officiated for Mʳ Coulton, to which Mʳ Naish agreed, and that he would do anything else the parish should ask of him.

1774. April 28. Further Church Rate of threepence in the £ for the last year to pay balance due to the late Churchwarden.

June 9. Church Rate Sixpence in the £.

That the thanks of this Vestry be given to Mʳ John Fasson late Churchwarden for his just and prudent conduct during his Churchwardenship.

October 6. The Beadle having attended Sir Martin Lumley's Lecture by order of the Churchwarden during the last Winter, he was directed to make him such satisfaction for his said attendance as in his discretion he shall think fit.

1775. January 12. Susannah Mynot, Singlewoman, now in the Workhouse with child by one Cornelius Chartress of the parish of Sᵗ Margarets Westminster, but who was willing to marry her, if the parish would pay the Fees and give him the sum of Four Pounds, on which the Churchwarden was directed to enquire if he did belong to that parish and in such case to pay the Wedding Fees and advance him the sum of Four Guineas.

February 23. That Mr Churchwarden Houston be at liberty to expend the sum of Four Pounds towards the expenses of the next Oyster Feast over and above the Forty Shillings given by the Will of Willm. Prior.

1775. April 20. Edward Bradley Parish Clerk acquainted the Vestry that he would undertake to wash and mend the Surplices and Communion Linen for which he has hitherto received the sum of Five Pounds ℔ Annum and to give up the yearly sum of fifteen shillings which he has heretofore claimed and received out of the devise made by the will of William Prior and the further sum of fifteen shillings which he has also received on the preaching of Three Sermons and not to collect any money for Christmas Box of the Inhabitants, provided the parish would pay him a salary of £24 ℔ Annum instead of the sum of £9 heretofore paid him. Resolved, That his proposal be agreed to, on condition that in future he does not charge for Pens, Ink, and Paper for the Vestry, and do officiate as Clerk at Sir Martin Lumley's Lecture. To all which he agreed and returned the Vestry thanks.

May 18. Church Rate One Shilling in £.

Churchwarden ordered to take necessary steps for the defence of the Poors Rate against which an Appeal was stated to have been lodged at the Quarter Sessions by the Excise Office.

July 6. It appearing that no Appeal had been lodged The Vestry Clerk ordered to have the opinion of counsel for the recovery of Poor and Church Rates.

That an Hand Engine be provided and that Mr Bristowe be employed effectually to repair the old one.

That a proper case lined with greenbaize be provided to put the Church Plate in.

August 24. Counsellor Dunning's opinion having been read, and the Church Warden having stated that if sufficient power was given to the Church Wardens he thought the rates might be settled to the satisfaction of the Parish Authority was accordingly granted to them to settle the arrears of Curch and Poor Rates now due from the Excise Office.

Thomas Maxwell applied to this Vestry and proposed to marry Mary Sandars a poor woman of this parish whom he stated was with child by him, if they would give him forty shillings, pay the Marriage Fees, and clothe her. And being asked if he had any settlement, he stated that he belonged to the parish of St Luke's Old Street. The Church Warden directed to enquire into the truth of his settlement and if found correct to give him the sum of Three Guineas on his marrying the said Mary Sanders.

1775. October 5. The Church Wardens reported that they had received and settled the several rates due from the Excise Office at the rate of £1600 ⅌ Annum. At which it was in future ordered to be assessed instead of £2000 as heretofore.

The Church Wardens empowered to contract with Mr Bristowe to clean and take proper care of the Engines.

December 29. Election for Beadle in room of Charles Chandler, deceased, by Ballot, when John Dickerson was elected the numbers being for

    John Dickerson 32
    Thomas Bolwell 15
    John Wells 2

Church Warden ordered to pay Mrs Chandler £3 for the Coat and Hat worn by her late Husband.

1776. April 11. That a Coat and Hat be provided for the Beadle not exceeding £3 and that he be excused from paying the poor's rate for the last year having pleaded inability to pay it.

June 27. Poor's Rate 3d. in £.

November 28. Thanks given to John Smith Esq.* for his Voluntary and Great Benefaction to this Parish, and that a copy of the deed of which the following is an Abstract, be deposited with the other deeds of the Parish and entered in the Vestry Book.

This Indenture made the 25th of September 16 George III. A.D. 1776 between the Governors of the Hospitals of Christ Bridewell and St Thomas the Apostle of the first part, John Smith Esq. of Great St Helens of the Second part, and Thomas Burfoot, Treasurer of Christ's Hospital London and William Brockett and Thomas Misenor on the third part Whereas John Smith, one of the Governors of the said Hospital proposed to transfer the sum of £2500 3 ⅌ C^t South Sea Ann^s of the year 1751, on condition

---

* 1783, June 29. John Smith, Esq., formerly a Lisbon Merchant and many years one of the directors of the South Sea Company.—*Gent. Mag.*, p. 629. (Deaths.)

that the Governors of the said Hospital would engage to pay his Nephew William Webber of Fursley in the County of Devon, Gent. aged 43 years an Annuity of £100 during his life; and after his decease to maintain and educate in the said Hospital two children perpetually to be taken out of the said parish of S*t* Helen and to be presented by a Publick Vestry, or by the major part of the Inhabitants present at such Vestry, which was approved by a Committee of the said Governors the 14*th* of August last and by them recommended to a General Court held for the said Hospital the 12*th* of September and unanimously agreed to be accepted. And whereas the said sum has been transferred and doth now stand in the names of the said Tho*s* Burfoot, W. Brockett & T. Misenor for the use of the poor Children educated in the said Hospital Now this Indenture witnesseth, That the said Governors in consideration of such transfer do hereby for themselves, Successors and Assigns, covenant with the said John Smith &c. that they will well and truly pay or cause to be paid to the said William Webber, one yearly payment of £100 clear of all deductions during the term of his natural life, by quarterly payments, the first payment to be made at Michaelmas 1777. Provided and it is hereby agreed between all parties, that if the said William Webber shall at any time assign or dispose of such Annuity or any part thereof, that then such Annuity or such part or parts thereof as shall be so assigned or otherwise disposed of shall cease and the said £2500 applied to the benefit of the poor children in the said Hospital as if the said W. Webber was actually dead. And the said Governors covenant, that from the decease of the said W. Webber or after the said Annuity shall otherwise cease, they, shall and will from time to time for ever, Maintain and Educate in the said Hospital Two Poor Children of persons who shall be Inhabitants of the said parish of S*t* Helen, to be chosen by the majority of a Vestry of the said parish, and on the death or discharge or other removal of every such Child or Children within three months then next to receive and admit other or others, in his, her, or their room. Provided, that the parent or parents of such Child or Children so to be maintained and educated shall have been an inhabitant or inhabitants of the said parish One whole Year next immediately before such choice shall be made, and every Child so to be chosen shall be upwards of Seven Years of age, Born in lawful Wedlock, of Honest & Reputable parents; And the Minister and Church Wardens of the parishes whereto such Child or Children shall respectively belong, shall comply with and be subject to the forms generally in use for the admission of Children into the said Hospital. In Witness whereof to the one part to remain with the said John Smith, the said Governors have caused their Common Seal to be affixed. And to the other part to remain with the said Governors, the said John Smith hath set his Hand and Seal, the day and year first above written.

Mr Church Warden Potter reported that on perusing one of the Books belonging to the parish, he had discovered that the application of the gift of Cicely Cyoll and also of Thomas Hutchins of Wheaten Bread to the poor of this parish had been discontinued from or about the year 1693.

Resolved, That the benefactions above mentioned be restored to the several poor persons belonging to this parish under the descriptions mentioned in the said Wills.

Dr Orme applied for leave to cut away each side of the Steeple of the Church that he might have the benefit of a better view from the Top of his House, and Mr Gosling assured this Vestry that the parts of the Steeple intended to be cut away would do no harm to the Steeple, and that in case leave should be given to cut away the same, he would make good and finish the Steeple in such manner as would be an ornament thereto, and he makes good the places that shall be so cut away.

Thanks to Thomas Houston late Churchwarden for his great care and integrity in the execution of the said office.

That W. Clarke's Salary for looking after and taking care of the Church Clock be raised from 40s. to 45s. ℗ ann.

1777. January 2. The Church Wardens and Vestry Clerk having waited on Mr Smith with the Thanks of the last Vestry, Mr Smith desired them to give his best respects to the Inhabitants of this parish and thanked them for the respect they had shewn him, and that his motives for doing what he had done was on account of the great respect they had shewn him during 27 years that he had been an Inhabitant, and to make some provision from time to time for two poor children and that he thought he could not do it in a better way and requested that his Benefaction might not be inserted in the list of Benefactors at present.

1777. April 3. William Sibley of the parish of St Olive Tooley having by Bond dated July 14 1776 stood bound to the parish in the sum of £40 for a female Bastard Child which had been sworn to him by Sarah Bawcomb of this parish, and the child having become chargeable, the Church Warden has agreed to receive 3s. ℔ Week for its support and had received £1 4s. 0d. in full to the 4th Sepr last, but had not been able to get any more money by reason that the said Sibley has a wife and family and was very poor. And the wife of the said W. Sibley had informed him that in case this parish would accept of a sum of money and deliver up the Bond, she would endeavour to raise it provided time was given for that purpose. Resolved, That upon payment of £10 including the sum of £1 4s. 0d. already paid within the period of Six Months from this date, the said Bond shall be given up.

May 1. Church Rate 9^d in £.

Mrs Bradley had leave to lay a flatt stone over the Grave of her late brother Joseph Bryant with an inscription in the Church Yard with the usual reservation.

That John Jennings late an Inhabitant of this parish have leave to take away the cushions placed by him in the pew where he formerly sat in this Church.

That Catherine Green, Sextoness be allowed from henceforth a salary of £18 p^r annum in lieu of the salary heretofore paid her, and also of all other charges which she hath been accustomed to make, and likewise in lieu of the Annual Collection made for her at the Oyster Feast.

That the parish Clerk and Sextoness do in future oblige all persons who shall hereafter bury in the Church or Church Yard to clear and take away all the rubbish that shall remain after the graves are filled up at their own expense.

That the Common Council and Church Wardens consult with those of the adjoining parishes about the necessary steps to be taken to procure a constant passage through the Excise office at seasonable hours.

May 29. Thanks given to John Smith Esq. the Church Warden having reported that Mr Smith had at his own expense painted the doors and door cases of the Church and also the Iron Rails round the Church Yard.

July 17. That a New Surplice be provided for Revd Mr Toovey.

1777. October 2. William Sibley having paid Two Guineas since the Order of Vestry of April 3 being out of work and unable to pay any further sum, and the Child being dead, he was released from further payment and the Bond given up.

The House occupied by Mr Henry Ward held jointly by this parish and the Carpenters' Company being in bad repair which by estimate would require the expenditure of £80 and which he was willing to undertake to do, if they would grant another lease at the expiration of the present term for 21 Years with liberty to quit at the end of 7 or 14 years and allow him One Year's rent towards the said repairs. This Vestry agreed thereto and the Churchwardens were directed to wait upon the Carpenters' Company and request their concurrence.

That for the future the Churchwardens have liberty to expend the sum of Six Pounds at the Oyster Feast over and above the 40s. given by Mr William Prior and that in future the Bill of Expenses be called for and settled at Eleven of the Clock.

1778. January 8. The Carpenters' Company agreed to grant the lease for 21 Years at the rent of £34 per Annum on condition that £80 be laid out in substantial repairs within two years but without any other allowance to which Mr Ward assented.

The Churchwarden stated that he had unavoidably expended £1 11s. 6d. at the last Oyster Feast more than is allowed. Ordered, That he be at liberty to charge the said sum in his account.

That Mr Bristow be discharged from the care &c. of the parish Engines and John Dickerson the Beadle be appointed thereto.

John Dickerson was appointed to look after and take care of the Church Yard at the Yearly Salary of £2.12.6.

Mr. Henry George had leave to lay a flat Stone in the Church over the grave of his late wife, with an inscription thereon, with the usual reservation.

February 12. Plan and proposal was received from the Surveyor of the Excise office for granting part of their Premises to make a passage for the accommodation of the inhabitants of St Helen and of St Peter le Poor, Broad Street Upon condition that the two parishes would purchase other premises named in the plan and grant them to the Excise in lieu of the other premises proposed to be granted for the passage; the said plan and proposals being answer to the Petition which had been preferred by the two parishes on the subject. To which the following reply was agreed on.

"That having maturely considered the said plan and proposals are extremely sorry to find themselves obliged to decline them. The premises required to be purchased by the parishes greatly exceed those offered in lieu thereof and the expense of purchasing would greatly exceed the sum of £3000, exclusive of an Act of Parliament &c. &c. All that your Petitioners requested was that the time of the Office Gates being kept open should be extended a few hours longer, and also on Holidays, and trust that upon reconsideration you will indulge them with the liberty they formerly enjoyed of passing through the office gates daily at seasonable hours."

1778. April 23. The Beadle to have £3 13s. 6d. Pr Ann. to look after the Engines, and that they be cleaned, oiled and played at least four times every year.

That every Under Church Warden for the future do see that the Engines are kept in good condition and that the above order is complied with.

The Beadle also appointed Organ Blower at a Salary of 40s. Pr Annum.

In reply to the Memorial, The Commissioners of Excise were sorry that they could not comply with the request set forth in their Memorial, as they did not think it consistent with the safety of the office.

That John Smith, Esq., had promised to get Charles Oxtoby a poor boy belonging to this parish into Christ's Hospital and had given the Churchwarden Five Guineas to divide among the poor pensioners also belonging to this parish, for all which the Thanks of the Vestry were ordered to him.

May 21. Church Rate Ninepence in £.

Thanks of Vestry to Joseph Potter late Church Warden for his upright conduct and unwearied application in promoting the interest of this Parish.

August 27. Thanks voted to John Smith, Esq., the Church Warden having reported that he had made the parish a present of a large folio Bible, also a Silver Cup and Cover Gilt with the following inscription engraved thereon, viz., The Gift of John

Smith, Esq., to the Parish Church of St. Helen, London, for the use of the Communion Service. 1778.

That the two Silver Cups usually made use of at the Communion Service be Gilt.

1779. January 21. Church Warden informed the Vestry that the Inhabitants present at the last Oyster Feast were very numerous, and on that account he had unavoidably expended £6 13s. 8d. more than is allowed, Ordered That he be at liberty to charge the same in his account.

April 8. That John Smith, Esq., be excused from serving all parish offices in consideration of the many favours received by this parish from him.

W. Clarke and Timothy Corp to take care of Church Clock at 45s. ℞r Annum.

June 16. That the time of any persons quitting or dying in this parish be entered in the Parish Book.

August 5. Necessary steps to be taken to recover the arrears due from Mrs Martin of the Four Pounds ℞r Annum given by the will of Joyce Featly.

October 14. Mrs Martin being dead, enquiry ordered to be made to whom the copyhold property at Kennington has descended.

That the London Workhouse Rate be not paid out of the rate made for the support of the poor for the present year.

Church Warden allowed to charge the extraordinary expenses at the last Oyster Feast amounting to £1 14s. 4d.

1780. January 5. John Smith, Esq., having expressed his desire of having the remainder of the Communion Plate belonging to this parish Gilt, and having desired the Church Warden to acquaint this Vestry, That in case this parish would cause it to be done, he would be at one half the expense thereof. This Vestry taking into consideration the many benefits received by this parish from the said Mr. Smith, doth order that his said desire be complied with.

Repealed next Vestry March 30.

It appearing that a pint of wine only, was allowed by this parish for the Vestry on a Sunday, but of late a Bottle has been constantly taken thereto, Ordered That a pint of Wine only be allowed the Vestry on a Sunday as heretofore from henceforth.

Complaint being made of the foulness of the Pump Water in

Great St. Helen's, Ordered That the Church Wardens do cause the well of the pump to be inspected, and give such directions as shall be found necessary to prevent the water being foul in future.

That the sum of £20 P^r annum be paid to the Revd Geo. Toovey by the Under Church Warden by quarterly payments, and continue during the pleasure of this Vestry.

The above grant is meant as a proof of the personal esteem which this Vestry entertain for the Rev^d Mr. Toovey who has been Curate to this parish Twenty-two years, and is not to be considered as a precedent for any future Minister to expect the same.

1780. March 30. Timothy Cork to look after the Church Clock at 45s. P Annum.

A Letter from Lord George Gordon President of the Protestant Association dated Welbeck Street January 1780 was read, and also a petition therein enclosed was also read, and Ordered to lie on the Table.

June 15. That the thanks of this Vestry be given to John Smith, Esq. for having presented the Parish with three new Bells and the hanging thereof in the Steeple of this parish church.

1781. January 3. Thos Sowerby had leave to lay a flat Stone over the grave of his late wife and children in the Church, with the usual reservation.

March 29. That the sum of Three Guineas be distributed on Xmas day next amongst the poor belonging to this parish who shall not be in the workhouse.

April 19. That a new Umbrella be provided for the use of the Minister.

That the sum of £3 3s. 0d. ordered by the last Vestry and the like sum of £3 3s. 0d. be given & distributed amongst such poor, yearly from henceforth in the following manner, That is to say, That there be given on Christmas Eve next and on every Christmas Eve in every year thereafter, unless Christmas day shall fall on a Monday & then on the Saturday preceding as follows.

To every grown person including the Husband or Wife if actually living with the pauper who shall apply for the same.

Two Pounds of Good Beef or Mutton.
One Two Penny Loaf ... One Pound of Flour.

> Four Ounces of Suet ... Four Ounces of Raisins.
> One Penny for an Egg ... One Peck of Coals or
> Money to buy them. ... One Pint of Porter or
> Two Pence to buy it.

And for every Child actually living with & maintaining by the Pauper in addition to the above,

> Half a pound of good beef or Mutton,
> One Twopenny Loaf, and One pound of Flour.

And that the said provisions be purchased & distributed by the Under Churchwarden for the time being, and that the Upper Churchwarden for the time being do furnish a list of the persons meant by the said Order, with the number of children each person has, and which are actually maintained by the said person one week before Christmas-day. And that no Servant of this parish receive any part of the said gift. And that the Beadle do give publick notice of the said gift to the poor, three several Sundays preceding Christmas Eve next ensuing and of the time of giving it away.

1781. May 17. A Bill of Costs presented signed R. Hughes for £41 17s. 0d. for prosecuting Charles Oxtoby a pauper of this parish for assaults committed on two female children. Referred to the Vestry Clerk to peruse and give his opinion thereon.

October 4. The Vestry Clerk reported that he had conferred with Mr Hughes upon certain items in his Bill, which were considered unwarrantable, and that Mr H. had proposed to take £18 for this parishes proportion thereof, which was acceded to.

1782. January 17. Petition ordered to be presented to the Court of Common Council that this parish conceived themselves aggrieved by the election of Mr Wm Falkner to be one of the Common Councilmen for this Precinct and praying relief against the said election.

April 4. Thos Carrington to look after the Church Clock at 45s. ℘ annum.

May 30. That the Revd Mr Naish do preach or cause to be preached the several Sermons directed by the respective wills of the Benefactors to this Parish on the several and respective days on which they are appointed to be so preached, and that Mr Naish be furnished with a copy of this order.

1783. September 18. The Auditors having refused to allow the late Churchwarden what he had unavoidably expended more than the £8 allowed by this parish for the Oyster Feast, Ordered That the Auditors do allow him the same.

This Vestry being desirous of showing their gratitude and respect to the memory of John Smith, Esq. deceased, for the many favors received from him while living, Doth resolve, That in case his Executors shall at any time hereafter be desirous of erecting or putting up a Monument to his memory in any part of this parish Church, they shall be at liberty to do so without paying any sum of money whatsoever to this Parish for the same.

Thomas Watkins elected Churchwarden for the remainder of the year. Vacant by the death of Mr Henry Frome.

October 1. The above election declared null and void.

1784. January 29. Mr Churchwarden Butt reported that he had attended a meeting of the Creditors of the late Mr Frome, when a proposal was made by the Executrix to give security for payment of Nine Shillings in the £ on their respective debts on the 25th of March next, and that it appeared to be the sense of the Creditors present to accept such proposal. Resolved, That the Churchwarden be at liberty to sign an agreement to accept thereof on the Balance of £55 2s. 4d. due to this parish, and on payment thereof to give a discharge in full for the same.

That a Pick Axe be provided for taking up the Fire Plugs in this parish.

February 12. John Smith, Esq. having by his Will left £20 to be distributed amongst the most necessitous poor Inhabitants of this parish at the discretion of a Vestry to be called for that purpose The following persons were recommended as proper objects and the legacy divided amongst them as follows:

	£	s.	d.
William Baker	4	15	0
Roger Robarts	2	2	0
Richard Whitehead	4	4	0
Mrs Doxey	4	4	0
George Bertie	2	13	0
John Dickerson	2	2	0

This Vestry taking into consideration the distresses of the Poor who are not in the workhouse, on account of the severity of the

Weather, doth order, That Mr Churchwarden do give to Thomas Dod One Guinea, to Elizabeth Chipps One Guinea, to Matthew Bishop Three Guineas, to Mary Guy Half a Guinea, and to Catherine Sinclair Five Shillings. And that he do also give to each of the Pensioners One Shilling ℙ week, and to such of them as have Children the further sum of Sixpence per Week for each and every Child, over and above what is at present paid them during the continuance of the present Frost.

1784. April 15. This Vestry request the Overseer to be aiding and assisting the Church Wardens in the management of the poor for the Year ensuing.

Complaints having been made that Edward Bradley, Parish Clerk, had received more for Burials than the Table of Fees approved at a Vestry held April 8, 1681, or the Order of Vestry made January 13, 1757, warranted. Ordered That the said Order be repealed and that the Parish Clerk for the future make no other charge than what is mentioned in the said Table of Fees upon any pretence whatsoever. And that the Vestry Clerk do from henceforth yearly and every year make and deliver to the Under Churchwarden a Copy of the said Table of Fees.

June 3. Church Rate 1s. 3d. in £.

June 17. The Auditors having examined the Accounts of Mr John Butt, there appeared a balance due from him of £199 9s. 4d., the whole of which he confessed he had applied in payment of his own debts, and that he was now unable to pay the said balance to this parish, Whereupon the Beadle was directed to desire Mr Butt to attend the Vestry immediately. To which Mr Butt returned answer that he could not think of coming to the Vestry. Whereupon the Vestry adjourned to that Se'nnight when they expect Mr Butt will attend and propose such terms and security as they may approve, and in default thereof, the parish will take the most effectual steps against him to enforce payment.

June 24. The Vestry Clerk stated that Mr Butt had desired him to state that he could not attend the Vestry, but was ready to enter into an obligation to pay £100 at the end of 12 Months and the remainder at 12 Months after, and that was the utmost he could do.

After consideration, Ordered, That the Vestry Clerk do forthwith proceed against Mr John Butt late Church Warden for the recovery of the said balance of £199 9s. 4d. due from him to this parish.

Mʳ George Hickes had leave to erect a small Stone not exceeding 2 feet in height to the memory of his late Wife with an inscription thereon on the side of the footway leading to the Church in the Church Yard.

Committee of Gentlemen who have passed the Chair, to inspect the Standing Orders relative to the expenditure of the Parish Money.

1784. October 14. The above Committee reported, That they were of opinion that the Swearing-in Dinner and Supper in future should be provided at 3s. 6d. ℞ Head, including Bread, Beer, &c., Wine and Punch only excepted. And that the Beadle and Sextoness should be allowed a Crown each instead of attending to receive the broken victuals.

That on Ascension Day there should be only Wands and Favors provided for those Children of the Inhabitants who walked with the Gentlemen, and that Dinner and Supper on that day should be provided for the inhabitants at 4s. ℞ Head including everything, excepting Wine & Punch. And that the Beadle and Sextoness be allowed a Crown each instead of attending to receive the Broken Victuals.

Also, That the Supper at the Oyster Feast should be provided at 2s. 6d. ℞ Head including everything except Punch and Wine, and on which the Church Wardens should not expend more than £4, And that the Beadle and Sextoness be allowed 2s. each instead of attending to receive the broken victuals.

That the said Committee were also of opinion All Money collected by Virtue of Briefs or the King's Letter should in future be paid over to the person appointed to receive the same, and no part thereof be applied to any other use whatsoever.

Ordered, That the several regulations proposed by the said Committee be carried into execution by the present and future Church Wardens of this Parish.

The Committee having also caused extracts to be taken from the Vestry Books of Several Orders necessary to be known by the Church Wardens for the time being, they were Ordered to be fairly entered in two Books to be provided for that purpose, and delivered to each of the present Church Wardens and by them to their respective successors.

That an Order of Vestry made April 15, 1773, for erasing the Arms of James Townsend, Esq. late Lord Mayor of the City of London, put up in this Parish Church be repealed.

Mr John Butt proposed to enter into a Bond together with Messrs John & William Felton as his Sureties for payment of £100 in twelve months from this time, provided the Parish would accept the same in full for the balance due from him. And to pay the costs of the Action brought by this Parish against him. Whereupon Mr Houston moved and Mr Greenaway seconded, That this Parish do agree to accept the offer now made, and the question was carried in the Affirmative.

1785. January 27. That no person whomsoever who is not an inhabitant of this Parish be permitted to remain in the Vestry Room at any Vestry hereafter to be held for the same Parish.

March 10. Application was made on behalf of one Richard Low who stands committed to the Poultry Compter . . . .
. . . .
. . . and offering to pay £7 in case this Parish would release the said Richard Low and consent to his being discharged, but such offer was rejected.

Mr George Archdale Low had leave to lay a flat Stone over the graves of his father and mother in the Church Yard with the usual reservation.

March 31. Mr John Hardwicke and Mr William Moore being put in nomination for Under Church Warden and Mr Hardwicke being elected, Mr Moore informed the Vestry that it was impossible for Mr Hardwicke to serve the said office on account of his business, but if they would elect Mr Joseph Potter in his stead, he would enter into an obligation for his faithful discharge of the duties of the Office. Whereupon it was agreed, That the Election of Mr Hardwicke be vacated, And that Mr Potter be elected in his room. On condition that Mr Hardwicke doth enter into an obligation with this Parish for said Mr Potter's faithful discharge of the duties of the said office.

April 28. Church Rate 9d. in £.

September 1. That no Churchwarden of this parish shall in future permit or suffer the Beadle of this parish in any manner to act in the discharge of the duties of the office of Churchwarden of the said parish. New Surplice for the Minister.

1785. October 27. A proposition was made by Mʳ Butt and his Sureties to pay the sum of £50 on account of their Bond for £100 and requested twelve months time to pay the remainder with interest, which was acceded to.

1786. January 12. It appearing that Sir Martin Lumley's Gift of £4 ⅌ Ann. had not for several years been distributed according to his Will, Ordered, That the present and future Churchwardens of this parish do from time to time from henceforth distribute and give the said £4 ⅌ Annum amongst the poor householders inhabiting within the said parish at the times and in manner directed by the said Will.

March 30. Committee appointed to inspect the outside of the Church and Church Steeple, and to report the several repairs wanting thereto.

Mʳ Kuhff had leave to lay a flat stone over the grave of his child in the Church, with the usual reservation.

That every person who shall hereafter be buried in the Church in Lead, and shall not be a parishioner and an Inhabitant of this parish, shall pay a sum of Five Guineas for the use of the said parish, over and above all other the accustomed fees now paid.

April 6. The Committee having recommended certain repairs, Mʳ W. Gosling and Mʳ Schooling were added to the Committee for the Superintendence thereof, and they were directed to employ the following persons to do the said repairs.

John Upwood,	Throgmorton Street,	the Plasterer's Work.
Wix & Poynder,	Bishopsgate Street,	Bricklayers.
Booth,	Lothbury,	Painter.
Phillips,	Camomile Street,	Smith.
John Scidmore,	Bishopsgate Street,	Plumber.
W. Gosling,		Carpenters.
Mʳˢ Lupton,	Old Broad Street,	Glazier.
and Tysen,	Tooley Street,	Slater.

April 27. That the present and every future Under Churchwarden of this parish, do deliver in an account of his Churchwardenship, to the Auditors of this parish within fourteen days after he or they shall be out of the said office.

June 29. That the present and all future Churchwardens of this parish do at the time their respective accounts shall be signed by the Auditors, deliver up the Several Church and Poor Rate Books, and all the vouchers in their respective custody or power, relating to the said Accounts, and that the same be deposited with the records and other papers belonging to this parish.

1786. August 3. Negatived. That the Swearing In and Ascension dinner be in future discontinued.

October 26. Mr. Churchwarden Potter stated that the Benefactions given by Cicely Cyoll, Thos Hutchins, Sir John Lawrence, Mary Clapham, and Robt Dingley amounted to £590, and that the moiety of the rent of the house given by Edward Fenner, and of the house given by William Prior, and also of the house given by Thomas Fenner had not for some time past been applied according to the Wills of the respective donors, Ordered That the Trustees of the parish stock do from time to time from henceforth pay the interest of the said sum of £590 (part of the sum of £650 3 ⅌ C^t Bank Annuities 1726 possessed by the parish) to the Churchwardens for the time being, to be by them and the Overseers of the poor applied as directed by the said Benefactors, And that the said Churchwardens from henceforth receive the rents and profits of the said Messuages or Tenements and apply the same as directed by the respective Wills of the donors.

It appearing by a Computation made of the Interest of the said sum of £590 and of the rents of the said Messuages, there will be a surplus (after application of so much as is directed by the wills of the said donors) of £54 or thereabouts. This Vestry doth therefore further order and direct, That the Churchwardens and Overseers of the parish do from henceforth lay out £8 ⅌ annum in the purchase of Sea Coal and the further sum of £35 in Wearing Apparel out of such surplus and distribute the same amongst the poor of this parish, and also the remainder of the Surplus in such manner as they in their discretion shall think fit.

Application having been made to Messrs Felton requiring payment of the sum of £50 and In^{tr} and no answers having been received, the Vestry Clerk was directed to proceed against them for the recovery thereof.

1787. January 18. The Vestry Clerk reported that he had brought actions against John Felton and William Felton and in consequence thereof, had recovered the principal and interest amounting to £52 10s. which he was directed to pay to the Churchwardens.

Vestries, A.D. 1787. 195

1787. June 7. That the several repairs wanting to the inside of this Church (and whereof particulars and estimates were produced at a former Vestry) be done forthwith.

Committee appointed to see the several repairs effectually performed, and that they do employ the several Tradesmen who made out the particulars of the said several repairs to do the same.

That the Churchwardens do provide and cause to be fixed up in this Church, Two Stoves to warm the said Church so as the expense thereof doth not exceed the sum of £50.

Church Rate 1*s*. 3*d*. in the £.

That the Trustees of this parish of the sum of £750. 3 ⅌ C^t Bk Anns 1726 now standing in their names and belonging to the said parish, do sell out and transfer £160 thereof, being so much remaining after setting apart the sum of £590 for the purposes mentioned in the Order of Vestry of the 26th of October last and pay the same to the Under Churchwarden.

The Inhabitants of St Peter-le-Poor Broad Street having of late years on their procession on Ascension day, gone through a considerable part of St Helens Parish, and as the continuance of such practice might beget an idea of a right to do so, a Letter was written to the Church Warden of that parish, stating, that if the gentlemen of the parish of St Peter-le-Poor could not conveniently get a view of their Bounds within their own parish, The parish of St Helens was willing to accommodate the Church Wardens and a few of the Gentlemen with a passage for that purpose on a request of the Vestry of St Peter-le-Poor, the said request to be in writing, in order that it might remain among the records of this parish as an evidence of their right—At the same time the parish of St Helens desired to assure the parish of St Peter-le-Poor that a wish to prevent the possibility of any dispute arising between the said parishes in future, was the sole motive that induced them to make the said application.

To which the following answer was returned and ordered to be entered in the Vestry Book and the Originals deposited with the records of the parish.

Old South Sea House, Oct. 20, 1876.

Sir,—Mr Thornton Churchwarden of St Peter-le-Poor having laid your Letter of the 26th of September last to him before the gentlemen of the Vestry of such parish, I have their directions to inform you that it is their request that St Helens parish will accommodate the Churchwardens and a few of the Gentlemen of the parish of St Peter-le-Poor with a passage through St Helens parish for the purpose of obtaining a view of their Boundaries on their annual perambulation.

I am Sir, Your Most Obed^t Servant

To Mr. Joseph Potter, Churchwarden of the Parish of St. Helen's, London.

Nich. W. Lewes Vestry Clerk of the Parish of St. Peter-le-Poor.

1787. July 5. That the Vestry Clerk do deliver to Mr John Hardwicke his Bond bearing date the 1st April 1785 in the penalty of £499 and executed by him to this parish for Mr Joseph Potter's faithful discharge of the duties of the office of Churchwarden of the said parish in pursuance of an Order of Vestry bearing date the 31st March, 1785, the said Mr Potter having executed the said office to the satisfaction of this Vestry.

Mem. Mr Potter was still in office and continued to March 1788.

That the Churchwardens do pay the Revd Mr Naish 5 Guineas out of Sir John Lawrence's gift to this parish for the last year, ending Lady-day last.

That the annual payment of Ten Shillings to the Vicar of this parish and 2s. 6d. to the Clerk and claimed by them as the gift of Diana Astrey be from henceforth discontinued. It not appearing that the said parish has any funds to pay the same.

October 11. The several Tradesmen's Bills for the repairs of the Church amounting to £206 1s. 8½d. having been examined and found correct, were ordered to be paid.

1788. January 10. That the Morning Service on a Sunday in this parish Church do in future begin at a quarter of an Hour before Eleven o'clk.

March 27. The order of Vestry April 19 1781 that three guineas should be annually distributed among the poor was repealed, Mrs Mary Clapham having in the year 1736 left a fund for that purpose.

May 23. Church Rate Sixpence in £.

That the present and every future Church Warden do keep a distinct and separate account of all monies received and disbursed on account of the charitable donations, and that the Under Churchwarden for the time being do receive as heretofore all rents and annuities on said account and thereout pay the gifts left by Sir Martin Lumley and Mr Hanson to poor housekeepers. The said Sir Martin Lumley's gift for a Lecture, the sums directed to be paid for sermons by the Wills of Joyce Featley, William Prior and Thomas Fennor, such part of Sir John Lawrence's gift as this Vestry shall from time to time order to be paid to the Vicar of this parish, the forty shillings left by William Prior for a drinking, the Insurance of the house left by the said William Prior, the Baker's bill for Bread left to the Poor by John Robinson, William Robinson, Joyce Featley, Cicely Cioll, Thomas Hutchins and John Dingley, and that he do also pay to the Upper Churchwarden out of the before mentioned rents and annuities, the sum of £40 in the month of August and the further sum of £22 in the month of February following, and what shall remain in his hands after such payments as aforesaid in the last Week of his office as Under Churchwarden.

That the Upper Churchwarden do apply the Several Sums received by him from the Under Church Warden on account of the said charitable donations in such manner as is directed by the Wills of William Prior, Edward Fennor, Thomas Fennor, Mary Clapham and an Order of Vestry of October 26, 1786.

That the Under Churchwarden do annually pay the Revd Mr Naish £5 5s. 0d. out of Sir John Lawrence's gift during the pleasure of this Vestry.

1788. June 25. That a Vestry be held on Wednesday next to chuse a Sextoness in the room of Catherine Green, deceased, and that such choice be by ballot to commence at 5 and close at 7 o'clk. in the afternoon.

July 2. The Candidates having appeared and offered themselves for the place of Sextoness for the remainder of the Year, upon casting up the numbers found for

| Elizabeth Baylis | . 31 | Elizabeth Dickerson | 16 |
| Ann Whitehead | . 30 | Ann Green . . . | 2 |

Whereupon Elizabeth Baylis was declared duly elected.

1789. May 14. Election for Beadle, Engineer and Organ Blower vacant by the death of John Dickerson. Richard Whitehead being the only Candidate was unanimously elected for the remainder of the year.

1789. June 18. Church Rate 9d. in £.

That the sum of Five Guineas be paid to the Revd John Naish for his attention to the wishes of this parish in the appointment of a Morning Preacher.

That the like sum be paid to the Revd Mr Edmonds as a testimony of this parish's respect and approbation.

Mr S. R. Gaussen applied for leave to erect a Monument against the wall of the Church 10 f^t high by 5 or 6 wide, near the grave of the late Peter Gaussen, Esq. which was granted on his making good all damage that may be occasioned thereby, and paying all expenses attending the same.

October 15. The order of April 15 1784 directing the Vestry Clerk to deliver yearly to the Under Churchwarden a copy of the Table of Fees was repealed.

1790. January 7. Mr Saml Margerum had leave to lay a flat stone over the grave of his late wife in the Church with an inscription thereon, with the usual reservation.

That the Churchwardens of this parish do not in future enforce the payment of the Church Rate against the Quaker Inhabitants more than once in two years unless occasion shall require it.

June 11. This Vestry taking into consideration that the Revd John Naish, Vicar of this parish, has ever shewn himself ready and desirous to oblige the Parishioners by employing such Clergymen to officiate in this parish church as they have approved; and that the Collection annually made by or for him the said Vicar has of late fallen considerably short of its former amount, Doth resolve and order that the said Collection be discontinued and that in lieu thereof, the Under Churchwarden do pay the sum of £50 to the said Revd John Naish in the month of July next, And that the Under Churchwarden for the time being do pay the like sum of £50 annually in the month of July to the said Revd John Naish until otherwise ordered by the Vestry of this parish.

That the Under Churchwarden do in the month of July next pay the Revd Mr Edmonds the sum of Ten Guineas as a testimony of this parish's respect and approbation.

July 22. The Church Rate Book being incomplete could not be signed by this Vestry which was therefore adjourned to the 28th

Inst and notice of such adjournment was ordered to be given in the church on Sunday next, and summonses delivered out for such adjournment.

1790. October 21. That an additional Key of the doors of the Church be provided and delivered to Mr Thomas Houston in order that Ladders provided in case of Fire may be more readily obtained, and a board with Notice where the same may be obtained to be put in some conspicuous place without the Church.

1791. June 23. Holmes Hall and Co ordered to be summoned for Poor Rates.

August 25. Application made on behalf of Rose Christian Barnard who was old and infirm and (as was alledged) belonged to this parish, and proposed to pay to the use of this parish the sum of £100 of which she was possessed if this parish would accept the same and provide for the said Rose Christian Barnard with the rest of the poor belonging thereto. Agreed to.

October 20. Mr Houston moved, and was seconded by Mr Churchwarden Greenaway, That the swearing in dinner and the dinner on Ascension day be in future discontinued. Agreed to, but repealed at the next Vestry.

That the sum of Ten Guineas be presented to Revd Mr Edmonds as a donation from this parish.

That a reward of Two Guineas (increased to Five Guineas at the next Vestry) be given to any Watchman or other person, who shall apprehend any person or persons who has broke open, or shall be found in the act of breaking open the House, Shop, or Warehouse of any inhabitant of this parish, the same to be paid on conviction of the offender or offenders by the Under Churchwarden for the time being, and that Notice of such reward be fixed up in such conspicuous places within the parish as the Under Churchwarden shall direct.

1792. April 12. Mr Geo. Grove appointed to look after Church Clock.

June 14. Proceedings ordered to be taken against the representatives of Joyce Featley.

July 12. That the Sextoness of this Parish for the time being do not in future place any Inhabitant of this parish or other person or persons in any Pew or Seat in this parish Church, but under the direction of the Under Churchwarden.

September 27. Mrs Goodall, widow of Richard Goodall, Esq., had leave to lay a flat stone with an inscription over the grave of her late Husband in the Church with the usual reservation.

1793. April 4. New Lease granted to Mr Ward for 40 years at £34 ₽ ann. on his agreement to spend £250 in repairs, the parish allowing him the first year's rent towards the expense of the repairs.

June 13. The Engines to be played twice only in the course of the Summer, in every year, instead of four times as heretofore.

The Churchwarden stated that by virtue of a Pass Warrant, Rose Christiana Barnard aged 70 years had been removed from the parish of St Ann Westminster to this parish. That the friends of the said pauper had applied to him and requested that the weekly sum which would be paid by this parish for her maintenance in the workhouse might be allowed to her, in which case her said friends would take due care of her. And this Vestry having taken the said request into consideration as also the age and infirmities of the said Rose Christiana Barnard, Doth order that the sum of Four Shillings ₽ week be paid for her during the pleasure of this Vestry.

July 18. Ten Guineas to Revd Mr Edmonds.

1794. April 24. Mr Greenaway informed the Vestry that the Trustees of the Society called the Ethelberga Society with a view of promoting the interests thereof, requested leave of this parish that a part of the Charity Children belonging to the said Society might attend Divine Service in this Parish Church and be placed in the Gallery to sing the accustomed Psalms. The said Society being at the expense of providing and keeping necessary Seats for them and of any other incidental charges. And this Vestry having taken the same into consideration doth order that the said Society have leave to send such Children accordingly.

October 9. Ten Guineas to Revd Mr Edmonds.

That in case the Revd Mr Middleton shall think proper to preach the Lecture directed by the Will of Sir Martin Lumley at Six o'C^{lk} in the Evening, there shall be allowed Candles for that purpose by the parish. Repealed at the next Vestry.

1795. January 8. In consequence of the high price of coals, the Poor Pensioners to be allowed Six Pence a Week extra.

June 18. Pursuant to an Act of Parliament for raising a certain number of Men for the service of His Majesty's Navy and by an Order of General Sessions appointing three men to be levied and raised for this parish and the parish of St Martin Outwich A meeting of the Inhabitants of the respective parishes was called, and it was agreed that this parish should raise at its own expense, two of such men, and the parish of St. Martin Outwich should at its own expense raise the other of such men. That in consequence of such resolution, the Church Warden procured such two men and got them enrolled, and in order to defray the expences of raising them, a rate was made on the Inhabitants by virtue of the said Act. The application whereof appears in the Church Warden's Accounts.

1795. September 3. Revd Mr Naish late Vicar having departed this life and a debate arising on the right of presentation a Committee was appointed to wait on the Dean & Chapter of St Paul's and request leave for the Inhabitants of this parish to name a minister to be collated and inducted to the Vicarage of this parish, and that Mr. Bradley the Impropriator be requested to accompany the said Committee.

September 10. The Committee reported that they had attended at the office of Mr Jenner the Register to the Dean and Chapter on the 4th ins^t, but Mr Jenner not being in town, they acquainted his partner Mr Bush that they were a deputation appointed to solicit permission for the Inhabitants to nominate a Preacher for the approbation of the Dean and Chapter, to be by them collated to the living of St Helen in the room of the Revd Mr Naish deceased, the living being exceeding small, unless aided by the generosity of the Parish towards the Incumbent.

That Mr Bush replied, the absolute right of presentation was completely vested in the Dean and Chapter by usage of more than a century, and that they would not receive anything in the form of a nomination from the parish as that would imply a right, but that he had no doubt of a recommendation from the Vestry meeting with a favourable attention.

That on the same day the Committee also attended Dr Jackson, one of the Canons Residentiaries of St Paul's and requested his consent to such recommendation, when Dr Jackson enquired whether they were prepared to recommend any particular person, which being answered in the Negative, he said he would confer with the Dean and Jenner, and give his answer accordingly.

The Committee attended Dr Jackson again this day who told them he could not give a final answer till a meeting of the Chapter had been held, there being divers applications and several interests involved in the business, and mentioned particularly the Minor Canons, and likewise that he had received a Letter signed Edwd Bradley in which as Impropriator but not presuming on any right of presentation he desired to recommend the Revd William Edmonds (who had officiated for some years for the late Revd Mr Naish) to be collated to the Vicarage, he having the good wishes of the Parishioners.

Dr Jackson then desired to know who Mr Bradley was, and the Committee informed him that he was the Clerk of the Parish, who had also purchased the Tythes many years. That as to Mr Edmonds it was true he had officiated as represented, but that the parishioners were not by any means unanimous respecting him. Dr Jackson then informed them that as soon as the Dean and Chapter had determined on the business, they would transmit their sentiments to this parish.

That the Five Guineas received on account of the interment of the late Revd Mr Naish in Lead, be returned to his representatives.

1795. October 8. Ten Guineas to Mr Edmonds.

That One Hundred Copies of the Table of the Tythes payable by the inhabitants of this parish be printed and distributed amongst such inhabitants.

November 12. The Church Wardens reported that they had received a Letter from the Dean & Chapter of St Paul informing them that Mr. Watts had been collated by them to the Vicarage of this parish, and that Mr Watts had taken possession of the Vicarage in consequence thereof.

That the sum of £4 4s. 0d. be paid to Mrs Naish Widow of the late Vicar as a proportion of the sum of £50 ⅌ Ann^m heretofore paid him from the month of July last to the time of his death.

The Vestry then proceeded to consider of the right of the inhabitants to elect an afternoon preacher, and resolved, That the said inhabitants shall elect an afternoon preacher, and that the sum of £35 ⅌ Annum be allowed and paid as his salary. And that such persons as shall deliver in their names to the Church Wardens on or before the 29th instant and no other shall be admitted Candidates for the said Office, and that the Church Wardens do apply to the

Vicar for the use of the Pulpit in the forenoon of those days on which the Candidates shall preach their probationary Sermons, and on the Thursday next after the preaching of the last of the said Sermons, the Election of a preacher, by Ballot, shall take place.

1796. January 21. Mr. Churchwarden Boughey informed the [Vestry] that he had applied to Revd Mr Watts for the use of the pulpit for the Candidates for the intended Lectureship in preaching their probationary Sermons, and received for answer that his patrons had desired he would not admit of any alteration in the duty of the Minister, and he being willing to do the duty as it had heretofore been done, could not accede to their request.

Resolved, That the Election of a Lecturer be postponed.

That the Table of Fees for Burials, Christenings and Marriages be removed from the Vestry and placed in some conspicuous part of the void part of the Church.

Repealed next Vestry.

That the Parish Clerk do on all applications for Burials make out an account, particularising all the parish dues, and that such account be signed by the Churchwardens or one of them, and rendered previous to the breaking up of the ground for any funerals.

That a fine of £30 shall be paid by every person who shall hereafter desire to be, and be excused from serving the office of Churchwarden.

March 30. Order of April 20, 1775. Salary of Parish Clerk Repealed.

Repealed at Next Vestry.

In consequence of the increased price of provisions the allowance ℙ Head for the dinners on Ascension Day and Swearing in day. Resolved, That in future the sum of 4s. 6d. ℙ Head be allowed for the dinners and suppers on those days including everything except Punch and Wine, and that no invitations be given to the swearing in dinner to any persons who shall not have passed the Chair, except the Sidesmen, the late Sidesmen, and the Minister or Ministers Vestry Clerk and Organist, for the time being.

George Venables to look after the Church Clock.

May 26. Church Rate 1s. 3d. in the £.

Five Guineas to be annually paid to Rev^d Mr. Watts out of Sir John Lawrence's gift.

1796. June 30. Letter of thanks from Mr. Watts "With his best wishes for the prosperity of the parish and an assurance of my faithful endeavours to discharge my duty towards them as far as my poor abilities will enable me."

October 6. Letter from Mr. Thomas Trundle resigning the office of Vestry Clerk which he had held for 26 Years.

Election to be on the 20th Ins^t. The Ballot to be open from 4 to 6 o'clk.

October 20. Election.

   For Mr. Abbiss. Bishopsgate St Hardwareman . 53
     Mr. Finch. Little St Helens Attorney . . 17
                 Majority . . 36

Thanks of the Vestry to Mr. Trundle for the faithful discharge of the duties of the office for 26 Years to be fairly transcribed and presented to him.

The Churchwarden having on consultation with some of the Senior Inhabitants allowed the Exe^{rs} of Peter Kuhff to make a brick arched grave in the Church on payment of £40 This Vestry approved thereof.

November 10. Leave given for a Monument on payment of the further sum of £20.

The situation of Parish Clerk being vacant by the death of Mr. Bradley, the Rev. Mr. Watts was asked if he would accept the choice of the Vestry, who answering in the affirmative, the Election ordered to be by Ballot on the 24th Ins^t from 4 to 6 o'Clk.

December 8. Election postponed to this day.

Candidates. Richard Whitehead, of Little St. Helen's.
    James Bradley, Sun Street.
    William Pocock, Bishopsgate Street.
    — Godson, Clerkenwell.

Motion having been agreed to, Memorandum drawn up and signed by the Candidates.

" We whose names are hereunto subscribed being Candidates for the office of Parish Clerk do sincerely and unequivocally promise that in case of the Election of either us to the said office, that we will not procure a licence to hold the same till the further pleasure of this Vestry is made known."

Ballot for Whitehead	46
Bradley	27
Pocock	7
Goodson	0

Whereupon Mr. Whitehead resigned his previous office of Beadle and an Election for Beadle ordered by Ballot on the 15th Ins^t from 5 to 7 o'Clk.

Some of the poor having pawned their Clothes, Ordered That the Linen and Apparel of the poor be in future marked or stamped, agreable to the order of the Churchwarden.

Messrs Blake, Hobson, and Allfrey had leave to erect a Tablet against the wall near Sir John Robinson's Monument to the memory of a West India Gentlemen, size 2 feet 6 in. by 2 feet, on payment of £10.

1796. December 15. Thomas Watkins being the only Candidate for the offices of Beadle, Engineer, and Organ Blower, was unanimously elected.

1797. January 2. St. Helens parish having to furnish 3 Men for the service of His Majesty's Navy, resolved, That the Churchwardens procure the said Men on the best terms they possibly can.

On account of the increased expense of the Oyster Feast, resolved, That in future every inhabitant attending at the Annual Oyster Feast, do pay the sum of 2s. 6d., Except the Minister Clerk, Organist and Vestry Clerk.

March 7. This Vestry being of opinion That the Poor Law Bill now before Parliament, a great increase in the Poor's Rate must be the result, The Churchwardens & Overseers were authorised to sign in the name of the parish the petition to be presented to Parliament against the said Bill.

April 20. That Mr. Thos Fasson takes his seat in this Vestry as Common Councilman of this precinct.

June 1. Church Rate 9d. in £.

August 3. This Vestry observing the good conduct of Richard Whitehead since the time of his being elected Parish Clerk and relying that his future behaviour will correspond with his past, are of opinion that he is at liberty to procure himself to be licensed.

October 19. Committee appointed to inquire into the number of Vaults and where they are situated.

1797. November 23. The Upper Churchwarden being dead, M'r Jon'n Punshon undertook the office for the remainder of the year, except collecting Poor Rate.

1798. March 1. Resolved Unanimously

That at the present awful crisis, when an inveterate and implacable foe has openly declared a determination, not only to subvert the civil and religious constitution of our country, but also to annihilate its very existence as an independent nation It is the bounden duty of every Briton, whatever his rank or condition may be, to use his utmost efforts in order to frustrate the malevolent design of so determined an enemy, that the wages and subsistance of the Servant, the earnings of the Mechanic, the profits of the Shopkeeper, the capital of the Merchant, the funds of the Stockholder, and the estate of the landed proprietor, are alike interested in the issue of the present contest, and that the exertions of all are due to their country, their families and themselves.

That it is the opinion of this meeting a Book be opened to receive the voluntary contributions of those Inhabitants who agree with the aforesaid resolution and remain in the Vestry room from Friday, March 2nd to Thursday March 8th inclusive, and that the aggregate amount be paid into the Bank of England as the Voluntary Contribution of the parish of St Helens, London.

That a Committee be appointed for conducting the said business, and that they do attend every day Sunday Excepted from 12 to 2 o'clock in the Vestry room to receive the Subscriptions of the parishioners.

That these resolutions be signed by the Chairman printed and distributed at every house in the parish, and also inserted in the *Morning Chronicle, True Briton*, and *Johnson's Sunday Monitor*.

April 12. That this parish discontinue the Annual Perambulation of the boundaries of this parish and of dining together as heretofore on Ascension day, and that the same be from henceforth but once in every three years.

That from henceforth the sum of Two Guineas be allowed for all Quarterly Vestrys, and the sum of One Guinea for all other Vestries.

April 19. This Vestry being informed that a public notice had been given in the Church, whereby the hours of Divine Service are altered, and also that the Revd Mr Watts had discontinued the usual Sunday Afternoon Sermon highly approve of the same.

1798. June 28. £158 received as Fines in the last two years.

That this parish do petition the Court of Common Council to widen the entrance of Great St Helens into St Mary Axe.

Richard Sumner to look after the Clock.

1799. July 11. Ten Guineas to Revd Mr Ellis for his past services.

August 29. R. Whitehead the parish Clerk applied to be excused paying the taxes for the house he resides in a part of, until the party Wall is rebuilt and the house put into a tenentable repair, which was agreed to.

October 17. That the Land Tax on the house belonging to this parish and occupied by Mr Whittenbury be redeemed.

That the Trustees for this parish of the sum of £590 3 ℔ C^t do transfer so much of the said capital sum as shall be necessary to redeem the Land Tax. £126 16s. Stock for redemption of £3 6s. 0d. ℔ annum.

Five Guineas to be paid annually to the Revd J. Blenkarne out of Sir John Lawrence's gift.

1800. January 16. Church Rate 4d. in £.

April 17. Ja^s Abbiss to look after the Clock.

That this Vestry direct the Under Church Warden to pay the Revd Jas^s Blenkarne, Vicar of this parish, the sum of Seventy Pounds in the month of July next and also in the month of July in every year, during the pleasure of this Vestry, as a testimony of their esteem and approbation.

That the dinner on the day of swearing in the Churchwardens be discontinued.

June 5. First entry of Mr. Williams' Senr. name as present at Vestry. Church Rate 1s. in £.

1801. January 15. That a petition be presented to the Honble East India C^o, That the Gates might be replaced at the entrance into St Helens from St Mary Axe as formerly, they being taken away by the said Company's orders.

February 10. To which the East India Company returned for answer that in taking down the Old Ones and giving twelve feet of ground to the public, they had removed a considerable nuisance, and could not pay further attention to the application.

October 22. That in case any Church Warden shall hereafter

permit the respective rates to be in arrears and uninforced, he shall be proceeded against, as the Law has provided.

1802. February 4. The relatives of Thos Carter permitted to make a Brick Grave in the middle Isle of the Church on payment of £40.

July 22. Vote of Thanks to Mr Powell late Churchwarden passed at last Vestry not confirmed.

1803. April 14. Gift of John Smith, Esq. ordered to be inserted on the Table of Benefactors in the Church.

October 27. New Lease for 21 Years to Mr Whittenbury at £42 ℔ annum.

1804. April 5. The Beadle Thos Watkins being very old and infirm the Church Warden was ordered to pay him 10s. 6d. ℔ Week during pleasure, and the Vestry adjourned to Thursday next the 12th ins^t to choose a Beadle. To begin at One and finally close at 2 o'clk. the same day.

April 12. There being no other Candidate John Ward was unanimously elected Beadle of this parish.

1805. February 14. It was prayed by Mr Deputy Greenaway that this Vestry do grant him an extension of Seven Years in addition to the term in the lease heretofore granted to Mr James Stone deceased which expires at Midsummer 1823, the said Thomas Greenaway having resided therein thirty years and the sole property for the residue of the present term being vested in him. Agreed to.

April 19. That the Salary of the parish Clerk be increased from £25 to £30 ℔ Annum, subject to the same restrictions as ℔ order of Vestry April 20, 1775.

That no Corpse be in future buried within the Walls of this Church, unless it is contained in a leaden Coffin.

May 1. J. G. Saggers, unanimously chosen Vestry Clerk in the room of Mr Abbiss resigned.

August 8. The thanks of the Vestry to Mr Abbiss for his faithful discharge of the duties of Vestry Clerk and that the sum of £20 be presented to him as a further testimony of their approbation.

September 5. That the assessment of the Church Rate on Mr Whitehead the Parish Clerk and Mrs Baylis the Sextoness be in future discontinued during the pleasure of this Vestry.

October 17. The office of Preacher of Sir Martin Lumley's

lecture having become vacant and no appointment having been made, the Churchwarden appointed the Revd Mr Blenkarne the Vicar to assume the duties, of which the Vestry approved.

1806. April 10. Richard James had leave to place a Tablet to the memory of his two children in the void of the Church on payment of Three Guineas.

That in future the sum of Two Guineas be allowed for the expenses of the Supper of every Vestry of this parish.

June 19. Church Rate 1s. 6d. in £.

July 24. That the Salary of the Vestry Clerk be in future £30 ℔ annum, but that no charge shall be made for examination of Paupers, or any other business than what is expressly ordered by the Churchwarden or the Vestry.

1807. April 30. The Revd Mr Cooke having purchased the Tithes and made demands to the extent of 2s. 9d. in the £, a Committee appointed to examine the records, &c. of the parish relative to the subject and to take such legal advice &c. as they shall deem necessary.

June 11. The Committee having an interview with Mr Cooke he adverted to a copy of a decree of the Court of Exchequer made many years since, and which he requested to be permitted a perusal thereof. To which this Vestry resolved That his request cannot with propriety be complied with.

July 1. A Committee having been appointed for the repairs of the Church appointed Mr Chapman their surveyor who recommended that the several repairs should be done by contract & stated that the gross amount of the repairs of the church, the outside being rough cast instead of cemented, and including the enclosure of the Organ Loft, would be £973.

That such sums of money as should be necessary in addition to the Church Rate for the time being, to defray the charges of the aforesaid repairs, should be raised by loan of the Inhabitants in shares of £50 each, to be repaid from monies from time to time accruing in the hands of the Churchwardens with interest at 5 ℔ C^t per ann. the priority of payment to be ascertained by lot.

The opinion of Mr Chitty an eminent special pleader as to the right of assessing houses which have been subdivided and inhabited by different families which becoming thereby several tenements were so rateable whilst so inhabited.

1807. July 16. Letter from the Impropriator Revd Mr Cooke in consequence of his not having been applied to respecting the repairs of the Church, denying the right of the parish to interfere with the Chancel for repairs &c. without his previous consent and approbation, it being his personal freehold.

October 15. Opinion of Sir Thos Plumer Solicitor General on a case submitted to him respecting the Tithes of this parish.

The Impropriator has the same right as an Ecclesiastical Rector, and will be entitled under the statute of Henry 8th and the decree* therein referred to, to the sum of 2s. 9d. in the £ upon the rent of all Houses &c. in the parish, unless the parish can protect themselves under the 17th Article of the decree by shewing that at and prior to the 37th Hen. VIII. a less Sum had been accustomed to be paid for Tithes. The circumstances disclosed in this case, afford ground to contend that this was the case in respect to the ancient Houses in the parish, not including Crosby Square. The occupiers of these Houses should insist upon the unchangeable validity of these accustomed payments in lieu of tithes, and should offer to continue to render them. If refused, they can only stand on the defensive and resist any suit that may be instituted against them upon this ground. In their answer they should rely on this defence and set forth the proceedings in the suit referred to, for discovering which every search should be made. They should also state the further documents in support of their claim, some of which I think may be received in evidence, and all of which should be offered.

The case and the Solicitor General's opinion were afterwards laid before Mr Chitty to point out cases relevant to the Solicitor General's opinion.

The case of Bennett *v* Trespass reported in 2 Gwyllim on Tithes 633, and 2 Browns Parl. Cas. 437, appears to me very favorable to the parishioners of the parish of St Helen. In that case on a Bill brought for tithes of houses in London after the rate of 2s. 9d. in the twenty shillings rent the Court of Exchequer directed an issue to try whether any less sum or sums of money than such customary payment set up by the defendants had ever been paid,

---

* Exchequer, Feb. 9, 1662. Langham *v.* Lawrence and others. St. Helen's Tithes.

and that too, though there was no *proof* of any regular Modus, and tho' the payments of the annual sums for tithes appeared to have varied, yet the Court of Exchequer considered the payments of less than 2s. 9d. in the pound though not proved to have been made for 8 years *before* the passing of the Act as sufficient evidence of accustomed payments within the meaning of the 18th Sec^n. The decree alluded to, if it can be established in evidence will be conclusive,—See the observations in 2 Gwyllim 641, and I apprehend that by minute search in the Court of Exchequer the Original decree may be obtained, but if not, I think the evidence referred to in the case will suffice. It does not **appear** to me that any step is necessary to be taken by the parishioners, excepting that they should respectively tender the sums which they insist they are liable to pay, immediately after the days of payment. I apprehend the tithe at the rate of 2s. 9d. in the pound upon the *improved* rent is payable by the occupiers of all houses *newly* erected. Gwyllim $505 = 1426 = 1314$. The Court of Chancery and the Court of Exchequer have jurisdiction immediately over the subject of Tithes in London.

The Committee seeing the necessity of establishing the present payments as ancient ones went round the parish to collect the sums correctly then paid in order to assimilate to the ancient payments. Mr Cooke having summoned several Inhabitants before the Lord Mayor on the 2^d September the Committee employed Counsel to attend, who insisted that the accustomed duties had never been denied as Mr Cooke himself admitted. The complaint was dismissed with Costs and the 5th Septr was fixed for hearing any further Complaint, that thereupon Mr Cooke served summonses on several inhabitants to answer on that day why they refused to pay the tithes, and on hearing Mr. Cooke and the Counsel for the respondents, his Lordship thought proper to declare it was a matter more fit for the decision of the Lord Chancellor and declined to give any judgment thereon.

1808. April 21. John Williams, Elected Sidesman.

May 10. That in future the fine for Sidesman be increased to Five Pounds.

July 1. Vestry's held in the room of the Leather Sellers Company in St. Helen's Place, the Vestry Room being under repair.

1809. February 9. That in consideration of the great inconvenience arising from Pryor's Bequest commonly called the Oyster Feast being kept as a Supper, the inhabitants shall instead thereof in future dine together on the first clear Thursday in Lent, the Under Churchwarden and each Gentleman attending to pay 5s. and the Bill to be called at 9 o'Clk in the Evening, and that the Vicar and Organists be the only non-residents invited.

April 27. That a Vestry be held on Friday May 12th at 4 o'Clk precisely in the afternoon for the choice of an Organist for the remainder of the year (in the room of Mr George Griffin deceased) by ballot to commence at the time above mentioned and close at 6 precisely, That the Upper Churchwarden have the casting vote if necessary. That the several Candidates do declare themselves such on or before Saturday the 6th May and be permitted to play probationary tunes a quarter of an hour each on Wednesday the 10th May to commence at 4 o'Clk precisely in the afternoon.

May 12. Election.   Master Cutler*   36
                    Miss Rodd   29
                    Miss Naish   1

Whereupon Master Cutler was declared duly elected.

---

* "William Henry Cutler, Mus. Bac. Oxon., was born in the year 1792, of respectable parents, in the City of London. Shortly after the birth of this their second child, the father obtained a spinet at a sort of lottery sweepstake, and after the business of the day was over would frequently strum to his two little boys on this instrument. He had then, however, very little knowledge of music; but, possessing industry and perseverance, overcame every difficulty in the science, so as to enable him to superintend his second son through all his subsequent exertions in practice. A friend relates that, one time when he entered the father's parlour, he saw him with this little boy on his lap, teaching him his notes; at another time, the same friend has seen father and son on the carpet playing with pieces of card, on which the notes of music and their names and lines, &c. appeared, corresponding with papers pasted on the keys of the spinet. At that time the child could not have been much above two years of age, certainly not three years old. His father, conceiving that the boy had a taste for music, next engaged a master to teach him the violin, when he improved so rapidly as to play a concerto of Jarnowich before he was five years old. He performed on the little Amati violin, which was once Dr. Crotch's, and which his father bought of the late Mr. Betts. Still, however, the spinet appeared to be the child's favourite, and J. H. Little was for some time his instructor on that instrument, which was at length changed for a pianoforte, G. E. Griffin being engaged as the boy's master. About the year 1799, the child had lessons of singing and thorough-

That the sum of £5 5s. 0d. be presented by this Vestry to Miss Rodd.

That the salary of the Organist for the remainder of the year be at the rate of Twenty Guineas ₽ ann.

That Mr England be appointed to tune the Organ for the remainder of the year at a salary of Six Guineas ₽ Annum.

1809. July 13. Application having been made on behalf of Mr. W.

---

bass from Dr. Arnold, who expressed his approbation of his talent by repeated gifts of small silver two-penny and three-penny pieces. Shortly after this, he played a concerto of Viotti on the pianoforte, at the Haymarket theatre, for the Choral Fund Concert, and received universal applause: he has played concertos, &c. several times since for the same fund. He sang also at the oratorios under Dr. Arnold.

"In 1801, when Dr. Busby took his degree of doctor of music, young Cutler went to Cambridge to sing the principal airs in that exercise; and under this gentleman he would have been placed, but his father objected to his being other than a concert-singer, while the doctor wished him to be brought out in theatrical performances. In 1803, he was placed in the choir of St. Paul's. He sang also at Harrison's concerts, the concerts of ancient music, the glee club, (generally) Wykhamists, &c. &c., and private concerts. Previously to this, he had also appeared before the public as a composer, his first publication being a march for the full band of the sixth regiment of Loyal London volunteers, in the rifle company of which regiment his father was an officer. Soon after this, he sang in the solemn services, dirge, &c. of three of the greatest men of the day, being summoned to attend the funerals of Lord Nelson and Messrs. Pitt and Fox. After leaving the choir of St. Paul's, he was placed under the instruction of the late W. Russell, Mus. Bac. Oxon., for the theory of music, and was, in 1818, elected organist of St. Helen's, Bishopsgate; he also taught in several private families. In the year 1812, he took his bachelor's degree at Oxford, highly complimented by letter from the professor of that university [Dr. Crotch]. In 1818, when Logier came to England from Dublin, W. H. Cutler, influenced by Kalkbrenner's advertisement, applied to Logier and paid one hundred guineas to learn his system. He then took a house in Broad-street-buildings, and opened an academy on the Logierian plan; but, after between two and three years' trial, finding it not advantageous to keep up the requisite establishment, he relinquished that house, though he still teaches the theory of music according to Logier's system. In 1821, Cutler was engaged to sing at the oratorios at Drury-lane, under the direction of Sir George Smart; but want of nerve prevented his giving full power to his voice, and determined him to relinquish altogether singing in public. In 1825, a part of the exercise for his bachelor's degree was performed at the oratorios under the direction of Bochsa. He has lately resigned the situation of organist of St. Helen's, and been appointed organist of Quebec Chapel, Portman-square."
—See "Dictionary of Musicians," vol. i. pp. 195-6. Ed. London, 1827. No record of W. H. Cutler's death has been discovered.

Gosling on the death of his Wife for the purchase of a Vault in the void of the Church immediately behind the pew of the Churchwardens for himself and family and that in consequence the Churchwardens had agreed to sell the same to him for the sum of Fifty Guineas which sum had been received by them. This Vestry approved thereof and confirmed the Contract.

1809. October 12. A List of the persons who made advances by way of Loan of £50 each towards defraying the expense of the repairs amounting to £1200.

Application having been made on behalf of the family of the late Mr. Morgan for the purchase of a Vault in the void of the Church near the small tomb of Robinson, the Churchwardens agreed to sell the same for Eighty Guineas.

Application having been made on behalf of the family of the late Mr. Galindo for the purchase of a Vault opposite the Vestry door marked on the keystone with the letter E. The Churchwardens agreed to sell the same for One Hundred Pounds.

This Vestry approved and confirmed the said Contracts and gave leave to lay a flat stone respectively with inscriptions thereon and also over the Vault lately sold to Mr. Gosling.

That the two Guineas allowed for a Vestry Supper be retained in the hands of the Churchwarden and expended during the summer in a dinner, in lieu of Suppers to those Gentlemen who attend their duties in the Vestry four times in the Year.

The Committee to whom it had been referred to consider of the propriety of increasing the Fees for Christenings, Marriages, and Burials, and making arrangements with respect to future interments in the Church reported that on due deliberation and having consulted Ecclesiastical Authorities, they were of opinion that any alteration should for the present be deferred.

1810. January 25.

	£	s.	d.
Ordinary repairs of the Church amounted to the sum of	2552	1	9
Surveyor's Commission and extraordinary expenses	392	15	6
	2944	17	3
Of which had been paid in part	2352	16	6
Balance	592	0	9

It was the opinion of the Committee for repairs that the sum of £500 would be sufficient to enable the Churchwarden to defray such balance, and it would be advisable to raise the same in the manner the £1200 had already been raised. Agreed to.

That the expenses of the Committee during the said repairs be allowed by the Auditors not exceeding £20.

1810. April 26. That the Sacramental Plate be insured by the Churchwardens to the amount of Two Hundred Pounds in the Eagle Insurance Office as doubly hazardous.

That the Churchwardens do in future provide and deliver to the inhabitants, receipts, on payment of the Church and Poor Rates, respectively.

May 2. That the names of the several Inhabitants be fairly transcribed in the Register Book of Parishioners with the period of their becoming resident, and that the Book be laid on the Table every Vestry.

Eleven Gentlemen fined for Sidesmen.

June 28. That the Under Churchwarden for the time being do pay the Revd Ja^s Blenkarne the sum of Ten Pounds in the month of July next in addition to the £70 heretofore granted making £80 and the like sum of £80 in the month of July in every succeeding Year during the pleasure of this Vestry.

The names of those who subscribed the add^l £500.

Particulars of repairs, &c.

On the North side (External) a number of Stone Steps were discovered leading as supposed from the ancient convent into the Church, the roof was incrusted with Smoke, the Steps much worn and the Wall above extremely decayed, the whole was fitted up firm with Stone and brick.

Interior.

In stripping the South Side behind the Table of Benefactions a large Pointed Window was discovered completely glazed but stopt up by the Wall of the House immediately behind.—This Window was filled up with brickwork, and also another found on the west side from which the Glass had been removed.

A large screen of timber covered with Stucco was erected to the ceiling of the Church and completely surrounded the external of the Organ loft.

The pews were all taken down and erected on a complete new

flooring on oak joists supported by brickwork and made single that all the congregation might turn towards the Minister, whose desk and that of the Clerk were removed and a new one erected on a more elevated plan. The pulpit also completely repaired and the sounding Board removed.

The whole pavement of the Church was taken up and laid about 4 inches higher than before.

Crosby's ... Gresham's ... and I suppose Pickering's Vault, as it is not mentioned, were not opened.

In Spencer's his Coffin was discovered.

List of Bills for Repairs.

	£	s.	d.		£	s.	d.
Tyson & Co., Slaters	2	6	6	Ashton, Stationer	27	5	0
Evans & Co., Ironmongers	10	4	0	Catherwood, Brazier	9	14	10
Dempsey & Co., Ironpipes	44	6	0	Heriot, do.	32	15	7
A. Roskell, Plumber	72	9	0	Cooper, Upholsterer	96	9	2
T. Clarke, Plasterer	464	13	6	Philp, do.	65	5	6
T. Knight, Bricklayer	311	4	2	Chapman, Surveyor	144	17	6
W. Roper, Carpenter	818	4	7	Hayes, Oil Cloth	3	17	6
J. Richards, Mason	296	12	6	Tinkler, Hassocks	2	15	0
Halsey, Painter	245	11	1	Varty, Linen	5	4	0
Stewardson, Glazier	68	7	4	Abbiss, Silversmith	9	5	6
Clarke, Smith	230	2	9	Shepherd, Box Maker	2	1	6
England, Organ Builder	66	10	0	Saggers, Vestry Clk. % Contracts	18	17	8

That the Salary of Mr Cutler the Organist be increased to £25 ⅌ ann^m, and that the Salary of Mrs Baylis be increased from £18 to £23 ⅌ annum.

1810. July 12. That the Salary of the Beadle be increased to £10 ⅌ annum.

1811. January 31. Propositions from Revd Mr Cooke Impropriator.

That in consideration of all Arrears being paid up to Midsummer 1810, except in St Helen's Place where the new rate takes place from the commencement of the occupation of each new house, and of an annual rent of £560 to be divided between the Rector and Vicar and to be made perpetual as the Rector and Committee shall determine, the Tithes be indefinitely leased to Trustees for the use of the parishioners at their expense.

That if this be unanimously assented to, A piece of Plate not exceeding the value of £10 be given as a friendly present on each side.

That Crosby Square be not included in this arrangement, but be allowed to accede to it, on contributing a proportionate share of annuity.

That if no general agreement could be effected Mʳ Cooke was ready to treat with any individual for his own Tithes.

Application having been made on behalf of Thoˢ Trundle Esq. for the purchase of Bond's Vault, the Church Warden had agreed to sell it for £94 10s., which this Vestry approved and confirmed.

1811. March 6. Report of Committee on Tithes with Sir Thomas Plumer's further opinion on Case and questions submitted to him. That the inhabitants of Sᵗ Helen's Place could not defend themselves against the claim of 2s. 9d. in the £.

That the inhabitants of a house built upon and within the limits of an old site or sites will be protected by proving the customary payment in respect of such site or sites, or the building lately standing thereon.

That in cases of customary payment there is no fixed period of time. Such a continued usage must be proved as tends to establish the fact that the payment contended for was a customary payment at the time of the Statute and decree.

That in case the original decree cannot be found the copy thereof which appears in the very old parish Book will not be admitted as evidence.

That if it should appear that any of the customary payments although uniformly made for a number of years last past, yet differ from those stated in the old Lists of Documents, I think it very doubtful whether the variance between the old list and the practice in this case, will not be fatal to the plea of a fixed customary payment. The settled usage however would I should think be more likely to prevail than the old list without any usage in favor of it.

The Committee conceive that such inhabitants as can prove an ancient payment for the premises they respectively occupy, and more particularly if such inhabitants identifying their premises, can shew such premises to correspond with the ancient Tithe Lists or Tables, will be a good answer to Mʳ Cooke's claim.

March 14. On the recommendation of a Committee who had conferred with Mʳ Cooke it was moved,

That the sum of £500 ℔ ann. be paid to Mʳ Cooke the Impropriator and £60 ℔ ann. to the Vicar in lieu of all tithes, oblations, offerings, and payments heretofore paid, such sums to be raised by an equal pound rate on the Inhabitants of this parish (except the

East India Company's Warehouses and Crosby Square) the amount to be regulated by the Assessment to the Property Tax Letter A, and that the said sums be legally and effectually secured without delay (at the expense of the parish) to the Impropriator and Vicar by equal quarterly payments, and that this motion be not put in the usual way by shew of hands, but that declarations of Assent and Dissent lay in the Vestry for the subscription of individual inhabitants To-morrow and Saturday.

1811. April 18. The declaration of Assent was signed by Thirty Three Inhabitants (Fifteen of whom residing in St Helens Place) and of Dissent by Thirteen.

  July 17.   Population of the Parish.

  Families. Males. Females. Total. Inhabited Houses.
  130 ... 295 ... 357 ... 652 ... 115

1812. January 30. That in future no Churchwarden of this parish shall grant the privilege to any individual (parishioner or not) to erect a Tomb over a Vault, affix a Tablet in or on the Walls of the Church, or lay a flat stone over any grave in the Church or Church Yard with any inscription on it, without first receiving the sanction of this Vestry.

That this Vestry recommend to the Church Wardens to take an early opportunity of informing the friends of   Pitts lately interred, That the leave given to them by the Churchwardens to lay down a flat stone with an inscription thereon cannot be acceded to or confirmed by this Vestry.

  April 2. Mr Churchwarden Whittenbury become Insolvent.

That the Overseers should once in every quarter visit the poor in the Workhouse.

Application for the purchase of a Vault on behalf of Mr. Burrows. Negociation left to the discretion of the Church Wardens and three others.

April 21. Mr. Rawson had leave given to put up a Marble Tablet 2 feet 6 in. by 1 ft. 10 in. on payment of £50.

June 15. £311 3s. 1d. due from Mr. Whittenbury's Estate which was paid by his assignees in consideration of a lease of the house being granted to them or their nominee Mr. Arman who wished the lease to be extended to 21 Years and offering £50 ℔ Annum, on which the parish had the opinion of a Surveyor and agreed to grant the lease at £55 ⅌ Annum. The Assignees having paid for the use of the parish £390.

1812. August 13. Five Guineas to be paid to Mr Abbiss for his Services in collecting Poors Rate &c. since Mr. Whittenbury's stoppage.

That Twenty Guineas be presented to Mr Saggers the Vestry Clerk for his great attention and care in the late proceedings relative to the premises occupied by Whittenbury.

August 20. Election for Sextoness in the room of Mrs Baylis deceased.

For Eliz^h Bradley 41
Mary Wright 15
Rebecca Harvey 2

Whereupon Mrs. Bradley was declared duly elected, and the Sum of Two Guineas ordered to be presented to each of the unsuccessful Candidates to pay her expenses on the present occasion.

October 1. That the Under Churchwarden do provide a curtain for the Vestry Window.

Extracts from Church Wardens' Accounts.

	£	s	d
1563. Collections made in the Parish towards the relief and succour of the poor harboured in the Hospitals, £2 12s. 0d. out of the Collection allowed to the Parish for their poor. This was continued every Year till 1571 and again in 1584. The first collection was £13 8s. 4d.			
1563. Sexton's Wages	1	0	0
Keeping of the Clock for a hole year . . .		6	8
1564. March 21. Paid Mr. Colshill for the charge of the Lease of this parsonage as appereth by his acquittance and according to an order taken in Vestry	20	0	0
To Father Howe for his fee for the Organs for a hole year		2	0
1566. German Cioll. 1567. Thomas Colshill, Church Wardens.			
Paid to Underwood the Clerk for his hole year's wages	2	0	0
1569. Paid ffetler the Carpenter for layeing the great beame in the west ende of the roofe of the Church, and for ij. new pieces of timber on the syde wall and for removing the hole steeple to the corner of the Church	6	6	8

		£	s	d
Mem. That the xxiii. daye of December 1570. By appointment of the parishioners of this parish, the Chalice that lately appertayned to this parish, wayinge 24½ oz. which was sold for 5s. 4d. the oz. is now newly and altered into a newe Communion Cuppe of solid and gilt, which with the Cover, wayeth xx. oz. and a little more which with the 6s. 8d. per oz. And as there is more layde out than the Chalice came to by 3s. 4d. which is paid by Peter Dod, Churchwarden.				
1571. William Kerwin, Church Warden.				
1575.* Received of Sir Thomas Gresham, Knight, for his lycense to eat flesh, and put into the Poor Men's Box according to the statute			6	8
1580. Paid Mr. Gardener for the Lector	12		0	0
1581. Paid to Mr. Gardner and to the parson of St. Ethelborowe's parish for redding the Lector for one hole year	12		0	0
1582. Candles for the Lector			7	6
1584. Received towards Charge of the Lector, as appeareth by the booke appynted for the same		9	6	0
1585. Paid to Mr. Curtis for one Quarter for reading of the Lector		3	0	0
Pain to Mr. Lewys for three Quarters		9	0	0
1586. Laid out for Barber's sonne by consent of divers of the parish, for a Dublett, a pair of Stockinge, a pair of Shoes, & a Cap.			8	0
Itm. More paid for the keping of the said boye unto one Girton his Nourse for one month after he first brought him to the parish			4	0
Itm. Paid more for the keping of the said boye unto Widow Robinson for his meate, drink and lodging being sick the space of 36 daies			12	0
Itm. More given unto the said boye when he went to my Lady Gresham's. A new shirt and his showes mended			1	8
1587. Proceedings commenced respecting Lease.				
1589. Paid for Petition to the Lord Treasurer about the parsonage			1	0

---

* "1550-1. The ix day of Marche was a proclamasyon that no man or woman shuld nott ett no flesse in lent, nor fryday nor wednesday thrught the yere, nor ymberying days, nor no days, nor no days that ys condemned by the chyrche up one payne of forfyte."—"Diary of Henry Machyn," p. 4. Ed. Camden Society, Lond. 1848.

		£	s.	d.
1589.	Paid to a Pursuivant at Sir Walter Mildmey's that took paynes about our lease		2	6
	Paid to Mr. Vagan for his dutys for the lease of the parsonage	3	7	8
	Paid Mr. Lewis, Minister for the rent of his house	2	0	0
	Paid Mr. Lewis for his half year's farme due at our Ladyday	10	0	0
1590.	Lecture only Six Months	5	0	0
	The charge of £20 for the Vicar, bringing the parish in debt.			
1591.	Lecture only three months	2	10	0
1592.	Lecture the whole year			
	1591-2. Two Accounts of Under Church Warden.			
	Paid for fittinge out of Soldyers as apeareth	3	2	10
1594.	Received for 4 Grave Stones sold by consent	8	2	6
1595.	First Account of Money for Poor. In the Poor Men's Box	1	10	0
1598.*	Itm. To the Soldier in his purse whom the parish sent out		3	0
1600.	First Collection for Tythes.			
	Itm. he chargeth himself with the some of £14 15s. 6d.	14	15	6
	Gathered for Tythes for half a yeare ending at the feast of St Michael the Archangel last past as by the particulars appeareth.			
	Paid Mr. Oliver for serving the cure one Q^r	5	0	0
	Paid to Mr. Stanhope for half a yeares farme ending at Mich last	4	8	0
1601.	Tythes	30	8	0
1603.	Item to a preacher when Mr. Lewis was in prison		5	0
	Item given to Mr. Morley when preached Mr. Lewis being suspended		3	6
	Item for our bot hire to Fulham, from thence to Braynford and back again for the procuring Mr. Ball to be our Minister		12	0
	Church Wardens chosen at Michaelmas till after 1603, when the same Wardens served until 1605.			
	Lecture discontinued.			
1607.	Item to Sir John Spencer Knight, or his farm rent for a Yere	8	16	1
1609.	Item for vi. gallons and iii. quarts of Clarett Wyne at ijs & iiijd the gallon and ijs the rondlett		16	9

* "In an Assessment Roll for levying Subsidies dated Oct. 1st, 40th Elizabeth, 1598, the name of William Shakspeare occurs in connexion with that of Sir John Spencer and other inhabitants of the Parish of St. Helens with the sum of 5l. 13s. 4d., the Assessment against the Poet's name; arising it is said from the Bull Inn."—Timbs' "Curiosities of London," pp. 238-9.

	£	s	d
Item for a Sugar loafe waying vii lbs & x. ounces at xviijd the pound for my Lord Bishop of Gloucester		11	4
1613. Item of Mrs. ffountaine for a legacy given to the parish by her late Husband's Will . . . Sir Henry Rowe, K^t and Mr. James Ellyott, Exe^{rs} of Mrs. Cioll.	10	0	0
Item for trymming the Vyne		1	0
1612. Decr 23. First Account.			
The Accompte of the Poore's Stock.			
Imprimis receaved for the foote of the last accompte	40	0	0
Item of Mr. Phillips and Mr. Wardner, Collectors for their foote	10	0	0
Item gathered at the Church dore 27 Dec^r .		9	0
Item of Mr. Awdley for a free guift . . .		10	0
Item of Mr. Wardner for a free guift . . .		5	0
Item receaved at vi Comunions beginning the 3 of January as by the Booke of Comunicants appeareth	3	4	0
Item of the Company of Ironmongers . . .		2	0
Item of Mr. Hickley from the Inquest . . .		6	0
Item of Mr. Awdley for a free guift 3 April 1613		3	4
	54	19	4
Imprimis. Given to the Poor 3 April 1613, being Easter Eve as by the books appeareth . . .	1	0	0
Item, disbursed for the poor Children according to an order agreed uppon at a Vestry which is added to my former accompt £3 19s. 4d. . . . . Sum total	4	19	4
1614. Itm p . . . . Balance	50	0	0
1614. Itm for the guift of Mr. Edward Bryerwood, Reader of the Astronomy Lecture in Gresham Howse	10	0	0
Itm of Mrs. Olyver for her husband's guift to our Poor	2	0	0
1616. Itm for a runlett of Canary Wyne presented unto my Lord Bishop of Worster, and for the runlett and carriage.	1	16	6
Countess of Pembroke lived here.			
1620. Itm for vi dozen of points to give to the children.		1	6
Allowed for the Audit dinner		15	0
1622. Lecture } but no charge except for No Collection } Clerk 13s 4d. Sexton 6s. 8d.			
1624. Item for opening the grounde att Leathersellers Garden to see if the water offended not the foundation with the viewers of the Church .		7	4

Extracts from Church Wardens' Accounts. 223

		£	s.	d.
1630.	Paid the Bell Founder for changing our great Bell and New Mettell added	7	6	0
1631.	Received for the tithe of our parish and other things belonging to ye parson for one whole yeare endinge at Lady Day	69	8	9
	Paid for ye remainder of yeares of our parsonage (being 4½ yeares) unto Mr. Ball £160. The charges of a journey thither is £4 10s. 9d. the drawing of wrighting £1 3s., and the charges paid for the whole yeare £30 2s. is the somme of	195	15	9
1632.	Received for the tithe of our parish over and above all ordinary charges concerning it . .	37	10	3
	The assessment made by the Committee appointed by the Vestry in St Hellens Parish towards ye repairing of the Church	372	0	0
	The names of the Parishioners which have paide five years Tythes beforehand beginning at Christmas Anno 1632	205	1	0

Collected in free Contributions towards the repairing of our Church, of divers Companies and particular persons as followeth:—

	£	s.	d.			
Out of the Chamber of London for Gresham College	66	13	4			
of the Companie of Mercers in respect of College	66	13	4			
of the East India Companie in respect of Crosbie House . .	50	0	0			
of ye Companie of Merchant Tailors in respect they make so much use of our Church . .	20	0	0			
of ye Companie of Skinners in respect of their Almshouse in our parish	10	0	0			
of ye Companie of Leathersellers in respect their Hall is in our parish	25	0	0			
of Sir Julius Cæsar a free gifte	20	0	0			
of Mr. Thomas Audley his free gifte at 3 several times . . .	18	0	0			
of Mr. Richard coming from East India his free gifte . . .	4	0	0			
of Mrs. Meynon her free gift before her death	5	0	0			
of Mr. Abell Gwilliams his free gift before ye assessment .	2	0	0			
of Mr. Clutterbuck his free gift	4	0	0			
of Mr. Hatlie his free gift . .	1	0	0			
of Mr. John Blunt his free gift	1	2	0	293	8	8

Additional Subscriptions:—

		£	s.	d.
1632. Received from Sir Henry Machin		10	0	0
„ from the East India Company over and above £50 formerly given		50	0	0
„ from the Company of Leathersellers		10	0	0
„ from Mr. John Slany		5	0	0
„ from ye wors^d Companie of Merchants trading to ye East Indies, principall & interest since Novr 1630 in all		399	4	4
„ Daniell Williams for his fine being free from all offices		13	6	8
„ Thomas Hutchin do. do.		13	6	8
„ by the book for the tithe this yeare cleare of ye charge		29	9	5

Repairs:—

	£	s.	d.			
Paid for the New Font & Cover	20	0	0			
to Mr. Boone for curing the laborer that broke his legge in our Church Work	2	0	0			
for 10½ Ells of Canvas for ye Commandments		11	4			
Bricklayers & laborers as apears by Bills	35	0	5			
ye Carpenters for ye roofe & Clock Tower as ℞ Bills	122	0	9			
ye Smith for Iron Work & Nails	35	17	0			
for paving tiles for ye Church	10	9	9			
ye plummer in full	139	9	6			
ye painters in full	78	1	6			
in full for whiting the Church	6	6	8			
ye masons in parte of their demand	299	13	5			
ye masons for Church porch	23	10	9			
ye Joyner	463	9	11			
ye Glass painter	15	16	6			
ye Glazier in part of his work	16	0	0			
for carving as by bills appeareth	10	5	6			
for mending and painting divers tombs	5	0	0			
unto two Men that sett up Queen Elizabeth; tomb that was to be sold		2	0			
ye Smith's bills for all woorke	3	19	2			
for the Clock	21	0	0			
for paveing the Church Yard and Street nere ye Church and for Gravell	7	2	4			
the plaistering of the Church in part	6	6	8	1322	3	2

Year	Entry	£	s	d
1636.	Received of the Right Honble the Earl of Northampton towards ye repairinge of our Church	30	0	0
	Paid Earl of Northampton a years Rent for the Tythe of our Parish	10	0	0
1637.	Received of the Lady Ceaser for Composition for the setting up Sir Julius Ceaser's Tomb. The Reader paid £5 Pr Annum	20	0	0
1638.	Received of several persons for Pew monies 6s. 8d. and 13s. 4d. each			
1643.	Paid for taking down the Cross upon the Belfry		1	6
	Received of Mr. North 200 of lead taken of the Cross on the Belfry		18	8
	Paid for writing the names of those that tooke not the Covenant and carrying it to Westminster.		3	0
1644.	Received for 13^lb of ould brass of Mr. Bromage at 5^d ℔ lb.		5	6
	Paide a Carver for defacing the superstitious inscriptions	1	2	0
	Paide for the Covenant which hangs upp in the Church		1	6
	Paide for a Sunne Dyall and setting it uppon the Church	1	6	8
1647.	Paide severall Ministers to officiate from Mich's 1646 to Mich's 1647 as ℔ Acc^t	50	15	3
	Paid Mr. Barum Lecturer & Subscription Money	20	19	2
	Paid Mr. Barrum for his Ministry from the 20th of 7ber 1647 till the 25 March 1648 is ½ a year and come to	19	0	10
1648.	Paid our Minister Mr. Barrum this Year	80	0	0
1681.	Payd to Mr. Cokayne for curing the Sexton's head		17	0
	No charge for Vine after this period.			
1685.	Payd the Ringers and for a Bonfire & Faggots		6	6
1686.	Payd for a Book Entituled the Bishop of Rochester's History of the Presbiterian's Plot		9	0
1690.	Payd for a Coach to carry the Vestry Table to Doctors Commons		1	0
	Bill for Oyster Feast.			
	Sir John Lawrence lived at Putney.			
	Rev^d Mr. Hesketh's kind gift from the parish ℔ Ann.	6	0	0
1699.	Rate for Repair of Church	120	2	4

1700.		£	s	d
	Poors Rate	121	14	8
	Rents, &c.	99	9	0
	Sacrament	3	15	6
	Burials	15	10	0
	Balance due to Church Warden	19	19	10
		260	9	0

		£	s.	d.
1700.	Arrears of Poors Rate	4	16	5
	Paid for Poor	110	19	5
	Paid for Parish	144	13	2
		260	9	0

1705. Mar. 25. Paid for a Banquet of Confectionary for the Bishop* 3 4

Received upon a Six Months Assessment rated on this parish pursuant to a statute 13-14 Car. 2, for better reliefe of the poor, and an Act of Common Council 29 June 1704 for better putting that Statute in execucon by raising money for a supply towards further employing ye poor of this City and liberties thereof:—

	£	s.	d.			
of Gresham College City and Mercers	1	5	0			
of the Leathersellers Co.	1	10	0			
of Wellcome Roblis & Co.		17	0			
of the East India Warehouse	1	5	0			
of Moses Newnes	1	1	0	5	18	0

Note.—The rest of the Inhabitants of the parish were eased of paying anything to that assessment in respect the parish by agreement in Vestry paid out of their Parish Stock the Quota enacted by the said Act of Comon Council for the Parish to pay.

1707. Collected only of unusefull Members of the Parish for the Corporation Poor:—

	£	s.	d.			
of Gresham College	1	5	0			
of Leathersellers Co.	1	10	0			
Mr. Grosvenor's Meeting House	1	0	0			
Mr. Robinson's Meeting House		16	0			
East India Co.	1	5	0			
Moses Newnes	1	1	0	6	17	0

Received by a quarter of an Ell of Holland remainder of the Linnen bought for the Surplice more than was used 1 8

1709. An assessment made on the Inhabitants by a Pound Rate of Nine pence in the Pound for repairing the Parish Church 177 12 0

---

* "Henry Compton, youngest son of the Earl of Northampton, was translated from the Bishopric of Oxford to that of London, 18th Dec. 1675, and confirmed at Chelsea, 6th Feb. 1675-6. He died at Fulham, 7th July, 1713, aged 81, and was buried in the churchyard there." Le Neve's Fasti, vol. ii. p. 304. Ed. (Hardy) Oxon. 1854.

CHAPTER VIII.

"WORTHIES" CONNECTED WITH ST. HELEN'S.

SIR JOHN CROSBY.

> " 'Tis great pity
> Such a gentleman as my master (for that title
> His being a citizen cannot take from him)
> Hath no male heir to inherit his estate,
> And keep his name alive.
> * * * * *
> Happy were London, if, within her walls,
> She had many such rich men!"—MASSINGER.*

AMONG the many eminent citizens of London whose wealth and extensive dealings when trade was in its infancy contributed to lay the foundation of that commercial pre-eminence for which this kingdom is celebrated, was Sir John Crosby. That his family was ancient and highly respectable is certain, although a silly tradition respecting him was current in the time of Stow,† who says, "I hold it a fable said of him, to be named Crosby, from his being found by a cross." This absurdity is effectually negatived by the following pedigree:—

Johan de Crosbie, King's Clerk in Chancery, *temp.* Edward II.

Sir John Crosbie, *temp.* Edward III., Knight, and Alderman of London.

John Crosby, Esq., called, in a patent of Henry IV., the "King's Servant."

Of the earlier members of the Crosby family. "In the year 1406, the 7th of Henry IV., the said King gave to his servant John Crosby the wardship of Joan, daughter and sole heir to *John Jordaine*, Fishmonger, &c. Stow considers this Crosby to have been the father or grandfather of the before mentioned Sir John Crosby. And in the reign of Edward III., Edward Prince of

---

* "The City Madam," act i. scene 1, and act iv. scene 1.
† Stow's Survey, vol. i. p. 435. Ed. Lond., 1754-5.

Wales, Duke of Cornwall, granted to Thomas Rigby, 'the custody of the Manor of Haneworth, and the advowson of the Church of Haneworth, which was lately Sir John Crosby's,' which he held of the same Prince Edward, the day wherein he died, to have and to hold until the lawful age of John, his son and heir, called John Crosby." This Hanworth is placed on the River Thames, not far from Hampton Court . . . . and was so pleasantly situated, that Henry VIII. delighted in it, saith Camden, "above any other of his Houses."*

The first mention that occurs of John Crosbie in our records is in the will of Henry Lord Scrope, of Masham, who was beheaded at Southampton for being concerned, with Richard, Earl of Cambridge, the King's own cousin, and others, in the plot against Henry V., in 1415, and who left Crosbie "a woollen gown without furs, and one hundred shillings."

In the records at Guildhall we find, under date April, 1466, 7th Edward IV., "In this *Common Council*, John Crosby, Grocer, was elected a Member of Parliament." The names of the four members stand thus:—R. Josselyn, Knight, Alderman; Thomas Urswyk, Recorder; John Ward, Mercer, and John Crosby, Grocer, Commoners. In the same year, in this *Common Hall*, John Crosby, Grocer, was elected one of the auditors of the City and Bridge House." 1468.—9th Edward IV.—In this *Court of Aldermen*, out of four persons named, John Crosby was elected Alderman of Broad-street Ward. He also served the office of Sheriff in 1470; was twice warden of the Grocers' Company, to which he made some considerable bequests in his will,†

---

* Stow's Survey, vol. i. p. 435. See also Camden's Britan., vol. ii. p. 2. Ed. (Gough) Lond. 1789.

† One instance of the distribution of Sir John Crosby's property remains in the Church of Theydon Gernon, in Essex, where there is the following, engraved in Mr. Pegge's Sylloge of Inscriptions from a copy taken by him Oct. 21, 1786. The first line probably began, Pray for the soules of . . . . . which has been studiously erased, as has also been the sum given. It may be read thus:—

* * * *

| Arms of Grocers' Co. | Sir John Crosbie, Knight, late Alderman and grocere of London, and a . . . . of Dame Anne and Annes his wyves of whos godys was gevyn . . . . li towards the makyng of thys steepyll . . . . v. o. que d'ni 1520. | Arms of Crosby. |

and finally, was promoted to the important post of Mayor of the Staple at Calais.

Although Sir John Crosby inherited a liberal patrimony, he early embarked in trade, and by his success considerably augmented his wealth. The extent of his dealings is proved by his intimacy and connexion with the Friscobaldi of Florence, who, with the Medici, were the great bankers and engrossers of the commerce of Europe.

Sir John Crosby appears to have distinguished himself amongst the party attached to the House of York, and was knighted by Edward IV., May 21, 1471, when, as Alderman and Sheriff of London, he, with the Mayor, Aldermen, and other citizens, went out to meet that prince between Shoreditch and Islington on his coming to London. Stow says that he was knighted on the field with twelve Aldermen and the Recorder, for their brave conduct "when Thomas Nevil, the bastard Falconbridge, with a riotous company, set upon this city."*

In the reprint of Heywood's *Edward IV.*, by the Shakspeare Society,† Crosby is represented as the Lord Mayor when Falconbridge, having raised a rebellion, marched on to London, encouraging his forces to restore King Henry (who had been lately deposed) from the Tower. On arriving at the gates of London Bridge, they demand entrance, which is refused by the Lord Mayor and citizens, with the City apprentices, who enact prominent characters on the occasion. Matthew Shore, the goldsmith, is also of the party, and having answered Falconbridge's appeal, is asked his name, and Falconbridge replies, "What! not that Shore that hath the dainty wife? the flow'r of London for her beauty?"

The rebels having been valiantly repulsed, the Mayor addresses the victors:—

> "Ye have bestirred yourselves like good citizens,
> And shown yourselves true subjects to the king.
> You worthily, prentices, bestirr'd yourselves,
> That it did cheer my heart to see your valour."

In the second scene of act iv., at the Mayor's house. Enter

---

* Stow's Survey, vol. ii. p. 222. Ed. Lond. 1754-5. And Chronicle, p. 425. Ed. Lond. 1631.

† First Part, pp. 16, 23, 58. Ed. Lond. 1842.

the Lord Mayor (having been knighted by the King) who soliloquizes:—

> "Ay, marry, Crosby! this befits thee well.
> But some will marvel that, with scarlet gown,
> I wear a gilded rapier by my side."

Jane Shore is represented as officiating as the Lady Mayoress, whereby the King first becomes acquainted with her. The whole play is very interesting, but, unfortunately for the facts, Sir John never served the office of Lord Mayor. Sir John Stockton, one of the Aldermen knighted with Sir John Crosby, was the Lord Mayor at this period.

In the following year a most delicate commission was given to him, in common with Sir John Scott, Knight, Marshall of Calais, Master William Hatclefe, the king's secretary, Dr. John Russell, Archdeacon of Berkshire, and other eminent persons. Their chief ostensible object was to arrange various matters then in abeyance between the Duke of Burgundy (who had married Elizabeth of York, the king's sister) and the King of England, and we presume to form a treaty of alliance against France, which Edward then meditated attacking. From thence they passed to the court of the Duke of Brittany, where, besides concluding a similar treaty, they were, says Stow,* "To have gotten there the two Earls of Pembroke and of Richmond." Had they succeeded in this object, in what very different channels might not the history of this country have run! Soon after the defeat of the Lancastrians at the battle of Tewkesbury, the Earl of Pembroke had fled with his young charge to France. A storm drove his vessel on the coast of Brittany, and the two nobles were detained by Francis, the reigning duke. Edward now claimed them as enemies and fugitive traitors, but in vain; he could get no other assurance than that they should never be allowed to disturb his Government. This was far from satisfactory; hence the secret mission given to Sir John Crosby and his companions, who, by profession of friendship for the exiles, succeeded at last in persuading both them and the duke of the propriety of returning to England. The future conqueror of Bosworth Field was already at St. Malo, on the point of embarkation, when Landois, the minister of the duke, suddenly arrived, and prevented

---

* Stow's Chronicle, pp. 426, 429.

his sailing on various pretexts, till Richmond took the alarm, and fled from the agents of the man who had probably the same fate in store for him that had awaited Henry VI.

Stow,* in describing the magnificent house in Bishopsgate Street known by the name of Crosby Place, says, "It was built by Sir John Crosby, Grocer and Woolman"—in the time of King Edward IV.—" in the place of certain tenements, with their appurtenances, let to him by Alice Ashfeld, Prioress of St. Helen's, and the convent, for the term of 99 years, from the year 1466 to the year 1565, for the annual rent of 11*l*. 6*s*. 8*d*. This house he built of stone and timber, very large and beautiful, and the highest at that time in London." Sir John "died in 1475 : so short a time enjoyed he that large and sumptuous building !" The mansion is described as a residence fit for a prince, and soon after its founder's death was actually inhabited by royalty itself, in the person of the Duke of Gloucester, Lord Protector, afterwards Richard III.

Sir John Crosby was twice married. By his first wife, Anney, he had several children, who are supposed to have died during his lifetime. Mention is, however, made of a daughter, whom he styles Johanna Crosbie, otherwise Talbot, who was living when he made his will, 6th March, 1471, four years before his death, and by which his affection for his first wife appears to have been much greater than for her who survived him. With reference to his widow he says, "And if the said Anne, my wife, hold her not contented or pleased with my bequest, then I will and ordain that all my said bequests to the said Anne, my wife, be utterly void, and that the said Anne have such part only as the law will then give her, without any other manner of favour to be showed to her." He also directs, "My body to be buried in the Chapel of the Holy Ghost, within the parish Church of St. Helen, in the same place where the body of Anney lieth buried, in case it fortune me to decease within the realme of England; and I bequeath to every of the four, five, or six persons of the livery of my craft, that shall bear my body to the church, 6*s*. 8*d*.; and if it fortune me to decease out of the realme of England, then I will that my body be buried in some honest sepulture of Holy Church beyond the sea,

---

* Survey, vol. i. p. 434.

where it shall please Almighty God to provide for me. And if it fortune me to be buried within the Chapel of the Holy Ghost afore rehearsed, then I will that my executors, as soon as they can after my decease, provide an honest tomb of marble, to stand over the bodies of me and the said Anney late my wife, with Scripture, and images of me, my said late wife, and my children, to be made thereon, making-mention of our persons, and of the day and year of my decease, and all other things according to our degree. And if I am buried beyond the sea, I will that my executors provide some tomb of stone in the place where it shall be my fortune to be buried, and one other tomb of stone in the said Chapel of the Holy Ghost, where my wife layeth buried, and that on my tomb be made an image and Scripture, according to my degree, and on her tomb an image and Scripture, making mention of her and our children there buried. And after that my body be buried and my debts paid, then I bequeath to the said high altar of St. Helen's for my offerings restrained or forgotten, if any so have been done, in discharging of my soul, 66*l*. 1*s*. 4*d*.

"I will that all the torches and tapers that shall be occupied about my body the daye of my interment and months mind, be held by poor people without any other candlestick. Every man to pray for me, and to have for his labour 12*d*."

After bequeathing considerable sums to the nuns of St. Helen's, Holywell, Stratford, and Sion, the Friars, Minores, Preachers, and Carmelites, the Hospitals of St. Mary Spittle, Bethlehem, and gaols of London and Southwark, for their prayers and relief, he bequeathed "400 marks sterling" (equal to about 5000*l*. of our day), for a priest of good fame "to say mass and to pray for my soul," and all Christian souls in the Church of St. Helen's, for forty years after my decease, and the said priest, or others succeeding him, during all the time my wife resides in St. Helen's, to be obedient to her in all things lawful and honest, and give his attendance in singing divine service before her at such times as she shall desire him, and if the said priest be found debateful or of unclean life, to be removed by my executors and another chosen." The said obite to be holden every year on the anniversary of his death, and for it he bequeathed 100 marks sterling. The Master, Wardens, and all the Commonalty of the Grocers' Company, to attend the said obite yearly for the said forty years, and to be trustees of the said 500 marks after the decease of his executors. "Also considering the great damages that the prioress of St. Helen's and convent stand in by means of the great duties they owe; of my pure charity and good zeal that I bear toward them, I bequeath Forty Pounds to be applied in diminishing their debts. Also upon the renewing and reforming the said Church 500 marks sterling."

He further directs his executors to do the costs of the glazing, garnishing, and appariatying of the chancel of the parish church of Haneworth, Middlesex, though the cost extend unto 40*l*., or somewhat more; to the repairs of Bishop's Gate and the walls adjoining, 100*l*.; to making a new tower of stone at the south end of London Bridge, 100*l*.; to the repairs of Rochester Bridge, 10*l*.; to the Grocers' Company, two large pots of silver, half-chased, half-gilt, weighing 13lbs. 5oz., troy weight, and desiring the same to remain in the treasury to the use of the Company, and to be occupied in the worship of God, and of the same Commonalty in their Hall, to the intent that the Commonalty might have mind of his soul.

Various legacies are also left to his relations and friends, as well as to his *apprentices* and servants, and in the event of his leaving no child which should attain full age, or marry, &c., he directs the residue of his estate to be disposed of by his executors, for the benefit of his soul, "in deeds of charitie and pittie; in making or buying of books, chalyces, and other apparalment of the church, and to be given to poor churches; in relieving of poor persons; in marriage of poor maidens of good name and fame, to each 40*s*.; to amending of broken bridges, and of foul, noyous, and perilous high waies, and in other deeds of alms."

Thomas Rygby, of London, gentleman, and William Bracebridge (M.P. for London 1478 and 1483), citizen and draper, were appointed executors, with a legacy of 60*l*. each, on condition that they undertook the execution of the will, which was proved in the Prerogative Court of Canterbury, 6th February, 1475.

JOHN LEVENTHORPE.

The Leventhorpes of Hertfordshire were a branch of a most ancient family of that name, formerly seated at Leventhorpe Hall, in the West Riding of Yorkshire, which migrated into

Herts so early as the reign of Richard the Second. The name of John Leventhorpe, of Sabbesford, Esquire, appears in the original roll of the Gentlemen in the county of Herts who could dispend 10*l*. per annum in the time of Henry VI., and also as having served in Parliament as member for the County in the first and third years of Henry V., and first of Henry VI. He bought the manor and lands of Shingey Hall, and was one of the executors named in the will of King Henry V. John, his son and heir, was further enriched by Henry VI. by grants of neighbouring territory to a very great extent, with free warren in all his lands, so that no man might enter into those manors, to hunt and chase in them, or take anything that pertained to the warren, without his licence and good will. By another charter, dated Feb. 14th, 1447, the same king granted to him and his heirs a market to be held on every Wednesday in the week and two fairs in every year, with all things belonging to such markets and fairs. Also licence to enclose 400 acres of land, 40 acres of meadow, and 40 acres of wood, with pales or piles in Sawbridgeworth and Thorley to make a park, and to hold the same imparked to him and his heirs for ever. He died May 31, 1484, leaving a son, Thomas, who had issue, *John Leventhorpe*,* who died in the first year of King Henry VIII., and was buried in St. Helen's Church, the inscription on his tomb describing him as one of the four keepers of the Chamber to King Henry VII. The estates descended in a direct line to Sir John Leventhorpe, who was knighted in 1603, and created a Baronet in 1622, and whose son and heir, Sir Thomas Leventhorpe, became the father of Mrs. Cæsar. Her husband, Charles Cæsar, Esq., being grandson of Sir Julius Cæsar.

SIR WILLIAM HOLLES.

Sir William Holles was born at Stoke about the year 1471. He was made free of the Mercers' Company Sept. 17, 1499, and became Master of the Company in 1538. 21st Henry VIII. was chosen Sheriff of Middlesex, by the Commonalty Aug. 31, 1527, for of the two Sheriffs of London and Middlesex, that for London was then chosen by the Mayor, the other by the Com-

---

* His wife was Jane Clovell, of the county of Essex, descended from the heir of the Lord FitzAucher.

monalty. On the 31st March, 1528, he was elected Alderman of Aldgate Ward, in the room of John Rudston, who chose the ward of Candlewyck Street after the decease of John Kyme, late Alderman there. The inhabitants nominated to the Mayor and Aldermen, Sir John Mylburne, Knt., Sir John Aleyn, Knt., William Hollyes, and William Roch, and they chose William Holyes, as the name is wrote in the register at Guildhall. . . . . He received the honour of Knighthood 25th Henry VIII., and about six years after was elected Lord Mayor of London on St. Edward's Day; which election, entered at large amongst the registers at Guildhall, sets forth, that William Holleis, Mercer, and James Spencer, Vintner, aldermen, were nominated by a great and immense multitude of the Commonalty, and that the Lord Mayor and Aldermen chose the said William Holleis Lord Mayor. During his mayoralty he caused the Moore ditch to be cleansed, which, as Stow observes, " happened in his remembrance, and not long before from the Tower of London to Ealdgate."* At this time also Henry VIII. married the Lady Anne of Cleves, " who was received into London," says Baker, " Jan. 3 (A.D. 1540), by Sir William Hollice, then Lord Mayor, with orations, pageants, and all compliments of State, the greatest that ever had been seen."† Hall saith, " The 4th February next ensuing the King and she came to Westminster by water, accompanied with many nobles and prelates in barges, on whom the Mayor and his brethren in scarlet, and twelve of the chief companies in the City, all in barges garnished with banners, pennons, and targets, richly covered, and replenished with minstrelsy, gave their attendance," &c.‡ And both Hall and Holinshed tell us that, the King issuing forth of the Park at Greenwich to meet the Lady Ann, then arrived at Blackheath, the Barons proceeded first after the King's servants, the youngest first, "and so Sir William Hollis, Knt., Lord Mayor of London, rode with the Lord Par, being youngest Baron."§ Hence may be observed the dignity of the Mayor of London, who out of his own proper jurisdiction was ranked amongst the Barons of England.

Somewhat west of Sir Thomas Gresham's dwelling was another

---

* Stow's Survey, vol. i. p. 13.
† Baker's Chronicle of the Kings of England (Henry VIII.), p. 50. Ed. Lond. 1643. ‡ Hall's Chronicle (Henry VIII.), p. 837. Ed. Lond. 1809.
§ *Id.* p. 834. Holinshed's Chronicles, vol. iii. p. 812. Ed. Lond. 1807-8.

very "fayre house," wherein Sir William Holles kept his mayoralty. Sir Andrew Judd also kept his mayoralty there.

Somewhat more than a year after his mayoralty, and about a year before his death, Sir William Holles made his will whilst yet in perfect health and memory, as follows :—

"In the name of God, Amen, the 25th day of the moneth of December, in the year of our Lord God 1541, and in the 33rd yeare of the Raigne of our most dread Soveraigne Lord Henry VIII. I, Sir William Holles, Knt., and late Lord Mayor of the City of London, whole of mind and of good and perfect remembrance (laud and praise be to Almighty God) make and ordeine this my present testament and last Will concerning the disposition of my movable goods in this wise following :—That is to say, First, I bequeath and commend my soule unto God Almighty, my Maker and Redeemer, to the glorious Virgin Mary his mother, our lady St. Mary, and to all the Holy Company of Heaven ; and my body to be buried in Christian burial (where it shall please God to provide for it) at the discretion of my Executors underwritten; that is to say, of Dame Elizabeth, my well-beloved wife, of Mr. Andrew Judde, Alderman of the City of London, and mine especial friend, Mr. Anthony Bonewise, Merchant, whom I ordein and make my true and lawful executors, And I bequeath unto the said Andrew Judde and Anthony Bonewise for their paynes and labours in that partie to be had, and to accomplish this my present Testament and last Will as hereafter followeth, eyther of them Ten Pounds Sterling. . . . . . . Item. I will that if any Person or Persons what degree he, she, or they shall be, will come after my decease to my Executors, which, upon a credible information by themselves, or true and faithful witness, will or can depose by his or their oathes, how that they have suffered, susteined, or had any hurt or harme, wrong or any losse by me, or my occasion: I desire, will and charge my said executors, that they will make to every such person or persons, due restitution and satisfaction of the same according to right and conscience in that behalfe. And moreover I will and desire my said Executors to give unto certain Aldermen, and unto certain Commoners of the City of London, and to others of my lovers and friendes (whom they shall think best and convenient) Black Gownes : and also to every one of my servants, menservants, and women servants, black gownes, and every of them Five Shillings, over and above their wages. And furthermore, I give and bequeath unto the Mayor and Aldermen of the City of Coventry, and to the Commons of the same £200 Stg. to this intent and purpose hereafter ensuing; that is to say, to make a new Crosse within the said City. . . . . . Also I give and bequeath unto Sir Thomas Moore, my Chaplain, a black gowne and twenty marks in money, to be payd him, or his assigns, in full restitution and recompense of all old reckonings en him and me. And whereas it hath alwayes beene, time out of minde, accustomed and used, that whensoever any freeman within the City of London departes out of this miserable worlde, the goods, moveables and debtes of him or her so departed, ought and hath been alwayes used to be divided and parted into three parties, that is, th' one thirde parte to the wife, the seconde thirde to be equally parted and divided amongst the children, if they were not sufficiently advanced before; and the other thirde parte, for the accomplishment and fulfilling of the deathe's Will. Wherefore know all men unto whom my present will and testament shall come to see, heare, or read, that I the said Sir William Hollis, Knt. hath highly and singularly preferred and set forth my three sonnes in my lifetime: and I have given and assured unto every of them Mannors, Lands, Tenements and Hereditaments, and which of them hath least, cost me fower thousande Marks, and above which I have already given them, and assured them, for the full advancement of them my three sonnes; and for that intent and purpose, that they, nor none of them, should hereafter, make clayme, nor demande any part of goodes, or debtes, nor at any time hereafter, sue, vexe, molest, nor trouble my said executors for no parte nor parcell of my goods, chattels, ne debtes; Forasmuch as I have singularly preferred, set forth, and advanced every of them in my life time, Yet, nevertheless, for the great zeal, love and favour that I beare towards my sonnes, and the unity, peace, and love hereafter to encrease betweene the right good lady their Mother, and them to be had, more and more. Therefore, I will, that the third parte of all my Goods, Chattels and debtes be equally truly and justly parted and divided amongst my sonnes according to the laudable custome of this Honorable City of London, although that they be highly advanced and preferred, as aforesaid. Furthermore I charge and command my said three sonnes, upon my Blessing, that they, and every of them during their lives, one to love another; and in so doing, I doubt not but God himself shall worke in them the world also shall prosper with them. And moreover, I will and heartily desire my trusty and well-beloved wife, and my singular good friends Mr. Andrew Judde and Anthony Bonewise to be good and favorable friendes unto my said sonnes, even as you would I should be to yours, in case I were as ye be now . . . . . Also I give and bequeath unto the Parishioners of St. Helyns, towards the reparation and other Ornaments to the said Church belonging £20 sterling. . . . . . .

"Moreover, I will, that my said executors shall give to certain poor maydens marriages, such parcels of money as they shall think best for the welth of my soule, which I instantly desire them so to do, as they would be done unto. Also I will that my said Executors shall find an honest priest, not beneficed, of good conversation, name, and fame, to sing and say Masse when he shall be disposed within the Church called Thomas Beckkets, or else within the Parish Church where it shall fortune my Body to be buried at the discretion of myn Executors; and other divine service, &c., specially praying for my soule, my wife's soule, and all Christian soules; which priest to serve the term of Twenty years next after my decease, and I will that the said priest shall be always named, and put into the said service by Dame Elizabeth, my wife, she paying for him, for his salary and wages £6 13s. 4d. sterling, at four usual terms in the year, and after her decease the same priest shall always be named and put in by Thomas Hollys and his heirs. . . . . Also, I will, by this present Testament, that my said executors during the term of twenty years after my decease, shall keep and find yearly, within the Parish Church of St. Hellyns, on the day of the month that it shall fortune me to decease, upon the day before, or upon the day next ensuing, a yearly obite or anniversary, solemnly by note for my soule, my wife's soule, and all Christian soules. That is to say, Placebo and Diridge, to be done over evening, and mass of requiem on the morrow then next ensuing. And, I will, that my Executors, during the term of 20 years, shall expend every year, yearly, at every of the said obites, so to be kept 4 marks sterling: that is to say, that the Master of the mistery of the Mercers for the time being, who shall be present at my said Obite shall have 3s. 4d. Item. To every other of the said Wardens of the said Mercers, coming to my said Obite 2s. 0d. Item. To every one of the livery of the said company being at my said Obite 4d. Item. To the Clerk of the said company 12*d*. Item. To the priest that shall sing the Mass of Requiem 10*d*. and to every other priest there being 6*d*. Item. To the Parish Clerk 6*d*. Item. To the Sexton 4*d*. To every child there during service 2*d*. The residue to be dealed amongst poor people, and deeds of alms at the discretion of myn Executors; Also, I will, that my Executors shall deliver every year, during the term of 20 years next after my decease, unto the Fellowship and Company of Mercers £4 sterling, for to have a dinner for their loving assembly together, at my said Obite, or anniversary, there remembering and praying for my soule, Dame Elizabeth my wife's soule, and all Christian soules." . . . . .

"Sir William Holles died at his house in London, Oct. 13, 1542, and was buried at St. Helen's Church, where a becoming Monument was erected and stood in the middle of the North Aisle.*
He married Elizabeth, daughter of —— Scopeham who did not long survive him, dying in London, March 13, 1543. By her Will, dated Feb. 17, 1543, she directs her body to be buried in the same Monument with her Husband in the parish of St. Ellyns. Besides other legacies, she requires her Executors, Andrew Judde, Alderman and her brother Thomas Scopeham to erect Six Almshouses for men or women in the said parish of St. Elyns and endow them with £10 ⅌ ann. out of which every one of the Almspeople to receive 7*d*. weekly, and the remainder to buy them coals. These Almshouses were accordingly erected and attributed to Sir Andrew Judde.†

"Sir William Holles had by her three Sons and a daughter Anne, who died before her parents, having been married to John Whiddon of the Inner Temple who in 1st Edward VI. was the first of the seven sergeants who kept their feast in Lincoln's Inn and was made a Judge of the King's Bench. It is said that he was the first Judge who did ride to Westminster Hall on a Horse the Judges before his time riding on Mules.

"Sir Thomas, the eldest son, was by his lavishness and imprudence, the ruin of his family. His father left him a fair estate, yet he lived to spend it all and die in prison. His taking a wife from Court was part of his undoing. He married Catherine Payne who was Maid of Honour to Queen Catharine first Wife to Henry VIII. He had the honour of Knighthood conferred on him

---

* No vestige of this **monument remains**. † See pp. 249 *et seqq*.

at the same time with his brother William, viz., two days after the Coronation of King Edward VI., at which he is said to have been present with threescore and ten followers.

"Sir William, the second son, married Anne, eldest daughter of John Densel of Densel, in the county of Cornwall, and after her death he married Jane, daughter of Sir Richard Grosvenor, Knt., whom he also survived. He was by Edward VI. made one of the Knights of the Carpet, with several others of great note, February 22nd, two days after the coronation; all those summoned being to be made Knights of the Bath, but for want of time the ceremonies were omitted. He was elected one of the knights for the county of Nottingham, and was twice High Sheriff. His daughter he married to Walter Stanley, a cadet of the illustrious house of the Earls of Derby. George, Lord Clifford, that brave and active Earl of Cumberland, made application to have her for his wife, but could not gain her father's consent; and when his friends endeavoured to persuade him, stating what an advancement it would be for his daughter, he answered 'Sake of God' (his usual mode), 'I do not like to stand with my cap in my hand to my son-in-law; I will see her married to an honest gentleman, with whom I may have friendship and conversation,' which accordingly he did to Mr. Stanley, January 20th, 1578. He was usually styled the 'good Sir William;' he began his Christmas at Allhallow tide, and continued it until Candlemas, during which time any man was permitted to stay three days without being asked whence he came, or what he was. And the proportion which he allowed every day during the twelve days of Christmas was a fat ox, with sheep, and other provision answerable. Besides, it was certain with him never to sit down to dinner till after one of the clock, and being asked why he always dined so late, he answered for aught he knew, there might be a friend coming twenty miles to dine with him, and he would be loth that he should lose his labour. He died January 18th, 1590, and was succeeded by his grandson, who was created Baron Houghton and Earl of Clare, and married Anne, only daughter of Sir Thomas Stanhope, July 9th, 1616. His grandson, having married the daughter of the Duke of Newcastle, who left him his whole estate, was advanced by King William III. by the title of John Holles, Duke of Newcastle and Marquis of Clare."

RICHARD WILLIAMS.

Richard Williams, *alias* Cromwell, great grandfather to the protector, Oliver Cromwell, was the eldest son of Morgan Williams, gentleman of the Privy Chamber to Henry VII. His mother was sister to Thomas Cromwell, afterwards Earl of Essex, and Vicar-General, the great favourite of Henry VIII. Leland, in describing the county of Glamorgan,* says :—" In the south side of this hill, six miles from the mouth of the Remny, was born, Richard Williams, alias Cromwell, in the paroche of Llan-Ishn." He was introduced by his uncle, Thomas Cromwell, to the king, whose favour he soon obtained by his active spirit and various accomplishments. His preferment was forwarded by the zeal with which he engaged in the suppression of a dangerous insurrection that began in Lincolnshire, when the king's enemies first evinced a determined intention to abrogate the institutions of the Papacy. In the following year, on the passing of the Act for the Dissolution of the Monasteries, &c., he was appointed one of the visitors of the religious houses, and very quickly obtained a full share in the rich harvest of abbey lands, which were divided among the promoters of the Reformation. Previously to this he had superadded the name of Cromwell to his own, in honour of his uncle, then Earl of Essex, and on the recommendation of the king, who had strongly enjoined the adoption of family names to all his Welsh subjects, in preference to the mode which then prevailed. In March, 1537-8, he had a grant of the nunnery of Hinchinbrook, near Huntingdon,† with its appurtenances. The other grants in this county included the Monastery of Saltry-Judith, lands at Eynsbury, &c., belonging to the late dissolved chantry of Swasy, in Cambridgeshire. The site of the rich abbey of Ramsey, and the several meres and lakes belonging to it, and generally its possessions in this country, the annual revenue of which was estimated at 1987*l.* 15*s.* 3*d.*, St. Mary's Monastery, in Huntingdon, St. Neot's Monastery, and also the abbey of Grey Friars, at Yarmouth; the priory of St. Helen's, Bishopsgate, the castles, lordships, and manors of Manerberc and Penalle, both in Pembrokeshire, and by exchange for

---

* Leland's Itinerary, vol. iv. p. 38. Ed. Oxon. 1769.

† See Noble's Memoirs of the Protectoral House of Cromwell, pp. 5-9. Ed. Lond. 1787.

other lands, the Abbey of Neath, in Glamorganshire. The annual value of these estates was at that time estimated at 30,000*l*. It is expressed in the grant, that " it passed in consideration of his good service and the payment of 4963*l*. 4*s*. 2*d*., to be held in capite by knight's service."

The bravery and prowess which he displayed, at a great triumph at jousting, at Westminster, in 1540, which jousts had been proclaimed in France, Flanders, Scotland, and Spain, for all comers that would, against the challengers of England, still further advanced him in the king's favour. Stow says,* " The challengers came into the lists that day richly apparelled, and their horses trapped all in white velvet .... and all their servants in white doublets and hosen, cut all in the Burgonian fashion; and there came to joust against them forty-six knights all richly apparelled .... and after the said jousts were done, the said challengers rode to Durham-place, where they kept open household. The 2nd May, Anthony Kingston and Richard Cromwell were made knights. On the 6th May, the said challengers broke up their household. In the which time of their housekeeping they had not only feasted the king and queen, with their ladies and the whole Court, but, on the Tuesday in Rogation week, they feasted all the knights and burgesses of the Commons House in the Parliament; and on the morrow after, they had the Mayor of London, the Aldermen, and all their wives to dinner." Henry was so much delighted with the skill and courage displayed by Richard Cromwell, that, according to a family tradition, preserved by Fuller,† he exclaimed, " Formerly thou wast my Dick, but hereafter shalt be my diamond, and thereat let fall his diamond ring unto him. In avowance whereof, these Cromwells have ever since given for their crest a lion holding a diamond ring in his fore-paw."

In 1541 Sir Richard was appointed High Sheriff for the counties of Huntingdon and Cambridge. He was also member for Huntingdonshire, in the Parliament which met in January, 1542. In this year he was also made one of the Gentlemen of the Privy Chamber. In 1543 he was appointed " Capteine of the Horssemen,"‡ in the expedition sent into France, under Sir John

---

* Stow's Chronicle, vol. i. pp. 579-80.
† Fuller's Church History, Book VI. p. 370. Ed. Lond. 1655.
‡ Holinshed's Chronicle, vol. iii. p. 832. Ed. Lond. 1807-8.

Wallop and Sir Thomas Seymour, which consisted of 6000 men, "right hardie and valiant," including the flower of the English chivalry. The following year he was made Constable of Berkley Castle, Steward of the Lordship of Archinfield, with the Constableship of Castle of Goderyche, in the march of Wales, with the power of appointing the Master-Sergeant and Porter belonging to those offices, during the nonage of the Earl of Shrewsbury. Sir Richard Cromwell married in 1518, Frances, daughter of Sir Thomas Mirfyn, Lord Mayor of London. Lady Frances died at Stepney, and was there buried, Feb. 20th, 1533, leaving two sons, Henry, the eldest and heir, and Francis, who was one of the knights for the county of Huntingdon, 15th Elizabeth. By his will, dated 25th June, 1545, Sir Andrew Judde, who had also married a daughter of Sir Thomas Mirfyn, was appointed one of the executors. He there directs that his body shall be buried in the place where he should die. The will was proved 28th Nov. 1546.

Sir Thomas Mirfyn was a native of Ely, in Cambridge, member of the Skinners' Company, Sheriff in 1511, and Lord Mayor in 1518. Stow observes, "that after his time it was usual to knight the Lord Mayor when elected."*

The energetic action taken by Thomas Cromwell in the progress of the Reformation may be judged by the following extract from Stow's Chronicle, September, 1538.† "Thomas Cromwell, Lord Privy Seal, Vicegerent, to the King's Highness, sent forth Injunctions to all bishops and curates throughout the realm, charging them to see that in every parish church, the Bible, of the largest volume, printed in English, were placed, for all men to read on, and that a book of register were also provided and kept in every parish church, wherein shall be written every wedding, christening, and burying within the same parish for ever." Arms: Sa. a lion rampant, argent. The crest, a demi-lion, rampant, double tailed, argent. In his dexter gamb a gem ring, or.

THOMAS BENOLTE.

Thomas Benolte, Clarenceux King at Arms, appears to have been of foreign extraction. At the time of his appointment he was in Spain to proclaim war against Charles V. At his return he

---

* Stow's Survey, vol. ii. p. 224.   † Pp. 574-5.

consented that his commission should be the same as his predecessor had accepted, empowering Garter King at Arms jointly with him to grant arms, and do other things belonging to his province.* In 1516 he was sent to Scotland to confirm the truce for one year. It is stated that he was placed there as a spy upon the conduct of the Regent Albany. King Henry sent him in 1519 to the Courts of France, Burgundy, Germany, and Italy to proclaim the jousts intended to be solemnized by the Kings of England and France, between Ardres and Guisnes, which he attended in 1520. The following year he went to Scotland, and in 1522 was sent thither again, to accuse the Duke of Albany, Regent of that kingdom, of a design to marry the Queen Mother and usurp the Crown, and to defy him if he did not immediately leave the realm. He was joined with Sir Francis Pointz, Knt., in a commission to go to Spain in 1526, to demand half the ransom which the Emperor Charles V. had received for setting Francis I. of France at liberty, whom the Spanish General had taken prisoner at the Battle of Pavia; and to demand that one of the two sons of that monarch pledged as hostages for the payment, should be sent to England. In the following year he went with Guienne, King at Arms for France, to defy and carry the lie to the Emperor and bid him combat. They found the Court at Burgos, and having obtained leave of audience, were admitted to the presence of the Emperor, who was surrounded with his princes and nobles, at about nine o'clock in the morning of January 27th. They entered bareheaded, with tabards hanging upon their right arms. Having permission to deliver their message, with assurance of safe conduct to the confines of France, Clarenceux defied his Majesty, in the name of his Royal Master, by sea and land, and delivered to him the lie in writing, signed Clarenceux, King at Arms, and having received the Emperor's answer to the alleged provocation of having arrested and detained the Pope and the Sacred College of Cardinals, took his tabard and put it on his body. The same ceremonies were observed by Guienne, who defied the Emperor in his sovereign's name. On his return to

---

* The earliest commission known for an Heraldic Visitation was that given to Benolte in 1528-9, empowering him to visit the counties of Gloucester, Worcester, Oxford, Wilts, Berks, and Stafford.—Coll. of Arms, Appendix, xxi.

England Clarenceux was very near suffering undeserved disgrace, the King being exasperated at his declaring war, and the Council threw all the blame upon him. In this dilemma he went to Hampton Court, and by the friendship of Sir Nicholas Carew had a private audience of his Majesty, and producing his instructions, signed by Cardinal Wolsey, exculpated himself, the King properly transferring his indignation from him to his Minister.

In the year 1529 Henry gave him a new commission, under the Great Seal, inhibiting Garter and all others from interfering in granting arms in his province. He was deservedly a favourite with this monarch, who in his ninth year gave him a grant of the bailiwick of St. Botolph and the duty arising from weights for the term of his natural life, and in his thirteenth year, conferred upon him the important office of receiver of all profits belonging to the honours and castles, appointed to pay the wages of all captains, officers and soldiers in the town of Berwick and in several other places, and likewise gave him the profits and revenues of the town of Berwick. Some of his services abroad have been noticed, but it appears probable that he was engaged in many others, as he told Sir Thomas Wriothesley, that he spent more time abroad than at home. He died in 1534,* and was buried in St. Helen's Church under the effigies of himself and his two wives, one of whom was Mary, daughter of Lawrence Richards *alias* Fermour, of Minster Lovel, in Oxfordshire, Esquire, ancestor of the Earls of Pomfret, by whom he had two daughters, Eleanor, married to —— Jones, of Caerleon, in Monmouthshire; and Ann, who had two husbands, Sir John Radcliffe and Richard Buckland. Mr. Benolte's other wife is not mentioned.

ANTONIO BONVISI.

Antonio Bonvisi, an Italian gentleman, born at Lucca, resided many years in London. He came to England about 1505. The Bonvisi family, from which many Cardinals and other distinguished personages had proceeded, were, in fact, very famous in England at this period, and seem to have been friends of the Gresham family, with whom they were at different times associated

---

* In the partition fees is 10*l*. at St. George's Day, 1534, "Mr. Clarenceux Thomas Benolte absent, seke, and dyed the 8th of Maie, next ensuing, on whose soule God have mercie."

in public business. Antonio Bonvisi, however, far excelled his relatives, both in personal endowments and fortuitous advantages. In 1542 Bonvisi bought Crosby Place of Sir Thomas More, and had it afterwards bestowed on him by Henry VIII.,* and resided there for many years. He will be remembered with interest for the extraordinary affection borne him by Sir Thomas More. The latter, during his confinement in the Tower, a short time previous to his execution, being deprived of the use of writing materials, made shift with a coal to unburthen his heart to Bonvisi, and sent him a Latin epistle full of tender eloquence. He is said to have assisted Sir Thomas More with many conveniences while he was a prisoner. He afterwards retired to Louvain—having been excepted out of the general pardon of Edward VI., A.D. 1552—where his house was open to all the English that resorted thither, in the beginning of Queen Elizabeth's reign.

NICHOLAS HARPSFIELD.†

Nicholas Harpsfield, brother to Dr. John Harpsfield, Bishop Bonner's chaplain, was first educated in Winchester School, and thence sent to New College, Oxford, where he was admitted Fellow in 1536. Having chiefly distinguished himself in the Canon Law, in 1544 he was chosen Principal of an ancient house of civilians called Whitehall, upon the site whereof Jesus College was afterwards erected. In 1546 he was made Royal Professor of Greek, and in 1553, the first year of Queen Mary, having taken the degree of Doctor of Law, had considerable practice in the Court of Arches. In 1554 he was made Archdeacon of Canterbury, in the place of Edmund Cranmer, who was deprived on account of his marriage, and took a very prominent part in the trial of Archbishop Cranmer at Oxford, in 1555. When Queen Elizabeth obtained the crown, he was one of the divines called upon to defend the Papist cause in a conference; and afterwards, refusing to submit to the Queen's injunctions, he was deprived of his preferments and committed to the Tower, where he remained above twenty years, and died in 1583. He spent the time of his confinement to the benefit of his own party, and his life was in

---

* See Stow's Survey, vol. i. p. 435.

† See Strype's Annals of the Reformation, vol. i. pp. 139, 40; vol. iv. pp. 600, 607. Memorials of Archbishop Cranmer, pp. 24, 472. Life of Archbishop Parker, vol. i. p. 103. Ed. Oxon. 1812-28.

accordance with his character. He was an excellent Grecian, poet, and historian.

SIR ANDREW JUDDE.

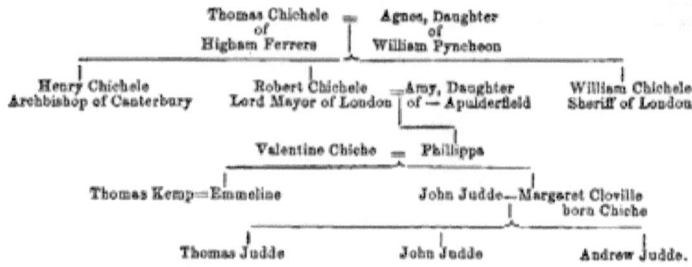

Sir Andrew Judde, Knight, was born at Tunbridge, in Kent. His ancestors are stated to have been returned by the Commissioners in the reign of Henry VI. among the principal gentry flourishing in that county in 1434. Sir Andrew inherited from his father some considerable estates between Tunbridge Town and Tunbridge Wells. His mother was a member of a Kentish family (Chiche) of great antiquity. She was twice married. Her first husband was Henry Colville, Esq. of Colville Hall, in Essex—a person of note and large property in that county. The Chiches were seated at Goodneston, near Faversham, in Kent. Thomas Chiche is mentioned in Philpot's Survey as being a great benefactor to the Church of St. Mary Bredin, in Canterbury. His name, effigies, and coat of arms are still to be seen in stonework. He was bailiff of Canterbury (the same officer as mayor at present) in 1259. His grandson was Sheriff of Kent in the 15th year of Richard II., and was grandfather of Valentine Chiche, who married Phillippa, daughter and heiress of Sir Robert Chichele, next brother of Henry Chichele, Archbishop of Canterbury, the munificent founder of All Souls' College, Oxford. He was "Lord Mayor of London, both in the years 1411 and 1421."*

Of Sir Andrew Judde's two brothers nothing is known, except that Thomas was a Fellow of All Souls' College. It is probable that the family is extinct in the male line, as from the fact of all the kin of the founder of All Souls being, until the last few years, entitled to the very desirable fellowships of that College, claims must in recent times have been made to them by some branches of it (if any had existed), which, however remote, must have been

---

* See Hasted's History of Kent, vol. iii. p. 814.

allowed, and none appear to have been preferred by any persons of the name of Judde.

Being destined to commercial life, Sir Andrew was in early youth sent to London, where he acquired a splendid fortune by a most extensive trade in furs—an article at that time in great request. He served the office of Sheriff of London in 1544, and of Lord Mayor in 1550, during which he displayed a princely magnificence and hospitality at his house in Bishopsgate Street, situated, according to Stow, "somewhat to the west of Sir Thomas Gresham's."* At this period the sweating sickness visited England for the last time, and carried off great numbers of persons of all ranks. During his Mayoralty, also, in consideration of the sum of 647*l*. 2*s*. 1*d*., the City obtained a charter, by which they became entitled to the manor, &c., of Southwark, and in consideration of 500 marks, the assize of bread, wine, beer, and ale, and a fair for three days; also the office of Coroner and Clerk of the Market were for ever vested in the Lord Mayor for the time being.

The necessities of Edward VI. having compelled him to borrow considerable sums of money from Anthony Fugger and Nephews, of Antwerp, the Lord Mayor and Corporation were joined as collateral security; and in King Edward's Book of Warrants there is a recognisance granted to Sir Andrew Judde, Mayor of London and Commonalty of the same, that the King shall discharge them, their successors, lands, possessions, and goods whatsoever, as well beyond the seas, as on this side, for the payment of certain sums of money they stood bound for, to Anthony Fugger and Nephews, dated April, 1551, to be paid at Antwerp.†

Sir Andrew was greatly in favour with their Majesties Philip and Mary, particularly for his spirited conduct during Wyatt's rebellion. Being Lord Deputy and Mayor of the Staple of Calais,‡ he received Philip when he passed over to that place September 4, 1555, and on that occasion presented his Majesty with a purse containing a thousand marks in gold—a most liberal offering for those times from an individual. Philip lodged that night at the Staple Inn, at Calais, and set out the next morning to visit his father, the Emperor Charles V., who then kept his Court at Brussels. So pleased was his Majesty with his reception at Calais

---

* The same house "wherein Sir William Holles kept his Mayoralty." See Stow's Survey, vol. i. p. 435.

† See Strype's Mem. Eccl., vol. ii. pt. 2, p. 242.   ‡ See Appendix.

and the liberality of Sir Andrew Judde, that, previously to his departure, he gave a thousand crowns to the soldiers of that place, and displayed every mark of respect for the pious founder of Tunbridge School, the worthy Skinner of London.*

Sir Andrew died September 4, 1558, and was buried with great pomp in the church of St. Helen's. His funeral was adorned with twelve escutcheons and other heraldic ornaments of the fashion of that day. A great number of poor men in new mourning gowns attended the procession, and two heralds, deputed by the Earl Marshal, preceded the corpse.

Sir Andrew lived universally esteemed and died equally lamented. Among many things recorded to his honour, it is mentioned that the good Sir Thomas Whyte—for so he was universally named—a Lord Mayor of London and founder of St. John's College, Oxford, loved him. In the statutes of St. John's College Sir Thomas Whyte expressly says, " I give one of my Fellowships for ever to Sir Andrew Judde's newly-erected School at Tunbridge. —Propter eximium amorem in Andream Judde."

Sir Andrew is styled in the old documents which have recorded his history, Citizen Skinner, and Merchant of Muscovy. The trade to Muscovy for furs had then been recently commenced, and had become the source of great emolument to the merchants of London in consequence of an exclusive patent obtained by Queen Mary from the Czar, for the whole trade to Muscovy, to which country the communication had been lately opened by the discovery of the passage to Archangel.

There is reason to believe that in building the Alms Houses in Great St. Helen's,† Sir Andrew acted only as the Executor of

---

* See Holinshed's *Chronicles*, vol. iv. p. 80.

† SIR ANDREW JUDDE'S ALMS-HOUSES:
Great St. Helen's, Bishopsgate Street Within.

" In the *Historical Collections of the Noble Families of Cavendishe, Holles, Vere, Harley, and Ogle*, Ed. Lond. 1752, folio, compiled by Arthur Collins, there is a passage denying that this charitable establishment was in reality founded by the benevolent and magnificent Citizen whose name it uniformly bears. Its original design and endowment are there attributed to the testamentary directions and bequests of Elizabeth, daughter of John, or Thomas Scopeham, and wife of Sir William Hollys, of St. Helen's, Alderman and Mercer,[1] who died March 13th, 1543, and whose last Will is dated Feb-

[1] " The Sir William Hollys was the ancestor of the noble family of Holles, Dukes of Newcastle. He was Sheriff of London in the 19th Year of

Dame Elizabeth Hollys, who died in 1554, and who was his cousin and the widow of Sir William Hollys, Lord Mayor of London. She left sufficient funds to build the Alms Houses and to endow them. By his Will, dated Sept. 2, 1558, a short time only before

---

ruary 17th, in the same year, and the Probate March 28th, 1544.[1] 'She therein orders,' says Collins, page 33, 'her body to be buried in the same monument with that of her husband, Sir William Hollys, in the Parish of St. Ellyn's, London. She bequeaths, beside other legacies already mentioned, to her brother, Thomas Scopeham; 100 marks. To Joan Wedon, her granddaughter, 50*l.*; and requires her Executors, Andrew Judde, Alderman of London,[2] and her brother, Thomas Scopeham, to erect six Alms-houses, for men or women, in the said Parish of St. Elyn's, and endow them with x lib. per annum; out of which every one of the Alms-people to receive 7d. weekly, and the remainder to buy them coals. Which alms-houses were accordingly erected; yet Stow and others[3] attribute the work wholly to Sir Andrew Judde, not mentioning this pious lady who was the true founder of them. But it appears clearly, by her Will, that she was the foundress of six alms-houses, which, perhaps, the dishonesty of Sir Andrew Judde hath defrauded her the honour of; our histories ascribing them only to himself. However, Dugdale in his *Warwickshire*,[4] after giving his relation of Coventry-Cross, hath these words: 'And having thus taken notice of his magnificence in

---

Henry VIII., 1527; was knighted in the 25th of the same Sovereign, 1533-34; was elected Mayor of London on St. Edward's day, in the 31st Year of the same, Oct. 13th, 1540; and died in October, 1542, and was buried in St. Helen's. The beautiful Cross of Cross-Cheaping at Coventry, was erected at the sole expence of Sir William Hollys, and was begun in the 33rd Year of Henry VIII., 1541, and finished in his 36th, 1544; as recorded in a MS. Chronicle of Mayors belonging to the Corporation, cited by Dugdale in his Antiquities of Warwickshire, p. 143. Ed. Lond. 1730. By the Will of Sir William Hollys [see above, pp. 236-9, where the references to St. Helen's are only noticed], dated Dec. 25th, 33rd Henry VIII., and proved Dec. 18th, 1542, registered in the Prerogative Office, Spert, Quire 14, the sum of 200*l.* was also bequeathed to the Mayor and Aldermen of Coventry, to make a new Cross: of which 20*l.*, in ready money, had been delivered to Mr. Warren, Draper, in that City, on the preceding 24th August; 70*l.* to Mr. Over, by the hands of — Salt, Sir William's Bailiff of Yoxall; and the remaining 110*l.* were to be paid to the Corporation within one year after the Testator's decease.

[1] "Register in the Prerogative Office, Pynnyng, Quire 5.

[2] "Sir Andrew Judde had been also Executor to the above mentioned Sir William Hollys. See Sir N. H. Nicolas' Testamenta Vetusta, vol. ii. p. 710. Ed. Lond. 1826. They had likewise held their Mayoralty in the same 'fair house' on the West side of Gresham College. See Stow's Survey, vol. i. p. 435. Ed. Lond. 1754.

[3] "Survey of London, vol. i. p. 435.

[4] "Antiquities of Warwickshire, p. 145. Ed. Lond. 1730.

he died, he directed that the Master and Wardens of the Skinners' Company should for ever, weekly, pay unto the six poor Almsmen inhabiting in his Alms House within the close of St. Helen's, for their relief, four shillings, that is to say, to each of them Eight Pence

erecting so noble a monument, I hope the mention of his lady's charity, though the poor of London were the object thereof, will not be thought impertinent, considering that it is not elsewere taken notice of. Which was, that, by her testament Six Alms-houses, &c., as before specified, were erected in St. Hellen's Parish, by Andrew Judde, Alderman of London, &c. Howbeit it hath hitherto not been publicly known that she was the foundress; forasmuch as Stow and others do attribute the work wholly to the same Sir Andrew Judde, passing by this pious lady without any memorial for the same.'[1]

"It is generally stated that Sir Andrew Judde established these Almshouses and his celebrated Free-School at Tunbridge, under the authority of the same Letters-patent, dated May 16th, in the 7th Year of Edward VI., 1553; but, independently that such an instrument was probably not required for the foundation in St. Helen's, the record of the original license for that School in the Rolls Chapel, contains no reference to the former charity. Whether Sir Andrew were the actual founder of this establishment or not, it is evident, by the ensuing extract from his Will, that he considered himself as such; and that he at least augmented the original endowment of the members, and vested the funds and government in the Company of Skinners of London. This instrument is dated September 2nd, 1558, and was proved the following October 15th; and is recorded in the register of the Prerogative Office, 58 Noodes, Quire 22.

"'Also I will that the said Master and Wardens, for the time being, shall for ever weekly pay, or cause to be paid, unto the Six poor Alms-men inhabitants in *my Alms-Houses within the Close of St. Helen's* aforesaid, for their relief, 4s.; that is to say, to every one of them 8d., weekly: and I will the

---

[1] In the account of the Charitable foundations belonging to the Skinners' Company, contained in the Eighth Report of the Commission appointed to enquire concerning Charities, page 359, it is stated that "it appears that there are Alms-houses in the Parish of St. Helen, *which are called Sir Andrew Judde's.*" In Little St. Helen's, Bishopsgate Street, on the site of which the present St. Helen's Place is erected, there also stood seven Alms-houses for poor Widows of Members of the Company of Leathersellers, the original institutor of which appeared formerly to be in as much obscurity as that of the present establishment; as Edward Hatton in his New View of London, vol. ii. p. 746, Ed. Lond. 1708, says, "the founder's name the clerks think fit to conceal, for some reasons, I suppose, best known to themselves." The Alms-houses, however, were endowed out of a donation made to the Company for that purpose, called "Hasilwood's Gift" mentioned in the Will of John Hasilwood, dated Jan. 16th, 1544, amounting to 300*l.* sterling, a silver bason and ewer, valued at 20 marks (13*l.* 6s. 8d.), a cup valued at 6*l.*, and 11¾ cwt. of lead. Farther Report (Tenth) of the Commissioners appointed to enquire concerning Charities, dated 28th June, 1823. Page 242.

weekly, and that the same be paid every Sunday by the Renter Warden of the said Company, who was to have for his pains Ten Shillings yearly. The Alms Houses consist of two apartments for each of six old men who receive the above allowance quarterly,

---

same to be paid every Sunday in the year, by the hands of the Rent-Warden of the said Company of Skynners for the time being. And I will that the said Rent-Warden for his pains to be taken in and about the payment of the said Six Alms-men, as is aforesaid, shall have yearly out of the rents and profits of the premises 10s. And farther I will that the Rent-Warden of the said Company of Skynners, shall bestow yearly out of the rents and profits of the said premises 25s. 4d. upon Coals; which Coals so bought, I will shall be yearly distributed and divided, by the said Rent-Warden, to and amongst the said Six Alms-men, for their farther relief and comfort. And I will the residue of all the rents, issues, and profits, yearly coming and growing of the said messuages, tenements, lands, gardens, and other the premises bequeathed to the said Master and Wardens, shall be employed by the said Master and Wardens for the time being, upon the needful reparations of the messuage or tenements aforesaid; and the overplus thereof remaining I will shall be to the use and behoof of the said Company of Skynners to order and dispose at their wills and pleasures.'

"As there is not any distinction between the property left for the support of the Tunbridge School and that intended for these Alms-houses,—a description of the whole as given in another part of the same Testament, will be found in the notices of the life and principal charitable establishment of Sir Andrew Judde, attached to the Engraving of his Monument in St. Helen's Church . . . . . Forty years after his decease the Alms-houses in St. Helen's received an additional endowment by the Will of Alice, his only surviving daughter and heiress, who was married to Thomas Smythe, Esq., of Westenhanger in Kent, Farmer of the Customs under the Queens Mary and Elizabeth. That instrument is dated July 10th, 1592, and was proved May 12th, 1598; it is recorded in the register of the Prerogative Office, 42 Lewyn, and the passage relating to this establishment is as follows:—

"'Item. I will that of the first money that afterward shall come to the hands of my Executors, that they do bestow, with all convenient expedition, so much upon the purchase of lands, as will buy to the value of 15l. per annum, at the least, of estate of inheritance in fee-simple; which I will to be conveyed and assured to the Company or Corporation of the Skinners of London, and their successors, for this intent: That after such assuring shall be passed to the same Corporation, whom I put in trust for it, I will that of the said 15l. per annum, to be purchased as aforesaid, there shall be bestowed and given to them the sum of ten pounds and eight shillings per annum, to the increasing of the pensions of the *Five poor Alms-houses in Great St. Helen's founded by Sir Andrew Judde, my Father;*[1] to wit, to every such

---

[1] "In Stow's abstract of this Will given in Strype's edition of the Survey of London, vol. i. p. 435, it is stated that the bequest was 'for

amounting to Eight Shillings and Eight Pence per Quarter, and in addition they were also to receive at the same time another sum of Eight Shillings and Eight Pence each, being a donation to them under the Will of his daughter, Mrs. Alice Smythe, dated July 10, 1592.

By a resolution of the Court of Assistants, July 23, 1730, the Company added to the above donations a gift of Twenty-Four

---

house eight pence a week. Item. Moreover out of the said 15*l*. per annum of lands to be purchased, I will to be given the sum of thirty and six shillings per annum for the relief of three poor women in the Parish of All Saints in Lombard Street, by twelve pence a piece, every month to be paid unto them. And for that purpose the Church Wardens of the same Parish for the time being to call for it of the Wardens of the Corporation aforesaid. Item. More out of the said 15*l*. per annum, I will that there be the sum of twenty and four shillings per annum paid by the Wardens of the said Corporation to the Church-Wardens, for the time being, of the Parish Church called Gabriel Fen Church, in London, to be bestowed upon two poor women of the same Parish, having most need, by twelve pence a month to each of them; and the rest and residue of the said 15*l*. per annum I will shall be bestowed by the Wardens of the Corporation aforesaid, to and among the poor of the said Corporation.'

"In the statement relating to this Charity given by the Skinners' Company in answer to the enquiries of the Parliament Commissioners, it is observed concerning the above bequest, that 'there is nothing in the books of the Company to show that any such purchase or conveyance was ever made, as directed by the Will of Alice Smith, nor does it appear that any annual receipt of a sum of 15*l*. is distinctly applied as Mrs. Alice Smith's donation; but the several payments as directed by the Will of Mrs. Alice Smith, are, in fact, made by the Company. They pay annually the sum of 1*l*. 16*s*. to the Churchwardens of the Parish of All Saints, who receive the same at Skinners' Hall; and at the same time and place the other sum of 24*s*. given by the Will to the Parish of St. Gabriel, is paid to the Church-wardens of that Parish.'[1] The present benefactions of this charity as related in the same Report, are stated to be 8*s*. 8*d*. per quarter, to each pensioner, in conformity to the Will of Sir Andrew Judde; and 8*s*. 8*d*. paid at the same time under the Testament of Alice Smith. 'By a resolution of the Court of Assistants,' continues the same authority, 'on the 23rd July, 1730, the Company added to the above donations a gift of 24*l*. per annum, out of their own funds; and another of 54*l*. 12*s*. per annum, was resolved to be given to the Alms-house, by an order of Court, dated 20th April, 1792, being

---

the augmenting of the pensions of certain poor, inhabiting in *eight* Alms-houses erected by Sir Andrew Jud, Knt., her father.'

[1] "Farther Report (Eighth) of the Commissioners for enquiring concerning Charities, dated 13th July, 1822 : City of London, Chartered Companies : Skinners. Pages 358, 359.

per Annum out of their own funds; and another addition of Fifty-Four Pounds Twelve Shillings per Annum was resolved to be given to the Alms House by an order of Court dated April 20, 1792, making the total yearly amount 99*l*. 8*s*., but the money given by the Company is understood to depend entirely on their own pleasure.

---

together 78*l*. 12*s*., and making the amount of the total yearly sum enjoyed by the alms-people 99*l*. 8*s*.; but the money given by the Company out of their own purse is understood to depend entirely on their own pleasure. The Company also take the repairs upon themselves, the expense of which is defrayed out of their own funds.' In satisfaction of the sum of 25*s*. 4*d*. directed by Sir Andrew Judde's Will to be laid out in coals, 'the Company give one chaldron of coals to each alms-man, annually; which, of course, must greatly exceed the amount given by the Will.'[1] The inhabitants of the Alms-house consist of poor and aged freemen of the Skinners' Company, appointed by the Court of Assistants as vacancies occur.

"A small Ground-plan exists showing the presumed site of the original Alms-houses, as it appears to be indicated in the large four-sheet Map of London by Radulphus Aggas, about the year 1560; wherein at 'St. Elen's' is shown a line of small low buildings, under a connected roof, with a centre house having a gable-front rising above them. But whatever might be the original site and form of these dwellings, as they stood considerably beyond the extent of the ravages of the Great Fire, they remained until they fell into decay with years; and in 1729 the Skinners' Company erected the present Alms-house, on the west of the former, and on the north side of the approach to Great St. Helen's from Bishopgate Street, opposite the back of Crosby Hall. It seems probable that this spot immediately adjoined to the old buildings, and that it was fixed there that the pensioners might remain undisturbed until the new Alms-house were quite completed. In its arrangements the increased value of the ground on which it stands is made particularly evident, since the Alms-men are placed in distinct apartments and floors only, instead of separate dwellings. The rooms are six in number, three on each side of the door-way and passage in the centre; and consist of a bed-chamber and sitting-room for each person, with closets and other conveniences. Upon entering, the doors of the apartments on the ground-floor are on the right and left of the passage, and those to the upper-chambers are from the landings of staircases ascending from the back part of the house, communicating with a paved yard behind. The apartments of the basement-story are used for coal-cellars."

---

[1] "In 1512 a chaldron of the best coals was sold for 5*s*., and an inferior kind at 4*s*. 2*d*.; and in 1551 a load of coals was 12*s*. It is observed by Dr. William Fleetwood, Bishop of St. Asaph, in his very curious Chronicon Preciosum, p. 95, Ed. Lond. 1745, that 'whenever you meet with coals, in old accounts, you are to understand thereby *charcoal*, not *seacoal*; which has not been in common (as well as I can guess) 150 years; at least not in London: though I find them in M.Paris, under the name of *Carbo Marinus*,

It further appears by the abovementioned Will that the sum of Twenty-Five Shillings and Four Pence was directed to be laid out in Coals for the further relief of the said Alms people. The Company, however, give one ton of Coals to each Almsman annually, which of course greatly exceeds the Amount given by the Will.

Sir Andrew Judde was three times married, but no particulars are known of his first or second wife. His third, Mary, who was the heiress of Sir Thomas Mirfyn,* Lord Mayor of London in 1518, survived him upwards of forty years. He had two sons, John and Richard (both of whom died without issue), and one daughter, Alice, who inherited her father's wealth. Dame Mary Judde married, secondly, James Altham, Esq., of Mark Hall, in Latton, Essex. He was Sheriff of London in 1577, of Essex in 1570, and died in 1585. His widow erected a stately tomb for him in Latton Church, and died at an advanced age in 1602. She appears to have been animated with the same spirit of benevolence that distinguished her first husband. During her widowhood she established and endowed an excellent institution for the industrious poor at Colchester, the benefits of which are still enjoyed: it is styled The Lady Judde's Charity.

Alice Judde married Thomas Smythe, Esq. (of an ancient Wiltshire family), who in 1562 settled at Westenhanger, in the parish of Stanford in Kent. The mansion-house was a magnificent structure. Thomas Smythe possessed very extensive property, which he largely increased by his marriage. His wife possessed the bounteous disposition of her family. By her Will she gave to the Almsmen in St. Helen's, as has been already mentioned, lands to the value then of 15*l.* per annum, but which now produce a handsome income. She also gave some considerable legacies to various charitable uses; among others, to the support of scholars at the Universities.

---

in the time of H. III. *in Additament.*' In 1512 seacoal appears to have been little used, since the main stratum was not then arrived at, and many complained that it would not burn without wood; and in the seventeenth century the consumption of it was confined to blacksmiths and poorer persons, who could not afford to procure wood."

* See above, p. 67, and the account of Richard Cromwell, who married Frances, daughter of Sir Thomas Mirfyn, above, p. 243.

Thomas Smythe and Alice Judde were the parents of twelve children—six sons and six daughters. The eldest son, Sir John, was Sheriff of Kent in the 42nd of Elizabeth : he died in 1608, leaving an only son, Thomas, who was made a Knight of the Bath in 1625, and created a Peer of Ireland by the title of Viscount Strangford in 1628, from whom the present Viscount Strangford is the direct lineal descendant.

The second son, Sir Thomas Smythe, was Governor of the Company trading to the East Indies and Treasurer for the Colony of Virginia. He was Ambassador also to the Court of Russia, and served the office of Sheriff of London in 1600. He died in 1625, and left estates for the benefit of Tunbridge School; bequeathed bread to the poor of Tunbridge, which is still distributed to them weekly; besides bread, money, and cloth for wearing apparel, to be given by the hands of the Master and Wardens of the Skinners' Company every year for ever on the day of their annual visitation.

Alice, one of the daughters of Thomas Smythe and Alice Judde, married Sir Christopher Hatton, by whom she was mother to Christopher Lord Hatton, from whom the Earl of Winchilsea is descended.

By his Will, executed September 2, 1558, a short time only before he died, Sir Andrew Judde devised certain lands and houses to the Skinners' Company, "for the perpetual maintenance of the School that he had erected at Tunbridge." Among his estates are the "Sandhills," formerly demised, at a small rent, to the Dukes of Bedford, but now let on building leases for long terms. Judd Place (East and West), Tunbridge Place, Burton Crescent, Mabledon Place; Bidborough, Hadlow, Speldhurst, and Leigh Streets, and many others, are situated on this property. For a long period this property, ample as it has now become, yielded an income little more than sufficient to defray the specific charges made upon it by the Founder's Will. During the time that the surplus rents were comparatively small, it was unimportant whether the Skinners' Company held this property under the Will or as Governors of the School under Fisher's deed (whom Sir Andrew had appointed a Trustee); but when the building leases upon the property at St. Pancras (about 30 Acres) and the improvements in Leadenhall Market raised the revenue to some thousands per annum, it became necessary to decide this question, because in the former case the surplus rents were applicable to the general purposes of the Company, but in the latter to the purposes of the School exclusively. The words of the Charter, which was granted by King Edward VI. in the 7th year of his reign (1553) are—" And we will, and by these presents ordain, that all the issues, rents, and revenue of all the lands, tenements, and possessions hereafter to be given and assigned towards the support of the School aforesaid, from time to time, shall be converted to the support of the Master and Usher of the School aforesaid for the time being, and to the reparation of the said lands and tenements, and not otherwise, nor to any other uses or intents." The cause was heard before the Vice Chancellor, who decided that the Skinners' Company were Trustees for the benefit of the School, and the Lord Chancellor confirmed this decision. A scheme was directed to be prepared for the future appropriation of the property to the purposes of the Foundation. With regard to the property that passed by the Will *alone* to the Company, the Lord Chancellor decided that the Skinners' Company are entitled " to order and dispose of the overplus" (subject to the charges to which it is made liable by the Will), in the terms of the devise " at their wills and pleasures."

SIR WILLIAM PICKERING.

"William Pickering, son and heir of William Pickering, Knight-Marshal to Henry VIII., was born about 1517, and educated at Cambridge, where he acquired a good knowledge of classical literature, but does not appear to have graduated. He is mentioned as one of the eminent Greek scholars here who adopted Cheke's new mode of pronouncing that language. He served Henry VIII. in his wars, and was made a Knight of the Carpet immediately after the coronation of Edward VI. He was despatched to France as resident ambassador in 1551. Soon after he was joined in the commission for presenting the Garter to Henry II. In August the same year he was made steward of the lordship of Sheriff-Hutton in Yorkshire, and constable of the Castle there, obtaining also a grant of the herbage and poundage of the Park thereunto belonging. A letter from him to the Privy Council, dated Melun, 4th Sept. 1551, gives a masterly sketch of the policy of France and England at that period in relation to the great enterprises of Charles V. and the condition of Italy and the Empire. In November, 1551, Sir William Pickering was joined in commission with Lord Clinton for the negotiation of a marriage between Edward VI. and the Princess Elizabeth, daughter of the King of France. Queen Mary on her accession recalled him from France, but afterwards sent him as ambassador to King Philip in Flanders, and he was employed in mustering 3000 Germans, whom it was proposed to add to the English army. He was a ripe scholar, of elegant manners, and an uncommonly handsome man of a tall stature and dignified presence, so that in the early part of Queen Elizabeth's reign he was very commonly mentioned as one whom her Majesty was likely to marry. He retired from the public service at a comparatively early period of his life, and during the remainder of his days applied himself to literary pursuits. He had an estate at Oswald Kirk, Yorkshire, and a mansion called Pickering House in the parish of St. Andrew Undershaft, London, where he died 4th Jan. 1574-5."*

SIR JOHN SPENCER.

Sir John Spencer, usually called "Rich Spencer," was the son of Richard Spencer, of Waldingfield, in Suffolk. Sir John was an Alderman and Clothworker of London, Sheriff in 1583-4, and elected Lord Mayor, Michaelmas, 1594. He appears to have possessed much public spirit, loyalty, and patriotism, and though connected with many of the leading characters of the Court, was extremely tenacious of the rights and privileges of the City. The year 1594—the year of his Mayoralty—was one of great scarcity, and in order to provide against a dearth in the City, the Companies were, by the Lord Mayor's means, ordered to buy, each of them, a certain quantity of foreign corn, and lay it up in their granary in the Bridge House. Before this object could be effected, Sir John Hawkins, Admiral of the Fleet, required the Bridge House for the laying up the provisions for the Navy, and the ovens also there for baking their ship bread. In this strait Sir John sent an earnest message to the Lord Treasurer Burleigh, telling him that they

---

* See Athenæ Cantabrig., vol. i. pp. 325-6. Ed. Lond. 1858.

could not spare them, and praying the Lord Treasurer's good favour, that the Granaries, being the property of the City, might be employed for their use, that there might be no want nor outcry of the poor for bread, or else, that if there fell out a greater want or dearth than there was at that time, and that the City was unprovided, his Lordship would be pleased to hold him excused.

In the year 1595 the tumultuous proceedings of the populace, who drew in the London Apprentices to join them, produced such repeated and alarming riots, that it was thought necessary by the Lord Mayor to lay the case before the Lord Treasurer for her Majesty's protection. In consequence of this, on the 4th of July, a proclamation was issued, wherein her Majesty appointed a Provost Marshal with power to apprehend all rioters, and by order of martial law to punish them accordingly. Sir Thomas Wilford, who was appointed Provost Marshal, patrolled the city, with a numerous attendance on horseback, armed with pistols, and apprehended many of the rioters, whom he took before the justices for their examination. On the 22nd July they were tried at Guildhall, and five of them being condemned, were, agreeably to their sentence, executed on Tower Hill two days afterwards. This example had the desired effect, for the rest were so intimidated that they immediately dispersed, and peace was again restored in the City.

As a further example of his firmness, it being reported that the Queen intended to take the Recorder into her service, and the Lord Keeper having stated that her Majesty desired the Lord Mayor to send to her the names of such persons as were put in nomination for that office, the citizens alarmed at such an extraordinary proceeding nominated only one person. With this nomination Sir John Spencer, in a letter to the Lord Treasurer, July 23, 1595, stated "that very urgent suit was made in Common Council on behalf of the City, whereof I thought it my duty to advertise your Lordship, most humbly desiring you to be a means that we may herein have our own free election, according to our ancient custome; and for mine own opinion we have one born and dwelling among us whom we have great experience of, and think very able to do us service; his name is James Altham, son of Mr. Altham, late of Essex, Esq.; he is a bencher of Grays' Inn, and one of our ordinary sworn Councillors of the City, well acquainted with our customs, and very well thought of for his honesty and skill in law . . . . . . And therefore as a well willer to the City, and one that desireth that the continual business may be attended to as it ought, I am as far as I may, a most earnest and humble petitioner to your good Lordship to farther us and him therein" . . . . . . There was, however, no new election, for Sir J. Crooke continued in office until 1603, and was then succeeded by Sir Henry Montague, afterwards Earl of Manchester.

In a curious pamphlet, entitled "The Vanity of the Lives and Passions of Men, by D. Papillon, Gent.," 1651, the following remarkable passage occurs from a private record: "In Queen Elizabeth's days, a pirate of Dunkerk laid a plot, with twelve of his mates, to carry away Sir John Spencer; which if he had done, fifty thousand pounds had not redeemed him. He came over the seas in a shallop, with twelve musketiers, and in the night came into Barking Creek, and left the shallop in the custody of six of his men, and with the other six came as far as Islington, and there hid themselves in ditches, near the path in which Sir John came always to his house; but by the providence of God, Sir John upon some extraordinary occasion, was forced to stay in London that night, otherwise, they had taken him away; and they fearing they should be discovered, in the night time came to their shallop, and so came safe to Dunkerk again."

Sir John's country-house, to which reference is here made, was Canonbury, of which he had purchased the Manor of Thomas Lord Wentworth in 1570, his town residence being at Crosby Place, which he had bought of the representatives of Antonio Bonvisi. When Sir John took possession of Crosby Place, he found it in a state of considerable dilapidation. In this noble mansion he is said to have lived in great state, and here, as was then the civic custom, he kept his Mayoralty.

Sir John Spencer had by his lady, Alice Bromfield, one sole daughter and heiress, Elizabeth, of whom it is said that she was carried off from Canonbury House in a baker's basket, by the contrivance of William, the second Lord Compton, to whom in the year 1594 she was married. There is a tradition that the Knight was so much incensed at the elopement of his daughter that he totally discarded her, until a reconciliation took place through the kind interposition of Queen Elizabeth, of which the following graphic description is taken from *Chambers's Edinburgh Journal*, April 16, 1842 :—

" Let us in idea go back two centuries and a half, and step into the presence-chamber of Queen Elizabeth. The walls are hung with rich tapestry, while the floor is strewed with fresh hay. At the door leading to the queen's apartments stands an usher dressed in velvet, with a gold chain around his neck, the badge of his office. In the chamber may be seen, besides, a great number of councillors, officers of the crown, and clergymen of high rank—for the queen, after giving passing audience to those present, proceeds to chapel, the day being a holiday of the church.

" The mid-doors are thrown open, and the coming of the queen is announced. Gentlemen, barons, earls, and knights of the garter, all richly dressed and bareheaded, are the first to enter the presence-chamber from her apartments. They are followed by the lord-chancellor, bearing the seals in a silk purse ; and on each side of him walks a nobleman, one bearing the royal sceptre, and the other the sword of state in a crimson scabbard. Queen Elizabeth follows. A small golden crown is upon her head, and rests on a profusion of thick curled hair, of a colour too deeply sanguine to countenance her early flatterers when they called the hue golden. The locks now worn by Elizabeth are, however, but a close imitation of what her natural tresses were in her younger days. Rich pearls hang from her ears, and a necklace of fine jewels is thrown over her shoulders. A white silk robe, bordered with large pearls, adorns her person, and the long train is borne by a marchioness of the realm. Elizabeth is now, as has been hinted, past the meridian of her days, yet is her gait erect and majestic, and her small dark eye retains its clear and vivid expression. A sharpening of the lines of her naturally acute lineaments is all that speaks of the advance of years.

" On the occasion when this scene, here described in the present tense, was to be witnessed, foreign ministers were in the presence-chamber, and to each Elizabeth spoke in his own language, whether that were Spanish or Italian, French or Dutch. Whithersoever she turned her eye, all knelt down before her. Whosoever had the honour of a word from her, remained kneeling, unless the great queen raised him. She passed along slowly through the large chamber, conversing to those on one side and another, and sometimes receiving strangers presented by the usher. She came at length to a gentleman advanced in years, who knelt at her look. He was richly dressed, but not in the robes of office or nobility. 'Ha!' said the queen, stretching out her hand, and raising this personage; 'our good citizen, Sir John Spencer. Welcome! Thou wert informed of our wish to converse with thee?' 'I had the honour,' answered the citizen, 'to receive your majesty's commands to that effect.' 'Thou hast ever indeed, good Sir John, regarded our slightest wish as a command,' continued Elizabeth; 'and well thy loyalty beseems thee. Thou hast paid dearly, too, for thy affectionate regard to our person.' The old citizen sighed as if involuntarily, showing well that he understood the queen's allusion. She went on, however, to refer more plainly to the subject, while all around fell respectfully back, marking her low tones. 'It was while an attendant on our train that my young Lord Compton first saw thy daughter, and the issue was the rash marriage which thou deplorest. Sir John, we would remedy the evil thou hast sustained.' The face of the citizen-knight grew suddenly flushed, and then left him more pale than before. He knelt down after a moment of apparently agitated thought, and said, in a low and hurried voice, 'I hope—I trust your majesty does not mean to lay your commands on me to pardon——' The queen interrupted him. 'Listen to us, Sir John Spencer. Your paternal resentment will be respected by us It is a *favour* which we have now to require of thee, and the granting of which may partly remedy the misfortune which you have suffered. An infant boy has somewhat strangely fallen to our particular guardianship. He is of such rank and birth that we conceive thee to be a fitter person to act as his sponsor than any of the nobles of our court. Thy civic position suits thee much more for serving the future fortunes of this boy; and, God's bread, Sir John, thou shalt have a queen for a partner in the office.'

"Doubt had gradually disappeared from the citizen's brow during this speech, and had been supplanted by a feeling of the highest gratification, as was clear and apparent in his looks. 'Your majesty,' said he, 'does me an honour which kings might be proud of. And by life, madam, I shall prove, by my conduct to the boy, that your majesty has not so honoured one who is ungrateful for it. I have no child,' continued the citizen, more slowly—' I have no child now, and my godson shall supply the place which has been wilfully vacated.' The queen was obviously pleased with what had passed. As she looked on Sir John, who had cast down his eyes in closing his speech, there was a sparkle of passing pleasure in her quick dark eye. 'Farewell, for the present, Sir John Spencer,' said she; 'due tidings shall reach thee when it becomes necessary to assume thy new duties.' The knight stooped to kiss the hand extended to him, and the queen passed on, leaving the citizen to follow, and finally wend his way homewards.

"Sir John Spencer, commonly called 'Rich Spencer,' was in his day the wealthiest and most influential citizen of London. The mayoralty and shrievalty had been both served by him more than once, we believe. He was a great favourite with the queen, being noted for his public-spiritedness, and his anxiety to sustain the honour of his sovereign and his country. Such a feeling was peculiarly evinced by the opulent clothworker, as he was by profession, on the occasion of the Marquis of Rosny's visit to England, as ambassador from Henry IV. of France to Elizabeth. The Marquis (afterwards Duke of Sully) was lodged and entertained by Sir John in the most sumptuous manner, at his own private cost. He was understood to be worth a million sterling, and had but one child, a daughter, his sole heiress. Having fixed upon a son-in-law in his own rank in life, the worthy citizen had been deeply irritated by the elopment of his daughter with the young Lord Compton; and though, at the period referred to in our story, more than a year had elapsed since the event, Sir John's anger seemed to have increased rather than diminished by the lapse of time. Various attempts had been made to bring about a reconciliation, but unsuccessfully. So stood the family affairs of Sir John Spencer, when the good Queen Bess intimated her wish to honour him in the manner related.

"Of that honour the citizen continued to think with pride, up to the time of his receiving a message from the queen, requiring a second visit from him at Greenwich Palace. Thither, accordingly, Sir John wended his way, meditating how he might best show, in a marked manner, his sense of the high favour bestowed on him by the queen. When ushered into the presence of the latter, he found her with a goodly company of ladies and courtiers; and in presence, also, was her majesty's household chaplain. 'Welcome, Sir John,' said the queen, as the citizen paid his duty on entrance; 'thou art punctual, yet we have been for some time in readiness. The ceremony shall be private, as best befits the condition of our poor little charge.' Sir John bowed in silence; and the company, at a motion of the queen's hand, proceeded to the small chapel, where her majesty was accustomed to perform her private devotions.

"We shall suppose the child baptized, and the whole ceremony over. Increasing the amount of the honour, the queen gave to the child the Christian name of 'Spencer.' This unexpected circumstance, and the uncommon beauty of the infant, seemed to determine the knight in its favour. 'Madam,' said he to the queen, with tears in his eyes, 'I have resolved to show my sense of this honour by adopting this child, now my name-son. He shall be my *sole heir;* and, that no foolish relentings may afterwards affect this resolve, I here solemnly vow, before the holy altar, and in presence of your majesty and this fair company, to settle irrevocably my estate by deed in this child's favour, and to place it immediately in your majesty's possession, if you will honour me by accepting such trust.'

"The eyes of the queen sparkled with unaffected pleasure. ''Tis well, Sir John Spencer,' said she; 'we are witnesses to your promise, and know that it will be kept.' She then turned round, and exclaimed, looking to a side door, 'Without there! You may enter.' In an instant the door was thrown open, and Sir John Spencer beheld his daughter, the Lady Compton, and her husband, kneeling at his feet. Before the agitated citizen could speak, the queen addressed him. 'Sir John, the child whom thou hast here adopted is thine own grandchild. Take these his parents also to your favour, and make this one of the happiest hours in a queen's life.' 'Pardon, dearest father, pardon!' cried the weeping daughter of the knight; 'pardon,' continued she, taking her child from an attendant, and raising it in her arms —'pardon, for this child's sake!' Sir John Spencer could not resist these appeals. 'Heaven bless you, my children!' said he, embracing them by turns; 'I do forgive all the past; and I heartily thank her majesty, who has brought about this happy event.'

"Our anecdote is told. Many glorious acts signalize the reign of Elizabeth, but it may be questioned if any recorded deed of hers places her character in a more pleasing light, than the little ruse by which she reconciled Sir John Spencer and his daughter."

In 1599, August 1. Q. Elizabeth gave the Manor of Brooke Hall, once belonging to St. Osith's Monastery, to John Spencer, Esq., born at Waldingfield in Suffolk, and died March 30, 1609.

Same date. Q. Elizabeth granted the Manor of Bower Hall, formerly belonging to St. Owen's Priory, to John Spencer, Esq. Elizabeth, his only daughter and heir, brought it to her husband, William, Lord Compton. He kept his first Court here, October 14, 1617.

Same date. Q. Elizabeth granted the Manor of Bocking with appurtenances and the site of the same, and marsh and lands 18 acres, called Le Rey, and 20 acres more, parcel of this manor, to John Spencer to hold of the Queen, of the Honour of Hampton Court by the 20th part of a Knight's fee and not in capite. It descended to his daughter.

Sir John Spencer died at an advanced age, March 3, 1609, and was buried in St. Helen's Church.* The following particulars are part of a letter, from Mr. John Beaulieu to Mr. Trumbull, resident at Brussels, dated Mar. 22 (April 2), 1609-10.†

"Upon Tuesday the funerals of Sir John Spencer were made, where some thousand men did assist in mourning cloakes, or gowns, amongst which there were 320 poor men, who had every one of them, a basket given them, stored with the particular provisions as follows, a black gowne, four pounds of beef, two loaves of bread, a little bottle of wine, a candlestick, a pound of candles, two saucers, two spoons, a black pudding, a pair of gloves, a dozen of points, two red herrings, four white herrings, six sprats, and two eggs, but to expound to you the mystical meaning of such an anticke furniture, I am not so skillful an Œdipus, except it doth design the horn of abundance which my Lord Compton hath found in that succession. But that poor Lord is not like (if God do not help him) to carry it away for nothing, or to grow

---

* See above, p. 70.
† Winwood's State Papers, vol. iii. p. 136. Ed. London. 1725.

very rich thereby, being in great danger to lose his wits for the same; whereof being at the very first newes, either through the vehement apprehension of joy for such a plentiful succession, or of carefulness how to take it up and dispose it, somewhat distracted and afterwards reasonably restored, he is now of late fallen again (but more deeply) into the same frenzy, so that there seemeth to be little hope of his recovery. And what shall these thousands and millions avayle him, if he come to loose, if not his soul, at least his wits and reason? It is a faire and ample subject for a Divine to course Riches, and a notable example to the world not to wooe or trust so much in them. It is given out abroad that he hath suppressed a will of the deceased's, whereby he did bequeath some 20,000*l.* to his poor kindred and as much in pious uses; for the which the people do exclaim that this affliction is justly inflicted upon him by the hand of God, for a punishment of such an impious deed. But whether that suppression be true or not, it is not yet very constantly reported."

Sir Thomas Edmondes, in a letter to Sir Ralph Winwood, March 17, 1609, expresses himself to the same effect. "The Lord Compton hath been so transported with joy for the great fortune befallen him by the death of Sir John Spencer, his father-in-law, as the overworking of the same in his mind did hinder him from taking any rest, whereby he was grown half distracted, but now he is reasonably well recovered again."*

"Mr. Beaulieu in a precedent Letter to Mr. Trumbull," which is only quoted by Winwood, states "that Sir John Spencer died worth at least 300,000*l.*, some said 500,000*l.*, others 800,000*l.*"† And in a subsequent letter, dated March 29, 1610, he gives the following account: "Here is dead within these two days, the old Lady Spencer, following the heels of her husband; who gave away amongst her kindred 13,000*l.* of the 15,000*l.* which she was to have of my Lord Compton; who is now altogether distracted and so franticke as that he is forced to be kept bound. The administration of his goods and lands is committed to the Lords Chamberlaine, Privy Seal, and Worcester; who coming the last week into the City, took an Inventory (in the presence of the Sheriffs) of the goods, amongst which (it is said) there were bonds found for 133,000*l.*"‡

---

* Id. p. 137. † Id. p. 136. ‡ Id. pp. 145-6.

It appears that the distraction before mentioned was only temporary, as on the 19th July, 1618, this noble Lord was created Earl of Northampton. His death, however, happened on a sudden, of which S. Meddus, in a letter dated July 2, 1630, has given the following account:—" Yesterday seven-night, the Earl of Northampton, Lord President of Wales (after he had waited on the King at supper and had also supped), went in a boat with others to wash himself in the Thames, and so soon as his legges were in the water but to the knees, he had the collick, and cried out, ' Have me into the boat again, for I am a dead man !' and died a few howers after at his lodgings in the Savoy, within the suburbs of London, on June 24, 1630 (6 Car. I.), and was buried at Compton with his ancestors."

The Earl had issue a son, Spencer, before mentioned, and two daughters. His son succeeded him in the title and estates; and having raised a regiment of foot and a troop of horse, commanded the royal army at the battle of Hopton Heath, but fell in the moment of victory by a severe wound from an halbert at the back of the head, March 19, 1642.

The following Letter from the daughter of Sir John Spencer to her husband, was copied from the original by the Hon. Mrs. Boyle Walsingham, and communicated to the Antiquarian Repertory by the Earl of Essex. Written probably about 1617.

" My Sweet Life,—Now that I have declared to you my mind for the settling your Estate, I supposed that it were best for me to bethink what allowance were best for me; for considering what care I have ever had of your estate, and how respectfully I dealt with those which, both by laws of God, Nature, and Civil Policy, Wit, Religion, Government, and Honesty, you my dear, are bound to. I pray and beseech you to grant to me, your most kind and loving wife, the sum of 1600*l.* per ann., quarterly to be paid.

" Also I wou'd, besides that allowance for my apparel, have 600*l.* added yearly for the performance of charitable works; those things I would not, neither will be, accountable for.

" Also I will have three horses for my own sadle that none shall dare to lend or borrow; none lend but I, none borrow but you.

" Also I wou'd have two Gentlewomen, lest one should be sick; also, I believe it is an indecent thing for a Gentlewoman to stand mumping alone, when God have blessed their lord and lady with a great estate.

"Also when I ride hunting or hawking, or travel from one house to another, I will have them attending; so for each of these said women I must and will have a horse.

"Also I will have six or eight gentlemen; and will have my two Coaches, one lined with velvet to myself, with four very fair horses; and a coach for my women, lin'd with sweet cloth, o'erlaid with gold; the other, with scarlet and laced with watched lace and silver, with four good horses.

"Also I will have two coachmen, one for myself, the other for my women.

"Also, whenever I travel, I will be allowed not only carroches and spare horses for me and my women, but such carriages as shall be fitting for all; orderly; not pestering my things with my women's, nor theirs with chambermaids', nor theirs with washmaids'.

"Also, laundresses, when I travel, I will have them sent away before with the carriages, to see all safe; and the chambermaids' shall go before with the grooms, that the chambers may be ready, sweet, and clean.

"Also, for that it is indecent to crowd up myself with my gentleman usher in my coach, I will have him have a convenient horse to attend me either in city or country. And I must have four footmen. And my desire is that you will defray all the charges for me.

"And for myself, besides my yerely allowance, I would have twenty gowns apparel, six of them excellent good ones, eight of them for the country, and six others of them very excellent good ones.

"Also I would have to put in my purse 2000*l*. and 200*l*., and so you to pay my debts.

"Also I would have 8000*l*. to buy me jewels, and 6000*l*. for a pearl chain.

"Now, seeing that I have been and am so reasonable unto you, I pray you to find my Children apparel and their schooling, and all my servants, men and women, their wages.

"Also I will have all my houses furnished, and my lodging chambers to be suited with all such furniture as is fit; as Beds,

Stools, Chairs, Cushions, Carpets, Silver Warming Pans, Cupboards of Plate, fair hangings, &c. So for my drawing chambers in all houses, I will have them delicately furnished with hangings, Couch, Canopy, Cushions, Carpets, &c.

"Also my desire is, that you would pay your debts, build up Ashby House, and purchase lands, and lend no money (as you love God) to the Lord Chamberlain, which would have all, perhaps your life from you: remember his son, my Lord Walden, what entertainment he gave me when you were at the Tilt Yard. If you were dead he said he wou'd be Husband, a Father, a Brother, and said he wou'd marry me. I protest I grieve to see the poor man have so little Wit and Honesty to use his friend so vilely; also he fed me with untruths concerning the Charter House, but that is the least; he wished me much harm, you know how: God keep you and me from him, and any such as he is.

"So now that I have declared to you my mind, what I wou'd have, and what I wou'd not have, I pray you, when you be an Earl, to allow me a 1000*l.* more than I now desire, and double attendance.
"Your loving Wife,
"ELIZ. COMPTON."

DANIEL FEATLEY.[*]

His right name was Fairclough, and by that name he was ordained both Deacon and Minister, but by the ignorance and corruption of the times the name varied and altered to Featley, which he first owned in print of all the family. He was son of John Featley (sometime cook to Dr. Humphrey, President of Magdalen College, Oxford) by Marian Thrift, his wife, was born at Charlton-upon-Otmore, near Oxford, March 5, 1582; educated in the Grammar School adjoining Magdalen College, admitted Scholar of Corpus Christi College, 13th December, 1594. His admirable disputations, his excellent sermons, his grave, yet affable demeanour and rare accomplishments, induced Sir Thomas Edmonds, on being appointed Ambassador to France, to make him his chaplain, where he resided three years. During that time he became the honour of the Protestant religion and the

---

[*] See Newcourt's Repert. Lond., p. 571, and Wood's Athenæ Oxoniens., vol. iii. col. 156—160. Ed. Lond. (Bliss) 1813-20.

English nation. Upon his return to England he took the degree of Bachelor of Divinity, 1613, and soon after became Rector of Northill, in Cornwall. He was scarcely settled at that place, when he was sent for to be domestic chaplain to Dr. Abbot, Archbishop of Canterbury, by whom he was speedily preferred to the Rectory of Lambeth, in Surrey. In 1617 he proceeded in divinity and puzzled Prideaux, the King's Professor, so much with his learned arguments, that a quarrel thereupon being raised, the Archbishop was in a manner forced to settle it for his chaplain's sake. The Archbishop of Spalato* being present, was so much taken with Dr. Featley's arguments, that he forthwith gave him a brother's place in the Savoy Hospital, near London, he being then Master thereof. .... About that time he had given him the Rectory of Allhallows Church in Bread Street, which he soon after exchanged for the Rectory of Acton in Middlesex, and at length became the third and last Provost of Chelsea College. On the 15th September, 1623, the Doctor married Mrs. Joyce Holloway, relict of Mr. Holloway, and formerly relict of Mr. Thompson (both merchants of London), who lived in a handsome house of her own, with a beautiful garden at Kennington. This marriage Dr. Featley for some time concealed, and continued to reside with the Prelate. In the year 1625, the time of a raging pestilence, the Archbishop removed with his whole family to Croydon, for fear of infection, and the Doctor being taken ill, removed to his wife's house at Kennington, where he soon recovered. He then removed his books, &c., from Lambeth Palace, and wholly devoted himself to piety and charity. In November, 1642, after the King had encountered the Parliament soldiers at Brentford, some of the rebels took up their quarters at Acton, who, after they had missed the Doctor (whom they took to be a Papist, or at least that he had a Pope in his belly), drank up and eat his provisions, burnt down a barn full of corn and two stables, the loss amounting to 211*l.*; and at the same time did not only greatly profane the Church with their beastly actions, but also burnt the rails, pulled

---

* Mark Anthony de Dominis, born at Arba, about 1561, and educated at Padua, came to England, and conforming to the Protestant religion, was made Dean of Windsor, Master of the Savoy, and Rector of West Ilderly, Berks. He returned to Rome in 1622, and abjured his opinions and died there in 1625. Biograph. Dict., vol. xii. pp. 231-2.

down the font, broke the windows, &c. In February following they sought after him in Lambeth Church on the Lord's day, to murder him, but he escaped them. In 1643, when the Bishops were disabled from performing their office, and thereupon the Assembly of Divines was constituted by the "blessed Parliament," as some called it, Dr. Featley was appointed a Member thereof. But being a main stickler against the Covenant, in a letter to the learned Dr. Usher, Primate of Ireland, then at Oxford, he showed to him the reasons why he excepted against it. A copy thereof being treacherously obtained from him, was first carried to the Close Committee, and afterwards to the House of Commons. Whereupon being adjudged to be a spy and a betrayer of the Parliamentary cause, he was committed prisoner to the Lord Petre's House, in Aldersgate Street, on the 30th September, and deprived of his rectories, "that of Acton being bestowed on the Independent, Philip Nye, and that of Lambeth on John White of Dorchester"—called "the old instrument of sedition,"—who afterwards got an order to obtain and keep his library of books, till such time as he could get his own back, which had been seized a short time previously at Dorchester, by Prince Rupert. In the said prison house he continued until the beginning of March, 1644-5, and then after much supplication made to the Parliament in his behalf (he being then very ill with the dropsy), he was removed for his health's sake to Chelsea College, of which he was still Provost, for six weeks upon good bail; but it pleased God to take him, April 17, 1645, being the last day of the six weeks limited for his return. He was generally esteemed as one of the most resolute and victorious champions of the Reformed Protestant religion in his time, a most smart scourge for the Church of Rome, a compendium of the learned tongues, and of all the liberal arts and sciences: also, that though he was of small stature, yet he had a great soul, and had all learning compacted in him.

SIR THOMAS GRESHAM.

The family from which Sir Thomas Gresham was descended, like most other old Norfolk families, derived its name from a little village where it had been settled for many generations. His father, Sir Richard, and his uncle, Sir John, who were the third and fourth sons of his grandfather, John Gresham of Holt, in that county, were bred to trade, acquired great wealth, and each of them served the offices of Aldermen and Lord Mayor. He was the third and youngest son of Sir Richard Gresham by his first wife Audrey, daughter of William Lynn, of Southwick, in Northamptonshire. Of his youth we know nothing except that he had the misfortune to be deprived of a mother's care at the tender age of three years, and that he was subsequently sent to Cambridge and admitted a pensioner of Gonville Hall. Richard Gresham was agent to King Henry VIII., or, as it was sometimes called, King's Merchant or Factor, an office of early origin. In the year 1531 he received the honour of knighthood, being then Sheriff of London. The merchants of London used at that time, for the transaction of business, to assemble every day in Lombard Street, where they were exposed to all the inclemencies of the weather. Sir Richard had been at Antwerp, where a Bourse had been newly erected, and while he was in office wrote to the Lord Privy Seal, "that if certain houses were purchased and pulled down, a handsome Bourse might be erected, which he supposes would cost 2000*l.*"* In the year 1537 he was Lord Mayor of London, and in 1541 was with his brother, Sir John Gresham, put into commission for heresies done in the city and diocese of London. He dwelt at Bethnal Green; and dying February 20, 1548, was buried in the church of St. Lawrence Jewry, where there is an ancient Tomb with an inscription on the east wall to his memory.†

The office of agent for the Crown with the trading interest was of the highest importance, inasmuch as it united the duty of raising money for the royal occasions by private loans, with that of protecting and cherishing the sources from which they were derived. In this, as well as in his own great commercial concerns, it is quite evident that he designed his son Thomas for his successor, by binding him to his uncle, Sir John Gresham, as an apprentice; in consequence of which he was, in 1543, admitted a member of the Mercers' Company, being then in the 25th year of his age. Ten years afterwards, writing to the Duke of Northumberland from Antwerp concerning commercial matters, he says, "To the wyche syence I myselfe was bound prentisse viii

---

* See Ward's Lives of the Professors of Gresham College, &c. Ed. Lond. 1748.
† See Stow's Survey, vol. i. p. 563. Ed. Lond. 1754-5.

yeres, to come by the experyence and knowledge that I have. Neverthelesse I need not to have been prentisse, for that I was free by my Father's coppye: albeit my Father Sir Richard Gresham being a wyse man, knew, although I was free by his coppye, it was to no purpos, except I were bound prentisse to the same; whereby to come by the experience and knowledge of all kinds of merchandise."

The earliest contemporary notice of Sir Thomas Gresham occurs in one of the despatches of Seymour and Wotton to King Henry VIII., written from Brussels, 18th June, 1543 :—" The Regente hathe also granted a lycence for the gonne-powder and salt-peter, bought for your Highnes, the whyche we have delyveryd to yonge Thomas Gresham, solycitour of the same."[*] Allusion is here made to Henry's preparations for war with France, which led to the taking of Boulogne in the ensuing year. He is again mentioned in March, 1545, by Secretary Paget, who writes to Petre from Brussels concerning an arrest of merchandize which had taken place by order of Charles V. This unjustifiable step was occasioned by Henry's having received certain Flemish ships which were carrying assistance to the French, and the writer is speculating on the consequences likely to result to the merchant adventurers.

Between the writing of these two letters his marriage occurred. His wife, Anne,[†] was the daughter of William Ferneley, Esquire, of West Creting, in Suffolk, and widow of William Read, a gentleman of good family, whose ancestors were settled at Beccles, in the same county. Read styles himself in his will "citizen and mercer of London," and appears to have been on terms of intimacy with the Gresham family, for he appointed Sir Richard overseer of his will, and left him a legacy of 10*l.* and a black gown. He died in the beginning of 1544; and that his widow was married to Thomas Gresham in the same year appears from a curious full-length portrait of the latter formerly preserved at Weston Hall, in Suffolk. The painting is in Holbein's best manner, and represents a well-proportioned young man, rather above the middle height, clad entirely in black. Holbein has given him an intellectual brow and a mouth full of expression. His features are regular and eminently hand-

---

[*] State Papers, temp. Henry VIII. vol. ix. p. 418. Ed. Lond. 1830–52.

[†] Her younger sister, Jane, was married to Sir Nicholas Bacon, the Lord Keeper.

some, and his general aspect singularly mild and engaging. The beard and moustache are short; on either hand he wears a ring—in that day a mark of distinction—and in his right hand he holds a pair of gloves; at his feet, on the pavement, the artist has thought proper to introduce a skull. On the right of this portrait, which is about the size of life, is written—

"A.D. 1544.
"THOMAS GRESHAM, 26;"

and on the left, the initial letters both of his wife's name and his own, with the following motto—

"A. G.   Love, Serve, and Obei.   T. G.;"

while on each side of the black frame is inscribed, in letters of gold the motto, DOMINUS . MIHI . ADIVTOR, followed by the letters T.G. The Thruston family, to whom this portrait formerly belonged, resided at Hoxne Abbey, in Suffolk, and there the picture had probably hung ever since the priory of Benedictine Monks at Hoxne was granted to Sir Richard Gresham.*

The supposed wedding-ring of Sir Thomas Gresham is in the possession of Granville William Gresham Leveson-Gower, Esq., of Titsey Park, Surrey, who is lineally descended from Sir John Gresham, the younger brother of Sir Richard Gresham, father of Sir Thomas Gresham. It opens horizontally, thus forming two rings, which are nevertheless linked together, and respectively inscribed on the inner side with a Scripture posy, QUOD . DEUS . CONIVNSIT being engraved on one-half, and HOMO . NON . SEPERAT on the other. The ring is beautifully enamelled and contains two stones, corresponding with which in a cavity inside the ring are two minute figures of loves or genii; one of which has disappeared.

---

* 38 Henry VIII. This portrait is now in the possession of the Gresham College Committee, which is constituted by the Mercers' Company and the Gresham Committee of the Corporation of the City of London. By means of the indefatigable exertions of the late Edward Taylor, Esq., Gresham Professor of Music, the gift of this portrait was made to the College in 1845, by its then possessor, John Thruston, Esq., and now hangs in the Library of that Institution with the following inscription subjoined:—

"1845.—JOHN THRUSTON, Weston Hall, Suffolk.
Clarissimi Fundatoris hanc claram imaginem ex opere Holbein
in usum Collegii,
JOANNES THRUSTON,
de Weston Hall in agro Suffolc.
Armiger A.D. MDCCCXLV."

How many children Sir Thomas had by his wife is not known: we hear but of one, Richard, who must have been born before 1548, since in that year his name appears in his grandfather's will; but an incidental mention of " my powre wiffe and children" in 1553-4 leaves it reasonable to suppose that he had others, who must have also died at an early age.

About the end of the year 1551 Thomas Gresham was called upon to serve the King Edward VI., and that he might the better attend to the important duties that now devolved upon him, he removed with his wife and family to Antwerp. The English merchant adventurers are said to have established a factory there as early as the year 1296; but it was not until 1558 that the Hotel Van Lyere, or residence of the Burgomaster of that name, was finally ceded for their accommodation, and at this house our Ambassadors, journeying to or from foreign courts, were usually domiciled on their arrival at Antwerp.

It appears from the written statement of Gresham's transactions, which he presented to Edward VI. on his return from Antwerp, August, 1552, that between the 1st March and the 27th July his payments had amounted to 106,301*l*. 4*s*. 4*d*., his own expenses 102*l*. 10*s*., and he had concluded his mission by giving his friends a feast, which forms the last item in the account "Paid for a supper and a banckett that I made to the Fugger* and to the Schetz,† and other that I have had to do withall for your Majesty, sens your Hightnes haythe comytted this great charge unto me, the 28th July 1552, 26*l*."

On the accession of Queen Mary Gresham found himself suddenly supplanted in his office of Royal Agent, a circumstance easily accounted for when it is remembered that the Duke of Northumberland, his great patron, was most hostile to the Queen's succession, and that he was personally obnoxious on the score of his religious opinions. Conscious, however, that his abilities to execute the duties of his office were unrivalled, and fearful that the fruition of his projects should be delayed by the mismanagement of ignorant competitors, he ventured instantly to present to the Queen a memorial stating, with a boldness of expression very unusual at that time, his service to her late brother, and conceived

---

* Anthony Fugger and Nephews were then believed to be the wealthiest merchants in Christendom.

† Another of the most distinguished families at Antwerp.

with such force and dexterity, that, while it concluded without any direct request, it left her scarcely at liberty to do otherwise, in common prudence, than to reinstate him. The evidence of what passed during the first few weeks of Queen Mary's reign, is not sufficiently circumstantial to enable us to trace the early movements of her Privy Council. It is, however, certain that they took upon themselves to procure supplies by writing directly to the Fuggers at Antwerp, and commissioning certain persons to negotiate the required loans. The council, however, soon became sensible of the evils which awaited them through the inefficiency of their agents, and in this emergency seem to have turned to Gresham for assistance, as, in the Record Office at the Rolls— removed thither from the late State Paper Office—there is a paper dated Nov. 13, 1553, entitled, "A Memoriall gyven by Thomas Gresham to the Queene's Majestie," which sets forth the terms on which he was willing to resume his office. From his instructions, which are dated the same day, it is only necessary to mention that his orders were to proceed immediately to Antwerp and borrow the sum of 50,000*l*. for the space of a year, on interest at the rate of 11 or 12 per cent. on the security of the Queen's bond, and that of the city of London under the great seal, as had been customary in King Edward's time.

Whether in consequence of the intrigues of Paulet, Marquis of Winchester, the lord treasurer, who, jealous of Gresham's weight and influence in all matters of finance, showed himself his enemy on more than one occasion, or from whatever other cause, his occupation of the office of Royal Agent was frequently interrupted during Mary's reign. That nobleman, he says, sought to ruin him by "informing the sovereign with half a tale .... once in King Edward's time and once in Queen Mary's time."

Upon Queen Elizabeth's accession to the crown, in 1558, he was immediately taken into her service, and employed to provide money and buy up arms. The year following he was directed to repair to the Court of the Regent of the Netherlands, as temporary ambassador, on which occasion the honour of Knighthood was conferred upon him. At this period Sir Thomas Gresham resided in Lombard Street, and like all other bankers and merchants living in that street, kept a shop,[*] and over his door was his crest,

---

[*] Now the banking house of Messrs. Martin & Co., 68, Lombard Street.

a grasshopper by way of sign. The original sign was in existence so late as 1795, when, on the erection of the present building, it disappeared. A German traveller, who visited England in 1593, says, that he saw in Lombard Street "all sorts of gold and silver vessels exposed for sale, as well as ancient and modern coins, in such quantities as must surprise a man the first time he sees and considers them."* At the period of Gresham's death a considerable portion of his wealth consisted of gold chains.

During his protracted periods of absence from England, Gresham ever and anon expresses his concern for the welfare of his wife. " I shall most humbly beseech your highness," he said, addressing Queen Elizabeth in 1560, " to be a comfort unto my pore wife in this my absens in the service of your Majesty," and similar passages are comparatively of frequent recurrence in his correspondence with Secretary Cecil and Sir Thomas Parry, to whom he alternately recommends her, or returns thanks for the kind attentions she had experienced at their hands.

By this time some idea must have been formed of the nature and extent of the services which were continually required of Sir Thomas Gresham. That he not only discharged the duties of Agent, negotiating loans for the State, and of Queen's Merchant, in which capacity the task of furnishing the country with military and other stores continually devolved upon him, but that he corresponded with Sir William Cecil, as the ambassadors at foreign courts were accustomed. In truth, the very best proof of the opinion which was entertained of his abilities by Queen Elizabeth and her ministers is afforded by a mere inspection of the Flemish correspondence of the period. Many and interesting are the proofs supplied by the correspondence of these two eminent men of the watchfulness with respect to occurrences, and the system of espionage over persons which they maintained. But Gresham's most " delicate stratagem" was corrupting King Philip's servants, for he did not scruple to obtain the co-operation, subserviency, or connivance of persons in office, by a bribe or any other means within his power. Not altogether on strangers, however, did he depend for his own intelligence, like his illustrious friend Cecil, of whom Hoby said, " you come so by starts, as tonight you are here, and to-morrow you are gone;" he would be

---

* Hentzner's Travels, p. 31. Ed. 1797.

to-day at Antwerp, and on the slightest summons, in less than
four days in London; or, as was often the case, he was found
writing from Brussels and other towns, where he judged his
presence desirable. On such occasions the only mode of travelling
was by post horses; and on one of his hasty journeys, he met
with a fall, by which his leg was broken. This was in October,
1560, and the injury seems to have been serious, for the Queen,
four months afterwards, alludes to the accident in the following
terms:—"We trust after the prolongation of this February dett,
your legg will be hable to carry you a shipboard, to return to us;
where both for your recovery and for intelligence of your doings,
we shall be glad to see you." It appears from his subsequent
correspondence that he continued lame ever after.

During Gresham's residence at home the management of his
affairs was confided to Richard Clough, a Welshman, whom he
left behind him at Antwerp, and in whose zeal and ability he re-
posed entire confidence. This interesting individual belonged to
a family which had been settled from an early period in North
Wales. No evidence of the events of his early life exists except
the indubitable fact that, in the fervour of youthful zeal, he performed a pilgrimage to Jerusalem, where he was created a Knight
of the Holy Sepulchre. Having entered the service of Sir Thomas
Gresham in 1552, he contrived by his industry and ability to
amass a large fortune, and chose for his wife that remarkable
woman, Katharine Tudor, better known as Katharine of Berain,
great granddaughter of King Henry VII. Of the charms of this
lady her numerous portraits give indisputable evidence. Tradition
has been ill-natured enough to preserve an anecdote which if true,
however creditable to her charms, reflects little credit on her heart.
Her first husband was John Salusbury, at whose funeral, it is said,
she was led to church by Richard Clough, and afterwards conducted home by the youthful Morris Wynn, who availed himself
of that opportunity to whisper his wish to become her second
husband. She is said to have civilly informed him that on her
way to church she had accepted a similar proposal from Richard
Clough: but she consoled Wynn with the assurance that if she
survived her second husband, he might depend on becoming her
third; which he accordingly did, and when left a widow for the
third time, had still smiles left for a fourth and last husband,
Edward Thelwall, of Plâs y Ward, Esquire.

The active mind of Gresham was ever on the watch for opportunities to benefit the State; and as during his long residence at Antwerp he had witnessed the superiority of the Custom House regulations of that city, he now wrote to Clough to obtain complete information of the system pursued in Flanders, and in a very few days received for answer an epistle covering more than twenty sides of folio paper, and entering into all the details of those regulations with the utmost minuteness. The most interesting point in Richard Clough's letter was his suggestion relative to an Exchange for merchants, although the honour of having originated that project rests, as we have seen, with Sir Richard Gresham. He says, " Indede it is marvell that wee have so gude orders as wee have, consyderying what rulers wee have in the sittey of London, suche a company that do study for nothyng ells butt for their own profett. As for insampell; consyderyng what a sittey London ys, and that in so many yeares they have nott founde the menes to make a Bourse! but must wallke in the raine, when ytt raineth, more lyker pedlers than marchantes; and in thys countrie, and all other, there is no kynde of pepell that have occasion to meete, butt they have a plase meete for that pourpose. . . . . . In dede and yf your besynes were done, and that I myghtt have the lesure to go about ytt. . . . . I wyll nott doutt to make so fere a bourse in London as the grett bourse is in Andwarpe."

On the 2nd August, 1563, on the breaking out of the plague, in order to escape the infection, Gresham hastened with his family down to his "poor house at Intwood near Norwich," which was for a long time his only country seat, and where he seems to have been for many years in the habit of occasionally retiring with his family. Few traces of the old Hall now exist; the garden, however, retains its ancient raised terrace walks and turreted walls. Here, too, the ivy covered ruins of the red brick porch have been suffered to remain, and in the spandrils over the doorway are found the arms of Sir Richard Gresham, and his initials encircling the family crest, a grasshopper.

During the intervals between his late journeys, Gresham may be presumed to have been busy in the erection of the mansion in Bishopsgate Street. It is doubtless to this edifice that Clough alludes in the following passage which occurs in a letter addressed to his master in the beginning of 1563 " as towching the galary and the stones for the wyndose and walls, they are all shippyd in the shippe of John Ryke, who departyth from hens within two or three days at the furthemost."* Stow, speaking of the houses occupied by men of worship in St. Helen's and the neighbourhood, mentions Gresham House as " one the most spacious thereabouts, built of brick and timber."† Like the exchange it consisted of a square court, surrounded walk, or piazza, with spacious offices adjoining, the whole being surrounded by pleasant gardens, which extended from Bishopsgate Street on the one side to Broad Street on the other. Vast as the proportions of this mansion were, its inmates were merely himself and his lady, Richard, his only son, and Anne his natural daughter.

In 1564 we find Gresham writing from his " powre dowffe ‡ housse at Oystreley," and here he generally lived ever after. Norden, who wrote in 1593, calls Osterley House "a faire and stately building of bricke," and says of the extensive park which is still abundantly supplied with wood and water, that it was formerly "garnished with manie faire ponds, which afforded not only fish, and fowle, and swannes, and other water fowle, but also great use for mills, as paper mills, oyle milles, and cornmilles." The old manor house had been taken down by Gresham and rebuilt on a grander scale, but no drawing of it appears to be met with, nor can anything be added to the foregoing meagre description. About this period (1564) he lost his only son, who must have been between sixteen and twenty years of age. This must have been a heavy calamity, and perhaps in his estimation even counter-balanced the splendid results of a life of enterprise and ability.

Towards his daughter, Anne, whose mother is said to have been a native of Bruges, Gresham made the only reparation in his power, by bestowing upon her all the advantages of a careful education and an ample dower. She married into a family of high distinction, for the great Lord Bacon was her brother-in-law. Her husband was Sir Nathaniel Bacon, second son of Sir Nicholas, the Lord Keeper, by his first wife, Jane, the sister of Lady Gresham, so that his daughter Anne married one who should have been her cousin.

From the minutes of the Court of Aldermen, January 4, 1564-5, it appears that a proposal was made to the Court by Sir Thomas Gresham that a Bourse or Exchange should be built in

---

* See Burgon's Life of Sir Thomas Gresham, vol. i. p. 417. Ed. Lond. 1839.
† Stow's Survey, vol. i. p. 435.
‡ "'Dowffe' is the Scotch word for dull or melancholy." Burgon's Life of Sir Thomas Gresham, vol. ii. p. 77.

London at his expense for the accommodation of merchants, provided a site was found to build upon. A subscription was readily entered into for that purpose, and the ground on which the Exchange now stands was conveyed to him. In Stow's Chronicle it is stated that " upon good advice the citizens of London bought divers times, houses and many small tenements in Cornehill, and pulled them downe, and made the ground faire and plaine to build upon."*

On the 9th February, 1565-6, Sir Thomas Gresham being at the house of Alderman Ryvers, most frankly and lovingly promised that within a month after the Bourse should be fully finished, he would present it in equal moieties to the City and the Mercers' Company. In token of his sincerity he gave his hand to Sir William Garrard, and in the presence of his assembled friends drank a carouse to his kinsman, Thomas Rowe.

When the site on which it was intended the edifice should stand had been made clear, the length of the area from east to west on the Cornhill side was found to be 161 feet 6 inches. From Cornhill to Broad Street on the Swan Alley side, was 198 feet, and on the New Alley side, 149 feet 6 inches. The City paid to the proprietors of the soil for the whole number of houses 2208*l.* 6*s.* 8*d.*, to the tenants for their leases 1222*l.* 14*s.* 0*d.*, and in legal and other expenses 101*l.* 16*s.* 6*d.*, making in all 3532*l.* 17*s.* 2*d.* Towards defraying which, the City possessed 204*l.* 13*s.* 4*d.* The materials of the houses pulled down were sold for 478*l.* 3*s.* 4*d.*, and twenty of the principal Companies contributed 1685*l.* 9*s.* 7*d.* On the 13th September, 1566, an account was rendered by Sir Thomas Rowe of the proceedings of the Commissioners up to that day; by which it appears that their receipts had about equalled their disbursements.

No one can have compared the view of the Royal Exchange with the Bourse at Antwerp, without being struck with the extraordinary resemblance which those edifices bore to one another, which is sufficiently explained by the fact that a Flemish architect was employed to superintend the progress of the building. In Clough's letters to his master, this individual is termed Henryke, as in the following passage, dated July 22, " Towching the steves and other thyngs you wryte for, they are in hand, and shall be sent to you as soone as they are done: beying glad that you do so

---

* Stow's Chronicle, p. 667, ed. Lond. 1631.

well lyke Henryke, and that your works go so well forwards. So that, when he comyth over, I wyll follow your order for the rest." From this, and other passages, it would appear that the artist was in the habit of migrating from London to Antwerp, for the purpose of providing in the latter city the materials necessary for the prosecution of the work he had in hand in London. "Henryke and his men arryved here, and the carpendere also, whom I do mene shortly to retourne," says Clough, writing from Antwerp, August 4, 1566. It is quite surprising to perceive, from the incidental notices contained in his correspondence, to what an extent at this period an English edifice was indebted to continental artificers, not merely for its decorations, but for its most material features. "And as touching your things belonging to the Burse, they shall be provyded here, and sent away as soon as they shall be ready."—"And wyll not fayle but to send both the wainscot and the glass by the fyrst ship that shall depart for those parts. And for that he shall be well servyd of his wainscot, I do now send one to Amsterdam to provyde wainscot for the Bourse." And in April, 1567, " your Worship's man and his fellow . . . . . be here, ready to pass (in) these next ships for London ; wherefore, I mean to send them in one of the shippes layden with stone for the Borsse, for the which there ys three ships readie to depart from hence, as tomorrow, yf that the wynde serve them." The erection of the Bourse thus went forward; and in the course of a few months sufficient progress had been made to render it desirable to introduce the statues, all of which, with the exception of Queen Elizabeth's, appear to have been made in England. "I have received the pictures you wryte of," says Clough, " whereof I wyll cause the Queene's Majestie's to be made, and wyll sende you the rest back againe with that, so soon as yt ys done."

"A.D. 1570, on the 23rd of Januarie, the Queene's Majestie, attended by her nobilitie, came from her house at the Strande, called Somerset House, and entered the city by Temple Bar, through Fleete Streete, Cheapside, and so by the North side of the Burse, to Sir Thomas Gresham's in Bishopsgate Street, where she dined. After dinner, her majestie returning through Cornhill, entered the Burse on the south side, and after that she had viewed every part thereof above the ground, especially the pawne, which was richlie furnished with all sorts of the finest wares in the citie; she caused the same burse, by a heralde and a trompet, to be proclaimed the ROYAL EXCHANGE, and so to be called from thenceforth, and not otherwise."—Brief Memoir of Sir T. Gresham, p. 8, ed. Lond. 1832.

The last passage in Clough's letters, where the slates for the Bourse are mentioned, is October, 1567, which corresponds with

Stow's narrative—"By the month of November, in the year 1567, the same was covered with slate, and shortly after fully finished."*

The haste in which the Royal Exchange had been built (begun June 11, 1566, and covered in November, 1567) seems to have been inimical to its due stability, for the Ward Book of Cornhill, under so early a date as 1581, contains a copy of a supplication presented by the Ward Inquest to the Lord Mayor and Aldermen, requiring them "to take speedy orders for repayring the upper parts or arches of the Royal Exchange, being on the S.W. and S. parts thereof within the said Warde, whereunto the Merchants do commonly resorte, have accesse, and do walke," &c. Another entry in the Ward Book, under the date 1594, gives some intimation as to the manner in which the Vaults were appropriated:— "Presented William Grimbel for keping typlinge in the Vaults under the Exchange and for broyling of herringes, sprots, and bacon, and other thinges in the said Vaults, noisome to the Merchaunts and others resorting to the Exchange."

The Exchange having been destroyed at the great fire of London, it appears by the books of the Mercers' Company that on the 2nd November following estimates were ordered to be prepared for its rebuilding:—Feb. 1666-7. The joint committee of the Corporation and the Mercers' Company directed the ground to be cleared and prepared. May 3. That artists having applied for instructions, the committee agreed that the new Exchange should be built upon the old foundations, &c. On Oct. 23 King Charles II. laid the base of the column on the west side of the north entrance. His Majesty and suite were regaled under a temporary shed upon the "Scotch Walk" with a chine of beef, fowls, ham, dried tongues, anchovies, caviare, and wines. On the 31st of the same month the first stone of the eastern column was laid by the Duke of York, who was regaled in the same manner; and Nov. 18 following Prince Rupert laid the first stone of the pillar on the east side of the south entrance.

During the rebuilding the Merchants held their meetings at Gresham College. The New Exchange was opened September 28, 1669: from the books of the Mercers' Company it appears that the total cost was 58,962*l*.

Sir Thomas Gresham had for some years meditated the foundation of a school for the sons of the Citizens of London, but

---

* See Burgon's Life of Sir Thomas Gresham, vol. ii. pp. 115-121.

seems to have been undetermined where to establish it. Each of the Universities addressed him on the subject; he, however, resolved to convert his dwelling house in Bishopsgate Street into a College: to endow it with the revenues arising from the profits of the Royal Exchange, and to place it under the care of the same Trustees. The situation of the College, the accommodations of the Professors, the open courts and walks, with the offices, stables and gardens, were all well adapted for the purpose; the stipends for the Professors were also considered liberal for the period, the stated annual payments as directed by the will,* amounted to 603*l*. 6*s*. 8*d*., while the yearly rents of the Exchange received by him were 740*l*., but the Lady Anne Gresham was to enjoy both the Mansion and the Exchange during her life, in case she survived him.

Sir Thomas having thus settled his affairs, was at liberty to enjoy the fruits of his past labours, but the manner of his death discovered his prudence in not having deferred the performance of his good intentions to a sick bed, for upon Saturday, Nov. 21, 1579, between six and seven o'clock in the evening, coming from the Exchange to his house in Bishopsgate Street, he suddenly fell down in his kitchen, and died immediately afterwards. His obsequies were performed in a very solemn manner in the Church of St. Helen, where he had prepared a sumptuous tomb, without any epitaph or inscription.† The funeral was attended by 100 poor men and the like number of poor women, whom he had ordered to be clothed in black gowns of five shillings and eight pence per yard. The charges of the funeral amounted to eight hundred pounds.

By the inventory of his goods taken after his decease his chief seat appears to have been at Mayfield in Sussex, one room of which was called the Queen's Chamber, and the furniture, &c., belonging to it, were estimated at 7553*l*. 10*s*. 8*d*.

Sir Thomas is stated to have been generous and kind in all his actions. He was the great friend and patron of the Martyrologist John Foxe. Hugh Gough, who dedicated a book to him, particularly acknowledges his great liberality. His house was some-

---

* Pepys's Diary, vol. ii. p. 282, ed. Lond. 1848. "Sept. 7, 1666. This day our Merchants first met at Gresham College, which, by proclamation, is to be their Exchange." For Sir T. Gresham's Will, see Appendix.

† See Holinshed's Chronicle, vol. iv. p. 426. Until A.D. 1736, the monument bore no inscription. Then the following words from the Register were inscribed:—" Sir Thomas Gresham, Knight, bury^d Decem^b the 15th, 1579."

times appointed for the reception of foreign princes upon their first arrival in London. The most shining part of his character appears in his public benefactions, nor ought his charities to the poor, his eight almshouses, and liberal donations to the ten prisons and hospitals of London be forgotten.

Dame Anne Gresham continued to reside after his decease in the Mansion in London in the winter, and at Osterley in the summer season. In 1581 an Act of Parliament was passed for establishing an agreement between Lady Gresham and Sir Henry Nevill, and confirming the good uses and intents of the will, Lady Gresham still receiving the rents and profits, which then amounted to the yearly value of 751*l*. 5*s*. 0*d*. The leases of twenty-one years granted by Sir Thomas Gresham being nearly expired, she prevailed upon the tenants to take fresh leases of her for the like term at the old rents, with the addition of premiums amounting to 4000*l*. This was done a few months only before her decease, which took place Nov. 23, 1596, at Osterley Park, from whence she was brought to London, and buried in the same vault with her husband on the 14th December,* leaving one son, William, by her former husband, who was knighted and lived to a great age, as appears from a remarkable cause in which he was engaged in the year 1621, for being then outlawed upon an indictment for not repairing a bridge, he was afterwards admitted to his Writ of Error, and moved to pursue it by his attorney; but as this was against the rule of the Court, all the lawyers agreed that he must appear in person, and therefore being brought from his house, ten miles from London, in a horse litter, and upon men's shoulders into Court, he there assigned his error and put in bail. He was then eighty-three years old, and had kept his bed upwards of a year. His son, Sir Thomas Reade, married Mildred, the second daughter of Thomas Cecil, Lord Burghley, died at Osterley, July 3, 1595, and was buried July 14 in Sir Thomas Gresham's vault in St. Helen's Church.

About 1645 several ingenious men who resided in London, and were interested in the progress of Natural Philosophy, agreed to meet once a week to discourse on subjects connected with those

---

* "The funeral of Dame Gresham, wyfe of Sir Thomas Gresham, Knyght, who was buryed the 18th of Dec. 1596, at the Chryche of St. Ellens, London. The officers serving then were Clarencieux and Rouge Croix, pursuivants-at-arms, who received for their ffees fourtye pounds. T. Rouge Croix." Harleian MS. No. 6033.

sciences. The Meetings were held sometimes in Dr. Goddard's lodgings in Wood Street—because he kept in his house an operator for grinding glasses for telescopes—sometimes in Gresham College. In the year 1648-9 several of the gentlemen who used to attend these meetings being appointed to situations in the University of Oxford, they instituted a similar society in that city. The greatest part of these Oxford gentlemen coming to London in 1659, held their meetings twice a week at Gresham College. These meetings were continued till the Members were scattered after the resignation of Richard Cromwell, when their place of meeting was converted into quarters for soldiers; but after the restoration of King Charles II. in 1660, these meetings were revived and still more numerously attended. On the 28th Nov. 1660, a number of gentlemen met in Mr. Rooke's apartment in Gresham College, and agreed to constitute themselves into a Society for the Promotion of all kinds of Experimental Philosophy. Regulations were drawn up, and a weekly contribution of a shilling was collected from each of the Members, in order to defray the expenses of their experimental investigations. At first the number was limited to fifty-five, but it was afterwards extended, and finally admission was left open to every proper candidate. Such was the origin of the Royal Society of London. On July 15, 1662, a Royal Charter was granted by Charles II.; their first meetings were held at Gresham College. They afterwards removed to Crane Court, Fleet Street, where they continued to hold their meetings until 1780, when apartments were provided for them in Somerset House, where they always afterwards met until their removal in 1874 to Burlington House, Piccadilly, rebuilt for the Royal Academy of Arts, and other learned Societies.

CÆSAR ADELMARE.

Cæsar Adelmare* was the second son of Peter Maria Adelmare and Paola Cæsarino. The family was of Italian origin, and had

---

* The following details have been supplied by Miss F. E. Cottrel-Dormer, of Danes Dyke, Flamborough, a lineal descendant of the Cæsar family:—
"The facts relating to the family of Adelmare were taken from a Latin MS. (brought with an English translation) by my great-grandmother to Renshaw, Oxfordshire, on her marriage to Sir Charles Cottrell-Dormer, Knight, from MS. written by Nicholas Maurus, of Treviso, 1598.

"The Adelmary, Adelmari, or Adimari, came from Florence: but in the wars between the Houses of Guelph and Gibeline, they being adherents of

been long seated in the city of Treviso, near Venice, in the rank of nobility. P. M. Adelmare was a Doctor of both laws, and particularly eminent as a civilian. He had three sons, of whom the second having been educated for the medical profession, in which he had taken his degree of Doctor in the University of Padua, came into England in the year 1550. Italy at that time produced many eminent medical men. Having practised for some time in London, Dr. Adelmare was appointed Physician to Queen Mary; and in the following reign was at the head of the medical department at Court. His reputation long survived him, for we find among the Sloane Manuscripts in the British Museum a volume of recipes inscribed " Ex. Manuscriptis D. Dris Cæsar Excerpta," 1683, of 240 pages, which Sir Hans had taken the pains to transcribe very neatly. However his skill might have been esteemed at Court, we do not find that he experienced any extraordinary degree of liberality from either of the princesses whom he served. He had a lease for twenty-one years from 1566 from the Crown of the prebend of Higher Hayne and other lands in the county of Devon, which were leased to him at 24*l.* 8*s.* 4*d.* ℞ ann. He had also a lease for twenty-one years from Michs. 1568 jointly with Thomas Coleshill at the yearly rent of 8*l.* 16*s.* 1*d.* of the rectory of St. Helen's,* in which parish he had on the 21st May, 1561, purchased of the son of Balthasar Quercy an estate which had been granted to that Balthasar, by letters patent of the 21st April, 1539, and therein denominated, the neat house† and gardens, late part of the dissolved priory of St. Helen's, situate within the close of the said priory. Here Dr. Adelmare fixed his residence, and in 1569 died, and was buried in the Chancel of the parish church.

---

the Guelphs, settled at Treviso in the reign of Frederic II., where we find them A.D. 1240, and they remained there some 300 years. . . . . Peter Maria, son of Bonfrank, many years Judge at Treviso, and also Ambassador to the Emperor Maximilian, married Paula, daughter and heiress of John de Paulo Cæsarino, of the ducal family of that name. Their second son seems simply to have called himself Cæsar Adelmare, Cæsar in his case being probably his baptismal name. He settled in England, and became physician to Queen Mary Tudor, and after her death to Queen Elizabeth, the latter queen having, it is said, expressed her wish that he should take an English wife: he married a Mrs. Margaret Perrin." The information supplied by Miss Cottrell-Dormer is distinguished by the initials F. E. C.-D.

* See above, p. 48.

† This house was No. 29, Great St. Helen's, which has long since been demolished. The ground is now covered with modern offices.

Dr. Adelmare married Margaret, daughter of Martin Perin or Perient, who is styled in the visitation of Kent made in 1619, Treasurer in Ireland. By this Margaret he had five sons and three daughters. His widow was afterwards married to Michael Lock of London.

Julius Cæsar was born at Tottenham in 1557, and baptized at St. Dunstan's on the 10th February in that year by the names of Julius Cæsar, the latter of which he afterwards adopted as a surname, almost wholly abandoning that of his ancestors, while some of his brothers and their issue even to a late period in some measure retained it by using the designation of Cæsar, alias Adelmare. The exalted rank of his Sponsors at the font affords a sufficient proof of the estimation in which his father was held at Court. They were William Powlett, Marquis of Winchester and Lord Treasurer; Henry Fitzalan, Earl of Arundel, and the Queen herself, represented by the Lady Montacute. It would have been strange if the son of an Italian, who was in the service of the most bigoted popish Sovereign in Europe, had received the rudiments of religious education in any other faith; but he lost his father when he was only twelve years old, and his mother remarrying a zealous Protestant, his youthful mind was easily turned to that persuasion, and he became a student at Magdalen Hall, Oxford, where he took his degree of Bachelor of Arts, 17th May, 1575, and that of Master of Arts at Midsummer Term, 1578.*

He remained at the University until the end of the following year, when he went to Paris, to finish the study of his profession as a civilian, and on the 15th, 18th, and 22nd April, 1581, was admitted there Bachelor, Licentiate, and Doctor of both Laws, having had the last of those degrees conferred on him also at Oxford on the fifth of the preceding month. On the 10th May, 1582, he received the complimentary appointment of advocate in the Parlement of Paris, and a few weeks afterwards returned to England, which he seems never again to have quitted. On the 9th October he received his first public professional employment,

---

* Lodge says, "We learn many of these facts, &c., particularly those to which dates are affixed, from a paper among the MSS. of Dr. Birch, preserved in the British Museum, indorsed—' Extracts of a MS. in vol. v. of the MSS. of Sir Julius Cæsar:' 'A short memorial or brief chronicle of things past concerning my father, myself, my wives and children.'" Lodge says that the papers of Sir Julius were sold for 20*l.* by his great-great-grandson, Charles Cæsar. F. E. C.-D.

which was, to use his own words, that "of Justice of the Peace in all causes of piracy, and such like throughout the land," an office no longer known, and the precise duties and faculties of which it might perhaps be difficult to define. On the fifteenth of the same month he was appointed Chancellor to the Master of the Royal Peculiar of St. Katharine's, near the Tower. He now laid the surest foundation for his advantage by a most prudent match with Dorcas, daughter of Richard Martin, an Alderman of London, who was afterwards knighted, filled the office of Lord Mayor, A.D. 1593, and was Master of the Mint in the reigns of Elizabeth and James I. To this lady, who, although scarcely twenty years old, was already the widow of Richard Lusher, a student of the Middle Temple, he was married February 26th in the same year, according to the old style of calculation.

In 1583, as we are informed by his journal, he was nominated Counsellor to the City of London, and on the 26th of the following December was made Commissary of Essex, Herts, and Middlesex. "These were his several gradations towards the Bench, and he became Judge of the Admiralty Court, April 30th, in the following year. It seems strange that this dignified promotion should have been almost immediately succeeded by his acceptance of a very inferior appointment, as, on the 21st June, he was sworn in a Master in Chancery, of the class which is denominated 'extraordinary,' since he afterwards tells us, Oct. 9th, 1588—'I was admitted a Master in Chancery in Ordinary;' but it was one feature of the rudeness of those times for persons to hold offices widely dissimilar in their character and in the degrees of dignity and profit."

"On the 15th September, 1584, his first child was born, and named after her mother, Dorcas. She was married, when very young, to Thomas Anderson, Esq., a barrister, and died childless, at her husband's house at Thames Ditton, in Surrey, of an imposthume or dropsy, April 1, 1608. His second child, Charles, who died at a month old, was born Oct. 3rd, 1586; and his third, Julius, on the 14th February, 1587, of whose premature death he has the following note in his minutes for the year 1607. Jan. 8th, says he:—'My second son and third child, Juley, being upon the point of twenty years of age, was slain in Padua, an University of Italy, upon a private quarrel between another and himself.' His third son, Charles, who thus became his heir, was born the 27th January, 1589."

"The slenderness of the profits of his respectable office induced him about that time to solicit some aid to support its dignity, and he is found in this year, 1589, making the heaviest complaints of the hardships of his situation, the circumstances, however, of which it is impossible precisely to conceive. A Judge relieving the wants of poor suitors in his Court from his own purse; expending four thousand pounds more than his profits (a sum equal at least to ten thousand now) in seven years, on occasions of actual public service; and sacrificing his interests and his comforts to a high sense of duty, are phenomena which we cannot hope to solve, and which in these days must be utterly incomprehensible."

"On the 10th January, 1590, Dr. Cæsar was sworn into the much-coveted office of Master of Requests, and thus became a medium of communication between the Crown and the petitioning suitors of his Court, being now enabled to obtain, or rather to give, prompt answers, and to procure from the Sovereign those occasional extra-judicial boons, the distribution of which from his private means had nearly dried up the sources of his own liberality. These, however, were almost the only advantages attending his present appointment, which was that of a Master Extraordinary, and probably with very little, if any, emolument." About five years afterwards, August 17th, 1595, however, his suit was fully granted; for he says in his minutes—" Being the Lord's day, her Majesty delivered me Bills offered to her, and received going to the Chapel, and so possessed me of my *ordinary* place of Master of the Requests attendant on her person."

"On the 16th July, 1591, Elizabeth signed a patent to him for the reversion of the Mastership of St. Katharine's Hospital, near the Tower. On July 25th, in the next year, he was put into the commission of the peace for the county of Middlesex; was chosen Treasurer of the Inner Temple, November 11th, 1593, and soon afterwards, December 6th, appointed Governor of the Mine and Battery Works throughout England and Wales."

"On the 30th May, 1595, his fourth son, Richard, was born and baptized at Hornsey, where Dr. Cæsar then lived. The birth of this child, who did not survive twelve months, was fatal to the mother, who died on the 16th of the ensuing month, at the age of thirty-four, and was buried in the Temple Church. Dr. Cæsar did not remain a widower quite a year. April 10th, 1596, he says in his minutes, 'I married my second wife, Alice Dent, of London, widow, at her house at Mitcham, where for many years after this date he fixed his rural abode. This lady died May 23rd, 1614, and was buried with great pomp, June 30th, at St. Helen's.'"

"In 1596 he succeeded to the Mastership of St. Katharine. A letter from Dr. Cæsar to Lord Burghley, relative to this appointment, furnishes an anecdote of singular curiosity. It appears, not only that Dr. Cæsar gave 500*l.* to Archibald Douglas, the Scotch Ambassador, as a bribe for his interest with Elizabeth to procure the appointment, but that the Ministers, and even the Queen herself, had known from the beginning that it had been obtained by means of a bargain of that kind, though they were not previously informed of the amount of the sum. Elizabeth, who neglected no means of keeping her servants in a state of dependence on herself, was particularly careful to prevent their becoming rich. She had been informed that he had paid a larger douceur to Douglas than he really had, and determined to stop his further preferment; he was therefore obliged to make this candid avowal, and by her subsequent conduct it appears that the Queen was satisfied."

On the 29th October, in the same year, Elizabeth signed his patent for 100*l.* a year fee, for his attendance on her person and in the Court of Requests. He now made his London residence at St. Katharine's, where his fifth son, John, was born, October 20th, 1597.

"Having thus become at least independent, and perhaps growing wealthy, Elizabeth honoured him with the fearful distinction of a visit. Tuesday, September 12th, 1598, he says, "The Queen visited my house at Mitcham, and supped, and lodged there, and dined there next day. I presented her with a gown of cloth of silver, richly embroidered; a black network mantle, with pure gold; a taffeta hat, white, with flowers; and a jewel of gold set therein with rubies and diamonds. Her Majesty removed from my house after dinner, the thirteenth of September, to Nonesuch, with exceeding good contentment, which entertainment of her Majesty, with the charge of the former disappointment, amounted to Seven

Hundred Pounds sterling, besides mine own provisions, and whatever was sent me by my friends."*

"On May 10th, 1600, Dr. Cæsar was promoted to the post of eldest Master of the Court of Requests; on the 17th of March following his sixth son, Thomas, was born, as was on the 9th October, 1602, his seventh son and last child, Robert."

"The Queen died March 24th, in the same year. During her reign his life had been invariably marked by anxiety and discontent. A better fate awaited him under her successor," James I., by whom he was knighted at Greenwich, May 20th, 1603. "In this instance the title was honoured rather than the man."

April 7th, 1606, George Hume, Earl of Dunbar, resigned the offices of Chancellor and Under Treasurer of the Exchequer. On Friday, the 11th, the King gave those offices to Sir Julius Cæsar. "The principal duties at that time of a Chancellor of the Exchequer were performed in the capacity of Chief Judge in that Court, the peculiar province of which was to administer justice in all controversies which related to the King's revenues, strictly so called. His secondary occupation was in the private and extra-judicial conservation and management of the sources of those revenues, and in the application of them to the public and private disbursements of the Crown." Sir Julius now grew rapidly into favour. "'On Good Friday, May 13th, 1607,' say his minutes, 'I was licensed to come into the Withdrawing Chamber, next to the Privy Chamber, where the Privy Councillors stay, and there

---

* See Nichols' Royal Progresses, vol. iii. pp. 428-9. Ed. Lond. 1823.

A portrait at Rensham, Oxfordshire, represents Lady Cæsar Adelmare at the time when the Queen came to visit her husband. She shortly afterwards had a child, who, so says that babbling Dame Tradition, was wrapped in a chemise of the virgin Queen, left behind for that purpose, which garment, alas! was lost within the memory of man by the Chester family. This Lady Cæsar was a divorced wife, daughter of Mr. Christopher Grant, and widow of a Mr. Dent of London. Sir Julius had first married Mrs. Dorcas Martin, who died 1595. The child above-mentioned was John Cæsar, who died 1647. Sir Julius married, thirdly, Mrs. Anne Hungate, widow, daughter of Sir Henry Woodhouse or Wodehouse, of Waxham, Norfolk. I do not know when she died. She was niece to Sir Francis Bacon, Lord Verulam, her mother, Lady Wodehouse, having been the daughter of Sir Nicholas Bacon, Master of the Rolls, and the great Bacon died in the arms of Sir Julius Cæsar, who was sent for to the bedside of his wife's uncle at the house of Lord Arundel, at Highgate, 1626.—See Life of Lord Bacon, by Lord Campbell, pp. 425-6. Ed. London, 1846.—F. E. C.-D.

to stay likewise at my pleasure.' This distinction was perhaps an accustomed prelude to that dignity, for he was sworn of the Privy Council on the 5th of the succeeding July."

On the 16th January, 1610, the King had given him by patent under the Great Seal, the reversion of the office of Master of the Rolls, after the death, forfeiture, or surrender of Sir Edward Philips, and on his death, September 11th, 1614, he was accordingly promoted to it. He was sworn in two days afterwards. He had lately removed from St. Katharine's to the Strand, nearly opposite the Savoy, where with his wife he laid the foundation of a New Chapel, August 10th, 1613, which, as we are informed by Stow,* received the name of Cecil Chapel, and was consecrated on the 8th May following by the Bishop of London.† Fifteen days after this date Lady Cæsar died, at the age of forty-four years and eleven months, and was buried at St. Helen's.

To recur to the private life of Sir Julius Cæsar: his love of domestic society induced him, though now somewhat advanced in years, to take a third wife. On April 19th, 1615, he was married at the Rolls Chapel to Mrs. Anne Hungate, a widow, of an age not unsuitable to his own. " Her hand was given to Sir Julius at the nuptial ceremony by her uncle, the great Sir Francis Bacon, then Attorney-General; and the friendship which had long subsisted between these two eminent persons was strengthened and confirmed by this marriage. That glorious and melancholy instance of the extent of human wisdom and weakness, the philosopher Bacon, found, after his disgrace, an asylum in the bosoms of his nephew and niece, composed many of his immortal works in an utter retirement in the house of Sir Julius Cæsar; became dependent upon his beneficence for a becoming support, and expired in his arms."

"December 12th, 1615 (as we are informed by the curious and very extensive Common Place Book of his grandson, Mr. Charles Cæsar), ' the Earl of Essex after his divorce, having been sentenced to pay back his Lady's portion, to raise part of it, sold his hunting house, with a large park of deer, and his Manor of

---

* Survey, vol. ii. p. 108.

† " John King, S.T.P., Archdeacon of Nottingham and Dean of Christ Church, was confirmed Bishop of London, Sept. 7th, 1611, consecrated at Lambeth, Sept. 8th, and died March 30th, 1621, ætat. 62."—See Le Neve's Fasti, vol. ii. p. 303. Ed. (Hardy) Oxon, 1854.

Bennington, in Hertfordshire, to Sir Julius Cæsar for the sum of fourteen thousand pounds.'"

"The remainder of his life affords few circumstances to the biographer. The history of his last twenty years is for the most part written in the records of his Court. His own minutes, preserved in the Lansdowne Collection,* present us, after this period, with little beyond the usual records of an old man's pen—complaints of decaying health, and lamentations for the loss of friends."

"Sir Julius Cæsar died on Easter Day, April 18th, 1636, O.S., in the seventy-ninth year of his age, and was buried on the 28th in the Chancel† of St. Helen's Church, where his Monument (executed, as we are informed, by Mr. Walpole), at a charge of One Hundred and Ten Pounds, with its curious device and inscription, designed and written by himself, remains in a state of high preservation."

"His Will, dated February 27th, 1635, was proved the day after his death. It contains scarcely any except charitable legacies, for his affection for his children, his natural disinterestedness, and his professional experience, had united to induce him to settle his real estates on them in his lifetime, which he had done, as he there informs us, 'many years before, by good assurances in the law.' He desires to be buried in the parish church of St. Helen's, where his 'father, mother, first son Charles, only daughter Dorcas, brother Sir Thomas, and second wife Alice lye, in the upper part of the Chancel,' and with a strict charge that ' all manner of superfluities commonly spent on funerals may be avoided;' and that his body may be buried ' whole and unopened,' the evening after his death, or with all convenient expedition. Then, having spoken of the settlement on his children, he adds, 'And I beseech God to bless respectively my said three sons, Charles, John, and Robert, and their wives and children, with a zeal for His glory, with a perfect love and practice of godliness and righteousness, peace and truth, all their days; with a good conscience, to walk painfully, soberly, justly, and religiously, in their several callings; to hate idleness, the mother of all vices; to abhor all excess and riot, in meat, drink, apparel, and vain delights; to be humble, meek, and gentlehearted, doing unto all men as they would be done unto, avoiding quarrels, and all occasions of quarrel, all the days of their lives;

---

* Lansdowne MSS., vol. clxi. No. 329.

† This is a mistake. The monument is in the South-transept.

that so living in the fear of God, they may so die in His favour, and enter at their deaths into the eternal life of glory, by the only free mercy of God, in the merits and passion of our Saviour Jesus Christ.'"

"He then bequeaths to the poor of Saint Helen's 5*l*., to the three Brethren and three Sisters of the Hospital of St. Katharine, 3*l*. each, and to each of the ten poor Beadeswomen 40*s*.; to the poorest of the precincts of St. Katharine 10*l*.; to the Hospitals of St. Bartholomew and St. Thomas in Southwark and to the two Compters and the prisons of Ludgate, Newgate, and the Fleet, the King's Bench, Marshalsea, and the White Lion in Southwark, and the Gatehouse in Westminster, and to Bethlehem Hospital 5*l*. each."

"He gives to his son, Sir Charles Cæsar, of Bennington, his written book called Polyanthea Cæsaris, in folio, and his Enchiridion, both written by his own hand; and a moiety of all his written books to be found either in his study at Hackney, or in the two great presses at the Rolls; and also his written book of the Ten Commandments, the Lord's Prayer, and the Three Creeds in Six Languages, with divers Psalms of David and Verba Verbi-Incarnati in Greek, written all with his own hand."

"To his son Sir John Cæsar, of Hide Hall, all the books in the Chapel of his house at Hackney, to remain to that house so long as it shall continue in his name and family; and to his son Robert, one of the Six Clerks in Chancery, his written book called the Register of the Chancery, and the other moiety of his written books in his studies at Hackney and at the Rolls. The residue, plate, jewels, mares, horses, coaches, caroches, household stuff, implements of house, ready money, silver vessels, debts, &c., he bequeaths to his wife, Anne Cæsar, whom he constitutes sole executrix, appointing as overseers his friends, Sir Edmund Bacon, of Redgrave in Suffolk, Bart., and Sir Henry Marten, Judge of the Prerogative Court, Canterbury, to each of whom he gives 30 oz. of gilt plate."

"His character presents to us a picture of the most perfect integrity, sweetened and adorned by great mildness of temper, and a constant benevolence. 'He clothed his very denials,' says Lloyd,[*] 'in such robes of courtship, as that it were not easy discernible whether the request or denial were most decent; and

---

[*] State Worthies.

was a person of such prodigious bounty to all persons of worth or want, that he might seem to be Almoner General of England. A Gentleman,' continues the same writer, 'once borrowing his coach, which was as well known to the poor as any hospital in the kingdom, was so followed and encompassed with the London beggars, that it cost him all the money in his purse to satisfy their importunity, so that he might have hired twenty hackney coaches on the same terms.'" Isaac Walton, in his Life of Sir Henry Wotton,[*] who had been promised the reversion to his place, states "that Sir Julius Cæsar was said to be kept alive beyond Nature's course by the prayers of those many poor whom he daily relieved." His conduct on the Bench displayed the most earnest desire to do justice, the most unwearied patience in the pursuit of it, and a sympathy in the sufferings of the unfortunate who came under his judicial observation, of which no parallel instance can be found.

"Somewhat of his more private and domestic character may be inferred from some verses written by himself, and to which the following entry in his minutes may properly serve as an introduction. 'This,' he says, 'was the answer of my godfather, William Poulet, Knt., Lord St. John, Earl of Wiltshire, Marquis of Winchester, Lord High Treasurer of England, being demanded by an inward friend, how he had lived in the times of King Edward IV., King Richard III., King Henry VII., King Henry VIII., King Edward VI., Queen Mary, and Queen Elizabeth, in all times of his life increasing in greatness of honour and preferment.

> "'Late supping I forbear;
> Wine and Women I forswear;
> My neck and feet I keep from cold:
> No marvel then though I be old,
> I am a willow, not an oak:
> I chide, but never hurt with stroke.'"

In the Commonplace Book of his grandson, Mr. Charles Cæsar, we find the following continuation, entitled by him "Sir Julius Cæsar's Notes."

> "Never let wrath dwell in thy house,
> Wrath reason doth subdue;
> It breeds sharp fevers, and by it
> May sudden death ensue.

---

[*] P. 92. Ed. Oxford, 1824.

>Awake with joy, arise with speed;
>Attire thyself as thou hast need;
>Wash hands and face, and comb thy head;
>Pray, and peruse the holy read;
>Then to thy calling thee apply;
>Let not extortion gain thereby;
>So that thou do to every wight
>As thou wouldst him to do thee right.

>"If thou be free, become not bound;
>If wrapt in debt, or likewise found
>Deceived by choice of wicked wife,
>Thank God, but still beware of strife.
>If she do chide, no answer give,
>Her wants supply, her griefs relieve;
>Rejoice in her, and please her still,
>And always let her have her will.
>But, above all, fear God above;
>And live and die in perfect love;
>And seek for bliss in Christ alone,
>Who died to rid thee from all grone."

Sir Julius Cæsar sold the house No. 29 in Great St. Helen's in 1581 to William Harrington, from whom it passed in 1590 to William Bond, and from him in 1595 to William, Thomas, and William Hewitt. It was conveyed by the Hewitt family in 1674 to George Finch, and passed from his son William Finch in 1716 to Edward Browne, in whose family it remained till 1788, when Elizabeth Browne sold it to Thomas Woodroffe Smith, of Stockwell Park, in the county of Surrey.

Sir Thomas Cæsar, Knight,* the third son of Dr. Adelmare, was born in 1561. He became a Barrister of considerable fame and practice, and was raised to the dignity of a Baron of the Exchequer on the 26th May, 1610, and was knighted at Whitehall on the 25th of the following month.

He was thrice married. His first wife died about the end of June, 1590, as appears by her will, made with the consent of her husband. She there styles herself Susan, "wife of Thomas Dalmare, alias Cæsar, of the Middle Temple, Gent.," and bequeaths to her mother, Chapman, a ring of gold with a red stone; and to her son Thomas, and her daughters Ellen and Margery, 6l. 13s. 4d. each,

---

* The memoirs of the several members of the Cæsar family, although not in direct succession to the period, when other "Worthies" of St. Helen's lived, here follow in order to preserve a continuous reference to the particulars concerning them.

all of whom died infants. His second wife was Anne, daughter of George Lynn of Southwick, in the county of Northampton, Esq., and widow of Nicholas Beeston, a Lincolnshire gentleman, who died childless.

Sir Thomas Cæsar married thirdly, at Stepney, January 18th, 1592, Susan, daughter of Sir William Ryther, Knight, an Alderman of London. This lady and her sister Mary, the wife of Sir Thomas Lake, one of the Secretaries of State to King James I., became by the death of their only brother, Ferdinando, in 1603, co-heirs to their father, and jointly inherited his great wealth. This lady brought Sir Thomas three sons and five daughters.

" Of Sir Thomas Cæsar's public and professional life we have no account, beyond his general reputation as a sound lawyer, an able pleader, and an upright judge. Some opinion of his domestic character may be formed from the following short extract from a letter to his brother, Sir Julius, marking so strongly the honest good-humour and kindness of the writer:—

" . . . . There are offered me now to be sold three mannors in this Countie for 4000*l*. If the price, title, and assurance thereof, after good and deliberate view aud consideracʼon thereof (for I have not yet surveyed them) shall like me, I pray tell my swete sister, yoʳ diamonde, that I will not forget the imployment of hir stocke to the ratable benefite of so muche money; and if it returne under 20 in the 100 gayner, tell hir I shall think my paynes ill imployed for hir : but, if wee deale, how great soev'r the gayne shalbe, it shalbe hir's, according to the proporcʼon of hir adventure. I hope yoʳ jointe and sev'rall issues be well: God blesse them all, and make you happy parents of them. My sweet harte and I, with my brothers Beck and Peck, and their wives, doe all of us recomʼend oʳ duties to yoʳself, and my sweete sister yoʳ wief, and do pray you to remembʳ us to my brother Charles, and my brother Henry, when you shall see them. And so, readie to doe you or my Sister any service in theis pᵗˢ or elsewhere I comʼend you to the m'cifull p'teccʼon of the Almightie. From Eastmeaue, this 17 of M'che 1597.

"Yoʳ most assured loving brother,

"Thoˢ. Cæsar."[*]

---

[*] Lansdowne MSS., vol. clx. No. 169.

Sir Thomas Cæsar died June 9th, 1621, and his widow remarried to Thomas, second son of Sir John Philpott, of Compton Wascelin, in Hants, Knight, and died in the year 1640.

Of the other sons of Dr. Adelmare, Charles, the second son, was a military man of high reputation, and died childless. Of the fourth son, William, we have no further intelligence than that he was an eminent merchant; and the fifth son, Henry, studied at Oxford, and also at Cambridge. When a very young man he was presented to the Vicarage of Lostwithiel, in Cornwall, and took his degree as Doctor of Divinity at Oxford, Nov. 6th, 1595. Soon after which he was presented by the Queen to the Rectory of St. Christopher-le-Stock, Lothbury; he afterwards held several other livings, and in 1614 succeeded Dr. Tyndall in the Deanery of Ely, where he died 27th June, 1636, in his 72nd year, and lies buried on the north side of the Presbytery of Ely Cathedral.*

Sir Charles Cæsar, Knight, the third son of Sir Julius in order of birth, became his heir, Charles, the eldest, having died in infancy, and Julius, the second, having been snatched away by a violent and premature death when he had just attained to manhood.† Sir Charles was educated at All Souls' College, Oxford,‡ was admitted D.C.L. A.D. 1612, and was knighted at Theobald's, Oct. 6th, A.D. 1613. Having practised the profession of the Law, he became a Master of the Court of Chancery on the 30th September, 1619, and at length rose to the important office of Master of the Rolls, in which he succeeded Sir Dudley Digges.§ "True it is, however strange it may appear in our day, that he purchased the appointment of Charles I. in the commencement of that unfortunate Prince's distresses. We find in the MSS. of his second son, Mr. Charles Cæsar, the following Memorandum:—" June 14, 1640.—Sir Charles Cæsar, Kn^t. was sworn Master of the Rolls in Chancery, or Assistant Judge to the Lord High Chancellor of England; for which high and profitable office he paid to King Charles the first Fifteen Thousand Pounds, broad pieces of old gold; and lent the King two thousand more when he went to meet his rebellious Scotch Army, invading England." . . . . " He enjoyed the fruit of his purchase little more than two years, for on the 6th of December he fell

---

* See Le Neve's Fasti Eccles. Anglican., vol. ii. p. 348. Ed. Oxford (Hardy), 1854. † See above, p. 289.
‡ See Lodge's Lives of the Cæsars, p. 49. Ed. Lond. 1827.
§ See Lodge's Lives of the Cæsars, p. 49.

a prey to the Small Pox, a malady peculiarly fatal in his family." The following extract is from his Nuncupative Will, which was made only two days previous to his death : " I have now gotten the Small Poxe after I am three and fiftie years of age, though I had them heretofore in my younger daies."*

---

* Archbishop Laud in his notes of the 6th day of his trial says :—"There was a fling at Sir Charles Cæsar getting of the Mastership of the Rolls for money, and that I was his means for it ; and so it was thence inferred that I sold places of Judicature, or helped sell them. For this they produced a paper under my hand : but when they had thrown all the dirt they could upon me, they said they did only show what probabilities they had for it, and what reason they had to lay it in the end of the fourth original article, and so deserted it. And well they might ; for I never had more hand in this business than that when he came to me about it, I told him plainly, as things then stood, that place was not likely to go without more money than I thought any wise man would give for it. Nor doth the paper mentioned say any more but that I informed the Lord Treasurer what had passed between us." See History of Archbishop Laud's Troubles and Trials, p. 279.—F. E. C.-D.

Extract from Lodge's Lives of the Cæsars, in Cur. Prerog. Cant. Memorand. :—"That on Sunday, Dec. 4th, 1642, Sir Charles Cæsar, Kt., &c., lying sicke in his bedd, in an upper chamber att his house called The Rolles, in Chancery Lane, having notice that David Budd was in the said howse, and come to visite him, sent for him to come into the chamber where he lay sicke, and being come, the said Sir Charles used these words:— 'David I have now gotten the smalle-poxe after I am three and fifty years of age, though I had them heretofore in my younger daies, but I thanke God, I am reasonable well; yet if I growe worse, if you bee not afraide to come to me, I will send to you to make my will in writinge;' and then further said these words : ' As I have often declared that my sonne Henry shoulde have all my lands at Toseland, soe it is my will still ; and I doe will that all those lands, and all my lands in Yelling, I meane both the Yellings, shall bee for Henry and his heires ; and that all my lands in Gransden shall be for my sonne Charles and his heires ; and, for my lands at Bennington, and in Lincolnshire ; I have already settled them on my sonne Julius. The lands at Toseland and Yelling are worth fower hundred and fifty pounds a yeare, and Gransden is worth about twoe hundred pounds a yeare; which will be somewhat for younger Brothers.' Which words the said Sir Charles uttered and spake with an intention to settle his estate and to declare his will, before credible witnesses, his Ladie beinge then likewise p'tent in the same chamber : and the same Sir Charles was att all p'misses in good mind and memorie, and talked and discoursed sensibly. This was saide on the Sunday aforesaid, about two of the clocke in the afternoone in p'sence of us whose names are underwritten, and then presently put into writing before Evening Prayer began. RICHARD EDWARDS.
DA. BUDD.

"Julius, the short-lived heir, rather to his father's contagious disease than to his estates, died five days after Sir Charles, Dec. 11th, 1642. A daughter,

Sir John Cæsar, Knt., the second surviving son of Sir Julius, attended James I. in his journey to Scotland in 1617, and received there, in his minority, from that prince the honour of knighthood. In 1625 his father settled him in an independence suited to his station by a grant of estates in Hertfordshire. In Chauncey's history of that county " that writer informs us, oddly enough, that Sir John Cæsar was a justice of the peace for that county divers years, being qualified with a strong constitution, and ready smart parts." He died at Hyde Hall, May 23rd, 1647, in the fifty-fourth year of his age.

Jane, had died of the same malady about a month before, aged two years."—Lodge, pp. 50, 51.

Sir Charles Cæsar Adelmare's first wife was Anne Vanlore, daughter of Sir Peter Vanlore, Knight. We read in Murray's Handbook for Berks, Bucks, and Oxon:—" From Reading 3 m. on N. 1½ m. *Tilehurst*. The Church preserves the monument of Sir Peter Vanlore, ——, a rich Merchant, 1627, and his lady." P. 54. The portrait of this lady is at Rensham, Oxon. She wears most magnificent lace, elaborately painted, and handsome jewels, one on the thumb of one hand. The second wife is represented in her portrait, also at Rensham, in the dress of a widow, at that time seemly having performed her devotions, and the monument of her husband in the background. She was the daughter of Sir Edward Barkham, Knight (Alderman of London) who had served the office of Mayor, 1622. She died in the house of her son, Charles Cæsar, at Much Hadham, Herts, 1661. She had passed most of the years of her widowhood at Linwood, in Lincolnshire. To her favourite son, Charles, she left " the great jewel which was left her by her mother, Lady Barkham." Her will is Reg. in Cur. Prerog. Cant.

Sir Henry Cæsar Adelmare, Knight, succeeded his father, Sir Charles Cæsar, and being within age at the death of the former, his wardship was granted to Jane Cæsar, his mother. He spent some time in the study of logic and philosophy at Jesus College, Cambridge, thence was removed to the Inner Temple, and shortly after married Elizabeth, sole daughter and heiress of Robert Angell, of London, Merchant, by whom he had issue—Charles and Jane, who married Sir Thomas Pope, Knight and Bart., of Tittenhanger, Herts. Sir Charles served his country faithfully in that Parliament which called King Charles II. to his Crown, was active there to repress the Court of Wards and Liveries, and to ease the people of the hardships and changes which accrued to them by the tenure of Knight-Service, and from the composition which was yearly paid for corn and victual. He was a Justice of the Peace, of the Quorum, and Deputy-Lieutenant of the County of Herts. Was knighted 7th July, 1660, at Whitehall, and at the next succeeding Parliament was returned for the County of Herts. In 1667 he caught the small-pox from sitting next Sir R. Hare in the House of Commons, while sick of this disease he also made a will concerning the guardianship of his children. " The words," says the Probate, " were spoken by Sir Henry Cæsar, on Sunday evening, January 5th, 1687, in the presence of John Lightfoot, D.D., Susannah Riccard, and others." He died the next day, and his lady, who was buried with him at Bennington, followed him in the year 1670.—F. E. C.-D.

Of Thomas, the third surviving son of Sir Julius Cæsar, we can learn little more than that he was born March 17th, 1600, and baptized at St. Katharine's; that he was educated in the University of Oxford, and became a Doctor of Divinity in that of Cambridge; that he was married, but died without issue.

"Robert Cæsar, fourth surviving son of Sir Julius Cæsar, was born Oct. 9th, 1602. He, too, was destined to the profession of the law, and became early in life one of the Six Clerks in Chancery. Most of the little that can be collected relative to him is to be found in the following extract from Lord Clarendon's History of the Great Rebellion," with which that illustrious writer concludes the character of Richard Weston, Earl of Portland, and Lord High Treasurer:—

"Sir Julius Cæsar was then Master of the Rolls, and had inherent in his office the undubitable right and disposition of the Six Clerks' places, all of which he had for many years bestowed upon such persons as he thought fit. One of these places, upon any vacancy, was designed by the old man to his son Robert Cæsar, but the Lord Treasurer procured the King to send a message to him, expressly forbidding him to dispose of that place until his Majesty's pleasure should be further made known. This was felt by the old man very sensibly. The Treasurer had no great difficulty so far to terrify him, that for the King's service, as was pretended, he admitted for a Six Clerk a person recommended by him, Mr. Fern—who paid six thousand pounds ready money. The depriving Sir Julius of his right was successfully represented to the King himself, who was graciously pleased to promise, that if the old man should die before any other of the Six Clerks, that office, when it should fall should be conferred on his son, whoever should be Master of the Rolls; and the Lord Treasurer obliged himself to expiate the injury, to procure some declaration to that purpose under his Majesty's sign-manual, which, however easy to be done, he long forgot or neglected.

"One day the Earl of Tullibardine, being with the Treasurer, asked him whether he had done that business? to whom he passionately answered, with a seeming trouble, that he had forgotten it, for which he was heartily sorry; and if he would give him a little note in writing for a memorial, he would put it with those which he would dispatch with the King that afternoon. The Earl presently writ in a little paper, 'Remember Cæsar!' and gave it to him; and he put it into that little pocket, where he said he kept all his memorials which were first to be transacted. Many days passed, and Cæsar never thought of;" until looking over his notes and papers "he found this little billet, '*Remember Cæsar!*' and which he had never read before, and knew not what to think or make of it.—After much serious deliberation with his friends, it was agreed that it was a warning from some friend of a conspiracy against his life, and they all knew Cæsar's fate by contemning or neglecting such animadversions; and therefore they concluded that he should pretend to be indisposed, that he might not stir abroad all that day, nor that any might be admitted to him but persons of undoubted affection; and that the gate-porter and servants should watch all night, and that they and some other gentlemen would remain and wait the event. Such houses are always in the morning haunted by early suitors, but it was very late before any could now get admittance into the house, the porter excusing himself to his acquaintances by whispering to them that 'his Lord should have been killed that night, which had kept all the house from going to bed.' And, shortly after, the Earl of Tullibardine asking the Treasurer whether he had remembered Cæsar, he quickly remembered the ground of his perturbation;" and so the whole affair of his fright was settled.

Mr. Robert Cæsar was married at the Rolls Chapel, December 7th, 1630, to Elizabeth, daughter of John Manning, an eminent merchant of London. He died childless at his house in the Strand on Sunday, October 27th, 1637, and was buried in the Church of St. Helen's.

The following information, which is not without interest, has been kindly furnished to the Editor by Miss Cottrell-Dormer:—

" Sir Charles Cæsar Adelmare married Susanna, daughter and heiress of Sir Thomas Bonfoy, Knight, merchant of London, by whom he had issue.— Charles, Henry, Elizabeth, and Thomas. Lady Cæsar died in childbed, 1693, and Sir Charles in the prime of life, August 13th, 1694. The arms of this gentleman were—Gules, three roses, argent, on a chief of the second, as many more of the field: crest—on a wreath, a dolphin, embowed, naiant, in water, proper. His son, Charles Cæsar, Esq., was born in London, Nov. 21st, 1673, and succeeded to his property when he was twenty-one years of age. He married Mary, daughter of Ralph Freeman, Esq., of Aspeden Hall, Herts, 'with a fortune of 5000*l*.' This lady seems to have had a taste for books, and to have been honoured with the friendship of distinguished men. In a copy, now at Rensham, of the Poetical Works of Matthew Prior, we find written as follows:—

"'To the best wife, the most careful mother, and most obliging friend, Mrs. Cæsar. This book is most humbly presented by her most obedient and most humble servant, Matthew Prior, 1718-19.'

"In the Odyssey of Homer, translated by Alexander Pope, also at Rensham, published by subscription, MDCCXXV., by Lintot, we find the following MSS. letter:—

"'Madam, you will see by ye enclosed I have obeyed you in some articles as to Lord Stafford, Lady Sarah, &c. I took another liberty with your own name, which you knew nothing of, nor I daresay could have suspected, and have made a star (sic) of Mrs. Cæsar, as well of Mrs. Fermor.' [Note the name of Fermor, which is that of Pope's Belinda.] 'If anybody asks you the reason of this, quote to them this verse of Virgil:—

"'Processit Cæsaris Astrum.'—Eclogue 5.

"'I am daily in hopes of waiting on you when I hear you are in town.

"'Your obedient servant,
"'A. POPE.'

"Mr. Cæsar was sent to the Tower of London a prisoner for his Jacobite opinions, and there are at Rensham two MS. letters written from thence to Mrs. Cæsar:—

"'Date, January 30th, 1716-17.—I writ this morning to Mr. Secretary Stanhope to desire that my dearest might have the pleasure of being a prisoner with me whilst I am one, but that is a thing not to be granted till after I have been examined by a committee of the Councell, and this being a day all Englishmen ought to spend in devotion, it is not thought proper ye committee should meet till six o'clock, when that is over I do not doubt but they will be so humain as to let me have ye comfort of a loveing wife, if they do not set me immediately at liberty. I have a very good lodgeing, and never slept better in my life than last night and have taken care of some victuals in a proper time. I beg of my dearest to be as easy as is your loveing husband.

"'My blessing to my children. "'C. C.'

"In the second letter he says:—'Feb. 1st. Being deprived of liberty cant but be uneasy to any man that has a just value for it but ye want of your company is much ye worst part of my confinement.'

"Mr. Cæsar died April 1st, 1741, and was buried at Bennington, April 5th, so was his Relict on July 12th, 1741.

Epitaph addressed to Mrs. Cæsar, written by John Boyle, Earl of Orrery.[*]

"'Why flow those tears, or why those sighs arise?
Why dim the lustre of those radiant eyes?
The parts well acted both of friend and wife,
Thro' ev'ry scene of thy all-blameless life;

---

[*] Gentleman's Magazine for 1741, p. 325.

Let conscious virtue cank'ring griefs controul,
And calm each struggling passion in the soul.
Think, if departed spirits aught can know,
In upper regions, of the world below,
How can the man for whom those tears are shed,
(Dear as he was, irrevocably dead!)
How can he deem his state compleatly blest,
While sorrow reigns unconquer'd in your breast?
Ah! let your wisdom be to fate resign'd,
Take comfort in the blessings yet behind:
Nor is your heart of ev'ry joy bereft,
Your daughters live, and still one Cæsar's left.'

"Mr. and Mrs. Cæsar's eldest son, Charles, born early in the 18th century, died young, in 1740. This gentleman had married a Miss Jane Long, a Ward of Chancery, under circumstances told in the following ballad, communicated by the Rev. W. Elwin, editor of Pope's Works.

"'UPON THE ROYSTON BARGAIN;

OR,

ALE-HOUSE WEDDING, *i.e.*,

Marriage of Mr. Charles Cæsar to Miss Long, October, 1729.

I.

Yᵉ fathers and mothers,
Yᵉ sisters and brothers
  That have a rich heiress in guard,
I'll tell you a tale,
If you mind, it wont fail
  To preserve in all safety your Ward.

II.

Never keep her at Hammels
In traces and trammels,
  Nor think an old man and his cat
Are company fit
For a girl that has wit,
  And is eager to know what is what.

III.

While Ralph and his spouse
Were employed in the house
  With Wiseman, their chief Secretary,
Away went the gay thing
In search of a plaything,
  And so she began the vagary.

IV.

Quoth he then to his wife
I'll venture my life
  She's gone to the Ale-house at Munden.
And who can be there,
As I honour small beer,
  But Cæsar *aut nullus* from London.

V.

I've told you, dear Ralph,
If you'd keep that girl safe,
  Ne'er let her alone with Miss Cremer;
And as for Miss Jenning,
Her ways are so winning,
  She'll make her as gallant a schemer.

VI.

Just as she had said
Came in the poor maid
  With message and face most importune.
That Cæsar with forces,
And coach and six horses,
  Had stolen away their great fortune.

VII.

You see you old fool,
You are made a mere tool,
  And duped by Cæsar and your sister—(say *his* sister).
You thought the girl safe
By the care of son Ralph,
  But the booby cracked walnuts and missed her.

VIII.

Then out went the scouts
To the towns thereabouts,
  In hopes to have luckily found them.
But Saygrace the Parson
Had carried the farce on,
  And in a cottage had just before bound them.

IX.

And now turn your face
To Bennington Place,
  And see with what joy this is taken;
Whose Madam does chatter
To all that come at her,
  And cries "we have now saved our bacon."

X.

Now my foes I despise,
And my grotto shall rise,
  Though some folks may call it my folly.
And when all is sold
The rest shall be told
  'Twixt Julius, Betty, and Molly.'

Mary Granville, Mrs. Delany, speaks of a pleasant party at young Mrs. Charles Cæsar's house, but she appears to have died young, in 1737, leaving only two children, daughters, ultimately coheiresses to the Cæsar name and what remained of the property. Of my great grandmother, the eldest daughter, I can only say that those who knew her seem to have felt a strong love for her, and I must quote the following passage from Horace Walpole's correspondence, in which he speaks of his visit to Rensham:—" Had I as pretty a house and as pretty a wife, I would let King George send to Herrnhausen for a Master of the Ceremonies." She was born 1732, and christened Jane. She married Charles Cottrell-Dormer, Esq., only surviving son of Sir Clement Cottrell-Dormer, Knight, Master of the Ceremonies, and of his wife, Bridget Sherborne, only daughter and heir of Davenant Sherborne, Esq. This gentleman succeeded his father as Master of the Ceremonies. He had two children by his wife, Jane Cæsar Adelmare. Clement, born 1757, died 1808; succeeded his father as Master of the Ceremonies, which office he resigned to his cousin, Sir Stephen Cottrell, Knight; and Jane, who died 1768, and is buried with her father and brothers at Rensham, Oxfordshire. Traditions still lingered in my childhood as to her beauty and grace. She was only eleven when she died in a room still called 'the nursery.' Lady Cottrell-Dormer became a widow 1779, and married, secondly, 1782, the Hon. Lieut.-Gen. George Lane Parker, second son of George, second Earl of Macclesfield, who died 1791, and his widow, 1802.

Her only sister, Harriet, married 1758, Robert Chester, Esq., of the Middle Temple. Her first son, Robert, succeeded Sir Stephen Cottrell, Knight, as Master of the Ceremonies. He died 1848. He married Eliza, third daughter of John Ford, Esq., of the Chauntry, near Ipswich. Their second son, Charles Colonel Chester, was killed in the Indian Mutiny, 1857, and their third son, Harry Chester, died 1868. He was Clerk to the Privy Council, and will be remembered for his exertions in the cause of education and the good of the people.

I will now, in conclusion, revert for a moment to the other three children of Mr. and Mrs. Cæsar, the Julius, Betty, and Molly mentioned in the Ballad. These ladies died unmarried, and at an advanced age, I believe. Julius, of whom there is a portrait at Rensham, which represents him as having been a handsome man, became a Major in the Foot Guards, in the 1st Regiment. He became a Major-General, 1759, and in 1760 was nominated a member of the Court for the trial of Lord George Sackville. He saw some foreign service, and died unmarried, 1762. We find the following notice of him in The Life of David Garrick, by Percy Fitzgerald, vol. i. p. 344, Ed. Lond. 1868:—" Wilkinson's mimicry of Woffington's shrill voice had made the Dublin audience scream with laughter, and, it was hoped, would have the same effect here.... A Colonel Cæsar of the Guards ... now came to wait on Mr. Garrick, to protest against any mimicry, adding he should be obliged to hold Mr. Garrick responsible as a gentleman and a man of honour." Mrs. Margaret Woffington was then suffering from the effects of a paralytic stroke, from which she soon afterwards died, without, as was expected, leaving her fortune to General Cæsar, who, it is reported, had promised her all his in case he died first." See Lodge's Lives of the Cæsars, p. 63.—F. E. C.-D.

MATTHEW AND ALBERIGO GENTILI.*

"The name Gentili was borne by two noble Italian families,† distinguished respectively as the 'Red' and the 'White' families. To the former of these belonged Matteo Gentili, a physician settled at Castello di San Genesio, a small but ancient town in the march of Ancona. He was a grave and stern man, devoted to science, but not sufficiently in advance of his age to be prevented from discussing the question whether or no diseases are the work of dæmons. His wife, Lucrezia, bore him seven children, of whom the eldest, Alberigo, and the youngest but one, Scipio, are known to fame. Albericus was born in 1551, and was in due course sent over the Apennines to the neighbouring University of Perugia. It so happens that the aspect which the city must have presented during his student days is made known to us by a bird's-eye panorama of

---

* The following information respecting these "Worthies" is obtained from An Inaugural Lecture on the latter, delivered at All Souls' College, Oxford, November 7th, 1874, by Thomas Erskine Holland, B.C.L., Barrister-at-Law, Chichele Professor of International Law and Diplomacy in the University of Oxford, formerly Fellow of Exeter College, and is here inserted by that gentleman's permission.

† "The Gentili Rossi bore for arms 'un Saracino colla benda rossa in su gli occhi.' In those of the Gentili Bianchi the bend was white. The name had been for many generations eminent in public employment, law, and medicine. Albericus, in the *Laudes*, describes himself as one 'cui pater, frater, patruus, patruelis, duo avunculi, iidemque agnati, maioresque avunculi duo, atavi duo, doctores numerantur.'

"MATTEO GENTILI, a physician, had a son—

"LUCENTINO, who had, by Clarice Mattheuci, (1) Vincenzo, (2) Pietro, (3) Gregorio, (4) Pancrazio (physician at Ascoli), and (5) Matteo. This

"MATTEO, born 1517, married 1549 Lucrezia (ob. 1591), daughter of Diodoro Petrelli, and by her had (1) Alberigo, (2) Manilio, (3) Antonio, (4) Vincenzo, (5) Quinto (studied at Padua—an interlocutor in the *Dialogi Sex*), (6) Scipio, and (7) Nevida (who married Venanzio di Ottaviano Bevilacqua, 1573. She was buried with her father in London).

"ALBERICUS married, about 1589, Hester de Peigni, of French extraction, who survived till 1648. Their children were

"(1) Robert, born Sept. 11th, 1590; matriculated at Christ Church æt. 9; B.A. Jesus College, 1603; of St. John's College; Probationary Fellow of All Souls, in 1607, by his father's influence, who 'got him sped into that house by an argument in law as being under statutable years'—Wood; B.C.L. 1612.

"(2) Matthew.

"SCIPIO married in 1612 Magdalen, daughter of Cæsar Calandrinus."

it, taken just at that time. 'Old College,' 'New College,' and the then recently founded 'Bartolus College,' are represented in this curious print. The University had then been established nearly three centuries; and had been fortunate in a succession of eminent teachers. Bartolus, the greatest name of the 'Scholastic,' or second, school of Jurists, had been professor there; and was succeeded by a pupil of whom it was said:

"'Qui Baldum iuris negat accendisse lucernam
Ille potest medio sole negare diem.'

"Gentilis boasts that the honour of the Law Faculty of Perugia had been well maintained since the days of these great men, and he gives the names of his own teachers; of whom Rinaldo Rodolfini was the most famous. Thanks to the industry of local archæologists, we have the fullest information as to the history of the University, its statutes, and the succession of its professors. In the time of Gentilis seventy doctors of law were resident in the town, of whom twenty-five gave lectures. The exercises requisite to graduation were so difficult that candidates often migrated to some other University, where there was more likelihood of their passing.

"The degree of Bachelor, and the intermediate status of licentiate, were alike unknown at Perugia. Albericus therefore, on completing his studies, became full Doctor, and a few months afterwards was elected 'practor,' or judge, of Ascoli; where his father at this time held the office of city physician. For some reason or other both father and son resigned before long their respective appointments, and returned to their native San Genesio; where they were held in much honour. Albericus was admitted to be an advocate there in 1577, and was employed in negotiations affecting the interests of the town, and upon a revision of its statutes.

"The career thus opening was interrupted by a cause which broke up the whole family circle. The father, we are told, 'from the reading of the divine oracles, and the conversation of good men, obtained some taste of heavenly truth,' or—as the same fact is represented from another point of view—'he was swept away by the rage of the Reformation, falsely so-called, by which that age was deluded.' Such a change of opinion had been by no means uncommon, especially in the higher classes of Italian society, a few years previously; but by this time the Inquisition had succeeded in breaking up the little centres of Protestantism which existed, for instance, at Modena, Ferrara, and Venice; and an exodus of hundreds of thoughtful people had taken place, which has been compared in its effects to that which followed the Revocation of the Edict of Nantes. The emigration was permanently Protestantising the Valtelline and the Engadine, but little bands of fugitives were scattered through Switzerland, Germany, and even England. Mathew Gentilis found that his only chance of safety was in flight, and proposed it to his wife. Lucretia's reply, as preserved by family tradition, was to the following effect: 'I not only permit, but bid you go, for I see your danger. As to accompanying you, pardon me when I say I cannot do it. I am accustomed to the air, the food, and the religion of my native land. If you take me hence, you take me to death. Recompense my self-denial in letting you go by consenting to my staying behind. We shall be as devoted to one another in our separation as we have ever been. Take Albericus with you, but leave the younger children with me.' Mathew consented, bade adieu to his wife, and set off, accompanied only by Albericus, who had long shared his father's opinions. A pious fraud was however practised upon the mother; and the fugitives were joined, soon after leaving home, by the young Scipio, who was about sixteen years old. Lucretia not unnaturally wrote to her husband upon this subject with a certain 'dulcis amaritia.'

"Just then, and for a few years longer, Protestantism was the predominant faith in the Austrian dominions, and the exiles accordingly found a temporary resting-place in Carniola, where Mathew was honoured with the title of 'Archiater' of the Duchy. It may have been at this time that, while the three were seated one winter evening round the fire, the father said to his sons: 'Take each of you a piece of coal. I will give you a sentence in prose, and do you turn it into verse, which you can write with the coal on the stove.' While Scipio expressed the idea in three lines, Albericus nearly covered the stove with poetry. The father encouraged Scipio to go on writing verses, but made Albericus promise to give up the practice. The prosperous physician did not keep his sons with him in Carniola, but sent Scipio to pursue his studies in Germany, and Albericus to turn his learning to account in England.

"A few words only can be spared to the subsequent histories of the father and the younger son. Matthew Gentilis before long found that the Austrian policy had changed. He must either 'Romanis placitis stare, aut migrare.' He chose once more the latter alternative, and followed his eldest son to England. For a long time before his death, which occurred in 1602,* he was only able in the intervals of suffering to gratify his love of knowledge by devouring the contents of all the new books on theology, medicine, or philosophy.

"Albericus must have reached England in 1579. He tells us that on his arrival nothing was further from his thoughts than to seek the society of the great; but that he was irresistibly attracted by the fame of Sir Philip Sidney. He doubtless brought introductions to the little congregation of Italian Protestants worshipping in London, to which belonged, or had recently belonged, Contio (Acontius), famous as the author of the 'De Stratagematibus Satanae,' Julio Borgarucci, physician to the Earl of Leicester, and suspected of misapplying his knowledge of drugs in the Earl's service, and Battista Castiglioni, Italian master to the Queen. It seems to have been through the good offices of the last named, and of Dr. Tobie Mathew, in 1579 Vice-Chancellor of Oxford (subsequently Bishop of Durham and Archbishop of York), that Albericus came to the notice of Leicester, Chancellor since 1564 of this University, and obtained from him a commendatory letter to the authorities here, which describes him as one who 'had left his country for religion sake,' and whose 'desire was to bestow some time in reading and other exercises of his profession in the University.' He was received into New Inn Hall, and was granted small stipends by Merton and other Colleges, and afterwards from the University Chest. He was also incorporated D.C.L.

"In 1584 Gentilis and John Hotoman were consulted by Government as to the proper course to be pursued with Mendoza, the Spanish Ambassador, who had been detected in plotting against Elizabeth; and it was by their advice that he was merely ordered to leave the country. That the opinion given by Gentilis was the right one is now universally admitted; but it was directly

---

* See above, p. 96.

in the teeth of one which had been given by the English civilians fifteen years before in the case of Leslie, Bishop of Ross. Albericus chose the topic to which his attention had thus been directed as the subject of a disputation when Leicester and Sir Philip Sidney visited the schools at Oxford in the same year; and the disputation was six months later expanded into a book—the 'De Legationibus' —dedicated to Sir Philip Sidney.

"Gentilis was still at Oxford in the early part of 1586, but in the autumn of the same year he is at Wittenberg, where he dedicates books to the Duke of Brunswick and others. . . . . He had left England, desponding probably of success in this country, with apparently no intention of returning; and by the influence of Walsingham had accompanied Horatio Palavicino in his embassy from Elizabeth to the Elector of Saxony. It was through the same influence, even more than that of Leicester, that Gentilis was recalled from the Saxon Court in 1587, and was appointed Regius Professor at Oxford.

"The last three years of his life were mainly engaged in the discharge of the office of Advocate to the Spanish Embassy ('honorifico salario constituto'), to which, with the permission of King James, he was nominated by the Ambassador, Don Petrus de Zunica. England was at that time neutral in the war which was going on between Spain and the Netherlands, and many cases in which Spaniards were interested came before the English Court of Admiralty. Gentilis must not only have been consulted on such cases, but must also have argued them; for he mentions an occasion on which, when the junior advocate and the proctor had given up a point, he insisted upon it, and brought round the judge to his opinion. These forensic engagements of Gentilis explain the fact that his will was made in London.

"His last wish was to be buried as near as possible to his father, of his affection for whom this is one among many proofs. He commends his children to the care of his brother Scipio, and begs that he will destroy all his MSS., except those relating to the Spanish advocacy, which are not in so imperfect a state as the rest. These were accordingly published by Scipio, under the title 'De Advocatione Hispanica,' in 1613. It is stated by Wood,*

---

* *Athenæ.* In *Hist.*, Gutch, ii. p. 858, he had given 1609 as the date.

and after him in the Biographical Dictionaries, that Gentilis died in 1611, and was probably buried in Christ Church Cathedral. Wood, however, expresses himself with some uncertainty on the point." He died in London, on the 19th of June, 1608, five days after the date of his will, and was buried on the 21st* near to his father, in the graveyard of St. Helen's, Bishopsgate. Not a trace of the locality where his father's remains were interred can now be discovered. The following "epitaph"—of which G. M. Konigius, Librarian of the University of Altdorf, in his Bibliotheca Vetus et Nova, Altdorfii, 1678, s. v. Albericus Gentilis, says: Epitaphium eius tale circumfertur—has also disappeared :—

D. O. M. S. ALBERICO GENTILI ICTO CLARA ATQUE PRAESTANTI FAMILIA IN PROVINC. ANCONITAN. NATO . ANNO AET. XXI DOCTURAE ORNAMENTA PERUSII ADEPTO . PAULOQUE POST IN NOBILISSIMA ITAL. CIVITATE ASCULO IUDICI . ALIISQVE HONORIBUS MAGNA LAUDE PERFUNCTO . POSTREMO REGIAE (sic) ACAD. OXONIENSIS PER XXVI ANNOS LEGUM PROFESSORI . PLURIMIS EDITIS INGENII MONUMENTIS . CELEBERRIMO OPTIMEQUE DE REP. MERITO . REGIAE CATHOLICAE HISPAN. MAIESTATIS SUBDITORUM CONSTITUTO (OB EXIMIAM VIRTUTEM ET DOCTRINAM) ADVOCATO IN ANGLIA PERPETUO . HOC IN LOCO UNA CUM OPTIMO ET CLARISSIMO PATRE D. MATHAEO GENTILI . CARNIOLAE DUCATUS ARCHIATRO . FILIOLAQVE DULCISSIMA IN CHRISTO JESV REQVIESCENTI . H. M. S. ESTHERA GENTILIS DE PEIGNI MAR. OPT. CHARISS. ET HONORATISS. OBIIT LONDINI ANNO MDC VIII. D. XIX IUNII . AETATIS LVIII." †

EDWARD BRERE WOOD.

Edward Brerewood was born and educated at Chester. His father, Richard Brerewood, was thrice Mayor of that city. In 1581 he was sent to Brasenose College, Oxford, being then about sixteen years of age, where he had the character of being a very hard student. In the year 1590 he took the degree of

---

* See above, p. 96.

† This epitaph is about to be restored by means of a tablet, within St. Helen's, Bishopsgate.

Master of Arts,* while in that College, but afterwards removed to St. Mary Hall. In 1596 he was chosen the first Professor of Astronomy in Gresham College, being one of the two, who at the desire of the electors, were recommended to them by the University of Oxford. He loved retirement, and wholly devoted himself to the pursuit of knowledge. He died November 4th, 1613, and was buried in the chancel of St. Helen's Church, near the reader's pew, without any memorial. He had collected a large and valuable library, which he left with his other effects to his nephew, Robert Brerewood, and was the author of a great many works, but which were not published until after his death.

PETER MAUNSELL.

Peter Maunsell, a native of Dorsetshire, was entered at Brasenose College, Oxford, in the year 1587, where he took the degree of Bachelor of Arts in 1591, and that of Master in 1594. After this he pursued the study of physic four years, and then travelling abroad for about five years, resided first at Paris, and afterwards at Padua. Upon his return to England he went again to Oxford, and employed the two succeeding years partly there, and partly at London among the Gresham Professors. He then made a second tour, and having visited the Universities of Basil and Strasburg, came back by Leyden in 1607. While he was abroad he took the degree of Doctor of Physic. In the month of September in that year he was chosen to succeed Dr. Gwynne in his Professorship in Gresham College. This settlement proving agreeable and a good situation for his practice as a physician, he continued there until his death. He was buried in St. Helen's Church, October 18th, 1615.

RICHARD BALL.

Richard Ball was educated at Magdalen College, Oxford, where he took the degree of Bachelor of Arts in 1590, and of Master in 1594. Upon the settlement of Gresham College (1596) Mr. Ball and Mr. Caleb Willis were recommended by the University of

---

* Being a candidate for a fellowship and losing it, he applied himself seriously to his studies, and became a most accomplished scholar. He maintained against Mr. Byfield that we are not bound to a Jewish exactness in the observation of the Sabbath.

Oxford, for one of them to be chosen to be the first Professor of Rhetoric on that foundation. Mr. Willis was chosen, but being in a bad state of health, by leave of the Gresham Committee he appointed Mr. Ball to read for him, who was afterwards chosen as his successor. In 1603 he became Vicar of St. Helen's Church, where he established a lecture in 1606. Upon January 14th, 1613, he resigned his Professorship, and about the same time was succeeded in his vicarage of St. Helen's by Mr. Thomas Downing. He must then have been about forty years of age, but whether he died, or had some other preferment that occasioned his removal, is uncertain.

ARTHUR BARHAM.

Arthur Barham was born at Buckstead, in Sussex, November 22nd, 1618. He was first designed for the Law, but upon his father's death he sold his law books and went to Cambridge, where he studied divinity with great diligence and delight. When he left the University he was first chosen lecturer of St Olave's, Southwark, from whence he removed to St. Helen's, to which he was presented by Sir John Langham, to whom he was related by marriage. There he continued about ten years, preaching with great success, until his ejectment in 1662. He then removed with his family to Hackney, where he continued until the Five Mile Act passed, when he left his family and retired into Sussex. Upon the indulgence in 1672, he took out a licence and preached in his own house twice every Lord's Day, catechized in the afternoon, and expounded some portion of Scripture in the evening. Besides which he preached a Lecture every Friday, catechized two days in the week, and performed family duty every morning in two, and sometimes in three, families besides his own. But this was not suffered long, for no sooner was the King's declaration recalled than he was informed against, and his goods were seized until he had paid a considerable fine. About six weeks afterwards a second warrant was issued out against him, though he had not preached since the first; but being beloved by his neighbours they gave him notice of it, so that he removed his goods to London and took lodgings. Not long after he was seized with apoplectic fits, which took away his memory, and quite disabled him for further service. For the last two years of his life he lived with his son-in-law, Mr. John Clark, a bookseller in the City, and exchanged this life for a better, March 6, 1692, aged seventy-four years. He was a sincere, godly, humble man, of a mild and peaceable disposition, and was generally beloved by those who knew him.

THOMAS HORTON.

Thomas Horton, son of Lawrence Horton, merchant, was born in London, and admitted a member of Emmanuel College, Cambridge, July 8th, 1623. In the year 1637 he was appointed one of the twelve University preachers. In 1638 he was chosen Master of Queen's College; and July 12th, in the same year, minister of St. Mary Colechurch, London (in the gift of the Mercers' Company), which he resigned in 1640. Was elected Professor of Divinity in Gresham College, October 26th, 1641, and in 1647 Preacher to the Honourable Society of Gray's Inn, and shortly after created Doctor of Divinity, and the ensuing year (1650) Vice-Chancellor of Cambridge. In Easter Term Dr. Barnard succeeded him as Preacher at Gray's Inn, and Dr. Horton marrying about that time, to secure his continuance in the Divinity Professorship at Gresham College, had procured an order from the Committee of Parliament for reforming the Universities and other colleges, that he should not be disturbed from that place, nor removed from it on account of his marriage. This Order the Doctor laid before the Gresham Committee, who then resolved to apply to the Committee of Parliament and acquaint them with the Will of the Founder as to that case, and in 1652 they declared the Professorship vacant, but did not immediately proceed to an election. In this year also Dr. Horton was incorporated Doctor of Divinity in the University of Oxford, and the year following nominated one of the Triers or Commissioners for the approbation of young ministers. In 1656 the subject was resumed by the Gresham Committee, who proceeded to a new election, and chose Mr. George Gifford. This obliged the Doctor to apply to the Protector Cromwell for a fresh dispensation, and an order was made by the Protector in Council in his favour. After this Dr. Horton remained in quiet possession of his Professorship until the restoration of King Charles II. in 1660, and held with it the Headship of Queen's College, Cambridge, from which he was removed in August of this year to make way for the return of Dr. Martin, who had been ejected in 1644. Dr. Horton had, however, sufficient interest at Court to obtain a new dispensation to retain his Professorship.

This was, however, soon revoked, and Mr. Gifford re-chosen June 7th, 1661. The year following Dr. Horton was in the number of those Divines who were silenced by the Bartholomew Act, but he afterwards conformed, and on June 13th, 1666, was admitted to the Vicarage of St. Helen's, which he held till his death. He was buried March 29th, 1673, in the chancel of the Church, under the communion table.

Dr. Wallis, who published a volume of his sermons, states that " He was a pious and learned man, a hard student, and a sound divine, well accomplished for the work of the ministry, and very conscientious in the discharge of it."

From a MS. of the ecclesiastical parties in the reign of Charles the Second:—

" Doctor Horton is Minister of St. Helen's, he hath a very great congregation of half-conformists, in whom he hath much interest. He is a man of very good learning, and a constant, laborious preacher."

JONATHAN GODDARD.

Jonathan Goddard was born at Greenwich. In the year 1632, being then fifteen years of age, he was admitted a Commoner of Magdalen Hall, Oxford, where he took the degree of Bachelor of Arts, and then travelled, as was the practice at that time, for his improvement in the knowledge of physic. After his return he took the degree of Doctor of Physic at Catherine Hall, Cambridge, January 20th, 1642, being then a probationer in London; and was elected a Fellow of the College of Physicians November 4th, 1646. He had then lodgings in Wood Street. He was afterwards Physician to Cromwell, and attended him on his visit to Ireland. In 1651 he was appointed Warden of Merton College, Oxford, by the Parliament, on the resignation of Sir Nathaniel Brent, and also incorporated Doctor of Physic there. The year following, Cromwell, being then in Scotland, did, by an instrument bearing date Oct. 16th, constitute him, with Dr. Owen, Dr. Wilkins, Dr. Goodwin, and Mr. Peter French, or any three of them, to act as his delegates (he being then Chancellor of the University of Oxford) in all matters relating to grants or dispensations that required his assent; and in 1653 Dr. Goddard was chosen singly to represent the University in Parliament, and also one of the Council of State. Nov. 7th, 1655, he was elected Professor of Physic in Gresham

College. He continued the Headship of Merton College until the restoration of Charles II., 1660, when he was removed by a letter from his Majesty, who, claiming the right of nomination during the vacancy of the see of Canterbury, appointed Dr. Reynolds, his chaplain at that time, and soon afterwards Bishop of Norwich, to be Warden of Merton College, as successor to Sir Nathaniel Brent. After this Dr. Goddard settled himself at Gresham College, and was continued a Fellow of the College of Physicians by their new charter in 1663, and being likewise nominated one of the first council of the Royal Society in their charter of the same year, he became very zealous and active in promoting the design of that institution. Upon the dreadful conflagration of the City of London in 1666, Dr. Goddard removed from Gresham College, with the other Professors, to make room for the public business, which for some years till the City was rebuilt was transacted there. After this he again returned to the College, where he remained till his death, which was very sudden and unexpected, being seized with apoplexy in the street, March 24th, 1675, and lies buried in St. Helen's Church, on the north side of the chancel, near the rails of the communion table, without any monument or inscription.*

ROBERT HOOKE.†

Robert Hooke was born at Freshwater, in the Isle of Wight, July 18th, 1635. His father was minister of the parish. He was at first intended for the ministry; but his frequent fits of headache so interrupted his learning, that his father laid aside all thoughts of making him a scholar. He had great fondness for making mechanical toys, and also for drawing; and after the death of his father in 1648 he was placed with the celebrated

---

* An excellent character has been given of Dr. Goddard by Seth Ward, afterwards Bishop of Salisbury, who commends him for his benevolence to all good and learned men, for his extensive knowledge and skill in his profession, and observes particularly that he was the first Englishman who made telescopes.

† Dr. Robert Hooke was the discoverer and inventor of the isochronal balance-spring and other contrivances for the production of that most important instrument for ascertaining the longitude at sea, the chronometer, and the dead-beat clock experiment, now generally known as Graham's, from which emanated the slide valves, and hence, by their alternate action, the means of controlling the power of steam. His invention of the air-pump is also to be seen on every steamboat.

painter Sir Peter Lely; but the smell of the colours increasing his headache, he was removed to the College School at Westminster, and lived with the famous Dr. Busby as a scholar in his house, and was afterwards sent to Christ Church College, Oxford, where he assisted Mr. Thomas Willis in his Chemistry, and afterwards for some years the Hon. Robert Boyle in the same manner. In 1663 the degree of Master of Arts was conferred on him by the favour of Sir Edward Hyde, then Chancellor. The founding of the Royal Society in 1660 afforded numerous opportunities for the display of his uncommon genius; and upon November 12th, 1662, he was appointed curator to the Society, which then met at Gresham College, and was to furnish several new experiments at every meeting. The journals of the Royal Society show how well he discharged his duties. Upon the establishment of that illustrious body by Royal Charter in 1663, he was one of the first Fellows nominated by the Council, and was exempted from all charges. In 1664 Sir John Cutler having founded a Mechanic Lecture, settled it upon Mr. Hooke for life, with a salary of fifty pounds per annum. On March 20th, 1664, he was chosen Professor of Geometry in Gresham College. At the time of the Great Plague he accompanied Dr. Wilkins and Sir Henry Petty to the seat of the Earl of Berkeley, near Epsom; and immediately after the Great Fire Mr. Hooke produced to the Royal Society a model designed by himself for rebuilding the City; and Sir John Lawrance, who was present (the late Lord Mayor) acquainted them that the Court of Aldermen greatly preferred it to that of the City Surveyor, to which office Mr. Hooke was shortly afterwards appointed, and laid out the ground to the several proprietors for rebuilding the City, by which office he acquired most of his riches. In 1674 the Royal Society resumed their meetings at Gresham House, and the Gresham Committee allowed him 40*l*. to erect a turret over part of his lodgings for the purpose of making observations. In 1678 he styled himself Secretary to the Royal Society, which he resigned in 1682, and from this time became more and more reserved. The death of his niece, Mrs. Grace Hooke, in the early part of 1687, who had lived with him several years, affected him very much. The year following he grew very weak and ill, but read lectures occasionally. At the same time he was engaged in a Chancery suit with Sir John Cutler respecting his salary for reading the Cutlerian Lectures, which also tended to increase his disorder. In December, 1691, he was created Doctor of Physic, by a warrant from Archbishop Tillotson. About the same time he was employed in forming the plan of the Hospital at Hoxton, founded by Alderman Aske. This was generally considered a handsome building; but Dr. Hooke was greatly blamed for exceeding the sum at first allotted for it, and by that means lessening the revenue. March 27th, 1695, his Chancery suit still continuing, the Council of the Royal Society granted a certificate of the full performance of his duties, and the suit was decided in his favour July 18th, 1696. His satisfaction thereat was thus expressed in his diary:—" DOMSH.L.G.ISS.A. Deo optimo maximo summus honor, laus, gloria, in sæcula sæculorum. Amen. I was born on this day of July, 1635, and God has given me a new birth; may I never forget His mercies to me; while He gives me breath may I praise Him." For more than twelve months previously to his death he became nearly helpless, though he seldom went to bed, which doubtless caused the mortification in his legs; and he died in Gresham College, March 3rd, 1702. He was buried in St. Helen's Church, all the members of the Royal Society attending his funeral. In person he was of mean appearance, being short, very crooked, pale, lean, and of meagre aspect. He used to say that he was straight until about sixteen years of age, when being of a thin and weak habit, he first grew awry by frequently using a turner's lathe. He frequently pursued his studies the whole night. He seldom received any benefit or made any valuable discovery without expressing his thankfulness to the Divine Providence. He had intended to promote the objects of the Royal Society by building a handsome fabric for their use, with a library, repository, laboratory, &c., and by founding a physico-mechanical lecture. But whatever might have been his intentions, he did not live long enough to fulfil any one of them.

SIR MARTIN LUMLEY.

The family of Lumley or Lomeley, originally written Lomelin, was of Italian extraction, of great antiquity, and reckoned to be nobly descended. They took their surname from the Laumelin, in the Duchy of Milan. Domenico Lomelini, the first who settled in England, was Gentleman of the Privy Chamber to King Henry VIII., and commanded a troop of horse at the siege of

Boulogne. Queen Elizabeth, August 5th, 1560, granted him an annuity of 200*l*. His son, James Lomelin or Lumley, was an eminent merchant of London, and died in 1592, aged eighty-eight years. By his wife, Joane, daughter of — Litton, of Derbyshire, he had his son, Sir Martin Lumley, Knight, Sheriff of London in 1614, and Lord Mayor in 1623. He purchased the Manor of Great Bardfield, in Essex, where he built an elegant house in a delightful situation. He died July 3rd, 1634, and was magnificently interred in St. Helen's Church, the funeral directed by Sir Henry St. George, Sir William Leneve, and others of the Heralds. By his will, dated Sept. 1st, 1631, he gave an annuity or rent-charge of 20*l*. per annum for the establishing a lecture or sermon for ever, to be preached on Tuesday evening weekly, from Michaelmas to Lady Day, and also bequeathed an annuity of 4*l*. per annum for the use of the poor of the said parish. He married Margaret, daughter of — Witham, and had by her a daughter, married to Sir Stephen Anderson, Bart.; and also a son, Martin, born in 1604; High Sheriff of Essex 1639; created a Baronet January 8th, 1640, and one of the Knights for that shire in the Parliament which met November 3rd, 1640. He married first, Jane, daughter of John Meredith, of Denbighshire, by whom he had only a daughter, married to Sir Roger Mostyn, Bart. His second wife was Mary, daughter of Edward Alleyn, Alderman of London, and by her he had Martin, Thomas, and James.

Sir Martin, the eldest son, was Sheriff of the County in 1663. He married Anne, daughter of Sir John Langham, Knight, Alderman of London, by whom he had Martin, and a daughter who died young. He departed this life in August, 1702. Sir Martin Lumley, his son, who had three wives, was Sheriff of the County in 1710, and died the same year, being succeeded by his son and heir, Sir James Lumley. In 1725 an Act of Parliament was passed for vesting his several estates in trustees, to be sold for the payment of his own and his father's debts and legacies.*

SIR JOHN LANGHAM.

Sir John Langham, of Cottesbrooke, in Northamptonshire, was descended from William, son of Henry de Langham, who

---

* The Lumley family is now believed to be extinct.

held three carves of land in Langham, in Rutland, 10 Edward I. He was knighted by Charles II. at the Hague (with James his eldest son), being one of those principal citizens deputed by the City of London to wait on his Majesty at Breda, in Holland, "to invite him to take possession of his Kingdoms." Here he received the honour of Knighthood, and was created, after the Restoration, a Baronet by letters patent, June 17th, 1660. He had contributed largely towards the support of the Royal family during their exile. Sir John was born at Northampton in 1584, and married Mary, sister of Sir James Bunce. He was Sheriff of London in 1642, Member of Parliament for the same city in 1654, and for Southwark in 1660; and was one of those Aldermen sent to the Tower with the Lord Mayor, in 1647, and also in 1648, for refusing to publish an Act, entitled "An act for the exheredation of the Royal Line, The abolishment of monarchy in the kingdom and the setting up of a Commonwealth." Sir John Langham was a Turkey merchant, and acquired a large estate, but not greater than his generosity and charity. He founded a free school at Guilsborough, in Northamptonshire, which he endowed with 50*l.* per annum; and for the maintenance of six poor widows he settled 36*l.* per annum on St. Thomas's Hospital, in Northampton; and 25*l.* per annum on Christ's Hospital, London, for placing out yearly six poor children of that house; but his charity was most extended towards the rebuilding of churches and public edifices which had been consumed by the dreadful fire of London, particularly 500*l.* towards the rebuilding of St. Michael's Church, Cornhill, and his large contributions to the poor sufferers by that calamity. He died at Crosby House, May 13th, 1671, in the eighty-eighth year of his age, and was buried with his lady at Cottesbrooke, where a table monument of marble with their effigies is erected to their memory. They had issue (besides eight children who died in their youth), Sir James Langham, Bart., Sir William and Sir Stephen Langham, Knights; Elizabeth, married to Sir Philip Boteler, Knight; Anne, married to Sir Martin Lumley, of Essex, Bart.; Rebecca, married to Sir Thomas Lake, of Middlesex, Knight, and Sarah, married to Sir Thomas Hussey, of Lincolnshire, Bart.*

---

* See Bridges' Hist. of Northamptonshire, vol. i. pp. 554-7. Ed. Oxon. 1791.

SIR JOHN LAWRENCE.

> "So when contagion with mephitic breath
> And withered famine urged the work of death;
> . . . . . . London's generous Mayor,
> With food and faith, with medicine and with prayer,
> Raised the weak head and stayed the parting sigh,
> Or with new life relumed the swimming eye."—DARWIN.*

John Lawrence, Alderman, of Bishopsgate Ward, Sheriff in 1658, and received the honour of Knighthood June 16th, 1660, on the occasion of King Charles II., accompanied by his brothers the Dukes of York and Gloucester, and several of the nobility, coming to sup with the Lord Mayor. Before supper the Lord Mayor brought to his Majesty a napkin, dipped in rose water, and offered it kneeling, with which when his Majesty had wiped his hands, he sat down at a raised table, the Duke of York being at his right hand, and the Duke of Gloucester on his left; and was served with three several courses. The nobility and gentry were seated at another table. His Majesty conferred the honour of knighthood on Alderman Lawrence and Mr. Cutler, two loyal citizens, the two first that his Majesty bestowed that honour on in the City of London.

Sir John Lawrence was elected Lord Mayor in 1664, and Evelyn states that "this was the most magnificent triumph by water and land.† I dined at Guildhall at the upper table, placed next to Sir H. Bennett, Secretary of State, opposite to my Lord Chancellor and the Duke of Buckingham, who sate between Mons. Comminges, the French Ambassador, Lord Treasurer, the Dukes of Ormond and Albemarle, Earl of Manchester, Lord Chamberlaine, and the rest of the great officers of state. My Lord Maior came twice up to us, first drinking in the golden goblet his Majesty's health; then the French King's, as a compliment to the Ambassador; then we returned my Lord Maior's health, trumpets and drums sounding. The cheere was not to be imagined for the plenty and raritie, with an infinite number of persons at

---

* The Loves of the Plants, canto ii. p. 88. Ed. Lond. 1790.

† "The printed title of the Pageant was London's Triumphs, celebrated the 29th of October 1664, in honor of the truly deserver of honour, Sir John Lawrence, Knight, Lord Mayor of the honourable City of London, and performed at the costs and charges of the Worshipful Company of Haberdashers." Written by John Tatham, Gent. Ed. London Pageants, p. 109.

the rest of the tables in that ample hall. The feast was said to have cost 1000*l*. I slipt away in the crowd, and came home late."*

Sir John Lawrence kept his Mayoralty at his house in Great St. Helen's, and continued in the metropolis during the whole time of the Great Plague. He sat constantly as a magistrate; "heard complaints and redressed them; enforced the wisest regulations then known" respecting the prevention of the pestilent contagion, ".and saw them executed" himself; appointed physicians and surgeons for the relief of the diseased poor; and particularly requested the College of Physicians to publish directions for cheap remedies for the poor in all circumstances of the distemper. This was done by a consultation of the whole College, and copies given gratis to all who desired it. The day after the disease was known with certainty to be the plague, above 40,000 servants were dismissed and turned into the streets to perish, for no one would receive them into their houses, and the villagers near London drove them away with pitchforks and firearms. "Sir John Lawrence supported them all, as well as the needy who were sick, at first by expending his own fortune till subscriptions could be solicited and received from all parts of the nation."

This dreadful distemper broke out about the beginning of May, and in the first week it was discovered carried off nine persons. In June the weekly number having increased to 470, all that could immediately left London. In July, the number increasing to 2010, all the houses were shut up, the public places deserted, and grass growing in the streets. There was a general calmness in the weather, there having been neither wind nor rain for many weeks. Innumerable public fires were lighted, for purifying the infected air. They were, however, kept burning but a few days, being considered by some of the physicians as a nourisher of the plague. Coffins, pest carts, red crosses upon the doors, with the inscription, "Lord have mercy upon us," were everywhere seen, and scarcely any sounds were to be heard but from the windows of "Pray for us!" and the dreadful call of "Bring out your dead." Pepys states, August 12th, "the people die so, that now it seems they are fain to carry the dead to be buried by day-

---

* Evelyn's Memoirs, vol. i. p. 369. Ed. Lond. 1809.

light, the nights not sufficing to do it in; and my Lord Mayor commands people to be within at nine at night, all, as they say, that the sick may have liberty to go abroad for ayre."*

Under these dreadful circumstances the citizens were deserted by their parochial ministers; the Nonconformist ministers considering it their indispensable duty, though contrary to law, repaired to the deserted pulpits, where the people of all sects joyfully attended, in such numbers that the ministers were often obliged to clamber over the pews to get at the pulpits; and in a letter from Mr. Bing to Dr. Sancroft, August 3rd, he says, "We had on the fast day a laudable sermon by Mr. Risden, minister in Bread Street, My Lord Mayor being present, Sir Richard Brown, and Sir J. Robinson, and other Aldermen, with a great congregation."

In September the burials reached their highest weekly number, 7165, and then gradually decreased, having carried off 68,596 persons.

Sir John Lawrence died August 23rd, 1718, at his house at Chelsea, where his family had long been settled. The chapel at the end of the north aisle contains monuments of the Lawrence family for many generations.

This ancient and respectable family first came into England with William the Conqueror, and settled at Ashton Hall in the county of Lancaster, where they resided for three hundred years, and possessed an immense property, which in 1591 included thirty-four manors, the rental of which amounted to £6000 per annum. The family has been honoured with fifteen titles, and among those who have signalized themselves in the service of their King and country we find the following :—

Sir John Lawrence, made Knight Banneret at the Siege of Ptolemais, anno 1191.

William Lawrence, slain at the battle of St. Albans, 1451.

John Lawrence, who, with Sir E. Howard, commanded a wing at the battle of Flodden Field, 1513.

Oliver Lawrence, knighted at the battle of Musselburgh, 1547.

Sir Robert Lawrence, Governor of York Castle during the Civil Wars.

Sir John Lawrence, Lord Mayor of London.

---

* Pepys's Diary, vol. iii. p. 68. Ed. Lond.

The following pious contemplation of the Arms of the family is written on the margin of their pedigree, which in 1810 was in the possession of William Morris, Esq., of Gloucester, being supposed to have been written about 1664.

The Cross in General.	Christ's Cross a mistique mirable may be, His blood was there let loose to set us free; To wash our stains away, He shed his blood, And dying He thus dyed the blushing wood. Our parents from a tree received their fall That gave us death, this doth lost life recall, This is the Lignum Vitæ to us all.
The Field Argent.	The Field is Argent and the Charge a Cross, Riches without Religion are but dross. White, like this field, O Lord, his Life should be Who bears the Cross, follows and fights for Thee. Those, therefore, who for Ermines, Argent yield, Carelessly spot the Honour of the Field.
A Cross Gules.	Who to the field of War his courage bends, Let every bloody charge have pious ends. Success, for a religious sword makes room; Great Constantine in this did overcome By the Cross, when Holy Blood had changed its hue, The Lamb the roaring Lion did subdue.
Raguly or Notched.	The way to Heaven is not with roses spread, But thronged with Thorns, as was Thy sacred head. Our peace is hack'd, and hew'd, our life's a war, We for our Cross must many Crosses bear. Or a red sea,* our passage doth withstand; Or fiery serpents† or a barren sand,‡ Ere we can reach the truly Holy Land.
In imitation of a Scaling ladder.	Christ's Cross the ladder is that leads to bliss, Blest Jacob's vision was a type of this. Who climbs by other steps is at a loss, To Heaven the only ladder is the Cross.

Judith, daughter of Sir John Lawrence, married Sir Stephen Anderson, Bart., by whom he had Sir Stephen Anderson, Bart., who married Anne, only daughter of Sir Martin Lumley, of Bardfield, Essex, Bart. Elizabeth, another daughter, was married to Sir Wm. Loraine, Bart., but she died in about three years, leaving no issue.§

---

* Persecutions.   † Afflictions.   ‡ Want.
§ Kimber's Baronetage, vol. ii. pp. 294, 297.

SIR PHILIP BOTELER.

Sir Philip Boteler, who was made a Knight of the Bath at the coronation of Charles II., died in the thirty-third year of the same reign, and was buried in the family vault at Watton. His father, Sir John Boteler, had been made Knight of the Bath at the coronation of Charles I. In 1642 he was one of the Commissioners of Array for the county of Herts, and was so zealous in supporting the Royal cause that he drained his private fortune to carry on the war, and when no more was to be done than suffering, he had his share of ill usage from those in power—a long imprisonment in Ely House and the plundering and sequestering his estate.

SIR JOHN EYLES.

Sir John Eyles was descended from a family long settled in Wiltshire. He never served the office of Sheriff, nor was he a freeman of London. He received the honour of knighthood from King James II., by whom he was appointed Lord Mayor of London in the last year of his reign, but resigned on the news of the arrival of the Prince of Orange. He was buried July 6th, 1703, in St. Helen's Church, leaving three daughters, whereof Sarah was married to Joseph Haskin Styles, of London, Esquire.

SIR FRANCIS EYLES.

Sir Francis Eyles, Bart., brother of Sir John, was an eminent merchant, many years a director of the East India Company, Alderman of Bridge Ward, Sheriff in 1711, created a Baronet Dec. 1st, 1714, was Governor of the Bank, and died June, 1716. By Elizabeth, his wife, daughter of Mr. Ayley of London, he had six sons and four daughters. Joseph,* the fourth son, was knighted by George I., was Sheriff of London in 1726, chosen Alderman of Cheap Ward in 1738, and member in the last Parliament of George I. for Devizes, and in the first Parliament of King George II. for the Borough of Southwark.

---

* "1728. Contract made with Sir Joseph Eyles for the Herbage of the Artillery Garden, at a rent of 36*l.* per Annum, and by an under lease granted for sixty-one years for building at 1*s.* 6*d.* per foot.
"1710. Alderman Eyles, Lieut.-General of the Artillery Company.
"1733. Sir Joseph Eyles elected Treasurer."
Highmore's *History of the Artillery Company*, p. 194.

SIR JOHN EYLES.

Sir John Eyles, Bart., Citizen and Haberdasher, eldest surviving son of Sir Francis Eyles, Bart., Lieut.-General of the Artillery Company 1710, elected Alderman of Vintry Ward June 14th, 1716, Sheriff in 1720, Lord Mayor in 1727, was translated to Bridge Ward Without in 1737, and was appointed one of the joint Postmasters-General in 1739. He was also Sub-Governor of the South Sea Company, a Director of the East India Company and of the Bank of England, Colonel of the White Regiment of the London Militia, and member in the last Parliament of Queen Anne, and in the first and second Parliaments of King George I. for Chippenham, and in the first Parliament of King George II. he represented the City of London. He married Mary, the daughter of the above mentioned Joseph Haskin Styles, by whom he had a son and a daughter. Sir John died March 11th, 1745,* and was succeeded by his son, Sir Francis Haskin Eyles Styles, Baronet, having taken that surname on being made heir to his uncle, Benjamin Haskin Styles, Esq.†

Arms of Eyles.—Ar. a fess, engrailed, sable, on a chief, three fleurs de lis, on the second.

---

* His country residence was at Gidea Hall, Romford.

† In the Steward's Room of Guy's Hospital is a whole length picture of Sir John Eyles, Bart., Lord Mayor at the Coronation of King George II., President of this Hospital, 1737, painted by Vanloo. A moderate wig powdered, the coat purple, the stockings brown, the robe lined with satin, the sword and mace on a table.

The large chandelier, formerly in the centre of the Ladies' Chamber at Drapers' Hall, was the gift of Sir John Eyles.

1727, June 16th. On this day the Lord Mayor, Sir John Eyles, and Aldermen, attended George II. at Leicester House on the demise of the late King, when an address of condolence and congratulation was presented by Sir W. Thomson, the Recorder.

CHAPTER IX.

CROSBY PLACE.

This mansion, as has already been stated,* was built by Sir John Crosby, in the reign of King Edward IV. Crosby Hall as it now stands formed but a very small portion of the magnificent structure of Crosby Place, by which appellation it was generally known. In its original splendour it must have appeared more like a stately palace than the town residence of a British merchant. The principal remains consist of three apartments—viz., the Hall, the Council Room, and an ante-room, forming two sides of a quadrangle. The Hall has on the east side eight beautiful flat-pointed windows, and on the west side six, with another handsome octangular bay or oriel window, whose finely-executed roof is constructed of stone from Caen in Normandy. The Hall ceiling is a flat pointed arch, with three longitudinal and nine transverse beams highly ornamented, whose intersections form twenty small flat-pointed arches, with the same number of conical drops, of which the centre one is far superior to the rest; but all are most exquisitely wrought. The intermediate spaces are simply filled in with stiles and Gothic mouldings on the edges. There is a chimney in good preservation, ten feet six inches wide and seven feet high. The Hall is of stone, fifty-four feet in length, twenty-seven feet in width, and forty feet in height. The floor was originally paved with stone, chequerways, but it is now almost all destroyed. The Council Chamber has a very rich flat-pointed arched ceiling, entirely of oak, composed of six transverse beams or principal rafters, highly ornamented with enriched half-circles. In the compartments are square sunk panels, filled in with quatrefoils. The room measures forty feet in length and twenty-two in width. Originally there were two small and two larger windows of the same description as those in the Hall.

Crosby Place was built upon the site of certain tenements, with

---

* See above, p. 230.

their appurtenances, which were let to Sir John Crosby by Alice
Ashfield, prioress of St. Helen's, for ninety-nine years, at the
annual rent of 11*l*. 6*s*. 8*d*. What were the contents and particulars
therein granted to Sir John Crosby may be understood by the
grant of Crosby Place, &c., made by Henry VIII. to Anthony
Bonvisi, the Italian merchant—" Rex omnibus," &c. &c., " cum
Alice Ashfield," &c.—wherein are mentioned, first, the great messuage or tenement now commonly called Crosby Place, with a
certain venell—*i.e.*, lane or passage—that extended in length
from the east end of a certain little lane north, bending unto the
Priory close; also nine messuages, situate and lying in the said
parish of St. Helen's, whereof six were situate and lying between
the front of the Bellhouse or Steeple of the said Church; and
another messuage of the said nine messuages, which Catherine
Catesby, widow, formerly held, situate within the gate and steeple
aforesaid, and the six messuages mentioned before; together with
a certain void place of land situate in the said parish, extending in
length towards the east by the said messuage, which the said
Catherine Catesby formerly held, from the outward part of the
plat or post of the Bellhouse abutting upon the north part of the
said six messuages and the King's Street unto the Churchyard
there, five foot and a half assize, and thence extending in breadth
towards the south directly unto a certain tenement there, formerly
in the tenure of Robert Smith; and two messuages more of the
said nine messuages jointly, situate within the close of the said
Priory; of which one was heretofore in the tenure of John Crosby
by the demise of Alice Woodhouse, late Prioress, and the other
heretofore in the tenure of the said Robert Smith; and these were
the tenements and appurtenances held of the Priory of St. Helen's
by Sir John Crosby.

Sir John Crosby, in his Will, dated March 6th, 1471, states,
"that whereas he had done great and notable cost in building in
and upon certain lands and tenements which he then held of
the Prioress and Convent of the house of St. Elyne's; and
whereas they then stood greatly indebted to divers creditors, to
their right grievous charge and paine, out of his very pure charity
and good zeal he left them £40 towards paying such creditors;
provided they should when required seal and deliver, under their
common seal, such writings sufficient in law and approved by

counsel, as should for them and their successors approve, ratify, and confirm, the remainder of his estate and term of such lands," &c. And by the same Will he bequeaths such residence to his wife, Ann, by the description of all his household, whole as it is, in St. Helen's; and all his estate and term to come in the same, with all his wares and merchandize therein, his plate of gold and of silver gilt and of silver white, with all his armours, broaches, beads, rings, &c.

Richard, Duke of Gloucester and Lord Protector, afterwards King by the name of Richard III., was lodged in this house, while his nephew Edward V. reigned, and here the citizens came to him with their professions of acceptance, and desiring him to accept the Crown. This duke must have had early possession of Crosby Place, after the death of the founder, there being only ten years difference in the period of their lives, Sir John Crosby dying in 1475, and Henry VII., after his victory and the death of Richard, ascending the throne in 1485. Crosby Place was doubtless the scene of his plots and conspiracies against the lives and fortunes of his brother Clarence, the Earls Rivers, Grey, &c., and where, in council with Buckingham, Catesby, Lovel, and other ambitious minions, he premeditated the destruction of Lord Hastings, and the bastardizing and subsequent murder of his nephews, thus depicted by Shakspeare :—

> "*Buckingham.* Good Catesby, go, effect this business soundly.
> *Catesby.* My good lords both, with all the heed I can.
> *Glo'ster.* Shall we hear from you, Catesby, ere we sleep?
> *Catesby.* You shall, my lord.
> *Glo'ster.* At Crosby Place, there shall you find us both."

And in the admirable scene between Gloucester and Lady Anne, widow of Prince Edward, the following reference also occurs :—

> "*Glo'ster.* If thy poor devoted suppliant may
> But beg one favour at thy gracious hand,
> Thou dost confirm his happiness for ever.
> *Anne.* What is it?
> *Glo'ster.* That it may please you leave these sad designs
> To him that has more cause to be a mourner,
> And presently repair to Crosby Place:
> Where—after I have solemnly interr'd
> At Chertsey monast'ry this noble king,
> And wet his grave with my repentant tears,—
> I will with all expedient duty see you."
>   *Richard the Third*, act i. sc. 2, and act iii. sc. i.

All this, however, appears to have been a chronological error of the poet. The grant from the prioress of St. Helen's being made in 1466, and the building completed in 1472, it does not appear probable that it came into the Duke of Gloucester's possession until after the decease of Sir John Crosby, which took place in 1475, whereas Henry VI. died May 23rd, 1471. It having however been discovered that the name of William Shakspeare appears as one of the inhabitants of St. Helen's, in an assessment roll for levying subsidies, bearing date October 1st, 1598, the 40th Queen Elizabeth, in connexion with Sir John Spencer and others,* with the assessment of 5*l*. 13*s*. 4*d*. against his name, it is therefore probable that he was well acquainted with the building, and thereby associated it with the stirring events of his drama, and thus it will never fail to be recorded that Crosby Place was actually the residence of the aspiring and ambitious Richard III.

In 1502 Crosby Place was assigned by the surviving executors of Sir John Crosby to Sir Bartholomew Reed, Lord Mayor of London. It subsequently devolved to John Best, Alderman of London, and from him by purchase to Sir Thomas More, Lord High Chancellor in the time of Henry VIII. Sir Thomas sold his remaining interest in the lease of the "great tenement of Crosby Place" to his intimate and valued friend Antonio Bonvisi, the same to whom, when deprived of pen and ink, during his imprisonment in the Tower, he wrote with a piece of charcoal that most touching letter, published in the life of Sir Thomas More, by his son-in-law, Roper.†

In 1538, at the dissolution of the Monasteries, the freehold in Crosby Place was surrendered to the Crown; but it appears that Antonio Bonvisi was confirmed in his possession by an express grant from the King in the year 1542, as follows:—

" Know you, that we, of our special grace, certain knowledge, and mere motion, give and grant unto the said Anthony Bonvice, the reversion and reversions of the said messuage and tenement, with the appurtenances, commonly called Crosby Place, and of all the said houses, solars (cellars), gardens, lanes, messuages, tenements, void places of land, and all other and singular premises, with the appurtenances, lying and situate in St. Helen's, and

---

* See above, p. 246, and Stow's Survey, vol. i. p. 435.   † See above, p. 245.

parcel of the said late Priory, &c.—Teste Rege apud Westmonast. 9 die Sepr. An. Reg. Henrici Octavi 34."

German Cioll was the next inhabitant, and was succeeded by Alderman Bond, who " increased the house in height by building a turret on the top thereof. He died in the year 1576, and was buried in St. Helen's Church. Divers ambassadors were lodged there—viz., in the year 1586, Henry Ramelius, Chancellor of Denmark, Ambassador to the Queen of England, from Frederick II., King of Denmark; and an ambassador from France, &c. Sir John Spencer, Alderman, made great reparations therein, and kept his Mayoralty there, in 1594." .... "In the first year of King James I. (1604), when divers ambassadors came into England, Monsieur de Rosny (Sully), Great Treasurer of France, with his retinue, which was very splendid, was there harbored, the house then belonging to Sir John Spencer." Also "the same year were lodged the youngest son of William, Prince of Orange, Monsieur Fulke, and the learned Monsieur Barnevelt, who came from the States of Holland and Zealand."* In the time of the Civil Wars Crosby House was made a temporary prison for the Royalists. It was afterwards inhabited by Alderman Sir John Langham,† in whose time a great fire happening, probably consumed so much of it as rendered it unfit for a domestic habitation. In the reign of Charles II. it was first appropriated to the Nonconformists, the Hall being fitted up as a Chapel, who retained it as a place of worship upwards of a century. The first religious society assembling in Crosby Square was collected soon after the Act of Uniformity by the Rev. Thomas Watson, the ejected minister of St. Stephen's, Walbrook. Doctor Grosvenor, another pastor, had a congregation so numerous and opulent, that the annual collection used to exceed that of any Presbyterian Church in London. This church dissolving itself in 1769, a lease of the building was taken by the celebrated Antinomian, Mr. James Kelly, who preached here to a society of his own formation till his death. To the above tenants Messrs. Holmes and Hall succeeded in 1778, who made many alterations and spoliations, in order to adapt it to the purposes of their business. Part of the south wing was converted into private dwellings; both the bow windows on the

---

* Stow's Survey, vol. i. p. 435.   † See above, p. 322.

south side of the Council Room were taken down, to form a staircase to the adjoining dwelling-house, then the residence of a Mr. Hall. Very small vestiges of its former splendid character distinguish the upper part and once ornamented roof of the Council Chamber. Of the oak carvings not the smallest fragment is left.

A late Duke of Norfolk* (A.D. 1816) employed an artist to make correct drawings of Crosby Hall, and built his celebrated banqueting-room at Arundel Castle precisely on the same model. In the early part of 1816 the whole of the beautiful stonework, pillars, and ornamental masonry of the Council Room were taken down by order of the proprietor, Strickland Freeman, Esq., and removed to his seat at Henley-upon-Thames, to adorn a dairy he was then building! The masons were employed six weeks on this occasion, and all the fragments injured in the dilapidation were carefully cemented, and safely packed previously to removal.

The apartments, which were formerly the Withdrawing Room and Throne Room of the mansion, and which had for some time ceased to be occupied as a dwelling, afterwards became "warehouses in the occupation of the Company of Merchants of London, trading to the East Indies." About the same time, the present houses in Crosby Square were built upon the site of that part of the ancient mansion which had been destroyed by fire in the year 1678; and in 1683 the house beyond the Hall on the north was erected on part of the "void piece of land" described in the old deeds as abutting on the Priory Close.

Thus progressively had Crosby Place assumed the appearance of decay after having passed through one or two intermediate tenancies, whilst the freehold still remained with the Freemans, the late occupiers being Messrs. Holmes and Hall, Packers, whose lease expired in 1831, when the Hall became once more untenanted.

During the occupation of these tenants, the many alterations made to adapt the premises to the purposes of their business, caused more serious injury to the building than at any period since its erection. In addition to the floor at the level of the south gallery, erected probably at the time the Hall was first used

---

* Bernard Edward Howard, 15th Duke, K.G., born Nov. 21, 1765; died March 16, 1842. See Burke's Peerage, p. 873. Ed. Lond. 1876.

as a meeting-house, a second floor was inserted just below the springing of the roof, and much of the carving and ornamental work was injured or removed. In this state it continued till the year 1831, not unnoticed, however, nor unknown; for even in its lowest state of neglect and humiliation, it was visited by the antiquary, the historian, the man of letters, and the artist, not of this country only, but foreigners also; and there were not wanting zealous friends of the structure, anxious to draw the public attention to its forlorn condition, and to co-operate in its restoration. This feeling at length assumed a more practical bearing. The premises then untenanted had been for some time rapidly falling still further and further into a state of dilapidation and decay. Being pronounced incapable of substantial repair, it was proposed to sell the old materials, and to erect modern houses on the site; at the same time a placard was issued, announcing the premises " to be let on a building lease." At this crisis, through the zealous interference of two or three neighbouring families, anxious to avert such a loss to the arts, and such a discredit to the age, a few gentlemen met together, and resolved to make a public appeal on behalf of the venerable fabric. The appeal was not made in vain. A Committee was formed, and on Tuesday, the 8th May, 1831, a meeting was held at the City of London Tavern, William Taylor Copeland, Esq., M.P., and Alderman of the Ward, in the chair, to take into consideration the best means to be adopted for preserving and restoring Crosby Hall. The result was most encouraging; a Committee of gentlemen was formed, and subscriptions were opened. About this period William Freeman, Esq., the proprietor, attained his majority; and a new lease for ninety-nine years was granted. The work of restoration was then commenced, under the direction of E. Blore, Esq., F.S.A., who gratuitously afforded his valuable services, Messrs. Ruddle and Clarke being the contractors, who for the sum of 728*l.* contracted to do the substantial reparations of the Great Hall—to provide for which was the first care of the Committee. In the meantime negotiations were carried on with the Mercers' Company and the Joint Gresham Committee, as to the practicability and expediency of appropriating Crosby Hall, when completed, to the use of the Gresham Professors, but without success. A treaty was also entered into with the Choral Harmonists' Society, who were willing to take the lease of Crosby Hall, and to finish the

Great Hall agreeably to the designs of Mr. Davies, the architect; but the negotiation did not take effect. At this period, March, 1835, the funds at the disposal of the Committee being exhausted, and but little having been done beyond the substantial repair of the Great Hall, the removal of the floor which encumbered the Hall, &c., there was danger apparently of the work of restoration remaining incomplete. It was then that a lady, Miss Hackett,[*] whose name will never be forgotten in connexion with Crosby Hall, came forward and proposed to take the lease upon herself, with all the clauses, covenants, and options contained therein; and so to uphold the fabric according to the terms of that lease, and the resolutions of the Committee, as to preserve its ancient character; to carry into effect the engagements of the Committee, by making an entrance from Bishopsgate Street; and to offer the Hall at a moderate annual rental to the Gresham Committee, for the use of the Professors, under the will of Sir Thomas Gresham; or to appropriate the same to some other public object, or objects, connected with science, literature, or the arts. Miss Hackett further agreed to discharge all the outstanding liabilities and debts incurred by the Committee in the execution of their trust, beyond the amount of the subscription. This proposal was approved and accepted by the Committee, who thus devolved upon Miss Hackett the further carrying out the anxious wish of all parties, that Crosby Hall might be restored to its pristine beauty, and devoted to some useful public object. This lady, with admirable public spirit and good taste immediately continued the work of restoration. On Monday, June 27th, 1836, the first stone was laid of the new works, in that portion of the building known by the name of the Council Chamber and Throne Room, and forming the north boundary of the quadrangle, under the direction of Edward L. Blackburn, Esq., architect, the author of an architectural and historical account of Crosby Place, London—a work of great research and antiquarian lore. Under the superintendence of that gentleman, the south wall of the Throne and Council Room, with its elegant windows, was rebuilt, as well as the two north windows of the same apartments, and the substantial repairs of the roof were effected.

All hope of the realization of Miss Hackett's most earnest

---

[*] This lady died in 1875 at a very advanced age.

wish that Crosby Hall should be appropriated to the use of the Professors under the will of Sir Thomas Gresham, being at an end, matters relating to the final destiny of the Hall remained in abeyance for some considerable time; until at length two or three influential and public-spirited individuals, with the aid of friends whom their zeal enlisted in the good cause, formed themselves into a Company of proprietors, purchased Miss Hackett's interest, appointed Mr. John Davies, of Devonshire Square, their architect, and in good earnest set about the completion of the repairs and restoration, with the object of adapting the Hall and premises for the use of "The Crosby Hall Literary and Scientific Institution," which speedily failed. It was then occupied by "The City of London Evening Classes," and finally came into the possession of Messrs. F. Gordon and Co., who having restored the whole building with considerable taste and at a great outlay, have converted it into one of the best conducted restaurants within the City of London. Since the occupation of the old premises those gentlemen have also annexed to it a large and spacious building, which, although wholly different as to its architectural details, is an ornament to the locality.

CHAPTER X.

NONCONFORMIST DIVINES, OCCUPANTS OF CROSBY HALL, FROM A.D. 1662 TO A.D. 176-.

The following is as accurate a list of the Ministers who were connected with the Presbyterian Church in Crosby Hall, whether as Pastors or Assistants, as it seems possible to obtain, a brief outline of whose career cannot be without a certain amount of interest :—

MINISTERS' NAMES.	PASTOR from	to	ASSISTANT from	to
Thomas Watson, M.A.	1662	1689		
Stephen Charnock, B.D.	1675	1680		
Samuel Slater, M.A.	1680	1704		
John Reynolds,			16—	1691
Daniel Alexander,			1693	1704
Benjamin Grosvenor, D.D.	1704	1749		
Samuel Wright, D.D.			1705	1708
John Barker,			1708	1714
Clerk Oldsworth,			1715	1726
Edmund Calamy, Jun.			1726	1749
John Hodge, D.D.	1749	1762		
Richard Jones,	1763	1769		

THOMAS WATSON, M.A., was educated at Emmanuel College, Cambridge. In the time of the Civil Wars he became rector of the parish of St. Stephen, Walbrook, A.D. 1646, where he filled the office of a faithful pastor for nearly sixteen years.* During the commotions that agitated the nation in his time, Mr. Watson showed great loyalty and attachment to the person of King Charles I., and totally disapproved of the methods made use of by the Army to bring him to trial. He also joined the Presbyterian ministers in a remonstrance to General Cromwell and the Council of War against the death of that monarch. After this, in 1651, he was concerned with some other persons in carrying on a correspondence with the Scots, for the purpose of bringing in Charles II., which being discovered, he was apprehended and committed to the Tower with Dr. Drake, and others. These after some time, on their petitioning for mercy, and promising submission to the Govern-

---

* See Allibone's Dictionary of British and American Authors, vol. iii. p. 2608. Ed. Lond., 1859-71.

ment, were released, but Mr. Christopher Love, an eminent Presbyterian minister, was publicly executed.

Mr. Watson continued at his living till St. Bartholomew's-day 1662, when he was ejected for Nonconformity; he, however, continued the exercise of his ministry in private, as he was enabled to find opportunity. After the fire of London in 1666, when the churches were burnt and the parish ministers unemployed for want of places of worship, the Nonconformists fitted up large rooms with pulpits, seats, and galleries, for the reception of those who had an inclination to attend. Of this number was Mr. Watson; and upon the Indulgence, in 1672, he licensed the great Hall in Crosby House, then belonging to Sir John Langham, who patronized the Nonconformists, where he preached for several years, till at length, his strength wearing away, he retired into Essex, where he died suddenly in his closet, whilst at prayer.

Mr. Watson published a variety of books upon practical subjects, but his principal work was "A Body of Divinity" in 176 sermons upon the Assembly's Catechism.

STEPHEN CHARNOCK, B.D., descended from an ancient family in Lancashire, was born in 1628 in the parish of St. Katherine Cree, London, where his father, Richard Charnock, practised as a solicitor. At a proper age he was sent to Emmanuel College, Cambridge, where he had for his tutor Dr. William Sancroft, afterwards Archbishop of Canterbury.* Upon leaving Cambridge he went to reside in a private family, and afterwards spent some time in the exercise of the ministry in Southwark. About 1649 he proceeded to Oxford, and in the following year obtained a fellowship in New College. In 1652 he was incorporated Master of Arts, as he had before stood at Cambridge. Two years afterwards he became Senior Proctor of the University, "being then taken notice of," (says Wood),† "by the godly party for his singular gifts, and had in reputation by the then most learned Presbyterians." Upon the expiration of his Proctorship, in 1656, he went over to Ireland, and resided in the family of Henry Cromwell. In Dublin he con-

---

* William Sancroft, S.T.P., Dean of St. Paul's, consecrated in Westminster Abbey, Jan. 27th, 1677-8, deprived Feb. 1st, 1690-1, and retired to Fressingfield, in Suffolk, where he died, Nov. 24th, 1693. See Le Neve's Fasti, vol. i. pp. 27, 28. Ed. (Hardy) Oxford, 1854.

† Athenæ Oxoniens., vol. iii. col. 1234. Ed. (Bliss) Oxford, 1813-20.

tinued the exercise of his ministry about four or five years, being held in high esteem by the most serious and judicious Christians, of different denominations. While he resided in that City, it is apprehended, he received the degree of B.D. from Trinity College. The Restoration putting an end to his ministry in Dublin, he returned to London, where he spent fifteen years in retirement; and for his further improvement took a tour occasionally in France and Holland. At length, in 1675, he accepted a call to become joint pastor of the congregation in Crosby Square, with the Rev. Thomas Watson. In this connexion he continued till his death, which took place July 27th, 1680, in the fifty-third year of his age. On the 30th of the same month his remains were conveyed from Whitechapel, the place of his decease, to Crosby Square, and thence to St. Michael's Church, Cornhill, where they were deposited, and where a funeral sermon was delivered on the occasion by his fellow collegian, the Rev. John Johnson.

"Mr. Charnock was a man of excellent abilities, strong judgment, and singular genius. His attainments in learning were of the first order, having been through life a most diligent and methodical student, and a great redeemer of time, rescuing not only his restless hours in the night, but even time that was spent in walking, from those impertinences and fruitless vanities which so often fill up the minds of men, and steal away their hearts from those nobler objects that more justly challenge their regard."

Mr. Charnock published nothing in his lifetime excepting a single sermon on "The Sinfulness and Cure of Thoughts," in the supplement to the "Morning Exercise" at Cripplegate. His other valuable writings were published after his death. Their merit can scarcely be rated too high, as for strength of reasoning, solidity of judgment, and sublimity of genius, they are equalled by few and excelled by none. Mr. Toplady says, "I have met with many Treatises on the Divine Perfections, but none equal to that of Mr. Charnock; it is indeed considered one of the most inestimable productions that ever did honour to the sanctified judgment and genius of a human being." The first collected edition of his works was published in two vols. folio, 1684.

SAMUEL SLATER, M.A.—This pious and excellent divine was the son of the Rev. Samuel Slater, Minister of St. Katharine's, near the Tower, who, after passing through his elementary studies, was sent to Cambridge, where he took his degree. The first place of his stated labours was at Nayland, in Suffolk, where he continued several years; and thence removed to St. Mary's, Bury St. Edmunds, where he exercised his ministry with great diligence and success till the first assizes after the Restoration, when he and Mr. Claget, his fellow-labourer in that town, were prosecuted for not reading the Book of Common Prayer. Thus early did he begin to feel the storm which on St. Bartholomew's-day, 1662, drove him and many other ministers of the Established Church into obscurity.

Mr. Slater being vigorously opposed for Nonconformity at Bury St. Edmunds, removed to London, where he took advantage of the indulgence granted by the king, and cheerfully embraced every opportunity of public service and usefulness. On the death of Mr. Charnock he became pastor of this congregation, where he laboured with great acceptance and fidelity until his death. "The last Sacrament he administered," says Dr. Grosvenor in his Diary, "I received with him: he looked upon himself as near his end. At the close he took a solemn leave of the congregation, and ended with these words, which were delivered with the solemnity of a dying patriarch blessing his children and with the authority of an Apostle—'I charge you before God that you prepare to meet me at the day of judgment, as my crown of joy, and that not one of you be found wanting to meet me there at the right hand of God.'

"During his long weakness he enjoyed uninterrupted peace and tranquillity within, and like the bright luminary of the morning, who after cheering us for a while with his benignant rays, leaves us gradually at night, so did this good man calmly descend into the Valley of Death, and died May 24th, 1704, it having pleased God to prolong his life to an advanced period."

JOHN REYNOLDS, at the Restoration, was Minister of Roughton, in Norfolk, from which preferment he was ejected for Nonconformity. Coming afterwards to London, he was chosen colleague with Mr. Slater, at Crosby Square. He was one of the ministers who, on the part of the Presbyterians, went up to King James II. with the address of thanks for his indulgence in 1687. Mr. Slater, who preached his funeral sermon, speaks of him as a person of considerable abilities and learning, as a truly gracious, humble Christian, a profitable preacher, and a faithful friend. Mr. Reynolds died November 25th, 1691.

DANIEL ALEXANDER.—With the history of this gentleman previously to his settlement in Crosby Square, we are entirely unacquainted. In 1693 he was chosen assistant to Mr. Slater, and was happy in this connexion till Mr. Slater's death, when some uneasiness arising in the congregation occasioned his leaving Crosby Square. Of this circumstance he thus speaks—"I had the honour and advantage to be an assistant to Mr. Slater near eleven years, in all which time not the least tincture of jealousy or suspicion obtained to hinder our usefulness; but I was always treated by him with that unparalleled candour, affability, kindness, and sincere respect, which rendered my work much more pleasant and desirable than it otherwise would have been, as is now manifest from the quite contrary treatment I have met with since his death." About 1704 Mr. Alexander removed to Armourers' Hall, where he preached to a congregation till his death, September 3rd, 1709, when he was forty-nine years of age. He was buried in Bunhill Fields.

BENJAMIN GROSVENOR, D.D.—This eminent and truly excellent divine was born in London, January 1st, 1695. His father was an upholsterer. At an early age he became impressed with the importance of Divine things, which were strongly inculcated by his pious parents. When only ten years old he had such an awful view of the evil of sin, that his life became quite a burden; till at length, through the providence of God, he heard a sermon from a minister whose name he never knew, that satisfied his doubts and gave him clear views of the Gospel method of salvation. From this time his soul found its true rest, and henceforward the duties of religion were his greatest delight. He no longer relished the diversions of youth; but after school hours retired to his closet, spending many hours in prayer and devout meditation.

With the consent of his parents he entered upon a course of studies suited to the profession he had chosen; and in 1693 was placed under the tuition of the celebrated Mr. Timothy Jollie, at Attercliffe, in Yorkshire.

In very early life he connected himself with the Baptists, and continued with them for seven or eight years. Soon after his return from the Academy he declared his opinion in favour of infant baptism and the Presbyterian form of Church government; also that unordained persons ought not to preach. These things moved the Church, and, after much time spent in controversy, they were necessarily obliged at his request to dismiss him from his membership with them.

In the year 1699 Mr. Grosvenor entered upon his public work, and was chosen assistant to Mr. Oldfield, at Maiden Lane, Southwark; and was ordained July 11th, 1704, to succeed the venerable Mr. Slater as pastor of the congregation in Crosby Square.

The popularity of Mr. Grosvenor as a preacher recommended him to some of the most considerable of the Lectures about London. Besides the one at the Old Jewry, he was one of the first preachers of the Friday Evening Lecture at the Weigh House; and in 1716 he was chosen into the Merchants' Lecture upon a Tuesday morning, at Salters' Hall. The University of Edinburgh conferred upon him, in 1730, the Degree of Doctor in Divinity; and in 1735, when the nation was under the alarm of Popery, some Dissenting ministers undertook a course of sermons at Salters' Hall against the principal errors of the Church of Rome. It fell to the lot of Dr. Grosvenor to discuss the subject of persecution, which he exposed in very strong colours.

Dr. Grosvenor continued in the faithful discharge of his pastoral office till 1749, when age and infirmities compelled him to relinquish his charge, having been a minister in London during the period of fifty years. The remainder of his life he spent in devout retirement, and being at the funeral of Dr. Watts, a friend said to him, "Well, Dr. Grosvenor, you have seen the end of Dr. Watts, and you will soon follow: what think you of death?" "Think of it?" replied the Doctor; "why, when death comes, I shall smile upon it, if God smiles upon me." He was confined to his chamber for seven weeks, with much suffering. He lost his speech some days, but not his senses, till he slept in Jesus on Lord's-day morning, August 27th, 1758, in the eighty-third year of his age. His remains were interred in Bunhill Fields, and an excellent discourse upon the occasion of his death was preached at Crosby Square by the Rev. John Barker, who had been his assistant, and intimate friend for nearly half a century.

SAMUEL WRIGHT, D.D., Dr. Grosvenor's first assistant, a minister of great reputation and celebrity in the City of London, was born January 30th, 1682-3, and was the eldest son of the Rev. James Wright, of Retford, in Nottinghamshire.

Mr. Wright having lost his parents at an early age, the care of his education devolved on his grandmother and Mr. Cotton, of Haigh, in Lancashire, his maternal uncle. By them he was put to boarding-school at Attercliffe, under Mr. Jollie; and at the age of twenty-one he went to reside as chaplain with his uncle Cotton, at Haigh. But this gentleman dying, he removed to London, and was soon after invited by the congregation at Crosby Square to assist Dr. Grosvenor. He was also chosen, in conjunction with Mr. Hood, to preach a Lord's Day Evening Lecture at St. Thomas's, Southwark. In both these connexions he officiated a few years with great diligence and success till 1708, when he was chosen pastor of the Church Meeting at Blackfriars, but which afterwards removed to a more commodious and handsome building in Carter Lane, which was opened by Dr. Wright, December 5th, 1734; and by the blessing of God upon his ministry for the space of thirty-eight years, he had the satisfaction of preaching to as large an auditory and as distinguished for seriousness and affection as any in London.

About two years after his settlement at Blackfriars he married the widow of his predecessor, daughter of the Rev. Obadiah Hughes, of Enfield. Some years after he was chosen into the Tuesday Morning Lecture at Salters' Hall, and also into the Lord's Day Morning Lecture at Little St. Helen's.

After a lingering illness, Dr. Wright entered joyfully into his rest, April 3rd, 1746, aged sixty-four years. His liberality to the poor was regular and extensive. In his purse was found this remarkable memorandum:—"Something from all the money I receive, to be put into this purse for charitable and friendly uses. From my salary as a Minister, which is uncertain, a tenth part. From occasional and extraordinary gifts, which are more uncertain, a twentieth part. From copy money of things I print, and interest of my estate a seventh part."

JOHN BARKER.—Mr. Wright was succeeded in his office of assistant to Dr. Grosvenor by the Rev. John Barker, who was born about the year 1682; and after passing through the customary course of grammar learning, was placed for Academical instruction under the care of Mr. Timothy Jollie.

In 1709 Mr. Barker was chosen assistant to Dr. Grosvenor, and formed an agreeable and useful friendship with that minister and other valuable persons; and, after a lapse of more than forty years, publicly declared, "that he viewed their former connexion with pleasure, and accounted it his honour."

Shortly after the death of the pious and excellent Matthew

Henry, in June, 1714, Mr. Barker was chosen to succeed him as pastor of the congregation in Mare Street, Hackney, where his preaching, which was then without notes, was accompanied with a considerable share of popularity.

Mr. Barker, to the no small dissatisfaction and surprise of the whole Church, resigned his charge in the year 1738, and went to reside at Epsom in Surrey, where he lived about three years, without any stated employment, but was on all occasions ready to assist his brethren. On the death of the Rev. John Newman, of Salters' Hall, in July, 1741, Mr. Barker, who was then nearly sixty years of age, was invited to preside over that congregation, with which invitation after a short time he complied.

Mr. Barker retained his connexion with the congregation at Salters' Hall so long as he was able to perform the duties of his office; but severe affliction, which attended his declining years, compelled him to resign his charge in the spring of 1762. His death took place May 31st, 1762, when he was eighty years of age, and he was interred in Hackney churchyard, in a vault near the south wall.

CLERK OLDSWORTH, Dr. Grosvenor's next assistant, received his education in the College of Glasgow, upon what may be called Dr. Williams's foundation. He was ordained at the Old Jewry, January 11th, 1721. After this he continued to assist Dr. Grosvenor till his death, which happened in the prime of life about the year 1726.

EDMUND CALAMY, B.D., son of the celebrated Dr. Calamy.—It is probable that he was educated for the ministry, first in Scotland and afterwards in Holland, at both which places his father possessed considerable connexions. Returning to London, he was chosen in 1723 to preach a Tuesday Lecture at the Old Jewry, in conjunction with several other ministers of the younger class. In the year 1726 he was chosen assistant to Dr. Grosvenor, in which situation he continued till the Doctor's resignation in 1749, when he also declined preaching. After this he lived a few years in retirement, till his death, which happened in St. John's Square, June 13th, 1755. He was a learned and ingenious man, of great worth, and much respected in his day.

JOHN HODGE, D.D., received his academical education at Taunton under the learned Mr. Henry Grove, and the first years of his ministry were spent, as we believe, at Deal, in Kent. Thence he removed to Gloucester, where he laboured with considerable reputation. Dr. Grosvenor having resigned the pastoral office in 1749, Dr. Hodge accepted an invitation to succeed him in Crosby Square. At this time the congregation was in a very low state; and notwithstanding his discourses were very sensible and devotional, he was not so happy as to raise its numbers, but, as the old members died or families removed, it continued sinking. The infirmities of advanced life obliged him to resign the pastoral charge about the year 1761 or 1762. After this he lived for some time in retirement, until removed by death, August 18th, 1767.

RICHARD JONES.—Upon the resignation of Dr. Hodge the principal members invited the Rev. Richard Jones, formerly a pupil of Dr. Doddridge, to succeed him. Mr. Jones had been settled for some years with the Presbyterian Congregation in Green Street, Cambridge. Hopes were entertained that the congregation in Crosby Square would revive under his ministry, but the experiment did not succeed. The lease of the meeting-house expiring about six years afterwards, the state of the Society was too discouraging to warrant a renewal; so that they agreed to dissolve their church state, and the remaining members dispersed into other Societies. This event took place October 1st, 1769, when Mr. Jones delivered a farewell discourse suited to the occasion, from Titus ii. 13, " Looking for that blessed hope, and the glorious appearing of the great God and our Saviour Jesus Christ."

In this sermon, which was afterwards printed, Mr. Jones takes leave of his Church in the following words: " I close my public services among you with the profession of my sincere respect and esteem for you, and with my wishes for your happiness, temporal and eternal. With this discourse and the celebration of the Lord's Supper, my relation to you, as a pastor and teacher, will expire; but there is one relation that I shall ever bear you, in whatever place or station of service I may be hereafter fixed; for I shall always be yours to the utmost of my power, in all the offices of friendship, love, and gratitude. I have no doubt that the future charges of my life will be under the direction of that Great Being, in whose favour I hope to make my final remove out of it; and if I had been more useful to you during the short time of my connexion with you, it would have afforded me a very exalted pleasure at parting. Make a serious business of religion wheresoever you go, now that our gates are desolate; nor let it ever appear that you have hitherto heard in vain. . . . . Such of you as knew this place in its prosperous days must for many late years have experienced similar emotions with those old men amongst the Jews, who wept at seeing the sad difference between the second Temple and the first. The Church of Christ, though not of this world, will in some measure partake of its changes and variations; and we of this Society must be reconciled to the disagreeable alterations that time and death have made amongst us." Mr. Jones afterwards settled at Peckham, where he preached for many years, and was succeeded by the Rev. W. B. Collyer.

Besides the assembly of Nonconformists in Crosby Hall, a meeting-house existed in Little St. Helen's*—a building erected about the time of King Charles's Indulgence, in 1672—of a moderate size, with three galleries, and being conveniently situated, was often made use of for Lectures and other public services among the Dissenters. The first public ordination held by the Nonconformists, after the Bartholomew Act, was performed at this place June 22, 1694, and lasted from ten in the morning until six o'clock at night. Hitherto, through the unfavourable spirit of the times, the ordination of Dissenting ministers had been carried on in private, and Mr. Calamy consulted several aged ministers in London respecting the propriety of a public service. Considerable difficulty, however, arose through the timidity of some of the elder ministers; the great Mr. Howe absolutely refused taking a part in this service, through fear of offending the Government, and Dr. Bates urged some other reasons to excuse himself. At length, however, the matter was accomplished, and Mr. Calamy was publicly ordained with six other young ministers. This was the first public transaction of the kind amongst the Dissenters in London, after the Act of Uniformity took place, 1662, and was conducted with peculiar solemnity.

The Friday Morning Lecture, founded by Mr. Coward, in 1726, was carried on at this place till the demolition of the meeting-house, when it was removed to Camomile Street. There

---

* Wilson's History of Dissenting Churches, vol. i. p. 363.

was also a Lecture here for many years, upon the Lord's Day Morning, at seven o'clock, during the summer season, in commemoration of the happy accession of George I. to the throne of these kingdoms. The Catechetical Lecture on a Wednesday evening, formerly at Lime Street, was removed to this place, and a casuistical exercise, on a Lord's Day evening, was conducted here for some years, by Mr. Pike and Mr. Hayward.

The congregation assembling in this place was collected by Dr. Samuel Annesley, and continued in a flourishing state for many years after his death. At length the congregation so far declined, that after the death of Mr. Kello in 1790, they dissolved their church state. The meeting-house was then occupied by Mr. William Brown, who after preaching there a short time, removed his people, in 1792, to Cumberland Street, Shoreditch. The place was then taken by the Rev. C. F. Triebner, a German Lutheran divine, who had raised a small society in Brown's Lane, Spitalfields, but in consequence of a division, conducted part of the people in 1792 to Little St. Helens. Mr. Triebner occupied the place about two years, when the lease expiring, he removed to the meeting-house in Eastcheap. A Mr. Underwood then occupied it for about a twelvemonth till the place was shut up. In October, 1794, a Lecture on a Sunday evening was opened here by Mr. David Rivers, who for a short time entertained his hearers with some pulpit essays, and then removed to Monkwell Street. The last sermon preached here was at Mr. Coward's Friday Lecture, May 15th, 1795, by the Rev. Samuel Palmer, of Hackney. This ancient building was then shut up for a few years; but in 1799 was entirely taken down, and some handsome houses erected on its site.

The ministers of the old Presbyterian Congregation were as follows:—

MINISTERS.	PASTOR		ASSISTANT	
	from	to	from	to
Samuel Annesley,	1672	1696		
John Woodhouse,	1697	1701		
Benjamin Robinson,	1701	1724		
Harman Hood,			17—	1720
Edward Godwin,	1722	1764	1721	1722
Thomas Prentice,	1764	17—		
George Stephens,	17—	1780		
James Kello,	1781	1790		

SAMUEL ANNESLEY, LL.D., was born of religious parents at Kenilworth, near Warwick, Ann. Dom. 1620. He was first cousin to Arthur Annesley, Earl of Anglesey, Lord Privy Seal in the reign of Charles II. His father dying when he was only four years old, the care of his education devolved upon his mother, a prudent, pious woman. He was so early under serious impressions, that he often declared that he never knew the time when he was not converted, and this religious disposition strongly inclined him to the ministry from his very infancy. At Michaelmas Term, 1635, being fifteen years of age, he was admitted a student in Queen's College, Oxford, where he took his degrees in Arts, and was particularly remarkable for temperance and industry. In 1644 he became chaplain to the Earl of Warwick, the Admiral of the Parliament's Fleet. In process of time he was promoted to the valuable living of Cliff, in Kent, worth 400*l.* per annum. Here he succeeded Dr. Higges, the sequestered minister. At the commencement of his labours he met with considerable difficulties, the people being rude and ignorant. So high did they carry their opposition, as frequently to assault him with spits, forks, and stones, often threatening his life; but he declared, "Let them use him as they would, he was resolved to continue with them, till God had fitted them by his ministry to entertain a better who should succeed him; but solemnly declared, that when they became so prepared, he would leave the place." In a few years his ministry met with surprising success, and the people were greatly reformed.

In July, 1648, Mr. Annesley was called to London to preach the Fast Sermon before the House of Commons, which by their order was printed. But, though greatly approved by the Parliament, it gave much offence to others, as reflecting upon the King, then a prisoner in the Isle of Wight. It was about this time that he was honoured by the University of Oxford with the title of Doctor of Laws, conferred on him at the instance of the Earl of Pembroke. August 25th, in the same year, he again went to sea with his patron, the Earl of Warwick, who was employed in giving chase to that part of the English navy which went over to the then Prince, afterwards Charles II. After continuing at sea more than three months, he returned to London in the December following.

Some time after this, having procured a suitable successor, he resigned his Kentish living, much against the will of his parishioners. Not long after, in 1652, Providence directed his removal to London by the unanimous choice of the inhabitants of St. John the Evangelist, Friday Street. In 1657 he was nominated by Oliver, Lord Protector, Lecturer of St. Paul's, and in the following year the Protector, Richard, presented him to the living of St. Giles's, Cripplegate; but this presentation growing quickly useless, he in 1660 procured another from the Trustees for the maintenance of Ministers, being also a Commissioner for the approbation and admission of Ministers of the Gospel after the Presbyterian mode. His second presentation growing as much out of date as the first, he obtained, August 28th, 1660, a third presentation of a more legal nature from King Charles II. Yet even this did not keep him there long, for on St. Bartholomew's-day, 1662, he was ejected for Nonconformity, having been removed from his lectureship at St. Paul's about two years before.

Upon the indulgence in 1672, Dr. Annesley licensed a meeting-house in Little St. Helen's,* where he raised a flourishing society, of which he continued the pastor until his death, and as he possessed a considerable paternal estate he was enabled to do much good, not only providing for the education and subsistence of several ministers, but devoting a tenth part of his income to charitable purposes. In the early part of his life he is said to have been under darkness of mind, but he afterwards enjoyed uninterrupted peace, and laboured earnestly in the ministry for fifty-five years. At length he was attacked by a painful distemper, which after seventeen weeks of intolerable torture put a period to his life, December 31st, 1696, in the seventy-seventh year of his age.

The last time Dr. Annesley entered the pulpit, being dissuaded from preaching on account of his illness, he said, "I must work while it is day." His zeal to do good was equal to his ability.

---

* "There were also weekly meetings of ministers in a body, kept up at this time at Dr. Annesley's Vestry, at Little St. Helen's—now St. Helen's Place—in Bishopsgate Street. Once a month, there were Latin disputations upon such heads of divinity as were agreed upon. These were declined, and at length wholly dropped, as the heats and debates among the ministers grew warmer."—Calamy's Life, vol. i. p. 325. Ed. Lond. 1829.

Id. Account of Ordination of Seven Ministers, June 22nd, 1694, at Dr. Annesley's Meeting-house, Bishopsgate Within, near Little St. Helen's, p. 348.

The poor looked upon him as their common father. The celebrated Richard Baxter says of him:—"He is a most sincere, godly, humble man, totally devoted to God."

Dr. Annesley left a son, Benjamin, and two daughters. Judith, the eldest, married a Mr. James Fremantle, the other daughter, Ann, was married to the Rev. Samuel Wesley, father to the celebrated John Wesley. She was a sensible, pious woman, and bore nineteen children, of whom three were ministers.

JOHN WOODHOUSE, an eminent tutor and divine among the Nonconformists, received his education in the University of Cambridge; from thence, while but young, he removed into the family of Lady Grantham, as chaplain, where he resided several years.

When the Uniformity Act took place, Mr. Woodhouse appears to have resided in Nottinghamshire, as he is enumerated among the silenced ministers of that county by Dr. Calamy. He afterwards removed to Sherifhales, in Shropshire, where he opened an Academy for training young men for the ministry, and the many excellent persons who were educated under him gave proof of his ability for his office. He married the daughter of Major Hubbard, of Leicestershire, a lady of singular piety as well as handsome fortune.

Besides his employment as a tutor, Mr. Woodhouse exerted himself with great zeal as a minister of the Gospel. He dreaded a useless life, and when some unhappy circumstances occasioned him to break up the Academy, it was his frequent complaint— "Now every field is unpleasant for fear I shall live to no purpose." Not long afterwards, however, he received an invitation to succeed Dr. Annesley at Little St. Helen's, where he continued in the faithful discharge of his ministry till his death. Within a few days of that event he took a solemn leave of his people, in a sermon delivered with his usual warmth and affection. He enjoyed the exercise of reason till the last, prayed with great fervour, was full of inward comfort, and died without a groan in the year 1700.

BENJAMIN ROBINSON, a learned minister, and born of pious parents at Derby in the year 1666. His mother died a few days after his birth. At a proper age he was sent to the Grammar School at Derby, and was afterwards placed under the tuition of the Rev. John Woodhouse, at Sherifhales, where he finished his academical studies, and from thence removed into the family of Sir John Gell, where he applied so closely to study as greatly to injure his health. He there became acquainted with that great and good man, the venerable Richard Baxter. After some time he removed into the family of Mr. Samuel Saunders, of Normanton, as domestic chaplain. The conversation of this family and a valuable library, to which he had access, rendered his situation very agreeable.

Mr. Saunders dying, and Mr. Robinson altering his condition, he removed to Findern, in Derbyshire, where he was solemnly ordained to the work of the ministry, Oct. 10th, 1688. Notwithstanding the discouraging state of the times, he applied to his work with great labour and zeal. His learning, piety, and obliging behaviour introduced him to many worthy persons among the clergy and others, from whom he received such offers of preferment in the National Church as were not to be resisted, except upon a principle of conscience. At Findern he set up a private Grammar School in the year 1693, for which he was cited into the Bishop's Court; but upon personal application to Dr. Lloyd, then Bishop of Lichfield and Coventry,* with whom he was acquainted, he soon obtained relief. The good Bishop took this opportunity of entering into an amicable debate with him on the subject of Nonconformity, which continued till two o'clock in the morning, when Mr. Robinson was dismissed with particular marks of favour. About this time he became acquainted with the excellent Mr. John Howe, who, discovering his great worth, resolved to embrace the earliest opportunity of bringing him to London.

From Findern Mr. Robinson was called to Hungerford, in Berkshire, which invitation he accepted upon the recommendation of Mr. Howe, who conducted his settlement with a solemnity peculiar to himself. He exercised his ministry in this place with great acceptance for seven years, and at the earnest request of some of his brethren, in 1696, set up a private academy. This procured him enemies; and complaint being made to Dr. Burnet, Bishop of Salisbury,† he was sent for by that excellent prelate, then in his progress, on a visitation through Hungerford. Mr. Robinson gave the Bishop such satisfactory reasons for his Nonconformity,

---

* See Le Neve's Fasti, vol. i. p. 558.   † Id. vol. iii. p. 609.

and for that undertaking in particular, as laid the foundation of an intimate friendship ever afterwards.

In the year 1700, upon the death of Mr. Woodhouse, who had recommended Mr. Robinson to his people as a fit person to succeed him, he received an unanimous invitation to take the pastoral charge of the congregation in Little St. Helen's. In 1705 he was chosen one of the preachers of the Merchants' Lecture at Salters' Hall. As he approached his latter end his patience and resignation, through much suffering, were surprising to all around him—continually rejoicing in God, until, after eight weeks' confinement to his bed, he departed this life, April 30, 1724, aged fifty-eight years, and was interred in Bunhill Fields.

HARMAN HOOD.—Mr. Robinson was assisted several years by a Mr. Harman Hood, who also preached an evening lecture at St. Thomas's, Southwark, in conjunction with Dr. Wright; but increasing illness compelled him to relinquish both the services about the year 1720. He survived Mr. Robinson, and furnished several particulars relating to his life. His name (H. H.) is among the subscribing ministers at the Salters' Hall Synod in 1719, but no further particulars are known concerning him.

EDWARD GODWIN was born at Newbury, in Berks, about the year 1695. Being intended for the ministry, he was sent to the Rev. Samuel Jones's academy at Tewkesbury; and such was the high opinion entertained of him, that upon the death of his tutor he received a pressing invitation to succeed him in the important province of educating young men for the ministry. This, however, he modestly declined, and upon leaving the academy settled for a short time at Hungerford, and in the year 1721 became assistant to Mr. Robinson in Little St. Helen's. In the following year he was ordained co-pastor, and upon Mr. Robinson's death in 1724 succeeded to the whole charge. As Mr. Godwin was a very lively and ready preacher, the congregation, which had declined under his predecessor, soon experienced a considerable revival, and he was speedily called to preach at some of the most popular lectures among the Dissenters. The first he was called to engage in was at the Old Jewry on a Tuesday evening, about the year 1723; and upon the institution of Mr. Coward's Lecture in 1726, Mr. Godwin was one of the first ministers chosen to conduct it. After some time he was also chosen one of the Merchants' Lecturers upon a Tuesday morning at Salters' Hall, and likewise into the Friday Evening Lecture at the Weigh House.

The latter years of Mr. Godwin's life were embittered by many bodily infirmities, and after labouring in this part of the vineyard upwards of forty years with reputation to himself and usefulness to others, the lamp of life was almost insensibly extinguished on the 21st March, 1764, in the sixty-ninth year of his age.

His remains were interred in Bunhill Fields, and Dr. Langford delivered a funeral discourse to his afflicted Church, from John xii. 26—"If any man serve me, let him follow me; and where I am, there shall also my servant be."

Mr. Godwin married the widow of his tutor, Mr. Jones, and by her had two sons, the eldest, though not trained to the ministry, preached a short time in Mr. Whitefield's connexion, but died in early life. The other son was educated under Dr. Doddridge, and settled at Wisbeach.

THOMAS PRENTICE received his education at Mile End, under Drs. Conder, Walker, and Gibbons, and was chosen Assistant to Mr. Godwin in 1762, and succeeded him in the pastoral office. In this situation he continued but a short time, when embracing the Sandemanian sentiments his connexion with the Church was dissolved. After this he joined the Sandemanian Society in Bull-and-Mouth Street, but after a few years retired to Nottingham and carried on a manufacturing concern.

GEORGE STEPHENS, M.A.—After the departure of Mr. Prentice, the Rev. G. Stephens, a Scotchman, was invited to undertake the pastoral office, which he accepted. In this situation he remained until his death, about the end of the year 1780. Mr. Stephens had the misfortune to be blind of one eye; but this was not his greatest defect, he was an imprudent man, and became involved in his circumstances.

JAMES KELLO, brother to Mr. Kello, of Bethnal Green, was born about the year 1755, in the City of London, and pursued his academical studies at Homerton. On leaving the Academy he settled with a congregation at Hertford, whence he removed to London to succeed Mr. Stephens. Here he preached for the space of eight years, when he was removed by death in the midst of his days, February 4th, 1790, aged but thirty-five years. His remains were interred in Bunhill Fields, and with his death the Church over which he was pastor may be said to have died also.

Not long after the dissolution of the Presbyterian Society in Crosby Square, the meeting-house was taken on lease by Mr. James Relly, the leader of a religious sect whose distinguishing tenets have received the name of Antinomianism.

JAMES RELLY was born at Jefferson, in the county of Pembroke, North Wales, in the year 1720. His parents were respectable persons, and placed him for education at the Grammar School of that town. At the usual age he was put apprentice to a cow-farrier, in which occupation he is said to have excelled. Relly was a wild ungovernable youth, and addicted to bad company. On a certain Sunday he agreed, with some other lads of his own stamp, to go and hear Mr. Whitefield preach, that he might have an opportunity of laughing at the Methodists. They commenced their sport by making a noise and ridiculing the preacher, to the disturbance of the congregation. At length Mr. Whitefield's discourse so riveted the attention of young Relly, that when his companions wished him to retire, he resolved to stay behind, and from that time became serious. He now had many conflicts with himself on his past life and future expectations.

Mr. Relly having formed an acquaintance with Mr. Whitefield, became one of his most strenuous supporters, and in a little time commenced preacher. His first settled ministerial charge was in South Wales, where he continued to preach some years. During his residence in this place he took frequent journeys to Bristol, and on his way would often stop at Kingswood and other places to discourse with the colliers. At this time he was extremely popular; but a separation taking place between him and Mr. Whitefield, gave a new turn to his connexions. After this, Mr. Relly came to London, where he soon united himself with the Universalists. His first preaching-place was Coachmakers' Hall, where he had a numerous congregation. At this time he wrote several of his works; and his preaching and writings created no small stir in the religious world. The term Antinomian is said to have been first applied to him by Mr. John Wesley, and it has been fixed upon his followers ever since. The odium attached to his opinions, on account of the immoral tendency which they were represented to have produced a great influence upon his followers, who gradually deserted him till he had but few left. In process of time he took the meeting-house in Bartholomew Close, where he continued till the expiration of the lease at Midsummer, 1769. Soon after which he removed into the old meeting-house in Crosby Square, where he continued to preach till his death, which took place on the 25th of April, 1778, in the fifty-eighth year of his age. His remains were interred in the Baptist burial-ground, Maze Pond, Southwark, where a neat monument was erected to his memory.

In the vicinity of the Church in Great St. Helen's stood formerly a meeting-house, used for that purpose in the time of the Long Parliament by the famous Mr. Hansard Knollys. What became of the meeting-house after he quitted it we no where learn, but of this eminent man and of the church he collected, we have the following particulars.

HANSARD KNOLLYS was born about the year 1598, at Chalkwell, in Lincolnshire. He had the advantage of descending from religious parents, who maintained a tutor for him in their house till he was fit for the University, when they sent him to Cambridge, on leaving which he was chosen Master of the Free School at Gainsborough.

In June, 1629, Mr. Knollys was ordained. Soon after which he was presented by the Bishop of Lincoln to the living of Humberstone, in Leicestershire; but this he held only two or three years, when he began to scruple concerning the lawfulness of several ceremonies, and he accordingly resigned his living. About the year 1636 he renounced his episcopal ordination, and joined himself to the Nonconformists, which exposed him to many hardships. Being followed by persecution he sought shelter in New England, and is honourably mentioned by Mather as having a respectable character in the churches of that wilderness. Upon his arrival at Boston, he was apprehended by virtue of a warrant from the High Commission Court, and confined for some time to a private house; but by his serious discourse he so terrified the conscience of his keeper, that he set open his doors and suffered him to depart.

Mr. Knollys remained about five years in America, but being

recalled to England by his aged father, he arrived safely in London on the 24th December, 1641. At this time he was in great poverty, and for his better support he took under his care a few scholars till he was chosen Master of the Free School in St. Mary Axe, where, in the course of one year, he had one hundred and fifty-six scholars. But the benefits resulting from this employment he quitted to go into the Parliament army, and he preached freely to the common soldiers, till he perceived the commanders sought their own things more than the cause of God and his people, when he left the army and returned to London.

Episcopacy being now laid aside, Mr. Knollys preached for some time in the parish churches with great approbation; but the Presbyterians having gained the ascendancy, made as ill use of their power as their predecessors, proscribing all those who did not fall in with their particular sentiments; and Mr. Knollys being earnestly requested to preach at Bow Church, took occasion from his subject to speak against the practice of infant baptism: this giving offence, a complaint was lodged against him, and he was apprehended and kept several days in prison. At length being brought before the Committee, he was examined, and gave such satisfactory answers, that he was discharged without blame or paying fees.

Not long after this, Mr. Knollys went into Suffolk, and preached in several places; but being accounted an Antinomian, the virulence of the mob was excited against him by the High Constable. At one time he was stoned out of the pulpit; at another time the doors of the church were shut against him, upon which he preached in the churchyard. This was considered too great a crime to be excused, and he was taken into custody, and afterwards sent a prisoner to London, with articles of complaint against him to the Parliament. On his examination he proved that all the disorders which had happened were owing to the violence of his enemies. His answers were so satisfactory that he was not only discharged, but had liberty to preach in any part of Suffolk.

Mr. Knollys finding how much offence was taken at his preaching in the church, and to what troubles it exposed him, set up a separate meeting in Great St. Helen's, where the people flocked to hear him, and he had generally a thousand auditors; but this gave greater offence to his Presbyterian brethren than his former method. Now they complained that he was too near the church, and that he kept his meetings at the same times that they had their public worship; and first they prevailed upon his landlord to warn him out of the place. After this he had a large meeting-house in Finsbury Fields, and still continuing to preach, was summoned before a Committee of Divines at Westminster, who commanded him to preach no more. The life of this good man was a continual scene of trouble and vexation. Soon after the Restoration, Mr. Knollys was dragged to Newgate, with many other innocent persons, where he suffered eighteen weeks' imprisonment till delivered by an act of grace upon the King's coronation. After removing into different parts of England, Mr. Knollys went abroad, and on his return to London betook himself to his former employment of school teaching, by which he was enabled by the blessing of God to provide things honest and convenient for his family. He was also by no means negligent of that work which was the great labour of his life; but he continued in the faithful discharge of the pastoral office to gather congregations in various places till his death, at which time his meeting-house was in Broken Wharf, Upper Thames Street. He also preached a Morning Lecture every Lord's day at Pinners' Hall. The malice of man, however, occasioned frequent interruptions to his work. By virtue of an Act against Conventicles, commencing May 10, 1670, he was taken at a meeting in George Yard, and committed by the Lord Mayor to the Compter in Bishopsgate; but having favour in the eyes of the Keeper, was permitted to preach to the prisoners twice every week. Soon after, at the Old Bailey Sessions, he was set at liberty. He was, however, no sooner delivered from this trial than he was called to endure severe bodily affliction, and afterwards some domestic trials—first by the loss of his wife, who died April 13, 1671, followed by the death of his only son. After this his household affairs were managed by his granddaughter, whose prudent conduct rendered his declining years tolerably easy. He kept his bed but a few days, and dying Sept. 19, 1691, in the ninety-third year of his age, was buried in Bunhill Fields.

APPENDIX.

Page 6.—*Basing's Will.*

Prioratus S. Heleuæ, juxta vicum de Bishopsgate-streete, in civitate Londoniarum.

De constituendo Moniales in eadem.

[Ex cod. ms. penes Dec. et Capit. Eccles. Cath. S. Pauli, Lond., A. fol. 246.]

"Sciant præsentes et futuri, Quod ego Alardus Ecclesiæ S. Pauli Decanus et ejusdem Ecclesiæ capitulum, concessimus Willielmo fil., Willielmi Aurifabri patrono Ecclesiæ S. Helenæ, London., ut constituat in eadem Ecclesiâ moniales, Deo ibidem in perpetuum servituras, et Collegio ibidem constituto jus Patronatus ejusdem Ecclesiæ, quod à prædecessoribus nostris ei fuerat concessum, conferat. Ita quidem, quod quicunque ibidem nomine Priorissæ ministrabit, post electionem ab eodem Collegio factam, Decano et Capitulo London. præsentetur, et juret fidelitatem Decano et Capitulo tam de ipsâ Ecclesiâ, quam de Pensione dimidiæ Marcæ annue, infra octo dies Paschæ solvendâ et de jure patronatus non alienando, et quod nulli alio Collegio se subjiciet. Concessimus etiam, quantum in nobis est, quod Collegium ibi statutum omnes obventiones supradictæ Ecclesiæ, exceptâ dictâ pensione in usus proprios convertat. Idem quoque Collegium omnia onera Episcopalia ad Ecclesiam prædictam pertinentia sustinebit. Si autem in loco prædicto aliquo casu fortuito, conversatio monialium esse desierit, concessimus ut ibidem viri religiosi, absque contradictione, secundum formam de Monialibus superius expressam constituantur, et simili modo Decano London. et Capitulo obligentur. Ut autem hujus concessionis nostræ, nec non et totius conventionis tenor in perpetuum memoria firmiter teneatur, et firmiter observetur, ipsum totum sub formâ Chirographi scribi fecimus; cujus pars una nostro, pars vero altera ipsius W. et Monialium sigillis, ut omnis imposterum tollatur malignandi occasio, ad mutuam, hinc-inde cautelam roborata est. Hiis testibus Alardo Decano, et aliis."*

Page 6.—*Benedictine Rules.*

St. Benedict, the founder of the order of the Benedictine Monks, was born at Nursia, in Italy, about A.D. 480. He was sent to Rome when very young, and received there the first part of his education.

---

* Newcourt's Repert. Eccles., vol. i. pp. 363, 364. Ed. Lond. 1708. See also Dugdale's Monast. Anglican., vol. iv. p. 553. Londoni, 1817-30.

At fourteen years of age he removed to Subiaco, about fifty miles distant. Here he lived a most ascetic life, having shut himself up in a cavern, where nobody knew anything of him except St. Romanus, who used to descend to him by a rope and supply him with provisions. But being afterwards discovered by the monks of a neighbouring monastery, they chose him for their abbot. Their manners, however, not agreeing with those of Benedict, he returned to his solitude, where many persons followed him and put themselves under his direction, so that in a short time he was enabled to build twelve monasteries. In the year 528 he retired to Mount Casino, where idolatry was still prevalent, a temple to Apollo having been erected there. He instructed the people in the adjacent country, and having converted them, broke in pieces the image of Apollo, and built two chapels on the mountain; here he also founded a monastery, and instituted the order which in time became so famous and extended itself all over Europe. In this place he composed his "Regula Monachorum," so highly extolled by Pope Gregory. The period of his death is uncertain. He was looked upon as the Elisha of his time, and is reported to have wrought a great number of miracles.

The monks of this order were obliged to perform their devotions, which had reference solely to the passion and death of Christ, seven times in the twenty-four hours; they always went two and two together; every day in Lent they fasted until six in the evening, and abated of their usual time of sleeping and eating; but they were not allowed to practise any voluntary austerity without leave of their Superior; during meals they were obliged to attend to the reading of the Scriptures. For small faults they were shut out from meals or excluded from the chapel, and incorrigible offenders were expelled. Every monk had two coats,* a table book, a knife, a needle, and a handkerchief, and their cells were furnished with a mat, blanket, rug and pillow.

To the Benedictine Monks the greater number of the English owe their conversion from idolatry. In the year 596 Pope Gregory I., called "the Great," sent hither Augustine with several other Benedictine Monks. Augustine became Archbishop of Canterbury, and founded several monasteries.

Pope John XXII., who died in 1334, found after an exact inquiry, that since the first rise of this order it had produced 24 popes, near 200 cardinals, 7000 archbishops, 15,000 bishops, 15,000 abbots, above 4000 saints, and upwards of 37,000 monasteries. There have also been of the order 20 emperors and 10 empresses, 47 kings and above 50 queens, 20 sons of emperors and 48 sons of kings, above 100 princesses, besides dukes, marquises, earls, &c., innumerable; with a vast number of eminent writers and other learned men.

The Benedictine rule insisted upon "obedience without delay, silence, no scurrility, idle words, or such as excite laughter, humility,

---

* Loose gowns with large wide sleeves.

patience in all injuries, manifestation of secret faults to the Abbot, contentment with the meanest things and employments, not to speak when unasked, to avoid laughter, head and eyes inclined downwards, to rise to church two hours after midnight, every week the Psalter to be sung through—light in the dormitory; to sleep cloathed, with their girdles on, the young and old intermixed—to serve weekly and by turns at the kitchen and table—refection in silence and reading Scripture during meals—two different dishes at dinner, with fruit. One pound of bread a day for both dinner and supper. No meat but to the sick. Three quarters of a pint of wine *per* day—particular abstinence in Lent from meat, drink, and sleep; and especial gravity."[*]

There is reason to believe that no nunneries were formed after this rule until the year 620; it was at first somewhat mixed with other rules, but in the year 817 the Emperor Louis le Débonnaire caused the Council of Aix-la-Chapelle to be assembled, wherein an uniform discipline was established. "St. Benedict did not decide of what colour the habit should be; but it appears by ancient pictures that the garment the first Benedictines wore was white and the scapular black." The nuns wore " a black robe, with a scapular of the same, and under the black robe a tunic of wool that had not been dyed. In the choir, or upon solemn occasions, they wore over all a black cowl," *i.e.*, hood. The scapular was a garment worn during the time of labour.

Page 11.—*Kentwode's Constitutions.*

The following document, having been accidentally omitted at its proper place, with reference to the text, is here given from the Rev. Thomas Hugo's " Last Ten Years of the Priory of St. Helen's, Bishopsgate:"—

" A fragment of the seal is appendant, of dark brown wax.

" The document is of parchment, measuring $20\frac{1}{2}$ inc. by 15 inc. and is endorsed ' Seint Poul,' ' sub altare x°,' ' Jniunccões Sc̄e Helene,' and, in a much later hand, ' Ordinances for regulation of the Nunnes of St Helens, neere Bishopsgate, in London.'

" Fastened to the upper left-hand corner is a small piece of the same material, on which is written, in a hand of the thirteenth century, a petition of the Prioress and Convent to the Dean, Archdeacon, and others, in defence of some contested property, belonging to the Priory. The Prioress ' D' was, I believe, the first of those dignitaries; and the dean and archdeacon were respectively Alardus de Burnham, dean of S. Paul's, 1204–1216; and Walter Fitzwalter, Archdeacon of London. The left edge is injured, but the following will be found a not inaccurate copy of a document, which, though hitherto unpublished, is of special interest and importance to an historian of the earlier years of the House :

---

[*] See Fosbrooke's British Monachism, pp. 66, 67; and 286–8. Ed. London, 1843' and Townsend's Manual of Dates, p. 136. Ed. Lond. 1874.

"'Viris Ven⁹abłibȝ. ⁊ dñis. A. dec'. W. Archid'. Lundoñ. ⁊ Cełis coarbiłs D. Humił. P⁹ orissa. ⁊ Couuent⁹ Ecclie Sc̃e Helene Salt̃ ⁊ obedienc̃. Diłci noḅ in dño W. fundatoris nr̃i laboribȝ ⁊ angustiis quas p 9t⁰uersia coram voḅ mota. M. fila sym̃. sup l̃ra. W. Wrhot. . . . . dem irrogauit injuste. debita compassione deferentes tam apllõi. q̃ᵃ ꝑhibicõi. ꝑ iurc ⁊ pos[sessio]ne nr̃a a. noḅ int̃põitis renũciam⁹. volentes. ⁊ concedñtes. vt juxᵃ formã 9pmissi. inł ptes pcedet arbił ̃u. Malum⁹. qᵈ si oportũit carere fundo. q̃ᵃ amico. spantes. nic̃homin⁹. de justicia [vr̃]a q' indempnitati Ecclie nr̃e qᵃntũ scdm̃ dm̃ połitis. eritis puisuri. Vałt.'

"T. H."

Page 27.

Adhuc de com̃ibȝ plitis tent⁹ in Hustengo Londoñ die lune pxᵒ ante fm̃ Sc̃i Dunstani Archiep̃i Anno R. R. E. ł⁰cij post conq: XLIX.

Dc̃is die & anno veñunt Gilbtus Chaumponeys Johes Fourneux Panna⁹ & Johes Vssher exec̃ Testĩ Ade ffraunceys & pbar⁹ fecerunt testm̃ p̃dc̃eAde quo ad articłos laic̃u feodũ tangenł p Johem Sybyle & Witłm Shirbõñe tesł iur⁹ ac diligenł & cepatim exãiãł qui dixunt qd p̃senł fuer̃) vbi dc̃us Adam suũ condidit testm̃ in hñc modũ. In dei nom̃ie Amen.   Ego Adam ffraunceys Ciuis & Mʲ⁾cerus Londoñ compos mentis mee & sanis in corpore ordiño & facio p̃sens testm̃ meũ de ℉ris tēn & reddĩtibȝ meis in Ciuitate Londoñ in hunc modũ vnm p̃ omĩbȝ in pmis lego & com̃endo aĩam meam Deo om̃ipotenti creatori & saluatori meo be qz Marie Virgini Matri sue ac omĩbz Sc̃is & Angelis eius corpus qz mc̃u ad scpeliend'⁾ in Capella Sc̃i Sp̃us in Ecclia sc̃e Elene infra Bisshopegate Londoñ. Itm̃ lego volo & ordino qd om̃ia debita mea in quibz teneor quibuscumqz psonis de bonis & catallis meis p̃mo & p̃ncipalił psoluanł. Et cum quidam Capellanus de cuiusdam denoc̃oe p̃ tcmpe sustentał⁾ totidie celebret & aliquandm̃ celebrare consuev̂it vnam missam de Sc̃a Maria p notam in ecclia conuentuali Sc̃e Elene p̃dic̃ł ad magnũ altare mane videł ̃ ante primam conuentualem ad quam quidm̃ missam de Sc̃a Maria sit celebrandam quedam monialium domᵍ p̃dce totidie inłfĩnt & consuev̂int inłesse. Ac cũ quidam alius capellanus consimiliłł sustentatᵉ totidie in dc̃a capella Sc̃i Sp̃us infra eandm̃ eccliam vnam aliam missam sive nota similił consuev̂it celebrare qui quidm̃ capellani semp hacten⁵ p alt̃ius voluntate fuerunt amobiles nec ad eoɼ̃ sustentacõem ppetuam vnqᵃm prif aliquid ordinatū fůat aut p̃visum volens divini cultū p̃ut cuĩlt velle competit ad honorem Dei & salutem fideliū eoᴣ maxime qui migᵃrunt a scto ampliari. In nomĩe sancte & individue Trinitatis & p̃cipue Sc̃i Sp̃us ob cuius honorem dc̃am capellam fundavi & in nomĩe b̃e Marie Virginis gloriose ac om̃i scõᴣ vt huiusmodi misse temporibᴣ fut̃is p aĩa mea & aĩabᴣ prĩs mei matris mee, Agnetis vx̃is mee, Simonis, Ade, Thome, Petri, Rogɂi, Ric̃i, Johis, Matiłł, Sarre, Margɔte, Juliane, om̃i quibᴣ ñito teneõr & om̃i fideliu defunctoᴣ in forma p̃dc̃a imppm̃ celebrent⁹ qd qᴣ capełłi missas p̃dc̃ās & alia officia subscripta p aĩabᴣ p̃dc̃ĩs celebraturi & facturi ppetui sint & deceɾ̃o p altɂius voluntate sive causa roñabili nequeant amoveri quare lego & volo & in quanto Ciuiũ p̃dc̃õᴣ alicui p consuetudĩes laudabiles eiusdm̃ Civitatis hacten⁹ appb̃atas p testm̃ sũu dispoñe licet ex mea sincera & vltima voluntate ac denocõe integra lego ordina & assigno qd due Cantarie ppetue in forma sequenti fiant in Ecc̃lia sup̃dc̃a quaᴣ vnam cantariam b̃e Marie in ecc̃tia Sc̃e Elene infra Bysshopesgate Londoñ Alteram v̄o cantariam Sc̃i Sp̃us in eadm̃ Ecc̃lia volo ppetuis temporibᴣ nuncupari. Quaᴣ quidm̃ cantariaᴣ pronatf̃ executoribᴣ meis dũ vix̃int tm̃ et post mortem eoᴣdm̃ executoᴣ Priorisse & Conventui p̃dc̃e ecc̃tie Sc̃e Elene & Successoribᴣ suis in forma sbscripta lego imppm̃ optinend et quas quidm̃ Cantar fieri & fundari Capellanos qᴣ eisdm̃ Cantarɔ deservituros oñari & dotari lego similit̃ in forma sbsequenti lego videłt volo & ordino qd statim postqᵃm obiero duo Capellani idonei p executores meos p̃dc̃os vnus videłt ad Cantar b̃e Marie sup̃dc̃ām ałt̃ v̄o ad Cantarɔ Sc̃i Sp̃us p̃dc̃ām decano ecc̃tie Sc̃i Pauli Loudon qui p tempe fuɾ̃it si decan⁹ tunc huiusmodi heaɾ̃ et vacante decanatu eiusdm̃ ecc̃tie Sc̃i Pauli Capitło p̃sentent̃. Qui quidm̃ Capełłi ab eodm̃ decano si p̃senɔ fũit sui autem ab eiusdm̃ decani vicario si decan⁹ heaɾ̃ & vacante decanatu a p̃fato capitło admittanɾ̃ & in eisdm̃ cantarɔ instituanɾ̃ in forma iuris & sic quociens dc̃as cantarɔ p mortem cessionem resignacõem p̃vacoẽm amocõem in forma sbscripta vel alio modo legitimo vacarᴼ contiĝit durante vita exeɾ̃ meoᴣ aut alicui⁹ eoᴣdm̃ p eos & p eũ qui alios eoᴣdem supvix̃it post mortem alioᴣ p̃sentent̃ duo capełłi idonei ad easdm̃ cantarɔ sepatim vnus similt̃ capellan⁹ idoneus p̃senɾ̃ ad cantarɔ illam que eaᴣdm̃ sic vacav̄it ałt̃a plena existente & fiat huiusmodi p̃sentacõ infra quadraginta dies post

quamlt huiusmodi vacacōem post mortem p̃o dc̄oȝ execͫ meoȝ quociens dc̄as cãtarꝟ sic vacarꝟ contiḡit fiat p̃sentac̄o ad easdm̄ & ad
utͬmqȝ eaȝdm̄ cū vacaṽint in forma p̃dca infra quadraginta dies
similit post quamlt huiusmodi vacacoem de Capellanis idoneis
p̃dce ecctie Sc̄i Pauli Decano si decanꝗ heatͬ & vacante decanatu
eiusdm̄ ecctie Sc̄i Pauli Capit̃lo p priorissam & conventū p̃dc̄e
ecctie Sc̄e Elene qui p tempe fũint & p eoȝ successores imppm̄ & in
form p̃dc̄ā instituant & instituatͬ ille qui p̃sentatus fũit ad unam
eaȝdm̄ altͬa cantarꝟ p̃dc̄aȝ plena existente p decañu si p̃sens fuit sui
autem p eiusdm̄ decani vicarꝟ si decan⁹ heatͬ & vacante decanatu p
capitlm̄ sup̃dc̄m̄ aut p supiores suos ordinarꝟ gradatim & p successores suos imppm̄ si dc̄i Decanꝗ Vicarisͬ aut capitlm̄ sic p̃sentatū
admitte nolũint si p̃o dc̄i execuṱ durante tm̃io suo aut postmodū
p̃dc̄i Priorissa & conventꝗ aut successores sui negligentes fũint aut
remissi ita qd infra quadraginta dies aliquam vacac̄onum p̃dc̄aȝ
in forma p̃dc̄a pxᵒ sequentes ad Cantarias p̃dc̄as & ad utͬmqȝ eaȝdm̄
que sic vacaṽᵒit non p̃sentaṽint in forma pᵒdc̄a decanus sup̃dc̄us
si p̃sens fuᵒit sui autem eiusdm̄ decani vicarꝟ si decansͬ heatͬ sui
autem Capitlm̄ sup̃dc̄m̄ & successores sui ea vite conferant cantariam illam que eaȝdm sic vacaṽit & ad quam pᵒsentacio in forma
pᵒdca fc̄a non fũit cm̄c̄nqȝ volũint idoneo capellano salvo semp̃
alias pᵒfatis executorᵒ tota vita eoȝdm̄ & postmodū pᵒfatis Priorisse
& Conventui & successoribȝ suis iure suo pᵒsentandi ad cantarꝟ
pᵒdc̄as & ad eaȝdm̄ utmqȝ in quatt alia vacacōe cū infra tempus
deoȝ quadraginta dieȝ post huiusmodi vacacōēm idoneū capellm̄
volũint p̃sentarꝟ. Volo insup lego & ordino qd dc̄us capellūs ad
cantarꝟ be Marie sic admissus & successores sui impp̄m̄ unam
missam de Sc̄a Maria p notam ad magnū altarꝟ in ecctia pᵒdc̄a vel
ad aliud altarꝟ ubi post dc̄m magnū altarꝟ in eadm̄ ecctia com-
petenciꝗ fieri potͬit totidie celebret diebȝ cene Pascenes & Sabbi
Sancti dumtaxat exceptis & post dc̄am missam anteqͫm de
Stola fũit exutus comemoracōēm om̃i fideliū defunctoȝ videtͭ
Requiem etͬnam & cetͬa eidm̄ comemoracōi incumbentia sine
nota. Et post evangeliū quod incipit Inpᵒncipio &c. psalmū
dc̄m De pfundis cū orac̄oe dnīca p̃cibȝ & alijs orōibȝ conse-
quentͭ sequentibȝ que cōitͭ dici solent p defunctis & in fine anima
Adē ffraunceys & aīe om̃i fideliū defunctorȝ requiescant in pace
mane hora videtͭ consueta scitͭ ante horam p̃mam monialiū
dicat siliter om̃i die cuius quidm̄ misse celebrac̄oi & ad dc̄am

memoriam p defunctis una cū toto residuo ut p̄dicit̄ & quousqʒ
dc̄us capellanus de alba sua fuit exutus sex moniales de monialibʒ
ecclie Sc̄e Elene p̄dc̄e p priorissam que p tempe fuit & p successores suos imppm̄ in forma sbscripta limitandas volo lego &
dispono totidie psonalit̄ int̄esse quaʒ quidm̄ monialm̄ limitacoēm
p p̄mi sic fieri dispono videlt qd pxīo die sabbi postq̄"m deūs
capellanᵍ ad cantarᵢ be Marie sup̄ᵃdc̄am p̄mo fuit institut⁹
limitent̄ p Priorissam ecclie sup̄dce que p tempe fuit in capitlo
suo sex moniales domus sup̄dc̄e ad deserviend̄) cantar⁹ & capelto
p̄dcis in forma sequenti continue p septem dies sequentes et tunc in
alio p̄xiō die Sabbi tunc px sequenti sex alie moniales ecclie
sup̄dc̄e similit̄ limitent̄ loco p̄oʒ ad eisdm̄ cantar⁹ & capelto similit̄
deserviend p septem alios dies continue tunc sequentes. Et sic do
Septimana in Septimanam quolt die Sabbi imppm̄ limitent̄ sex
moniales de monialibʒ sup̄dc̄e ecclie que ultima septimana ante
huiusmodi limitac̄oēm cantar⁹ & capelto p̄dc̄is ñō deserviebant ad
eisdm̄ p septē dies tunc sequentes in forma p̄dc̄a deserviend si
numus monialiū in domo p̄dc̄a p tempe existent̄ ad tantas se
extendat & utrū in dc̄a domo tantus numus moniatiu videlt qd sex
moniales una septimana & sex alie sequenti septīā cantarie illi
deservire pot̄unt heat̄ an non volo lego & dispono qd cantar⁹ &
capellanᵍ pdc̄i p discrec̄oem Priorisse que p tempe fuit talit̄ a
monialiabʒ ȝviant̄ et qd limitacio & divisio monialiū illaʒ ita fiat
qd in labore eaʒdm̄ quo ad cantarie & capelto p̄dc̄is sic p p̄mi ȝviend
hīto respectu ad numu monialiu in domo p̄dc̄a p tempe existent̄
om̄es moniales eiusdm̄ dom⁹ in quantu competent̄ fieri pot̄it sint
equales. Et qd moniales ille om̄ia que competunt monialibʒ domᵍ
p̄dc̄e facienda in huiusmodi missis celebrand & que in alijs missis
p notam ibidm̄ solent fieri p alias moniales in p̄dce misse de Sc̄a
Maria celebrac̄oē totidie honeste faciant & denote & post misse
p̄dc̄e celebracoem expectent in choro dicendo quicquid eis ptinet
ad p̄dc̄ām com̄emorac̄oēm p defunctis & ad totu residuū supius
ordinatū & quousqʒ sacerdos post dc̄m̄ Evangeliū quod incipit
Inp̄ncipio &c et post dcm psalmū dcm De pfundis p̄dixit anima
Ade ffraunceys & āie om̄i fideliu defunctorʒ requiescant in pace et
moniales ille responderint Amen aliqualit̄ nō recedant alt̄ V̄o
capellanᵍ ad p̄dc̄ām cantar⁹ Sc̄i Spūs sic admissus & successores sui
imppm̄ unam missam in p̄dca capella Sc̄i Spūs una cū comemora-
c̄oe fideliū p̄dicta post dc̄ām missam nisi de dc̄a commemoracōē

celebravit et post dcūm̄ Evangeliū incipiens In principio etc totū psalmū dc̄m̄ De profundis et oīā sbsequencia supdc̄ā put alteri capetto supius est iniunctū celebret om̄i die pro aīab; supdcīs eisdm diebȝ cene Pascenes et Sabbi Sc̄i similit' exceptis. Et qd ut'qȝ Capellanoȝ p̄dcoȝ et successoȝ suoȝ imppm̄ psonalit' int'sit auxiliū suū et quod sibi imcumbit adhibendo decantac̄ōi totidie vesperoȝ decantac̄ōis vesptine de salve regina cū nota matutinaȝ missaȝ et aliaȝ singulaȝ horaȝ canonicaȝ et om̄i alioȝ divinoȝ officioȝ quæ p̄ pochianis in ecc̄tia p̄dca et sc̄dum usus eiusdm in eadm contigit celebrari quodqȝ similit' ut'qȝ dcoȝ Capellanoȝ et successoȝ suoȝ imppm totidie dicat officiū mortuoȝ in ecc̄tia Saȝ usitatu videt' Placebo et Dirige ccm̄endacōēm et omīa alia que eidem officio incumbunt septem spalmos (psalmos) penitentiales cū letania et quindecim psalmos g̊duū silit' p aiabȝ supdcis dicti v̊o capetti et eoȝ ut'qȝ et successores sui imppm̄ singtis annis p p̄dcum Decanū et si ip̄e absens fuit tunc p eius vicar° et vacante Decanatū p p̄sidentem capit'li supda infra tres dies p̄xōs post fm̄ Sc̄i Michis visitent° et si in aliquo dcoȝ capettoȝ aut successoȝ suoȝ imppm̄ septē defectus notorii p ip̄m̄ anno tunc p̄tito ppetrari inveniant' ita videt' qd ip̄o omiserit vel facere necglent' voluntarie id quod eidem in forma p̄dc̄ā fuit p istam ordinac̄oem iniunctū et sic p huiusmodi omissionem vel necgligenciam septem defectus in anno p̄cedenti com̄iserit nisi inde rōnabilem huit excusac̄oem et sic defect'] p Priorissam Suppriorissam Sacristam celerar° et capellanū pochialem ecc̄tie Sc̄e Elene supdce successores suos vel p tres deaȝ quinqȝ psonaȝ legitime pbent' et q"mvis in forma p̄dc̄a nō visitent tū dc̄oȝ capettoȝ aut successoȝ suoȝ huiusmodi septem defect'] quos infra spac̄m̄ uni'] anni voluntarie com̄iserit et defect'] illi ext° huiusmodi visitac̄oēm p p̄dcōs Priorissam Suppriorissam Sacristam celerar et capettm pochialem qui p tempore fuit vt p tres deaȝ quinqȝ psonaȝ dco Decano vel ei'] Vicar vt vacante Decanatu p̄sidenti Capit'li supdc̄i notificent' et p iuramentū triū eaȝdm̄ psonaȝ bona videt' fide et ȝelo justicie et non odii vel rancoris causa pbent' nisi dcus capettus qui huiusmodi defectus comiserit rōnabilem ut p̄dicit' inde heāt excusac̄oem aut si quem dc̄oȝ capettoȝ aut successoȝ suoȝ imppm̄ enormit' delinquere aut se male gerere contingat unde aliqua suspicio criminis in eodm potit legitime suspicari que conjectis v̊esitibȝ constac̄o potit et p p̄dcōs Priorissam Suppriorissam, Sacristam Celebrar° ac Pochialem Sacdotem aut successores suos aut

p tres eaȝdm̄ quinqȝ psonaȝ canonice ter monitu ipm̄ non corrige
vel a tali suspicōē sive excessu ipm̄ non sbtᵛhere tunc ille qñqȝ
psone vel saltem tres eaȝdm̄ deō Decano vel eius vicar v̄l p̃sidenti
sup̃dco decanatū vacante dc̄i capełłoȝ qui sic deliquerit crimina
excessus et suspicoem similit̃ notificent ac eiusdm̄ malos gestᵍ sibi
exponant. Cum quidem Decano eiᵍ vicarᵒ sive p̃sidenti si constarᵒ
poʳit aliquem dcoȝ capełłoȝ aut successoȝ suoȝ gᵃvit̃ deliquisse vel
male se hūisse unde scandalū eidm̄ dom̄m Sc̄e Elene ullo modo orisi
poʳit ex juramento eaȝdm̄ quinqȝ psonaȝ vel triū eardm̄ dumtaxat
accepto qđ nō odio vel rancore set una fide et ȝelo justicie et
honestatis contra aliquem dcoȝ capełłoȝ pponant tunc statim absqȝ
strepitu et figura judicii idm̄ capełłus tot huiusmodi defectᵍ sic
com̄ittens delinquens vel suspectus ħita huiusmodi inde p̃bacoe p
dc̄m Decanu vicarᵒ vel presidentem amoveatʳ et alius capełłūs
idoneus loco sui ad p̃sentacoem executoȝ meoȝ qᵃm̄dm vixint in
forma p̃dcā et postmodū ad p̃sentacoēm dc̄oȝ Priorisse et Conventus
infra quadraginta dies post huiusmodi defectum deliccoȝ gestᵍ
aut suspicōīs criminis notificacoem exposicoem et informa p̃dca
p̃bacoem fc̄as p dc̄m Decanu Vicar vel p capit1m ad Cantar ił unde
dc̄ūs Capellus qui huiusmodi defectus vel delicta sit com̄iserit extitit
amota admittatʳ et instituatʳ. Et nisi dc̄i execᵈ mei dū vixint et
post mortem eordm̄ nisi dc̄i Priorissa & conventᵍ & successores
sui infra p̃dcōs quadraginta dies ad cantarᵒ illam capellanū
idioneū p̃sentent tunc p p̃dc̄m Decanū si p̃sens fūit & si absens
p eiᵒ vicarᵒ aut p p̃dc̄m capit1m vacante decanatu cantarᵒ illa unde
dc̄ūs capełłus sic amoᵗ fūit illa vice ppʳ negligenciam dc̄oȝ execᵈ
in vita sua & postmodū dc̄oȝ Priorisse & conventᵍ ałti capełło
idoneo conferatʳ salvo semp iure dc̄oȝ execᵈ in vita sua tm̄ & postea
dc̄oȝ Priorisse & conventᵍ & successoȝ suoȝ in om̄i alia huiusmodi
vacatōe pᵒsentandi ad v̄tmqȝ dc̄āȝ cantarᵒ c̄ū necgligentes in
forma p̃dcā n̄o fūint nec remissi. Et si dc̄ūs Decanus vel eiˢ
vicarˢ si decanˢ fūit aut dc̄ūs pᵒsidens vacante decanatu capełłm̄ iłłu
qui huiusmodi defectˢ delicta vel causam suspicois sic ut p̃dc̄m est
p̃bata com̄iserit statim n̄o amovᵒit set huiusmodi amocōem distu-
lerit p sex dies iuridicos postqᵃm de huiusmodi defectubȝ delictis
aut causa suspicācōis modo & forma pʳdc̄is fūit informatᵍ tunc
liceat dictis execᵈ meis dū vixint & postmodū dc̄īs Priorisse & conventui & successoribȝ suis auctoritate ppia capełłm̄ iłłu qui huiusmodi defectᵒ delicta vel causam suspicōīs com̄iserit expellerᵒ &

amovere a cantar⁹ quam obtinuit & aliū capellm idoneū infra quadraginta dies p̃x post huiusmodi amōcōem & expulsionem loco sui p̃sentar⁹ dc̄ō Decano & vacante Decanatu dc̄ō capitlo qui quidm̄ capellus p̃sentatᵉ in forma p̃dca admittat et in Cantar⁹ quā Capellus qui sic amotus fuit priᵠ occupavit tanqᵃm vacantem instituatʳ ac si p mortem vel resignacōem illam priᵠ occupantis de facto vacaret. Et si contingat aliquem dcoᵹ Capelloᵹ p huiusmodi defectubᵎ delictis vel suspicio p dcm Decanū Vicar⁹ vel vacante decanatū P⁹sidente vel p dc̄ōs execᵘ Priorissam et Conventū post illos sex dies iūridicos in forma p̃dca fore amoᵖ. Et capellus ille ab huiusmodi amocōe sua vel p c̄essu inde ħendo appellar⁹ & suam p̃ sequi appellacōem tunc lego volo & ordino qd Capellus ille sic appellans tam a Cantar⁹ sua p̃dca prisᵉ obtenta qᵃm ab omī comodo quod p Cantar⁹ illa aliqualiᵗ esset pcepturus eo ño obstante qd ppetuus fuit seu in Cantar⁹ sua p ordinar⁹ institutᶠ amoveatʳ & penitᶠ excludatʳ & alius Capellus idoneūs modo & forma sup̃dcis loci ip̃ius subrogati ad Cantar⁹ qua sic amotᵠ occupavit p⁹seṅteᵖ admittatʳ & instituatʳ oña condicōes & p̃ficua in p̃senti testo constituta subiturus facturus & pcepturus in forma p̃dca. Et sic fiat de utroqᵎ capelloᵹ p̃dcōᵹ & successoᵹ suoᵹ imppm̄ quociens in forma p̃dca huiusmodi defectᶠ crimen excessus vel causam suspicois ip̄m incurrer⁹ contigit aut subire. Cui quidm̄ cantar⁹ illi videlt que Cantar⁹ be Marie ut p̃diciᵗ nuncupatᵒ & capello eidm̄ deservituro lego octo libraᵗ annui & quieti reddᵈ⁾ eidm̄ cantar⁹ be Marie dc̄ō qᵎ capellno dce cantar⁹ be Marie deserviᵗo & successoribᵎ suis imppm̄ obtinend⁹ & pcipiend de omibᵎ illis tr⁹ redditibᵎ & teñ meis c̄ū gardinis adiacenᵗ & suis ptiñ que quondam fuerñt dñi Johes de Veer Comitis Oxōn & Dñe Matill Uxᵎis sue in pochijs Sc̄i Martini Oteswych, Sc̄e Elene, Sc̄e Alburge, & Sc̄i Petri de Brade Strete in Ward de Bisshopegate & Bradestrete in Civitate Londoñ singlis annis ad quatuor tmīos p̃ncipales & in civitate Londoñ usuales p equales porcōes & qᵈ bene liceat dc̄ō capello dce cantar⁹ be Marie deservito⁹ & successoribᵎ suis imppm̄ p se & quosc̄ñqᵎ ministros suos distrigere in omibᵎ teñ p̃dc̄īs c̄ū ptiñ & in quall pte eoᵎdm̄ & districcōes capᵗ asportarᵖ abducᵉ & retiñe quociens p̃dcm annū redditᵗ in pte vl in toto ad aliquem tmīoᵹ p̃dcōᵹ aliquo modo imppm̄ aretrō fore contingat quousqᵎ de eodm̄ redditᵗ c̄ū omibᵎ inde arrerag̃ & de damp̄ñ & exp̄ñ occōne huiusmodi detencōis hītis dc̄ō capellno de tempe suo & successoribȝ suis de tempe suo imppm̄ plenarie satisfiat. Alteri v̊o cantar⁹ illi sc̄itt que Cantar⁹ Sc̄i Spūs sit vt p̄dicil̊ nuncupal̊ & capello eidm̄ Cantar⁹ deservīto lego quendam aliū annū redditꝰ Sepl̊ libraȝ dc̄o Cantar⁹ Sc̄i Spūs & eidm̄ Capelto eidm̄ Cantar⁹ Sc̄i Spūs deservituro & successoribȝ suis imppm̄ obtinend⁹ & pcipiencl singlis annis de om̄ibȝ & singlis ten sup͆dc̄is c̄ū om̄ibȝ & singlis suis ptin equis porc̄ōibȝ ad l̊mios supadc̄ōs. Ita qd bene liceat eidm̄ capellno dc̄ē cantar⁹ Sc̄i Spūs deservito⁹ & successoribȝ suis imppm̄ in om̄ibȝ & singlis ten sup̄dc̄ē c̄ū om̄ibȝ & singlis suis p̄tīn silicl̊ distring̊e & districc̄ōes cartas asportar⁹ abduce & retin̊e quociens dcm̄ aliū annū redd⁹ in pte vl̊ toto in forma p̄dc̄a ad aliquem l̊mioȝ p̄dc̄ōȝ aliquo anno imppm̄ aretro fore contingat quosqȝ de toto alio redd⁹ sup̄dc̄ō c̄ū om̄ibȝ inde arrerag̊ una c̄ū dampn̄ et exp̄n occ̄ōne detenc̄ōis huiusmodi hītis dc̄ō capello dc̄ē cantar⁹ Sc̄i Spūs deservito⁹ p tempe suo & successionibȝ suis p tempe suo imppm̄ plenar⁹ satisfiat Quociens insup dc̄i Annui redd⁹ aut vn͡q eoȝdm̄ in pte vl̊ in toto p unū mensem p̊ʀ sēqū aliquem l̊mioȝ p̄dc̄ōȝ aliquo anno imppm̄ & postq̄m post l̊mī illū p capellm̄ illu cui sic debet⸍ exactꝗ fūit apud ten p̄dc̄a detineantꝰ] & n̄ō solvantꝰ bene liceat illi capello cuiꝗ reddil̊ sic sbtʳhitʳ aut detineʳt & utriqȝ capelloȝ p̄dc̄ōȝ si amboȝ reddit⁹ sbtrahantʳ sepatim distn̊ge in om̄ibȝ & singtis ten p̄dc̄is c̄ū om̄ibȝ & singlis suis ptīn post mensem illū & districc̄ōes sic capl̊ abduce asportar⁹ & retiner⁹ quousqȝ de dupl⁹ illiꞌ quod sic aretro fūit de reddit sup̄dc̄is vt de uno eoȝdm̄ si unꞌ tantu detineal̊ capellis p̄dc̄is sepatim vel uni eoȝ illi vidett cuiꞌ redditꞌ sic detinel̊ p tempe suo & successoribȝ suis p tēpe plenar⁹ satisfiat & imppm̄. Item lego om̄ia & singla ten p̄dc̄a c̄ū om̄ibȝ & singtis ptīn suis p̄dc̄is in forma p̄dc̄a de p̄dicl̊ redditꞌ on̄ata Priorisse ecc̄tie Sc̄e Elene p̄dce & eiusdm̄ loc̄i conventūi simil c̄ū redditu hospic̄ quod Margareta Marsshal tenet ad l̊mi annoȝ quod quidm̄ hospic̄ pcella est eoȝd̄ ten statim postq̄m duo capelli in p̄dcas cantar⁹ instituantʳ & īp̄i capelli sint in seisina redditꞌ p̄dcoȝ ad cantar⁹ suas p̄dcas sic spectantꞌ p soluc̄ōem duoȝ denar⁹ vt ampliꝗ obtinend vidett dc̄is priorisse & conventui & successoribȝ suis & tenend de capital dn̄is feodi p ˆsvicia que ad p̄dc̄a ten ptinent imppm̄ excepta advocac̄ōe ecc̄tie Sc̄i Martini Oteswych p̄dicl̊ quam heredis meis imppm̄ volo spālil̊ reservari Reddendo inde annuatim capellis p̄dc̄is & successoribȝ suis impp̄m reddit⁹ p̄dc̄ōs in forma p̄dc̄a ad t̄m̄iōs sup̄dc̄ōs et solvendo quatt sep̄tia cūīlt illaȝ sex monialiū que p ministrac̄ōe celebrac̄ōis misse be Marie sup̄dc̄ē limitate fūint & p̄sentes ibm in forma p̄dca ultīō die Sabbi cū ͡sviciū Cantar⁹ illius p septimana p̄cedentem complev̄int modo sup̄dc̄o quatuoȝ denar̄⁾ & sic quott die sabbi de sep̄tīā in sep̄tīām cuīlt vidēt sex monialiū que sic ͡svicio Cantar be Mar̄⁾ sup̄dc̄ē fūint deputate si inf̄ūint & officiū illud complev̄int in forma sup̄dc̄a quatuoȝ denar solvent' per septimana illa tn̄c finita p Priorissam dom⁹ sup̄dc̄ē que p tempe fūit & p eiusdm̄ loci conventū & successores suos impp̄m de ten̄ sup̄dcis. Et inveniendo vestimenta appat⁹ p altari calices missalia panem viñū & luminar̄⁾ p cantar⁹ p̄dc̄is & p capellanis eisdm̄ deservituris p successoribȝ suis impp̄m Inveniendo eciam & sustinendo quandam lampadem die & nocte impp̄m continue ardentem coram altari in capella Sc̄i Sp̄us sup̄dca. Lego p̄rea & dispono q̄d ijdm̄ Priorissa & convent⁹ & successores suis singlis añnis impp̄m in Vigilia dici videlt annīvsar⁹ mei faciant pulsac̄ōem campanaȝ modo p mortuis consueto ac plenu ͡sviciu de Placebo & Dirige cū nota dicant in choro videlt eaȝdm̄ & extrius in ecctia pochiati Sc̄e Eleñe sup̄dce cū nota similit̄ dic̄i faciant p alios seculares & in crastino dicto videlt annīvsar⁹ die quot missas rōnabilit̄ potunt & unam p̄cipue missam ad minus cū nota ad magn̄u altar⁹ ibidem de officio mortuoȝ p aiabȝ p̄dc̄is impp̄m faciant cū denoc̄ōe solempnit̄ celebrari. Volo insup lego & dispono q⁴ singt̄is annis eodm̄ die annīvsar⁹ mei dc̄i Priorissa & convent⁹ & successores sui impp̄m tresdecim paupos egenos in cibar⁹ & potubȝ oportunis ad uñu repastū sufficient̄ in p̄dc̄a domo Sc̄e Elene p eisdm̄ similit̄ aiabȝ cibar⁹ faciant competent̄. Preterea lego volo & dispono q̄d quociens p̄dc̄ōs anu⁹ reddit⁹ Cantarijs p̄dcis & capettis eisdm̄ deservituris in forma p̄dc̄a sepatim dispositos & legatos ad aliquem t̄mioȝ p̄dc̄oȝ in pte vel toto aretro fore aut p̄dc̄ōs quatuor denar⁹ quott die sabbi singlis septimanis impp̄m cūīlt sex monialiū que Cantar⁹ be Marie sup̄dc̄ē p septīām diem illū px̄ p̄cedent̄ deservierint sic solvent̄ alicui eaȝdm̄ sex monialiū detineri aut vestimenta appat⁹ altar⁹ calices missalia panem viñū aut luminar⁹ p Cantar⁹ & Capettis p̄dcis aut lāpadem in forma p̄dc̄a n̄o inveniri vel pulsac̄ōem aut ͡sviciū p̄dc̄a in vigilia die annīvsar⁹ mei singlis annis non fieri aut missas in crastino modo p̄dco n̄o celebrari vel tot paupes quot p̄mittent̄ singlis annis modo silic̄ sup̄dc̄ōs n̄o cibari aliquo tempe imppm contingat tunc bene liceat tam capellis supdcīs & vtriqʒ eoʒdm̄ & successoʒ suoʒ qᵐ eciam heredibʒ meis imppm̄ distringe in omibʒ teñ supdcis cū omibʒ suis ptiñ & in qualt pte eoʒdm̄ & districcōes capl̄ asportarᵉ abduce & retine quousqʒ tam videll vtriqʒ capelloʒ p̄dcoʒ qui p tempe fuint de eo quod de reddil̄ illo sibi competit in hac pte aretro fuit & cuilt sex monialiū p̄dcaʒ de eo quod de p̄dcīs quatuor denarᵉ p quatt. septimana p quam Cantarᵉ de Marie supdc̄e & Capello eiusdm̄ deservierit in forma p̄dc̄a simill̄ sibi fuit detentū plenarᵉ fuit satisfiem̄ qᵃm eciam quousqʒ vestimenta appatᵏ callices missalia panis viñū luminarᵉ & lāpas supᵃdc̄ā competenl̄ inveniantᵉ & eciam quousqʒ p quoll defectuū pulsacōis & ᵃsviciū mortuoʒ in vigilia diei anniᵛsarᵉ mei & missaʒ in crastino quadraginta solid & p quoll defectū cibacōis paupū eodm̄ die viginti solidi p aīābʒ supdcīs p eosdm̄ Priorissa & conventū aut successores suos imppm̄ alijs paupibʒ erogentᵏ. Et ne p neegligenciam monialiū aut successoʒ suoʒ p̄sens mea vltima voluntas in aliquo supᵏ contentoʒ infringatᵏ aut aliqua de p̄dicl̄ ordinalᵏ imppm̄ casualil̄ omittatᵏ volo lego & dispono qd tam Priorissa qᵃm quell monialiū in p̄dc̄ā domo Sancte Elene existens sup Sc̄a Evanglia corpale faciant iuramentū qd ipe et quell eaʒdm̄ om̄es ordinacōes supdc̄as & singulás eaʒdm penes se facient & ᵃsvabunt & quo ad alios quantū in ipis est facient simill̄ fidelil̄ observari & qd ipe om̄es & singlas moniales que deceᵗo de domo supdc̄a habitū religionis assumᵉe & in eadm̄ contingint pficeri tanqᵃm p quodam articlo pfessionis sue sup eadm̄ pfessione sua facient conferre consile iuramentū. Ita qd om̄es & single moniales in dc̄a domo iam existentes ac om̄es ille que in futoro imppm̄ moniales ibm fore contigint ad faciend tenend & observand om̄es & singlas ordinacōes supdc̄as quantū in ipis fuit & qd facient imppm̄ om̄es & singulas successores suos in & sup pfessione sua sup Sc̄a Evanglia palam coram videll Priorissa & toto conventu ecclie supdc̄ē consimile face iuramentū p huiusmodi iuramentū fidelil̄ astringant. Itm̄ lego p̄dcīs Priorisse & conventū domᵏ Sc̄e Elene p̄dc̄e totam shopam meam cū omibʒ suis ptiñ que quondam fuit Wall̄i le Bret Civis & Zonarij Londoñ & Cristine vxis eius situaᵗ in venella vocata Sopereslane in Londoñ videll intᵉ teñ Thōm de Granthᵃm ex ptibʒ boriali & orientali & quandam Shopam ptinenl̄ ecclie Sc̄i Pancracᵉ Londoñ expᵗe australi ad dc̄ām venella vocaᵗ Sopeslane ex pte occidentᵉ tenend eisdm̄ Priorisse & conventui & eoʒ successoribʒ imppm̄ De capitaɫ dñīs feodi illiꝗ p ſvicia inde debita & consueta solvendo inde annuatim Kaꞇine Wolf Moniali domꝗ Sc̄e Elene pdc̄c̄ ad ꞇm̄i vite sue quadraginta solid sꞇlinꞡ ad quatuor anui ꞇmīōs pncipalēs & in Civitate Londoñ usuales p equales porc̄ōes. Itm̄ lego eisdm̄ Priorisse & conventui p̄dc̄c̄ domꝗ Sc̄e Elene omīa illa ꞇras & teñ cū omibʒ & singꞇis suis ptiñ que Joħes de Cantebrigg Civis Londoñ & ego nup coniunctim huimꝗ ex dono & feoffamento Thoṁe de Ecton Rectoris ecc̄tie Sc̄i Nichi de Geñlaco in Com̄ Eboʒ executoris testi dñi Joħis de Ecton cꞇici & que quondam fueꝏ eiusdm̄ dñi Joħis in Moggewelstrete infra Crepulgate Londoñ heñd & teñd oṁia p̄dicꞇ ꞇras & teñ cū oṁibʒ suis ptinj p̄fatis Priorisse & conventui & eoʒ successoribʒ de capital Dñīs feodi illiꝗ p ſvicia inde debita & de iuꝏ consueta imppm̄. Et quoniam piū & deo placabile fore constat aliquod quod ad honorem sūu & saꞇtm̄ fideliū competit stabiliri maiꝗ tamen piū reputo & salubre huiusmodi stabilita si p̄fecta ñō fuīnt pficꞏe et in augmentū divini cultꝗ & auxiliū univsale ut ppetuo sustententur talia ampliaꝏ volo igitꞌ lego & dispono in honorem Dñi nr̄i Jħu Xp̄i omīqʒ sc̄oʒ suoʒ ac in salutem aīaʒ oṁi fideliū defunctorʒ sp̄aliꞇqʒ p aīa Petri ffaneloꞌ & in suaʒ penaʒ alleviac̄oem quandꞋm Cantarᵒ de duobʒ capeꞇꞇis una cū quodam lampade die ac nocte continue imppm̄ ardente in quada capella infra ecc̄tiam eoʒdm̄ Sc̄oʒ Oṁi de Edel-meton quam idu Petrus de novo nup edificavat duratꞋm̄ ppetualiꝑ ordinari. Et eandm̄ Cantariam Cantariam Petri ffanelo, ppetuis temporibʒ nuncupari. Et eiusdm̄ cantarie Patronatū p̄sentac̄oem & donac̄oem quantū ad patroñu ptinent vicarᵒ eiusdm̄ ecc̄tie de Edelmetoñ & suis successoribʒ qui p tempe fuīnt lego imppm̄ possidend Lego eciam & ordino qd vicariꝗ eiusdm̄ ecc̄tie de Edel-metoñ qui p tempe fuīt duos Capeꞇꞇos idoneos ad cantaꝏ illam p nomen Cantaꝏ Petri ffaneloꞌ in ecc̄tia de Edelmetoñ celebrande p ꝟba que in consimilibʒ p̄sentac̄oibʒ contineri solent Ep̄o Londoñ qui p tempe fuīt p̄sentet qui ad cantaꝏ illam p eundm̄ Ep̄m admittantꞌ & in eadm̄ canonice put in alijs Cantarijs institui moris est instituantꞌ capeꞇꞇi de eadm̄ Cantaꝏ ppetualiꝑ pmansuri. Et ijdm capeꞇꞇi extunc p aiabʒ p̄dc̄is totide celebrent in capella p̄dc̄a & oṁia & singꞇis officia ecc̄tiastica ac oñia faciant & important que p capellanos huiusmodi sc̄dm sacras canones & singꞇas alias constituc̄ōes in ecc̄tia Saʒ usitatas fieri competñt in hac pte. Et cedentibʒ vt decedentibʒ capellis illis seu eoʒ alt̃o duo alij idonei seu unus secd̃m casus exigenciam p vicar̃ dc̃ē Eccl̃ie de Edelmet̃on p tempe existente p̃fato Ep̃o tunc simili͠t existenti q°mciti⁹ fieri polit competent̃ p̃sentent' aut p̃sentet' p eund̃m Ep̃m admittendi & instituendi sive admittendus & instituendus in forma iuris. Et ip̃i eid̃m Cantar̃ deserviant & in forma p̃dcā faciant & celebrent ppetuali͠t in capella p̃dc̃ā. Et sic imppm̃ fiat quociens Capellos p̃dc̃ōs seu alt̃um eoʒ cedere decedere resignare vt privari contingat. Ita qd Cantar̃ illa ñnq°m̃ cesset sec qd in ead̃m capella fideli͠t a duobʒ capellis in forma p̃dcā p̃sentatis admissis ac institutis om̃ia & singla p̃missa facientibʒ & supportantibʒ cantaria illa continue fiat et imppm̃ celebret'. Quibʒ quid̃m capellis sic p p̃dcm vicar̃ p̃mo p̃sentandi p sustenc̃õe eoʒdm lego illas duas marcal & dimid'] annui liberi & quieti reddit̃ cū ptin quas nup adquesivi coniunctim cū Joh̃ne Osekyn de Anna Relicta Witti fit Witti de Leyr nup civis Londoñ Hugone Lu & Joh̃e Montveron executoribʒ testi p̃dc̃ī Witti fit Witti que singlis annis ad t̃m̃iös in Civitate Londoñ usitatos levari debent & solui de toto illo ten̄ cū domibʒ supedifical & omibʒ ptin̄ suis quod Joh̃es de Redyng Allutar⁹ Londoñ tenuit ex dimissione quondam Rād̃i Balle & Isabell de Sc̃ō Albano vX̃is ei⁹ in poch Sc̃ī Martini Pomer̃ Londoñ in Ismongereslane in quo quid̃m ten̄ Adam Stable postmodū comoravit nec non & illas viginti solidal annui libi & quieti reddit⁹ cū ptin quas simili͠t adquesivi coniunctim cū p̃fato Joh̃e Osekyn de p̃dcis execl p̃dc̃ō Witti fit Witti de Leyre que singlis annis ad t̃m̃iös antedc̃ōs levari debent & solui de toto illo ten̄ quod Joh̃es de Horsford nup h̃uit in pochia om̃i Scoʒ pvū Sup celar̃ in vico de Thamestrete Londoñ quod quid̃m ten̄ situ est int̃ ten̄ quondam Dñe Johanne Parmenters ex p̃te orient̃ & ten̄ quondam Nich̃ī Ffarndon ex p̃te occident̃. Et eciam sexdecim marcal annui reddil pcipiend singlis annis ad t̃m̃iös sup̃dcos de omibʒ ter̃ & ten̄ cu ptin̄ in Londoñ que quondam fuer̃ p̃dc̃ī Witti fit Willi de Leyre nup civis Londoñ quoʒ quodam sita sunt in pochia Om̃i Scõʒ pvū sup celar̃ in latitud̃iē vidett int̃ venellam que ducit de cimit̃io Sc̃ī Laurencij usqʒ vicu Reg̃ñi de Thamestrete ex p̃te orient̃ & ten̄ quondam Rād̃i de la More ac ten̄ hospital Sc̃ī Bart̃h̃ī de Smethefeld London ex p̃te occident̃ & extend̃nt se in longitud̃iē a ten̄ quondam Salamonis de la More v̄sus aquilon̄ vsqʒ vicu Regni de Thamestrete v̄sus ausl quedam eciam & shope

eisdm tenementᵗ p̄astantes sita sunt in venella & pochia Scē
Laurencij in judaismo Londoñ que p p̄dc̄m Wiłłm filiū Wiłłi
de dño Rado Gorges Milite quondam fuerñt adquesita similiᵗ
quedam sita sn̄t in vico de Milkstrete in pochia Scē Marie Magdalene & quedam massenta quond vx̄ Wiłłi de Wyntoñ nup civis
Londoñ ea tenuit ad ťmi vite sue hend & teñd tam p̄dc̄ās duas
marcaᵗ & dimidiam & viginti solidaᵗ annui libī & quieti reddᵗ]
qᵉm p̄dc̄ās sexdecim marcaᵗ reddiᵗ c̄u p̄tīn & in forma p̄dc̄ā ad
ťmīōs antedc̄ōs pcipiend eisdm vid’t capełłis postqᵉm ab Epō
admissi fuint & vt p̄dicitʳ instituti & suis successoribȝ capełłis in
dc̄ā Capella apud Edelmeton sic celebratuc̄ʳ imppetuum. Lego
eciam eidm̄ vicac̄ʳ ac p̄dc̄īs Capełłis quendam annūu reddiᵗ uniᵠ
marce eisdm̄ sciłt vicac̄ʳ & capełłis & successoribȝ suis p ppetua
invenc̄ōe & sustentac̄ōe uniᵠ lampadis in eadm̄ capella apud Edel-
metōn die & nocte continue ardentis imppm̄ obtinend’] & pcipiend’]
singłis annis ad ťmīōs antedc̄ōs de omibȝ & singłis tēn & shopis
sup̄dc̄īs c̄u p̄tīn in Londoñ que fuec̄ʳ p̄dc̄ī Wiłłi fił Wiłłi. Volo in
sup lego & ordino qd bene liceat eisdm̄ vicac̄ʳ ac capełłis & eoȝ
cuiłt & successoribȝ suis imppm̄ in omibȝ p̄dc̄īs tēn c̄u p̄tīn que
sic fueñrt p̄dc̄i Wiłłi fił Wiłłi distꝭgē quociens p̄dc̄m̄ annūu
reddiᵗ sexdecim marcaȝ ad sustenac̄ōem p̄dc̄oȝ capełłoȝ sic dis-
pocitū et eciam quoc̄iens p̄dc̄m̄ annūu reddiᵗ uniᵠ marce ad
invenc̄ōēm & sustentacōēm uniᵠ lampadis in forma p̄dc̄ā ardentis
aretro fore contingat & districc̄ōes sic capᵗ quocunqȝ voluint
abduce asportac̄ʳ & retinec̄ʳ quousqȝ tam de p̄dc̄ō redd Sexdecim
marcaȝ eisdm̄ sciłt capełłis qᵉm de p̄dc̄ō reddiᵗ uniˢ marce p
sustentacoe lampadis sup̄dc̄ē eisdm̄ sciłt vicac̄ʳ ac capełłis c̄u om̄ibȝ
inde arreragijs ac dampnis p detenc̄ōe seu ño soluc̄ōe p̄dc̄oȝ
eisdm̄ plenarᵉ fuit satisfc̄m̄. Lego eciam om̄īā tēn sup̄dc̄ā c̄u p̄tīn
que sic fuec̄ʳ p̄dc̄i Wiłłi fił Wiłłi de p̄dc̄m̄ redd sexdecim m̄rcaȝ
& uniᵠ mᵉrce sic oñate execᵈ meis infra scriptis ad vendend eadm̄
tēn c̄u p̄tīn postqᵉm p̄dc̄i capełłi in Cantac̄ʳ p̄dc̄ā fulint instituti
& possessionem p̄dc̄e redditˢ sexdecim marcaȝ optinerint &
postqᵉm p̄dc̄ā lampas ad ardend fuit constitute & denac̄ʳ p tēn
p̄dc̄ās sic vendendis pcipiendos volo & lego fore distribuendos in
missis celebrandis aut alijs pijs opibȝ pficiend pāīā p̄dc̄ī Petri &
aiabȝ sup̄dc̄īs sedm̄ dispoc̄ōēm & arbitriū execᵈ meoȝ p̄dc̄oȝ. Et
cum Katʳina que fuit ux̄ Johis de Donyndon quondam civis &
appotecarᵉ Londoñ teneat ad ťmī vite sue septem libratis & duo-

Appendix.

decim denaraꝛ reddiꝉ de diᵥsis teñ in Civitate Londoñ exeunꝉ ac eciam cū Stepħus Kyng Civis & Zonarᵒ Londoñ & Alicia uẋ eius teneant ad ꝑmī vite eoꝛ quoddam tēñ cū domibȝ supedificaꝉ shoꝑ solaꝏ & suis ptin in venella & pochia Sci Laurencij in veꝉ Judiaisimo Londoñ necnon cū Witts Goderich ffound' & civis dcē Civitatis & Isabella uẋ eius teneant ad ꝑmī vite eoꝛ quoddam tēñ cū shoꝑ Celaꝏ solaꝏ & suis ptiñ in venella & pochia ꝑdictōs reᵥsonibȝ dcōȝ reddiꝉ & teñ cū ptin michi & heredibȝ meis spectantibȝ. Que quidm̄ scitt reddiꝉ & teñ cū ptiñ cū aliqualiꝉ acciderint lego Ade ffraunceys Juniori de Londoñ filio meo & Margarete vẋi eius tēńd eisdm̄ & ħedibȝ de corpibȝ eoȝ legitē pereaꝉ de capitaꝉ dn̄is p ᵥviꝉ inde debita & de iure consueta imppm̄. Et si idm̄ **Adam** sive heꝏ de corpe suo ƚic pcꝏ obierit **lego** dcā reddiꝉ & tēñ cū **ptin** cū ut ꝑdc̄m est **acciderint** Matiꝉꝉ fit mee tenend **eidm̄ & here-dibȝ** de corpe suo ƚic pereaꝉ de capitaꝉ dn̄is p ᵥvicia inde debita & de iuꝏ consueta imppm̄. Et si eadm̄ Matiꝉꝉ sine heꝏ de corpe suo ƚie pcꝏ obierit tunc volo & lego qd eadm̄ reddiꝉ & teñ cū ptiñ cū **acciderint** ut suꝑdc̄m est rectis hered meis integre reᵥtant' & remaneant imppm̄. Tenend de **capital** dn̄ı̄s p ᵥvicia **inde** debita & de iure consueta imppm̄. Itm̄ **lego** Agneti uẋi mee om̄ia teñ mc̄a cū ptiñ situata in poch Scē **Mildrede in Poletria Londoñ** ac eciam totu illud teñ cū ptin quod Joħes de Metford de me tenet in pochia Scē Marie Magdalene in Westchepe Londoñ. Teñd eadm̄ teñ cū ptin eidm̄ Aḡñ ad ꝑmī vite suē de Capital dn̄ı̄ꝉ feodi p ᵥvicia inde debita & de iure consueta. Que quidm̄ teñ cū ptiñ post decessū ꝑfate Aḡñ lego ꝑfato Ade ffraunceys Juniori. Lego eciam eidm̄ Ade statim post decessū meū ceꝉ teñ mea & redd supius n̄ō legata scitt om̄ia & singƚa cū suis ptiñ de quibȝ scisit' sū in dn̄icō meo ut de feodo die Obiꝉ mei in Civitate ꝑdcā & in suburbijs eiusdm̄ Tenend tam dcā teñ cū ptiñ ꝑfate Agneti ad ꝑmī vite sue legata cū post eius decessū acciderint qᵃm ceƚa teñ & redditꝗ cū ptin ꝑnōıata statim post decessū meū vt ꝑdc̄m est eidm̄ Ade & heredibȝ de corpe suo ƚie pereaꝉ de Capital dn̄ı̄ꝉ p ᵥvicia inde debita & de jure consueta imppm̄. Et si idm̄ Adam sine **herede** de corpe suo exeunꝉ obieri tunc lego & volo qd tam dcā teñ cū ptı̄ñ ꝑfate Agneti ad ꝑmī **vite** sue legata cū post eius decessū acciderint ut ꝑdc̄m est qᵃm ceƚa teñ & redditꝗ suꝑdcā cū ptiñ integre remaneant ꝑfate Matiꝉꝉ & ħeꝛ de corpe suo legitē pereaꝉ. Teñd de Capital Dn̄ı̄s p ᵥvicia **inde debita** & de iure consueta imppm̄. Et si eadm̄ Matill sine herede de corpe suo exeunte obierit lego eadm̄ ten̄ & reddit꞊ cū omibȝ suis p̃tin̄ scilt tam ten̄ cū p̃tin̄ p̃fate Agneti ad t̃mi vite sue legata cū post eius decessu acciderint ut sup̃dc̄a est q°m cetᵃ ten̄ & reddit꞊ om̄ia & singla p̃notata cū omibȝ suis p̃tin̄ executoribȝ meis aut eoȝ executoribȝ vel execᵈ p̃dcoȝ execᵈ p eosdm̄ vendenda p visū Maioris & Recordatoris Londoñ qui p tempe fuint & ad ulliu aliu usū fore convᵗtenda Ita qd ijdm̄ execᵈ vel eoȝ executoƩ gᵃdatim nup eadm̄ ten̄ & reddit꞊ cū p̃tin̄ scilt omia & singla p eosdm̄ ad venend ut p̃mittit̃ legata integre vendant q°m cito optime polunt postq°m urqȝ dc̄oȝ Ade & Matill obierint sine heredibȝ de corpibȝ eoȝ leg̃ic pereat̃ si eos talit̃ decedeƩ contingat et om̄es denaƩ inde pvenient̃ lego eisdm̄ exec-distribuendos p visū dc̄oȝ Maioris & Recordatoris qui p tempe fuint ut in missis celebrandis paupibȝ cibandis puellis e gentibȝ maritand̃ Prison p debit̃ capt̃ & minus sufficientibȝ delibandis ecclis hospitalibȝ & domibȝ religiosis ad inopiam divᵛsis relevand̃ Pontibȝ & iteneribȝ piculosis emendand̃ & in alijs opibȝ caritativis imponend̃ sedm̄ discrec̄ōem exēc p̃dc̄oȝ & p visu dc̄oȝ Maioris & Recordatoris qui pro tempe fuint. Ita qd om̄es denaƩ illi circa aliqua alia nisi circa ea que ad honorem dei & salutem āiaȝ p̃dc̄aȝ concerñnt nullaten꞊ expendant͛ Huius autem testi mei meos facio & constituo executores videlt Johem Piel, Willm de Halden, Gilbᵗum Champoneys, Johem ffourney, Pannar, & Johem Ussher. In cuius rei testioñu huic testo Sigillu meū apposui, Dat̃ Londoñ Vicesimo Sexto die Augusti Anno Dn̄i Millesimo tricentesimo Septuagesimo quarto. Et regni regis Edwardi t̃cij post conquestū Anglie quadragesimo octavo.

Page 39.—*Restoration* 1865-8.

From the several preceding statements of the text, it will be seen that various sums had from time to time been expended for substantial repairs of the fabric of St. Helen's, and which, judging from their magnitude, should have afforded but little scope for the labours of the Restoration Committee of 1865-8. Such, however, was not the case, and a description truthfully depicting the sad state of the Church at that time would be regarded as apocryphal. "The plaster walls, smoke-begrimed and saturated with damp, had in many places given way; the decayed timbers of the roof had been mended with brown paper, painted to resemble wood—in one of the columns of the nave arcade no less than seventeen incisions had been made;—the two westernmost bays were separated from the body of the Church by a clumsy, deep gallery containing the organ, many of the windows had lost their tracery, and the floor of the Church was so honeycombed with vaults that it was a matter for wonderment that the whole held together as it did.

"To remedy this state of things a Committee, consisting of parishioners and other gentlemen (including the then Master of the Merchant Taylors' Company, Mr Foster White) interested in preserving the fabric from becoming a thorough ruin, was formed, and subscriptions for that purpose were publicly solicited, and although the by no means inconsiderable sum of 1400*l.* was through their instrumentality collected, apart from the many stained glass windows that were introduced, yet this sum was totally inadequate to meet the requirements of such a heavy work. Then it was that the parishioners came forward, and by means of a rate collected upwards of 2000*l.* to meet the deficiency.

"To the labours of this Committee may be attributed the following works :—The removal of the organ gallery and screen, and of Sir John Spencer's* monument (A.D. 1609) from the south transept to the south side of the parochial nave, the substitution of the present oak benches in lieu of the previous high pews, the reparation of the carved miserere seats, and their adaptation for the use of the quire, the removal of the accumulated earth in the transept and Chapel of the Holy Ghost, thereby opening out the bases of the pillars and tomb of Sir John Crosbie, the repaving the Chancel and parochial nave with encaustic tiles, re-roofing one-half of the nun's quire, together with the erection of a reredos and the organ.

"Works of as great utility as these just enumerated and undertaken by the parishioners were the filling in and hermetically closing the large vaults which existed throughout the building, and the thorough repair of such portions of the roofs as the Restoration Committee had been unable to accomplish, and also providing the apparatus for warming the Church.

"The numerous stained glass windows must not be passed by without mention, in that they add materially to the beauty of the Church. The names of the donors are appended to this sketch. Other windows there are which require to be filled in a similar manner; and here it may not be amiss to reply to the criticisms which have been made by archæologists and others, as to the texture and deep tones of some of the modern glass, whilst admitting that glass of a lighter texture, and approaching the 'cinque-cento' period, would be more in accordance with the style of the architecture of the building, and certainly more conducive to the transmission of the light so requisite in a city church, that the fact ought not to be overlooked that, as the pious gifts of individuals, it is frequently impossible to attempt interference with the cherished project of the donor. Could

---

* This was done at the expense of the Marquis of Northampton (the lineal descendant of the Earl of Compton, who clandestinely married the only child of the deceased), and two splendid arches, highly decorated in rich blue and vermilion colours—now much faded—were exposed.

it have been foreseen by the Committee that so many costly gifts would have been subsequently added, a scheme embracing a regular iconographic series might have been prepared for that purpose.

"In addition to contributions to the Restoration Fund several of the City Companies with their characteristic liberality undertook the renovation of the monuments of their predecessors; the Worshipful Company of Grocers rescued from decay the beautiful tomb of Sir John and Lady Crosby; the Mercers' Company, that of Sir T. Gresham; the Haberdashers, that of Captain Bond; and the Skinners, the quaint little tablet to the memory of the founder of Tunbridge Grammar School, Sir Andrew Judde.

"Such is the history (in outline) of the church of St. Helen's, until it became, under the Order in Council of 5th May, 1873, the church of the united parishes of St. Helen's and St. Martin's. Under the scheme for union, the glass of the east window of St. Martin's was removed to and placed partly in the window of the newly discovered Lady Chapel, and in the eastern dormer windows of the south transept of St. Helen's. All the monuments were also removed thither; and, as far as possible, were restored and replaced in St. Helen's, in sites shown on the ground plan of the church. The names connected with these monuments are as under:—

"John Oteswich and wife, *cir.* 1400; Hugh Pemberton, *cir.* 1500; Richard Staper, *cir.* 1608; Langham, *cir.* 1694; Clutterbuck, *cir.* 1697; Goodman, *cir.* 1714; Teasdale, *cir.* 1804; Edwards, *cir.* 1810; Simpson, *cir.* 1827; Rose, *cir.* 1821; Grant, *cir.* 1836; Ellis, *cir.* 1838; Atkinson, *cir.* 1847; Simpson, *cir.* 1849.

"John Bruex, 1459, and Nicholas Wotton, 1483, being the brass effigies of two rectors on a gravestone; Thomas Wight, 1633, a brass plate on a gravestone; Tufnel, 1686, a large gravestone.

"The annual value of St. Helen's will be 800*l.* and Easter offerings, and the patronage of the united benefice is vested in the Company by Part III., Sec. 3, which enabled the Master and Wardens as patrons to restore, as was much deserved, the Lady Chapel and that of the Holy Ghost. During the restoration, the vestry room, which had filled up the entire Lady Chapel, was pulled down, and there were brought to light two early perpendicular windows, *temp.* Richard I., several elegant niches, piscinas, sedilia, &c., all of which have been carefully restored.

"The monumental effigies of John Otewich and his wife (A.D. 1400 to 1428), being first cleansed and revived by Mr. Poole, have been placed upon a plain and simple table, between the two east Chapels, *i.e.*, the Lady Chapel and that of the Holy Ghost.

"The accession of these monumental effigies and tablets from the neighbouring Church of St. Martin Outwich, further enhance the quaint but solemn dignity of the fabric, rendering it still more worthy of its rightly-accorded title of 'the Westminster Abbey of the East.'

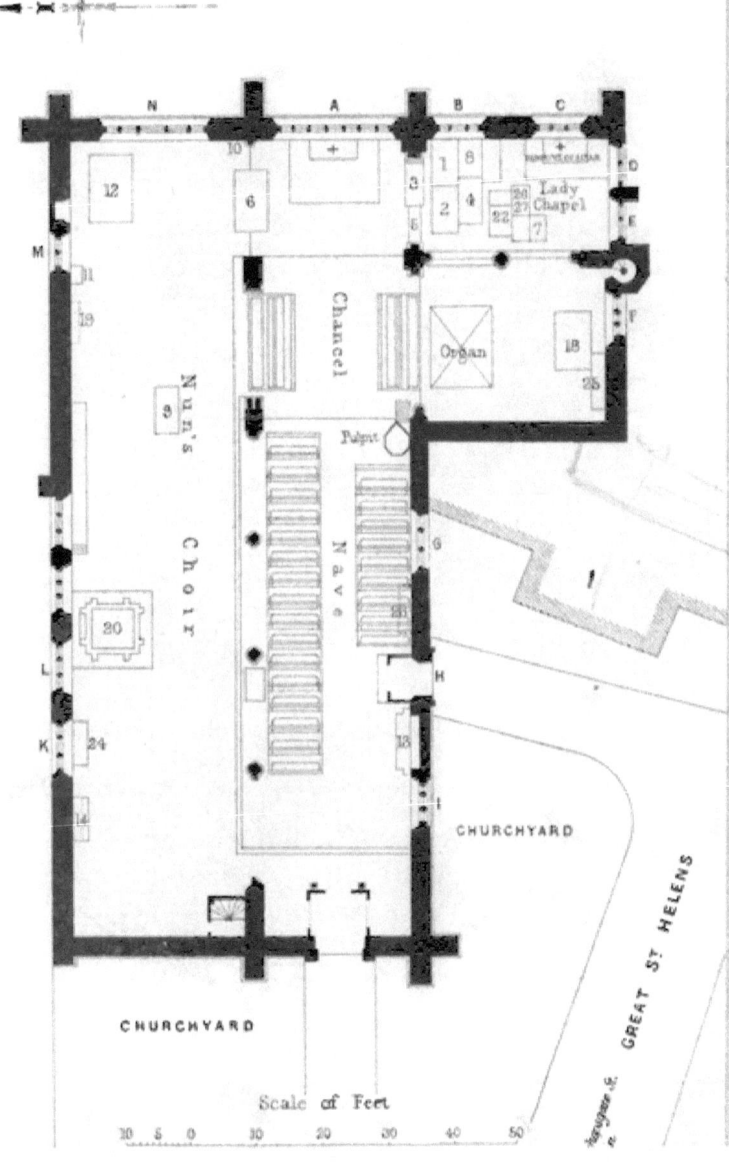

Appendix

STAINED GLASS WINDOWS.

Subjects.	Gifts of
"A.—In the parochial nave, east, consisting of 7 lights with traceried head: 'The Ascension'*	Kirkman Daniel, and **James** Stewart Hodgson, Esqs., in memory of their late father, John Hodgson, Esq.
B.—In the chapel of the Holy Ghost, three lights*	Made up of ancient glass preserved from the other windows, at the expense of Churchwardens Rolfe and Richardson.
C.—Three lights in the Lady Chapel: 'The Conversion of Constantine'*	The Merchant Taylors' Company.
D. and E.—The upper part filled with Emblematical Glass.*	
F.—A window of 3 lights...	William Jones, Esq.
G.—In the south aisle adjoining pulpit, 3 lights: 'St. Alban, St. Michael, and St. Edmund'†	Mr. Alderman Colonel Wilson.
H.—In the same aisle over the south door, 3 half lights: 'Christ's Charge to St. Peter'†	Messrs. **MacDougall**.
I.—In the south aisle, by Sir John Spencer's monument, 3 lights: 'The Finding of the Cross by St. Helena'†	William Meade Williams, Esq., in memory of his father and mother, John and Susan Williams.
J.—In the parochial nave, west, 5 lights: 'The Crucifixion'†	Subscription window in memory of Alderman Copeland, M.P., &c.
K.—In the north-west corner of the Nuns' Quire, single lancet: 'A Bishop in Pontificals'	J. F. Wadmore, Esq., in memory of Bishop Robinson.
L.—In the north aisle, 3 lights: 'Faith, Hope, and Charity'†	Messrs. MacDougall.
M.—Abbess' window, of 2 lights, north wall of Nuns' Quire: 'Christ healing the lame man, and Receiving little Children'†	Dr. **Cox, in** memory of 3 of his children.
N.—In the Nuns' Quire, 5 lights and traceried head: 'St. Helena,' flanked by three of the Evangelists and their symbols‡	The Gresham Committee, in memory of Sir Thomas Gresham."

BRASSES AND MONUMENTS IN ST. HELEN'S CHURCH, BISHOPSGATE.§

1.² A brass of a merchant and his wife, date about 1400, names unknown. See "Fairholt," p. 183. (Lost.)

2. Brass of *Joana*, daughter of Henry Seamer, wife of Richard, son and heir of Lord Poynings. The account of this brass given in Stow's "Survey," adds, "Died a virgin in 1420." This figure is now lost, but an impression of it taken by the late Mr. E. R. Mores when it was preserved in the Church chest, represents her habited in a mantle, surcoat, and kirtle with mitten sleeves,

---

* By Heaton, Butler & Co.   † By Gibbs.   ‡ By Powell & Co.
§ Supplied by Dr. Cox for Clode's Memorials of the Merchant Taylors' Company, pp. 341-4. Ed. Lond. 1875.

and on her breast a large "I. H. U. Mercy," her headdress of the veil kind with the bosses of reticulated hair above the ears. Mr. Mores has written under it "Obiit Virgo, 1420." See Gough's "Sepulchral Monuments," vii. ii. p. 55.

3. Monument to *Alderman Sir John Crosby and Anne, his wife*, 1475–6.
4. Brass to memory of *Thomas Williams*, gentleman, and Margaret his wife. The former died January 16th, 1495. The date of wife's death not inserted.
5. Brass, very elaborate, of a Lady Abbess of the peroid of Henry VII., the costume that of the aged ladies of that day, who not unfrequently ended their days in a nunnery as Lady Abbesses or even as mere sisters, to the no small emolument of the Church. See "Fairholt," p. 238.
6. Monuments to *Sir William Pickering—Father and Son*, 1542–47.
7. Brass to memory of *John Leenthorp* [or *Leventhorpe*], *Esq.*, one of the four Keepers of the Chamber to Henry VII.: died August 16th, 1510.
8. Brass to memory of *Mr. Robert Rochester*, Sergeant of the Pantry to Henry VIII., who died May 1st, 1514.
9. *Thomas Benolte*, sometime Windsor Herald to Henry VIII., otherwise Clarenceux King of Arms, died May 8th, 1533. Figure in Herald's Tabard, bearing arms of England and France quartered, on each side two female figures; that of later date in more elaborate costume than the former (lost, but stone remaining).*
10. Monument to *Sir Andrew Judd*, Lord Mayor, Citizen and Skinner, 1551.
11. Monument to *William Bond*, Alderman, Sheriff of London, 1576.
12. Monument to *Sir Thomas Gresham*, Citizen and Mercer, 1579, and William his Son, 1560.
13. Monument to *Sir John Spencer*, 1609. This monument before the restoration of the Church in 1865 stood on the west side of the Lady Chapel.
14. *John Robinson*, Alderman and Merchant Taylor, Merchant of the Staple, 1599.
15. *William Kerwin*, Freemason, 1594.
18. *Sir Julius Adelmair* (alias *Cæsar*), Knight, Doctor of Laws, Judge of the Court of Admiralty, 1636.
19. Monument to *Martin Bond*, Captain of the City Train Bands. Commanded in the camp at Tilbury in 1588. Died 1634, aged 85.
20. Monument to *Francis Bancroft*, an Officer of the Corporation of London, 1727.

---

* In Nuns' Quire, between No. 6 and No. 11.

Appendix. 381

From St. Martin's.

22. *The Otewich effigies.* **Removed from the Church of St. Martin** Outwich in 1874.
23. *Richard Staper*, Alderman, 1608. Removed from the **Church of** St. Martin Outwich in 1874.
24. *Hugh Pemberton*, Merchant Taylor and Alderman, 1500. Also Katherine, his wife. This monument was removed from the Church of St. Martin Outwich in 1874.
25. *William Bernard*, 1746. Removed to this position in 1874 from the north wall of a Vestry **which** formerly stood on the site of the Lady Chapel, which Vestry was removed in 1874.
26. A Brass of *John Breieux*, Rector, 1459.
27. A Brass of *Nicholas Wotton*, Rector, 1483. An Honorary Member of the Merchant **Taylors'** Company. } on one stone.

Page 46.—*An Act for Tithes in London.*

Where of late Time **Contention, Strife and Variance** hath risen and grown within **the** City **of** *London*, **and the Liberties** of the same, between the Parsons, Vicars **and** Curates **of the** said City, and the Citizens and Inhabitants of the same, **for and concerning** the payment of Tithes, Oblations, and other Duties **within** the said City and Liberties: **For** appeasing whereof, a certain **Order and** Decree was made thereof **by the** most Reverend Father in **God** *Thomas* [Cranmer] Archbishop **of** *Canterbury*, Metropolitane, Chief Primate of all *England*, *Thomas Audley* Knight, Lord *Audley* of *Walden*, and then Lord Chancellor of *England*, **now** deceased, and other of the King's Majesty's **most** Honourable **Privy** Council; and also the King's Letters Patents **and Proclamation was** made thereof, and directed to the said Citizens concerning the same; whereupon it was after enacted in the Parliament holden at *Westminster* by Prorogation the Fourth Day of *February* in the Twenty-seventh Year of the King's Majesty's most noble Reign, by **Authority of** the same Parliament, that **the Citizens and the Inhabitants of** the same City should, at *Easter* then next coming, **pay unto the** Curates of the said City and Suburbs, all such and like Sums of Money for Tithes, Oblations and other Duties, **as the said Citizens and Inhabitants by** the Order of the said late Lord Chancellor, **and other of the** King's most honourable Council, and the King's said **Proclamation, paid or ought** to have paid by Force and Virtue of the said **Order at** *Easter*, which was in the Year of our Lord God **MDXXXV, and the same** Payments so to continue from Time to Time, until such **Time as** any other Order or Law should be made, published, ratified **and** confirmed by the King's Highness, and the Two and Thirty Persons **by** His Grace to be named, as well for the full Establishment, concerning **the Payment of** all Tithes, Oblations, **and other Duties** of the Inha-

bitants within the said City, Suburbs and Liberties of the same, as for
the making of other Ecclesiastical Laws of this Realm of *England*, and
that every Person denying to pay, as is aforesaid, should, by the Commandment of the Mayor of *London* for the Time being, be committed
to Prison, there to remain until such Time as he or they should have
agreed with the Curate or Curates for their said Tithes, Oblations and
other Duties, as is aforesaid, as in the said Act more plainly appeareth:
Sithen which Act divers Variances, Contentions and Strifes are newly
risen and grown between the said Parsons, Vicars and Curates, and
the said Citizens and Inhabitants, touching the Payments of the
Tithes, Oblations and other Duties, by reason of certain Words and
Terms specified in the said Order, which are not so plainly and fully
set forth, as is thought convenient and meet to be; for appeasing
whereof, as well the said Parsons, Vicars and Curates, as the said
Citizens and Inhabitants, have compromitted and put themselves to
stand to such Order and Decree touching the Premises, as shall be
made by the said Right Reverend Father in God *Thomas* Archbishop
of *Canterbury*, Metropolitane and Primate of *England*, the Right
Honourable Sir *Thomas Wryothesly* Knight, Lord *Wryothesly*, and
Lord Chancellor of *England*, the Right Honourable *Thomas* Duke of
Norfolk, Lord Treasurer of *England*, the Right Honourable Sir
William Paulet Knight, Lord *St. John*, Lord President of the Council,
and Lord great Master of the King's most Honourable Household,
the Right Honourable Sir *John Russel* Knight, Lord *Russel* and Lord
Privy Seal, the Right Honourable *Edward* Earl of *Hertford*, Lord
Great Chamberlain of *England*, the Right Honourable *John* Viscount
Lisle, High Admiral of *England*, Sir *Richard Lister* Knight, Chief
Justice of *England*, Sir *Edward Montague* Knight, Chief Justice of the
Common Bench at *Westminster*, and Sir *Roger Cholmely* Knight, Chief
Baron of the Exchequer, for a final End and Conclusion to be had and
made touching the Premises for ever. And to the Intent to have a
full Peace and perfect End between the said Parties, their Heirs and
Successors, touching the said Tithes, Oblations and other Duties for
ever, be it enacted by the Authority of this present Parliament, That
such End, Order and Direction, as shall be made, decreed, and concluded by the forenamed Archbishop, Lords and Knights, or any Six
of them, before the First Day of *March* next ensuing, of, for, and concerning the Payments of the Tithes, Oblations and other Duties
within the said City, and the Liberties of the same, and inrolled in the
King's High Court of Chancery of Record, shall stand, remain, and be
as an Act of Parliament, and shall bind as well all Citizens and Inhabitants of the said City and Liberties for the Time being, as the said
Parsons, Vicars, Curates, and their Successors for ever, according to
the Effect, Purport and Intent of the said Order and Decree so to be
made and inrolled; and that every Person denying to pay any of his or
their Tithes, Oblations, or other Duties, contrary to the said Decree
so to be made, shall, by the Commandment of the Mayor of *London*
for the Time being, and in his Default or Negligence, by the Lord
Chancellor of *England* for the Time being, be committed to Prison,

there to remain till such Time as he or they have agreed with the Curate and Curates for his or their said Tithes, Oblations and other Duties as is aforesaid.

The DECREE.

II. As touching the Payment of Tithes in the City of *London*, and the Liberties of the same, it is fully ordered and decreed by the most Reverend Father in God *Thomas* Archbishop of *Canterbury*, Primate and Metropolitane of *England*, *Thomas* Lord *Wryothesly*, Lord Chancellor of *England*, *William* Lord *St. John*, President of the King's Majesty's Council, and Lord great Master of His Highness Household, *John* Lord *Russel*, Lord Privy Seal, *Edward* Earl of *Hertford*, Lord great Chamberlain of *England*, *John* Viscount *Lisle*, High Admiral of *England*, *Richard Lister* Knight, Chief Justice of *England*, and *Roger Cholmely* Knight, Chief Baron of His Grace's Exchequer, this present Twenty fourth Day of *February*, *Anno Domini*, *secundum cursum et computationem Ecclesiæ Anglicanæ*, *millesimo quingentesimo quadragesimo quinto*, according to the Statute in such Case lately provided, that the Citizens and Inhabitants of the said City of *London* and Liberties of the same, for the Time being, shall yearly without Fraud or Covin for ever pay their Tithes to the Parsons, Vicars, and Curates of the said City, and their Successors, for the Time being, after the Rate hereafter following, that is to wit, Of every x.s. Rent by the Year of all and every House and Houses, Shops, Warehouses, Cellars, Stables, and every of them within the said City and Liberty of the same, xvi. d. ob. And every of xx. s. Rent by the Year of all and every such House and Houses, Shops, Warehouses, Cellars, and Stables, and every of them within the said City and Liberties, ij. s. and ix. d. And so above the Rent of xx. s. by the Year, ascending from x. s. to x.s. according to the Rate aforesaid.

III. Item, That where any Lease is or shall be made of any Dwelling House or Houses, Shops, Warehouses, Cellars or Stables, or any of them, by Fraud or Covin, reserving less Rent than hath been accustomed, or is, or that any such Lease shall be made without any Rent reserved upon the same, by reason of any Fine or Income paid beforehand, or by any other Fraud or Covin; that then in every such Case the Tenant or Farmer, Tenants and Farmers thereof shall pay, for his or their Tithes of the same, after the Rate aforesaid, according to the Quality of such Rent or Rents, as the same House or Houses, Shops, Warehouses, Cellars or Stables, or any of them were last letten for, without Fraud or Covin, before the making of such Lease.

IV. Item, That every Owner or Owners, Inheritor or Inheritors of any Dwelling House or Houses, Shops, Warehouses, Cellars or Stables, or any of them, within the said City and Liberties, inhabiting or occupying the same himself, or themselves, shall pay after such Rate or Tithes as is abovesaid, after the Quantity of such yearly Rent as the same was last letten for, without Fraud or Covin.

V. Item, If any Person or Persons have taken, or hereafter shall take any Mease or Mansion Place by Lease, and the Taker or Takers thereof, his or their Executors or Assigns, doth or shall inhabit in any Part thereof, and have or hath within Eight Years last past before this Order, or hereafter will or shall let out the Residue of the same ; that then in such Case the principal Farmer or Farmers, **or first Taker or Takers** thereof, his or their Executors or Assigns, shall pay his or their Tithes after the Rate aforesaid, according to his or their Quantity therein, and that his or their Executors, Assignee or Assignees, shall pay his or their Tithes after the Rate abovesaid, according to the Quantity of their Rent by Year.

VI. And that if any Person or Persons have, or shall **take divers Mansion Houses, Shops, Warehouses, Cellars or Stables, in One Lease,** and letteth or shall let out One or more of the said **Houses, and** keepeth or shall keep One or more in his or their own Hands, and inhabiteth or inhabit in the same ; that then the said Taker or Takers, and his and their Executors or Assigns shall pay his or their Tithes after the Rate abovesaid, according to the Quantity of the yearly Rent of such Mansion House or Houses, retained in his or their Hands ; and that his Assignee **or** Assignees of the Residue of the said Mansion House or Houses, shall pay his or their Tithes **after** the Rate abovesaid, according to the Quantity of their yearly **Rents.**

VII. Item, If such Farmer or Farmers, **or his or their** Assigns of **any** Mansion House or Houses, Warehouses, Shops, **Cellars or Stables,** hath at any Time within Eight Years last past, **or shall** hereafter, let over all the said Mansion House or Houses **contained in his or** their Lease, to One Person or to divers Persons ; **that then the** Inhabitants, Lessees or Occupiers of them, and every of them, shall pay their Tithes after the Rate of such Rents **as the** Inhabitants, Lessees or Occupiers, and their Assignee or Assignees have been or shall be charged withal, without Fraud **or** Covin.

VIII. Item, If any Dwelling House, within Eight Years last **past,** was or hereafter shall be converted into a Warehouse, Storehouse, **or** such like, or if a Warehouse, Storehouse, or such like, within the **said Eight Years,** was or hereafter shall be converted into a Dwelling **House ;** that then the Occupiers thereof shall pay Tithes for the same, after the Rate above declared of Mansion House Rents.

IX. Item, That where any Person shall demise any Dyehouse or Brewhouse, with Implements convenient and necessary for Dyeing or Brewing, reserving a Rent upon the same, as well in respect of such Implements, as in respect of such Dyehouse or Brewhouse ; that then the Tenant shall pay his Tithes **after** such **Rate as** is abovesaid, the Third Peny abated ; and that **every** principal House or Houses, with Key or Wharf, having any Crane or Gibet belonging **to** the same, shall pay after the like Rate of their Rents as **is** aforesaid, **the** Third Peny abated ; and that other Wharfs belonging to Houses having no Crane or Gibet, shall pay for his Tithes as shall be paid **for** Mansion Houses, in **Form** aforesaid.

X. Item, **That** where any **Mansion House with a Shop, Stable,**

Warehouse, Wharf with Crane, Timber Yard, Teinter Yard, or Garden belonging to the same, or as Parcel of the same, is or shall be occupied together, that if the same be hereafter severed or divided, or at any Time within Eight Years last past were severed or divided; that then the Farmer or Farmers, Occupier or Occupiers thereof, shall pay such Tithes as is abovesaid, for such Shops, Stable, Warehouses, Wharf with Crane, Timber Yard, Teinter Yard or Garden aforesaid, so severed or divided, after the Rate of their several Rents thereupon reserved.

XI. Item, That the said Citizens and Inhabitants shall pay their Tithes quarterly, that is to say, at the Feast of *Easter*, the Nativity of St. *John Baptist*, the Feast of St. *Michael* the Archangel, and the Nativity of our Lord, by even Portions.

XII. Item, That every Householder paying **Ten Shillings Rent** or above, shall, for him or herself, be discharged of their **Four Offering-days**: But his Wife, Children, Servant, or others **of their Family, taking the Rights of the Church at** *Easter*, shall **pay Two-pence for their Four Offering days yearly.**

XIII. Provided always, and it is decreed, That if any House or Houses which hath been or hereafter shall be letten for Ten Shillings Rent by Year or more, be or hath at any Time within Eight Years last passed, or hereafter shall be, divided and leased into small Parcels or Members, yielding less yearly Rent than Ten Shillings by the Year; that then the Owner or Owners, if he or they dwell in any Part of such House, or else the principal Lessee and Lessees, if the Owner or Owners do not dwell in some Part of the same, shall from henceforth pay for his or their Tithes after such Rate of Rent as the same House was accustomed to be letten for, before such Division or dividing into Parts or Members: And the under Farmer and Farmers, Lessee and Lessees, to be discharged of all Tithes for such small Parcels, Parts or Members, rented at less yearly Rent than Ten Shillings by Year without Fraud or Covin, paying Two-pence yearly for Four Offering-days.

XIV. Provided alway, and it is decreed, That for such Gardens as appertain not to any Mansion House, and which any Person or Persons holdeth or shall hold in his or their Hands for Pleasure, or to his own Use; that the then Person so holding the same, shall pay no Tithes for the same: But if any Person or Persons, which holdeth, or shall hold any such Garden, containing Half an Acre or more, doth or shall make any yearly Profit thereof by way of Sale; that then he or they shall pay Tithes for the same, after such Rate of his Rent, as is herein first above specified.

XV. Provided also, That if any such Gardens now being of the Quantity of Half an Acre, or more, be hereafter by Fraud or Covin divided into less Quantity or Quantities, then to pay Tithe according to the Rate abovesaid.

XVI. Provided alway, That this Decree shall not extend to the Houses of great Men, or noble Men, or noble Women, kept in their own Hands, and not letten for any Rent, which in Times past hath paid no Tithes, so long as they shall so continue unletten: Nor to any Halls or Crafts or Companies, so long as they be kept unletten, so that the same Halls in Times past have not used to pay any Tithes.

XVII. Provided always, and it is decreed, That this present Order and Decree shall not in anywise extend to bind or charge any Sheds, Stables, Cellars, Timber Yards, ne Teinter Yards, which were never Parcel of any Dwelling House, ne appertaining or belonging to any Dwelling House, ne have been accustomed to pay any Tithes; but that the said Citizens and Inhabitants shall thereof be quit of Payment of any Tithes, as it hath been used and accustomed.

XVIII. Provided also, and it is decreed, That where less Sum than after Sixteen Pence Halfpenny in the Ten Shillings Rent, or less Sum than Two Shillings Nine-pence in the Twenty Shillings Rent, hath been accustomed to be paid for Tithes; that then in such Places the said Citizens and Inhabitants shall pay but only after such Rate as hath been accustomed.

XIX. Item, It is also decreed, That if any Variance, Controversy, or Strife, do or shall hereafter arise in the said City for Non-payment of any Tithes; or if any Variance or Doubt arise upon the true Knowledge or Division of any Rent or Tithes, within the Liberties of the said City, or of any Extent or Assessment thereof, or if any Doubt arise upon any other Thing contained within this Decree; that then upon Complaint made by the Party grieved, to the Mayor of the City of *London* for the time being, the said Mayor, by the Advice of Council, shall call the said Parties before him, and make a final End in the same, with Costs to be awarded by the Discretion of the said Mayor and his Assistants, according to the Intent and Purport of this present Decree.

XX. And if the said Mayor make not an End thereof within Two Months after Complaint to him made, or if any of the said Parties find themselves aggrieved, that then the Lord Chancellor of *England* for the time being, upon complaint to him made within Three Months then next following, shall make an End in the same, with such Costs to be awarded as shall be thought convenient, according to the Intent and Purport of the said Decree.

XXI. Provided always, That if any Person or Persons take any Tenement for a less Rent than it was accustomed to be letten for, by reason of great Ruin or Decay, brenning, or such like Occasions or Misfortunes; that then such Person or Persons, his Executors or Assigns, shall pay Tithes only after the Rate of the Rent reserved in his or their Lease, and none otherwise, as long as the same Lease shall endure.

Page 46.—*An Act for the Relief of certain Incumbents of Livings in the City of London.*

WHEREAS by an Act, passed in the Twenty-second and Twenty-third Years of the Reign of his late Majesty King *Charles* the Second, intituled, "An Act for the better Settlement of the Maintenance of the Parsons, Vicars, and Curates, in the Parishes of the City of *London*, burnt by the late dreadful fire there. AFTER reciting, that the Tythes in the City of London were levied and paid with great Inequality, and were, since the late dreadful Fire there, in the rebuilding of the same, by taking away of some houses, altering the Foundations of many, and the new erecting of others, so disordered, that, in case they should not for the Time to come be reduced to a Certainty, many Controversies and Suits at law might thence arise; IT was Enacted, That the Annual certain Tythes of all and every Parish and Parishes within the said City of *London* and the Liberties thereof, whose Churches had been demolished or in part consumed by the late Fire, and which said Parishes, by virtue of an Act of that Parliament, intituled, "An additional Act for rebuilding of the City of *London*, uniting of Parishes, and rebuilding of the Cathedral and **Parochial** Churches within the said City," remained and continued **single as** theretofore they were, or were by the said Act annexed **or united** into one Parish respectively, should be as followeth (that is **to say**) The Annual certain Tythes **or Sum of** Money in lieu of Tythes,

Of the Parish of Alhallows **Lombard Street, One hundred and Ten Pounds;**
Of Saint Bartholomew Exchange, One hundred Pounds;
Of Saint Bridget *alias* Brides, One hundred and Twenty Pounds;
Of Saint Bennet Fink, One hundred Pounds;
Of Saint Michael Crooked Lane, One hundred Pounds;
Of Saint Christopher, One hundred and Twenty Pounds;
Of Saint Dionis Back Church, One hundred and Twenty Pounds;
Of Saint Dunstan in the East, Two hundred Pounds;
Of Saint James Garlick-Hythe, One hundred Pounds;
Of Saint Michael Cornhill, One hundred and Forty Pounds;
Of Saint Michael Bassishaw, One hundred and Thirty-two Pounds Eleven Shillings;
Of Saint Margaret Lothbury, One hundred Pounds;
Of Saint Mary Aldermanbury, One hundred and Fifty Pounds;
Of Saint Martin Ludgate, One hundred and Sixty Pounds;
Of Saint Peter Cornhill, One hundred and Ten Pounds;
Of Saint Stephen Coleman Street, One hundred and Ten Pounds;
Of Saint Sepulchre, Two hundred Pounds;
Of Alhallows Bread Street, and Saint John Evangelist, One Hundred and Forty Pounds;
Of Alhallows the **Great and Alhallows** the Less, Two hundred Pounds;

Of Saint Albans Wood Street and Saint Olaves Silver Street, One hundred and Seventy Pounds;

Of Saint Anne and Agnes and Saint John Zachary, One hundred and Forty Pounds;

Of Saint Augustin and Saint Faith, One hundred and Seventy-two Pounds;

Of Saint Andrew Wardrobe and Saint Ann Blackfriars, One hundred and Forty Pounds;

Of Saint Antholin and Saint John Baptist, One hundred and Twenty Pounds;

Of Saint Benet Gracechurch and Saint Leonard Eastcheap, One hundred and Forty Pounds;

Of Saint Bennet Paul's Wharf and Saint Peter Paul's Wharf, One hundred Pounds;

Of Christ Church and Saint Leonard Foster Lane, Two hundred Pounds;

Of Saint Edmond the King and St. Nicholas Acons, One hundred and Eighty Pounds;

Of Saint George Botolph Lane and Saint Botolph Billingsgate, One hundred and Eighty Pounds;

Of Saint Lawrence Jury and Saint Magdalen Milk Street, One hundred and Twenty Pounds;

Of Saint Magnus and Saint Margaret new Fish Street, One hundred and Seventy Pounds;

Of Saint Michael Royal and Saint Martin Vintry, One hundred and Forty Pounds;

Of Saint Matthew Friday Street and Saint Peter Cheap, One hundred and Fifty Pounds;

Of Saint Margaret Pattons and Saint Gabriel Fenchurch, One hundred and Twenty Pounds;

Of Saint Mary at Hill and Saint Andrew Hubbard, Two hundred Pounds;

Of Saint Mary Woolnoth and Saint Mary Woolchurch, One hundred and Sixty Pounds;

Of Saint Clement Eastcheap and Saint Martin Orgars, One hundred and Forty Pounds;

Of Saint Mary Abchurch and Saint Lawrence Pountney, One hundred and Twenty Pounds;

Of Saint Mary Aldermary and Saint Thomas Apostle, One hundred and Fifty Pounds;

Of Saint Mary Le Bow, Saint Pancras Soper Lane, and Alhallows Honey Lane, Two Hundred Pounds;

Of Saint Mildred Poultry and Saint Mary Cole Church, One hundred and Seventy Pounds;

Of Saint Michael Wood Street and Saint Mary Staining, One hundred Pounds;

Of Saint Mildred Bread Street and Saint Margaret Moses, One hundred and Thirty Pounds;

Of Saint Michael Queenhythe and Trinity, One hundred and Sixty Pounds;

Of Saint Magdalen Old Fish Street and Saint Gregory, One hundred
and Twenty Pounds;
Of Saint Mary Somerset and Saint Mary Mounthaw, One hundred and
Ten Pounds;
Of Saint Nicholas Coleabby and Saint Nicholas Olaves, One hundred
and Thirty Pounds ;
Of Saint Olave Jewry and Saint Martin, Ironmonger Lane, One hundred and Twenty Pounds ;
Of Saint Stephen Walbrook and Saint Bennet Sheerhog, One hundred
Pounds;
Of Saint Swythin and Saint Mary Bothaw, One hundred and Forty
Pounds ;
Of Saint Vedast *alias* Forsters and Saint Michael Quern, One hundred
and Sixty Pounds;

Which respective Sums of Money to be paid in lieu of Tythes within
the said respective Parishes, and assessed as thereinafter is directed,
should be and continue to be esteemed, deemed, and taken, to all
Intents and Purposes, to be the respective certain Annual Maintenance (over and above Glebes and Perquisites, Gifts and Bequests to
the respective Parson, Vicar, and Curate of any Parish for the Time
being, or to his or their respective Successors, or to other Persons for
his or their use) of the said respective Parsons, Vicars, and Curates,
who should be legally instituted, inducted, and admitted, into the respective Parishes aforesaid : And that the said several Sums of Money
for Tythes might be more equally assessed upon the several Houses,
Buildings, and all other Hereditaments whatsoever within all the said
respective Parishes, It was Enacted, That the Alderman of such respective Ward or Wards within the said City wherein any of the said
Parishes respectively lay, and his or their Deputy or Deputies, and the
Common Councilmen of such respective Ward or Wards, with the
Churchwardens and One or more of the Parishioners of such respective
Parish wherein the Maintenance aforesaid was respectively to be
assessed, to be nominated by such respective Alderman, Deputy,
Common Councilmen, and Churchwardens, or any Five of them,
whereof the Alderman or his Deputy to be one, should in the Manner
therein directed, assemble and meet together; and that they, or the
major Part of them so assembled, should proportionably assess upon
all Houses, Shops, Warehouses and Cellars, Wharfs, Keys, Cranes,
Waterhouses, (which Waterhouses should pay in their respective
Parishes where they stood, and not elsewhere) and Tofts of Ground
(remaining unbuilt) and all other Hereditaments whatsoever (except
Parsonage and Vicarage Houses) the whole respective Sum by that
Act appointed, or so much of it as was more than what each Impropriator was by that Act enjoined respectively to allow, in the most
equal way that the said Assessors, according to the best of their Judgments, could make it; and such Regulations were made for effecting
the Purposes of the said Act as therein are mentioned: And it was
amongst other Things further Enacted, That for the surer and better
Payment of the said respective Sums of Money so to be assessed

and taxed towards the raising of the said Maintenance of the respective Parsons, Vicars, and Curates of the said respective Parishes as aforesaid, all and every such respective Sum and Sums of Money so to be assessed and taxed as aforesaid towards the raising of the said Maintenance of the said respective Parsons, Vicars, and Curates of the said respective Parishes, should be paid to the said respective Parsons, Vicars, and Curates, and their Successors respectively, at the Four usual Feasts (that is to say) at the Annunciation of the Blessed Virgin Mary, the Nativity of Saint John the Baptist, the Feast of Saint Michael the Archangel, and the Nativity of our Blessed Saviour, or within Fourteen Days after each of the said Feasts, by equal Payments: And in any Parish or Parishes where any Impropriations were, It was Enacted, That all and every the Impropriator or Impropriators of any of the said Parishes, should pay and allow what really and *bonâ fide* they had used and ought to pay and satisfy to the respective Incumbent of such respective Parish, at any Time before the said late Fire, and that the same should be esteemed and computed as Part of the Maintenance of such Incumbent, notwithstanding that Act or any Clause or Matter or Thing therein contained:

And whereas, since the passing of the said recited Act the Rectory of the aforesaid Parish of Saint Christopher hath, by an Act passed in the Twenty-first Year of the Reign of His present Majesty, been united to the Rectory of the aforesaid Parish of Saint Margaret Lothbury, and there is now but one Incumbent of the said united Rectories:

And whereas the said recited Act hath failed in providing a proper Maintenance for the Parsons, Vicars, and Curates in the said Parishes, inasmuch as the respective Incomes being by the said Act fixed at very low Rates, the same are, by the decreased Value of Money, the enhanced Price of all the Necessaries of Life, and by various other Circumstances peculiarly attached to the Incumbents of the City of *London*, become greatly insufficient for the due Support of their Situation and Character; it hath been therefore deemed expedient for their Relief to make such Alterations in the said in part recited Act as are hereinafter expressed and contained;

Be it therefore Enacted by the King's Most Excellent Majesty, by and with the Advice and Consent of the Lords Spiritual and Temporal, and Commons, in this present Parliament assembled, and by the Authority of the same, That, instead of the Annual Tythes of all and every Parish and Parishes within the City of *London* and the Liberties thereof, whose Churches were demolished or in Part consumed by the Fire mentioned in the said recited Act, the Annual certain Tythes or Sums of Money in lieu of Tythes, of and for the Parish and Parishes within the said City and Liberties hereinafter enumerated, shall, from and after the Twenty-ninth Day of September One thousand Eight Hundred and Four, be as follows (that is to say)

Of the Parish of Alhallows Lombard Street, Two Hundred Pounds;
Of Saint Bartholomew Exchange, Two Hundred Pounds;

Of Saint Bridget *alias* Brides, Two Hundred Pounds;
Of Saint Bennet Fink, Two Hundred Pounds;
Of Saint Michael Crooked Lane, Two Hundred Pounds;
Of Saint Dionis Back Church, Two Hundred Pounds;
Of Saint Dunstan in the East, Three Hundred and Thirty-three Pounds Six Shillings and Eight Pence;
Of Saint James Garlick Hythe, Two Hundred Pounds;
Of Saint Michael Cornhill, Two hundred and Thirty-three Pounds Six Shillings and Eight Pence;
Of Saint Michael Bassishaw, Two hundred and Twenty Pounds Eighteen Shillings and Four Pence;
Of Saint Mary Aldermanbury, Two hundred and Fifty Pounds;
Of Saint Martin Ludgate, Two Hundred and Sixty-six Pounds Thirteen Shillings and Four Pence;
Of Saint Peter Cornhill, Two hundred Pounds;
Of Saint Stephen Coleman Street, Two hundred Pounds;
Of Saint Sepulchre, Three hundred and Thirty-three Pounds Six Shillings and Eight Pence;
Of Alhallows Bread Street and Saint John Evangelist, Two hundred and Thirty-three Pounds Six Shillings and Eight Pence;
Of Alhallows the Great and Alhallows the Less, Three hundred and Thirty-three Pounds Six Shillings and Eight Pence;
Of Saint Albans Wood Street and Saint Olaves Silver Street, Two hundred and Eighty-Three Pounds Six Shillings and Eight Pence;
Of Saint Anne and Agnes, and Saint John Zachary, Two hundred and Thirty-three Pounds Six Shillings and Eight Pence;
Of Saint Augustin and Saint Faith, Two hundred and Eighty-six Pounds Thirteen Shillings and Four Pence;
Of Saint Andrew Wardrobe and Saint Anne Blackfriars, Two hundred and Thirty-three Pounds Six Shillings and Eight Pence;
Of Saint Antholin and Saint John Baptist, Two hundred Pounds;
Of Saint Bennet Grace Church and Saint Leonard East Cheap, Two hundred and Thirty-three Pounds Six Shillings and Eight Pence;
Of Saint Bennet Paul's Wharf, and Saint Peter Paul's Wharf, Two hundred Pounds;
Of Christ Church and Saint Leonard Foster Lane, Three hundred and Thirty-three Pounds Six Shillings and Eight Pence;
Of Saint Edmond the King and Saint Nicholas Acons, Three hundred Pounds;
Of Saint George Botolph Lane and St. Botolph, Billingsgate, Three hundred Pounds;
Of Saint Lawrence Jewry and Saint Magdalen Milk Street, Two hundred Pounds;
Of Saint Margaret Lothbury and Saint Christopher, Three hundred and Sixty-six Pounds Thirteen Shillings and Four Pence;
Of Saint Magnus and Saint Margaret New Fish Street, Two hundred and Eighty-three Pounds Six Shillings and Eight Pence;

Of Saint Michael Royal and Saint Martin Vintry, Two hundred and Thirty-three Pounds Six Shillings and Eight Pence;

Of Saint Matthew Friday Street and Saint Peter Cheap, Two hundred and Fifty Pounds;

Of Saint Margaret Pattons and Saint Gabriel Fen Church, Two hundred Pounds;

Of Saint Mary at Hill and Saint Andrew Hubbard, Three hundred and Thirty-three Pounds Six Shillings and Eight Pence;

Of Saint Mary Woolnoth and Saint Mary Woolchurch, Two hundred and Sixty-six Pounds Thirteen Shillings and Four Pence;

Of Saint Clement Eastcheap and Saint Martin Orgars, Two hundred and Thirty-three Pounds Six Shillings and Eight Pence;

Of Saint Mary Abchurch and Saint Lawrence Pountney, Two hundred Pounds;

Of Saint Mary Aldermary and Saint Thomas Apostles, Two hundred and Fifty Pounds;

Of Saint Mary le Bow, Saint Pancras Soper Lane and Alhallows Honey Lane, Three hundred and Thirty-three Pounds Six Shillings and Eight Pence;

Of Saint Mildred Poultry and Saint Mary Colechurch, Two hundred and Eighty-three Pounds Six Shillings and Eight Pence;

Of Saint Michael Wood Street and Saint Mary Staining, Two hundred Pounds;

Of Saint Mildred Bread Street and Saint Margaret Moses, Two hundred and Sixteen Pounds Thirteen Shillings and Four Pence;

Of Saint Michael Queenhithe and Trinity, Two hundred and Sixty-six Pounds Thirteen Shillings and Four Pence;

Of Saint Magdalen Old Fish Street and Saint Gregory, Two hundred Pounds;

Of Saint Mary Somerset and Saint Mary Mounthaw, Two hundred Pounds;

Of Saint Nicholas Coleabby and Saint Nicholas Olaves, Two hundred and Sixteen Pounds Thirteen Shillings and Four Pence;

Of Saint Olave Jewry and Saint Martin Ironmonger Lane, Two hundred Pounds;

Of Saint Stephen Walbrook and Saint Bennet Sheerhog, Two hundred Pounds;

Of Saint Swithin and Saint Mary Bothaw, Two hundred and Thirty-three Pounds Six Shillings and Eight Pence;

Of Saint Vedast *alias* Fosters and Saint Michael Quern, Two hundred and Sixty-six Pounds Thirteen Shillings and Four Pence;

And be it further Enacted, That the said respective Sums of Money to be paid in lieu of Tythes within the said respective Parishes, shall be and continue to be esteemed, deemed, and taken, to all Intents and Purposes, to be the respective certain Annual Maintenance (over and above Glebes and Perquisites, Gifts and Bequests, to the respective Parson, Vicar, and Curate of any Parish for the Time being, or to his or their respective Successors, or to other Persons for his or their Use) of the said respective Parsons, Vicars, and Curates, legally instituted, inducted, and admitted into the respective Parishes aforesaid.

And in order that the said several Sums of Money in lieu of Tythes, may be more equally assessed upon the several Houses, Buildings, and all other Hereditaments whatsoever, within all the said Parishes; BE it further Enacted, that the Alderman or Aldermen of such respective Ward or Wards, within the said City, wherein any of the said Parishes respectively lie, and his or their Deputy or Deputies, and the Common Councilmen of such respective Ward or Wards, with the Churchwarden or Churchwardens, if there should be only One, and any One or more of the Parishioners of the respective Parish wherein the Maintenance aforesaid is respectively to be assessed, to be nominated by such Alderman or Aldermen, Deputy or Deputies, Common Councilmen and Church Wardens, or Church Warden, or any five or more of them, whereof the Alderman or Aldermen, or his or their Deputy or Deputies, to be One or Two, shall at some convenient and seasonable Time before the Thirty-first Day of July next after the passing of this Act, assemble and meet together in some convenient Place, within every of the respective Parishes, wherein the Maintenance aforesaid is to be assessed, and the said Alderman or Aldermen, Deputy or Deputies, Common Councilmen, and Churchwardens or Churchwarden, and Parishioner or Parishioners to be nominated as aforesaid, or the major Part of them so assembled, shall proportionably assess upon all Houses, Shops, Warehouses, and Cellars, Wharfs, Keys, Cranes, Waterhouses (which Waterhouses shall pay in the respective Parishes where they stand, and not elsewhere), and Tofts of Ground remaining unbuilt, and all other Hereditaments whatsoever (except Parsonage and Vicarage Houses), the whole respective Sum by this Act appointed, or so much of it as shall exceed what each Impropriator is hereinafter by this Act enjoined respectively to allow in the most equal Way that the said Assessors according to the best of their Judgment can make it; which said Assessments shall be made and finished before the twenty-first day of August then next ensuing.

And be it further enacted, That if any Doubt or Variance shall happen to arise about any Sum so assessed as aforesaid, or if any Parishioner or Parishioners, or Owner or Owners of any House or other Hereditaments hereby directed to be assessed within any of the said Parishes, shall find himself, herself, or themselves aggrieved by the assessing of any Sum or Sums of money, in Manner and Form aforesaid, then upon complaint made by the Party or Parties aggrieved, to the Lord Mayor and Court of Aldermen of the said City, within Fourteen Days after Notice given to the Party or Parties of such Assessment made, the said Lord Mayor and Court of Aldermen summoning as well the Party or Parties aggrieved, as the Alderman or Aldermen, or Deputy or Deputies, Common Councilmen, Churchwardens or Churchwarden, and such others as shall make the said Assessment, or the Survivors of them, shall hear and determine the same, in a summary Way, and the Judgment by them given shall be final and without Appeal; and if no such Parishioner or Parishioners shall be nominated in the Manner and for the Purpose aforesaid, or being so nominated, if the said Alderman or Aldermen, Deputy or Deputies, Common Councilmen, Churchwardens or Churchwarden, and Parishioner or Parishioners so appointed, shall after Summons and Request made in that Behalf unto them, by the Lord Mayor and Court of Aldermen, or the Incumbent or Incumbents of any of the said respective Parishes, refuse or neglect to meet and make such Assessments as aforesaid, then and in either of such Cases it shall and may be lawful to and for the Lord Mayor and Court of Aldermen of the said City, and they are hereby required, on Application of the Incumbent or Incumbents of the said respective Parishes, to authorise and appoint any other Person or Persons to make such Assessment or Assessments for the Purposes aforesaid.

And be it further Enacted, That if in all or any of the aforesaid Parishes, it shall appear necessary to the Parishioners specially convened by the Churchwardens or Churchwarden for the Purpose, and assembled in Vestry, at the End of Seven Years from the Time of passing this Act, and so from Time to Time at the Expiration of every Seven Years, afterwards to review and alter the respective Assessments to be made in pursuance of this Act, and to make in all or any of the said Parishes, a new Assessment and Rate, or Assessments and Rates, in lieu of the then preceding Assessments for the Purpose of raising the Sum and Sums of Money by this Act directed to be raised and paid as aforesaid, then that the Alderman or Aldermen of the respective Ward or Wards within the said City, wherein such Parish or Parishes shall respectively lie, and his or their Deputy or Deputies, and the Common Councilmen of such respective Ward or Wards, with the Churchwardens or Churchwarden, and One or more of the Parishioners of the respective Parish wherein such Assessment shall appear necessary (which Parishioner or Parishioners shall be nominated as before directed) shall in like manner as hereinbefore is mentioned, assemble and meet together within Fourteen Days after such Nomination, and they or the major Part of them so assembled shall then and there proportionably assess and rate upon the respective Houses and other Hereditaments hereby directed to be assessed, the respective Sums by this Act directed to be raised and paid as hereinbefore is mentioned, and that every such new Assessment and Rate shall be liable to the like Appeals as aforesaid, and shall be collected, levied, and paid in like Manner as the first Assessment or Rate mentioned in this Act may or ought to be collected, levied, and paid.

And be it further enacted, That the said Assessors within Fourteen Days after any Assessment shall have been made, and the respective Appeals (if any be) determined, shall make four Transcripts thereof in Writing, containing the respective Sums to be payable, or appointed to be paid out of all and every the Premises assessable within such respective Parish, and subscribe the same with their respective Names, and that within Twenty Days after such Subscription as aforesaid, One of the said Transcripts shall be sent to the Lord Mayor of the City of *London*, and deposited in the Town

Clerk's Office of the said City, and there kept and preserved among the Records of the said City, for a perpetual Memorial thereof; another of the said Transcripts shall be deposited in the Registry of the Consistory Court of the Lord Bishop of *London*, to be kept and preserved as aforesaid; another of the said Transcripts shall remain and be kept in the Vestry of such respective Parish, for a perpetual Memorial, as before mentioned, and the remaining Transcript shall be delivered within Three Days after such Subscription to the Incumbent of such respective Parish, and the said Assessment shall continue in force and be acted upon until any new Assessment shall be made in pursuance of this Act.

And, for the further and better Payment of the said respective Sums of Money so to be assessed or taxed, towards raising the Maintenance of the said respective Parsons, Vicars, and Curates of the said respective Parishes as aforesaid; BE it further Enacted, That all and every such respective Sum and Sums of Money so to be assessed and taxed as aforesaid, towards the raising of the said Maintenance, shall be payable to the said respective Parsons, Vicars, and Curates of the said respective Parishes, and their Successors respectively, or their Agents, Receivers, or Collectors, on the following Days in every Year, that is to say, the twenty-fifth day of December, the twenty-fifth Day of March, the twenty-fourth Day of June, and the Twenty-ninth Day of September, or within Thirty Days after each of the said Days, by equal Payments, free and clear of all Manner of Taxes, Assessments, and Deductions whatsoever, affecting the said respective Sums of Money.

And whereas in certain of the Parishes hereinbefore named there are Impropriations; and the Impropriators were, as hereinbefore is mentioned, by the said recited Act directed to pay and allow what really and *bonâ fide* they had used and ought to have paid and satisfied to the respective Incumbents of the said Parishes before the said Fire, which said Payments were to be esteemed and computed as Part of the Maintenance of such Incumbents; BE it therefore further Enacted, That in the Parishes of Saint Bridget otherwise Saint Bride's, Saint Bennet Finck, Saint Mary Aldermanbury, Saint Stephen Coleman Street, Alhallows the Less, Christ Church, Saint Lawrence Jewry, Saint Lawrence Pountney, and Saint Mary Cole Church, the Impropriators shall continue to allow and pay to the respective Incumbents of the same Parishes what they have been accustomed to allow and pay before and since the passing of the said recited Act of the twenty-second and twenty-third Years of the Reign of King *Charles* the Second, which said Sums shall be paid to the Incumbents of the same respective Parishes, in part of the respective Sums hereinbefore appointed to be the certain Annual Maintenance of the same respective Incumbents.

And whereas Two-third Parts of the Impropriate Tythes of the Parish of Saint Sepulchre are vested in Trustees, in Trust for the Parishioners of that Parish; and the Vicar of the said Parish is endowed with the remaining Third Part of the said Impropriate Tythes; BE it therefore further Enacted, That the said Vicar shall from and after the twenty-ninth Day of September One Thousand Eight hundred and Four, receive the full Sum directed by this Act to be paid him for his Maintenance, in lieu of the Third Part of the said Impropriate Tythes, to which by virtue of his Endowment he is entitled, from the several Inhabitants, of or from or out of, or for or in respect of the several Houses, Tenements, and other Hereditaments situated within that Part of the said Parish of Saint Sepulchre, which lies within the Liberties of the City of *London*, but exclusive of and over and above the Third Part of the Tythes to which he is entitled, from the Inhabitants, of or from or out of, or for or in respect of the several Houses, Tenements, or other Hereditaments situate within that Part of the said Parish which lies within the County of *Middlesex;* and that from and after the said twenty-ninth Day of September, One thousand Eight hundred and Four, the said Third Part of the said Impropriate Tythes, due from the Inhabitants, of or from or out of, or in respect of the several Houses, Tenements, or other Hereditaments situate within that Part of the said Parish of Saint Sepulchre which lies within the said Liberties of the City of *London*, shall cease and determine, and be no longer paid or payable.

And whereas in several of the aforesaid Parishes divers Houses and other Buildings have been taken down, for the Improvement of the City of *London*, by Order of the Lord Mayor, Aldermen, and Common Council of the said City, or have been taken down or altered by other Corporate Bodies or Public Companies or Persons, for other Purposes; and as a Compensation in respect thereof, certain Yearly Sums have been regularly paid by the Chamber of the said City, or by such Corporate Bodies or Public Companies, or Persons, to the Incumbents of the Parishes wherein the House and Buildings so taken down were respectively situate, which Yearly Sums are equal to the Yearly Sums paid under the before recited Act to the said Incumbents, in respect of the said Houses and other Buildings so taken down; and it may happen that other Houses and Buildings may be hereafter taken down or altered for similar Purposes; BE it therefore further Enacted, that the several Yearly Sums of Money, which such Incumbents respectively have been accustomed or are or may be entitled to receive from the Chamber of *London*, or from any other Corporate Body or Bodies, Company or Companies, or from any Person or Persons whomsoever, in respect of the said Houses and other Buildings so taken down, shall respectively be and continue to be paid and payable to the said Incumbents respectively, and their respective Successors, in Aid and as Part of the several Sums hereinbefore authorized to be raised by Assessments, for the Benefit of the said Incumbents respectively, but so nevertheless as not to exonerate any Dwellinghouse, Shop, Warehouse, or other Building, in the Occupation of any private Person or Persons, from the Payment of the Sum or Sums for Tythes or in lieu of Tythes to be assessed by virtue of this Act; but that the said Sum or Sums to be so assessed and paid for or in respect of any such Dwellinghouse, Shop, Warehouse, or other Building, shall be received and taken by the Incumbent of any Parish in which the same shall be situate, in part of the Sum or Sums by this Act authorized to be raised for the benefit of such respective Incumbent.

And be it further Enacted, That if any of the Inhabitants in any of the respective Parishes aforesaid, shall refuse or neglect to pay to the respective Incumbents of any of the said respective Parishes any Sum or Sums of Money to him or them respectively payable, or appointed to be paid by virtue of this Act, or any Part thereof, contrary to the true Intent and Meaning of this Act, (being lawfully demanded by the said respective Incumbents, or their Agents or Receivers, or Collectors, either in Person or by Writing left at the House or Houses, Wharf, Quay, Crane, Cellar, or other Premises out of which the same is payable) that then it shall be lawful for the Lord Mayor or any other Magistrate of the City of *London* for the Time being, upon oath to be made before him of such Refusal or Neglect, to give and grant Warrants for the Officer or Person appointed to collect the same, with the Assistance of a Constable, in the Day Time, to levy the same Sums of Money so due and in Arrear and unpaid, by Distress and Sale of the Goods and Chattels of the Party or Parties so refusing or neglecting to pay, or the Goods and Chattels of the Occupier or Occupiers for the time being of the Tenements or Hereditaments in respect whereof such Arrears shall be due or owing, restoring to the Owner or Owners the Overplus of such Goods, or the Overplus of the Monies produced by such Sale, over and above the said Arrears of the said Monies so due and unpaid, and the reasonable Charges of making such Distress, which he is to deduct out of the Monies raised by Sale of such Goods.

Provided always nevertheless, and it is hereby further Enacted and Declared, That notwithstanding any thing hereinbefore contained, in case, and when and so often as all or any of the respective Annual Maintenances or Sums by this Act appointed to be raised and paid, or so much of them respectively, or any of them, as shall exceed what the respective Impropriators before mentioned are by this Act enjoined respectively to allow, shall respectively be assessed and raised, by the Ways and Means and in the Manner hereinafter authorized and directed, and paid to the said respective Incumbents, or their respective Agents or Collectors, or Receivers, within Thirty Days next after the several Quarterly Days hereinbefore appointed for the Payment thereof, without any Deduction or Abatement whatsoever, then and in every such Case, from Time to Time, such of the same respective Annual Maintenances or Sums, or such Part or Parts thereof respectively as shall be so paid, shall not be raised or paid as hereinbefore is directed but by the Ways and Means, and in the Manner hereinafter authorized and appointed in that behalf.

And be it further Enacted, That it shall be lawful for the Churchwardens or Churchwarden (if but one) of the respective Parishes wherein the Maintenances aforesaid are respectively to be assessed, and to and for any One or more of the Parishioners, to be Yearly appointed in Vestry by the Inhabitants of such respective Parishes (the first of such Vestries in each Parish to be summoned by the said respective Churchwardens or Churchwarden, and held within twenty-one Days next after the passing of this Act) to assemble and meet together Yearly and every Year at some convenient and seasonable Time before the thirty-first Day of July next after such Appointment, in some convenient Place within every of the respective Parishes wherein the Maintenances aforesaid are to be assessed; and the said Churchwardens or Churchwarden, and the Parishioner or Parishioners to be appointed as aforesaid, or the major Part of them, so assembled in and for each respective Parish, are hereby authorized and empowered Yearly before the twenty-first Day of August in every Year, by an equal Rate upon all Houses, Shops, Warehouses, Cellars, Wharfs, Quays, Cranes, Waterhouses (each Waterhouse to be paid for in the Parish where it stands only) Tofts of Ground, remaining unbuilt, or other Hereditament or Hereditaments whatsoever (except Parsonage and Vicarage Houses) within such respective Parish, to assess the whole of the respective Sum by this Act appointed to be paid in lieu of Tythes within such respective Parish, for or towards such Maintenance as aforesaid, or so much of it as shall exceed what the respective Impropriators (if any) are hereinbefore by this Act enjoined respectively to allow, together with the Charges of making such respective Rate or Assessment, and collecting the Money so assessed, and all other incidental Charges relating thereto, the same to be payable and paid Quarterly on the several Days first hereinbefore appointed for the payment of the said Maintenance; and the said Churchwardens or Churchwarden, and Parishioner or Parishioners, to be Yearly appointed as aforesaid, or the major part of them so assembled in and for each respective Parish shall and they are hereby further authorized to collect and receive the sums so by them to be assessed, as and when the same shall become due, and with or out of the same or otherwise, to pay and discharge the respective Maintenance for and in respect whereof the same shall have been assessed respectively, within Thirty Days next after each Quarterly Day of Payment first hereinbefore appointed for the payment of such Maintenance, without any Deduction or Abatement whatsoever and thereupon also to retain, pay, and discharge all such incidental Charges and Expenses as aforesaid.

And be it further Enacted, That in case any Person or Persons shall think himself, herself, or themselves aggrieved by any Rate or Assessment to be made as last aforesaid, it shall be lawful for him, her, or them respectively, to appeal to the Court of Mayor and Aldermen of the said City, whose decision shall be final and conclusive: Provided always, that Notice of such Appeal shall be left in Writing at the Office of the Town Clerk of the said City, and also at the House of the Churchwarden, or of the Vestry Clerk of the respective Parish for which the Assessment complained of shall be made, within Ten Days next after the Sum so rated and assessed shall be demanded, and such Appeal shall be made to the next Court of Mayor and Aldermen of the said City, after such Notice shall be so left as aforesaid.

And be it further Enacted, That if the Owner or Owners, or Occupier of any House or other Hereditament which shall be rated and assessed by virtue or in pursuance of this Act, by the Ways and Means and in the Manner last hereby authorized and directed, shall refuse or neglect by the Space of Fourteen Days next after his, her, or their respective Rate or Rates, Assessment or Assessments shall be due, and shall be demanded by the Churchwardens or Churchwarden, and Parishioner or Parishioners to whom the same ought to be paid (such Demand being left in Writing, at the House, Shop, Warehouse, Cellar, Wharf, Quay, Crane, Waterhouse, Toft, or other Hereditaments or Premises possessed, rented, or occupied by him, her, or them so rated and assessed) to pay such Rate or Rates, Assessment or Assessments, so demanded as aforesaid, unless Notice of Appeal shall have been left as last before mentioned; or if any such Notice be left, and if such Appeal shall not be made accordingly, to the next Court of Mayor and Aldermen as aforesaid, then and in every such Case it shall be lawful for such Churchwardens or Churchwarden, and Parishioner or Parishioners, every or any of them, having a Warrant or Warrants under the Hand and Seal of the Lord Mayor, or any other Magistrate of the said City (which Warrant or Warrants the said Churchwardens or Churchwarden, and Parishioner or Parishioners, is and are hereby required to apply for; and the Lord Mayor or any other Magistrate of the said City, is hereby authorized and required to grant,) and with the Assistance of a Constable, or any Peace Officer of the Ward, County, City, or Liberty where the Person or Persons, Party or Parties, so refusing or neglecting, shall reside, there to seize and distrain any of the Goods and Chattels of the Person or Persons, Party or Parties so refusing or neglecting to pay, or to seize and distrain any of the Goods and Chattels of the Occupier or Occupiers for the Time being of the Tenements or Hereditaments, in respect whereof such Arrears shall be due or owing; and if the same shall not be replevied, or such Rate or Assessment paid within Five Days next after such Distress made, together with the Costs and Charges thereof, then to appraise and sell so much of the said Goods and Chattels as shall be sufficient to pay the said Rate or Assessment, and the Costs and Charges attending such Distress and Sale, returning the Overplus (if any) to the Owner or Owners of such Goods and Chattels, the said Costs and Charges to be settled and allowed by the said Lord Mayor, or other Magistrate who shall have granted such Warrant or Warrants respectively: Provided always, that no such Distress shall by virtue of this Act be made out of the Limits of the said City and Liberties thereof, unless such Warrant or Warrants respectively shall be first backed or countersigned by some Magistrate of the County, City, or Liberty where such Distress is proposed to be made; which Warrant or Warrants any Magistrate, who shall be applied to for that purpose, shall forthwith and is hereby authorized and required to back or countersign without Fee or Reward.

And be it further Enacted, That when and so often as any

Quarterly Payment of any Annual Maintenance or Sum by this Act authorized to be raised and paid, or so much thereof as shall exceed what any Impropriator before mentioned is by this Act enjoined respectively to allow, shall happen to be in Arrear and unpaid to the said respective Incumbent entitled to the same, or his respective Agent or Collector, or Receiver for the space of Thirty Days next after any of the Quarterly Days hereinbefore appointed for the Payment thereof, then and in every such Case, from Time to Time, every such Quarterly Payment so in Arrear and unpaid shall and may be raised or levied and paid by the Ways and Means, and according to the Assessment, and in the Manner first hereinbefore authorized and directed in that behalf.

And be it further Enacted, That nothing in this Act contained shall be construed to compel or oblige any Person or Persons, being of the People called Quakers, to collect any of the Monies to be raised under or by virtue of this Act, but such Person or Persons is and are hereby excused and exempted from collecting the same.

And be it further Enacted, That all and singular the Powers and Authorities in and by the said recited Act of the twenty-second and twenty-third Years of King *Charles* the Second, given to and vested in the Lord Mayor and Court of Aldermen of the City of *London*, shall be and the same are hereby from henceforth given to and vested in the said Lord Mayor and Court of Aldermen for the Time being, for and in respect of all and singular the Matters and Things in this Act contained, or by this Act enacted, so far as the Case is or shall be applicable; and that in case the said Lord Mayor and Court of Aldermen shall refuse or neglect to execute any of the respective Powers to them by this Act granted, or to perform all and every such Things relating either to the assessing or levying of the respective Sums aforesaid, as they are by this Act authorized and required to perform, either expressly or by Reference, that then it shall be lawful for any Two or more of the Barons of His Majesty's Court of Exchequer, by Warrant or Warrants under their Hands and Seals, to do and perform what the said Lord Mayor and Court of Aldermen, according to the true Intent and Meaning of this Act, might or ought to have done, and by such Warrant either to empower any Person or Persons to make the respective Assessments as aforesaid, or to authorize the respective Officers or Persons appointed to collect such Assessments, to levy the same by Distress and Sale of the Goods of any Person or Persons that shall refuse or neglect to pay the same, in Manner and Form aforesaid.

Provided always, That no Court or Judge Ecclesiastical or Temporal, shall hold Plea of or for any the Sum or Sums of Money due or owing or to be paid by virtue of this Act, or any Part thereof, other than the Persons hereby authorized to have Cognizance thereof; nor shall it be lawful for any Parson, Vicar, Curate, or Incumbent, to convent or sue any Person or Persons assessed as aforesaid, and refusing or neglecting to pay the same, in any Court or Courts, or before any Judge or Judges, other than what are authorized and appointed by this Act for the Hearing and determining the same in Manner aforesaid.

And be it further Enacted, That this Act shall be deemed, adjudged, and taken to be a Public Act, and shall be judicially taken Notice of as such by all Judges, Justices, and other Persons whomsoever, without specially pleading the same.

Page 50.

ST. HELEN IN BISHOPSGATE STREET IN THE CITY AND DIOCESE OF LONDON.

Special Commission.

Laid before the Board 9th Feb. 1778, and a Ticket ordered, made out Do.

Lot, 6th February, 1810.   *No.*

Set aside same day   *Certified above £80.*

To THE REV. WILLIAM MORICE, D.D.
  "   "   GEORGE GASKIN, D.D.
  "   "   HENRY FLY, D.D.
Mr. James Pearson, Mr. Thomas Loggin, Solicitors, and Mr. Thomas Simpson, Secretary to Sion College.

WHEREAS the Governors of the Bounty of Queen Anne, &c., have judged it necessary, pursuant to the statute of 1st George 1st, chap. 10th, to be more fully informed both of the nature and of the yearly value of the Vicarage of St. Helen in Bishopsgate Street in the City and our Diocese of London, and how such yearly value doth arise, with the other circumstances thereof, NOW KNOW YE, that for putting in execution the said Act of Parliament and by virtue thereof, we trusting to the Integrity and skill of you, the several Gentlemen above named, Do by these presents nominate, substitute, and appoint you, or any three or more of you Commissioners in our stead, as well by the oaths of two or more credible Witnesses as by other lawful ways and means to inform yourselves both of the nature and yearly value of the said Vicarage of St. Helen, as well such part thereof as is fixed and certain, as also such part thereof as is voluntary and gratuitous, distinguishing the same as far as may be, and how such yearly value doth arise, with the other circumstances thereof, agreeably to the printed heads of Inquiry hereto annexed, and having so informed yourselves, you are hereby required to certify to us, under your respective Hands, the several particulars above mentioned, by way of answer to the several printed Queries hereto annexed. To the end that we may Certify the same to the said Governors. IN WITNESS whereof we have hereunto set our Hand and Seal the 21st day of May, in the year of our Lord 1797, and in the tenth year of our Translation.

                                                B. LONDON. (Seal)

Directions for the better Execution of the within Commission.

THAT the Commissioners take what care they can that the Witnesses, whether brought in by the Minister or called by themselves, be credible Persons, and that they do avoid as much as possible, giving any Oath to the Minister himself, and that in their Inquiry into the nature of the Living, they do ask only such Questions of the several Witnesses upon their Oaths, as do relate to mere matters of fact.

That in forming their Judgments touching such part of the value of the said Living as is fixed and certain, they do not consider voluntary subscriptions, gifts, or contributions, or anything of that kind, but only such things as are perpetually annexed thereto, and which can legally be demanded, and that in making deduction thereout, they do not consider the charges of the King's Tax, nor Poor Rates, nor Repairs, but only Pensions, Procurations and Synodals, and such other Things as are certain and perpetual Charges and outgoings.

WE whose hands are hereunto subscribed, and set, being four of the Commissioners nominated and appointed by the Commission hereto annexed, do humbly Certify unto the Right Honourable and Right Reverend Father in God, Beilby, Lord Bishop of London, that in pursuance of such Commission, We, by the Oaths of Thomas Greenaway of Bishopsgate Street, in the Parish of St. Helen's, Hatter, and Jonathan Punshon of Bishopsgate Street, Oil and Colourman, and by all other lawful ways and means, have used our utmost endeavours to inform ourselves both of the Nature and of the yearly value of the Vicarage of St. Helen in the City of London, agreeably to the printed Heads of Inquiry annexed to the said Commission, and that the several answers subjoined to the several printed Queries do contain the best and truest Information we have been able to get concerning the premises.

IN TESTIMONY whereof we have hereunto subscribed our names this second day of January, in the year of our Lord One thousand seven hundred and ninety-eight.

         WILLM. MORICE, D.D.
         GEO. GASKIN, D.D.
         HEN. FLY, D.D.
         THOS. LOGGIN.

1st Query. Is Saint Helen in London a Rectory, Vicarage, or perpetual Curacy; or is it a Donative exempt from all Ecclesiastical Jurisdiction? and who is the Patron; or is it a Chapel of Ease to any, and what Church?

Answer. A Vicarage under the Patronage of the Dean and Chapter of Saint Paul's.

2nd Query. If a Rectory or Vicarage, Is it united to, or consolidated with, any other, and what Church? If a perpetual Curacy or Donative, Is it a Parish of Itself? If a Chapel of Ease, Is the Incumbent of the Mother Church obliged to do the Duty himself, or to provide a Curate to do it for him?

Answer. It is not united to, nor consolidated with, any other Church.

3rd Query. What is the ancient and accustomed duty which has usually been done at Saint Helen?

By whom is divine service there performed, and how often, and at what particular stated times?

Answer. By the Vicar, on Sundays, in the morning and afternoon, and on Good Friday, Ascension-day, and Christmas-day.

4th Query. If St. Helen is a Rectory or Vicarage, has the incumbent been duly instituted and inducted thereto? or does the present minister hold it by sequestration, and on what ground was such sequestration issued? If it is a perpetual Curacy, or a Chapel of Ease, has the Minister been duly nominated by the Patron, and been thereupon licenced by the Bishop? And if a Donative, does the minister serve it by virtue of any grant or appointment in writing from the patron?

Answer. The Incumbent has been duly collated and inducted.

5th Query. What is the present clear improved yearly value thereof, distinguishing what part is fixed and certain, and set forth how the whole doth arise, whether from glebe land, tythes, composition of tythes, or in what other manner? and what part is uncertain, as surplus fees, Easter offerings, &c.; and in case there is any stipend, set forth by whom the same is paid, and for how long time past, and what security there is that the same will be continued?

Answer. The Vicar receives from Mr. David King, the Impropriator, a yearly pension of Twenty pounds, reserved and made payable out of the rectory of St. Helen's by letters patent granted by Queen Elizabeth in the year 1599, for a stipend or salary to a sufficient preacher of the Word of God from time to time in the said church to be allowed by the Bishop of London. Also from the Company of Skinners in the City of London a yearly payment of three pounds. Also, for preaching two annual sermons, in pursuance of the Will of William Prior, deceased, the yearly sum of thirteen shillings and fourpence. Also for preaching an annual sermon, in pursuance of the Will of Thomas Fenner, deceased, the yearly sum of ten shillings. Also, for preaching an —— in pursuance of the Will of Joyce Featley, deceased, twenty shillings. Also, the yearly sum of twenty shillings for preaching a sermon, in pursuance of the Will of Francis Bancroft, Esquire, deceased. Also, the yearly sum of ten shillings for examining and catechising the children of the Charity School founded by the said Francis Bancroft on the day such sermon is preached, in pursuance of his Will. Also, part of the yearly sum of Twenty pounds granted by Sir John Lawrence Knight, deceased, to the parish of St. Helen, to be applied towards the encouragement of the Minister, and for the use of the poor of the parish, at the discretion of the parishioners in Vestry assembled, which part or proportion for the Vicar is at present by order of Vestry Five Guineas per annum, to be paid during the pleasure of the Vestry.

The Minister of St. Helen is desired to add his proper Direction

ROBERT WATTS, M.A., Sion College, London.

{ The surplice fees arising to the Vicar for ten years last appear to have amounted on an average to about seven pounds fifteen shillings.

It does not appear that Easter Offerings have ever been paid to the Vicar.

A subscription has been lately made for the present Vicar, which amounts to eight guineas.

The Vicar is liable to pay to the Cathedral Church of St. Paul the yearly sum of six shillings and eight pence.

So that the net certain annual income appears to be twenty-six pounds six shillings and eight pence. }

These are to Certify to the Governors of the Bounty of Queen Anne, &c., that after due examination and inquiry by the Oaths of four credible Witnesses, and by other lawful ways and means, into the nature and yearly value of the Vicarage of St. Helen in Bishopsgate Street, in the City and our Diocese of London, the same appears to be of the yearly value of Twenty-six pounds six shillings and eightpence.

IN WITNESS whereof we have hereunto set our Hand and Seal this fifth day of January, 1798, and in the eleventh year of our Translation.

B. LONDON. (Seal.)

Page 50.—*Queen Anne's Bounty.*

For the augmentation of the Stipend of the Vicar of St. Helen, the following Commissions were issued by the Bishops of London, Drs. Beilby Porteous and William Howley :—

"To the Reverend Dr. HAMILTON, Vicar of St. Olave, Jewry.
„ „ Mr. MEEN, Rector of St. Nicholas Cole Abbey.
„ „ Mr. WATTS, Rector of St. Alphage.
Mr. Deputy GREENAWAY, of Bishopsgate Street,
Mr. ABBISS, of do. do. } Churchwardens of
Mr. RUDD, of do. do. } St. Helen's.

"WHEREAS an Address of the House of Lords has been presented to his Majesty for an Account to be prepared and certified to the Governors of Queen Anne's Bounty of the clear improved yearly value of every Benefice with Cure of Souls in England and Wales, under the value of £150 per annum ; specifying how the same arises, and distinguishing such as have been augmented by the said Governors, from such as have not ; and also such as have been discharged from the payment of first fruits and tenths, from such as have not been so discharged. And whereas his Majesty has signified his pleasure, that directions be given for the said account being prepared and certified; NOW KNOW YE, that for carrying his Majesty's pleasure into effect, and in pursuance of the said Address, we, trusting to the integrity and skill of you the several gentlemen above named, do by these presents nominate, substitute, and appoint you, or any three or more of you, Commissioners in our stead, as well by the oaths of two or more credible witnesses, as by other lawful ways and means, to inform yourselves both of the nature and of the yearly value of the Living of St. Helen's, in the County of Middlesex, within our Diocese of London; as well such part thereof as is fixed and certain, as such part thereof as is voluntary and gratuitous, distinguishing the same as far as may be, and how such yearly value doth arise with the other circumstances thereof, agreeably to the printed Heads of Enquiry hereto annexed; and having so informed yourselves, you are hereby required to certify to us under your respective hands the several particulars abovementioned, by way of Answers to the printed Queries hereto annexed, to the End that we may certify the same to the said Governors. IN TESTIMONY whereof, we have hereunto set our Hand and Seal, this eighth day of February, in the Year of our Lord one thousand eight hundred and nine. "B. LONDON.

"*Directions for the Execution of the within Commission.*

"THAT the said Commissioners do take what care they can, that the witnesses, whether brought in by the Minister or called by themselves, be credible persons; that they do avoid as much as possible giving any oath to the Minister himself; and that, in their enquiry into the nature and value of the Living, they do ask only such questions of the several witnesses upon their oaths as relate to mere matters of fact. That in framing their judgments, touching such part of the value of the Living as is fixed and certain, they do not consider voluntary gifts or contributions, or any thing of that kind, but only such things as are perpetually annexed thereto, and can be legally demanded. And that in making deductions thereout, they do not consider the charges of the poor-rates nor repairs; but only pensions, procurations, synodals, and such other things as are certain and perpetual charges and outgoings. That the Commissioners do give clear and direct Answers to the Queries, and that two at least of the clergymen do act.

"WE, whose Names are hereunto subscribed, being five of the Commissioners nominated and appointed in and by the Commission hereto annexed, do humbly certify unto the Lord Bishop of London, that in pursuance of such Commission, we, by all lawful ways and means, have used our utmost endeavours to inform ourselves both of the nature and of the yearly value of the Vicarage of Saint Helen, in the City of London, within his Lordship's Diocese, agreeably to the following heads of Inquiry annexed to the said Commission; and that the Answers subjoined to the several printed Queries do contain the best and truest information we have been able to obtain concerning the premises.

IN TESTIMONY whereof we have hereunto set our hands, this sixteenth day of February, in the Year of our Lord, one thousand eight hundred and nine.

"R. HAMILTON, Vicar of St. Olave, Jewry, London.
H. MEEN, Rector of St. Nicholas Cole Abbey, London.
ROBERT WATTS, Rector of St. Alphage, London.
JAMES ABBISS, } Churchwardens of St. Helen's.
THOS. RUDD,

"N.B.—As satisfactory documents were produced, we did not find it necessary to examine any person upon oath.

"*1st Query.* What is the present clear improved yearly value of the Vicarage of St. Helen, London; distinguishing what part is fixed and certain; and set forth how the whole doth arise, whether from Glebe Land, Tythes, Composition for Tythes, or in what manner; and what part is uncertain, as Surplice Fees, Easter Offerings, &c.: and in case there is any Stipend, set forth by whom it is paid, and how secured, and for how long time past the same hath been paid.

"*Answer.* The Vicar receives from the Impropriator a yearly pension reserved out of the Rectory of St. Helen's, by letters patent dated 1599, for a stipend or salary £20 0 0
For five Gift Sermons 3 13 4
For an annual payment from the Skinners' Company 3 0 0

£26 13 4

Uncertain. As Surplice Fees, &c.

Surplice Fees on an average for three years... ... £10 10 0
Part of the yearly sum of £20 granted by Sir John Lawrance to the Parish of St. Helen: Anno 1684, to be applied towards the encouragement of the Minister, and for the use of the poor at the discretion of the Vestry 5 5 0
An annual donation during the pleasure of the Vestry, which has varied at different times, but is at present 70 0 0

£85 15 0

"*2nd Query.* Has it already been augmented by the Governors of Queen Anne's Bounty, and is it discharged from the payment of first-fruits and tenths?

"*Answer.* It has not been augmented, and is discharged from the payment of first-fruits and tenths.

"The Vicarage pays to the Cathedral Church of St. Paul's a yearly pension of 6s. 8d."

Page 50.

ST. HELEN'S IN THE CITY AND DIOCESE OF LONDON.
Pop. 1811.   652.
No.   .

Lot. 1815.   Pop.   .

Approved by Committee 1st November, 1815, for two Lots.
Confirmed 7th February, 1816.
Printed,   sent 19th April.

WHEREAS the Governors of the Bounty of Queen Anne, for the augmentation of the maintenance of the poor Clergy, intending to augment the Living of St. Helen's in the City of London, within my Diocese, if the same shall appear proper for augmentation, have desired me to certify to them the present nature and value of the said Living: Therefore in order that I may be able to make such Certificate, I do hereby desire you to make the necessary inquiries and answer the following queries, and to return the same to me under your hands.

To be directed to the Minister and one or two other Clergymen.

Dated, the 12th day of July, 1815.   W. LONDON.

To the Rev. JAMES BLENKARNE.
   ,,   R. WATTS, Rector of St. Alphage.
   ,,   G. A. HATCH, Rector of St. Matthew.

1st Query. Is St. Helen's a Rectory, Vicarage, or Perpetual Curacy; or is it a Donative, exempt from all Ecclesiastical Jurisdiction; and who is the Patron; or is it a Chapel of Ease to any, and what Church?

Answer. It is a *Vicarage,* is in the gift of the Dean and Chapter of St. Paul's Cathedral, London, and under their Ecclesiastical Jurisdiction.

2nd Query. Is it united to, or consolidated with, any other, and what, Church? Is it a Parish of itself? If it is a Chapel of Ease, is the Incumbent of the Mother-church obliged to do the Duty himself, or provide a Curate to do it for him; and, what distance is the Chapel from the Mother-church? What is the number of Inhabitants within the Parish or Chapelry, including the Hamlets, if any?

Answer. It is a Parish of itself, and not united to, or consolidated with, any other Church.

The number of Inhabitants is generally considered about a Thousand.

3rd Query. What is the ancient and accustomed Duty which has usually been done at St. Helen's; and how often, and at what particular stated times, is Divine Service there now performed?

Answer. Full *Duty on a Sunday, in the Morning and in the Afternoon, and at the usual Hours:* that is at eleven o'clock in the Morning, and at three o'clock in the Afternoon.

N.B.—There is no Lecturer; and on account of the Gratuity by Vestry, that is £90 a year, there is a sermon in the Afternoon.

4th Query. If St. Helen's is a Rectory or Vicarage, has the Minister been duly instituted and inducted thereto; or does he hold it by Sequestration, and if so, on what ground was the Sequestration issued? If it is a perpetual Curacy, or a Chapel of Ease, has the Minister been duly nominated, and by whom; and been thereupon licensed by the Ordinary; and whether as a perpetual Curacy, or only as a Chapel of Ease? If a Donative, does the Minister serve it by virtue of any Grant or Appointment in writing from the Patron?

Answer. It is a Vicarage; and the Vicar has been duly *instituted and inducted* and does the Duty *in Person.*

5th Query. Is there a House for the Residence of the Incumbent; and does he reside therein, or in the Parish, or where else, and at what distance from the Living? Is the Duty performed by the Incumbent himself, or by a Curate? If by a Curate, is he resident in the Parish or Chapelry, or at what distance from it?

Answer. There is no House belonging to the Vicarage; and the Vicar resides in the House appropriated for the Master of Queen Elizabeth's Free Grammar School of St. Olave, Southwark, as Master of the said School; which is about the distance of half-a-mile from the Parish of St. Helen aforesaid. And the Duty is performed by the Incumbent.

6th Query. What is the present clear improved yearly Value of St. Helen's, distinguishing what part is fixed and certain, and setting forth how the whole doth arise; whether from Glebe Land, Tithes, Composition of Tithes, or in what other manner; and what part is uncertain; as Surplice Fees, Easter Offerings, &c.? And in case there is any Stipend, by whom is it paid, and how secured, and for how long time past has the same been paid?

Answer. The Vicar receives from the Impropriator a yearly Pension reserved out of the Rectory of St. Helen's by Letters patent, dated 1599, for a Stipend or Salary £20 0 0

For five Gift Sermons 3 13 4

For an annual Payment from the Skinners' Company 3 0 0

£26 13 4

Uncertain. As Surplice, Fees, &c.

Surplice Fees on an Average for three years ... £10 10 0

Part of the yearly sum of £20 granted by Sir John Lawrence to the Parish of St. Helen, Anno 1684, to be applied towards the encouragement of the Minister, and of the use of the Poor at the Discretion of the Vestry 5 5 6

An annual Donation, during the Pleasure of the Vestry which has varied at different times, but is at present 90 0 0

£105 15 6

N.B.—The annual Donation was not given to the last Incumbent.

We believe the above to be an accurate statement.
{ JAMES BLENKARNE, A.M., Vicar of St. Helen.
ROBERT WATTS, M.A., Rector of St. Alphage.
GEO. AVERY HATCH, M.A., Rector of St. Matthew, Friday Street, and St. Peter's, Cheap.

Dated, July 17th, 1815.

The Incumbent of St. Helen's is desired to add his proper Direction

   The Reverend JAMES BLENKARNE,
    Tooley Street,
     St. Olave,
      Southwark.

N.B.—£85 15s. from Pension, Sermons, an annual Donation and &c.

I do hereby Certify to the said Governors that I believe the Answers to these Inquiries to be true.

To be signed by the Bishop   W. LONDON.

Page 50.—*Amount of Capital and how Obtained.*

In 1815 the Governors gave by lot £400—money—which in 1829 was invested in the purchase of £452 12s. 4d. Reduced.

Page 53.—*The Advowson of St. Helen's.*

At the Court at *Windsor*, the 5th day of May, 1873.

PRESENT,

The Queen's Most Excellent Majesty in Council.

WHEREAS the Ecclesiastical Commissioners for England have, in pursuance of the Act of the thirteenth and fourteenth years of Her Majesty, chapter ninety-eight, and of the Act of the twenty-third and twenty-fourth years of Her Majesty, chapter one hundred and forty-two, duly prepared and laid before Her Majesty in Council, a scheme, bearing date the first day of August, in the year one thousand eight hundred and seventy-two, in the words and figures following, that is to say:

"WE, the Ecclesiastical Commissioners for England, in pursuance of the Act of the thirteenth and fourteenth years of your Majesty, chapter ninety-eight; and of the Act of the twenty-third and twenty-fourth years of your Majesty, chapter one hundred and forty-two, have prepared and now humbly lay before your Majesty in Council, the following scheme for uniting the benefice (being a vicarage), of Saint Helen, Bishopsgate, in the city of London, and in the diocese of London, with the benefice (being a rectory) of Saint Martin, Outwich, in the same city and diocese, and for effecting certain other measures hereinafter specified with respect to the said benefices.

"Whereas the Right Honourable and Right Reverend John, Bishop of the said diocese of London, has caused proposals for a scheme for effecting an union of the said two benefices to be laid before us, such proposals being prepared under the seventh and eighth sections of the lastly-mentioned Act, and being finally approved by the said John, Bishop of London, and being assented to by the patrons and by the vestries of the parishes to be affected thereby, that is to say, by the said John, Bishop of London as patron in right of his see of the said vicarage of Saint Helen, Bishopsgate, and by the Master and Wardens of the Merchant Taylors of the Fraternity of Saint John the Baptist, in the city of London (who are hereinafter called the Merchant Taylors Company) as patrons of the said rectory of Saint Martin, Outwich, and by the vestries of the two parishes of Saint Helen, Bishopsgate, and St. Martin, Outwich.

"And whereas it appears to us to be expedient that the said proposed union shall be effected,

"Now, therefore, with the consents of the said John, Bishop of London (testified by his having signed and sealed this scheme), and of the said Merchant Taylors Company (testified by their having sealed this scheme with their common or corporate seal) and of the vestry of each of the said two parishes of Saint Helen, Bishopsgate, and Saint Martin, Outwich (testified in the case of each vestry by the signature attached to this scheme, in pursuance of a resolution to that effect of the chairman of a vestry meeting duly convened for the purpose of giving such consent), we, the said Ecclesiastial Commissioners, humbly recommend and propose all that is in this scheme set forth under the several parts or headings hereinafter mentioned, as follows :—

"*Part I.*

"As to the said proposed union itself and the immediate incidents thereof, we recommend and propose :—

"1. That the said benefice of Saint Helen, Bishopsgate, and the said benefice of Saint Martin, Outwich, shall be united and consolidated into and shall become and be one benefice by the name and style of 'The United Rectory of Saint Helen, Bishopsgate, with Saint Martin, Outwich.'

"2. That if, when this scheme shall have been ratified and confirmed by an Order of your Majesty in Council,* both of the said present benefices of Saint Helen, Bishopsgate, and Saint Martin, Outwich, shall be vacant, the union shall forthwith take effect, and if the benefice of Saint Helen, Bishopsgate, only shall be vacant, the union shall also forthwith take effect if the incumbent of the benefice of Saint Martin, Outwich, shall consent to become the incumbent of the united benefice, but if he shall not so consent, then that the union shall take effect upon the then next vacancy of his benefice, if at the time of such vacancy the benefice of Saint Helen, Bishopsgate, shall also be vacant; but if the benefice of Saint Helen, Bishopsgate, shall

---

* Here are omitted contingencies which did not happen.

not be then vacant, then that the union shall take effect upon the next vacancy of the said last-named benefice, and the then incumbent of the benefice of Saint Martin, Outwich, shall be the first incumbent of the united benefice ; and if, when this scheme shall be ratified and confirmed as aforesaid, the present benefice of Saint Martin, Outwich, only shall be vacant, the union shall take effect upon the then next vacancy of the benefice of Saint Helen, Bishopsgate ; and if, when this scheme shall be ratified and confirmed as aforesaid, both of the said present benefices shall be full, then that the union shall take effect upon the next vacancy of the said benefice of Saint Helen, Bishopsgate, if the incumbent for the time being of the said benefice of Saint Martin, Outwich, shall consent to become the incumbent of the united benefice, and that he shall be the first incumbent of the united benefice ; but if he shall not so consent, then that the union shall take effect immediately upon the first vacancy of the benefice of Saint Helen, Bishopsgate, which shall happen after the avoidance of the said benefice of Saint Martin, Outwich, and the then incumbent of the said benefice of St. Martin, Outwich, shall be the first incumbent of the united benefice ; and that in any case it shall be lawful for the Bishop to admit to the united benefice such first incumbent (if an incumbent for the time being of either of the existing benefices) without any form or fee of presentation, and he shall thereupon become the incumbent of the united benefice ; and that until the time of the union taking effect, the said two present benefices shall remain separate, and the rights and liabilities of each of them, and of the incumbent of each of them as such, shall remain unaffected.

"3. That if after this scheme shall have been ratified and confirmed as aforesaid, the present incumbents of the present benefices continuing to be the incumbents thereof respectively, the present incumbent of Saint Helen, Bishopsgate, shall retire from the incumbency of that benefice in order that the union may take immediate effect, and the present incumbent of Saint Martin, Outwich, shall be willing to become the first incumbent of the united benefice, the said present incumbent of the benefice of Saint Helen, Bishopsgate, shall be entitled, during the period hereinafter specified, to receive out of the annual income of the united benefice, and by way of compensation, the yearly sum of forty-two pounds nine shillings and ten pence (being a sum equal to the present net annual value of the endowments annexed to his incumbency), and also the Easter Offerings rendered in that portion of the united benefice which shall consist of or represent the present benefice of Saint Helen, Bishopsgate, and also the further annual sum of three hundred pounds; which annual sums of forty-two pounds nine shillings and ten pence, and three hundred pounds, shall respectively commence as from the day on which the union shall take effect, and shall be payable by equal quarterly payments in every year, the first quarterly payment to become due at the end of three calendar months next after the day on which the union shall take effect. The said annual sum of forty-two pounds nine shillings and ten pence, and the Easter Offerings above-mentioned, shall be respectively payable to the said present incumbent of Saint Helen, Bishopsgate, during the joint lives of himself and the present incumbent of Saint Martin, Outwich; and the said annual sum of three hundred pounds shall be payable to the present incumbent of Saint Helen, Bishopsgate, so long as he shall be able and ready and willing to perform in person, or by a substitute to be approved by the Bishop of London, the duties of curate of the united benefice; and whilst he shall so perform the duties of such curate he shall be styled and called the vicar in charge of the united benefice, but the performance of such duties by the vicar in charge shall not affect the obligation of the incumbent of the united benefice to reside on the benefice, unless such residence shall be duly dispensed with by licence from the Bishop, and such annual sums and Easter Offerings shall continue payable until the quarter-day next after the avoidance of the united benefice by such first incumbent thereof (being the present incumbent of Saint Martin, Outwich).

"4. That if such first incumbent of Saint Martin, Outwich, shall vacate the united benefice during the life of the present incumbent of Saint Helen, Bishopsgate, the annual sums and Easter Offerings aforesaid shall continue payable to the present incumbent of Saint Helen, Bishopsgate, until such one of the quarterly days of payment of the said annual sums as shall first happen after the united benefice shall so become vacant, and shall then cease to be payable; and from and after such quarterly day the present incumbent of Saint Helen, Bishopsgate, shall be entitled in lieu thereof to receive the annual sum of four hundred pounds during the remainder of his life, such annual sum of four hundred pounds to be payable by equal half-yearly payments in every year, the first half-yearly payment thereof to begin and be made at the end of six calendar months next after the quarterly day on which the said annual sum of forty-two pounds nine shillings and ten pence, the said Easter Offerings, and the said annual sum of three hundred pounds shall cease to be payable.

"5. That the said annual sums of forty-two pounds nine shillings and ten pence, and three hundred pounds, and four hundred pounds respectively, shall be charged upon the annual income of the united benefice, and shall be payable out of the same by the incumbent for the time being of the united benefice; and that, as between the incumbent for the time being of the united benefice and the retiring incumbent and his assigns, the said annual sums and each of them shall be a first charge at law and in equity upon the income of the united benefice, the incumbent of which benefice shall be deemed to have accepted the same, subject to a trust to pay to the retiring incumbent or his assigns the said annual sums out of the income of such benefice, and for that purpose shall use all due diligence to receive and collect the income of the said united benefice; and that if such annual sum, or any part thereof, shall at any time be in arrear and unpaid for more than twenty-one days after any of the said half-yearly days of payment, and the fact of the same being so in arrear shall be verified by the declaration of the incumbent who shall have so retired or his assigns, or in such other manner as shall be required by the Bishop, then that it shall be lawful for the Bishop to make an order upon the incumbent for the time being of the united benefice, requiring him to pay the amount in arrear within a time to be specified in such order, and if the same be not paid within such period, then that it shall be lawful for the Bishop to sequester the profits of the benefice until all such arrears and the costs of the sequestration shall have been paid and satisfied; but that the power to be so conferred upon the Bishop shall not in anywise abridge or interfere with the rights of the incumbent who shall have so retired or his assigns to recover the said annual sums and all arrears thereof by proceedings at law or in equity, or with the legal and equitable rights of the incumbent for the time being of the united benefice to recover from the preceding incumbent of the united benefice, his executors or administrators, any arrears of the said annual sums which ought to have been paid by such preceding incumbent.

"6. That upon the union taking effect, the present church of the parish of Saint Helen, Bishopsgate, shall become, and thereafter continue to be, the parish church of the united benefice.

"7. That after the union shall have taken effect, the expense of maintaining the fabric of the parish church of the united benefice, and providing the things requisite for Divine service therein, shall be defrayed by the two parishes of the united benefice, and shall, as between the same two parishes respectively, be provided as if the same were one parish, subject, nevertheless, to the provisions of 'The Church Rates Abolition Act, 1868.'

"8. That upon the union taking effect, the sacramental plate used in the church of the parish of Saint Martin, Outwich, shall be transferred to the parish church of the united benefice, but that if the whole of the plate of the two churches be more than sufficient for such parish church, then the vestry of each parish shall be at liberty to select so much as it pleases of the plate originally belonging to its own parish, to be tranferred to such other church or chapel within the diocese of London as the Bishop shall select, and that the font and communion table of the said church of Saint Martin, Outwich, shall be transferred to such other church or chapel within the diocese as the Bishop shall select.

"9. That upon the union taking effect, if the tables of fees used in the two churches be alike in all particulars, the table of fees used in the church which will become the church of the united benefice shall (until revised or altered by proper authority) be the table of fees for the two parishes of the united benefice; but if such tables of fees be not alike in all particulars, then that the same shall be of no authority, and a new table of fees shall be made by the proper authority for the use of the united parishes as if the same were one parish.

"10. That upon the union taking effect, the persons who at that time shall hold the offices of parish clerk of the parish of Saint Helen, Bishopsgate, and parish clerk of the parish of Saint Martin, Outwich, shall without any further appointment become the joint parish clerks of the united benefice; and that the persons who at the time of the union taking effect shall hold the office of sexton of the parish of Saint Helen, Bishopsgate, and sexton of the parish of Saint Martin, Outwich, shall, without any further appointment, become the joint sextons of the united benefice ; and that upon the death, retirement, or removal of either of the joint parish clerks, the other of them shall become the parish clerk of the united benefice, and upon the death, retirement, or removal of either of the joint sextons, the other of them shall become the sexton of the united benefice; and that the parish clerk of the united benefice shall afterwards, upon any vacancy in that office, be appointed by the incumbent of the united benefice, and that any future vacancy in the office of sexton shall be filled up by the joint vestry of the two parishes of the united benefice.

"11. That upon the union taking effect, the persons who at that time shall respectively hold the offices of clerk and sexton of the parish of Saint Helen, Bishopsgate, and who shall respectively become one of such joint clerks or sextons of the united benefice shall respectively cease to hold the office of clerk or sexton respectively of such last-mentioned parish, and that the clerk so ceasing to hold such office shall by way of compensation, so long as he shall be one of the joint clerks of the united benefice, receive from the vestry of the parish of Saint Helen, Bishopsgate, during the pleasure of such vestry, a salary equal in amount to his present salary; and that in like manner the sexton so ceasing to hold such office, shall, by way of compensation, so long as he shall be one of the joint sextons of the united benefice, receive from the vestry of the parish of Saint Helen, Bishopsgate, during the pleasure of such vestry, a salary equal in amount to his present salary, the receipt of such salary in the case of the said clerk and sexton respectively to be conditional upon the performance by such clerk and sexton respectively of such duties appertaining to the office of parish clerk or (as the case may be) of sexton in the parish church of the united benefice, or otherwise connected with such parish church, and the performance of the services therein as the rector and churchwardens of the united benefice may from time to time require, but that no parish clerk or sexton of the united benefice shall have any larger estate or interest in his office than he possessed in his original office before the union.

"12. That so long as a salary shall, under the provisions of this scheme, be payable by the parish of Saint Helen, Bishopsgate, to one of the joint clerks of the united benefice, that parish shall not be required to contribute any proportion of the salary of the other of the joint clerks of the united benefice, and that in like manner, so long as a salary shall, under the provisions of this scheme, be payable by the last-mentioned parish to one of the joint sextons of the united benefice, that parish shall not be required to contribute any proportion of the salary of the other of the joint sextons of the united benefice ; but that whilst such salaries, by way of compensation, shall continue payable to such joint clerk and joint sexton respectively, the salaries of the other joint clerk and joint sexton of the united benefice shall be paid exclusively by the parish of Saint Martin, Outwich.

"13. That upon the union taking effect, the persons who at that time shall respectively hold the offices of clerk and sexton of the parish of Saint Martin, Outwich, and who shall respectively become one of such joint clerks and joint sextons of the united benefice, shall respectively cease to hold the office of clerk and sexton respectively of such last-mentioned parish, and that the clerk so ceasing to hold such office shall, by way of compensation, so long as he shall be one of the joint clerks of the united benefice, receive from the vestry of the parish of Saint Martin, Outwich, so much as the same vestry shall see fit to apportion to him of the sum of one hundred and fifty pounds, which in the third section of the fifth part of this scheme it is recommended and proposed that we should pay to the said vestry, and that in like manner the sexton so ceasing to hold such office shall, by way of compensation, so long as he shall be one of the joint sextons of the united benefice, receive from the said last-mentioned vestry the remainder (after deducting the sum so to be apportioned to the clerk as aforesaid) of the same sum of one hundred and fifty pounds, the receipt by the said clerk and sexton of the sums so to be apportioned to them respectively to be conditional upon their undertaking, to the satisfaction of the said vestry, to perform such duties appertaining to the office of parish clerk or (as the case may be) of sexton in the parish church of the united benefice or otherwise connected with such parish church, and the performance of the services therein as the rector and churchwardens of the united benefice may from time to time require.

"14. That the present parsonage house of the said benefice of Saint Martin, Outwich, shall become and be the parsonage house of and for the united benefice.

"15. That upon the union taking effect as hereinbefore mentioned, all the properties which shall then constitute the endowments of the said present benefices of Saint Helen, Bishopsgate, and Saint Martin, Outwich, shall thereupon, without any conveyance or assurance in the law other than any duly gazetted Order of your Majesty in Council ratifying this scheme, become, and be the endowments of the united benefice, subject, nevertheless, to the annual payment thereout of the said annual sums of forty-two pounds nine shillings and ten pence, and three hundred pounds, or, as the case may be, of four hundred pounds, which are respectively hereinbefore mentioned, and made payable out of the annual income of the united benefice, and subject also to the three several rent-charges hereinafter mentioned, and proposed to be created as hereinafter is specified, in favour of the three intended new cures hereinafter mentioned, and subject also and nevertheless to this further proviso, that is to say, provided always that if the Reverend John Bathurst Deane, Clerk, now incumbent of the said benefice of Saint Martin, Outwich, shall become the first incumbent of the united benefice, he shall be entitled to receive and retain during such his incumbency the whole of the annual income of the united benefice, subject only to the said annual payment thereout of the said annual sums of forty-two pounds nine shillings and ten pence, three hundred pounds, and four hundred pounds (one or more of these sums), which are hereinbefore mentioned.

"*Part II.*

"As to the endowment of certain intended cures :—

"Whereas the aggregate endowments of the said present benefices of Saint Helen, Bishopsgate, and Saint Martin, Outwich, will, when they shall have become the endowments of the united benefice, as hereinbefore recommended and proposed, be in our opinion more than sufficient for the due maintenance and support of the incumbent of the united benefice and of any assistant curate or curates who may be by him employed.

"And whereas we intend, so soon as conveniently may be, having regard to the contingencies affecting the provision of endowments for such new cures as hereinafter mentioned, and with such consent as by law is required, to recommend and propose to your Majesty in Council the formation of three new cures within the diocese of London, that is to say, of a new cure to be taken wholly or partly out of the existing cure of Saint Philip, at Dalston, and to be called the District of the Holy Trinity, Dalston ; of a new cure to be taken wholly or partly out of the existing cure of Saint Dunstan, Stepney, and to be called the District of Christ Church, Stepney ; and of a new cure to be taken wholly or partly out of the existing cure of Saint Ann, at Limehouse, and to be called the District of Saint Peter Limehouse.

"And whereas the recommendation and proposal next hereinafter made is in accordance with, and is contemplated by, the proposals upon which this scheme is based, for uniting the said two present benefices of Saint Helen, Bishopsgate, and St. Martin, Outwich.

"Now, therefore, with respect to the endowments of the united benefice, we humbly recommend and propose :

"That a specified part of such endowments, that is to say, that the sum of two thousand two hundred and fifty pounds* per annum (being the amount of the annual fixed tithe, payable under the provisions of 'The London City Tithes Act, 1864,' subject to revision as in the said Act provided), and now constituting the endowment of the present benefice of Saint Martin, Outwich, shall over and beyond all payments thereout in respect of the three temporary charges (or any of them) of forty-two pounds nine shillings and ten pence, three hundred pounds, and four hundred pounds respectively hereinbefore mentioned, and also after and subject to such incumbency of the said John Bathurst Deane in the said united benefice as aforesaid, be subject to the three annual rent-charges next hereinafter specified, that is to say, to a rent-charge of six hundred pounds per annum, commencing as from the day hereinafter in that behalf mentioned (being a day subsequent to that on which the said John Bathurst Deane shall have avoided the said incumbency of the said united

---

* This presents a strange contrast to the value of the living as it was represented to the Company in 1603 by the then Vicar—viz., 30*l.* a-year. Mr. Lewis commenced a tithe suit which was stayed "by the mediation of divers worshipful and quiet men of the parish," upon the understanding that by contributions (the Company giving 5*l.*) the income was to be made up to 50*l.* per annum. See p. 54.

benefice) in favour of the minister or incumbent of the said proposed district of the Holy Trinity, Dalston, and his successors; to a rent-charge of three hundred pounds per annum, commencing as from the day hereinbefore and hereinafter in that behalf mentioned, in favour of the minister or incumbent of the said proposed district of Christ Church, Stepney, and his successors; and to a rent-charge of one hundred and ninety-two pounds nine shillings and ten pence, commencing as last aforesaid, in favour of the minister or incumbent of the said proposed district of Saint Peter, Limehouse, and his successors, such last-mentioned rent-charge, nevertheless, to be increased to five hundred and ninety-two pounds nine shillings and ten pence, when and so soon after the avoidance of the incumbency of the said united benefice by the said John Bathurst Deane, as the said annual sum of four hundred pounds hereinbefore proposed to be made payable to the present incumbent of the benefice of Saint Helen, Bishopsgate, shall cease to be so payable: but if the said annual sum of four hundred pounds shall before the same avoidance have already ceased to be payable, then such last-mentioned rent-charge to commence and continue at the full amount of five hundred and ninety-two pounds nine shillings and ten pence, each of the said three rent-charges to be payable half-yearly, and to arise and begin to accrue (subject as hereinbefore mentioned) as from the day of the date of the publication in the London Gazette of the Order of your Majesty in Council, whereby the district in favour of the minister or incumbent of which such rent-charge is to arise and accrue shall be created, and no one of the said three rent-charges to have priority over any other of them: and the minister or incumbent in whose favour any one of the said three rent-charges shall have been created to have, and we hereby recommend and propose that he shall have, all such remedies for the recovery of such rent-charge, the same being in arrear forty days, or upwards, after any half-yearly payment thereof shall have become due, as landlords have for recovery of rent being in arrear and unpaid: but nevertheless, and we hereby also recommend and propose, that if in any year the gross revenues of the said united benefice shall by means of variation in the amount of the said annual sum of two thousand two hundred and fifty pounds tithe rent-charge be increased beyond the sum of two thousand two hundred and ninety-two pounds nine shillings and ten pence, or shall be diminished below that sum, then and in every such year the said three rent-charges of six hundred pounds, three hundred pounds, and five hundred and ninety-two pounds nine shillings and ten pence, and each of them shall be increased, or (as the case may be) shall be reduced in proportion to their respective amounts in such manner that in that and every year the aggregate of the same three rent-charges shall be equal to the excess of the total revenues of the said united benefice above the sum of eight hundred pounds, the said three rent-charges if and whenever they be so reduced in amount to be receivable by the ministers or incumbents in whose favour they respectively arise and accrue in full substitution and satisfaction for the sums which but for such reduction would in that year have been receivable by them respectively.

E E

"*Part III.*

" As to the patronage of the united benefice :—

" Whereas we intend with such consents as are by law required, and in consideration of the endowments to be provided as hereinbefore mentioned to recommend and propose to your Majesty in Council that the patronage of the said intended new cure to be called ' The District of Christ Church, Stepney,' shall be assigned to the Bishop for the time being of the said diocese of London, and that the patronage of the said intended new cures to be called respectively ' The District of the Holy Trinity, Dalston,' and ' The District of Saint Peter, Limehouse,' shall, in like manner, be assigned to the said Merchant Taylors' Company and their successors.

"And whereas it is also a part of the consideration for such assignment in the case of the said intended district of Christ Church, Stepney, that the arrangement next hereinafter recommended and proposed should be effected.

" Now, therefore, with such consents, and so testified as aforesaid, we further recommend and propose that, as from the day on which the union hereinbefore proposed of the said two benefices of Saint Helen, Bishopsgate, and Saint Martin, Outwich, shall have taken full legal effect as hereinbefore mentioned, the patronage of the said benefice and vicarage of Saint Helen, Bishopsgate, which patronage is now vested in the Bishop of the said diocese of London and his successors, shall, without any conveyance or assurance in the law other than such duly gazetted Order of your Majesty in Council, as is hereinbefore mentioned by virtue of which Order the said union will have been so effected, be transferred from the said John, or other the then Bishop of the said diocese of London, and from his successors, to and shall thereupon become and be absolutely vested in the said Merchant Taylors' Company and their successors in such wise, that as the patronage of the said benefice and rectory of St. Martin, Outwich, is already vested in the said Merchant Taylors' Company and their successors, the whole advowson and patronage of the united benefice hereinbefore proposed to be created may be wholly and absolutely vested in the said Merchant Taylors' Company and their successors for ever.

" *Part IV.*

" As to the Church of St. Martin, Outwich :—

" With respect to the church of the said present benefice of Saint Martin, Outwich, we recommend and propose upon the said union taking effect as aforesaid :

" 1. That the same church shall (subject nevertheless to and in accordance with the provisions of the seventeenth section of the said Act of the twenty-third and twenty-fourth years of your Majesty, chapter one hundred and forty-two) be taken down, and its materials (except the glass in the east window) and site sold : the sale thereof, except so far as relates to that part of the premises which is to be purchased by the Commissioners of Sewers of the City of London under the provisions hereinafter proposed, to be by public tender or private contract, and to be made at one time, or at more than one time, as may be deemed most expedient by us, the said Ecclesiastical Commissioners, the pulpit, bells, clocks, organ, and other furniture, and fittings (other than the glass in the east window) being reserved to be appropriated (if required) for the use of such church or churches within the said diocese of London as the Bishop of the same diocese may select, but if the Bishop shall think it undesirable so to appropriate the same, then that the same (other than as aforesaid) be sold, and the produce dealt with in the same manner as the produce of the sale of the materials and site of the church.

"2. That before the said church of St. Martin, Outwich, is taken down, the glass in the east window thereof (which represents the armorial bearings of patrons and rectors of the same church) shall be carefully taken out, and shall be inserted in some window of the church of Saint Helen, Bishopsgate, at the cost of the fund created or to be created by the produce of the sale of the materials and site of Saint Martin's Church.

"3. That before the site of the said church of Saint Martin, Outwich, shall be sold as aforesaid, the said Commissioners of Sewers of the City of London shall have the option of purchasing at a price to be fixed as hereinafter mentioned, such a portion of the same site as the Surveyor of the said Commissioners of Sewers shall determine to be requisite or necessary for the purpose of widening the street fronting the said church of Saint Martin, Outwich, but the said Commissioners of Sewers shall declare such option within fourteen days next after the Bishop of the diocese of London shall have notified to them that the time for declaring such option has arrived, and if the said Commissioners of Sewers shall elect to make such purchase as aforesaid, the land so purchased shall be appropriated to the purpose of widening the street above mentioned, and to no other purpose.

"4. That the Surveyor of us, the said Ecclesiastical Commissioners for England, and the Surveyor of the said Commissioners of Sewers shall together determine and fix within fourteen days next after the said Commissioners of Sewers shall have elected to purchase under the option aforesaid, the price to be paid by the said Commissioners of Sewers for the land so to be purchased, and the said two Surveyors shall, before they proceed to determine and fix such price as aforesaid, agree upon a third surveyor to act as umpire between them, and to determine and fix the price as aforesaid, in case they are unable to agree, and the determination of such umpire shall be final, but if from any cause whatsoever the price to be paid as aforesaid by the Commissioners of Sewers for the land so to be purchased as aforesaid shall not have been determined and fixed, and shall not have been actually paid by the said Commissioners of Sewers before the expiration of two calendar months from the day on which the said Commissioners of Sewers shall have received notice from the Bishop as aforesaid, the option of purchase hereby proposed to be given to the said Commissioners of Sewers shall absolutely cease at law and in equity, and the site of the said church of St. Martin, Outwich, and every part thereof, shall as from the expiration of the said two calendar months be absolutely discharged from such option and from all right or claim of the said Commissioners of Sewers in respect thereof, and this provision shall take full effect notwithstanding that the cause of delay may have arisen from unavoidable accident.

"5. That the purchase money to be paid by the said Commissioners of Sewers for the land which they shall have the temporary option of purchasing as aforesaid shall, by the said Commissioners of Sewers, be paid to us the Ecclesiastical Commissioners for England, and the land to be therewith purchased shall, immediately after such payment, be conveyed to the said Commissioners of Sewers for the purpose aforesaid by us, under the authority of the Order of your Majesty in Council whereby this scheme will have been before such purchase ratified.

"*Part V.*

"As to the proceeds of the sale of Saint Martin, Outwich, Church :*—

"With respect to the monies to be realized by such sale or sales as aforesaid, of the materials, site, furniture and fittings (all or any of these things) of the said church of Saint Martin, Outwich, we recommend and propose:

"1. That, in the first place, such a sum as we may think necessary and reasonable shall be set apart by us out of the amount (so far as the amount can at the time of such setting apart be ascertained) of all monies received or receivable in respect of such sale or sales, and shall be added to the fund mentioned in the twenty-second section of the hereinbefore mentioned Act of the twenty-third and twenty-fourth years of your Majesty, chapter one hundred and forty-two.

"2. That, in the next place, out of the monies received or receivable as aforesaid, there shall be purchased by us such an amount of Three Pounds per Centum Consolidated Bank Annuities as will produce annual dividends or income to the amount of two hundred and fifty-two pounds, and that the dividends on the stock so purchased, that is to say, a sum of two hundred and fifty-two pounds per annum shall be paid by us as and when the same dividends shall become payable to the churchwardens for the time being of the parish of Saint Martin, Outwich, whose receipt shall be a sufficient discharge to us for every such payment; every sum so paid by us to be applied by the said churchwardens in payment of the annuities which, for the time being, may be payable under the provisions of a certain Act of Parliament passed in the thirty-sixth year of His late Majesty King George the Third, intituled 'An Act for Rebuilding the Parish Church of Saint Martin, Outwich, in Threadneedle Street, within the city of London,' and also, and equally in payment of a certain other annuity to commence and accrue as from the date of the publication in the London Gazette of any

---

* The sale realized 38,179*l.* 6*s.* 2*d.*, leaving (without any deduction for legal expenses) 25,185*l.* 16*s.* 2*d.* for the other parishes. 8000*l.* was assigned to each of the parishes of Dalston and Stepney.

Appendix. 421

Order of your Majesty in Council ratifying this scheme, to wit, an annuity of thirty-four pounds, to be payable and paid half-yearly by the said churchwardens to Louisa England, the present Organist of the said church of Saint Martin, Outwich, during her life : Provided, nevertheless, that no such payment by us to the said churchwardens shall be held to create as against us any trust, except in respect of the said churchwardens only : And provided also, that we may, if we shall see fit, sell from time to time any part of the stock so to be purchased as aforesaid, and pay over to the said churchwardens the amount realized by such sale or sales of stock if and whenever we shall be requested by the said churchwardens so to do, and if we shall be satisfied that the money to be realised by such sale and so paid will be applied by the said churchwardens in redemption of the said annuities or some or one of them respectively :—

" Provided also that if in any year the dividends for that year upon the stock then held by us under the investment aforesaid shall be more than sufficient (according to the testimony of the said churchwardens) to pay all the then subsisting annuities, the amount of the surplus shall be invested by us in the same securities and be added to the original principal sum thereof, and be subject to the provisions in this clause contained. And provided, lastly, that after the cesser, from whatever cause, of the said annuities, any balance remaining in our hands of the original and accumulated principal of the investment or investments made under this clause, shall be disposed of as in the eighth clause of this fifth part of this present scheme is provided with respect to the residuary monies therein mentioned.

" 3. That, in the next place, out of or in respect of the monies received or receivable by or in consequence of such sale or sales as aforesaid of the materials, site, furniture or fittings of the said church of Saint Martin, Outwich, there shall be paid by us to the vestry of the said parish of Saint Martin, Outwich, a sum of one hundred and fifty pounds, to be by the said vestry applied and apportioned as in the thirteenth section of the first part of this scheme is provided.

" 4. That, in the next place, out of or in respect of monies received or receivable by us as aforesaid from the sale of the materials, site, furniture or fittings of the said church of Saint Martin, Outwich, there shall be paid by us to the incumbent and churchwardens (whose receipt shall be a sufficient discharge to us for the same) of the said united benefice, a capital sum of three thousand pounds, the same capital sum or the interest thereof only, or some portion of the capital, with or without interest, to be applied by the said incumbent and churchwardens at their discretion in repairing and keeping in repair the church of the united benefice, that is to say, the said church of Saint Helen, Bishopsgate, and in putting the same into a fit and proper condition to become the church of the united benefice as aforesaid, and in reseating the same under the provisions of the twenty-eighth section of the said Act of the twenty-third and twenty-fourth years of your Majesty, chapter one hundred and forty-two.

" 5. That, in the next place, out of the monies to be received by us as aforesaid, such a sum as we may consider sufficient shall be set apart by us for, and shall be applied at our discretion in, the erection of a church within and for the said intended district of the Holy Trinity, Dalston: such church to be erected upon a site which shall have been duly conveyed to us in the manner provided by law.

"6. That, in the next place, out of the monies to be received by us as aforesaid, such a sum as we may consider sufficient shall be set apart by us for, and shall be applied at our discretion in, the erection of a church within and for the said intended district of Christ Church, Stepney: such church to be erected upon a site which shall have been duly conveyed to us as last aforesaid.

"7. That, in the next place, out of the monies to be received by us as aforesaid, such a sum as we may consider sufficient shall be set apart by us for, and shall be applied at our discretion in, the erection of a church within and for the said intended district of Saint Peter, Limehouse: such church to be erected upon a site which shall have been duly conveyed to us as aforesaid.

"8. Provided always, and be it clearly understood, that with respect to the sums to be set apart and applied as aforesaid for and in the erection of churches for the said intended districts of the Holy Trinity, Dalston, Christ Church, Stepney, and Saint Peter, Limehouse, such sums shall be so set apart by us in the order in which the said proposed churches are hereinbefore mentioned, and shall be so set apart by us only if and when and so far as the monies actually in our hands in respect of the proceeds of the aforesaid sale or sales of the materials, site, furniture and fittings of the said church of Saint Martin, Outwich, shall be sufficient, having regard to the provisions of this scheme and of the said Act of the twenty-third and twenty-fourth years of your Majesty, chapter one hundred and forty-two, to provide the same. And provided also that interest at the rate of three pounds per centum per annum shall be allowed by us upon any sums so set apart, and upon all balances from time to time in our hands applicable to the erection of the said churches, and all such interest shall be added to, and constitute part of, the principal of the same sums. And provided also, that each of such sums so set apart, when it has been increased by accumulation as aforesaid, and is therefore in excess of the sum set apart by us as sufficient for the purpose for which it was set apart may be by us reduced, if we shall see fit, to the amount originally set apart, but so that the surplus thus deducted may be by us, if we shall see fit, applied in aid of the sums or sum to be set apart and applied by us for and in the erection of the other two churches or one of them. And provided also, that if and when any of the said three sums shall have been by us set apart as aforesaid, the time for applying and expending the same sums or sum shall be ascertained by a certificate, to be addressed to us by the Bishop of the said diocese of London and by the Merchant Taylors' Company. And provided lastly, that all (if any) monies which, after satisfying the several appropriations in this fifth part of this present scheme mentioned and recommended and proposed to be made, shall remain out of or in respect of the proceeds of the sale or sales of materials, site, furniture and fittings of the said church of Saint Martin, Outwich, shall be by us added to the sum to be set apart by us under the first clause of this fifth part of this present scheme, and shall be dealt with accordingly.

"9. And provided also, that the scheme hereby proposed shall not take effect until the consents and approval which, by the seventeenth section of the said Act of the twenty-third and twenty-fourth years of your Majesty, chapter one hundred and forty-two, are made requisite to the sale or letting or appropriation under the powers conferred by that Act, of the site of any church shall be obtained to the sale and appropriation hereby proposed of the site of the said church of Saint Martin, Outwich.

"10. And provided also, that nothing hereinbefore contained shall prevent us from hereafter recommending and proposing any other measures relating to the matters aforesaid, or any of them, in accordance with the provisions of the said Acts of Parliament, or of either of them, or of any other Act of Parliament."

And whereas the said scheme has been laid before both Houses of Parliament for the space of two calendar months.

And whereas the said scheme has been approved by Her Majesty in Council: now, therefore, Her Majesty, by and with the advice of Her said Council, is pleased hereby to ratify the said scheme, and to order and direct that the same, and every part thereof, shall be effectual in law immediately from and after the time when this Order shall have been duly published in the London Gazette, pursuant to the said Acts ; and Her Majesty, by and with the like advice, is pleased hereby to direct that this Order be forthwith registered by the Registrar of the said diocese of London.

EDMUND HARRISON.

Page 64.

By an oversight the following particulars as to the monuments of William Bond and Thomas Benolte were omitted in the text:—

WILLIAM BOND. Here lyeth the body of William Bond, Alderman, and sometime Sheriff of London, a merchant adventurer, and most famous—in his age—for his great adventures both by sea and land. Obit. 30 die Maii 1576.

> Flos mercatorum, quos terra *Britanna* creavit,
> Ecce sub hoc tumulo, *Gulielmus Bondus*, humatur.
> Ille mari multum passus per saxa, per undas,
> Ditavit patrias perigrinis mercibus oras.
> Magnanimum *Græci* mirantur Jasona vates ;
> Aurea de gelido retulit quia vellera *Phasi*,
> Græcia docta, tace, *Graii* concedite vates ;
> Hic jacet *Argolico* Mercator *Jasone* major.
> Vellera multa tulit, magis aurea vellere *Phryxi*,
> Et freta multa scidet, magis ardua *Phasidos undis:*
> Hei mihi quod nullo mors est superabilis auro,
> Flos mercatorum, *Gulielmus Bondus*, humatur.*

---

* Behold, under this tomb WILLIAM BOND, "the flower of the merchants" which the land of Britain has produced, lies buried. He having suffered much amongst waves and rocks, enriched the shores of his country by means of foreign merchandize :

Page 74.

The following "circumscription" of the brass containing the effigies of Thomas Benolte, Clarenceux King of Arms, and his two wives—long since removed—is thus given in Maitland's Hist. of London, vol. ii. pp. 1607, Ed. Lond. 1775:—

"Here under lieth the Bodi of *Thõms Benolte*, Squyer, sometyme Servāt and Offycer of Armes by the name of *Windsore Herault* unto the right high and mighty Prince of   most drāde Soũaye Lod Kȳg Hẽry the viij, which Thoms Benolt, otherwyse namyd Clarenceux Kȳg of Armes decesid the viij. daye of May in the Yere of our Lord God Mvcxxxiiij in the xxvi Yere of our said Soveraȳe Lord."

Pages 67 and 248.—*Mayor of the Staple.*

"As the seas became safer, and the mercantile spirit of the Flemings rose, the great free cities of Flanders became as it were perpetual fairs, and were known as staples, from the German 'stapeln,' *to keep up.* In order that trade should be well under command, it was necessary that it should be carried on in few channels. The English Government had therefore chosen some of these Flemish towns, and ordered that all the chief productions of England, which have been already mentioned, should be sold in those towns, and nowhere else. These goods were therefore called staple commodities; the merchants who traded in them, the merchants of the staple. And this staple trade was put under an organization—there being a mayor, a constable, and courts of the staple. At these staple towns, the King's customers, or custom-house officers, by means of this organization, had every bargain under direct supervision; and every bargain thus supervised was obliged to be made for a certain sum of actual coin, the government thus securing a continual flow of silver into the hands of the English merchants. The staple towns were frequently changed. To reward any particularly faithful ally, or to raise the importance of any particular town, as for instance Calais, the staple was removed to that Prince's province, or to that town. The proportion of each bargain to be brought over in coin was also constantly varying. Indeed, the frequent interference of government in such matters was not among the least of the restrictions of trade. Edward III. was said, at one time of his life, to have had a different plan every month. Upon the whole, however, the principle was the same. Amongst the most remarkable plans of Edward III. was one for keeping the evident riches that

---

Grecian poets admire the mighty Jason, for his having brought the golden fleece from the icy Phasis. O learned Greece be silent! O Grecian poets yield the palm! Here lies a merchant far greater than the Grecian Jason. He carried away many fleeces more golden than those of Phryxis, and passed over many seas more rough than the waves of Phasis.

Alas! that death cannot be bribed by gold!
The Flower of Merchants—William Bond—is buried.

accrued to the staple towns within the limits of England.* In the twenty-seventh year of his reign he named nine towns in England which were to be the exclusive selling places of the English staple commodities. For an Englishman to carry such commodities beyond the seas was punishable by death. As Edward could not protect the foreign merchants visiting his staples, and as the additional trouble of purchasing goods at them naturally lowered prices, this plan did not answer. It was, in fact, suicidal for an island people, since it destroyed all object in the keeping up a mercantile navy. It was therefore speedily abandoned: and after the reign of Henry VI. Calais became the sole English staple town."†

Page 249.—*Merchant Adventurers.*

"This celebrated commercial company, said to have originated in the London Mercers' Company, obtained privileges from John of Brabant in 1296, and established themselves at Antwerp under the title of the Brotherhood of St. Thomas Beckett. In 1358 they were encouraged by Louis, Count of Flanders, who permitted them to form an establishment at Bruges; and in 1406 they received their first charter from Henry IV. of England. Edward IV. granted a new charter in 1466. Their importance was much increased by the celebrated treaty known as the *Intercursus magnus*, which was concluded between Henry VII. and Philip, Archduke of the Netherlands, Feb. 24, 1406; and in 1497 the company began to assume the title of the Merchant Adventurers. Henry VIII. granted them a charter in 1513; Queen Elizabeth granted them a charter in 1560, and a second July 8, 1564, confirming all former charters and privileges. Owing to the opposition of the Hanse Towns, they were temporarily expelled from Germany in 1597, but they were soon invited to return. James I. granted them a charter in 1617, and their privileges were confirmed by Charles I. in 1634. They settled at Dort in 1647, and made Hamburgh their principal staple about 1651. After 1661 Hamburgh became their only foreign station. In 1765 the company published a report, wherein they stated that their trade had been long declining."‡

---

* "Staple was regulated by 27 Edw. III. st. 2 (1353). The five chief or staple commodities of the kingdom were wool, woodfells (sheep-skins), leather, lead, and tin (butter, cheese, and cloth were sometimes added); which could only be sold for exportation by a corporation called Merchants of the Staple, and could only be sent from certain towns known as towns of the Staple. These towns were Bristol, Caermarthen, Calais, Canterbury, Chichester, Cork, Drogheda, Dublin, Exeter, Lincoln, London, Middleburgh, Newcastle-on-Tyne, Norwich, Waterford, and York. By 27 Edw. III. st. 2, c. 3 (1353), it was felony for any but authorised merchants to deal in staple goods. The Staple was the subject of numerous statutes." Townsend's Manual of Dates, p. 932. Ed. Lond. 1874.

† Bright's English History, vol. i. p. 257. Ed. Lond. 1875.

‡ Townsend's Manual of Dates, p. 649.

Page 271.—*Gresham Family Pedigree.*

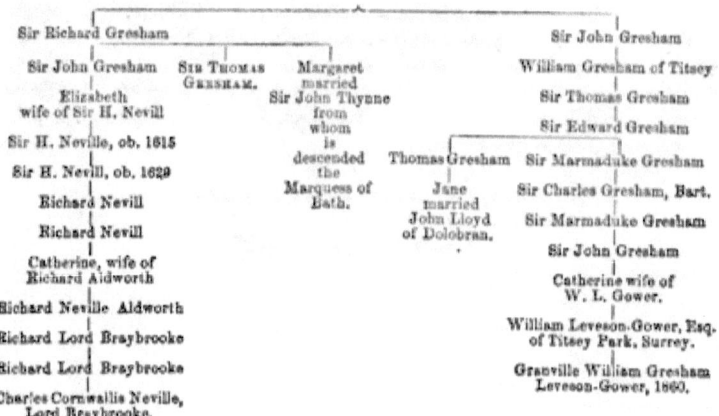

Page 284.—*Abstract of the Will of Sir Thomas Gresham.*

THIS IS THE LASTE WILL written and disposition of me, SIR THOMAS GRESHAM, of the cittye of London, Knight, concerning all my mannors, landes, tenementes, and hereditamentes, mentioned and conteyned in one quadripartite indenture, made betweene me the said Sir Thomas Gresham and Dame Anne my wife on the one partye, and Phillippe Scudamore, gent., and Thomas Celey on the other partie, dated the 20th day of May, in the seaventeenth yere of the raigne of our Soveraigne Lady, Queene Elizabeth.

First, concerninge the buildinges in London, called the ROIALL EXCHAINGE, and the pawnes, and shoppes, sellors, vawtes, messuages, tenementes, and other whatsoever myne hereditamentes, parcell or adjoyninge to the said Roiall Exchainge, I will and dispose, that after the expiration and determynation of the particular uses, estates, and interestes for life and entayle thereof, lymitted in the said indenture bearinge date the 20 of May, I will and dispose that one moietye thereof shall remayne, and the use thereof shall be unto the Maior and cominalty and citizens of London, by whatsoever especiall name or addition the same corporation is made or knowne, and to theire successors, for tearme of fiftye yeres then next ensuinge, upon truste or confidence and to the intente, that they doe performe the paiementes and other intentes in these presentes hereafter lymitted, thereof by them to be done and performed. And the other moietye of the said buildings, called the Roiall Exchainge, pawnes, shoppes, cellors, vawtes, messuages, tenementes, and other myne hereditamentes, with the appurtenances thereunto adjoyninge, shall remayne, and the use thereof shall be to the wardeins and cominalty of the mistery of the mercers of the cittye of London, viz., to the corporate body and corporation of the company of mercers in London by whatsoever especiall name or addition the same corporation is made or knowne, and to theire successors, for tearme of fiftye yeres next ensuinge, upon truste and confidence, and to the intente, that they doe performe the paiementes and other intentes in these presentes hereafter lymitted, thereof by them to be done and performed. And I will and dispose, that after such tyme as the one moitye of the said Roiall Exchainge and other premisses, according to the intente and meaninge of these presentes, shall come to the said maior and corporation of the said cittye, and from thence so longe as they and their successors shall by any means or tytle, hould, or enjoy the same, they and their successors every yere shall give and distribute to and for the sustentation, mayntenance and findinge foure persons from tyme to tyme to be chosen, nominated, and appointed by the said maior and cominalty, and cittezens and their successors, mete to reade the lecture of divynitye, astronomy, musicke, and geometry, within myne nowe dwelling-house in the parishe of St. Helynes in Bishopsgate Streete, and St. Peters the Pore in the cittye of London (the moitye whereof hereafter in this my last will is by me lymitted and disposed unto the said maior and cominalty and cittezens of the said cittye), the somme of 200l., of lawful money of Englande, in manner and forme followinge, viz. to every of the said readers for the tyme beinge the somme of 50l. of lawfull money of England yerely for theire sallaries and stipendes, mete for foure sufficiently learned to reade the saide lectures; the same stipendes and sallaries, and every of them, to be paid at two usuall tearmes in the yere yearly; that is to say, at the feastes of the Annunciation of St. Mary the Virgin, and of St. Mighell the Archangell, by even portions to be paid. And further, that the said maior and cominalty, and cittezens of the said cittie and their successors, from thenceforth, and so long as they and theire successors shall by any means have, hould, or enjoy the said moiety before in these presentes to them disposed, shall give and distribute the somme of 53l. 6s. 8d. of lawfull money of England yerely in manner and forme following, viz. unto eight almes folkes whome the said maior and cominalty and cittezens or theire successors, shall appoint to inhabite my eight almes houses in the said parish of St. Peters the Pore, to every of them the said almes folkes the somme of 6l. 13s. 4d. to be paid at foure usuall tearmes in the yere yearly, that is to say, at the feast of St. Mighell the Archangell, the Nativity of our Lord God, the Annunciation of the blessed Virgin Marye, and Nativitye of St. John Baptiste, by even portions. And further, that the said maior and cominalty and cittezens of the said cittye and theire successors, from thenceforth, and so longe as they and theire successors shall by any means have, hould, and enjoy the said moitye before in these presentes to them disposed, shall give and distribute at the tearmes aforesaid, to the reliefe of the pore persons and prisoners in the prisons and places called or knowne by the names of Newgate, Ludgate, the King's Bench, the Marshalsea, and Counter, now kept in Wood Streete, and wheresoever the same prison hereafter shall be kepte, 50l.

of lawful money of England in money, or other provision and necessaries for them, viz. to every of the same prisons or places, 10*l*., at the foure usuall feastes or tearmes of paimentes of rentes within the same cittye of London most accustomed, or within 28 daies next after, by even portions.

And as concerninge the other moitye, before in this my presente last will disposed to the said wardeins and cominalty of the corporation of the mercers, I will and dispose, that after such tyme as the same moitye, accordinge to the intent and meaninge of these presentes, shall come to the said wardeins and corporation of the mercers; and from thenceforth, so longe as they and their successors shall by any meanes or title have, hould, and enjoy the same, that they and theire successors, every yere yearly, shall give, and pay, and distribute to and for the findinge, sustentation and mayntenaunce of three persons, by them the said wardeins and cominalty and theire successors from tyme to tyme to be chosen and appointed, meete to reade the lectures of lawe, phissicke, and rhetoricke, within myne newe dwellinge-house in the parishe of St. Hellyns in Bishopsgate Streete, and St. Peters the Pore, in the said cittye of London, (the moitye whereof hereafter in this my presente last will is by me appointed and disposed to the said corporation of the mercers,) the somme of 150*l*. of lawfull money of England, in manner and forme followinge, viz. to every of the said readers for the tyme beinge the somme of 50*l*., for theire sallaries and stipendes, mete for three sufficiently learned to reade the said lectures, at two usuall tearmes in the yere, that is to say, at the feast of the Annunciation of the blessed Virgin Marye, and of St. Mighell the Archangell, by even portions to be paid. And that the said wardeins and corporation of the mercers and their successors, from henceforth, and so longe as they and theire successors shall by any means have, hould, or enjoy the said moitye before in these presentes to them disposed, shall yerely bestowe and expende 100*l*. of lawfull money of England, in manner and forme followinge, that is to say, severally at foure several tearmes in the yere, in and about the expences and charges of a feast or dinner for the whole company of the same corporation, to be had and made in the Mercers Haull in the said cittye of London, and in every their quarter day the somme of 25*l*.

[He further gives to Christ's Hospital, St. Bartholomew's Hospital, Bethlem Hospital, the Hospital of the poore in Southwark, and the Counter in the Poultry, to each 10*l*. per ann. And directs that the maior, &c shall place or put eight poore and ympotente persons into the eight alms houses.] AND, AS CONCERNINGE MY SAID MANSION HOUSE, with the gardeins, stables, and all and singular other the appurtenances in the said parishe of St. Hellyn's in Bishopsgate Streete, and St. Peter's the Pocre, in the citty of London, I will and dispose, that after the end, determynation, or expiration of the particular estates, uses, interestes, and entayles thereof lymitted by the said indenture quadripartite, dated the said 20 day of Maie, the same my mansion house, gardein, stables, and other the appurtenances shall remayne, and the use thereof shall be, to the maior and cominalty and cittezens of the said cittye of London, by whatsoever name or addition the same corporation is made or knowne, and to theire successors; and also to the wardeins and cominalty of the mistery of the mercers of the city of London : viz. to the corporate body and corporation of the mercers of London, by whatsoever name or addition the same corporation is made or knowne: to have and to hould in common for and during the tearme of 50 yeres, from thence next followinge full to be compleate and ended, upon trust and confidence, that they observe, performe, and keepe my will, intente and meaninge hereafter in these presentes expressed. And my will, intente, and meaninge is, that the said maior and cominalty, and cittezens, and theire successors, and that the said wardeins and cominalty of the mercers, and theire successors, after such tyme as the said mansion-house, gardein, and other the appurtenances, shall by vertue of these presentes come unto them, and from thenceforth, so longe as they and theire successors, or any of them, shall have, hould, or enjoy the same by any title or meanes, shall permitte and suffer seaven persons, by them from tyme to tyme to be elected and appointed in manner and forme aforesaid, meete and sufficiently learned to reade the said seaven lectures, to have the occupation of all my said mansion-house, gardeins, and of all other the appurtenances, for them there to inhabite, study and daily to reade the said and several lectures. And my will is, that none shall be chosen to reade any of the said lectures, so longe as he shall be married, nor be suffered to reade any of the said lectures after that he shall be married, neither shall receave any fee or stipend appointed for the readinge of the said lectures. And moreover I will and dispose, that if the said maior and cominalty, viz. the chief corporation of the said cittye, and the said wardeins and comiualty of the mercers, viz. the corporation of the mercers of the cittye aforesaid, before the end of the said fiftye yeres to them in forme aforesaid lymitted, shall procure and obteyne sufficiente and lawfull dispensations and lyssaunces, warraute and authority had and obteyned, shall have and enjoy the said Roial Exchainge, messuages, shoppes, pawnes, vaults, houses, and all other the premisses, with the appurtenances, for ever, severally by such moities, rates, and other portions, and in such manner and forme, as before in these presentes is lymitted, upon trust and confidence, and to the intente, that they severally for ever shall doe, maynteyne, and performe the paymentes, charges, and other intentes and meaninges thereof before lymitted and expressed, accordinge to the intente and true meaninge of these presentes. And that I do require and charge the said corporations and chief governors thereof, with circumspect diligence, and without longe delay, to procure and see to be done and obteyned, as they will answere for the same before Almightye God. For if they, or any of them, should neglect the obteyninge of such lyssaunce, or warrante, which I trust cannot be difficult, nor so chargable but that the overplus of my reutes and proffites of the premises hereinbefore to them disposed, will soone recompense the same, because to so good purpose in the commonwealth, noe Prince nor councell in any age will deny or defeate the same ; (and if conveniently by my will, or other conveyaunce, I might assure it, I would not leave it to be done after my death ;) then the same shall reverte to my right heirs whereas I do meane the same to the common weale. And then the defaulte thereof shall be to the reproach and condempnation of the said corporations afore God."

[Sir Thomas then leaves to the heirs of his niece, Elizabeth, the wife of Sir Henry Nevill, his manors of Mayfield and Wadhurst, Co. Sussex, and the residue of his property, to his wife, Dame Anne Gresham, and her assigns for ever.]

"In witness whereof, I, the said Sir Thomas Gresham, have written this will all with myne owne hand, and to each of the eight leaves have subscribed my name; and to a labell fixed thereunto all the eight leaves have set to my seale with the grasshopper, the fifth day of July, A.D. 1575.

Per me* THOMAS GRESHAM."

An Act of Parliament was soon afterwards obtained for confirming and ratifying the last will and testament of Sir Thomas Gresham. The clause relating to the College is in these words.

"The buildings in London, called the Royal Exchange, and all pawns and shops, cellars, vaults, messuages, tenements, and other whatsoever hereditaments, parcel of, or adjoining to the said Royal Exchange in London, some time the said Sir Thomas Gresham's, shall be to the said Dame Anne, during her life; and after her decease, the one moiety thereof to the mayor, commonalty, and citizens of London, by whatever special name or addition the same corporation is made or known, and to their successors for ever; and the other moiety thereof, to the wardens and commonalty of the mystery of mercers of the city of London, that is to say, to the body and corporation of the company of mercers of London, by whatsoever special name or addition the same corporation is made or known, and to their successors, to the good uses and intents in the said writing, last will and testament limited or appointed."—An. 23rd Elizabeth.

GRESHAM COLLEGE was one of the few buildings within the city that escaped the great fire in 1666; and there, for nearly half a century, the original founders and first members of the ROYAL SOCIETY held their meetings.†

"The place where they have hitherto assembled, is Gresham College; where, by the munificence of a citizen, there have been lectures for several arts endowed so liberally, that if it were beyond sea, it might well pass for an university. And, indeed, by a rare happiness in the constitution, of which I know not where to find the like example, the professors have been from the beginning, and chiefly of late years, of the most learned men of the nation; though the choice has been wholly in the disposal of citizens. Here the Royal Society has one publick room to meet in, another for a repository to

---

* This will was proved in the Perog. Court, Nov. 26th, 1579.

† "They received an additional benefit from the turret, erected by order of the Gresham committee over the apartment of the geometry professor, both for making observations in the heavens, and the trial of some instruments contrived by Mr. Hooke, who likewise read his Cutlerian lectures in the hall of the college."—Ward.

keep their instruments, books, rarities, papers, and whatever else belongs to them. And when I consider the place itself, methinks it bears some likeness to their design; it is now a COLLEGE, but was once the mansion-house of one of the greatest merchants that ever was in England. And such a philosophy they would build, which should first consist wholly of action and intelligence, before it be brought into teaching and contemplation."*

The whole constitution of the College having been altered under the authority of Parliament in the year 1767, an abridgment of the Act will conclude these brief memorials.

Page 285.

An Act for carrying into execution an agreement made between the mayor and commonalty and citizens of the city of London, and the wardens and commonalty of the mystery of mercers of the said city, and Stamp Brooksbank, Esq., secretary to the commissioners of his majesty's revenue of excise, for the purchase of Gresham College, and the ground and buildings thereunto belonging, and for vesting the same unalienably in the crown, for the purpose of erecting and building an Excise Office there; and for enabling the lecturers of the said College to marry, notwithstanding any restriction contained in the will of Sir Thomas Gresham, Knight, deceased.

WHEREAS the house and buildings now made use of for the managing and conducting the business of his majesty's revenue of excise, situated in the Old Jewry, London, and called or known by the name of the Excise Office, are, for want of necessary room for the officers and clerks, found very inconvenient for the well ordering and conducting the business of the said office, &c.

May it therefore please your majesty, and be it enacted, that from and after the 25th of March, 1768, the messuage called Gresham College, and all the ground, &c. thereunto belonging, containing on the west front, &c. with all rights and privileges belonging to, and enjoyed therewith, shall be vested in and annexed unalienably to the crown; in full satisfaction for which there shall be paid out of the revenue of the excise office to the city of London, and to the mercers company an annuity of 500*l.* per annum.

AND WHEREAS pursuant to the last will and testament of Sir Thomas Gresham of the city of London, Knight, deceased, four persons have from time to time been chosen, nominated, and appointed, by the mayor and commonalty and citizens of the city of London, to read lectures of divinity, astronomy, music, and geometry, within the said college; and also eight persons have been from time to time appointed by the said mayor and commonalty and citizens of London, to inhabit eight alms houses standing within, or adjoining to, and part of, the said college; and also three persons have from time to time been

---

* History of the Royal Society.

chosen, nominated, and appointed, by the wardens and commonalty of the mystery of mercers of the city of London, to read lectures in law, physick, and rhetorick, within the said college; and such seven persons so chosen, nominated, and appointed, to read such lectures, have, by the directions of the said will had apartments within the said college, for the purpose of residing there, and reading such lectures: and whereas the said several seven persons, so chosen, nominated, and appointed, to read the said lectures, and the said eight alms folks, the better to enable the mayor and commonalty, and citizens of the city of London, and the wardens and commonalty of the mystery of mercers of the city of London, to perform their part of the agreement entered into as aforesaid, have respectively agreed and consented to relinquish and quit their apartments and alms houses; be it enacted by the authority aforesaid, that the mayor and commonalty and citizens of the city of London, do and shall pay, or cause to be paid unto the four persons who now read the said lectures in divinity, astronomy, musick, and geometry, and to their successors, who shall from time to time be chosen, nominated, and appointed, to read the said lectures, and to each and every of them, the yearly sum of 50l. of lawful money of Great Britain, in lieu and instead of their respective apartments, so by them agreed to be relinquished and given up, and over and above the salaries and stipends found, provided and allowed to them for reading the same lectures. And in like manner that the wardens and commonalty of the mystery of mercers of the city of London, do and shall pay, or cause to be paid, unto the three persons who now read the said lectures in law, physick, and rhetorick, and to their sucessors, to each and every of them the yearly sum of 50l. in lieu and instead of their respective apartments, so by them agreed to be relinquished and given up, and over and above the salaries and stipends found, provided, and allowed to them for reading the same lectures.

AND BE IT FURTHER ENACTED, by the authority aforesaid, that the mayor and commonalty, and citizens of the city of London, and the wardens and commonalty of the mystery of mercers of the city of London, do and shall, from time to time, and at all times hereafter, find and provide sufficient and proper place or places for the present seven professors, and all succeeding persons to be chosen, nominated, and appointed for the reading the lectures in divinity, astronomy, music, geometry, law, physick, and rhetorick, to read the same in accordingly; and also like sufficient and proper place and places for the habitation of the eight alms folks, now and hereafter for the time being.

AND WHEREAS in and by the said last will and testament of the said Sir Thomas Gresham, the mayor, commonalty, and citizens of the city of London, and the wardens and commonalty of the mystery of mercers of the city of London were directed to permit and suffer the seven persons elected and appointed to read the seven lectures in the said will mentioned, to have the occupation of all the mansion-house, gardens, and other appurtenances, now called Gresham College, for them, and every of them, there to inhabit, study, and daily to read the said several lectures; and whereas in and by the said will it is directed, that no person chosen to read any of the said lectures, should be suffered to read any of the said lectures after that he should be married, nor should receive any fee or stipend appointed for the reading of the said lectures; and whereas in pursuance of this act the said college will be pulled down and taken away, and the collegiate life of the said lecturers, intended by the said Sir Thomas Gresham, will, by the pulling down of the said college, be put an end to; be it enacted by the authority aforesaid, that from and after the passing of this act, it shall and may be lawful to and for the said seven lecturers, or their successors, or any of them, to marry, notwithstanding any restriction contained in the said will, and each and every of the said lecturers, and their successors, shall, notwithstanding their being married, be suffered to read their said several lectures; and the mayor, commonalty, and citizens of the said city of London, and the wardens and commonalty of the said mystery of mercers, shall not be, or be deemed guilty of any misapplication of such sum or sums of money as shall be paid in fees or stipends to the said lecturers, though married; any restriction or limitation in the said will contained to the contrary notwithstanding.*

Page 62.—*Abstract of Francis Bancroft's Will.*

Francis Bancroft, grandson of Archbishop Bancroft, was for many years one of the Lord Mayor's officers, who in the execution of his office by informations and summoning the citizens before the Lord Mayor, upon the most trifling occasions, and for many things not belonging to his office, not only pillaged the poor, but likewise many of the rich, who rather than lose time in appearing before the magistrate, gave money to silence him, which together with his numerous quarterages from brokers, &c., annually amounted to a considerable sum of money. By these and other mercenary practices, he so effectually incurred the hatred and ill will of the citizens of all denominations, that the persons who attended his funeral, with great difficulty saved his corpse from being jostled off the shoulders of the bearers in the church by the enraged populace, who, seizing the ropes, rang the bells for joy at his unlamented death.

By his Will, dated March 18th, 1727, he directs "That my body may be embalmed within six days after my death, and my entrails to be put into a leaden box, and included in my coffin, or placed in my vault next the same, as shall be most convenient; and that my coffin be made of oak, lined with lead, and that the top, or lid thereof, be hung with strong hinges, neither to be nailed, screwed, locked down, nor fastened any other way, but to open freely, and without trouble, like to the top of a trunk. And I desire to be buried in a vault which I have made and purchased for that purpose under my tomb in the Parish Church of St. Helen's, London, within ten days after my decease, between the hours of nine and ten o'clock at night, and I do

---

* See Brief Memoir of Sir Thomas Gresham, &c., pp. 13-26. Ed. Lond. 1833.

direct that the whole expenses of my funeral shall not exceed the sum of two hundred pounds.

"I give my silver bason to the Church of St. Helen's, there to be used at the communion service, or otherwise in the service of that church, but for no other use or purpose whatsoever."

After numerous small legacies and annuities he bequeaths the whole of his real and personal property "as I compute the same to the value of 28,000*l*. to the Master and Wardens of the Company of Drapers, directing them to lay out and expend the sum of four or five thousand pounds in the purchase of a piece of freehold ground for the building thereon Almshouses for twenty-four old freemen of that company with a convenient chapel and schoolroom for one hundred poor boys, and two dwelling houses for two masters, with such other buildings, &c., as may be deemed necessary. The said twenty-four old men to have eight pounds per annum each by quarterly payments, and half a chaldron of coals each yearly, and a bays gown every third year.

"The two masters were to have thirty pounds a-piece salary and twenty pounds per annum to be allowed for coals, &c., for the use of the school and masters, with a sufficient allowance for books, pens, paper, and other necessaries. The boys to be clothed yearly with blue coats, caps, stockings, &c. And I desire the said Master and Wardens and such others of the Court of Assistants as are usually appointed for their visitations, once a year or oftener, to visit the said school and almshouses; to cause the said children to be publickly examined and catechised, and to enquire into the state, condition, and behaviour of the poor men, and to give orders for needful repairs, and that a sum not exceeding five pounds be expended on a dinner for the said committee, and that the two masters be invited to partake thereof.

"And I desire two sermons to be preached on a Sunday in the forenoon yearly for ever, in commemoration of these my charities; one in April in the Church of St. Helen's by the minister of that parish, the other in October in the Church of St. Michael's, Cornhill, or elsewhere. The said masters and children and old men to be present, and the children to be publicly examined and catechised. The ministers to have twenty shillings each for preaching the said sermons, and the readers ten shillings each for examining and catechising the children, and the clerks and sextons two shillings and sixpence each respectively.

"The children to leave the school at the age of fifteen years, and to be paid the sum of two pounds ten shillings, to buy them clothes to fit them for service, or four pounds to place them out apprentice. The Master, Wardens, &c., to have full power to displace the said masters or children or old men at their pleasure, in case they shall conceive sufficient cause for so doing.

"And whereas I have been at considerable expense in erecting my tomb in the Church of St. Helen's, I give and appoint the sum of two pounds per annum for ever, and more whensoever needful, for cleansing, preserving, taking care of, and repairing my said vault and tomb, it being my express intention and desire to have the same kept up in good order and repair for ever, whether the church be standing or not.

And to that end I hereby subject and charge all my estates with the payment and support thereof, before any of the charities herein before mentioned.

"And in case hereafter there shall appear any considerable overplus of my estate, then I desire it may be applied to the improving of this charity; and in case the said estate shall prove deficient to answer the purposes aforesaid, then a proportionate reduction to be made, not desiring that the said Company shall be in any way impaired by their acceptance of this trust."

Extract from an article entitled, "ST. MARTIN OUTWICH AND ST. ANTHOLIN," *contained in* "*The Argonaut,*" *edited by G. Gladstone,* vol. ii. pp. 25—27, Ed. London, n.d.

"St. Martin Outwich used to stand at the corner made by the junction of Threadneedle Street with Bishopsgate Street, just opposite to the large red brick building familiarly known in former times as the South Sea House, but now the rendezvous of the Baltic merchants. It was a dirty, shabby-looking building, and might have been supposed be much older than it really was, the late edifice having been erected in 1796. Its name and history, however, go very much further back. The parish is mentioned in public records as St. Martin's Otteswich as early as the year 1291; and what we may best call the old church was built in the fourteenth century. It is evident that in these early times it must have been the property of a family which gave its own name to the church, for the old building was erected by one Martin de Oteswich, at the cost of himself and other members of the family, and in its vaults some of their descendants were buried. It fortunately escaped the great fire of London, though not the ravages of time, but the old monuments it contained were transferred to the late building on its erection in 1796. Amongst these were two recumbent figures, in stone, representing John Oteswich and his wife, whose remains were found in the vault below; and another, bearing the following inscription: 'The Worshipful Richard Staper, elected Alderman of this Cittye ano (*sic*) 1594. Hee was the greatest merchant in his tyme, the chiefest actor in discovere of the trades of Turkey and East India,' &c.

"The contents of the vaults, which were very considerable in quantity, have been removed to Ilford Cemetery. Among these were the remains of a Mrs. Abigail Vaughan, who left a legacy of four shillings per annum to purchase faggots for the burning of heretics; and of a Mrs. Margaret Taylor, whose estate would in time have become very valuable, for it includes the South-sea House opposite. One of the vaults was remarkable for containing the bones of a family of giants, their dimensions being such as to show that the individuals to whom they belonged must have been over seven feet in height. The brasses, monuments, and recumbent figures have been removed to the neighbouring church of St. Helen's; and the large bell, weighing nine cwt., and bearing the inscription, 'John Boorlet made me, in 1623,' to Fulham.

"The parish records contain some curious entries. The following items will serve as specimens of churchwarden's accounts some three centuries and a half ago:—

'Relike Sonday, 1525. Payde for wyne on Relykys Sonday, 1d.

'Paschall or Hallowed Taper, Anno 1525. Paid to Thomas Vance, waxe chandeler, for makyng and renewyng of the beme lyght; and for makyng of the Paskall w^t the tenabur candell and Crosse candell xxs.; and for waste of the same Pascall, a pownd and halfe qrt.; viij$d$.

'License to eat flesh. Item. Received of the Lady Altham for the use of the poore, for a license to eat flesh, £0 13s. 4d.'"

Parish of St. Helen, Bishopsgate, in the Metropolitan Union of the City of London, in the City of London and Liberties thereof.

Gross value.	Rateable value.
£53,116 14 0	£44,289 0 0

Finally determined by Assessment Committee in accordance with the provisions of the Valuation (Metropolis) Act, 1869.

10*th December*, 1875.

INDEX.

ABBISS, James, 204, 208, 216, 219, 404, 406
Abbot, Archbishop, 270
Adelmare, Dr. Cæsar, 48, 286–8
Adelmare, Peter Maria, 286–7
Adelmare—see also Cæsar
Adylmar, Paulina, 96
Adynet, Johanna, 7
Agassiz, James John Charles, 95
Agassiz, Lewis, 95
Agassiz, Mary, 95
Aggas, Ralph, 254
Alard, Dean, 5, 6, 11
Alardus de Burnham, 361
Albany, Duke of, 244
Albemarle, Duke of, 323
Albinus the Priest, 5
Aldworth, Mrs., 123
Aldworth, Richard, 426
Aldworth, Richard Neville, 426
Aldworth, Thomas, 123, 124, 126
Alexander, Rev. Daniel, 338, 341–2
Aleyn, Agnes, 26
Aleyn, John, 26
Aleyn, Sir John, 235
Allen, —, 110, 121
Allen, Rev. —, 55
Allen, Dan, 113
Alleyn, Edward, 321
Alleyne, Ann, 26, 27
Alleyne, Edward, 26
Allibone, —, 338
Allin, Bridget, 97
Allin, Edmond, 97
Allin, Hellen, 97
Alston, Rev. Albert, 56
Alstone, Sir Edward, 97
Alstone, Lady, 97
Altham, James, 255, 259
Altham, Lady, 436
Althan, —, 175
Alwyne, Bishop, 4
Anderson, Anne, 326
Anderson, Stephen, 94
Anderson, Sir Stephen, 94, 321, 326
Anderson, Tho., 59
Anderson, Thomas, 289
Angell, Elizabeth, 301
Angell, Robert, 301
Anglesey, Arthur Earl of, 349
Anne, Lady, 331
Anne, Queen, 328

Annesley, Anne, 351
Annesley, Benjamin, 351
Annesley, Judith, 351
Annesley, Dr. Samuel, 348, 349–51
Ansty, Rev. James, 99
Apulderfield, —, 247
Apulderfield, Amy, 247
Arman, Edward, 78, 218
Armstrong, Thomas, 112, 113, 114
Arnold, Dr., 213
Arundel, Henry Fitzalan, Earl of, 288, 292
Arundel, Willoughby, 92
Ascough, Thomas, 91
Ashfield, Alice, 231, 330
Ashton, —, 216
Aske, Alderman, 320
Aspinwall, Elizabeth, 94
Aspinwall, Gilbert, 94
Aspinwall, Mary, 94
Asshfeld, Alice, 11, 12
Astley, John, 68
Astrey, Diana, 86, 196
Astry, Sir Ralph, 45
Atkinson, —, 378
Atkinson, Richard, 174
Atkyns, Richard, 33
Atwell, Ann, 95
Atwell, Mary, 95
Atwell, William, 95
Audley, Henry Lord, 35, 381
Audley, Thomas, 84, 223
Audley, Sir Thomas, 381
Augustine, St., 360
Aurelius, Abraham, 97
Auriol, Elisha, 95
Auriol, James David, 95
Auriol, John Lewis, 99
Auriol, Margaret, 95
Austen, Rice, 102
Austyn, Robert, 107
Awdley, —, 222
Ayley, —, 327
Ayley, Elizabeth, 327
Aylward, —, 122

BACKHOUSE, Alderman, 97
Backhouse, Julian, 97
Backhurst, Alderman, 131
Backwell, Richard, 131, 142
Bacon, Sir Edmund, 295
Bacon, Francis Lord, 280, 292, 293

438 Index.

Bacon, Gregory, 101
Bacon, Sir Nathaniel, 280
Bacon, Sir Nicholas, 273, 280, 292
Baker, —, 109
Baker, Elizabeth, 93
Baker, Sir Henry, 93
Baker, John, 87, 146
Baker, Katharine Lady, 93
Baker, Sir Richard, 235
Baker, William, 30, 33
Baker, William, 189
Baldwin, 4
Ball, Charles, 130
Ball, Elizabeth, 94
Ball, Rebecca, 94
Ball, Rev. Richard, 54, 78, 94, 221, 223, 314–15
Bancroft, Archbishop, 61
Bancroft, Francis, 60, 61, 62, 98, 136, 137, 162, 380, 403, 433
Barber, —, 220
Barbor, Rev. Thomas, 54, 106
Barham, Rev. Arthur, 54, 85, 94, 98, 225, 315–6
Barham, John, 94
Barham, Mary, 94
Barker, Rev. John, 338, 343, 344–5
Barkham, Sir Edward, 301
Barkham, Lady, 301
Barnard, Alderman, 155, 156
Barnard, Dr., 316
Barnard, John, 33
Barnard, Rose Christian, 199, 200
Barnard, Walter, 99
Barnevelt, Monsieur, 333
Barnwell, Henry, 135
Baronius, Cæsar, 1
Barrett, —, 132
Bartlett, —, 173, 174
Bartlett, Captain Edward, 97
Bartolus, —, 309
Basing, William, 6, 7, 359
Basings, Thomas, 7
Bateman, —, 110
Bates, Dr., 347
Bathurst, Henry Lord, 177
Bawcomb, Sarah, 183
Baxter, Richard, 351, 352
Baylis, Elizabeth, 197, 208, 216, 219
Beaulieu, John, 265, 266
Becha, 5
Beckett, St. Thomas, 425
Bedell, Francis, 136
Bedford, Duke of, 256
Beechcraft, —, 155
Beeston, Nicholas, 298
Bellby, Bishop, 402, 404
Bellows, John, 129
Benedict, St., 359, 360, 361
Bennett, Sir H., 323
Benolte, Ann, 245
Benolte, Eleanor, 245
Benolte, Mary, 245
Benolte, Thomas, 19, 32, 74, 243–5, 380, 423, 424
Bentham, —, 48
Benzelin, Francis, 113

Berchere, J. L., 160
Berde, Richard, 12, 13, 14, 15, 18, 27
Berkeley, Earl of, 319
Berkeley, Isaac, 86, 135, 137, 138, 141, 147, 149, 150, 151
Berkley, William, 97
Bernard, John, 17
Bernard, Mrs., 158
Bernard, Walter, 71
Bernard, Alderman William, 150, 151, 158, 162, 381
Bertie, George, 95, 189
Bertie, Mary, 95
Bertie, Thomas, 95
Best, John, 332
Betts, —, 212
Bevilacqua, Venanzio di Ottaviano, 308
Biddulph, Charlotte, 94
Biddulph, Mary, 94
Biddulph, Michael, 94
Bindle, Ann, 91
Bing, —, 325
Birch, Dr., 283
Bishop, —, 173
Bishop, Matthew, 190
Blackborow, Mrs., 159
Blackburn, —, 140, 142
Blackburn, Edward L., 336
Blake, Hobson, and Allfrey, Messrs., 205
Blenkarne, Rev. James, 55, 207, 209, 215, 407, 409
Blenkarne, Mary Ann, 99
Bliss, —, 269, 339
Blore, E., 335
Blunt, John, 223
Boardman, —, 133
Boddington, George, 86, 98, 114, 119, 131, 134
Boddington, Isaac, 135
Bodye, William, 35
Boeheme, Ann, 95
Boeheme, Clement, 95
Boeheme, Edward, 95
Boggi, —, 3
Bolwell, Thomas, 180
Bonard, Réné Marguerite, 93
Bond, Martin, 63, 64, 84, 97, 172, 217, 380
Bond, Rev. Richard, 55
Bond, William, 63, 64, 96, 297, 333, 378, 380, 423
Bonewise, Anthony, 236, 238
Bonfoy, Susanna, 303
Bonfoy, Sir Thomas, 303
Bonfrank, —, 287
Bonvixi, Antony, 21, 25, 34, 245–6, 260, 330, 332
Boone, —, 224
Boorlet, John, 435
Bootes, Hellen, 91
Booth, —, 176, 193
Booth, Henry, 92
Borgarucci, Julio, 311
Bosanquet, Anna Maria, 92
Bosville, Sir Robert, 91
Boteler, Sir John, 92, 327
Boteler, Philip, 92

Boteler, Sir Philip, 322, 327
Boucher, Alexander, 141
Boughey, —, 203
Boulter, —, 163
Boulton, Henry, 92
Bowcher, John, 93
Bowes, Sir Martin, 35
Bowsell, Henry, 23
Bowsfell, Henry, 23
Bowyer, Mary, 98
Boyfield, Richard, 160, 163, 174
Boyle, Hon. Robert, 319
Boynton, Catherine, 92
Bracebridge, William, 233
Bradley, —, 173
Bradley, Edward, 52, 164, 165, 179, 190, 201, 202, 204
Bradley, Elizabeth, 219
Bradley, James, 204, 205
Bradley, Mrs., 183
Bradley, Robert, 156, 176
Bradshawe, Lucretia, 92
Bradshawe, Obadiah, 91
Bradshawe, Suzan, 91
Braybrooke, Charles Cornwallis **Neville**, Lord, 426
Braybrooke, Richard Lord, 426
Breieux, John, 381
Brent, Amelia, 96
Brent, Sir Nathaniel, 317, 318
Brent, William, 96
Brerewood, Edward, 313-4
Brerewood, Richard, 313
Brerewood, Robert, 314
Brewer, Edmund, 30, 33
Bridges, John, 322
Briggs, —, 98
Bright, —, 425
Bristowe, —, 179, 180, 184
Brittany, Duke of, 230
Broadstreet, Rev. —, 54
Brockett, William, 180, 181
Bromage, — 225
Bromley, — 119
Bromley, Richard, 114, 123, 126
Broughton, Richard, 97
Brown, —, 175
Brown, Edward, 99
Brown, Rev. Joseph, 54, 94
Brown, Sir Richard, 325
Brown, William, 348
Browne, —, 136
Browne, Benjamin, 94
Browne, Edward, 297
Browne, Elizabeth, 297
Browne, Henrye, 100, 101
Browne, Suzan, 94
Browne, William, 173
Brownes, Elizabeth, 107
Bruex, John, 378
Brun, 5
Brunswick, Duke of, 312
Bryant, Joseph, 183
Bryerwood, Edward, 79, **222**
Bryscombe, Adrian, 33
Bryseley, Edward, 17, 33
Buck, James, 99

Buckingham, Duke of, 323, 331
Buckland, Richard, 245
Budd, David, 300
Bulleyn, Sir James, 15, 18
Bunce, Sir James, 322
Burdett, —, 171
Burdett, Rev. Charles, 95, 99, 148
Burdett, George, 95
Burdett, Mary, 95
Burdett, Thomas, 176
Burfoot, Thomas, 180, 181
Burgon, —, 280, 283
Burgundy, Duke of, 230
Burleigh, Thomas Cecil, Lord, 258, 285, 291
Burnet, Dr., 352
Burrows, —, 218
Busby, Dr., 213, 319
Bush, —, 201
Butler, Angell, 94
Butler, J., 141
Butler, Jane, 94
Butler, Sir Nicholas, 94
Butler, Rev. William, 55
Butt, John, 190, 192, 193
Byard, —, 85
Byfield, —, 314
Byngle, **John**, 96
Byscombe, **Andrew**, 17

CÆSAR (Adelmare) **Alice Lady**, 96, 291, 292, 294
Cæsar, Anne Lady, 70, 97, 225, 292, 293
Cæsar, Betty, 307
Cæsar, Charles (brother of Sir Julius Cæsar), 299
Cæsar, Charles (1st son of Sir J. C.), 96, 289, 294, 299
Cæsar, Sir Charles (3rd son of Sir J. C.), 290, 294, 295, 299-301
Cæsar, Charles (grandson of Sir J. C.), 234, 293, 296, 299, 300, 301
Cæsar, Sir Charles (great-grandson of Sir J. C.), 301, 303
Cæsar Charles (son of above), 288, 303, 304, 305, 307
Cæsar, Charles (son of above), 305, 307
Cæsar, Mrs. Charles, 234
Cæsar, Dorcas, 289, 294
Cæsar, Mrs. Dorcas, 289, 292
Cæsar, Ellen, 297
Cæsar, Harriet, 307
Cæsar, Henry, 299
Cæsar, Henry, 303
Cæsar, Sir Henry, 300, 301
Cæsar, Jane, 301
Cæsar, Jane, 307
Cæsar, Jane Lady, 301
Cæsar, Sir John, 291, 292, 294, 295, 301
Cæsar, Julius, 289, 299
Cæsar, Julius, 300
Cæsar, Colonel Julius, 307
Cæsar, Sir Julius, 69, 71, 83, 96, 97, 98, 123, 223, 225, 234, 288-97, 298, 301, 302, 380
Cæsar, Margery, 297
Cæsar, Mrs. Mary, 303, 304, 305, 307

Cæsar, Molly, 307
Cæsar, Richard, 290
Cæsar, Robert, 97, 292, 294, 295, 302, 303
Cæsar, Susan, 297
Cæsar, Thomas, 292, 302
Cæsar, Thomas, 303
Cæsar, Sir Thomas, 96, 294, 297-9
Cæsar, William, 299
Cæsarino, Paola, 286
Calamy, Rev. Edmund, 338, 345, 347, 350, 351
Calandrinus, Cæsar, 308
Calandrinus, Magdalen, 308
Calvert, Samuel, 97
Cambridge, Richard Earl of, 228
Camden, William, 228
Campbell, Lord, 292
Campion, Christopher, 35
Canham, —, 121
Canterbury, Augustine, Archbishop of, 57
Carew, Sir Nicholas, 245
Carewe, Frances, 91
Carey, Rev. —, 55
Carleton, Bigley, 94
Carleton, Marth, 94
Carleton, Samuel, 94
Carpenters' Company, 76, 123, 124, 126, 138, 184
Carrington, Thomas, 188
Carter, Anne, 98
Carter, Thomas, 208
Carvell, William, 156
Castiglioni, Battista, 311
Catesby, Catherine, 330
Catesby, Sir William, 331
Catherwood, —, 216
Cecil, Sir William, 277
Celey, Thomas, 426
Chamberlain, Mrs., 84
Chambrelan, Abraham, 79, 93
Chambrelan, Charles, 72, 126, 158
Chambrelan, David, 93
Chambrelan, Hester, 72
Chambrelan, Hester, 93
Chambrelan, Rachel, 72
Chandler, Charles, 161, 167, 171, 176, 180
Chandler, Mrs., 180
Chapman, —, 209, 216, 297
Charlemagne, 46
Charles I., 44, 46, 299, 338, 425
Charles II., 43, 51, 283, 286, 301, 316, 317, 322, 325, 333, 338, 349, 350, 387
Charles V., 243, 244, 248, 258, 273
Charnack, —, 111
Charnock, Richard, 339
Charnock, Robert, 114
Charnock, Rev. Stephen, 338, 339-40, 341
Chartress, Cornelius, 178
Chauncey, Sir Henry, 58, 301
Cheke, Sir John, 257
Chester, Anne, 95
Chester, Colonel Charles, 307
Chester, Granado, 95
Chester, Granodo, 95
Chester, Harry, 307
Chester, Col. Joseph L., 90
Chester, Mary, 95
Chester, Robert, 307
Chester, Robert, 307
Chesters, —, 134
Chewter, Math., 77
Chewter, Nathaniel, 116, 117, 127, 129
Chiche, Emmeline, 247
Chiche, Thomas, 247
Chiche, Valentine, 247
Chichele, Henry, 247
Chichele, Phillippa, 247
Chichele, Sir Robert, 247
Chichele, Thomas, 247
Chichele, William, 247
Chicheley, —, 45
Chichester, Eleanor, 95
Chichester, Henry, 95
Chichester, Henry William, 95
Chipps, Elizabeth, 190
Chitty, Abraham, 86, 113, 114
Chitty, Joseph, 209, 210
Cholmely, Sir Roger, 382, 383
Choral Harmonists' Society, 335
Chosroes I., 2
Churchill, R., 130, 134, 135
Clnget, —, 341
Clapham, Mary, 86, 146, 148, 194, 196, 197
Clare, Earl of, 240
Clarence, Duke of, 331
Clarendon, Lord, 302
Clark, —, 144
Clark, John, 315
Clark, William, 178
Clarke, —, 162, 216
Clarke, Charles, 94
Clarke, Elizabeth Lady, 94
Clarke, F., 216
Clarke, Francis, 98
Clarke, Sir Francis, 94, 98
Clarke, W., 182, 186
Clarke, William, 173
Cleves, Anne of, 235
Clinton, Lord, 258
Clode, Charles Mathew, 379
Clough, Richard, 278, 279, 281, 282
Clovell, Jane, 234
Cloville, Margaret, 247
Clutterbuck, —, 223, 378
Coel II., 1
Cokayne, —, 225
Cokayne, Francis, 156, 157, 160
Colby, David, 93
Colcel, Thomas, 48
Cole, Thomas, 149
Colepeper, John Spencer, 95
Colepeper, Martha, 95
Coleshill, Thomas, 287
Collins, —, 177
Collins, Arthur, 249, 250
Collyer, Rev. W. B., 347
Colshill, Thomas, 102, 103, 104, 106, 219
Colt, —, 135, 139, 149
Colton, Rev. —, 156, 160, 161
Colville, Henry, 247
Comminges, Mons., 323
Compton, Hon. Charles, 92
Compton, Henry, Bishop of London, 226

Compton, Lady, 264
Compton, William Lord, 70, 260, 262, 265, 266
Conder, Dr., 354
Constantine I., 1, 3, 4
Constantius Chlorus, 1, 3
Contio, —, 311
Cook, —, 83
Cook, Rev. Edward, 52, **209, 210, 211,** 216, 217
Cooke, Edward, 94
Cooke, Dr. Edward, 94
Cooke, John, 157, 158
Cooke, Mary, 94
Cooper, Rev. —, 54, 216
Cope, Sir Anthony, 91
Cope, Thomas, 92
Copeland, William Taylor, 335, 379
Corbett, Edward, 94
Corbett, Mary, 94
Corbett, Myles, 94
Cork, Timothy, 187
Corp, Timothy, 186
Costin, Ann, 93
Cotesbrok, Robert, 73
Cotton, —, 111, 122, 343
Cotton, Sir R. B., 55
Cottrell, Sir Stephen, **307**
Cottrell-Dormer, Charles, 307
Cottrell-Dormer, Sir Charles, 286
Cottrell-Dormer, Clement, 307
Cottrell-Dormer, Sir Clement, 307
Cottrell-Dormer, Miss F. E., 286, 303
Cottrell-Dormer, Jane, 307
Coulton, Rev. George, 55, 176, 178
Coventry, —, 109, 110
Coventry, Lady Ann, 98
Coventry, Thomas Lord, 91
Coward, —, 347, 348, 353
Coward, Thomas, 168
Cox, Dr. John Edmund, 56, 379
Crafford, Guy, 32
Crafford, Joan, 32
Craghead, —, 162
Crane, Margaret, 32
Crane, William, 32, **33**
Cranmer, Archbishop, 246, **381, 382**, 383
Cranmer, Edmund, 246
Crayford, Guy, 17, 33
Cremer, Miss, **306**
Criche, Thomas, **18, 27**
Crispe, —, 122
Crispe, Dorothy, 98
Croft, Thomas, 92
Cromwell, Frances Lady, 243
Cromwell, Francis, 243
Cromwell, Henry, 243, 339
Cromwell, Oliver, 241, 316, 317, 338, **350**
Cromwell, Richard, 286, 350
Cromwell, Sir Richard, 242, 243, 255
Cromwell, Thomas, 243
Cromwell—see also Williams, Sir Richard
Crooke, Anne, 94
Crooke, Hilkiah, 94
Crooke, Dr. Hilkiah, **94**
Crooke, Sir J., 260
Cropper, Thomas, 115

Crosbie, Johan de, 227
Crosbie, John, 228
Crosby, Agnes, 69
Crosby, Agnes Lady, 45, 68, 231, 232, 378
Crosby, Anne Lady, 231, 380
Crosby, Johanna, 69, 231
Crosby, John, 69
Crosby, Sir John, 11, 12, 40, 43, 45, 68, 69, 216, 227-33, 377, 378, 380
Crosby, Margaret, 69
Crosby, Richard John, 69
Crosby, Thomas, 69
Crosby Hall Literary and Scientific Institution, 337
Crosbye, John, 21
Crotch, Dr. —, 212, 213
Crue, Dorothy, 95
Crue, Dudley, 95
Cudden, John, 92
Culling, Peter, 98
Cumberland, George Earl of, 240
Curke, —, 109
Curling, Bunce, **93**
Curson, Robert, **35**
Curtis, —, 220
Cuthbert, 57
Cutler, —, 323
Cutler, Sir John, 319
Cutler, William Henry, 212, 213, 216
Cyoll, Cicely, 78, 79, 182, 194, 197, 222
Cyoll, German, 78, 101, 102, 219, 333

DALAMORE, Lord, 92
Dale, John, 169
Dalgarno, Rev. John, 55
Dalton, Margaret, 17, 33
Damaral, William, 33
Damerhawle, William, 17
Dane, Margaret, 75
Danvers, Frederick, 96
Danvers, Lucy, 96
Danvers, Thomas, 96
Darcy, Sir Arthur, 19, **32**
Dare, John, 135, 146, **149**
Dare, William, 132
Darrell, Elizabeth Lady, **92**
Davies, John, 336, 337
Davis, Rev. John, 93
Davis, Sarah, 93
Dawson, John, 95
Dawson, Sarah, 95
Day, R., 141
Dean, Rev. John Bathurst, 56, 415, 416, 417
Deane, Reginald, 33
Decosta, —, 117
De Dominis, Mark Anthony, 270
De Dompierre, Hector, 99
De Goltes, Philipp, 91
Dehoes, Andrew, 150
De la Chaumette, Francis David, 93
Delafield, Thomas, 78
De la Mare, Nicholas, 21, 27
Delany, Mrs., 305
Delavale, Elizabeth, 93
Delavale, Peter, 93

De Lillers, Jacob, 98
Dempsey & Co., Messrs., 216
Densel, Anne, 240
Densel, John, 240
Derby, Earl of, 240
Derrom, Steven, 101
Desleborough, Henry, 139
Dickerson, Elizabeth, 197
Dickerson, John, 180, 184, 189, 197
Digges, Sir Dudley, 299
Dingley, —, 166
Dingley, Charles, 99
Dingley, Elizabeth, 99
Dingley, John, 197
Dingley, Robert, 87, 134, 152, 158, 159, 160, 163, 194
Dingley, Susannah, 87, 159
Dingley, Susannah Cecilia, 92
Dod, —, 174, 178
Dod, Peter, 220
Dod, Thomas, 190
Dodd, Mrs., 151
Doddridge, Dr., 346, 354
Dodington, John, 18, 19, 20, 28
Donne, William, 107
Douglas, Archibald, 291
Downing, Rev. Thomas, 54, 315
Doxey, Mrs., 189
Drake, Dr., 338
Drapers' Company, 61, 434
Drax, William, 65
Drayton, Edward, 98
Drury, Drugo, 68
Dudley, Ann, 93
Dudley, Edward, 93
Dufresney, —, 140
Dugdale, Sir William, 6, 8, 11, 26, 35, 250, 359
Dunbar, George Hume, Earl of, 292
Duncomb, Charles, 95
Duncomb, Hannah, 95
Dunning, —, 179
Durand, —, 166
Durand, Ann, 95
Durand, John Baptist, 95
Durand, John Nicholas, 95
Durley, —, 55, 132
Durley, Richard, 129
Du Roveray, John Peter, 92, 93
Dymmocke, John, 35

EAST India Company, 76, 86, 135, 207, 223, 224, 226, 334
Eaton, Jane, 97
Edmondes, Sir Thomas, 266
Edmondes, Sir Thomas, 269
Edmonds, Rev. William, 55, 198, 199, 200, 202
Edmund the Martyr, 4, 39
Edward I., 10, 47
Edward II., 6, 227
Edward III., 7, 41, 227, 424
Edward IV., 228, 229, 230, 231, 296, 329
Edward V., 331
Edward VI., 27, 28, 47, 48, 68, 239, 240, 246, 248, 257, 258, 275, 276, 296

Edward, Prince of Wales, 228, 331
Edward, Richard, 300
Edwards, —, 378
Edwards, John, 101, 102
Edwards, Rev. Thomas, 54, 135
Egbert, Archbishop of York, 46
Eightshilling, Baldwyn, 96
Eightshilling, Peter, 96
Eleanor de Wyncestre, 11
Elizabeth, Queen, 48, 49, 63, 67, 68, 176, 224, 243, 246, 252, 256, 258, 261, 262, 263, 265, 276, 277, 278, 287, 288, 289, 290, 291, 292, 293, 296, 312, 321, 332, 403, 425
Elizabeth of York, 230
Ellis, —, 378
Ellis, Rev. J. J., 55, 207
Ellyott, James, 222
Elwin, Rev. W., 305
Emerson, —, 149
England, —, 213, 216
England, Louisa, 421
Entick, Rev. John, 4
Essex, Lady Catherine, 92
Essex, Earl of, 267
Essex, Thomas Cromwell, Earl of, 14, 241, 293
Estwicke, Rev. Sampson, 55, 121, 122
Eusebius, Bishop, 1
Evans, Benjamin, 163
Evans, Rev. Thomas, 54
Evans & Co., Messrs., 216
Evelyn, John, 3, 323, 324
Eyer, Edward, 95
Eyer, Elizabeth, 95
Eyer, Robert, 95
Eyles, —, 98
Eyles, Elizabeth Lady, 98
Eyles, Francis, 98, 113, 122
Eyles, Sir Francis, 98, 327, 328
Eyles, John, 84
Eyles, Sir John, 98, 99, 327, 328
Eyles, Joseph, 98
Eyles, Sir Joseph, 99, 327
Eyles, Mary Lady, 98
Eyles, Sarah Lady, 98, 99, 327
Eyre, Joseph, 82, 162, 166

FAIRFAX, Charles, 92
Fairfax, Ellinor, 92
Fairholt, F. W., 73, 379, 380
Falconbridge, —, 229
Falkner, William, 188
Farley, —, 165
Fasson, John, 177, 178
Fasson, Thomas, 205
Fawkner, George, 94
Fawkner, John, 94
Feake, Catherine, 95
Feake, Christopher, 95
Feake, William, 95
Featley, Dr. Daniel, 82, 83, 97, 115, 269-71
Featley, John, 269
Featley, Joyce, 82, 97, 115, 123, 125, 197, 199, 403

Felton, John, 192, 194
Felton, William, 192, 194
ffenner, —, 108
Fenner, Edward, 76, 123, 194, 197
Fenner, Thomas, 81, 403
Fennor, Thomas, 197
Fenwick, John, 95
Fenwick, Maria, 95
Fenwick, Maria Ann, **95**
Fermor, Mrs., 304
Fern, —, 302
Ferneley, Anne, 273, 280
Ferneley, Jane, 273, 280
Ferneley, William, 273
ffetler, —, 219
Finch, —, 109, 204
Finch, Esther, 65, 66
Finch, George, 297
Finch, Gulielmi, 64, 65
ffinch, Thomas, 122
Finch, William, 85, 93, **172**, 297
FitzAucher, Lord, 234
Fitzgerald, Percy, 307
Fitzwalter, Walter, 11, 361
Fitzwilliam, Earl, 5
Fitzwilliam, Sir William, 5
Flanders, Louis Count of, 425
Flavia Julia Helena, 3
Fleetwood, Dr. William, 254
Fly, Rev. Henry, 401, 402
Folkes, Martin, 92
Foot, —, 99
Foot, Ann, 98
Foot, Robert, 98, **110, 112, 113**, 130
Foote, —, 86
Ford, Eliza, 307
Ford, John, 307
Foster, Lady, 98
Fountain, —, 79
ffountaine, —, 222
Fox, Charles James, 213
Foxe, John, 284
Foxley, Thomas, 92
Framebreaking, Abraham, 96
Framebreaking, William, 96
Francis I., 244
Fraunces, Adam, 19, 27, 362–76
Fraunces, Julian, 25
Frederick II., 287, 333
Freeman, —, 52, 111, 121
Freeman, Mary, 303
Freeman, Ralph, 303
Freeman, Strickland, 334
Freeman, William, 335
French, Peter, 317
Friscobaldi, —, 229
Frome, Henry, 189
Fugger, Anthony, 248, 275, 276
Fulk the younger, 5
Fulke, Monsieur, 333
Fuller, Dr., 55, 120
Fuller, Thomas, 242
Fylio, Nicholas, 96
Fynes, Hellen Lady, 94
Fynes, Sir Henry, 94
Fynes, James, 94

G AITHORNE, Rev. John, 55
Galindo, —, 214
Gardener, Rev. —, 54, 220
Gardner, —, 164
Garrard, Sir William, 281
Garraway, Elizabeth, 94
Garraway, Richard, 94
Garraway, Thomas, 94
Garrett, —, 142
Garrett, Charles, 149
Garrett, Rebecca, 80
Garrick, David, 307
Gascoyne, Anne, 95
Gascoyne, John, 95
Gascoyne, Richard, 95
Gaskin, Rev. George, 401, 402
Gastrell, Francis, 92
Gates, John, 35
Gathurn, —, 142
Gaufrid, Nicholas, 4
Gaufrid the Constable, 4
Gaussen, Anna Maria, 99
Gaussen, Peter, 92, 99, 172, 198
Gaussen, S. R., 198
Gell, Sir John, 352
Gentilis, Albericus, 96, 308–13
Gentilis, Alberigo, 308
Gentilis, Antonio, 308
Gentilis, Gregorio, 308
Gentilis, Lucentino, 308
Gentilis, Lucrezia, 308, 310
Gentilis, Manilio, 308
Gentilis, Matteo, 308
Gentilis, Matthew, 308–13
Gentilis, Nevida, 308
Gentilis, Pancrazio, 308
Gentilis, Pietro, 308
Gentilis, Quinto, 308
Gentilis, Robert, 308
Gentilis, Scipio, 308, 310, 312
Gentilis, Vincenzo, 308
Gentyle, Albericus, 93
Gentyle, Hester, 93
Gentyle, Mathew, 96
Gentyle, Mathewe, 93
George I., 327, 328, 348
George II., 327, 328
George III., 180, 420
George, —, 171
George, Henry, 184
Gibbins, Edward, 132, 133
Gibbon, Edward, 134, 135
Gibbons, Dr., 354
Gibson, —, 130
Gifford, George, 316, 317
Gifford, Humfry, 94
Gifford, Philip, 94
Gilbert, —, 135
Giles, —, 84
Girton, —, 220
Gladstone, G., 435
Glassappe, Katherine, 26, 27
Gloucester, Bishop of, 222
Gloucester, Elizabeth, 7
Gloucester, Henry, 6
Gloucester, Henry Duke of, 323
Gloucester, Johanna, 7

Gloucester, John, 7
Gloucester, Margaret, 7
Gloucester, Richard Duke of, 231, 331
Gloucester, Wilhelmina, 7
Gloucester, William, 7
Glover, John, 130
Glyn & Co., Messrs., 81
Goddard, Captain George, 98
Goddard, Dr. Jonathan, 98, 286, 317-8
Goddolphyn, —, 101, 102
Godson, —, 204, 205
Godwin, Rev. Edward, 348, 353-4
Goodhall, Mrs., 199
Goodhall, Richard, 99, 199
Good-Inch, Richard, 98
Goodman, —, 378
Goodman, Charles, 134
Goodman, Reynald, 16
Goodman, Roland, 34
Goodwin, Dr., 317
Goodwin, William, 112
Goodwyn, Thomas, 35
Gordon, Lord George, 187
Gordon, John, 109
Gordon & Co., Messrs., 337
Goslin, Captain Francis, 95
Goslin, Richard, 95
Goslin, Sarah, 95
Gosling, W., 182, 193, 214
Gough, Hugh, 284
Gough, Richard, 74, 228, 380
Gould, John, 139
Gould, Nathaniel, 143, 148
Gower, W. L., 426
Graham, —, 119
Grant, —, 378
Grant, Christopher, 292
Grantham, Lady, 351
Granville, Mary, 305
Gray, George, 102
Graye, Elizabeth, 26, 27
Graye, George, 101
Graye, William, 101
Green, —, 173
Green, Ann, 197
Green, Catherine, 162, 183, 197
Green, Mary, 158, 162
Green, Mrs., 176
Green, Samuel, 142
Greenaway, Thomas, 82, 192, 199, 200, 203, 402, 404
Greene, Alice, 93
Greene, George, 93
Greene, John, 174, 175
Greene, Thomas, 93
Gregory the Great, 57, 360
Grene, William, 35
Gresham, Anne, 280
Gresham, Anne Lady, 96, 220, 273, 284, 285
Gresham, Charles, 95
Gresham, Sir Charles, 426
Gresham, Sir Edward, 426
Gresham, John, 96, 271, 426
Gresham, Sir John, 271, 272, 274, 426
Gresham, Sir Marmaduke, 426
Gresham, Martha, 95

Gresham, Mary, 95
Gresham, Richard, 275, 280
Gresham, Sir Richard, 271, 272, 273, 274, 279, 426
Gresham, Thomas, 426
Gresham, Sir Thomas, 35, 41, 45, 53, 66, 96, 97, 105, 216, 220, 235, 248, 271-86, 336, 337, 378, 379, 380, 426-33
Gresham, William, 426
Grevell, Anne Lady, 94, 97
Grevell, Sir Fouke, 94, 97
Grevell, Lettis, 94, 97
Grey, Earl, 331
Griffin, George, 175, 212
Griffin, G. E., 212
Griffin, Thomas, 152, 154, 155, 175
Grigman, —, 87
Grimbel, William, 283
Grindal, Edmund, 104
Grocers' Company, 45, 228, 378
Grosvenor, —, 226
Grosvenor, Dr. Benjamin, 333, 338, 342-3, 344, 345, 346
Grosvenor, Jane, 240
Grosvenor, Sir Richard, 240
Grove, George, 199
Grove, Henry, 345
Gurle, William, 35
Guy, Mary, 190
Guynand, —, 150, 160
Guynand, Henry, 162
Guyon, Samuel, 136, 138
Gwercy, Balthazar, 32
Gwillan, Amy, 162
Gwilliams, Abell, 223
Gwynne, Dr., 314

H ABERDASHERS' Company, 63, 378
Hackett, Miss, 336
Hagar, William, 101, 102, 103
Hailes, John, 102
Hale, —, 160
Hall, —, 334
Hall, Alice, 26
Hall, Edward, 235
Hall, Giles, 119
Hall, Henry, 99
Hall, Roger, 24, 26
Hall, Thomas, 130, 131
Halsey, —, 216
Hamerton, Henry, 139
Hamilton, Dr. R., 404, 406
Hanbury, John, 119, 120
Hanger, —, 131
Hanham, Elionor, 26, 27
Hanks, Mrs., 140
Hanson, Thomas, 80, 87, 173, 174, 197
Hardwicke, John, 192, 196
Hardwicke, Lord, 90
Hardy, —, 116
Hardy, Sir Thomas Duffus, 104, 121, 177, 226, 293, 299, 339
Hare, Sir R., 301
Harman, Richard, 17
Harpsfield, Dr. John, 246
Harpsfield, Nicholas, 246-7

Index. 445

Harrington, Sir John, 48
Harrington, William, 297
Harris, Edward, 134
Harris & Co., John, 154
Harrison, —, 213
Harrison, Edmund, 423
Harrison, Lancelot, 30, 33
Harrocke, John, 17
Harrope, John, 33
Harrys, Robert, 35
Harvey, Rebecca, 219
Harwood, Dr., 121
Hasilwood, John, 251
Haskinstells, Joseph, 92
Hastings, Lord, 331
Hastings, Walter, 96
Hatch, Rev. G. A., 407, 409
Hatclefe, William, 230
Hathaway, —, 128
Hattle, —, 223
Hatton, Sir Christopher, 256
Hatton, Christopher Lord, 256
Hatton, Edward, 251
Hawes, —, 162
Hawes, Dr. John, 95, 121
Hawes, Margaret, 95
Hawes, Tho., 114
Hawes, William, 95
Hawkins, —, 164
Hawkins, Sir John, 258
Haws, Rev. Thos., 55
Hawte, Alan, 15
Hawte, Alen, 17
Hawte, Elizabeth, 20, 30
Hay, George, 174
Haydn, Joseph, **177**
Hayes, —, 216
Hayward, —, 348
Haywood, Rev. Valentine, **55**, **99**, **142**, 146, 147, 149, 152
Heath, George, 114, 118, 121, 122
Hellen, Isaac, 136
Henchman, Anthony, 94
Henchman, Mary, 94
Henchman, Thomas, 94
Henneagius, Thomas, 68
Henry II., 257
Henry III., 10, 11
Henry IV., 227, 425
Henry IV. of France, **263**
Henry V., 228, 234
Henry VI., 10, 231, 234, 247, 332
Henry VII., 12, 41, 73, 234, 241, 278, 296, 331, 380, 425
Henry VIII., 7, 12, 13, 14, 15, 16, 17, 19, 20, 21, 22, 23, 24, 25, 26, 32, 33, 34, 35, 46, 47, 48, 51, 68, 73, 74, 228, 234, 235, 236, 239, 241, 244, 245, 246, 250, 257, 272, 273, 274, 296, 320, 330, 332, 380, 425
Henryke, 281, 282
Hentzner, —, 277
Heriot, —, 216
Herman, Richard, 33
Hertford, Edward Earl of, 382, 383
Hesketh, Rev. Henry, 55, 108, 109, 110, 111, 225

Hewitt, Thomas, 297
Hewitt, William, 297
Heylin, Rev. Peter, 54
Heyward, Johane, 17
Heywood, John, 229
Hickes, George, 191
Hickley, —, 222
Higges, Dr., 349
Higham, Roger, 35
Highmore, —, 327
Hill, Grace, 94
Hill, H., 85
Hill, Rowland, 94
Hill, Thomas, 149, **156**, **165**
Hilliard, —, 121
Hoare, Richard, 92
Hoby, —, 277
Hodge, Dr. John, 338, 345–6
Hodges, —, 150
Hodgson, Jacob, 166
Hodgson, James Stewart, 41, 379
Hodgson, Kirkman Daniel, 41, 379
Holinshed, Raphael, 235, 242, 249, 284
Holkomb, —, 121
Holland, Epiphanus, **95**
Holland, Susanna, 95
Holland, Thomas Erskine, 308
Holles, Anne, 239
Holles, Elizabeth, 250
Holles, Elizabeth Lady, 236, 238, 239
Holles, **Sir** Thomas, 239
Holles, **Sir** William, 234–40, 248, 249, 250
Holloway, —, 270
Holloway, Joyce, 270
Hollys, Thomas, 237
Holmes & Hall, Messrs., 199, 333, 334
Hood, Rev. Harman, 344, 348, 353
Hook, Rev. **Dr.**, 46, 47
Hooke, —, **430**
Hooke, Grace, **319**
Hooke, Robert, 318–9, 320
Horseley, John, 134
Horton, Lawrence, **316**
Horton, Rev. Thomas, 54, **316**–7
Hotoman, John, 311
Houghton, —, 108
Houghton, Lord, 240
Houston, Thomas, 179, **182**, **192**, **199**
How, Thomas, 134
Howard, Sir R., 325
Howard, Admiral Lord, **49**
Howe, —, 103, 104
Howe, Father, 219
Howe, John, 347, 352
Howell, William, 29
Howland, Sir Giles, **91**
Howland, John, 91
Howley, Bishop, 404
Howse, Anthony, 93
Howse, George, 93
Hubbard, Major, 351
Hughes, Rev. —, 54
Hughes, John, 170, 172, 176
Hughes, Rev. Obadiah, 344
Hughes, R., 188
Hughson, 4
Hugo, Hubert, 4

Hugo, Rev. Thomas, 11, 12, 16, 28, 32, 361
Humphrey, Dr., 269
Hungate, Anne, 292, 293
Hunt, —, 152, 160
Hunte, William, 35
Hunter, —, 83
Hussey, Sir Thomas, 92, 322
Hutchin, Thomas, 224
Hutchins, Thomas, 84, 182, 194, 197
Hutchinson, Harriet, 93
Hyde, Sir Edward, 319

INGRAM, Sir Arthur, 92
Iregonwell, Dorothy, 92
Ireson, Mrs., 77
Ironmongers' Company, 75
Iveson, Mrs., 134
Izard, —, 109

JACKSON, —, 141
Jackson, Dr., 201, 202
James I., 41, 46, 69, 289, 292, 293, 298, 301, 312, 333, 425
James II., 327, 341
James, Rev. Ptolomy, 55, 134, 141
James, Richard, 209
Jarnowich, —, 212
Jarrett, Sir Gilbert, 94
Jarrett, Mary Lady, 94
Jarrett, Robert, 94
Jarvis, Anne, 96
Jarvis, John, 96
Jarvis, Richard Beresford, 96
Jeckell, John, 93
Jekyll, Sir Joseph, 138
Jenner, —, 201
Jenning, Miss, 306
Jennings, John, 178, 183
Job rakt out of the Asshes, 93, 96
John, King, 6
John XXII., Pope, 360
John of Brabant, 425
Johnson, —, 172
Johnson, Rev. John, 340
Jollie, Timothy, 342, 343, 344
Jones, —, 99, 245
Jones, Inigo, 40, 44, 51
Jones, Joseph, 117, 118, 120
Jones, Dr. Richard, 338, 346-7
Jones, Rev. Samuel, 353, 354
Jones, William, 379
Jordaine, John, 227
Jordan, Abra, 152, 154, 155
Josselyn, R., 228
Judde, Alice, 255, 256
Judde, Sir Andrew, 66, 67, 236, 238, 239, 243, 247-57, 378, 380
Judde, John, 247, 255
Judde, Sir John, 256
Judde, Mary, 255
Judde, Richard, 255
Judde, Thomas, 247
Julian, Jane, 30, 33
Jurine, Captain Isaac, 97
Juxon, Bishop, 47

KALKBRENNER, —, 213
Katharine, Queen, 35, 239
Katharine of Berain, 278
Kello, Rev. James, 348, 354-5
Kellum, Major-General, 98, 144
Kelly, James, 333
Kemp, Thomas, 247
Kendall, Henry, 173, 174
Kentwode, Reynold, 8, 11, 14, 361
Kerwan, Andrew, 82
Kerwin, William, 59, 60, 82, 83, 131, 220, 380
Kettle, Clement, 114
Kimber, —, 326
King, David, 403
King, John, 293
Kingston, Anthony, 242
Kirk, —, 110
Kirk, Elizabeth, 81, 148
Kirke, Richard, 102
Kirkes, Thomas, 81
Kirwin, Benjamin, 60
Kirwin, Magdalen, 59
Knight, David, 143
Knight, T., 216
Knolls, Robert, 19
Knollys, Rev. Hansard, 356-8
Knowlys, Elizabeth, 93
Knox, —, 162
Knyght, Thomas, 12, 21
Koyll, William, 102, 105
Konigius, G. M., 313
Kuhff, Frederick Charles, 62
Kuhff, Henry Peter, 62
Kuhff, Peter, 62, 193, 204
Kylbye, —, 102
Kyme, John, 235
Kyrton, Richard, 35

LADYMAN, James, 141, 149, 150
Ladyman, John, 156
Lake, Attwell, 95
Lake, Sir Bybie, 95, 137
Lake, Mary Lady, 95
Lake, Sir Thomas, 298, 322
Lampon, Nicholas, 83
Landois, —, 230
Langford, Dr., 354
Langham, —, 378
Langham, Anne, 322
Langham, Dr., 97
Langham, Elizabeth, 92, 322
Langham, Henry de, 321
Langham, Sir James, 322
Langham, Sir John, 51, 84, 85, 92, 321-2, 333, 339
Langham, Lady, 97
Langham, Mary, 92, 94
Langham, Mrs., 97
Langham, Rebecca, 322
Langham, Sarah, 92, 322
Langham, Sir Stephen, 94, 322
Langham, William, 321
Langham, Sir William, 322
Langley, —, 109
Larke, Thomas, 13

Laud, Archbishop, 46, 300
Lawe, Emma, 33
Lawes, Nich. W., 196
Lawrence, Abigail, 60, 94
Lawrence, Lady Abigail, 98
Lawrence, Adam, 84, 108
Lawrence, Catherine, 99
Lawrence, Lady Catherine, **98**, **99**
Lawrence, Dorothy, 85, 146
Lawrence, Elizabeth, 326
Lawrence, John, 325
Lawrence, John, 94
Lawrence, Sir John, 325
Lawrence, Sir John, 43, 51, 60, 72, 85, 94, 98, 108, 142, 146, 147, 194, 196, 197, 203, 207, 225, 315, 319, 323-6, 403, 408
Lawrence, Judith, 326
Lawrence, Oliver, 325
Lawrence, Rebecca, 94
Lawrence, Sir Robert, 325
Lawrence, Rev. William, 54, 325
Leathersellers' Company, 7, 16, 36, 45, 53, 122, 138, 148, 211, 223, 224, 226, 251
Leicester, Earl of, 311, 312
Leigh, Richard, 91
Leithulein, —, 133
Leland, John, 241
Lely, Sir Peter, 319
Lem, Joseph, 109
Le Mesurier, Rev. J. M. L., 56
Lemm, —, 108
Le Neve, —, 105, **121**, **177**, **226**, **293**, **299**, **339**, 352
Leneve, Sir William, **321**
Lennox, Duke of, 94
Leonard, Chrisogon, 93
Leonard, Sir Henry, 93
Leonard, Pembrook, 93
Lepiper, —, 131
Leslie, Bishop, 312
L'Estrange, Lady Ann, 91
Leventhorpe, John, 73, 233-4, 380
Leventhorpe, Sir John, 234
Leventhorpe, Thomas, 234
Leventhorpe, Sir Thomas, 234
Leveson-Gower, Granville William Gresham, 274, 426
Leveson-Gower, William, **426**
Lewis, Rev. John, 54, **221**, **416**
Lewis, Joseph, 111
Lewys, —, 220
Licinius, 1
Lightbourn, —, 138
Lightfoot, John, 301
Lincoln, Bishop, 19, 356
Lintot, —, 304
Linus, 58
Lisle, John Viscount, 382, 383
Lister, Sir Richard, 382, 383
Little, J. H., 212
Litton, —, **321**
Litton, Joane, 321
Llandaff, Nicholas Bishop of, 17
Lloyd, Dr., 352
Lloyd, John, 426
Lloyd, William, 55

Lock, Sir John, 95, **139**
Lock, Martha, 95
Lock, Martha Lady, 95
Lock, Michael, 288
Locker, Stephen, **122**, **123**, **125**, **129**
Lodge, Edmund, 288, **299**, **300**, **307**, **334**
Lodge, George, 102
Lodge, John, 156, **161**, **169**, **177**
Loggin, Thomas, 401, 402
Logier, —, 213
Lomelin, James, 321
Lomelini, Domenico, 320
Lomelyn, Domenic, 22, 35
Londindine, Thomas, **156**
Long, Jane, 305
Long, Miss, 305
Lonondine, Margaret, 162
Looker, Rev. —, 161
Loraine, Sir William, 326
Lord, —, 163, 164
Louis le Débonnaire, 361
Love, Christopher, 339
Lovel, Lord, 331
Low, George Archdale, **192**
Low, Richard, 192
Lowe, Emma, 17
Lowe, Richard, **141**
Loyd, Richard, 136
Lubton, —, 171
Lucy, Mary, 92
Lumley, James, 321
Lumley, Sir James, 321
Lumley, Margery, 97
Lumley, Sir Martin, 54, 79, 80, 97, 120, 176, 178, 179, **193**, **197**, **200**, **203**, 320-1, 322, 326
Lumley, Sir Martin, **321**
Lumley, Thomas, 321
Lupton, Mrs., 193
Lusher, Richard, 289
Lynn, Audrey, 272
Lynn, George, 298
Lynn, William, 272

MACCLESFIELD, George Earl of, 307
McDougall, Alexander, 52, 379
McDougall, Alexander John, 52, 53, 379
Machin, Sir Henry, 224
Machyn, Henry, 220
Mackenzie, Rev. Charles, 56, 80
Mackin, Rafe, 74
Maden, Rev. Richard, **54**
Madox, Thomas, 12
Maitland, William, 424
Malatri, Richard, 5
Malcolm, James P., **7**, **15**, **16**, **30**, **37**, **55**
Malpas, Philip, 11
Manchester, Earl of, 260, 323
Manning, John, **303**
Manwaring, Jaell, 94
Manwaring, Roger, 94
Mapletoff, Elizabeth, 92
Mapletoft, Rev. —, 55, 176
Marchant, —, 160
Margerum, R., 160
Margerum, Samuel, 198

Marjoram, —, 163
Marsom, Jacob, 170
Marten, Sir Henry, 295
Martin, Dr., 316
Martin, Mrs., 186
Martin, Richard, 289
Martin & Co., Messrs., 276
Mary, Queen, 48, 68, 246, 248, 249, 252, 258, 275, 276, 287, 296
Mashedo, Thomas, 134
Masters, —, 81
Mather, — 356
Mathew, Dr. Tobie, 311
Mattheuci, Clarice, 308
Maundeville, Sir John, 3
Maunsell, Peter, 314
Mauras, Nicholas, 286
Maxwell, Thomas, 179
May, John, 134
Maynard, —, 149
Maynard, John, 169
Maynard, Thomas, 166
Mayo, Charles, 93
Mead, John, 109
Meddus, S., 267
Medici, —, 229
Meen, Rev. H., 404, 406
Melsham, John, 22, 25, 27
Mercers' Company, 45, 223, 234, 239, 274, 283, 316, 335, 378, 425
Merchant, Peter, 139
Merchant Taylors' Company, 41, 223, 377, 379, 381, 410, 418, 422
Meredith, Jane, 321
Meredith, John, 321
Meynon, —, 81
Meynon, Mrs., 223
Michael Angelo, 42
Middleton, Rev. —, 55, 200
Mildmay, Thomas, 29, 30
Mildmey, Sir Walter, 221
Miller, William, 130
Mills, —, 166, 172
Milward, Rev. Matthias, 54
Minton, Messrs., 44
Mirfyn, Frances, 255
Mirfyn, Sir Thomas, 243, 255
Misenor, Thomas, 180, 181
Montacute, Lady, 288
Montague, Sir Edward, 382
Montague, Sir Henry, 260
Moore, Sir Thomas, 237
Moore, William, 192
More, Thomas, 19
More, Sir Thomas, 246, 332
Mores, E. R., 74, 379, 380
Moreton, Mary, 164
Morgan, —, 214
Morgan, William, 92
Morice, Rev. William, 401, 402
Morley, Rev. —, 221
Morley, Anne, 93
Morley, Thomas, 93
Moseley, Elizabeth, 171
Moses, —, 167, 168
Mostyn, Sir Roger, 32
Mounsell, Peter, 96

Mountain, Mary, 92
Mulcaster, Robert, 109, 117, 120, 129, 130, 132, 135, 140, 141
Mullins, John, 104
Murray, John, 301
Murry, Patrick, 97
Mylburne, Sir John, 235
Mynot, Susannah, 178

NAISH, Rev. John, 55, 99, 177, 188, 196, 197, 198, 201, 202
Naish, Miss, 212
Naish, Mrs., 202
Necton, David, 21
Nelson, Admiral Lord, 213
Nelson, Mary, 95
Nelson, Captain Peyton, 95
Nesham, Agnes, 12
Nesham, Robert, 12
Netherlands, Philip Archduke of the, 425
Netley, David, 18, 27
Nevil, Thomas, 229
Nevill, Sir Henry, 285, 426, 430
Neville, Richard, 426
Newcastle, Duke of, 240, 249
Newcastle, John Holles, Duke of, 240
Newcourt, —, 4, 5, 6, 35, 51, 54, 269, 359
Newland, Mary, 145
Newman, Edwin, 53
Newman, Rev. John, 345
Newnes, Moses, 226
Newton, Henry, 95
Newton, John, 16, 34
Newton, Margaret, 95
Newton, Robert, 95
Newton, Dr. Thomas, 177
Nicholas IV., 47
Nicholas, Sir N. H., 250
Nichols, John Bowyer, 292
Niger, Roger, 46
Noble, Eustace le, 241
Norden, Fred. Lewis, 280
Norfolk, Bernard Edward Howard, Duke of, 334
Norfolk, Thomas Duke of, 382
North, —, 225
Northampton, Countess of, 94
Northampton, Spencer Earl of, 51, 94, 114, 225, 226, 267
Northampton, William Compton, Earl of, 267
Northampton, Marquis of, 70, 377
Northumberland, Duke of, 272, 275
Nye, Philip, 271

ODYLL, Thomas, 102
Offa, King of Mercia, 46
Oldfield, —, 343
Oldsworth, Rev. Clerk, 338, 345
Olivar, —, 79
Olivar, Rev. John, 54
Oliver, —, 221
Olyver, Mrs., 222
Orange, William Prince of, 333

Orme, Dr., 182
Ormond, Duke of, 323
Orrery, John Boyle, Earl of, 304
Orridge, B. B., 11
Osbert, 5
Osborn, Samuel, 165, 167
Oseley, Captain, 49
Oteswich, John, 378, 435
Over, —, 250
Owen, Dr., 317
Owterede, Robert, 22, 35
Oxtoby, Charles, 88, 185, 188

PAGE, John, 93
Page, Olympia Charlotte, 93
Paget, Sir William, 273
Paige, —, 109, 110, 111
Paige, Mrs., 86
Palavicino, Horatio, 312
Palmer, —, 142
Palmer, Rev. Samuel, 348
Palmer, William, 77, 134
Pamplyn, Joan, 26, 27
Papillon, D., 260
Par, Lord, 235
Parker, —, 148
Parker, Archbishop, 246
Parker, Hon. George Lane, 307
Parker, John, 32, 33
Parker, Richard, 17
Parker, Thomas, 101, 103
Parker, William, 52
Parry, Sir Thomas, 277
Parsons, John, 95
Parsons, Mary, 95
Pashley, Edward, 168
Paule, Alice, 33
Paulet, Sir William, 382
Paulo Cæsarino, John de, 287
Payne, Catherine, 239
Payne, Thomas, 159, 162
Pearson, James, 401
Peck, Ann, 97
Pegge, —, 228
Peirce, Mary, 94
Peirsen, Edmund, 94
Pelishall, Elizabeth, 91
Pelling, Rev. Edward, 54, 103
Pemberton, Hugh, 378, 381
Pemberton, Katherine, 381
Pembroke, Countess of, 222
Pembroke, Earl of, 230, 349
Penara, —, 137
Pennoyer, William, 80, 85
Penrice, James, 98
Pepper, Solomon, 165
Pepys, Richard, 92
Pepys, Samuel, 284, 324, 325
Percye, Thomas, 21
Perfect, Rev. —, 160
Perkins, Charles, 81
Perrin, Margaret, 287, 288
Persey, Thomas, 24
Petre, —, 273
Petrelli, Diodoro, 308
Petrelli, Lucrezia, 308

Pett, Thomas, 17
Petty, Sir Henry, 319
Pewterers' Company, 77
Philip of Spain, 248, 258, 277
Philips, Sir Edward, 293
Phillips, —, 193, 222
Phillips, William, 170, 172, 176
Philp, —, 216
Philpot, —, 247
Philpott, Sir John, 299
Philpott, Thomas, 299
Pickering, William, 67, 68
Pickering, Sir William, 44, 67, 68, 172, 216, 257-8, 380
Picketts, Thomas, 123
Pike, —, 348
Pilkington, William Boles, 99
Pinfold, Sir Tho., 118
Pitchford, Elizabeth, 91
Pitchford, William, 91
Pitfield, Alexander, 95
Pitfield, Elizabeth, 95
Pitfield, Winifred, 95
Pitt, William, 213
Pitts, —, 218
Pitway, John, 91
Plumer, Sir Thomas, 210, 217
Plumpton, William, 35
Plymley, Rev. —, 55
Pocock, William, 204, 205
Pointz, Sir Francis, 244
Pole, Cardinal, 27, 28
Pollard, Sir John, 96
Pollard, Lady, 96
Pomfret, Earl of, 245
Pontius Pilate, 2
Poole, —, 378
Poole, Nathaniel, 138, 144
Poole, William, 76, 126, 144, 157
Pope, Alexander, 304
Pope, John, 35
Pope, Sir Thomas, 301
Porteous, Bishop, 404
Portland, Richard Weston, 302
Potter, Joseph, 182, 185, 192, 194, 196
Poulet, Sir William, 296
Powell, —, 208
Powell, Elizabeth, 91
Powell, Susannah, 93
Powell, Sir William, 91
Poynings, Joane, 74
Poynings, Richard, 74, 379
Poynings, Robert Lord, 74, 379
Prentice, Rev. Thomas, 348, 354
Price, Ann, 144
Prideaux, —, 270
Prideaux, Ann, 98
Prideaux, Edmund, 98, 113, 114, 117, 123
Prideaux, Mrs., 86, 128
Prior, Matthew, 303
Prior, William, 77, 141, 143, 179, 184, 194, 197, 212, 403
Pritchard, —, 121
Pryor, —, 108
Punshon, Jonathan, 206, 402
Pyncheon, Agnes, 247
Pyncheon, William, 247

QUERCY, Balthasar, 287

RADCLIFFE, Sir John, 245
Radulf, 4
Ralph de Diceto, 5
Ramelius, Henry, 333
Rancoke, Thomas, 17
Ranulph, 4
Raper, Moses, 139
Rawdon, Elizabeth, 92
Rawson, —, 218
Raymond, Juliana, 92
Read, Elizabeth, 162
Read, William, 273
Reade, Ann, 91
Reade, Gertrude, 96
Reade, Mildred Lady, 285
Reade, Sir Thomas, 96, 285
Reade, William, 93
Reade, Sir William, 96, 285
Rebotier, Charles, 95
Rebotier, Esther, 95
Rebotier, Magdalen, 95
Rebow, Abigail, 72
Rebow, Lemying, 72
Reddaway, Richard, 134
Reed, Sir Bartholomew, 332
Reigni, Hester de, 308
Relly, Rev. James, 355–6
Reresby, Gervase, 71, 86, 126
Reynolds, Dr., 318
Reynolds, Rev John, 338, 341
Riccard, Susannah, 301
Richard II., 247
Richard III., 231, 296, 331, 332
Richard, —, 223
Richard de Winton, 4
Richard of Westminster, 2
Richards, J., 216
Richards, Lawrence, 245
Richardson, —, 379
Richmond, Earl of, 230, 231
Ridley, Bishop, 47
Rigby, Thomas, 228
Risden, —, 325
Rispe, Henry, 126
Rivaz, Frances Mary Rachael, 93
Rivers, David, 348
Rivers, Earl, 331
Rives, Brewen, 94
Rives, Joseph, 94
Robarts, Roger, 189
Robert, 4
Robert de Aco, 4
Robert de Amond, 4
Robert de Cadomo, 4
Robert the younger, 4
Robertson, J. C., 54
Robinson, Arthur, 75
Robinson, Rev. Benjamin, 226, 348, 351–3
Robinson, Bishop, 379
Robinson, Christian, 59
Robinson, John, 75, 59, 137, 197, 214, 380
Robinson, Dr. John, 98
Robinson, Sir John, 205, 325
Robinson, Mary, 98
Robinson, Mrs., 220
Robinson, William, 81, 197
Robson, Thomas, 27, 28
Roch, William, 235
Rochester, Bishop of, 225
Rochester, Robert, 73, 380
Rodd, Miss, 212, 213
Roe, —, 87
Roger, —, 126
Rolfe, —, 379
Rollesley, Alice, 12
Rollesley, Edward, 22, 27
Rollesley, Elizabeth, 12
Rollesley, John, 14, 17, 18, 22, 24, 27, 33, 35
Rollesley, Mary, 11, 12, 13, 14, 15, 26
Romaine, Rev. —, 162
Romanus, St., 360
Rooke, —, 286
Roper, —, 332
Roper, W., 216
Rose, —, 378
Roskell, A., 216
Rosny, Marquis of, 263, 333
Rougemont, John Henry, 93
Roulande, John, 28
Rowe, —, 155
Rowe, Sir Henry, 79, 222
Rowe, Sir Thomas, 281
Ruck, —, 142
Rudd, Thomas, 404
Ruddle & Clarke, Messrs., 335
Rudston, John, 235
Rupert, Prince, 271, 283
Russell, Dr. John, 230
Russell, Sir John, 17, 382
Russell, John Lord, 382, 383
Russell, W., 213
Rygby, Thomas, 233
Ryke, John, 280
Ryson, Thomas, 27
Ryther, Ferdinando, 298
Ryther, Mary, 298
Ryther, Susan, 298
Ryther, Sir William, 298
Ryvers, Alderman, 281

SACKVILLE, Lord George, 307
St. Botolph, 34
St. George, Sir Henry, 321
St. Helena, 1, 2, 3, 4
St. John, William Lord, 296, 382, 383
Saggers, J. G., 208, 216, 219
Salt, —, 250
Salusbury, John, 278
Sampson, Margaret, 26, 27
Sancroft, Dr. William, 325, 339
Sandars, Mary, 179, 180
Sanderson, Dr., 92
Sanderson, Dorcas, 96
Sanderson, Mary, 92
Sanderson, Thomas, 96
Sandys, George, 3
Saunders, Blase, 101, 102, 103, 104
Saunders, Mrs., 164

Saunders, Samuel, 352
Sayer, Edward, 95
Sayer, Elizabeth, 95
Sayer, Sarah, 95
Scattergood, —, 162
Schetz, —, 275
Schooling, —, 193
Scidmore, —, 193
Scopeham, Elizabeth, 249
Scopeham, John, 239, 249
Scopeham, Thomas, 239, 249, 250
Scott, Jane, 92
Scott, John, 134, 135
Scott, Sir John, 230
Scrope, Henry Lord, 228
Scudamore, Phillippe, 426
Seamer, Henry, 74, 379
Seayers, —, 131
Sem, Joseph, 86
Sewstre, John, 20
Seymour, Sir Thomas, 243
Shakspeare, William, 221, 332
Shakspeare Society, 229
Shelton, William, 13, 23
Shepherd, —, 216
Sherborne, Bridget, 307
Sherborne, Davenant, 307
Sherbrook, Richard, 99
Sherbrooke, John Brette, 99
Sherlock, William, 121
Sherly, Cicely, 91
Sheton, Jerome, 23
Shirborne, William, 35
Shore, Jane, 230
Shore, Matthew, 229
Shreife, John, 133
Shrewsbury, Earl of, 243
Shuckburgh, Anne, 94
Shuckburgh, George, 94
Shurburne, William, 18, 23
Shutt, —, 109
Sibley, William, 183, 184
Sidney, Sir Philip, 311, 312
Sikes, Rev. Thomas, 93
Simmons, William, 134
Simon of Durham, 3
Simpson, —, 378
Simpson, Rev. —, 55
Simpson, Thomas, 401
Sinclair, Catherine, 190
Skegge, —, 103
Skeres, Raffe, 102
Skinners' Company, 81, 223, 243, 251, 252, 253, 254, 256, 257, 378, 403, 408
Skipwith, Honnor, 94
Skipwith, Patrick, 94
Skipwith, Willoby, 94
Slade, —, 83
Slany, John, 224
Slater, Rev. Samuel, 338, 340-1, 342, 343
Sloane, Sir Hans, 287
Small, John, 35
Smart, Sir George, 213
Smith, Rev. —, 55
Smith, John, 62, 88, 89, 174, 180, 181, 182, 183, 185, 186, 187, 189, 208

Smith, John William, 99
Smith, Robert, 330
Smith, Thomas, 168, 171
Smith, Thomas Woodroffe, 297
Smith, William, 151
Smithson, George, 92
Smythe, Alice, 252, 253, 256
Smythe, Thomas, 252, 255, **256**
Smythe, Sir Thomas, 256
Snellinge, Sir George, 91
Society for Promoting the Gospel, 87
Somerset, Ann Duchess of, 50
Somerset, Charles, 91
Somerset, Edward Seymour, Duke of, 50, 273
Soulby, —, 122
Sowerby, Thomas, 187
Spalato, Archbishop of, 270
Sparrow, —, 150, 151
Spencer, Alice Lady, 70, 96, 260
Spencer, Lady Anne, 94
Spencer, Elizabeth, 98, **260**
Spencer, **James**, 235
Spencer, Sir John, 70, 93, 96, 114, 216, 221, 258-69, 332, **333**, 377, 379, 380
Spencer, Richard, 258
Spencer, Robert, 100
Sprackling, Mrs., 156
Spurstow, —, 86
Spurstow, Alderman, 99
Spurstow, Henry, 98
Spurstow, Susanna, 97
Stafferton, Richard, 19
Stafford, Lord, 304
Stampe, Isabel, 11, 12, 13, 22
Standish, Dr. John, 98
Stanhope, —, 221
Stanhope, Ann, 93
Stanhope, Anne Lady, 93
Stanhope, Edward, 93, 176
Stanhope, Sir Edward, 50
Stanhope, Elizabeth, 93
Stanhope, Michael, 50, 91, 93, 176
Stanhope, Sir Michael, 93
Stanhope, Secretary, 304
Stanhope, Sir Thomas, 240
Stanley, Walter, 240
Stanyer, Sir Samuel, 98
Staper, Richard, 378, 381, **435**
Staverton, **John**, 24
Staverton, Richard, **13**, **24**, **25**, **35**
Stephens, Rev George, **348**, **354**
Sterne, Anne, 91
Sterne, Robert, 91
Stert, Arthur, 99
Stert, Richard, **134**
Stevens, —, 157
Stewardson, —, 216
Stiles, Sir John Haskyns Eyles, 99
Stinton, George, 132
Stinton, Mrs., 132
Stockton, Sir John, 230
Stone, —, 77
Stone, Edmund, 102
Stone, James, 82, 208
Stone, John, 133

Stoughton, Mary, 92
Stow, John, 3, 5, 29, 35, 61, 74, 227, 228, 229, 230, 231, 235, 242, 243, 246, 248, 250, 252, 272, 280, 281, 283, 293, 332, 333, 379
Strangford, Viscount, 256
Strype, Rev. John, 48, 246, 248, 252
Sturdye, Guy, 30, 33
Styles, Benjamin Haskin, 328
Styles, Sir Francis Haskin Eyles, 328
Styles, Joseph Haskin, 327, 328
Styles, Mary, 328
Styles, Sarah, 98
Sully, Duke of, 263
Sumner, Richard, 207
Suzan, Cislye, 91
Sybbald, Rev. John, 54
Sympson, Rev. Peter, 99
Symson, Rev. Matthias, 99

TAME, —, 139
Tame, Captain, 140
Tate, Richard, 35
Tatham, John, 323
Taverner, Richard, 35
Tayler, Ferdinando, 93
Tayler, Richard, 93
Taylor, Edward, 274
Taylor, Margaret, 435
Taylour, George, 32
Teasdale, —, 378
Tennison, Ann, 95
Tennison, Bishop, 95, 110, 111
Tennison, Norbury, 95
Tennison, Dr. Richard, 55
Thelwall, Edward, 278
Theodore, 4
Thomas, Rev. Sir, 54
Thompson, —, 270
Thompson, Benjamin, **135**
Thompson, Lucy, 92
Thomson, Sir W., 328
Thornton, —, 195
Thrift, Marian, 269
Thruckstone, John, 145, 146, 161
Thruston, John, 274
Thurgood, John, 19
Thynne, Sir John, 426
Tilletson, Archbishop, 320
Timbs, John, 221
Tindal, Felix, 91
Tinkler, —, 216
Toovey, Dr. George, 55, 169, 170, 171, **178**, 183, 187
Toplady, —, 340
Townsend, Rev. —, 54
Townsend, George H., 46, 425
Townsend, James, 192
Townsend, Susanna, 99
Tracthall, Alice, 11, 12, 21
Triebner, Rev. C. F., 348
Tristram, John, 176
Troughton, Bryan, 95
Troughton, Martha, 95
Trumbull, —, 265, 266

Trundle, Thomas, 89, 174, 204, 217
Tryon, Moses, 84, 97
Tryon, Mrs., 86, 98
Tryon, Peter, 97
Tudor, Katharine, 278
Tuff, —, 157, 160
Tufnel, —, 378
Tullibardine, Earl of, **97**, **302**, **303**
Turner, —, 119
Turner, Bridget, 93
Turner, Peter, 93
Turner, Thomas, 92
Turner, Dr., **93**
Turstin, Archbishop, 4
Tyndall, Dr., 299
Tysen, —, 193
Tyson & Co., Messrs., 216

UMPTON, Jasper, 100, 101
Underwood, —, 219, 348
Underwood, Thomas, 102
Upwood, John, 193
Urswyk, Thomas, 228
Usher, Dr., 271

VAGAN, —, 221
Vance, Thomas, 436
Vanloo, J. Baptist, 328
Vanlore, Ann, 301
Vanlore, Sir Peter, 301
Van Mildert, Abraham, **95**
Van Mildert, Anne, 95
Van Mildert, Cornelius, **95**
Varty, —, 216
Vaughan, Abigail, 435
Vaughan, Hugh, 33
Venables, George, 203
Viner, Sir Thomas, 86, 98
Viotti, —, 213

WADMORE, J. F., **379**
Waghan, Edward, 17
Wakeman, Hanah, **131**
Walfrid, 4
Walker, —, 160, 165
Walker, Rev. —, 54
Walker, Dr., 354
Walker, William, **162**
Wallis, Dr., 317
Wallop, Sir John, 243
Walpole, —, 294
Walpole, **Horace**, 307
Walsingham, Mrs. Boyle, 267
Walsingham, Sir Francis, 312
Walter, Henry, 4
Walton, Isaac, 296
Warberton, Elizabeth, 94
Warberton, Robert, 94
Ward, Henry, 76, 184, 200
Ward, Henry William, 77, **96**
Ward, John, 208, 228, 272
Ward, Seth, **318**

Ward, Susan, 96
Ward, Susan Lydia, 96
Wardner, —, 222
Ware, Nathaniel, 77, 148
Warr, Thomas, 92
Warrand, —, 163
Warren, —, 129, 250
Warwick, Earl of, 349
Washbourne, Agnes, 94
Washbourne, Herriott, 94
Washbourne, Samuel, 94
Watkins, Thomas, 189, 205, 208
Watson, —, 102, 103
Watson, Elizabeth, 33
Watson, Rev. Thomas, 333, **338–9**, 340
Watts, Dr., 343
Watts, Rev. Robert, 55, 202, 203, 204, **206**, 404, 406, 407, 409
Webb, —, 142
Webber, William, 88, 181
Wedon, Joan, 250
Weever, John, 6, 7, 69
Wellcome, Robbis, & Co., Messrs., 226
Wells, —, 172, 173, 174, 175
Wells, John, 180
Wentworth, Thomas Lord, 260
Wesley, John, 351, 355
Wesley, Rev. Samuel, 351
Westcomb, —, 108
Whiddon, Anne, 239
Whiddon, John, 239
White, —, 125, 132
White, Foster, 377
White, Henry, 135
White, John, 271
Whitefield, —, 354, 355
Whitehead, —, 208
Whitehead, Ann, 197
Whitehead, Richard, 189, 197, 204, 205, 207
Whitlock, Boulstrod Lord, 94
Whitlock, Mary Lady, 94
Whitlock, Samuel, 94
Whittenbury, —, 78, 207, 208, **218**, 219
Whittingham, Henry, 85
Whyte, Sir Thomas, 249
Wight, Thomas, 378
Wilds, —, 85
Wilford, Sir Thomas, 259
Wilkins, Dr., 317, 319
Wilkinson, —, 28
Wilkinson, —, 307
Willes, Rev. Samuel, 54
William, 5
William I., **325**
William III., 240
William de Basing, 5
William de Cain, 4
William the Archdeacon, **4**
William the Founder, 5
William the Goldsmith, 5
William the Master, 4
Williams, —, 97, 115, 207
Williams, Daniel, 83, 224
Williams, Dr., 345
Williams, Dr. John, **111**

Williams, John, 211, 379
Williams, Margaret, 73, 380
Williams, Morgan, 241
Williams, Sir Richard, 33, 35, **47, 241–3**
Williams, Susan, 379
Williams, Thomas, 73, 380
Williams, William Meade, 379
Williamson, Thomas, 107, 108
Willimott, —, 160
Willis, Caleb, 314, 315
Willis, Elizabeth, 95
Willis, Joseph, 95
Willis, Rev. Thomas, 55, 95, 98, 111, 114, 118, 119, 120, 121, 319
Willmott, —, 156
Willoughby, Lady Anne, 93
Willoughby, Helen Lady, 96
Willoughby, Sir Rotherham, 93
Willoughby, William, 93
Willoughby, Sir William, 96
Wilson, —, 149, 347
Wilson, Alderman Colonel, **379**
Wiltshire, Earl of, 296
Winchester, Paulet Marquis **of, 276, 288,** 296
Winchilsea, Earl of, 256
Winfeild, Frances, 95
Winfeild, John, 95
Winfeild, Rev. Thomas, 95
Winwood, Sir Ralph, 265, 266
Wiseman, Elizabeth, 94, 97
Wiseman, Margaret, 94
Wiseman, Thomas, 94
Witham, —, 321
Witham, Margaret, 321
Wix & Poynder, Messrs., 193
Wodehous, Alice, 11
Wodehouse, Lady, 292
Wuffington, Margaret, 307
Wolsey, Cardinal, 5, 245
Wolverston, Richard, 19
Wood, Anthony à, 269, 312, 313, **339**
Woodhouse, Alice, 330
Woodhouse, Sir Henry, 292
Woodhouse, John, 348, 351, **353**
Woods, —, 77
Woods, Thomas, **113, 114**
Wooles, Thomas, **141, 142, 146**
Woolf, —, 99
Woolfe, —, 86
Woolfe, Alderman, **126**
Woolfe, John, 113
Woolfe, Sir John, 98
Woolfe, Joseph, 98, 131
Woolfe, Sir Joseph, 98, 127, 133
Worcester, Edward Earl of, 91, 96
Worster, Bishop of, 222
Wotton, Sir Henry, 296
Wotton, Nicholas, 273, **378, 381**
Wotton, Thomas, 68
Wren, Sir Christopher, **115**
Wright, —, 133
Wright, Rev. James, 343
Wright, John, 86
Wright, Mary, 92, 219
Wright, Dr. Samuel, 333, 343–4, **353**
Wriothesley, Lord, 352, 383

Wriothesley, Sir Thomas, 245, 382
Wyatt, Sir Thomas, 248
Wylde, Joane, 94
Wylde, Rebecca, 94
Wylde, Richard, 94
Wynarde, Hugh, 19
Wynestaneley, Thomas, 27, 28
Wynn, Morris, 278
Wynston, Thomas, 27

XIMENES, Manoel, 132

YORK, James Duke of, 283, 323
   Younge, —, 128

ZUNICA, Don Petrus de, 312

London: Savill, Edwards and Co., Printers, Chandos Street, Covent Garden.

www.ingramcontent.com/pod-product-compliance
Lightning Source LLC
Chambersburg PA
CBHW021420300426
44114CB00010B/573